IDEALISM AS MODERNISM

"Modernity" has come to refer both to a contested historical category and to an even more contested philosophical and civilizational ideal. In this important collection of essays Robert Pippin takes issue with some prominent assessments of what is or is not philosophically at stake in the idea of a modern revolution in Western civilization, and presents an alternative view.

Pippin disputes many traditional characterizations of the distinctiveness of modern philosophy. In their place he defends claims about agency, freedom, ethical life, and modernity itself that were central to the German idealist philosophical tradition and, in particular, to the writings of Hegel. Having considered the Hegelian version of these issues, the author explores other accounts as found in Habermas, Strauss, Blumenberg, Nietzsche, and Heidegger.

Any serious student concerned with the question of modernism and postmodernism will want this major collection of essays. Dealing with a wide range of modern theorists, the volume will interest philosophers, literary theorists, and social and political theorists.

MODERN EUROPEAN PHILOSOPHY

This series comprises a range of high-quality books on philosophers, topics, and schools of thought prominent in the Kantian and post-Kantian European tradition. The series is nonsectarian in approach and methodology and includes both introductory and more specialized treatments of these thinkers and topics. Authors are encouraged to interpret the boundaries of the modern European tradition in a broad way and to engage with it in primarily philosophical rather than historical terms.

IDEALISM AS MODERNISM

Hegelian Variations

ROBERT B. PIPPIN
University of Chicago

CAMBRIDGE
UNIVERSITY PRESS

PUBLISHED BY THE PRESS SYNDICATE OF THE UNIVERSITY OF CAMBRIDGE
The Pitt Building, Trumpington Street, Cambridge, CB2 1RP, United Kingdom

CAMBRIDGE UNIVERSITY PRESS
The Edinburgh Building Cambridge CB2 2RU, United Kingdom
40 West 20th Street, New York, NY 10011-4211, USA
10 Stamford Road, Oakleigh, Melbourne, 3166, Australia

First published 1997

Printed in the United States of America

Typeset in Baskerville

Library of Congress Cataloging-in-Publication Data
Pippin, Robert B., 1948–
Idealism as modernism : Hegelian variations / Robert B. Pippin.
p. cm. – (Modern European philosophy)
"The essays collected here have appeared in various journals and
collections" – CIP galley.
Includes bibliographical references and index.
ISBN 0-521-56025-X (hardcover). – ISBN 0-521-56873-0 (pkb.)
1. Idealism.   2. Modern, Philosophy.   3. Hegel, Georg Wilhelm
Friedrich, 1770–1831.   I. Title.   II. Series.
B823.P55   1996
190 – dc20   96-8627
CIP

*A catalog record for this book is available from
the British Library*

ISBN 0-521-56025-X hardback
ISBN 0-521-56873-0 paperback

CONTENTS

392

"see Xy" in Index

198-200

v

ACKNOWLEDGMENTS

The essays collected in this work have appeared in various journals and collections. I note here the first appearance of the articles, and express my gratitude to the editors and publishers for permission to reprint the following:

"Kant on the Spotaneity of Mind," *Canadian Journal of Philosophy* 17, no. 2 (June 1987): 449–75; "On the Moral Foundations of Kant's *Rechtslehre*," in *Studies in Philosophy and the History of Philosophy*, XII, *Kant*, ed. by Richard Kennington (Washington, D.C.: Catholic University Press of America), pp. 107–42; "Hegel, Ethical Reasons, Kantian Rejoinders," *Philosophical Topics* 19, no. 2 (Fall 1991): 99–132; "Avoiding German Idealism," *Proceedings of the 8th International Kant Congress*, I, pt. 3, (Milwaukee: Marquette University Press, 1996), pp. 977–97; "Hegel, Modernity, and Habermas," *Monist* 74, no. 3 (June 1991): 329–57; "On the Notion of 'Technology as Ideology': Contemporary Prospects," in *Sociology of the Sciences Yearbook, 1993: Technology, Pessimism and Postmodernism*, ed. by Yaron Ezrahi, Everett Mendlesohn, and Howard Segal (Dordrecht: Kluwer, 1994), pp. 93–113, copyright © 1994 by Kluwer Academic Publishers, reprinted by permission of Kluwer Academic Publishers; "The Modern World of Leo Strauss," *Political Theory* 20, no. 3 (1992): 448–72, copyright © 1992 by Sage Publications, Inc., reprinted by permission of Sage Publications, Inc.; "Being, Time, and Politics: The Strauss-Kojève Debate," *History and Theory* 22, no. 2 (Summer 1993): 138–61, copyright © Wesleyan University; "Blumenberg and the

Moderity Problem," *Review of Metaphysics* 40, no. 3 (March 1987): 535–57; "Modern Mythic Meaning: Blumenberg Contra Nietzsche," *History of the Human Sciences* 6, no. 4 (1993): 37–56; "Nietzsche's Alleged Farewell: The Modern, Premodern, and Postmodern Nietzsche," in *Cambridge Companion to Nietzsche,* ed. by B. Magnus and K. Higgins (Cambridge: Cambridge University Press, 1996), pp. 252–78; "On Being Anti-Cartesian: Heidegger, Hegel, Subjectivity and Sociality," in *Vernunftbegriffe in der Moderne,* ed. by H. F. Fulda and R. -P. Horstmann (Stuttgart: Klett-Cotta, 1994), pp. 327–46; "Hegel on the Rationality and Priority of Ethical Life," *Neue Hefte für Philosophie* 35 (1995): 95–126.

I am greatly indebted to scores of people over the last ten years or so for conversations about, and comments on, drafts of the following, and to many audiences at colloquia and conferences where versions were initially presented, too many people to list here. But I happily acknowledge special debts that cannot go unmentioned: to my e-mail interlocutor and friend Terry Pinkard for his generosity and help with many of the following pieces, all of which would have been more flawed than they undoubtedly still are were it not for his criticisms and suggestions; to Nathan Tarcov and the John M. Olin Center for Inquiry into the Theory and Practice of Democracy for very generous assistance in the final stages of the book's preparation; to R. Zuckert for preparing such an excellent index; to Terry Moore of Cambridge University Press for wise advice about the Modern European Philosophy series and much else; to my students and colleagues at the Committee on Social Thought at the University of Chicago; and to my wife, Joan Redd Pippin, for everything already actual and now possible.

ABBREVIATIONS

Kant

AA   *Gesammelte Schriften*, ed. Königlich Preussischen Akademie der Wissenschaften. Berlin, Leipzig: de Gruyter, 1922.

A/B   *Kritik der reinen Vernunft*, ed. R. Schmidt. Hamburg: Felix Meiner Verlag, 1954.

CJ   *Critique of Judgment*, trans. J. H. Bernard. New York: Hafner, 1968.

CJ1   *The Critique of Judgment*, trans. Werner Pluhar. Indianapolis: Hackett, 1987.

CPrR   *Critique of Practical Reason*, trans. L. W. Beck. Indianapolis: Bobbs-Merrill 1956.

DV   *The Doctrine of Virtue*, trans. Mary J. Gregor. Philadelphia: University of Pennsylvania Press, 1964.

F   *Foundations of the Metaphysics of Morals*, trans. L. W. Beck. Indianapolis: Bobbs-Merrill, 1969.

GW   *Grundlegung der Metaphysik der Moral*, Bd. IV of *AA*.

KdpV   *Kritik der praktischen Vernunft*, Bd. IV of *AA*.

KU   *Kritik der Urteilskraft*, Bd. V of *AA*.

MEJ   *Metaphysics of Morals: The Metaphysical Elements of Justice*, trans. John Ladd. Indianapolis: Bobbs-Merrill, 1965.

P   *Prolegomena to Any Future Metaphysics*, trans. L. W. Beck. Indianapolis: Bobbs-Merrill, 1950.

TP   "That May Be True in Theory but It Does Not Apply in Practice,"
          trans. H. B. Nisbet, in *Kant's Political Writings,* ed. H. Reiss. Cam-
          bridge: Cambridge University Press, 1970.
TL   *Gundlegung zur Metaphysik der Moral: Tugendlehre,* Bd. IV of *AA.*

Hegel

D   *Differenz des Fichte'schen und Schelling'schen Systems der Philosophie,*
          Bd. IV of *GeWe.*
Diff   *The Difference Between Fichte's and Schelling's System of Philosophy,*
          trans. H. S. Harris and Walter Cerf. Albany: SUNY Press, 1977.
FK   *Faith and Knowledge,* trans. W. Cerf and H. S. Harris. Albany: SUNY
          Press, 1977.
GeWe   *Gesammelte Werke,* ed. by Rheinisch-Westfälischen Akademie der
          Wissenschaften. Hamburg: Felix Meiner Verlag, 1968.
GPR2   Bd. VII of the *Jubiläumsausgabe in zwanzig Bände,* ed. H. Glockner.
          Stuttgart: Frommans Verlag, 1952.
GuW   *Glauben und Wissen,* Bd. IV of *GeWe.*
PhG   *Phänomenologie des Geistes.* Hamburg: Felix Meiner Verlag, 1952.
PhS   *Hegel's Phenomenology of Spirit,* trans. A. V. Miller. Oxford: Oxford
          University Press, 1979.
PR   *Grundlinien der Philosophie des Rechts.* Hamburg: Felix Meiner Ver-
          lag, 1955.
PRE   *Elements of the Philosophy of Right,* ed. Allen W. Wood, trans. H. B.
          Nisbet. Cambridge: Cambridge University Press, 1991.
PRE2   *Philosophy of Right,* trans. T. M. Knox. Oxford: Clarendon Press,
          1967.
PRG   *Grundlinien der Philosophie des Rechts.* Berlin: Akademie Verlag,
          1981.
SL   *Hegel's Science of Logic,* trans. A. V. Miller. London: George Allen &
          Unwin, 1969.
VPRN   *Die Philosophie des Rechts: Die Vorlesung von 1819/20 in einer
          Nachschrift,* ed. Dieter Henrich. Frankfurt a. M.: Suhrkamp, 1983.
VRP   *Vorlesungen über Rechtsphilosophie 1818–1831,* Bd. III, ed. Karl-
          Heinz Ilting. Stuttgart-Bad Canstatt: Frommann-Holzboog, 1974.
WL   *Wissenschaft der Logik.* Hamburg: Feliz Meiner Verlag, 1969.

Nietzsche

AD   *On the Advantage and Disadvantage of History for Life*, trans. Peter
      Preuss. Indianapolis: Hackett, 1980.

ASZ   *Also sprach Zarathustra*, Bd. IV of *G*.

BGE   *Beyond Good and Evil*, trans. W. Kaufmann. New York: Harper &
      Row, 1966.

BT   *The Birth of Tragedy and the Genealogy of Morals*, trans. F. Golffing.
      New York: Doubleday, 1956.

Da   *Daybreak*, trans. R. J. Hollingdale. Cambridge: Cambridge Univer-
      sity Press, 1982.

EH   *Ecce Homo*, in *On the Genealogy of Morals* and *Ecce Homo*, trans.
      Walter Kauffman. New York: Random House, 1967.

FW   *Die fröhliche Wissenschaft*, Bd. III of *G*.

G   *Werke. Kritische Gesamtausgabe*, ed. G. Colli and M. Montinari.
      Berlin: de Gruyter, 1972.

GD   *Götzen-Dämmerung*, Bd. VI of *G*.

GS   *The Gay Science*, trans. Walter Kaufmann. New York: Vintage,
      1974.

GT   *Die Geburt der Tragödie*, Bd. I of *G*.

HAH   *Human All Too Human*, trans. R. J. Hollingdale. Cambridge: Cam-
      bridge University Press, 1986.

JGB   *Jenseits von Gut und Böse*, Bd. V of *G*.

M   *Morgenröte*, Bd. III of *G*.

MAM   *Menschliches Allzumenschliches*, Bd. II of *G*.

OGM   *On the Genealogy of Morals*, trans. Walter Kaufmann and R. J. Hol-
      lingdale. New York: Vintage, 1969.

P   "The Philosopher: Reflections on the Struggle Between Art and
      Knowledge," pp. 3–58 in *PT*.

PT   *Philosophy and Truth: Selections from Nietzsche's Notebooks of the Early
      1870's*, ed. and trans. Daniel Breazeale. Atlantic Highlands, N.J.:
      Humanities Press, 1979.

PW   *Ueber das Pathos der Wahrheit*, Bd. I of *G*.

TI   *Twilight of the Idols*, trans. R. J. Hollingdale, Baltimore: Penguin,
      1968.

TSZ   *Thus Spoke Zarathustra*, trans. Walter Kaufmann. New York: Vik-
      ing, 1966.

VNN   *Vom Nutzen und Nachtheil der Historie für das Leben*, Bd. I of *G*.

WM   *Der Wille zur Macht*. Stuttgart: Alfred Kröner, 1964.

WP	*The Will to Power,* trans. Walter Kaufmann. New York: Vintage, 1967.
ZGM	*Zur Genealogie der Moral,* Bd. V of *G.*

Heidegger

BT	*Being and Time,* trans. John Macquarrie and Edward Robinson. New York: Harper & Row, 1962.
N	*Nietzsche.* Pfullingen: Neske, 1961.
STE	*Schelling's Treatise on the Essence of Human Freedom,* trans. Joan Stambaugh. Athens: Ohio University Press, 1985.
SZ	*Sein und Zeit.* Tübingen: Max Niemeyer, 1972.

Leo Strauss

Acc	"A Giving of Accounts." *The College* 22 (1970).
C	"On Collingwood's Philosophy of History." *Review of Metaphysics* 5 (1952): 559–86.
CCM	"Correspondence Concerning Modernity," trans. Susanne Klein and George E. Tucker, *Independent Journal of Philosophy* 4 (1983): 105–19.
CM	*The City and Man.* Chicago: University of Chicago Press, 1964.
LAM	*Liberalism Ancient and Modern.* New York: Basic Books, 1968.
NRH	*Natural Right and History.* Chicago: University of Chicago Press, 1968.
OCPP	"On Classical Political Philosophy." In *WIPP,* pp. 78–94.
OT	*On Tyranny,* ed. Victor Gourevitch and Michael S. Roth. New York: Free Press, 1991.
PAW	*Persecution and the Art of Writing.* Chicago: University of Chicago Press, 1980.
RCR	*The Rebirth of Classical Political Rationalism: An Introduction to the Thought of Leo Strauss.* Chicago: University of Chicago Press, 1989.
S	*Spinoza's Critique of Religion,* trans. E. M. Sinclair. New York: Schocken Books, 1965.
SPP	*Studies in Platonic Political Philosophy.* Chicago: University of Chicago Press, 1983.
TM	*Thoughts on Machiavelli* Chicago: University of Chicago Press, 1978.

TW "The Three Waves of Modernity." In *An Introduction to Political Philosophy: Ten Essays by Leo Strauss,* ed. Hilail Gilden. Detroit: Wayne State University Press, 1989, pp. 81–98.

UP "An Unspoken Prologue to a Public Lecture at St. John's." *The College* 30 (1979): 30–31.

WIPP *What Is Political Philosophy?* Chicago: University of Chicago Press, 1959.

FOR DREW AND LAUREN

INTRODUCTION: HEGELIANISM?

The essays in this collection refer to, defend proposals about, and attempt to link two topics that have become relatively unpopular and quite variously interpreted recently: "modernism" and "Hegelianism." The issues relevant to both terms have become so contentious that the following preliminaries are no doubt necessary.

I

Modernity has come to refer both to a contested historical category and to an even more contested philosophical and civilizational ideal, some historically distinct, collective human aspiration. Various defenses and dissatisfactions with this ideal have always involved a number of explicit or implicit philosophical claims. In the essays that follow, I take issue with some prominent assessments of what is or is not philosophically at stake in the idea of a modern revolution in Western civilization, and begin to suggest an alternate view.[1] A reconsideration of the original German Idealist formulations of the

---

1 These essays complement the general treatment defended in my *Modernism as a Philosophical Problem: On the Dissatisfactions of European High Culture* (Oxford: Basil Blackwell, 1991) and attempt either to extend that case to other modernity theorists, or to spell out in more detail the philosophical importance of the Kant–Hegel dispute and its relevance to such theories. For a general discussion of the issues raised in that book, and a response to criticisms by

problem of modern philosophy (which I interpret as the problem of free-dom), especially what I shall propose as Hegelian alternatives in such disputes, will form the basis of this discussion.

Such an approach and such a suggested response raise two immediate, potentially discussion-ending objections. To many, the idea of a topic like "philosophical modernism" is so vague and misleading that it is better avoided than embraced.[2] To others, perhaps the same skeptics, post-Kantian idealism is an episode in Western philosophy of interest only for historical reasons; the last attempt at systematic, a priori philosophy about "how things really are," the very excesses of which finally revealed the foolishness of such attempts. There is not, goes the skepticism, much of value in the vague category of modernism, certainly not much promising in speculative idealism, and much that now looks historically dated and quite naive.

Consider first the historical category. However contentious the issues, there is by now a long history of interpretations and assessments of Euro-pean modernism. Prominent among such narratives are explicitly philo-sophical treatments, and a broad consensus about the philosophical uniqueness of modern philosophy is thought to be well established. On the one hand, classic "Enlightenment" positions are marked out: the new con-ception of nature required by modern science; the post-Cartesian notion of mind as subjective consciousness; a political world of passion-driven but rationally calculating individuals, or a "post-Protestant" world of individually self-reliant, responsible agents; a new political language of rights and equal-ity; and, most of all, a common hope: that a secular, rational basis for moral and political order could be found and safely relied on, could inspire the allegiance and commitment necessary for the vitality and reproduction of a society. On the other hand, there are also romantic and generally "counter-Enlightenment" (if also hypermodern) positions, positions that celebrate the priority of the imagination in any sense-making, of an organic tradition and of some sort of creative "expressivity" in accounts of meaning; a consid-erably more relativist and heterogeneous spirit than any single notion of modernity could encompass; a fascination with novelty; an appreciation, even celebration, of instability and change (again, though, a complex of romanticism/nationalism/pluralism issues that, by their very anti-

---

Kenneth Baynes, William Blattner, and David Stern, see my "Hegelianism as Modernism," *Inquiry* 38, no. 3 (September 1995):305–327.

2 Cf. H. Schnädelbach, "Die Aktualität der 'Dialektick der Aufklärung'," and "Gescheiterte Moderne?" in his *Zur Rehabilitierung des animal rationale* (Frankfurt a.M.: Suhrkamp, 1992).

programmatic spirit, constitute a distinct modernist program). Besides all being matter-of-fact elements in a historical transition, raising the historian's questions about origins, precedents, and implications (and many revisionist doubts about supposed revolutionary status), each such element in a modern self-consciousness is clearly also motivated by philosophically contestable claims, and many extend a kind of philosophical promise about a better (worthier, more just, less illusory) future.[3] The idea of a philosophical contestation about modernity essentially involves a dispute about this sort of promise: the general claim for the universal normative superiority of distinctly modern institutions and practices.

Again, however vague the category itself, such claims have always been determinate enough to provoke grave doubts and objections. As old as the first inklings of a modern epoch is the "ancients–moderns" dispute: the insistence that the successful modern attack on many elements of premodern thought (or, in the original *Quarelle*, the abandonment of classical literary models) represents a great civilizational loss. In one way or another, such a theme has resurfaced in a number of twentieth-century writers (Voeglin, Strauss, Arendt, MacIntyre, certainly Heidegger) and will no doubt remain a perennial way of raising doubts about the sufficiency of modern civilization. The same could be said with respect to religious worries about the compatibility between traditional faith and modernization.

However, many later philosophical assessments of modernism went much further. These included sweeping characterizations of modernity as

---

3 Admittedly, hardly anything one can say about this topic is free of controversy. Many recent British and American treatments of the problems of liberalism and modernism (e.g., the work of Berlin, Taylor, Rorty, or Williams, or even the later Rawls) begin from a deep suspicion of any "philosophical program" or conceptually unified approach to these issues, and plead for philosophical modesty, pragmatism, and a more historically concrete approach. The rough idea is supposed to be that liberal or modernist aspirations are better understood against the concrete historical alternatives out of which they developed, and not as "grounded" on any world view or philosophical program. Simply a better chance here and now (or there and then) for a better collective life, informed by the historical experience of the wars of religion, monarchical power, technological change, economic efficiency, whatever, is supposed to be what is "enough." I am not familiar with any such view that avoids what it seeks to avoid, although I do not try to demonstrate that claim here. "Less pain and suffering," "more individual freedom," "more and more diversity," and so on: all are manifestly philosophical claims about *the* most defensible aspirations of modern European civilization and, I think, should be defended as such. Doing so inevitably involves one in the systematic problems tackled with such enthusiasm in the Idealist tradition: the notions of nature, agency, sociality, religion, death, finitude, art, and so forth, which must be made coherently compatible with any such aspiration. As difficult as such systematic problems are, I see no point in trying to pretend that, armed with sound common sense, we can avoid them.

essentially (and essentially objectionable) "Platonism," or "Christianity," or
the "philosophy of consciousness," or the "metaphysics of subjectivity" or of
"presence," or as the culmination of a "technological will to power," a grossly
hubristic humanism, and so forth. And, more recently, some have claimed
that the appeal to a progressive modern revolution could not be disentangled from the politics of Western imperialism, and represented only a
European rhetorical strategy for the sake of its own hegemonic interests.[4]

Still later, many such characterizations came to be associated with the
view not only that modernism was ending, much as classical Greek or Roman imperial culture ended, but that a new epoch is visible, a postmodernism. This topic has already, mercifully, pretty much been talked to death,
and postmodernism seems already to have suffered the fate of structuralism,
semiotics, poststructuralism, and deconstruction, edged out by the new historicism, social constructivism, feminist psychoanalytic theory, postcolonial-
ism, and so on. ("Fashion," Leopardi reminds us, "is the mother of death.")
But such discussions represent a continuing and intellectually unavoidable
reverberation of the constructions and explosions of the nineteenth century, and also count as more good evidence that such reverberations, self-
doubts, and dissatisfactions will likely be with us for some time to come and
cannot wholly be dismissed as academic fashion.

In other words, it is indeed true that there are so many different, often
not consistent or uniform elements in intellectual and social modernity that
it has taken a good while simply to sort out the meaning of rival claimants, to
understand what this vastly altered situation – in religion, social life, aesthetic experience, philosophical orientation – simply means. Modernity, far
from being over, has hardly had a chance to get started. And if it was true
that various practices and assumptions authoritative in premodern Europe
suffered a kind of crisis that made their continuation impossible, the question of what sort of response represented the best understanding of that
crisis and so the most promising response, which of the many possible
modern worlds would be worth the best bet, is another issue that we are still

4 I mean "philosophically disentangled." A matter-of-fact entanglement is beyond question.
  Hegel, for example, besides offering many sensible objections to such practices as the caste
  system, certainly did say many ignorant and proimperialist things about, for instance, India
  or Africa, especially in the *Lectures on the Philosophy of Religion: The Lectures of 1827*, ed. by
  Peter Hodgson, trans. by R. F. Brown, P. O. Hodgson, and J. M. Stewart, with assistance by H.
  S. Harris (Berkeley: University of California Press, 1988). But the philosophical issue concerns the issue now called "orientalism," or whether either the very possibility of the institutions Hegel wishes to defend or the ethical norms he wishes to establish as a matter of reason
  logically presupposes or entails some fabulous "construction" of an inferior "other." I know
  of no argument establishing such a philosophical point.

beginning to understand, rather than ready to be done with. And there is also something manifestly suspicious in the current popularity of *so many* classifications and categories, in the very categories that inform the title of this book. After so many recent "isms" and "posts," after so many movements and fads, so many rejoinders, so much camp warfare and sloganeering, it would be understandable if some historical nominalism now seemed more attractive, and individual authors were simply read as individual authors, contesting particular possibilities.

Although caution about the categorial issue is understandable and worthwhile, the issue itself (the sustainability, the very legitimacy of a modernist turn in philosophy) is not one that can be avoided by complaints about overly typological treatments of philosophical issues. There is, so goes the counter to such skepticism, no way to understand why even various academic problems in philosophy (like the mind–body, or other minds, or analytic–synthetic, or linguistic turn, or reductionist, or absent qualia or moral realism, or rational choice dilemma or contractarian problems) have become "our" problems, much less problems like race or gender or sexuality, without some account of who "we" have become, and that requires some position on radical historical change in philosophy, messy as that is, like it or not.

It is also true that the substantive questions at stake can lead any even vaguely "pro-modern" writer in a number of directions. Those substantive questions have to do with the right diagnosis of the putative normative or (broadly) ethical insufficiency of premodern life and the philosophical and practical/historical sufficiency of some preferred version of the modernist response. The issues are not so diverse and elusive that no comprehensive treatment is possible, and demonstrating such a possibility of comprehensive discussion is part of the task in what follows. These essays take their bearings from a particular understanding of such substantive questions, a version partly defended elsewhere, but that I hope to motivate further here. As in an earlier book, I want to continue to argue that much of the controversy about philosophical modernism, antimodernism, and postmodernism can still be profitably formulated within the framework first proposed in the German Idealist version of modernism, especially in Kantian and Hegelian discussions, especially in their discussions of agency, self-determination, and rationality, at least once many standard interpretations and dismissals of that tradition are successfully challenged. My claim throughout is a straightforward one: that various possible Idealist interpretations and justifications for foundational norms in modern thought (especially the central norm, autonomy) have not been sufficiently appreciated in many of the standard narratives and criticisms. So I hope to show that substantial elements of such a framework have been misinterpreted or ignored in a great many of the now relatively well known accounts offered by others, whether by Habermas, by Strauss or Blumenberg, or in various versions of Heideggerean postmodernism or Nietzschean *Kulturkritik*.

II

It is certainly controversial to maintain that some early-nineteenth-century German philosophers had diagnosed the real intellectual sources of a modernist break with the prior religious and intellectual tradition, and that they, not Machiavelli, or the Cartesians, or the early rationalists, or Hobbes, or the Scottish Enlightenment, or the French Encyclopedists, had correctly thought through the only consistent philosophical modernism.[5] And there is no simple way to summarize the ideal at the heart of their revolutionary aspirations, the ideal of a wholly critical, *radically* self-reflexive or rationally "self-authorizing" philosophy. At the time, of course, such proposals were certainly interpreted as radical and dangerous. Immediately, the countercharge, that such a project finally implied a groundlessness, a foolish human willfulness, a "nihilism," was first leveled against this version of modernism by a now relatively obscure polemicist named Friederich Heinrich Jacobi (who virtually invented the idea of slinging this particular sort of mud).[6] And the radical claim – that the consistent extension of the program would mean the end of all hope for rational norms, and again a kind of willful self-creation – would also soon appear. However, as noted already, if one treats the idea of modernity philosophically as well as historically, the question quickly becomes the basis for something like the moral authority of the allegiance demanded by modern institutions and practices: legal, scientific, aesthetic, as well as political and social practices. And the Idealists, Hegel especially, thought they had an answer for this question. Live this way, not that old, or these other ways, is the simple assumption that needs to be redeemed; the content of such a claim is just as easy to state. One need only

5 The writer whose work best illuminates the many dimensions of the "rival versions" of moral inquiry prominent in both the premodern and modern traditions is Alasdair MacIntyre. See especially *Three Rival Versions of Moral Enquiry: Encyclopedia, Genealogy, and Tradition* (Notre Dame: University of Notre Dame Press, 1990).
6 Good treatments of Jacobi's role can be found in Frederick Beiser's *The Fate of Reason: German Philosophy from Kant to Fichte* (Cambridge: Harvard University Press, 1987) and in Rolf-Peter Hortsmann's *Die Grenzen der Vernunft: Eine Untersuchung zu Zielen und Motiven des Deutschen Idealismus* (Frankfurt a.M.: Anton Hain, 1991).

quote Kant: *Sapere aude!* Dare to know! In broader terms: *live freely!* And so the justificatory question came down to the nature and possibility and, especially with Nietzsche, the meaning of such an aspiration to freedom. (Nietzsche would inaugurate much of the now familiar suspicion that we did not understand well what it was that we wanted when we wanted above all to live freely, and that we can see in modern, conformist, alienated, technology-dominated, anomic, and directionless societies the fruits of such an aspiration.)[7]

The claim to be defended concerns why this ideal, human freedom, understood ultimately as being a law, a compelling norm, wholly unto oneself, in a wholly self-legislated, self-authorized way,[8] should be touted as a supreme or even absolute ideal, or that the enjoyment of many manifestly satisfying human goods, like love, friendship, security, and peace, would not be worthwhile ends to pursue were they not "truly mine," truly legislated as ends by me. In this sense, the enemy of such a modernism (whether in the name of premodernism or postmodernism), its other, is ["dogmatism,"] the reliance on anything not redeemed by a reflexive account of the possibility of such reliance against possible objections, by rational justification.[9] The Idealists' case is for what they called "the reality," finally the absolute reality of such a self-determination, or freedom: that such a reflexive self- grounding could be realized systematically and in practical life. Particularly in the case of Hegel and the various left Hegelian and critical theory writers inspired by him, such an ideal was not understood as a moral claim, purely stipulated by reason, an ever distant ideal to be approximated by hopelessly irrational human beings. The claim was that modern societies themselves already depended, for the allegiance they required, the education and sanctions they legitimated, and their successful reproduction, on the realizability of such an ideal. Reality itself, modern social reality, had, in Hegel's famous phrase, become "rational," could only sustain and reproduce itself in a new way, by appeal to rational legitimacy and so to the capacities for free agency presupposed in such appeals. Coming to a final understanding of

---

7 In Nietzsche's famous charge, the most familiar (or "bourgeois") form of the modern aspiration – to be free from as many external constraints as possible in the pursuit of one's wants – is the aspiration of a slavish mentality, motivated by fear and resentment and unable to sustain a civilizational project.

8 Cf. my "Horstmann, Siep and German Idealism," *European Journal of Philosophy* 2 (1994):85–96.

9 Again, I am aware that at first pass, this characterization can seem a trivial acknowledgment of rationalism in any form. The radicality enters with the notions of completeness and so a wholly "self-authorizing" conception of rationality.

such a reality, and appreciating its living potential in the emerging modern social and political world, was, for the classical German tradition, the unimpeachable, irrevocable achievement of modernity.

In that tradition, the possibility of such freedom is linked both to the possibility of a wholly self-authorizing or self-grounding reason (and thereby the final destruction of dogmatism, and the realization of reason's complete or "absolute" self-reliance and so "maturity"), and the possibility of a practical rationality, and therewith practical autonomy or self-legislation. As understood by Kant, the early Fichte and Schelling, and Hegel and the left Hegelians, the modern enterprise is thus inextricably tied to an essentially practical goal, what one might call a kind of "metaphys-ical politics": working out, articulating, helping to defend and so to realize, the possibility of free self-determination, agency, spontaneity, activity, a self-directed "purposive life," eventually (in Hegel) a necessarily collective agency.[10]

Such an aspiration immediately raised two extremely complicated theoretical issues. One concerned the central notion of "spontaneous" or "free" activity already mentioned, and with it (at least in the reading I want to defend in the following) the possibility of a generally non-metaphysical and non-empirical (non-psychological) account of the human thinkings and judgings and intendings supposed to be the prior conditions for the possibility of any cognitive claim or intentional deed, a "critical" or a non-metaphysical account of mentality itself. The other concerns the right way to understand the normative dimensions of such activity, the kind of subjection to rules or normative constraints characteristic of such free activity (or what a "self-imposition of norms" amounts to and requires). Both issues, without benefit of metaphysical substances and necessary properties, and without reliance on generalized laws of association or empirical psychology, raised very quickly the vexing problem of determinacy or content in such accounts of activities and norms (why *in particular* we take up the world and regulate our conduct as we do, if that taking and regulating really are "due to us"). But first, both obviously lead back to the historical and philosophical origin of such a way of posing the problem.

10 This is probably as vague and imprecise an abstraction as is necessary to launch any summary of a common ideal in this tradition. The common cause of Schelling and Hegel against Kant and Fichte, the break between Schelling and Hegel, the abandonment (or at least radical reformulation) of idealism by both Fichte and Schelling, and, of course, all the details and individual arguments are another story altogether, arguably one that still needs to be written. But some details of common heritage, and so common thematic inspiration, at least if formulated in as abstract a way, can also be brought to bear.

There is no mystery about such an origin. The intellectual event that made possible such a claim for the priority of norm-governed activity in any account of experience or acting was Kant's 1781 *Critique of Pure Reason* and the inauguration there of a "transcendental" philosophy.[11] Kant's successors realized at once that the implication of Kant's argument was a more comprehensive and wide-ranging revolution in conceiving mind–world and subject–subject relations than ever before effected within the Western tradition. Kant had argued that, prior to attempting to answer any question, philosophical or empirical, about the world, or the mind, or the good, the original question on which all others depended must be that concerning the "possibility" of the mind's knowledge of anything. When that question is pursued rigorously, it turns out that the possibility of any objective representation must presuppose the active role of the subject in establishing its relation to the world. No mere interaction between the world and the mind, so went the case at its simplest level, could account for such a conscious intending.

For those caught up in such ideas, these claims thus immediately closed off two already popular modern alternatives. As noted, one was a model of the world's presence to the mind common to both the emerging empiricist and rationalist traditions, one wherein "priority" in accounting for the mind's directedness toward the world, its attentiveness to the world in such and such a way, was ascribed to a direct result of the interaction between the mind and world, including special objects within the world, "ideas." The other is an attempt to account for the mind–world relation in a way we would now call "naturalistic," as if that relation, like every other, is a matter-of-fact relation whose nature and dimensions ought to be explicable according to the best available canons of matter-of-fact explanation. The Kantian point in response was the now familiar "critical" one: that such accounts beg rather than resolve the question of the possibility of an epistemic (and so *normative*) mind–world relation in the first place. (For example, Fichte's remarks against dogmatism, highlighting this ineliminable normative problem, make this point very frequently and effectively.)[12]

The enormously complicated case deducing the "necessary forms" of such an active taking up and conceptualizing inaugurated the Idealist revo-

---

11 The reading I am suggesting, which heavily stresses the deep continuities in the later Idealists with Kant's anti-empiricist and anti-realist claims, is admittedly controversial. It has been accused of making the post-Kantians *too* Kantian. See Terry Pinkard, "How Kantian Was Hegel?" *Review of Metaphysics* 43 (1990):831–8, and my response in the same issue.

12 Cf. ch. 3 of my *Hegel's Idealism: The Satisfactions of Self-Consciousness* (Cambridge: Cambridge University Press, 1989), pp. 42–59.

lution. As with anyone who comes to believe that a classically empiricist or realist or naturalist account of the categorial structure of our experience was insufficient, that such conceivings cannot be said to be due wholly to the actual results of the world's impingement on our senses or mind, or due to the way the brain and body have evolved to work (that no such account could do justice to the normative status of such principles), such Idealists were faced with the task of accounting for such conceivings in radically new ways, as, somehow, results of the mind's normatively "determining itself" in its relations to nature and others. In its first manifestations, especially in the classic Kantian formulations, such a position appeared to have "cut us off" from the "world in itself," restricting claims to know our own representa-tions (as in the first misinterpretations of Kant as a Berkleyean), or restrict-ing cognitive claims to a "content" accessible only within a finite, distinctive "scheme." On the formal or subjective side, it wasn't long before the talk of a priority and subjective self-determination led to talk of mind itself as an intellectual intuition and of a fully systematic self-consciousness, seemingly spun out of thin air, all of which have little purchase today.[13]

But the philosophical problem at the heart of this enterprise, the implicit reliance by empiricist, realist, or naturalist approaches on the very nor-matively constrained activity denied by their positions, and its overall im-plications for the idea of a legitimate modern enterprise, does indeed still have a great deal of purchase. It remains a problem unavoidable for anyone dissatisfied with the resources within an empiricist or naturalist project to account for the normative dimensions of our sense-making practices, who, no matter the methodology or philosophical school, recommends, pro-poses, exhorts, dismisses, or even, as in the tone of some of the new natural-ists, preaches.

To be a "thinker," in other words, as understood within this post-Kantian context, is to be a "judger," a maker of claims with normative force, and so the logic or "logos" of thinking must involve the logic of such normativity, the basis of our entitlement to claim to have gotten something right, that others "miss" something they "ought not" miss in avoiding such claims (something that must be far stronger than, They don't go on as we do, or Their brains are not functioning normally). In terms of the basic mind–world relation at issue, this means that even the most direct presence of the

13 I attempt to block such an inference from these sorts of Hegelian objections in Chapter 5. See also "Hegel's Original Insight," *International Philosophical Quarterly* 33 (1993):289–95, and the response there to Sally Sedgwick's objections to my reading of Hegel on spontaneity–receptivity issues, (291–5).

world to the mind in sensation, what Kant called "intuitions," should not be understood to play any mere psychological or causal role in our justifyings and judgings, but that even such a direct presence must already play the role it plays normatively, within what has been called "the space of reasons."[14] And this simply means that neither the given content of experience nor some sequence of events in nature can be said to be responsible for our believing anything or acting in some way. We are responsible for what we take experience to constrain, and these constraints are rational, normative, not psychological or (in the modern sense of law-governed) natural. The deeper and the more radical the appreciation of the extent to which our thinking *is* such a "making up one's mind" or "taking" a stand, the more our philosophical attention shifts to the issue of the basis of, and the nature of the contestation about, such normativity itself and away from how the mind works, or even away from "the" transcendental structure of the understanding. (Kant, with his own strict dualism between spontaneity and receptivity, and so his own version of the scheme-content problem, only went part of the way toward such an appreciation, claimed the later Idealists, one of whom, Fichte, pressed this point above all others most effectively.)[15]

As already noted, such an "absolutization" of the self-legislating, normative domain had to introduce a great reconceptualization of the problem of human mentality itself. The Cartesian problems of mental substance, dualism, and interactionism (as well as the contrary positions of materialism or what we would now recognize as pragmatically inspired eliminitavism) were rejected as categorial misstatements of the issue and as dogmatic alternatives. Mentality itself was reconceived as a certain naturally possible *activity*, the capacity of such naturally embodied creatures to be receptive to, to subject themselves to, rational or putatively justifiable norms. Animals like us can play a certain kind of game, if you like, and being "minded" just amounts to such a capacity.[16] Mentality just *is* the capacity to engage others,

---

14 Cf. Wilfrid Sellars's classic "Meditations Hegeliènnes" (to use his words), "Empiricism and the Philosophy of Mind," in *Science, Perception and Reality* (London: Routledge, 1963), pp. 127–96, and John McDowell's variations on such a theme in *Mind and World* (Cambridge: Harvard University Press, 1994).

15 See my account of this element in Fichte in "Fichte's Alleged Subjective, One-Sided, Psychological Idealism," in *The Cambridge Companion to Fichte*, ed. by Gunther Zöller, in press.

16 I borrow this expression from Jonathan Lear. See "The Disappearing 'We,'" *Proceedings of the Aristotelian Society*, suppl. vol. 58 (1984):219–42, especially p. 229: "Let us say that a person is minded in a certain way if he shares the perception of salience, routes of interest, feelings of naturalness in following a rule that constitute being part of a form of life." See also "Leaving the World Alone," *Journal of Philosophy* 79 (1982):385. See, though, in the

with respect to the world or to actions, *normatively,* and the "problem" of such mentality came to be the nature and grounds of this possibly normative like-mindedness, rather than the traditional notion of "having a mind," or participating in a Group Mind, as in conventional readings. Or so, I want to claim, we should read Hegel on *Geist* and the essential sociality of human mentality.

This is admittedly a controversial direction, one that to some seems to avoid rather than answer the central question, What *kind* of beings are we? In many modern philosophical treatments, understanding the possibility of a strict distinction between the explanation and the justification of think-ings and actings is taken to be a metaphysical problem. Believing or acting on reasons is often treated as a distinct sort of event in the world, accom-plished by necessarily distinct sorts of beings, and thereby not subsumable under the causal laws that govern the motions of particles in space and time. Since Kant, though, a kind of Holy Grail for modern philosophy has been finding a way to argue that "our natures" are not properly accounted for by "subsumability to causal law" without basing such an argument on any meta-physical dualism, and, in the view I try to defend, that aspiration is enthusias-tically embraced by Kant's successors. But the new problem has always been coming up with the right way to state the *insufficiency* of such causal explana-tion.[17] Thus one can view functionalist accounts of the autonomy of the psychological, anomalous monism, the unique status of the subjective point of view, and so on, all as recent successors of the basic problem first ad-dressed in the post-Kantian German accounts of the status of human freedom.

It can be said that this sort of strategy has become more familiar recently, thanks to various contemporary anti-realist projects. The insufficiency of

former article, p. 230: "My experience of comprehension is legislated by my being like-minded with other 'cube'-users." From Hegel's point of view, this appeal to "being" like-minded conceals more than it reveals, conceals especially a possible history of coming to be like-minded, and the way in which a purposive (and challengeable) appeal to norms functions in human sociality. Compare the discussion of similar issues in Heidegger in Chapter 15, and the account of Habermas in Chapter 6.

17 I stress again the multiplicity of the strands of strategies Fichte was taking up and trying out in these early writings. One strategy in such an enterprise to which he was clearly attracted does go in the Kantian–Reinholdean direction. Room can be made for reference to actions and agents by insisting that nature itself is a result, a construct, a phenomenon; that the nonultimacy of our claims about it leave such room. But I am trying to point to another strategy, wherein the insufficiency of lawlike explanations for thinkings and doings is argued for more directly, within some comprehensive account of the place of the catego-ries of reason (*Geist*) and nature (*Natur*). In my view this would only finally become apparent in Hegel's formulation of the *Encyclopedia* project, but that is another story.

causal explanations, say, is not, in such theories, a case of some distinct ("spiritual") fact of the matter escaping a certain discriminatory scheme. On the contrary, any scheme makes possible or constitutes the objects for which it accounts. So its limitations are internal not external; making use of the scheme, as a sort of practice, reaches a point where it fails to satisfy the original purposes for which it was deployed, rather than fails to "match up" to something. All of this is obviously controversial, but, I want to argue, at work, if idiosyncratically, in Hegel.

Further, as already indicated, none of this insistence on a subject's establishing its relation to the world, especially its doing so freely or spontaneously, nor my own characterization of such a priority for agency and activity as a kind of metaphysical politics should be taken to imply that the door opened by Kant did or must lead to some measureless field of possible sorts of activities, to some creativity, to relativisms or historicisms, and so forth. It may be the most controversial and difficult to understand aspect of this tradition, but the original argument was always that such a central "spontaneity" *must* be conceived as law- or norm-governed, as itself possible (or possibly establishing any intentional relation to objects, or responsible activity) *only* if normatively constrained. The original form of this argument in Kant concerned what seemed a simple constraint, the "supreme condition" he called the "transcendental unity of apperception." All my experiences, my active intendings and conceivings, must belong to me, must be ascribable to a single subject over time. Simple enough to state, but requiring an argument complex enough to justify (or at least to provoke) several thousand Ph.D. dissertations. (Aside from the sheer difficulty of the claim and its variations, the deeper tension in the program is fully visible in Nietzsche's charge that there is, finally, no possible compatibility between such original activity and law or norm; to believe so is to reveal motives better described with terms like *cowardice* and *slavishness*.)

This argument form – that the mind–world relation is spontaneously established, or requires some active comportment underdetermined by such a world, in what must be a norm-governed way; or that such an original spontaneity could only be the spontaneity that *could* make experience or a practically intelligible life possible if realized as law, principle, categorical imperative, a *sensus communis* in the aesthetic domain; all in a way that displaces rationalist, empiricist, and naturalist alternatives – was to have many incarnations and reinscriptions, from Hegel's *Logic* to Lukács's reformulation of Kantian spontaneity as productive labor. But it is the Idealist argument form most at stake, most in need of attention in assessments of a possibly modern philosophy. And this is especially true of the concept at the center of everything, a notion of activity or of human doings and engagings and comportings not, supposedly, itself an empirical or material event, *or* a non-empirical or certainly not immaterial event, a condition not resistant to naturalist accounts because unnatural but because a different sort of philosophical *explicans* altogether.

It is certainly true that formulating and defending such a distinctive sort of *explicans* have been the source of the great difficulty in introducing such an alternative into contemporary discussions, and this for one reason above all. It is certainly true that any claim advocating anything like a philosophical transformation of

A) These S's are P's

into

A') We are so minded that S's count for us as P's[18]

invites a number of interpretations that lead straight to that number of dead ends, most of them psychologistic and empiricist misinterpretations, and I would add, metaphysical, logicist, and anti-philosophical misinterpretations and "misreactions" as well.

And, for all the qualifications and textual complications relevant to the issues, something like the sort of psychologism or subjectivism Frege worried so much about looks like what *is* being encouraged by the post-Kantians, and even by Kant. Hence all the criticisms. Such idealism is a one-sided philosophy of subjectivity or consciousness, as in the Heidegger–Adorno attack, even a way of framing the problem of the "thinkable" responsible for "technological" subjectivism and thoughtlessness. It suggests a dogmatic idealism, a viable enterprise only if committed to some view that objects depend on being thought (by our or some Divine Mind); else how could an investigation of "thinkability by us," of our mindedness, have any objective payoff. Or the idea that possible contents could be intelligible only with essentially finite schemes must lead to a kind of relativism or skepticism that makes for incommensurable and finally non–philosophically adjudicable alternatives. Or the only sense we could make of being-so-minded and of its centrality is psychological or psychosociological, and the philosophical questions should just be an introduction to such a Master Discipline, cognitive science, or cultural anthropology, or whatever. Or at least that we can

18 Cf. the reference to Lear, note 16.

resist such a direction only by the original Kantian strategy of trying to defend a purer notion of formality and so a priority, the original argument that inspired so much of the Fichtean and Hegelian attack against such a formalism as either empty (not action-guiding in morality) or question-begging (with tables of categories deduced from logical tables of forms of judgment).[19]

It will be unsatisfying simply to point to Hegel's position on these issues (as I am doing here), just to suggest that that position avoids these criticisms by not adhering to any such strict scheme–content distinction, by denying that there is any plurality of such schemes (that we could be radically other-minded), and yet by insisting that this does not all leave us with an introduction to some psychologism or sociologism, or with a radically anti-revisionary farewell to philosophy.[20] (It does not because Hegel maintains that any *such* response must itself be understood *within* the space of reasons, cannot be viewed as "about it," and therefore is continuous with, is inside, the self-reflection about such normativity constitutive of how we inescapably and interminably "go on.")

But this is only a statement of the desideratum: that Hegel is trying to provide a kind of internalist, radically "boot-strapping" theory of self-legislated normativity, of what is and what is not available to us in our deliberations in trying to Get It Right. And all such issues require an extensive independent treatment. I mean here only to outline the issues at stake and to sketch this sort of reading of the Hegelian issues (and to suggest that it has remained a neglected alternative in many well-known debates about philosophical modernism): a non-metaphysical, non-psychological account of the mentality and normativity without which cognitive claims would not be possible, and a similar account of the normative constraints on any possible agency. Both accounts will quickly lead to Hegel's theory of historical rationality and sociality, and the kind of historical justification of norms that requires, and such issues will come up frequently in the essays that follow.

It is probably fair to say that, however formulated, this is all not a project

19 I defend the original Hegelian case against Kantian formalism in Kant's *Theory of Form* (New Haven: Yale University Press, 1981).
20 On the scheme-content and realism issues, see the section on the *Phenomenology of Spirit* in my *Hegel's Idealism: The Satisfactions of Self-Consciousness* (Cambridge: Cambridge University Press, 1989), pp. 91–171. For a discussion of whether what is there called this "Kantianizing" interpretation can do justice to Hegel's full theory of truth, especially in the *Science of Logic*, see Ludwig Siep's criticisms in his review of *Hegel's Idealism*, "Hegel's Idea of a Conceptual Scheme," *Inquiry* 34 (1991): 63–76.

that many would now bet heavily on. On the one hand, versions of what Kant would have regarded as "pre-critical" dogmatism, that is, forms of naturalism, psychologism, empiricism, and materialism, have made quite a comeback. On the other hand, the general notions of autonomy and self-conscious subjectivity have been under steady and, in academic and cultural terms, successful attack for some time now. The notion looks naive to some, "gendered" to others (as if a striving for "autonomy" were inherently a patriarchal aspiration, not a human one), merely one sort of good among a variety of incommensurable goods (and very likely not even a good if considered in the light of my overall satisfaction and the satisfaction of my basic preferences). Things don't look much better if one also disagrees (as I do) with recent strategies for a defense of the modern tradition proposed by Habermas or Blumenberg.

And it has certainly never seemed a useful contemporary option to consider something as polysemous and controversial as "Hegelianism" to be a possible option in modernity's ongoing contention about itself. Doing so requires both an independent characterization of Hegel's basic position and a general statement of his relation to the complex modernity problem, something I have tried to do, or at least tried to begin, elsewhere.[21] But his basic well-known, oft-vilified claim – that the modern epoch represents some sort of rational culmination of perennial and unavoidable human aspirations, an unovercomable self-consciousness and so a kind of collective freedom – is so notorious that, it seemed to me, a more indirect consideration of his position, in the course of a direct assessment of competing accounts, might also help to motivate such a claim.[22]

21 I mean my *Modernism as a Philosophical Problem: On the Dissatisfactions of European High Culture* (Oxford: Basil Blackwell, 1991), and *Hegel's Idealism.*
22 Another very popular reason for a deep skepticism about Hegel: Many assume that Hegel's project is some sort of secular successor to forms of providentialism, and so is naively progressive and optimistic. In other words, How could anyone with the slightest knowledge of the history of the twentieth century take seriously the claim that the human species had reached some sort of absolute self-consciousness and completion? This seems to me the least worrisome, even if the most popular, of the sorts of objections to Hegel one regularly hears, because it is based on such a crude misinterpretation of his position. Trying to establish that modern Western history has resulted in some philosophically decisive and historically unavoidable collective aspiration for the institutions and practices that realize freedom, and trying to articulate the dimensions of such an aspiration, what we really must want in wanting to be free, all have nothing to do with trying to demonstrate that we have achieved some state of happiness, peace, or the end of human evil and misery. At least there is nothing in Hegel that implies such a connection. In some ways the achievement of such a realization is as much a tragic as a romantic completion.

III

It could, at least, in some climate where many traditional assumptions about Hegel are no longer taken so easily for granted. Accordingly, a few words about Hegel reception. Traditionally, apart from simply being an object of antiquarian historical interest (and periodic vilification), he was taken seriously mostly for his role in the emerging nineteenth-century historicist sensibility, and for his distinctive position in ethical and political theory. Until very recently, that is, there seemed little reason to take seriously any philosophical reconsideration of Hegel or his version of the provocations of, and justification for, modern moral life. This was so for a number of reasons.

Thanks originally to the world historical impact of Marxism, "Hegelianism" is most often associated with a "dialectical" theory of history, a theory that Marx supposedly "turned right side up." (Hegel supposedly had things upside down when trying to explain the course of historical events, the head or intellectual issues where the feet, or economic life, should have been.) Hegel, it is often held, inaugurated one of the most extreme versions of a historical theodicy, rationalizing past historical events as necessary developments in the inevitable coming to self-consciousness of what he called, in his lectures on world history, the World Spirit.

Also, thanks to the influence of, and the impact of, some famous attacks on early-twentieth-century British versions of Hegelianism (sometimes called "objective idealism"), a Hegelian theoretical philosophy is widely assumed to be committed to a monistic metaphysics, wherein the apparent distinctiveness or ontological uniqueness of individuals is denied, all in favor of an "internal relations" theory that asserts the metaphysical reality and even priority of relations and claims that anything "is what it is only in necessary relation to everything else."

Finally, thanks in some measure to suspicions of the entire German intellectual (especially romantic) tradition, suspicions largely inspired by reactions to World War II, Hegel's position on modern "ethical life" (*Sittlichkeit*), especially his theory of civil society and the state, has been understood as an organic and anti-individualist theory, inherently hostile to modern notions of civil liberties or even natural rights, displacing the priority of the modern rights-bearing individual with the priority of some militaristic, divine, all-consuming state.

Since it is very likely that there is a world composed of real individuals, existing independently of any human or divine mind, very unlikely that human history is a result of the necessary development of a World Spirit, and since very little seems divine or transcendentally significant about the modern nation state, such conventional views did not create a receptive context for the discussion of Hegel or his theory of modernity.

This situation has changed a great deal over the last forty years or so, roughly since the end of the Second World War. Partly this is due to the kinds of problems now on the intellectual agenda. One prominent one concerns altered views on the problem of conceptual change. As noted, Hegel is well known for accepting Kant's anti-empiricism and anti-realism, but for rejecting his hope for a transcendental account of human subjectivity and its necessary forms of thought and intuition. Once the hold of a kind of neopositivist progressivism in intellectual history and history of science was broken, a different take on and interest in Hegel's view were also possible. The Hegelian turn toward the problem of accounting for historical change, without such empiricist or realist assumptions, but with an attention to the deep interrelation among intellectual and social practices ("shapes of Spirit"), looked worth attending to. This was particularly so since Hegel's account was neither realist nor relativist, but promised some view of the rationality of at least basic or fundamental conceptual change.

Partly, such a more friendly climate has to do with the fate of liberal political thought and liberal society itself. Someone who believed that all ethical and political deliberation presupposed some sort of pre-deliberative attachments and involvements, that a starting point of wholly self-defining individuals was naive and when thought through and relied on in political life led to an anomic and barely political whole, but who was worried about the implications of the traditionalism or "communitarianism" suggested by this direction, might, it came to appear more reasonable, look to Hegel, who shared many such critical views of a liberal individualism, but who insisted that basic elements of modern ethical life could be shown to be "rational" not merely "our community's way of going on." (And in that sense, as well as many others, Hegel was no communitarian, as that term has come to be understood.)

Moreover, new critical editions of the works of Fichte, Schelling, and Hegel have begun to appear, together with an explosion of commentaries and monographs, many directly challenging the received narratives. The "neo-Hegelian" work of the Frankfurt school, the careful and philosophically astute work of a score of important postwar German scholars, more sympathetic treatments of Hegel's political philosophy, a general disaffection with the professionalized subfield approach in academic philosophy, and the whole modernity hubbub itself have all contributed to a greatly changed international Hegel discussion and a greatly renewed interest in Hegel. Hegel is now more often treated as a progressive, reformist, surely modernist political thinker, if not a standard liberal;[23] as a useful, not reactionary or traditionally religious critic of the cultural and social effects of "scientism" or "positivism" or "instrumental reason" within modernization, and as a sophisticated contributor to modern philosophical debates about the nature of self-consciousness, the mind–world relation, and social and conceptual change. In Habermas's apt phrase, Hegel was the first philosopher to make modernity itself a philosophical problem, and his doing so has now come to seem a landmark event in the Western tradition, not a regressive, or romantic, obscurantist turn.

His position, though, on any of these topics is a book-length subject in itself. The most fundamental elements of the Idealist version of modernism sketched previously – the priority of spontaneity, or an active "self-relation in relation to other" in our comportment toward the world and others, the claim that such spontaneity must be realized as norm, finally a rational norm (universally compelling), and, most critically, that some determinate content could be given to such norms – are all so controversial that it is difficult to state them in a way plausible enough to begin a reasoned discussion.[24] (It is all very well for Fichte, Schelling, and Hegel to accuse Kant of having pulled his categories and moral law and common sense out of thin air to solve such problems, but it is another thing to have kept to his own Idealist premises and resolved this determinacy problem. For many, what seemed to happen was that many descendants of Kant simply decided to pull a great deal *more* out of thin air, once the premodern notion of a purposive nature and the modern notion of a necessarily compelling nature were abandoned.) As noted, in the following, I try to raise what seems to me to be the Hegelian position (broadly conceived) on many modernism issues much more indirectly, by means of a consideration of several influential twentieth-

---

23 Cf. inter alia the different accounts given by Shlomo Avineri, *Hegel's Theory of the Modern State* (Cambridge: Cambridge University Press, 1972); Allen Wood, *Hegel's Ethical Thought* (Cambridge: Cambridge University Press, 1990); Steven B. Smith, *Hegel's Critique of Liberalism* (Chicago: University of Chicago, 1989); Terry Pinkard, *Democratic Liberalism and Social Union* (Philadelphia: Temple University Press, 1987); Harry Brod, *Hegel's Philosophy of Politics* (Boulder: Westview Press, 1992); Michael O. Hardimon, *Hegel's Social Philosophy* (New York: Cambridge University Press, 1994).

24 For example, it would obviously be a gross simplification, or at best very misleading, to describe Hegel as an "Enlightenment thinker." For all of his enthusiastic modernism he (in many ways like Kant) thought the early English and French statements of modern philosophy still wedded to a kind of dogmatism, and incapable of formulating properly the supreme modern norm, freedom.

century assessments of the modernity problem. This approach makes my use of Hegel ultimately dependent on readings and disagreements with other readings defended elsewhere. But each of the following was originally written as an independent article and can stand alone, even while, I hope, still suggesting a broadly based Hegelian (or perhaps a neo-Hegelian) variation on some major theme introduced by the figure under consideration. As I have been trying to stress here, I do so not to make historical points, or simply to point out what Hegel did or would have thought about this or that, but because Hegel's project, or its major elements, offers some chance for us simply to understand ourselves, and to understand why what has come to seem so familiar to us as worthy of respect in human life and of credibility in modern practices in fact is so worthy.

IV

I've included discussions in seven areas. Since the interpretation I defend depends heavily on a certain construal of the implications of Kantianism, I begin with a consideration of the theoretical and practical issues most important to that interpretation, and so with some seminal areas in the original dispute between Kant and Hegel. The key is obviously Kant's notion of spontaneity, so I begin with a defense of the reading of spontaneity that I rely on throughout. I am especially concerned there to defend the claim not only that the kind of inspiration that Fichte and Schelling and Hegel found in this doctrine is not foreign to Kant, but that appreciating its Kantian roots can help make clearer its role in later discussions. (It is not, I should also note, as if Kant alone is the only safe anchor in the swirling waters surrounding his basic position; as if philosophical respectability requires a Kantian lineage, however long the lifeline to that anchor. Rather, the problem with demonstrating an internal connection to, and internal development of, Kantian themes is important because of the basic persuasiveness of Kant's anti-dogmatism, and the force of his criticisms against empiricism and metaphysical realism; in a word, the force of his modernism. It is often assumed that those who wandered too far away from Kant in the Idealist tradition by doing so lost their purchase on such arguments, and relapsed into a form of essentially pre-critical metaphysics. The point of the "This is an internal development of Kant's basic insight" theme is to show that this is not so; that one can appropriate the force of Kant's critical turn and the radicality of his theories of activity, normativity, and freedom, but without many of the limitations and, let us say, religious implications Kant believed accompanied such moves.)

Since my intention is also to make use of such notions to understand the general Idealist assessment of the modernity issue and modern institutions, I then turn immediately to some of the practical and moral implications. I want, in Chapter 3, to show, mostly by means of an argument internal to Kant's position, how his own notion of freedom, when worked through a comprehensive "metaphysics of morals," begins already to create the kind of strains in his formalism, contractarianism, and proceduralism that will be very much at issue in Hegel's political and ethical thought, and in Hegel's well-known criticisms of Kant. This approach again is inspired by a claim quite often made by Kant's successors, that Kant's own position, when thought through, demands some sort of extension or expansion beyond what Kant had circumscribed as critical limits. In this chapter, I argue that this is the case with the mere existence of a political philosophy in Kant, or that to understand the normative force of such a position (or the reasons a moral position like Kant's should even require or be led to a political philosophy), Kant's own hints about the substantive and even historical basis of moral life must be pursued more aggressively. I continue this discussion in Chapter 4 by formulating more broadly the Hegelian position on ethical norms, especially considered as reasons for action, and contrasting that position in more detail with possible Kantian rejoinders. In Chapter 5, I try to provide more detail about how Idealists like Hegel were trying, once "inside" the Kantian project, to find their way "out" again by examining one of the most well known areas of contestation, and the one where Kant is leaning the most in the direction of his successors: Kant's account of our capacity to appreciate the beautiful and "estimate" life, and Hegel's rejoinders and extensions. My hope is that all these more scholarly accounts of Hegel and Kant, however introductory, will suggest in some detail the substantive ethical position Hegel associated with modern moral thought in general, and its presuppositions in an account of freedom and normativity.

The next section focuses on a "critical theory" account of modernization, Habermas's, and offers, first in Chapter 6, a general Hegelian rejoinder to Habermas's approach (and his understanding of the place of Hegel in the discourse of modernity), and in Chapter 7, what I consider a Hegelian response to Habermas's famous analysis of the "technology as ideology" thesis.

Chapters 8 and 9 take up the issue of Leo Strauss and attempt to rethink his influential analysis in terms of a tradition oddly underemphasized in his narrative of modernity, the Kantian and Hegelian. I especially try to do so in Chapter 9, where at least his interlocutor is a well-known, if incredibly eccentric Hegelian, Alexandre Kojève.

The work of Hans Blumenberg is still not terribly well known in the anglophone world, at least outside the subfields of history of science and intellectual history. This, together with the fact that his position is quite complicated, both subtle and formulated in terms of an exhaustingly wide range of figures and controversies, means that any responsible treatment of his position must be largely expository as well as analytic. Hence in these two pieces, concentrated on two of his most ambitious books (*The Legitimacy of Modernity* and *Work on Myth*), I deal almost exclusively with his own claims about the provocations of a modern intellectual revolution, and the relation between "mythic" thought and modernization. My own view is that my disagreements with both positions are consistent with the interpretation and defense of Hegel worked out elsewhere and indirectly in this collection, but I do not defend that claim here.

In Chapters 12, 13, and 14, I turn to a consideration of Nietzsche, and these essays, as I try to explain in Chapter 12, make up the most self-contained part of this collection. Like Hegel, Nietzsche treats the problem of modernity in terms that are essentially practical. The modern world, indeed the whole post-Socratic world, is assessed by Nietzsche in a way oddly continuous with the German tradition he held in such contempt: not as a "discovery" or the mere "product" of social forces, but as a proposed way of life, a promise or moral hope. In an approach with some affinity to the Hegel of the *Phenomenology*, Nietzsche also suspects the sufficiency of philosophical argument or empirical evidence, the sufficiency of the authority of a "pure" reason itself, in assessments of such a promise. These are all treated as in some sense derivative phenomena. The basic attraction of the promises of modernity can only be understood with a deeper and more comprehensive formulation.

Nietzsche, however, formulates the problem much more simply and radically: What is it that the modern revolutionaries *want*? What is there "worth loving" in such a project? Something worth presumably so much more than what had been capable of attracting and sustaining human eros. A Nietzschean "psychology," not a moral theory or a *Phenomenology of Spirit*, or an *Ideengeschichte*, or the human experience of the human, or a history of Being, is what is most of all needed. Since Nietzsche and Nietzscheanism have become immensely influential in much postmodernism, and since many commentators on Nietzsche tend to pose the Nietzschean challenge to the philosophical tradition in terms of a challenge to Hegel, I wanted to try to state Nietzsche's own views on both the nature of that question and his own answer to it as clearly as possible in these chapters. With respect to Chapter 14, clarity about Nietzsche's position seemed to me particularly important since the erotic dimension of Nietzsche's project has not been remotely well enough stressed.

Once it is stressed, the proper formulation of the Nietzsche contra Hegel alternative could then be forthcoming. In Chapter 13 I both dispute Habermas's characterization of Nietzsche as inaugurating some sort of "farewell" to modernity's hopes and try to show how Nietzsche's own genealogy of the modern moral tradition fails, and fails "internally," on its own terms, but in ways that would have been predicted from a roughly Hegelian point of view.

In the sixth section, in the case of the Heideggerean alternative, since I don't believe that his own treatments of Kant and Hegel allow what he calls a genuine "confrontation" (*Auseinandersetzung*) (mostly because his interpretations do not allow real alternatives to his own views to surface), I concentrate on basic Heideggerean claims and the kinds of Hegelian responses naturally provoked. (That is, I avoid for the most part the specific treatments of Hegel or Kant by Heidegger.) In Chapter 15 the issue is the competing accounts of sociality found in Hegel and Heidegger, or their differences over *Geist* and *Welt* and the respective role in each of the possibility of intelligibility in general. In Chapter 16, I concentrate on Heidegger's 1936 lectures on Schelling and try to suggest something of the differences between the "political metaphysics" inaugurated by Kant and the version that Heidegger notoriously ended up with.

All of the elements of the Hegelian variations presented here – the role of the spontaneity thesis, the nature of agency, the autonomy ideal, the realization of spontaneity as norm, the sociality of such norms, their historicity – are fit subjects for scholarly monographs or independent philosophical treatment. My hope here was that there might be something to Hegel's famous notion of "determinate negation," or that the limitations and *aporiai* of competing versions of modern possibilities might, just by virtue of these insufficiencies, both suggest and help motivate Hegel's many provocative suggestions. In order to provide some more determinate sense of what sort of ethical position such claims might help justify, I close with an attempt at a systematic restatement of Hegel's "ethical rationalism," the position that, I claim, is most at issue in Hegel's defense of philosophical modernism. Since so much of the criticism and suspicion about Hegel's position on modern society stems from views about what he meant when he proclaimed the "rationality" of modern "reality," I have undertaken to provide a somewhat non-standard account of that claim, one tied to recent and traditional work on the problem of moral motivation and the relationship between such themes and moral theory itself. Once Hegel's views are understood within such a tradition, one that goes back to Plato's claim that justice must be shown to "pay" but is most well known from Hume's moral skepticism, his account of modern ethical life will not be subject to such traditional suspicions.

These essays, then, present a somewhat indirect defense of a simple but fairly sweeping thesis: that the modern European intellectual tradition has not "culminated in nihilism," a technological will to power, or a thoughtless, hegemonic subjectivism. On the contrary the modern tradition is sustained by a defensible moral aspiration: to live freely. This is not a mere negative concession to the absence of any common civilizational ideal, but a positive aspiration. (As is sometimes pointed out, sometimes with some irony, many of the most suspicious and revisionist accounts of the Western canon are inspired by the same ideal, whether formulated negatively, as a freedom from oppression, even the oppression of "forms of discourse," or positively as the politics of identity and community.)

We are still engaged in a great contestation about such an ideal; it can still be called on to justify great sacrifices, even as we can only confusedly state what it is. To a large extent such a contestation has simply become *the* "discourse of modernity." And, in the Hegelian or Idealist view I want to defend, that discourse is also self-defining and practical, necessarily social and historical, not just academic or metaphysical. In the conversation about the status and implications of the ideal of autonomy we are deciding whom to become, as well as who we already "really" are. The current postmodernist suspicions about subjectivism and critical theory suspicions about the philosophy of consciousness have, I claim, become so extravagant and exaggerated that they have begun to make it impossible to understand the social subjectivity necessarily presupposed in such debates (often on both sides), the substantive norms any negative position must presuppose and promise, and the real social cohesion and common aspirations we still share.

If this is true, that these twin questions concerning what it is to live freely, and just why and whether that should be our highest aspiration, do pretty much define the distinctly modern landscape, my suggestion throughout is that our understanding of such questions can be deepened and broadened by attention to many of these founding disputes and their appropriation and misappropriation by later thinkers.

I am well aware of the suspicion that must greet any attempt to suggest that the things most important, that most need considering in the vast modernity issue, can be found in the rather arcane details of the Kant–Hegel relation and in Hegel's project. No amount of complaining that this suspicion largely stems from the inadequate versions of Kant and Hegel we've been accustomed to will allay such suspicions. It is the idea itself of recovery or revision that seems so utopian. For better or worse, many reason, we are just too well launched on this trip to worry all that much about how we got launched, and if the boat seems to be leaking we've just got to fix it one plank at a time, and not worry about the nature of the boat and its ultimate seaworthiness.

[handwritten margin note: asy- march of hist.]

This comforting Neurathean image is, however, highly misleading (as misleading as Heidegger's famous image of being simply "thrown" into the world). It assumes that we have some sense of where we are headed, or, if we do, whether that destination is preferable to any other, and that we should simply give up once and for all contestations about who is steering and under what authority or how work on the ship should be organized. Once such issues are raised and properly formulated, as they must be, just "going on as we do" will, I expect, seem an indefensibly smug response.

Part One

THE ORIGINAL OPTIONS:
KANT VERSUS HEGEL

2

KANT ON THE SPONTANEITY OF MIND

I

In the *Critique of Pure Reason*, Kant refers often and with no apparent hesitation or sense of ambiguity to the mind (*das Gemüt*).[1] He does so not only in his justly famous destruction of rationalist proofs of immaterialism, but throughout his own positive, transcendental account in the Transcendental Aesthetic and Transcendental Analytic. In the first edition of the *Critique*, he even proposed what he adventurously called a "transcendental psychology," and, although this strange discipline seemed to disappear in the second edition, he left in that edition all his frequent references to forms "lying in the mind," and to the mind, or the self, or the subject of experience, or the ego, doing this or that. Curiously, though, despite an extensive secondary literature, there is in that literature relatively little discussion of what these expressions, in a proper, strictly Kantian sense, are supposed to refer to. There are two imaginative, extremely suggestive articles by Sellars, some hints at connections with eighteenth-century psychology offered by Weldon,

---

1 References to the first *Critique* are to the standard first and second edition pagination. I have used R. Schmidt's edition of the *Kritik der reinen Vernunft* (Hamburg: Felix Meiner Verlag, 1954). Translations are from Norman Kemp Smith's *Kant's Critique of Pure Reason* (New York: St. Martin's, 1929), except where an alteration has been made and indicated by a *T* after the page citation.

a tenebrous book by Heidemann, and some recent attention to the general issue of "Kant's theory of mind" by Ameriks and Kitcher.[2]

By and large, however, if the question is, within the limits of transcendental philosophy, What should we say about the nature of the mind? or even more simply, What are thoughts? many commentators have rested content with the following answers, all clearly present in the text: (i) We do not know what thoughts or selves are "in themselves"; for all we know, they could, in themselves, be either material or immaterial, or neither (the noumenal ignorance thesis); (ii) as empirical events, thoughts or subjects of thoughts are known, like all empirical events, as "phenomena," as objects of experience. In this case, the events are primarily contents of inner sense, in time but not in space, and, like all alterations, they take place in "conformity with the law of cause and effect." Thus, empirically, a dualism of material and mental is true (the empirical dualism thesis); or (iii) transcendentally, thoughts and the subjects of thoughts are miscategorized if thought to raise any metaphysical problems. They are just "formal conditions for the possibility of experience"; for example, the logical subject of experience is just "that which experiences" and should not be construed as a type of being (the metaphysical neutrality thesis).[3]

The question I want to ask in the following is simply whether these well-established Kantian positions exhaust what Kant has to say about the "I that thinks," or the mind. I am especially interested in how we are to understand (iii), particularly in whether the distinction between the logical (or "transcendental logical") and the metaphysical is strictly adhered to by Kant himself. The main motivation for raising this issue is that when Kant defines thinking (for example, when it is opposed to intuiting) he not only makes use of such synonyms as "understanding," and "apperceiving" and "judging" and "synthesizing," he also calls thinking "spontaneity," and the issue I want

---

2 I discuss the work by Sellars, Heidemann, Ameriks, and Kitcher in the following notes. See also T. D. Weldon, *Kant's Critique of Pure Reason*, 2d ed. (Oxford: Clarendon Press, 1958). (Since this article was written in 1984, interest in Kant's philosophy of mind has grown significantly. A fuller survey of the literature would now also have to include, at least, Patricia Kitcher, *Kant's Transcendental Psychology* (Oxford: Oxford University Press, 1990); Thomas C. Powell, *Kant's Theory of Self-Consciousness* (Oxford: Clarendon Press, 1990); Wayne Waxman, *Kant's Model of the Mind* (New York: Oxford University Press, 1991), and Andrew Brook, *Kant and the Mind* (New York: Cambridge University Press, 1994).)

3 It should be noted that metaphysical neutrality by itself does not entail noumenal ignorance. We might think it possible to present an epistemology that involves no commitment to a position on what kind of thing thinks, without at all thinking that nothing can be said about that issue, as a separate topic.

to pursue is why he uses that term and what conclusions, logical and/or metaphysical, he draws from it.

After all, that characterization certainly leaps out from this list of equivalent terms. In many other contexts it is clear that for Kant a spontaneous activity is always a "self-causing" activity, as, for example, in the case of the "unconditioned causality" of freedom, also called the "causality of reason" (B561 = A446, where a cause of "absolute spontaneity" is said to begin "of itself"). Or, when God's intuition is said to be "spontaneous," Kant means that it "creates" (a sufficient but not necessary condition of spontaneity) the instances or objects it intuits; it is independent of any causal interaction with such particulars.[4] At the very least, then, the term suggests that, if it is logically necessary that the thinking involved in knowledge be a kind of spontaneity in order to be such a thinking, then although we may not know what a thinking subject is noumenally, we do know that whatever it is, it must be capable of spontaneous activity. And if that is true, then some recently suggested links between Kant's formal/material approach to epistemology and contemporary functionalism (or more broadly the software/hardware approach) cannot be made, at least not given any current hardware candidates.[5] That is, if the formal conditions of knowledge require that the content of cognition be actively conceptualized in a way that is finally, at some stage, causally independent of the causally produced reception of that material, and of any initial causal-series processing of that information, then a thinker cannot really be a causal system, whatever the system is made of. So the relevant questions are, Does Kant claim that epistemic mental activity must be spontaneous? Does he draw any substantive conclusions from that claim? Is he entitled to these conclusions?

Finally, there is another, very different but equally important reason for

---

4 Cf. *Kritik der Urteilskraft* (hereafter *KU*), in *Kants gesammelte Schriften,* Königlich Preussischen Akademie der Wissenschaften (Berlin: de Gruyter, 1922) (hereafter *AA,*), V, p. 406; *Critique of Judgment* (hereafer *CJ*), trans. J. H. Bernard (New York: Hafner, 1968), p. 254.

5 One of the first suggestions about such an approach can be found in Wilfrid Sellars, "Metaphysics and the Concept of a Person," in *The Logical Way of Doing Things,* ed. by Karel Lambert (New Haven: Yale University Press, 1969), pp. 219–52. See also Patricia Kitcher "Kant's Real Self," in *Kant on Self and Nature,* ed. by Allen Wood (Ithaca: Cornell University Press, 1985), pp. 111–45; and, for a much broader point of view, Daniel Dennett, "Artificial Intelligence as Philosophy and as Psychology," in *Brainstorms* (Cambridge: MIT Press, 1978), pp. 109–26, especially 111 and 122–6. I might note that a fuller demonstration of why Kant cannot be enlisted into Dennett's project would have to take account of what he says in ch. 5 of this book, his argument that the restriction of artificial intelligence (AI) to some form of mechanism is, given Church's theorem, no real restriction. See also p. 83.

pursuing the implications of the spontaneity characterization. I shall not be able to pursue the issue here in any detail, but it should at least be noted that it is by far the most important Kantian notion picked up and greatly expanded by later German Idealists. For Fichte, Schelling, and Hegel, it was Kant's characterization of the subject as spontaneously apperceptive that, more than anything else, convinced them that Kant had not simply destroyed the classical metaphysical tradition, but had begun a new kind of "philosophy of subjectivity," and the a priori restrictions set by such an apperceiving subject for what could count as an object of knowledge.[6] Primarily because such a thematic link has not received much of a contemporary hearing, there has been little carryover from the recent extensive attention to nearly all aspects of Kantian philosophy into post-Kantian areas. After Kant, it would seem, we face only romantic metaphysics, and uncritical speculation, as little up to its Kantian heritage as neo-Platonist theology was to Plato. So, for example, when Hegel remarks in his *Differenzschrift* "That the world is the product of the freedom of intelligence, is the determinate and express principle of idealism,"[7] his remark can seem like a distorted application of only a vaguely Kantian idea (the spontaneity of thinking). Part of what I want to begin to show is that the application is not distorted, and the idea is genuinely Kantian.

II

Although there are frequent references in the *Critique of Pure Reason* to the spontaneity of the mind, there is no independent discussion of that issue. The first definition of the term is typical.

> If the receptivity of our mind, its power of receiving representations in so far as it is in any wise affected, is to be entitled sensibility, then the mind's power of

6 This relation is quite an important subtheme in Ingeborg Heidemann's *Spontaneität und Zeitlichkeit* (Cologne: Kölner Universitäts-Verlag, 1958), although at times she makes Kant far more of a "dialectical" and "historical" thinker than he is, cf. pp. 13–14, 86, and 260. The issue pursued here – Kant's case against the possible phenomenality of the transcendental subject, and his denial that such a subject could be a causal system – is also an important element of her discussion, but is couched in terms of what she calls the *necessary* "duality" of "temporality" and "spontaneity," what she eventually calls the "Distanz der Spontaneität zur Zeitlichkeit," p. 222.

7 G. W. F. Hegel, *Gesammelte Werke* (hereafter *GeWe*), IV (Hamburg: Felix Meiner Verlag, 1968) (*Differenzschrift* [hereafter *D*]), p. 43; *The Difference Between Fichte's and Schelling's System of Philosophy* (hereafter *Diff*), trans. H. S. Harris and Walter Cerf (Albany: SUNY Press, 1977), p. 130.

producing representations from itself (*Vorstellungen selbst hervorzubringen*), the spontaneity of knowledge, should be called the understanding. (B75 = A51)

Later, concepts are said to be "based on the spontaneity of thought," sensible intuitions on the receptivity of impressions (B93 = A68). What is typical of such passages is that Kant leaves unexplained the meaning of such phrases as "producing representations from itself" and concepts being "based on" spontaneity, apparently confident that the contrast with receptivity clarifies what he's trying to get at. This contrast appears to commit Kant to the claim not only that our intellectual faculties cannot be receptive (no Aristotelian *nous pathetikos*), but that there is some kind of necessary discontinuity between the receptivity of sensation and the activity of thinking about sensory matter. Sensory impressions, it would appear, cannot be said simply to engage the mind in the sense of producing representations, with these representations subsequently producing or giving rise to "ideas." *We* (any thinker) produce something "from ourselves," and it is this initially somewhat metaphorical notion of spontaneity that Kant introduces so casually.

It is the nature of the epistemic claim that our minds are spontaneous in knowledge that looks so abruptly asserted. It is not, strictly speaking, a logical claim in the sense in which Kant usually uses his notion of transcendental–logical "formality." It may be a logically necessary attribute of the concept of experience that all experience involve both concepts and intuitions, that nothing can be a representation of mind unless it can be united synthetically with other representations, and that such synthetic unification cannot go on unless there are pure rules for such activity. But if in such arguments the notions of concept, synthetic unification, and application of pure concepts are to be truly formal, we should be neutral about such issues as whether the occurrence of sensations alone causally produces a certain conceptual activity (a specific unifying activity) or whether "we" do, in some causally independent way. All that should be important is that a connecting of representations *goes on,* a uniting not completely attributable merely to the occurrence of sensory impressions. Of course, if the spontaneity characteristic only means to refer to the necessity for some contribution by the subject over and above sensory receptivity, whatever the nature of this activity, then there is no problem to discuss. But, as befits the much stronger sounding implications of the term *spontaneity*, Kant struggles to find a way to express it so that it is stronger, and yet consistent with the tripartite division sketched previously.

Perhaps the most involuted claim occurs at a well-noted note at B158:

Now since I do not have another self-intuition which gives the determining in me (I am conscious only of the spontaneity of it) prior to the act of determination, as time does in the case of the determinable, I cannot determine my existence as that of a self-active being; all that I can do is to represent to myself the spontaneity of my thought, that is, of the determination; and my existence is still only determinable sensibly, that is, as the existence of an appearance. But it is owing to this spontaneity that I entitle myself an intelligence.

Kant seems aware in this passage that claiming the mind to be spontaneous involves much more than claiming that something must be contributed to experience beyond the reception of impressions. In this language, the spontaneity claim certainly appears to be a "determination of my existence" and it is against this obvious impression that Kant is working. But in doing so, he just muddies the waters. I do *not* have an "intuition" of my active "determining" capacities (although why I do not must await a later discussion), but I *am* "conscious of the spontaneity of it." What is that, particularly if it is an instance of *consciousness,* not a merely possible representation (as occurs, for example, in my representation of practical autonomy)? Further, I cannot determine my existence as a self-active (a nice Fichtean word here, *selbsttätigen*) being, but I am a self-active being. I can call myself an intelligence because that is what I am, although how I know I am, and what exactly that means, remain obscure.

At other points, Kant seems quite willing to wander far from the strict divide of formal–logical versus substantive. This passage from the *Antinomies* in which Kant seems to make quite a substantial claim about "man" (*Mensch*) is perhaps the strongest indication of such non-formalist temptations.

Only man, however, who knows all the rest of nature solely through his senses, knows himself also through simple apperception, and this indeed in acts and inner determinations which he cannot regard as impression of the senses, and is indeed to himself on the one hand, phenomenon, but on the other hand, namely in respect of certain faculties (because their action cannot at all be ascribed to the receptivity of sensibility), a simply intelligible object. (B574-5 = A546-7, T)[8]

Again the problem is the status of the claim that our being apperceptive beings establishes that we are "intelligible objects" or an *Intelligenz*.

Another indication of how far he is willing to go to make this claim, and how many of his own distinctions he is willing to hedge in order to make it, is

---

8 The original for the key concluding phrase is "ein bloss intelligibiler Gegenstand."

given (again in a footnote) at B422n. The whole footnote is an attempt to differentiate his own position from that of Descartes, and the main issue concerns what Kant regards as Descartes's "inference" from "I think" to "I exist." In denying that there could be such an inference, Kant is called on to present what he does think is given in what he admits is an "empirical proposition," "I think." This "I think," he says, "expresses an undetermined [unbestimmt] empirical intuition, i.e., perception (and therewith proves that sensation, which accordingly belongs to sensibility, already lies at the ground of this existential proposition)" (T).

Kant does not stop to explain why such a proposition expresses an undetermined empirical intuition if a self-perception really is involved. Presumably, such an inner sense could only be, determinately, of me. Instead he goes on to say that the category of existence in this existence claim ("I exist thinking") is not really a category. What then is an "indeterminate perception," presumably involved in all spontaneous apperception? It is "only something real [etwas Reales] that is given" and given only to thought in general, and so not an appearance, nor a thing in itself (noumenon) but as "something which actually exists, and which in the proposition 'I think' is denoted as such." This same suggestion of a fourth alternative to the transcendental position on mind (neither strictly phenomenal, noumenal, nor formal–logical) is hinted again a few pages later where Kant says that "in the consciousness of myself in mere thought I am the being itself [das Wesen selbst] although from this nothing is given to me" (B429).[9]

Similar, relatively confident references to what appear to be the metaphysical presuppositions of his epistemology also surface in the Prolegomena, when he writes, "When an appearance is given to us, we are still quite free as to how we should judge the matter,"[10] and in various Reflexionen, such as "In order to judge objectively, universally, that is, apodictically, reason must be free of subjectively determining grounds; for if they did determine reason, the judgment would be as it is only contingently, namely because of subjective causes."[11]

---

9 This passage has been the occasion for quite a number of rather speculative interpretations of the Critique on self-knowledge. See Heidemann, all of sect. 10, 207 ff.; Heinz Heimsoeth, "Persönlichkeitsbewusstsein und Ding an sich in der kantischen Philosophie," Studien zur Philosophie Immanuel Kants, Metaphysische Ursprung und Ontologische Grundlagen (Cologne: Kölner Universitäts-Verlag, 1956), pp. 229–55 and Gottfried Martin, Kant's Metaphysics and Theory of Science, trans. P. G. Lucas (Manchester: Manchester University Press, 1955), pp. 176–81.

10 AA, IV, p. 290. Prolegomena to Any Future Metaphysics (hereafter P), trans. L. W. Beck (Indianapolis: Bobbs-Merrill, 1950), p. 38.

11 Reflexion 5413, AA, XVIII, p. 176; see also 5441, 182.

Finally, to cite a passage that claims much the same thing as the B474–5 passage quoted earlier, but with all the hedging gone, there is this claim from the 1785 *Groundwork:* "Man now finds in himself a faculty by means of which he differentiates himself from all other things, indeed even from himself in so far as he is affected by objects, and that faculty is reason. This, as pure self-activity (*Selbsttätigkeit*) is elevated even above the understanding . . . with respect to ideas, reason shows itself to be such a pure spontaneity that it far transcends anything which sensibility can provide it."[12]

III

So much for many of the most intriguing, even if confusing, passages on spontaneity. I have been suggesting that Kant's apparent hesitancy in these passages stems from his uncertainty about the status of his claims about our spontaneous mind within the established transcendental triad. I want to start now considering what kinds of problems such remarks cause for that schema by considering the two most obvious issues that arise. Both could be considered instances of what I have tried to argue elsewhere is a very broad Kantian problem – the purported formality of transcendental knowledge itself.[13] But in this context, both issues can be raised specifically with respect to the spontaneity characterization.

The first reason for Kant's apparent discomfort with claims about the nature of the thinking subject could be methodological. That is, one reason why Kant might well be hesitant to count any result of transcendental reflection on the conditions for the possibility of experience as knowledge of the thinking subject, or mind (as an object of knowledge), however mentalistic his own language, would be his clear belief that knowledge of any object, including the subject of experience, presupposes transcendental conditions. Such *conditions* cannot be counted as properties of the "real thing which thinks" without vicious circularity. So, at B422:

> Therefore, the subject of the categories cannot, through the fact that it thinks, arrive at a concept of itself as object of the categories; for in order to think them, its pure self-consciousness, which is what ought to have been explained, must lie at the ground. (T)

---

12 *AA*, IV, p. 452. *Foundations of the Metaphysics of Morals* (hereafter *F*), trans. L. W. Beck (New York: Bobbs-Merrill, 1969), p. 80. Kant is here referring to a distinction he sometimes makes between the spontaneity of the understanding, which, however spontaneous, must still deal with the content of intuition, and the more unrestricted, purely spontaneous self-legislation of reason. Cf. sects. IV and V of the Introduction to the *Critique of Judgment.*
13 Robert Pippin, *Kant's Theory of Form* (New Haven: Yale University Press, 1981).

So, the nature of the subject of experience, we ought still to say, really is unknowable.

If this is what is making Kant uneasy, one might respond to it as Patricia Kitcher recently has. She claims that the passage quoted here confuses the "order of proof with what we might call the order of conceivability."[14] We cannot *know* that all human experience is apperceptive by relying on the necessity for categories in experience (and so the necessity of apperception to explain the possibility of categories), because we can only know that the structure of human experience is categorial if we already know, and rely on, the fact that human experience is apperceptive. "None of this implies that we do not use the categories in thinking about thinking, however. In fact, if Kant is right, then we must use the categories in thinking about thinking because the only way we can think at all is through the categories."[15] What Kitcher is out to show throughout her article is that Kant should not have said either that the subject of knowledge was unknowable or that it must be a non-phenomenal subject. And so, in the preceding, she is trying to block possible Kantian methodological concerns about how a subject could know itself if such knowledge always presupposed "a subject."

But I see no evidence that Kant was worried (mistakenly) about how transcendental reflection could arrive at a knowledge of the structure of all thought and knowledge, if such reflection had to make use of such a structure. The fact that in the *Amphiboly* such reflection by a subject on its own sources of knowledge is just what the *Critique* is said to be doing, and Kant's frequent claims that, in philosophical knowledge "reason is occupied with nothing but itself" (B708 = A680), belie that view of Kant's worry. Kant is not worried about how a subject could attain knowledge of the subjective structure of experience; what he wants to make sure we understand is that this knowledge should not be taken to be knowledge about what an experience is. Thus the B422 passage only reminds us again that the subject referred to in transcendental reflection is not, in any usual sense, an object of knowledge.

Moreover, apart from the issue of transcendental reflection, the passage and several of the others quoted so far clearly point to a second kind of worry Kant has, and it is this worry that is of much more interest for the spontaneity issue. When he speaks of the subject's possibly being able to "arrive at a concept of itself," or of a possible "self-intuition," or of the "indeterminate" empirical intuition involved in any "I think . . ." he is point-

14 Kitcher, "Kant's Real Self," p. 124.
15 Ibid.

ing to the fact that his own theory of experience involves the mind in a relation to itself in all experience that would seem to tell us a great deal about what a subject of experience is, especially about what it cannot be. This is, I want to suggest, Kant's motivation for so often denying that the subject of experience can simply be (that is, only be) phenomenal.

Since this is the issue of Kitcher's article, I can introduce this point by reference again to her strategy. Suppose the question is, Why isn't Kant willing to say that the "self" he is always talking about in the Transcendental Analytic is simply a phenomenal self, about which philosophical analysis may indeed discover necessary properties and capacities, even though it (analysis) cannot tell how these capacities are instantiated? Kitcher discusses at length why Kant might have been so unwilling, although the main reasons she suggests are the familiar ones. The first is a more sophisticated version of the methodology problem just mentioned. Since Kant seemed to believe that the subject of experience was responsible for the phenomenal world (there being such a subject is what makes the world phenomenal), he would find it impossible to consider that subject itself "really" phenomenal. Second, she discusses all the evidence that Kant, for reasons connected with the presuppositions of his moral theory, wanted to find a way to say that the real subject of experience is non-phenomenal, a thing in itself.

Now, what the spontaneity passages highlight, I believe, is a much more fundamental reason why Kant wanted to deny that the subject of experience was empirical or phenomenal, although, as already indicated, this reason also conflicts with the claims of metaphysical neutrality.[16] Kant, that is, surely did believe that the subject of experience, a thinker, could be phenomenal; could be considered as a possible object of empirical knowledge (cf. the empirical dualism thesis). And he certainly believed that there were qualities of any possible subject of experience that we did not come to know empirically, but by philosophical analysis (or "reflection," to use his term). So far, none of this is inconsistent with Kitcher's analysis. But what the

---

16 Moreover, there is fairly persuasive evidence that Kant fully realized after 1785 that he could get no moral mileage out of his transcendental philosophy, even though he continued to use such non-phenomenal terms as *Spontaneität* in the second edition of the *Critique*. However, establishing that, as a matter of fact, Kant did not argue against the possible phenomenality of the transcendental subject because he thought he thereby would establish some sort of noumenal agency does not of itself address Kitcher's central and quite appropriate question: Why did Kant not identify the transcendental and phenomenal subject, while admitting the difference between transcendental and empirical claims *about* this subject?

spontaneity passages reveal is that Kant also thought that such analysis revealed that there was one feature of any such subject that could never be the kind of property a phenomenal subject could have – spontaneity. (All phenomenal subjects are necessarily and completely parts of causal series.) And, as many of the previously quoted passages have already indicated (especially B422n.), Kant is eager to insist as well that proving in this way that the subject of experience cannot be exclusively phenomenal is not equivalent to proving that it is a thing in itself, and should not be inconsistent with the claim that the self is completely unknowable. But the potential violation of this classificatory schema is, I am arguing, the true source of his hedging.

IV

Understanding Kant's argument for this non-phenomenality claim involves coming to terms with another of his names for the spontaneity of thinking, introduced at B132. The representing or "act of spontaneity" that "cannot be regarded as belonging to sensibility," he calls "pure apperception." With that equivalence introduced, he can then move on to introduce the "highest" principle of knowledge, the transcendental unity of apperception. (A few pages later, Kant reminds us again of the equivalence between thinking, an act of spontaneity, and apperception by claiming, "Indeed, the faculty of apperception is the understanding itself" [B134n.].) Accordingly, the first task in uncovering Kant's mostly implicit argument for the spontaneity characterization involves understanding his view of thinking as "apperceiving."

Kant's clearest expression of the apperception thesis occurs in the same passage where the preceding definitions above occur, section 16 of the second edition of Deduction. There Kant states and explains the claim that "It must be possible for the 'I think' to accompany all my representations" (B131), and goes on to assert that "The principle of apperception is the highest principle in the whole sphere of human knowledge" (B135). I shall take this "absolutely fundamental" highest principle to assert that all human experience is ineliminably reflexive. It is reflexive because, according to Kant, whenever I am conscious of anything, I also "apperceive" that it is I who am thus conscious. And all the problems arise from trying to understand what he means by this. He at least means that, in any, say, remembering, thinking, or imagining, while the object of my intending is some state of affairs or other, I am also aware as I intend that what I am doing *is* an act of remembering, thinking, or imagining, and that I bring to these acts a subject identical with the subject of prior acts of intending. My asserting that *S is P* is not an assertion of mine unless I am aware that I am asserting, not entertaining the possibility of *S is P,* and no such complex judgment, requiring, as Kant thinks he can show, continuity over time is possible unless there is one continuous subject of experience over time, aware of its continuity in any conscious act. This apperceptive characteristic does not mean that the fact that I am perceiving rather than imagining is itself directly attended to, but that such an awareness is an inseparable component of *what* it is consciously to perceive, imagine, remember, and so on. Or: in trying to recollect the name of a friend who is approaching me, I am aware that I, the subject of all past instances of contact with the friend, am trying to recollect, without a second-order judgment, "I am recollecting," occurring. One could say that without my continuous act of recollecting somehow being "held in mind" the pursuits undertaken within that context would be unintelligible. (Or: I can "consciously follow" a rule without "always consciously applying" a rule. This must be possible if any rule following that is not an explicit constant application is to be distinguished, as it should, from behavior that ought to be explained by reference to natural laws.)[17]

Admittedly, at this point, a variety of thorny, long-debated problems arise. It is difficult, apart from a major commentary, to develop this line of interpretation adequately, as a plausible view of the issue itself, and as what Kant meant by the apperception condition. I should note, however, that this claim for an inherent reflexivity in consciousness should be distinguished from two other possible approaches that the cited passages have been taken to support. The first, most famously identified with Strawson, attempts an "austere," non-idealistic interpretation of the *Critique* by construing the Deduction argument to be based only on the logical possibility of the self-ascription of all my representations.[18] This approach, built around the problem of skepticism, makes no general claim about the nature of consciousness or "subjective conditions for the possibility of experience," but

---

17 Since apperception is a component of consciousness, or, as Kant says, the "vehicle" of concepts, and not itself a mental act accompanying consciousness (or the mental act that is consciousness), Kant is not committed to various claims about the self-conscious transparency of mental life, or its incorrigibility, and so forth. He is not, therefore, subject to the kind of complaints offered against his theory by Hans Georg Hoppe in *Synthesis bei Kant* (Berlin: de Gruyter, 1983), pp. 113–75. Indeed, the claim for the necessity of such an implicit self-construal in cognitive consciousness opens wide the door to realizing the profoundly mediated (and so corrigible) character of conscious activity, a fact that becomes the methodological fulcrum of Hegel's *Phenomenology of Spirit.*
18 P. F. Strawson, *The Bounds of Sense* (London: Methuen, 1966).

seeks a transcendental argument to show how the possibility of self-ascription requires the objectivity of certain pure concepts.

This interpretation has many problems, much discussed in other contexts, not the least of which is that it confuses just where and how the issue of skepticism about the external world arises for Kant, and so misconstrues the Deduction as a way of arguing Kant himself only introduces in the Refutation of Idealism. But at least the claims themselves, supposedly extracted from Kant, are plausible claims. At the other end of the extreme in interpretations about the role of apperception in the Deduction is the so-called conflation interpretation, the claim that Kant is somehow arguing that consciousness *is* self-consciousness, that in any conscious intending, I am aware of my own activity of creating or imposing my order on the world.[19] There are passages (e.g., A108, A116) that seem to support such a view, but almost all of them tend to drop out in the second edition, where there is a good deal more stress on the implicitly apperceptive character of all consciousness, and much less on some putative awareness of my identity and my constituting activity in every conscious representing. In that edition, instead, we find passages like "As *my* representations (even if I am not conscious of them as such) they must conform to the condition under which alone they *can* stand together in one universal self-consciousness, because otherwise they would not all without exception belong to me" (B132–3). In terms of this passage, the phrase "even if I am not conscious of them *as such*" indicates that Kant takes himself to be avoiding the conflation thesis, and the claim that *all* my representations must be subject to the conditions of "universal self-consciousness" indicates he is making a claim much stronger than the austere interpretation allows (i.e., he is not relying merely on what is required in any case of self-consciousness or self-ascription). As indicated earlier, the reason that all my representations must conform to such conditions is that consciousness itself is inherently even if not explicitly self-conscious.

Admittedly, relying on Kant's discussion of apperception to explain his characterization of thinking as spontaneous can appear a classic case of the

---

19 Dieter Henrich, *Identität und Objektivität* (Heidenberg: Carn Winter Universitäts-Verlag, 1976). Ulrich Pothast, in *Über einige Fragen der Selbstbeziehung* (Frankfurt a.M.: Klostermann, 1971), has tried to argue that Kant was simply ambiguous about whether apperception was an explicit self-perception or the implicit form of all thinking, cf. p. 13. I am claiming that Kant rather clearly intended the latter option, and do not see how the passages Pothast cites as evidence of the former view (A342 and A343) support his reading, since they are clearly preparing the way for what rational psychologists believe.

obscure through the more obscure. Not only is the textual material scanty, but, whatever Kant means by insisting on the requirement that any "φ-ing *x*" involves "My taking myself to be φ-ing *x*," he does not feel compelled to argue for the connection. There are some indications, from his infrequent discussion of animal consciousness, that he does not regard this reflexivity to be a necessary condition of consciousness per se, but only of cognitive consciousness: that is, cases of intentional awareness that can be said to be, and to be experienced as, possibly true or false intendings. In such cases, Kant appears to believe it is criterial that we must be implicitly aware of our having "taken" the world to be such and such, and thereby of its possibly not being such and such. The veridicality of, say, our sensory perceptions must be able to be, at least in some weak sense, held open, in cognitive conscious- ness, and that feature of such consciousness requires, Kant appears certain, that consciousness be apperceptive.

Further, there are some clarifications about what the apperception thesis does not claim, indications that Kant does not want his position on my continuously taking up and uniting my experiences to be confused with cases of empirical self-awareness or attempts at self-identification. The "identity" Paralogism states the latter point clearly, insisting in a way similar to that used by contemporary Wittgensteineans on self-awareness, that I can be aware that I am φ-ing without knowing who I am, or even if I am *mistaken* about my identity.[20] The detailed discussion in the second edition Deduc- tion on the "apperception–inner sense" distinction, as we shall see in more detail shortly, makes the former point, less clearly, but equally strongly. Roughly, that claim is that any attending to my own thoughts as empirical events is a cognitive claim like any other, and so already presupposes my taking myself to be attending to, and making claims about, my mental states. In fact, marking out these differences among self-awareness, self- identification, and apperception, all rests on a similar claim, what one could call an insistence on the non-isolatability of "apperception" as an event, that apperception cannot be a relation between me and my thoughts that "oc- curs" in addition to the causal and/or intentional relation between my thoughts and what they represent. It is because of this non-isolatability that this apperceptive component of experience cannot be regarded as, say, an inference I make about what I am experiencing, or as a caused result of some state or series of mental states. So, one could perhaps imagine an

20 Cf. G. E. M. Anscombe, "The First Person," in *Mind and Language,* ed. by S. D. Guttenplan (Oxford: Oxford University Press, 1975), pp. 45–65. For an excellent counter, see S. Shoemaker, "Self-Reference and Self-Awareness," *Journal of Philosophy* 65 (1968): 555–68.

unusual example where I do not know, say, whether I am perceiving or hallucinating, and where I try to infer from the evidence what I am doing or undergoing, but even in that example what I originally experience already includes my apperception of being in an unfamiliar state, and no later judgment about what is the case could be said to "add" apperception to my experience. One way of stressing this would be to suggest, in a Chisolmean way, that this apperceptive feature of experience is "adverbial," that when I perceive, think, imagine, and so forth, I *apperceptively* perceive, think, imagine.[21]

V

My claim thus far has been that understanding Kant's characterization of thinking as apperceptive might be of some help in filling out the meaning of his other enigmatic synonym for thinking, *spontaneity*. In the last section, I presented a brief interpretation of the apperception claim that both makes the most sense of the many different, often conflicting, things Kant says about apperception, and would begin to connect up with the claim for spontaneity. We have already seen one indication of the latter connection. Kant holds that experience requires my taking up a manifold and uniting its elements in judgment. But the way he describes such a condition makes it very hard to describe it as a kind of mental state–activity that could be regarded as produced by some other mental state or by some interaction with objects. To revert to a well-known *Reflexion* about this issue, apperceptive thinking cannot be said to be an "experience" at all, but a necessary component of any possible experience of *objects*.[22] Thinking may indeed be empty without intuitions, but, Kant appears to be assuming, nothing about my having intuitions, or the characteristics of the intuitions, can be said to provide a matter-of-fact explanation for my taking myself to be experiencing (intuited) objects of this or that kind. That, he keeps trying to find a way to say, is something I must *do*.

---

21 Although in such an account apperception is a necessary condition for conscious (cognitive) perception, one should not conclude that the position thereby limits all sentient interaction to such conscious perception. There can indeed be all sorts of "nonapperceptive" ways in which information of a sort about the external world is received and processed. But, even if the perception of such information might affect behavior, the position holds that it would not be conscious perception.

22 *AA*, XVIII, pp. 318–19. Cf. also the helpful discussion of the passage in Henry Allison, *Kant's Transcendental Idealism* (New Haven: Yale University Press, 1984), pp. 276–8.

It is *this* view of apperception that is, I submit, behind such claims as the B574-5 assertion that the apperceptive faculty "cannot be ascribed to the receptivity of sensibility," and thereby renders us an "intelligible object." Kant is claiming not only that thinking is not a kind of sensibility (contra both, say, Locke and Leibniz) but that it cannot be said to owe its *occurring* to sensibility, and is therefore "spontaneous." A similar remark could be made about the B158n. passage that mentions spontaneity as the "determining" in experience, never the determinable.[23] Finally, it is this view of apperception and spontaneity that seems to be involved in one of the few arguments about the claim. Again in the second edition Deduction, Kant's way of arguing that apperception must be spontaneous – not finally due to intuition or to the mental events caused by intuitions – is that apperception must not be confused with "inner sense."

To understand what Kant means by this claim, something needs to be said about what he means by the notion of inner sense. This doctrine is one of the darkest in Kant, but its basic elements can be sketched in this context.[24] Kant, as we all know, argued that the human intellect can supply itself with no content, but must be supplied it "from without." But it is obvious that what thought is about need not just be an object of the five senses of the body, or in Kant's more general terms, an object of outer sense (although Kant did believe that the content of all thought is ultimately supplied by outer sense). We can also think about, perhaps even formulate causal laws about, our thoughts, perceptions, memories, wishes, dreams, and so on; or about the contents of inner sense. But it is still true, according to Kant, that

---

23 In his recent *Kant über Freiheit als Autonomie* (Frankfurt am M.: Klostermann, 1983), Gerold Prauss has attempted a new, reconstructive interpretation of the theory of activity that Kant, it is claimed, late in his career realized was at the foundation of and unified his accounts of "knowing" (*Erkennen*) and "acting" (*Handeln*). For Prauss, that theory (sometimes called a theory of spontaneity) involves a complicated analysis of the intentional, purposive (*absichtlich*) character of knowledge claims; their possible "succeeding" or "failing"; and the derived status of practical actions that "depend" on the results of such intendings. My interpretation differs from his in presenting the problem of apperception as more fundamental to the issue of spontaneity, and so freedom, than intention, and in arguing that the chief reason Kant was hesitant and often confused about developing such a unified theory explicitly was his realization that it would require massive alterations in his transcendental program itself, and not a pre-critical allegiance to the "purity" of theory (cf. p. 110). In general, Prauss, it seems to me, takes off *from* Kant's claims on the "freedom" or spontaneity of thinking, and omits discussing whether Kant was entitled to such metaphysical sounding claims, and if so, how they would square with transcendental idealism.

24 Kant's discussion in the *Critique* should be supplemented by what he says in his *Anthropologie*, AA, VII, sects. 7 and 24. See also the account in Allison, *Kant's Transcendental Idealism*, pp. 255–71; the extensive discussion by Karl Ameriks, *Kant's Theory of Mind* (Oxford: Clarendon Press, 1982), pp. 241–55; and my *Kant's Theory of Form*, pp. 172–82.

although we do not sense these contents in the usual or straightforward manner, we must still consider our apprehension of such contents as analogous to such sensing – that we possess an "inner" sense. What Kant means to stress by this analogy is, as he puts it, that we are still "passively" affected by our own inner states when we are aware of them, they are still part of a given manifold, passively apprehended under the form of inner sense, time, and thereby still "phenomena," not things in themselves.

Now Kant admits that this notion of being passively affected by ourselves, in any way that is analogous to sensibility, is quite odd, and he tries to defend the notion in various complex ways that are not relevant here. What is relevant is Kant's claim that we must not confuse inner sense and apperception, more particularly that we must not confuse being reflectively aware of the objects of inner sense with the apperception that, for Kant, is implicit in all acts of awareness. That is, even in such direct, reflective awareness of the contents of inner sense, the synthetic unity of such awareness (say, the mere awareness of succession) cannot itself be a "content" that is apprehended. It too must be effected by the mind's activity, and so in such awareness there is both direct perception of, say, a stream of images now, and implicit apperception that I am attending to my mental states. Thus what Kant is pointing to in the passages where he distinguishes apperception and inner sense is crucial for understanding all the spontaneity passages quoted earlier. That is, I can not only be aware of, say, drums and then a noise produced with them; I can also be aware, from another point of view, of the empirical events that occur in my mind in such awareness – the *sight* of the drums and the *hearing* of noise (i.e., I can date, catalogue, and perhaps causally relate these contents of inner sense). But I can also *think together* these events ("spontaneously") in thinking *that* the drums produced the noise (or that the sound followed the sight in my experience). *This* cannot just be a passive awareness of a state or doing of my mind, conceptualized in judgment, since it is a thought made possible by my active understanding in the first place.[25]

Now these passages also create their own problems, since Kant seems perfectly willing to admit that all the mental states and activities of the empirical subject (including, for example, its judgings) occur because caused to occur, and seems content to say that, on this empirical level, there is no problem in claiming I am caused to represent *S* by the physical interaction between my body and *S*.[26] This generous admission appears flatly

---

25 Of course, in some obvious sense, such a "thought that . . ." could *be* such an event; in that case though, such a "happening" could not count *thereby* as a judgment.

26 Cf., for example, Kant's remarks about complete causal determinism for all appearances,

inconsistent with the claim that mind must be represented as a *Spontaneität*. Moreover, the passages about spontaneity might be admitting what Sellars has called only a "relative spontaneity" of the mental.[27] That is, Kant could admit that many states of mental life are causally necessary consequences of antecedent states, where all that means is that, *relative* to that antecedent state, it could not have been the case that the system did not come to be in its subsequent state. The system need not be directly caused to be in that state by some immediately antecedent "*foreign* cause." The mind could have a set of dispositions, much like a computer program, that requires external input to start whirring away, but once started would be, *and might appear to itself to be,* only relatively spontaneous. Or: I might see that drum, then think of all sorts of things, perhaps even seem to myself to be searching my memory actively for some other datum, or even to be actively investigating some other phenomenon, and it may turn out that these events are caused, though not caused along the direct, one-to-one foreign cause model. Sellars even goes on to point out that if Kant's arguments against the rational psychologists are considered here (their confusing what is true of our representings of the self with what is true of the self) *and* the First Analogy, interpreted by Sellars to mean that "all change is a change of (portions of) material substance,"[28] then Kant has no reason to hold to his empirical dualism or metaphysical neutrality thesis, and should, at least empirically, have been a materialist (broadly construed).

However, apart from that issue, the problem of reconciling Kant's willingness to treat mental events causally, and his claims about spontaneity must still be faced. And Sellars's "relative spontaneity" will not do. Kant, from all the passages we have seen, *also* wants to argue for a non-relative or absolute spontaneity in apperception, one in principle not susceptible to this kind of indirectly causal analysis. His apperception–inner sense discussion points this out, in a way deeply characteristic of his epistemological turn – for instance, arguing that even such mental events as described previously must finally also be considered as known *to a subject* as caused, and this is only possible by virtue of that subject and its thoughts not being considered part of the original causal order. This supreme condition for knowledge can be

---

B573 = A545, and his references to the present and future, hoped-for status of empirical psychology as a science, B874 = A846/B877 = A849. His position on this issue is not without its ambiguities, however. See Michael Washburn, "Did Kant Have a Theory of Self-knowledge?" *Archiv für die Geschichte der Philosophie* 58 (1976): 40–56.

27 Wilfrid Sellars, ". . . this I or he or it (the thing) which thinks . . ." *Proceedings of the American Philosophical Association* 14 (September 1971): 20.

28 Ibid., pp. 14–15.

called absolute spontaneity because Kant takes it as criterial for knowing whether this sequence (again, one of Sellars's relative spontaneity sequences) *is* a causal sequence that I be able to decide whether it is or not, to be able to distinguish objective from subjective succession, and this condition could not be satisfied if I were simply caused to represent some succession as objective. (That could occur, but it would not be *judging*.) Or, to invoke a limited version of the noumenal ignorance thesis, even if that (as a Sellarsian sequence) were true of all mental activity, I could not be said to *know* its truth, and in that sense, the sequence could not count as an object of knowledge, but as a non-knowable noumenal relation between a noumenal subject and things in themselves. Of course, some state or series of states in a causal system could be said to have truth conditions. But Kant would clearly challenge any claim that such conditions could constitute the state's being a case of knowing, or "empirical experience." The latter requires an explanation of how a representing or judging could represent an object or state of affairs independently of knowing whether the truth conditions are satisfied. For this to be possible, Kant argues, the judging must be self-conscious, not just another in a series of causally produced states.

Finally, this emphasis on the necessity of the spontaneity condition (as a condition of the possibility of knowledge, as opposed to causally produced mental states that, it might happen, correctly correspond to what is the case) also makes unlikely reconstructions of the synthetic unity of apperception claim that make it more consistent with recent functionalist research programs, that is, like the one offered in another article by Kitcher. She argues that we can recast Kant's claims about synthesis "in modern terminology," as

M1 and M2 stand in the relation of *synthesis*	$= def$	M1 is the synthetic product of M2, or M2 is the synthetic product of M1, or M1 and M2 are synthesized.

Or, "Put more simply, the relation of synthesis among mental states is a relation of contentual dependence."[29] On this view, then, the necessity for apperception or the "I think . . ." refers to the general anti-Humean point that representations, in order to be my representations, must be regarded as

29 This is the summary version of her thesis presented in "Kant's Real Self," 113. For a full exposition of her interpretation, see Patricia Kitcher, "Kant on Self-Identity," *Philosophical Review* 91 (January 1982): 41–72.

"belonging to a contentually interconnected system of mental states, an I that thinks."

The contrast with the "spontaneity" view of apperception is, I assume, clear-cut. On the latter view, there *can* indeed be a relation of existential dependence among mental states, such that a later (M2) could not be a mental state of a subject unless an earlier had occurred (M1), and psychology might eventually determine which kinds of such dependence there are. But on the spontaneity view, nothing about that relation of dependence accounts for M2's being a *representation of an object.* The dependence of M2's occurrence on other mental states is one thing, but M2's being a representation of, say, *m* is quite another. For that to be explained, I must be said to *take* the individual representation *to be* in a connection with other representations, or possible representations, as a condition of such possible intentionality. Or, for a judgmental representing to be an epistemic claim ("objective" in Kant's language), I must take up the contents of intuition and the mental states that can be said to be produced by such intuitions, and *make* such a claim. *It* cannot both be said simply to occur in a relation of existential dependence on other mental states, and to be "objective" (possibly true or false) representing of mind, unless I so "take" it. (Put a different way, even if it is empirically true that A causes both the representation B *and* my representation that A caused B [in my mental life], there would still be no knowable connection between the last representation and the first two unless I "take it" that the "A" and "B" of the last representation *were* the A and B that I had experienced and that a claim about *them* was being made.)

VI

All of which raises the question: If Kant is denying that apperceiving could ever be construed as a matter-of-fact or empirical relation among mental states (or as completely "instantiated" in a causal system of some kind), if he is arguing that spontaneity is a necessary property of any thinking subject, what could this be but a claim about our non-phenomenal natures, our noumenal selves, and what does that do to the noumenal ignorance thesis? I have been suggesting that the claims collected previously about spontaneity, and the scattered arguments in favor of it, do offer a claim about necessary features of any "subject of experience," but that such a claim does not violate Kant's restriction that we do not know our substantial "selves," when "self" is considered apart from all relation to finite conditions of knowability. These arguments could be said to admit a non-noumenal relativization of the spontaneity claim to "subject qua possible knowing subject," and so can be said not to violate that restriction on knowledge of the subject simply as it is in itself, even if all this does complicate Kant's official statements of the metaphysical neutrality thesis. (And, to recall an earlier point, understanding the status of this claim as a claim about what normative commitments and capacities are necessary in order for anyone to count as the subject of one's thoughts and deed, and not as a claim about a thinking being or substance, is all a necessary introduction to understanding later Idealist reflections on the subject, and to seeing them as following in this Kantian spirit, rather than as violating the noumenal restriction everywhere with talk of "egos," "absolutes," and "spirits.")[30]

However, coming up with a more positive way of explaining the transcendental status of these claims does invariably create problems within Kant's triadic separation of ways of talking about mind, and these should be noted and addressed. For one thing, there is ample evidence that Kant often thought one way to resolve the ambiguities was just to state flat out that the transcendental subject *was* the noumenal self. Perhaps his most famous such statement is the *Reflexion*, "The soul in transcendental apperception is *substantia noumenon*, hence it has no permanence in time, since this belongs only to objects in space."[31] The same identification between the "self proper, as it exists in itself," with "the transcendental subject" occurs in the *Critique* at B520 = A492. But this occasional identification has so many problems (many trenchantly pointed out by Strawson)[32] that it cannot (and, I have been arguing, need not) have been Kant's considered position. To cite the most obvious problem, it is completely inconsistent with the continually invoked anti-rationalist strategy of the Paralogisms. After all, the achievement of that justly praised section of the *Critique* was to show that

---

30 To be sure, this issue of Kant's positive philosophy of subjectivity was widely influential in the German tradition, even beyond Kant's Idealist successors. Its legacy is apparent in any number of contexts. Cf., for example, this typical claim by Alfred Bäumler: "Nach der *Kritik der reinen Vernunft* gibt es keinen mundus intelligibilis mehr. Aber es gibt eine rein intellektuelle Synthesis. Der Substanzenbegriff des noumenon hat sich in einer Funktionsbegriff verwandelt. Im Begriff der reinen intellektuellen Synthesis, dem Urbild der Kategorien, erkennen wir die letzte Sublimierung der Verstandeswelt im Gegensatz zur Sinnenwelt." *Kants Kritik der Urteilskraft; Ihre Geschichte und Systematic*, Band 1: *Das Irrationalitätsproblem in der Aesthetik und Logik des 18. Jahrhunderts bis zur Kritik der Urteilskraft* (Halle: Niemeyer, 1923), p. 346. I think the basic point expressed here is correct, but that Bäumler (and Heidemann) greatly confuse their own case by adopting a "noumenalist" language to refer to the subject's activity, and so they perpetuate the notion that post-Kantian idealism requires a pre-critical metaphysics.
31 *Reflexion* 6001, *AA*, XVIII, pp. 420–1.
32 Strawson, *Bounds of Sense*, pp. 248 ff.

(i) I am indeed aware of all my thoughts as one and all *my* thoughts, as belonging to one subject of experience (in the sense of: I could not doubt that they were all my thoughts, that some might be somebody else's),

but that (i) is not equivalent to, nor does it imply nor presuppose:

(ii) I am aware of myself as a simple, non-corporeal substance (i.e. that in being aware of all my thoughts as mine, I am aware of them as "determinations" of one simple, thinking substance),

or even

(iii) I am aware of my "personal identity" (the referent of my name) in being aware of my thoughts as belonging to one subject.

This strategy makes it imperative that Kant hold fast to the strongest statements on noumenal ignorance, as, perhaps most strongly, at A350.

Partly, this tendency to equate transcendental subjectivity with the noumenal self stems from Kant's not distinguishing between the claims that (a) the self in itself is unknowable because we do not have the proper "intellectual equipment" (intellectual intuition) for knowing it, and (b) the transcendental subject could not be, given its logical status, an object of *either* intellectual or sensible intuition.[33] And it is not hard to appreciate why Kant was reluctant to develop (b) into a separate kind of "transcendental knowledge," and why he alternated instead between strong claims of noumenal ignorance and equally strong but more infrequent claims of transcendental–noumenal equivalence. That is, Kant thought that his critical theory had forever destroyed the possibility of any purely rational determination of the real, so he would have obviously resisted the suggestion that his denial that a phenomenal theory could account for the epistemic subject, and his denial that we have any intellectual intuition of a non-phenomenal subject, still left open another possibility for an a priori deter-

---

33 For a fuller discussion of this distinction, see Allison, *Kant's Transcendental Idealism*, ch. 13, especially pp. 292–3. My differences with Allison on this issue turn on an ambiguity in his overall account of apperception: his willingness on the one hand to concede that apperception provides us with something that "cannot be accounted for in terms of the mechanism of nature or the empirical character of the subject" (323), and, like Kant, his continuing insistence on strict metaphysical neutrality (323–4). For a fuller discussion, see my review of *Kant's Transcendental Idealism*, *Kant-Studien* 77, no. 3 (1986): 365–71.

mination of what a subject of experience really must or could not be.[34] But, again, the argument of his successors was that this was just what his own version of transcendental reflection (later, for them, "absolute" reflection) had done.

Another noumenalism problem, though, is caused not by Kant's occasional tendency to make a direct claim about the noumenal subject, but by his very wide-ranging consideration of what it is logically possible for us to be, for all we know. That is, if we are truly noumenally ignorant, then it would seem possible that, within the analysis of transcendental reflection, what turns out to be spontaneity as a condition of experience could noumenally "turn out to be" (for God, or maybe Leibniz) *some* kind of causal system. We could perhaps be *automata spirituale*, though we could never know that, and transcendentally could only conceive of experience as necessarily inherently spontaneous. Indeed, Kant sometimes claims, what appears as extended matter in space might be noumenally identical with the noumenal analogue of nonextended thoughts in inner sense, and he demonstrates great willingness to offer all kinds of unusual examples about what a noumenal thinker could be like (cf. especially his billiard ball example for the communication of thoughts between substances, at A364n.).

These passages raise a number of different problems, but the difficulty they pose for the spontaneity thesis is apparent when one considers the following well-known example of Kant's noumenal speculation. The passage concerns practical spontaneity, or freedom, but its general import is clear.

> Whether reason is not, in the actions through which it prescribes laws, itself again determined by other influences, and whether that which, in relation to sensuous impulses, is entitled freedom, may not, in relation to higher and more remote operating causes, be nature again, is a question which in the practical field does not concern us, since we are demanding of reason nothing but the rule of conduct; it is a merely speculative question, which we can leave aside so long as we are considering what ought or ought not to be done. (B831 = A803)

However, from our point of view, the question cannot be set aside. If both reason's practical and theoretical self-legislation or self-determination can turn out to be nature again, even if a non-sensible nature in which there are only non-physical states causality producing other non-physical states, then

34 Cf. *AA*, V, p. 31; *Critique of Practical Reason*, (hereafter *CPrR*) trans. L. W. Beck (Indianapolis: Bobbs-Merrill, 1956), p. 31.

it *is* logically possible for a knowing subject to be instantiated in a causal system, even if an unknowably noumenal system, whose causality need not be the efficient causality specified by the Second Analogy.

I can only plead here that, from the evidence collected, this is not what Kant should have said. All that he should have said is perfectly analogous to what he eventually did say later in his practical rejection of the preceding noumenal possibility. That is, if it turns out we really are causal systems on the noumenal level, then the states, beliefs, and judgments produced by such systems would not be epistemic claims, even if the beliefs can be said to correspond to both phenomenal and noumenal reality. (The analogue in practical theory is the practical necessity for assuming that our noumenal agency could not turn out to be "nature again," could not, that is, if there still is to be practical agency.)

Thus Sellars, for whom the possibility of "noumenal science" is so important, is quite right to insist on the distinction between the "conceptual framework of which nature was the cause" and the "freely elaborate conceptual frameworks with which we now challenge Nature,"[35] and can even be right to suggest in his terms that the latter framework must be "free" because the noumenal reality about which it offers theories is in principle unobservable and incapable of effecting a causal alteration in theories. But this still cannot mean (for Kant) that the latter framework is "free" only *relative* to the objects it is about (uncaused by them) and in itself a really (noumenally) causal system in which its theories can be said to be "produced," that "In the Paralogisms Kant has kept the way clear for the view that in reality the 'I' is a system, and, in particular for the view that it is a system of scientific objects, the true counterparts of Kant's things-in-themselves."[36] Kant's remarks on spontaneity reveal that he would argue that no account of how such a system of scientific objects could know itself to be such a system could eliminate the characteristic of spontaneity from such a system. Although his own remarks often seem close to modern distinctions between "function" and "content," on this issue there cannot be a complete independence between them, something Sellars himself stresses when he admits that "we can conceive of the functionings in ways which abstract from specific embodiments, *though they lay down abstract requirements which any specific embodiments must satisfy.*"[37]

Finally, one might think that these arguments about transcendental spontaneity ought to have a noumenal payoff in Kant's moral theory, partic-

35 Sellars, "Metaphysics," p. 252.
36 Ibid.
37 Ibid., p. 248, my emphasis.

ularly since so many of the uses of "spontaneity" carry over from one domain to the other.[38] It can seem natural that Kant would argue that, since spontaneity is a condition for the possibility of knowledge, we have thereby proved that we must be free in a practically relevant sense, the kind of being capable of acting uncaused. And again, there are scores of indications in the Pölitz lectures, various and numerous *Reflexionen*, the 1783 review of Schulz's *Sittenlehre*, and in the *Grundlegung*, that Kant was confident that he could make such an argument.[39] But, first, nothing in what has been presented so far would either legitimate such an inference or necessarily tie the claim for transcendental spontaneity to such a practical issue. Simply put, it is quite possible that any action relevant to ethical judgment might be, say, "caused by sensual impulses," and yet that the spontaneity of the epistemic subject is a necessary condition for knowing that to be so. Proving that reason in one context must be assumed spontaneous does not prove that in other contexts, say where reason is a motive for action, it must be spontaneous there too.[40] Second, there is good evidence, cited persuasively by Ameriks and Allison, that Kant abandoned any such connecting arguments after 1785,[41] although he clearly did not abandon, in the second edition, his insistence on the spontaneous nature of thinking. If anything, that emphasis is stronger.

VII

Of course, the logical independence of these topics does not preclude the possibility that there might be interesting and important connections between the varieties of Kantian spontaneity. In the preceding, I have been concentrating only on defending an interpretation of the spontaneity of apperception and the implications of that interpretation for some contemporary reconstructions of Kant. But it should also be noted, as a brief conclu-

38 Heidemann is a typical example of someone who connects, somewhat quickly and carelessly, I think, the issues of *Spontaneität* and *noumenale Existenz*, pp. 212, 214, for example.
39 The best summary discussion of these passages can be found in Ameriks, *Kant's Theory*, pp. 193–203.
40 This is relevant to a point that Prauss often makes: that Kant ought to have altered his formulations about impulses', needs', and desires' simply determining behavior causally in heteronomous action, because his own theory commits him to the view that for an impulse to affect my behavior, I must freely "allow it to," and that what the desire is for can be understood only if the free self-determination of purposeful conduct is introduced (cf. pp. 224–5).
41 Ameriks, *Kant's Theory*, p. 195; Allison, *Kant's Transcendental Idealism*, pp. 310–29.

sion, that there are a variety of reasons for pursuing the issue of the more comprehensive account of subjectivity and spontaneous activity at the basis of what Kant wants to say in his different critical contexts. Understanding the similarities between Kant's views on apperceptive spontaneity and on autonomy, and eventually on the spontaneity of reflective judgment, might not only contribute to an understanding of the common view of subjectivity behind all of them, and might not only point to deep similarities in how Kant argues for the undeniability of such subjective conditions for experience, action, and reflection, but could clearly contribute to an understanding of the architectonic issue of the unity of all three *Critiques*, since so much in the enterprise of each is tied to the notion of spontaneity.[42]

Moreover, to return again to an earlier suggestion, attending to the fundamentality of the spontaneity of subjectivity in Kant's project can illuminate what we might vaguely call the direction of a post-Kantian philosophy. In investigating such matters as why we categorize the world the way we do, think we ought to direct our action the way we do, or reflect on the whole or unity of nature as we do, and whether any of those ways is legitimate or justifiable, viewing such ways as activities by a subject, or even a self-determination or "self-legislation" by a subject, at the very least suggests an explanatory category and justificatory strategy that cannot be completely exhausted by what we turn out to know about the laws of thought or the nature of the brain. What such a category ultimately does involve is, of course, impossible to state here. One can only note a similar kind of claim in all the Kantian contexts for its independence – that in any competing claim about the ways in which a subject is supposedly determined by something other than its own spontaneity (physical objects, sensuous impulses, beautiful things), there must always *also* be ways in which the subject takes itself to be so determined, at least if such a determination is to be known by a subject or experienced in a way relevant to its action or judgment. And, again, in all the contexts, this claim just raises the issue of what this spontaneous, self-determining subjectivity is supposed to be. Being able to demonstrate that such an activity could not be instantiated in a causal system tells us little about the positive nature of such activity, and it certainly does not entail that we ought to view that spontaneity as an arbitrary, or ex nihilo act of will. There may very well be inherently necessary constraints on such activity, such that it could count as an attempt at knowledge, or free action. And those constraints or norms might not be derivable from reflection on the

42 See the remarks at the end of the *Critique of Judgment* on the "causality of man" (*Kausalität der Menschen*), AA, V, p. 484; *CJ*, p. 337.

rules of thinking, as Kant thought, and might require a more comprehensive perspective on self-relating activity as such, as later German Idealists thought.[43] But the priority of spontaneous activity in such an account, and what that priority determines about the general kind of epistemic and practical explanation that could be given of such activity, would be clearly and importantly Kantian claims.

43 Prauss vigorously denies this, and argues that the post-Kantian Idealist tradition profoundly misses some of Kant's deepest insights (cf. pp. 308–26). I think he is wrong that that tradition ignored the purposive (and fallible, finite) character of human reason. Cf. Hegel's remark in the Jena *Phenomenology* that reason is "purposive activity," *Phänomenologie des Geistes, GeWe,* IV, p. 20. And, with more space, I would disagree strongly with the way he brushes aside Hegel's insistence on the inherently "negative," self-correcting, and self-transforming nature of thought. Such remarks seem to me to illuminate precisely what Prauss finds hidden in Kant.

3

ON THE MORAL FOUNDATIONS OF
KANT'S *RECHTSLEHRE*

I

In section 40 of *A Theory of Justice*, John Rawls wisely notes that it is a mistake to view Kant's ethics with undue emphasis on the problems of the generality and universality of the moral law, that Kant's moral theory "as a whole" must always be kept in mind, and that this latter goal requires attention to the later writings on politics, religion, and teleology.[1] It is certainly true that any fair inspection of the texts considered by Kant to be parts of his practical philosophy does reveal that he by no means regarded that philosophy as exhausted by the problem of the single, pure criterion by which the permissibility of individual actions could be judged. He obviously believed that he could produce a rich, rationally defensible theory of morals (*Sitten*) as well as a theory of morality, and Rawls is certainly right to suggest that we distort and cannot properly assess Kant's view of the foundations of this whole if we neglect to look to the "building" that these foundations were to support.

However, it is also fair to note that the chief reason commentators have concentrated so heavily on the logical problems of universalizability and moral judgment has not been willful neglect of the rest of Kant's moral theory, but the fact that it has never been clear how to put all the parts

---

1 John Rawls, *A Theory of Justice* (Cambridge: Harvard University Press, 1971), p. 251.

together. It is at least clear what problems must be faced in Kant's formulation of the categorical imperative, but it is far from clear how one is to understand the relation between Kant's foundational theory of morality and his philosophy of history, of religion, of law, of politics, of virtue, of education, of beauty, and of teleology, all of which are explicitly said to be parts, in sometimes various senses, of the practical or moral theory.

In short, when one attempts to follow Kant from his pure moral theory to his account of applied moral practice, it is often hard to isolate what is essential to the moral theory, either as a direct consequence of the moral law itself, or, apparently, as a necessary condition of its application in human life, and what is mere speculation *am Rande,* marginalia of no central importance to the core of the moral theory. Kant's account of what it is to live an actual life "worthy" of happiness just seems to range wildly over issues like justice and revolution, immortality and God, contracts between husbands and wives, the moral claims of taste, belief in progress, all the way to a discussion of why wigmakers should be allowed to vote, but not barbers.

However, there is one issue that is, I want to argue, a paradigm instance of at least the kind of relation Kant envisaged between the supreme moral law and the derived duties of human practice, an issue that may help to reveal the general form of that relation and thus the general shape of Kant's whole moral theory. That issue is Kant's derivation of specifically political duties. Primarily, this derivation is explained and defended in the first part of the *Metaphysics of Morals,* the "Metaphysical Elements of Justice," although important aspects of his account also appear in such essays as "On the Common Saying: That May Be True in Theory but It Does Not Apply in Practice" and "Perpetual Peace."

This issue in particular is the first and most important one to be confronted in any attempt to find the single thread that may run through the entirety of Kant's moral theory. For, when one turns to the work that best exhibits Kant's understanding of the relation between moral theory in general and a derived system of specific duties, one confronts first of all the fact that that system is in two quite distinct parts. It has taken commentators some effort, not always successful, to understand just how these two parts are to be differentiated, but it is undeniable that any interpretation of Kant's whole moral theory must begin by noting this duality between duties of "justice" and duties of "virtue," between a *Rechtslehre* and a *Tugendlehre.* Kant's whole understanding of the implications of obeying the moral law begins with this fact, this division between the specifically legal duties we owe others and the different ethical duties we owe ourselves and others.

This basic distinction is important for a number of philosophic as well as hermeneutic reasons. As an issue in political theory, what Kant's architectonic commits him to is a claim that may be his most important contribution to political theory (although he obviously shares credit with Rousseau): that political duties are a subset of moral duties.[2] This means that the bonds that tie us to others in civil society (and that thereby legitimate public authority) are distinctly moral bonds, rationally derivable from our general moral obligations to others.[3] They thus do not depend on any voluntary act, whether it be consent, tacit consent, or hypothetical consent (what I would choose if I were a hypothetical contractor in a fair, ideal choice situation), nor on "fair play" considerations derived from acceptance of benefits, nor from considerations of gratitude to others, and certainly not from any rational calculation of maximum utility. Although he would not use the term this way, Kant's claim is that there is what many contemporaries would recognize as a "natural duty of justice." Or, to state the point a different way, for Kant there is a moral duty to enter civil society (where Kant means by civil society "the rule of law"), and thus a moral warrant to coerce any who refuse. Even in a natural society of benevolent agents, who vote unanimously to remain in their state of nature, such a duty and warrant holds unequivocally.[4]

Now, of course, many so-called contract theories also presuppose a moral premise: that one ought to keep one's promises. But what I mean to stress here is that Kant does not explain political obligation exclusively in terms of this promise-keeping duty. Rather, he argues that there is an original, moral duty to collaborate with others in a state, a duty *to* promise.[5] Roughly, it is

---

2 Cf. sect. 4 of the Introduction to pt. 1 of the *Metaphysics of Morals: The Metaphysical Elements of Justice,* trans. John Ladd (Indianapolis: Bobbs-Merrill, 1965), pp. 21–30 (hereafter, references to this edition are abbreviated as *MEJ* and are followed by the page number of the Prussian Academy edition, VI, *Kants gesammelte Schriften,* Königlich Preussichen Akademie der Wissenschaften (Berlin, Leipzig: de Gruyter, 1922), (*AA*), pp. 221–28.

3 Obviously, a large problem looms for any such moral approach to political theory. Given the universal demands of moral obligation, how could one ever use a moral foundation to legitimate allegiance to a specific civil society? Would not one be bound, if one is, to all just regimes? To avoid this, it would seem that one would have to introduce empirical issues into any discussion of the locus of one's political duties. Contrary to the usual interpretation of Kant's formalism, I shall argue that that is just what he does. Cf. the discussion by A. John Simmons, *Moral Principles and Political Obligations* (Princeton: Princeton University Press, 1979), ch. 6, and his reference to the received view of Kant, p. 199.

4 *MEJ*, pp. 71–2; *AA*, pp. 307–8.

5 Kant, in fact, would agree with Hume's famous criticisms of the contractarian tradition (assuming that there is one). Cf. Jeffrie Murphy, "Hume and Kant on the Social Contract," *Philosophical Studies* 33 (1978): pp. 65–79. For a clear statement by Kant of his position, see the essay "That May Be True in Theory but It Does Not Apply in Practice," trans. H. B. Nisbet,

this claim that sets up the problem at issue in this essay – assuming we do have, say, a duty to "respect others as ends in themselves," why is it a consequence of that duty that I collaborate in a *Rechtsstaat*?[6]

Now, of course, even at this initial stage, there are further reasons to be wary of this claim. After all, the central problem in modern political philosophy has been and continues to be that concerning the basis for the use of state power to limit the liberty of others. In this context, it is understandable that one might be wary of crowning state power with some moral halo, of claiming that use of such power is warranted as a way of enforcing externally binding moral rules. That wariness stems from the suspicion that such moral claims are either too abstract, too controversial, or, especially, too liable to the abuses of self-righteousness, moral arrogance, or self-serving rationalizations, to serve this role. We are on the verge of turning the state into a paternalistic moral busybody with this view of duty and coercion, the objectors warn, and would be far better advised to begin with the clearest safeguard against such abuses: perhaps the supreme liberal maxim – *volenti non fit iniuria*, no injury can be done to the willing.

However, by noting the obvious architectonic fact that, for Kant, political

---

in *Kant's Political Writings*, ed. by H. Reiss (Cambridge: Cambridge University Press, 1970), p. 73 (hereafter *TP*, followed by *AA*, VIII, page numbers), *AA*, p. 289; and a helpful exposition by Manfred Riedel in "Herrschaft und Gesellschaft: Zum Legitimationsproblem des Politischen in der Philosophie," reprinted in *Materialen zu Kants Rechtsphilosophie*, ed. by Zwi Batscha (Frankfurt am M.: Suhrkamp, 1976), pp. 125–48, especially p. 135.

6 Of course, in other contexts, Kant distinguishes between legality and morality. But in this context, we can see that this is still a distinction between kinds of duties. The former are duties (part of our moral obligation) that can be said to exist and indeed to be fulfilled independently of any subject's motives. And, on the other hand, it is still true that we are morally bound to adopt justice as our end, but having or not having that as our end is not relevant to whether the act is (legally) just. A like answer could be given to someone who might object to this approach by asking how this notion of a "moral foundation" could possibly be appropriate in Kant, given his famous claim in "Perpetual Peace" that a race of intelligent devils could form what he explicitly calls a *just* state. Again, though, far from excluding a "moral foundation," such a hyperbolic claim just focuses attention on the nature of the Kantian view of political duty. That is, what Kant means to stress by this claim is that a state is just (if it is), has a certain moral authority, in a way that is independent of any *specific* ends desired by its citizens. He only means to insist that this moral authority can be said to exist even if allegiance to the state does not actually derive from pursuit of any moral ideal, even if devils simply realize that allegiance to the form of a *Rechtsstaat* is the most efficient means to satisfy their demonic desires. Such an association is not just because these devils contracted to obey it, or because it is efficient, and can be said to be just, to conform to our universal, juridical duties to others, regardless of the fact that its citizens happen to be devils. Kant himself seems to have discovered the importance of the difference between *Recht* and *Tugend* around the end of the 1760s and beginning of the 1770s, while formulating his differences with Baumgarten's *Initia Philosophiae Practicae Primae*.

duties, and thereby the authority of law, could be derived from a general moral basis, we are in no danger of interpreting him as some traditional natural law theorist, subject to the potential objections raised.[7] For the second feature of Kant's political theory that makes him directly relevant to many contemporary controversies is his claim to be able to show that the range of legitimate coercion by the state is precisely definable, and by no means ranges over all our moral duties to others. Indeed, as we shall see, that is the major force of the distinction between a *Rechtslehre* and a *Tugendlehre*, and indeed, or so I want to argue, Kant's second important contribution to political theory. There are only certain duties to others that we can, may, and ought to *compel* others to fulfill.

What is most important about this delineation is that it will, if successful, provide a firm basis for understanding an often-used notion in political thought – a right. For Kant, to specify a special class of duties to others, fulfillment of which may be compelled, is to specify those duties owed to others *by right,* as opposed to those owed, but not by right. Of course, in one sense, if A is duty-bound to B in some way, B has a "right" to expect fulfillment of that duty by A. But for Kant, this claim only goes so far as to mean, It is all right (or morally justifiable) for B to expect fulfillment by A. But it is a much stronger sense that, for Kant, is politically relevant, the sense in which B has a right to *demand* fulfillment by A, and to call on the law to guarantee such fulfillment. It is this sense that Kant promises to give us in his *Rechts-lehre,* and to do so, or so I shall interpret him, not (directly) because A in some way consented or promised to perform the act for B, but because of the moral duties anyone owes anyone else.

We can now see that the approach Kant takes will continually face two large problems. The first involves a clarification of what we might call Kant's moral interest in the state in the first place. After all, suppose one could rationally distinguish a special class of duties that exist and, given their special, formal characteristics, can be said to be fulfilled independent of motives – legal duties. That, by itself, would only entail that as an individual, I have a duty to treat others justly. And, again as an individual, I could

7 Admittedly, there is some controversy about Kant's relation to the tradition, especially in some recent German literature. The issues involved are complicated by some profound changes, apparently, in Kant's views on politics. I've only the space here to note that I find compelling Werner Busch's case for a genuinely "critical" *Rechtsphilosophie,* in his book *Die Entstehung der kantischen Rechtsphilosophie* (Berlin: de Gruyter, 1979), as opposed to the claims of Christian Ritter and Josef Schmucker. Cf. also the clear explanation of the difference between Kant and Aquinas by Alan Donagan in *The Theory of Morality* (Chicago: University of Chicago Press, 1977), p. 64.

attempt to fulfill that obligation in a thoroughly repressive, unjust regime, even though the consequences of my actions might be disastrous. All Kant does (in the body of the *Rechtslehre* itself) to get us from these individual duties to political obligation is to present a brief, inadequate argument that justice is "analytically united with the authorization to use coercion."[8]

However, that argument in section D of the *Rechtslehre* only establishes (if it can be said to establish anything) that punishment is consistent with the duty of justice; it does not establish that the coercive rule of law is a moral requirement. That is, he does not establish the stronger thesis that he elsewhere explicitly states – that we have a duty to collaborate in civil society, to institute, obey, and support a certain rule of law. We need to find his support for that stronger thesis.

And, second, we need to try to reconstruct his reasons for treating only some duties to others as political duties. That is, I shall claim that, in the "ideal case" at the center of most political philosophies, (i) Kant will try to prove that showing a state to be just depends on being able to show that the state's legal force or coercion is used to ensure fulfillment of certain duties to others, which duties are duties at all only within a moral framework that specifies in general what duties are owed others and why; but that (ii) for Kant those duties that justify coercion are a special, delimitable class, separate from ethical duties to others that do not warrant coercion and fulfillment of which it would be unjust to coerce. These juridical duties are those and only those for which others may claim corresponding rights. (As in: I have a right to be free from the murderous and larcenous acts of my fellow citizens, but no right to demand benevolence or esteem from them.)

I note immediately two qualifications on the scope of this project. First, from the fact that a state falls far short of this ideal, or approximates it not at all, nothing immediately follows about what I am duty-bound to do, or even, all things considered, what I ought to do. It is a fact that Kant himself thought that even in the latter extreme case I am still duty-bound to obey the law (there is no "right of revolution"), but that is a separate issue and one I shall not discuss.[9] Second, the general characterization given pre-

---

8 *MEJ*, pp. 35–6; *AA*, p. 231.

9 Several claims, although interconnected, must be kept distinct here. Kant's position commits him to claiming (1) that I have a duty to enter civil society and not leave it, (2) that a just state can be defined as one that best accords with the reasons behind (1), and (3) that I have an obligation to promote and support just institutions. For reasons we shall investigate, (1) is ranked higher in importance than (3) for Kant, but the moral force of both claims stems from a common source. Thus (1) and (3) are not the inconsistent pair critics of Kant on revolution often take them to be.

viously of justice is very abstract. As it stands it concerns only the state's role in protecting the "one natural right" – freedom.[10] There are also various "acquired rights," and corresponding duties, and in the course of our inquiry, more will have to be said about what kinds of rights can be justly acquired and how. However, since I have also claimed that how Kant derives his notion of juridical duties might provide a clue to the shape of his whole system of morality, the task at hand now is to turn to the *Rechtslehre* and examine how this derivation is attempted.

II

In the first subdivision of the *Rechtslehre*[11] (A. *"Was die Rechtslehre sei"*) Kant begins with a distinction stressed often throughout the opening pages, although it is far too broad for what he has in mind. "The sum of those laws for which outer legislation [*äussere Gesetzgebung*] is possible is called jurisprudence (*ius*)."[12] He had earlier stressed that the only kind of "legislation" possible for ethical duties was "internal." This difference in the types of possible legislation corresponds to a difference in the types of restraint possible in each case. "Right" actions continue to be right even if performed under external restraint, such as fear of punishment; "good" actions can only be good if the restraint is "inner," if the agent restrains himself out of respect for the moral law, and not fear of external consequences.

This distinction does not get us very far unless we can find a clear sense of just which actions can be externally legislated, which remain right even when externally coerced. In terms of legislative possibility alone, we can prohibit almost anything. Kant must mean "can be externally legislated" in a qualified sense; indeed the "can" must be qualified somehow by "in conformity with the moral law," here interpreted to mean "in conformity with the freedom of each." If this qualification can be defended, then Kant's several other descriptions of the distinction will have more force. It will, for example, help us to understand just what duties we can be said to have to others that bind independently of any motive we may adopt, versus our duties to

---

10   *MEJ*, p. 43 ("There is only one innate right"); *AA*, p. 237. Cf. also H. L. A. Hart, "Are There Any Natural Rights?" *Philosophical Review* 64 (1955): 179–200.
11   Much could be gained, prior to an examination of the text, by considering what is involved in each of the terms defining this domain of Kant's practical philosophy, a "Metaphysische Anfangsgründe der Rechtslehre," although such a consideration must lie outside the scope of this study. See Mary Gregor's helpful discussion in *Laws of Freedom* (New York: Barnes & Noble, 1963), pp. 1–33.
12   *MEJ*, p. 33; *AA*, p. 229.

pursue other ends or develop certain attitudes. And in turn we shall then be able perhaps to appreciate why, for the former class, external coercion is morally legitimate (not just possible), whereas for the latter class, external coercion is not just impossible but morally illegitimate. (The former would be those duties correlated with enforceable rights, the latter would be those duties not so correlated.)

Now, obviously, Kant has in mind here something like a list of basic or fundamental duties, a set of duties based on the very notion of a free agent – duties that, when violated, directly contradict the very notion of any agent acting freely. However, just where the move from the special nature of these duties to a political context occurs, and how the duties are to be defined, are both, oddly, given their centrality in Kant's *Rechtslehre*, hard to find. For the most part it is with regard to this distinction between duties to *act* in certain ways versus duties to *pursue* certain ends that Kant tries, however briefly, to spell out this latter division. He uses the distinction to point out either that juridical duties are "narrow" duties, duties to perform or forbear from specific actions, with no judgmental "leeway" for the agent, and are to be contrasted with ethical, "broad" duties to pursue certain ends, duties that always leave such interpretive leeway; or, preserving a distinction from the *Grundlegung* that occasionally seems identical to the narrow–broad distinction, that juridical duties are "perfect" duties (with the exception of perfect duties to oneself), whereas ethical duties are "imperfect."[13] This distinction is grounded, in turn, on the different ways in which the impermissibility of such duties is explained and defended. Juridical duties of action in some way directly contradict the moral law; they involve what one commentator has called a "contradiction in conception."[14] To do A, if B, if this claim is right, and A is to be legally impermissible, cannot pass the "law of nature" universalization test. Ethical duties, on the other hand, involve a "contradiction in willing," or can only be shown to involve a contradiction by showing how an agent could not consistently will that everyone adopt some end or policy. The maxim in question for such duties must be to do A, if B, in order to pursue C.

Finally, in one of the only passages in the *Rechtslehre* that specify the differences in some detail, Kant points out that the duties of justice can be said to be binding only with respect to actions that externally influence others, that this influence must be considered in terms of the *will* of the

---

13 Kant makes use of the perfect–imperfect terminology at *MEJ*, p. 46; *AA*, pp. 239–41.
14 Onora O'Neill, *Acting on Principle* (New York: Columbia University Press, 1975). I discuss her interpretation extensively in Section III.

other agent, not his needs or desires (which are the concerns of ethical duties); and, third, that this external relation of wills is to be considered only formally, that is, only with respect to the formal consistency of such actions and, again, not with regard to the ends pursued by the agents. With all of this in view, we have Kant's statement of the "universal principle of justice" (*Allgemeines Prinzip des Rechts*): "Any action is just that itself, or in its maxim, is such that the freedom of the will of each can coexist with anyone's freedom according to a universal law."[15]

So far, however, these distinctions, some of which coincide, some of which are identical, some of which follow from others, just give us a kind of shopping list of alternatives to try out: capable of external legislation and coercion, versus capable only of internal legislation and restraint; duties formulated with respect to actions only, versus duties to pursue certain ends; duties owed by right, versus those not so owed; duties for which external coercion is not only possible but morally legitimate, versus those for which coercion is impossible and illegitimate; narrow and perfect duties versus broad and imperfect duties; and finally, duties that affect the will (or liberty) of others, which effect is considered formally, with regard to a possible contradiction in conception, versus those duties to others that affect their needs or desires, with regard to a possible "contradiction in willing" some end or policy.

However, if we keep in mind what has been provisionally identified here as the core of Kant's doctrine of justice, that political duties must be understood as a subset of moral duties, but a limited, coercible subset, then the basic problem at the root of all the preceding distinctions is clear. Since the critical foundation of moral theory proclaims that there is one supreme moral law, understanding the distinctions comes down to understanding just why applying this law generates these two sets of duties. If the relation between the *Metaphysics of Morals* and the categorical imperative can be made out, we should be able to understand the moral legitimacy of law in its enforcing of specific duties, and why they are these specific duties. Obviously, for Kant, to understand why an action or the pursuit of a policy is morally impermissible is to understand why either violates the central prescription of the moral law, and, or so one hopes, perhaps understanding the different kinds of violation will give us our distinction between juridical and ethical duties, between what ought to be a matter of public legislation and what ought not to be.

15 *MEJ*, p. 35; *AA*, p. 230.

III

Commentators have addressed this issue in different ways. Of major concern, in commentaries on both the *Grundlegung* and the *Metaphysics of Morals,* has been whether anything specific can be said to be impermissible according to the standard of the categorical imperative. This problem has been so prominent in the literature that a good deal less attention has been paid to the issue central to the *Rechtslehre:* whether certain acts can be said to be impermissible in a distinct way, a way that explains and grounds the moral authority of public coercion. In those few discussions that tackle both problems, two distinct approaches can be found.

On the one hand, one can try to support Kant's claim that the categorical imperative itself, in what one might call its strictest formulation, can be used to generate specific duties, and the twofold division found in the *Metaphysics of Morals.*[16] (By the "strictest" formulation, I mean the second formulation given in the *Grundlegung:* "Act as though the maxim of your action were by your will to become a universal law of nature.")[17] On the other hand, others have argued that no system of duties, let alone the division in the *Metaphysics of Morals,* can be understood except by appeal to a derivative form of the moral law, one with more content already expressed in it. The most popular candidate for this version has of course always been the third version of the moral law in the *Grundlegung:* "Act so that you treat humanity whether in your own person or in that of another, always as an end and never as a means only."[18] We need to see, then, if either of these approaches can be used to justify the foundational divisions of the *Metaphysics of Morals.*

Kant himself has frustratingly little to say about the details of either approach, but a recent commentator has taken up what is the less popular of the two, the first, and tried to defend it in as rigorous a way as possible. Onora (Nell) O'Neill, in her book *Acting on Principle,*[19] argues that once we take seriously Kant's insistence that the impermissibility of certain maxims is based on a direct *self*-contradiction, visible when the universal "law of nature" corresponding to that maxim is produced, we shall have a clear criterion for showing the special contradictoriness of all violations of duties of justice. What I think she does not show is how that criterion can be used to

16 Most of Kant's early formulations of the *Recht–Tugend* distinction seem to rely on this strict or legalistic formulation. See *MEJ*, pp. 14–21; *AA*, pp. 214–21.
17 I. Kant, *Foundations of the Metaphysics of Morals*, trans. L. W. Beck (Indianapolis: Bobbs-Merrill, 1959), p. 39 (hereafter *F*), *AA*, IV, p. 422.
18 *F*, p. 47; *AA*, p. 429.
19 O'Neill, *Acting*. I shall be discussing chs. 4 and 5 of this book.

tell us precisely, or even generally, *which* duties are duties of justice and so subject to legitimate coercion.

She begins, appropriately, with Kant's clearest statement of the two ways in which the moral law may be violated:

> We must be able to will that a maxim of our action become a universal law: this is the canon of the moral estimation of our action generally. Some actions are of such a nature that their maxim cannot even be *thought* as a universal law of nature without contradiction, far from it being possible that one could will that it be such. In others this internal impossibility is not found, though it is still impossible to *will* that their maxim should be raised to the universality of a law of nature, because such a will would contradict itself. We easily see that the former maxim conflicts with the stricter or narrower (imprescriptible) duty, the latter with broader (meritorious) duty.[20]

She then notes that this distinction between ways of testing for contradiction gives us exactly the distinction between maxims of justice and maxims of virtue[21] and proposes to defend Kant's use of the former "contradiction in conception" test.

In doing so, she points out that the universalizability test can properly be used, not directly on a practical maxim but on a putative "natural law" that is the "*typic*" of the maxim.[22] That is, for a maxim like (a) To . . . if – we consider whether its "typified counterpart" (a′) Everyone will . . . if – , introduces a self-contradiction.[23] And that consideration is, of course, where all the classical problems arise. In trying to work out a clear test of universalizability that does not end up either permitting or condemning too much, the influential English-language commentaries (e.g., Paton and Beck) claim that in testing whether a maxim's counterpart could be a law of nature, we must have recourse to a notion of a lawlike harmony of natural *ends*. And, finally, this test will have to invoke the notion of human nature as a rational end in itself if we are even to discover which maxims are permissible for us. The ambitiousness of O'Neill's project is to reject this teleological notion of natural law in favor of a stricter test of self-contradiction. Aside from textual support, she does this for what is quite a good reason:

20 *F,* p. 41; *AA,* p. 424.
21 O'Neill, *Acting,* p. 61.
22 Compare Kant's discussion of the "typic" in his *Critique of Practical Reason,* trans. L. W. Beck (Indianapolis: Bobbs-Merrill, 1956) (*CPrR*), *AA,* V, p. 68.
23 The reason for this use of an analogous natural law is stated clearly by Kant, *CPrR,* p. 70; *AA,* p. 68.

Further, if purposiveness is to be introduced into every explanation of the role of typifying practical principles, then we may be at a loss to see what differentiates maxims that cannot be conceived as universal laws of nature (and so cannot be maxims of justice) from maxims that merely cannot be willed as universal laws of nature (and so cannot be maxims of any sort of duty).[24]

All of which obviously commits her to showing how this distinction can be made out, under the "stricter" interpretation. (We shall examine in a moment whether the teleological approach can successfully account for the basic division of the *Metaphysics of Morals*.)

Her strategy, in essence, is to follow the rough outline of the approach taken by Kemp and Dietrichson,[25] but to modify it so as to make clearer that Kant wants his criterion to test for the internal consistency of a possible natural law, not, for example, its inconsistency with assorted empirical facts. We thus do not want to show the impermissibility of false promising by showing that a consequence of false promising, given the empirical truth that humans remember and learn from the past, is to make the institution of promising impossible. Rather, she argues, in most of his famous formulations of the contradiction-in-conception test, Kant stresses that the contradiction is between my intention to act on a maxim (and thus also my willing the relevant means and foreseeable consequences) and the possible intention that the counterpart natural law be a natural law. I cannot, at the same time (without contradiction), intend to promise falsely and intend that it be a natural law that everyone falsely promise. If I intend to promise falsely, I must assume that all the relevant circumstances within which that act could be successful obtain, and, given that, I could not also will exactly the contrary situation.

O'Neill then deals with how her criterion could deal with problem cases always raised for any strict version of the universalizability test (e.g., maxims like "I will give presents, but not accept them," which should be permissible but might seem to be logically non-universalizable),[26] and goes on to show how her version of the test easily deals with our moral intuitions about bank robbery, embezzling, and the like. However, even though she later insists again that the results of the "test" Kant suggests in his "universal principle of justice" "are the same as those of the contradiction in conception test as

24 O'Neill, *Acting*, p. 65.
25 J. Kemp, "Kant's Examples of the Categorical Imperative," *Philosophical Quarterly* 8 (1958), and P. Dietrichson, "When Is a Maxim Universalizable?" *Kant-Studien* 55 (1964).
26 She does this, successfully I think, by showing a way in which such maxims would test, as we should expect, as permissible, neither obligatory nor forbidden. O'Neill, *Acting*, pp. 76 ff.

interpreted here,"[27] she nowhere tries to work this out in any detail. She even claims at one point, without elaboration or defense, that in the *Rechtslehre* "Kant is never . . . engaged in deriving individual duties of justice from the Categorical Imperative or directly from the Universal Principle of Justice."[28] If that is so, it is hard to see what relevance the principle of justice has at all to the Doctrine of Justice. O'Neill never asks what relevance failing her universalizability test has to *justice*.

Apart from this neglect, there are several other problems with her approach. The most serious is that her interpretation can yield a precise and clear test only at the cost of a loose and potentially ad hoc interpretation of an agent's "true intentions." If I intend to play soccer on Saturday morning, on O'Neill's interpretation, I must assume that all the relevant circumstances that make this possible obtain. But if that is so, then I cannot at the same time intend that there be a natural law such that everyone will play soccer on Saturday mornings. If the latter held, obviously, there would be no room to play, apart from other, potentially disastrous social consequences. A moralistic Kantian might then conclude that soccer playing is forbidden; it is possible only by "exempting" yourself, in a supposedly classically immoral way, from what is possible for all. Obviously, we would want to argue in response that the agent's true intention is not to play soccer "come what may," no matter what. If he were fanatically committed to playing, regardless of other overriding duties, commitments, fair distribution of playing time, and so on, we might then indeed be willing to say his maxim is forbidden. So, we claim, his true intention is to play soccer if . . . , and here we can fill in some relevant provisos that then make it consistent for him to hold this intention simultaneously with the intention to will that it be a natural law that everyone will play soccer if. . . .

But this all commits us to a potentially quite complex further test for determining just what an agent's true intentions are. O'Neill insists on honesty in reporting or describing intentions, but never gives an explanation of how to determine honesty, or what relation such a determination should have to law, or a way to prevent worries about the kind of ad hoc gerrymandering possible previously. (She does raise her own objections about this issue in her last two chapters.)

More to the present point, however, it is by no means clear that all acts forbidden by this test do coincide with what Kant would consider forbidden by public law. To take the obvious example, it is true, subject to a solution to the problems raised, that false promising is clearly forbidden on O'Neill's

27 Ibid., p. 72.
28 Ibid., p. 80.

interpretation. But it is by no means clear that all acts of false promising are thereby to be considered unjust, in the relevant legal sense, however clearly immoral they may be. (The account she begins with, Dietrichson's, obscures this point by discussing a *kind* of false promising that is simply intuitively close to our sense of a legally relevant false promising – false promising "to get oneself out of financial difficulties.")[29] Given O'Neill's identification of all maxims that fail the universalization test with violations of duties of justice, and given Kant's clear insistence that the right of coercion to prevent all violations of duties of justice follows directly from the concept of justice itself, we are left precisely with the "moral busybody" state worried about in part I, a state that makes any false promise, or even more extravagantly, any lie, a criminal offense. I see no evidence that Kant would regard this consequence as desirable, and no discussion by O'Neill to show just how it is preventable. In sum, although O'Neill's version of the distinction between a "contradiction in conception" and a "contradiction in willing" is relatively clear and straightforward, and can show at least one way in which different kinds of moral impermissibility can be made out, the contradiction-in-conception test is far too broad, both in itself (given the problem of intentions) and with respect to our central problem: Which obligations to others are duties of justice?

But there is a clear lesson to be learned from such problems, and it is the same one that has led many commentators to Kant's alternate formulation of the moral law. Namely, since it is clear that the major problem in using Kant's stricter version of "a possible natural law" is in deciding what could or could not be such a non-self-contradictory law, one that needs to go behind that legalistic criterion and examine why Kant is so insistent on this kind of generality. To do so is to see his trying to clarify his view of the root irrationality of all immoral acts, that they all presuppose for myself a kind of rational agency that is inconsistently denied to those who are equally fully capable of such agency. That is, it is to find a richer moral criterion, the notion of human being as a rational end in itself. Can this moral criterion be used to connect Kant's moral with his political theory?

IV

Those who have recently commented on Kant's moral theory, especially Murphy and Aune, certainly think so.[30] They attempted to show that, how-

29 Ibid., pp. 66–7.
30 Jeffrie G. Murphy, *Kant: The Philosophy of Right* (London: Macmillan, 1970); Bruce Aune, *Kant's Theory of Morals* (Princeton: Princeton University Press, 1979).

ever many difficulties one eventually encounters, there is little chance of defending Kant unless one admits that the only way to explain what counts as a "positive law of nature" is to introduce the teleological notion of a "harmony of ends." The use of law as a test of moral rightness is thus not a test of consistency (or, as in O'Neill, consistent intentions) but a test of a possible harmony of agents consistently pursuing their goals, with each agent assumed to be an "end in itself." However, to understand the importance of relying on the criterion of "treating humanity as an end in itself" as a way of defining the morally right (especially in its legally relevant sense), we need to step back a bit and consider again Kant's project in political philosophy.

   It is obvious that Kant wants to argue for a liberal defense of the state's coercive power (although as I have already argued, he does so on essentially moral grounds): that the only legitimate interference with the free activity of citizens is that which can be shown to secure or protect freedom. But what one always wants to know from any theorist who proposes such a view, including Kant, is how that definition can be defended, and what it entails: what "protecting freedom" amounts to. As we have seen, when Kant is interpreted to be answering the former question with some appropriate *moral* answer (based on a general theory of our duties to others) we can understand very little of that answer if we understand it just in terms of "acting consistently" or rationally. Rather, Kant's concern with these tests clearly stems from his prior fundamental commitment to autonomy as that which alone renders man worthy of respect and dignity, and respect for which we owe others. One then wants to know just how Kant goes from his metaethical reflections on any possible moral system directly to this supreme moral precept, and the details of this move, especially since they involve a full defense of Kant's understanding of teleology, are obscure. But it is at least clear that Kant defends the preceding liberal criterion because he thinks we have a moral duty to respect others as rational ends in themselves, where that means respecting their autonomy. Because of this interpretation of the moral law in human life, that for human beings acting rationally and consistently is acting consistently with the possibility of others acting rationally and so autonomously, we can get a clearer sense, in these terms, of the distinction at the heart of the *Metaphysics of Morals*. Respect for another's autonomy thus entails that we may not interfere with another's pursuit of her goals, so long as that pursuit does not, when considered universally, conflict with the possibility of all others' retaining their essential end, that which they must be assumed to want protected if they pursue any end at all – their rational nature, their ability to determine their own course in life. Duties of virtue, on the other hand, are duties to help *promote* others' (and our own) ends, or at least those ends Kant thinks (somehow) are necessarily tied to human nature as an end in itself, "happiness" and "perfection" or "culture."

But all of this is, of course, just a crude sketch. At first glance, it might seem to provide us with just a different vocabulary for what we have been discussing all along, and still to involve many of the same problems. But, initially, the new description gets us much closer, I believe, to the spirit of Kant's whole moral system. Given (to avoid controversy for the moment) a moral duty to treat others as ends in themselves, where this means respecting their autonomy, we have a duty of justice not to interfere with the free activity of others, as well as an obligation to interfere when another acts in such a way as to be inconsistent with respect for the autonomy of others.[31] Given also that we could not will freely to pursue any end without the cooperation of others, or without the development of our own talents, and given that we could not respect autonomy, either our own or others', without doing what is required as a means to accomplish what we set ourselves to do, we have a "duty of virtue" to help promote the happiness of others (their achieving their goals) and our own perfection.[32] This dual set of duties, expressed in this way, as an extension of respect for humans as ends in themselves, does appear to set out most clearly what Kant is after at the core of his practical philosophy.

Several metaphysical and metaethical issues are immediately raised by this account, but what is most important here is the question of what is involved in respecting another's autonomy. It is clear that Kant wants his argument to show that a duty of justice can be "narrowly" or "perfectly" determined because it involves an end no one could consistently sacrifice or compromise – her liberty or autonomy. Because of this moral ideal, and because it can be so strictly determined (no one could be presumed not to want this end protected), Kant seems at places to think that this kind of reasoning is sufficient to justify a *Rechtsstaat,* a legal institution the function of which is to protect such liberty, or to ensure non-interference with this necessarily presupposed end in itself of human life. On the other hand, although there are what Kant also calls (somewhat confusingly) "essential

31 To be sure, since this interference itself must be consistent with the equal freedom of each, it must be pursued in a procedurally fair way. Or, only the state may be the agent of interference. Cf. Murphy's clear contrast between Locke and Kant on the "right to punish," Kant, pp. 113–27.
32 I don't pretend that this is a derivation of Kant's two supreme virtues; it is only a sketch of his argument in the *Tugendlehre.*

ends" that we must also suppose as necessarily involved in any autonomous pursuit, there is no way universally to prescribe how these ends are actually to be pursued, and there is no defensible way to compel others actually to promote them. Again, these ends, the subject matter of the *Tugendlehre*, involve how I develop my own talents (or "perfect myself") and how I cooperate with others in achieving any goal (or "happiness").

Now, this basic distinction between *Recht* and *Tugend* is admittedly still obscure, but it at least allows us to see how much weight rests on a full explanation of just what is involved in securing the one necessary end-in-itself, autonomy.

For it is obvious that we are not morally bound never to interfere with the free activity of others, as if we are to stroll by rapists, muggers, and murderers out of respect for their freedom. It would be absurd to do so in the same way that it would be absurd to tolerate, out of a sense of duty to tolerate, brutal intolerance. Also, someone might claim that many actions of ours do restrict, impede, frustrate, limit, and perhaps even deny the free activity of others, without any prima facie moral problem. Economic competition, ownership of private property, various authority relationships, and so forth, would all be relevant examples of interference with the liberty of others that one might claim ought to be legally permissible. Thus, we need to know more precisely when this overriding respect for autonomy demands non-interference and when interference. More precisely, given this new moral test, the question becomes, What *counts* as an action that does not involve treating another as an end in itself? (We should note the parallel problem in the *Tugendlehre:* what counts as being unable to will to adopt a policy because such a willing would be inconsistent with treating others as ends in themselves?)

One way to achieve this clarification, the way taken by both commentators mentioned, is to invoke a more detailed concept of the essential ends of humanity. We know thus far that a just action is one that leaves secured the freedom of others, but not their freedom to do anything. We might then further qualify the duty of justice by claiming that we must then secure the freedom of agents only to pursue the *essential* ends of humanity, or to pursue ends that are in no way inconsistent with the pursuit of these ends. We would not be requiring the pursuit of those ends, nor specifying in any way exactly how they are to be pursued. But Kant does think that he can show that (i) autonomy is an end in itself and (ii) even when acting consistently with respect for autonomy, an agent can still not be presumed to be able to seek any material end unless that agent is able to develop his own talents, and able to pursue his own happiness or collaboration with others. So if our question is, What free activity must be secured? we can answer: the pursuit of these essential ends. Thus we get Jeffrie Murphy's reconstruction of Kant's criterion of just (or right) action.

> X is a right action if and only if the maxim of X would not, if a universal law, interfere with the freedom of any individual rational being to pursue his own ends in action *so long as these ends do not include the denial of freedom to others to pursue their essential ends – happiness and perfection.*[33]

Murphy is quite clear later that this qualification is to function in the relevant political or legal sense at issue throughout our preceding discussion. As he asks, "How are we to know when an abuse of freedom is severe enough to justify intervention?" And later he answers directly that "these ends (happiness and perfection) allow us to define a real violation of freedom."[34] Of course, if this is so, we face the difficult problem of proving that these are the essential ends of humanity, a case that would have to involve quite a complex defense of teleology and essentialism itself before it could be taken seriously. Bruce Aune, who in his recent book adopts, with slight differences, Murphy's teleological answer to the qualification problem sketched, argues persuasively that there is no morally neutral way to define these ends, and thus no way to apply the end-in-itself formula in the way Kant intended.[35]

However, it is at least roughly clear how an appeal to these ends is to function in the crucial ranking problem now before us. In the first place, as Murphy points out, Kant's whole approach, in a way typical of classical liberalism, throws the burden of proof on anyone arguing for interference with the activity of others. Now we can see that what I must show in such cases is that another's acts interfere with my pursuit of, or (in a way that will cause problems shortly) my ability to pursue, an essential end. Thus, I cannot claim that I have a right to demand that others dress neatly or uniformly because sloppy dress so upsets me that I cannot pursue my own ends. We place a strong burden of proof on such a person to show why being free of disgust at sloppy dress is essential to the pursuit of human happiness. Obviously, it is not, in a way quite different from cases where another, by stealing my possessions, beating or murdering me, cheating me or prohibiting me from educating myself, does deprive me of something essential in the pursuit of my happiness. He deprives me of my life; of the food, wealth,

---

33 Murphy, *Kant*, p. 103.
34 Ibid., p. 108.
35 Aune, *Kant's Theory*, p. 121.

shelter, and security necessary to maintain life; or the means to develop my talents so as to improve the kind of life I live – all of which can be said to be essentially involved in the pursuit of any specific goal.

Before examining the problems this account creates, it is important to stress its appeal and force. Murphy states this appeal well and succinctly at one point.

> What we need, obviously, is some way to bring the ideal of pure morality to bear on the concrete empirical contingencies of the human situation. For what is finally rational to do surely depends, at least in part, on the sort of creatures we are.[36]

Further, although there is little direct textual evidence for the reconstruction offered by Murphy, there is much indirect evidence, especially in the *Lecture on Ethics,* that Kant took the notion of these essential ends far more seriously than he often lets on.[37] And, finally, it is also instructive that Kant was forced to include this teleological criterion in his political philosophy at all. It is a fact that renders the standard strict textbook divisions between Kant and, say, Aristotle (or even Hegel and Marx) more than a little suspect.

However, noting this last fact just begins to highlight all the difficulties that must now be addressed. Ironically, Kant, by introducing this Aristotelian component, immediately introduces the classic problem with such an account. Murphy admits that Kant nowhere argues that, from the fact that these are our essential ends, it follows that they are therefore of moral significance. Even if one were to try to state the essentiality of these ends along lines that preserved Kant's insistence that only a will can be good, that problem would still have to be faced. That is, even if one argued that these are not natural ends, but ends I could not but *choose,* the inference to some claim about their moral status needs more development than Kant provides. And, of course, as indicated earlier, it is by no means clear why these two are our essential ends, or even more broadly, exactly what the whole status of teleology is in Kant's architectonic.

Given the interpretation of Kant I want to develop shortly, there are more revealing and interesting problems in Murphy's approach. Recall that all along we have been searching for the moral foundation of legal coercion or authority in the first place. We have been looking for an explanation not just

---

36 Murphy, *Kant,* p. 88.
37 Cf. Murphy's presentation of this evidence, *Kant,* p. 98.

of what I am obliged to do with respect to others, but of on what basis I can be said to be obliged to support the rule of law, which coerces others to do or forbear from doing. Second, we have been searching, within Kant's general moral context, for the scope of the state's authority: in Kant, for the ground of the *Recht–Tugend* distinction. Helpful as his account is, I don't believe Murphy's interpretation gets us any closer to answering these questions.

He himself points out that Kant's brief argument that law analytically contains the authority (*Befügnis*) to compel is not supported by any specific moral argument in Kant. Murphy goes on to suggest that a justification of such authority might be made directly "from the Categorical Imperative." He asks, "Could the maxim 'Permit the abuse of freedom' be a universal law?" and claims that it could not because "as a finite rational creature, I necessarily desire that others not interfere with my freedom."[38] Here we can already see that Murphy's notion of some "essential" facts about human nature has already entered the argument. It may be true that I "necessarily desire that others not interfere with my freedom," or, as he says later, that "I would want others to come to my aid in the event of someone attempting to deprive me of my rights as a man,"[39] but the most this could establish is that I have a duty of virtue to assist others when their freedom is being interfered with (I could not consistently will that abuses of freedom go unchecked). If it were a law of nature that abuses of freedom are permitted, the most that could be said is what Murphy does say, "one would have no security,"[40] and it is still unclear why I have a moral obligation to ensure that this does not happen. Even in such chaos, as Kant often points out, I am unequivocally obliged to obey the moral law, and still "can." We clearly need an additional premise before we can move from the categorical imperative to our duty to collaborate in a state, and I shall try to supply one in a moment.

Also, it can still be asked whether, if certain ends can be established as essential, and if the moral relevance of that fact can be defended, such a fact can function as a criterion to define serious injuries to freedom in the politically relevant sense. In part this question is connected with the former. Even if we can establish that some injuries to another's freedom are more serious than others, or deny his essential ends, we still need to show just why that is politically relevant and other, less serious but still immoral injuries are not. We can say that it would be "odd" to admit that such serious injuries are

38 Ibid., p. 95.
39 Ibid.
40 Ibid.

wrong and "not do anything about it," but why exactly we should do something and what we should do are still left open. Moreover, in part, this question asks whether the "essential ends" criterion does in fact establish the *Recht–Tugend* distinction itself. To see this, consider how many classical problems involved in defining an injury to freedom are still left open by this criterion. If I may not directly interfere with another's pursuit of his essential ends (and may be forcibly prevented from doing so), may I indirectly interfere by impeding his ability to pursue those ends? That is, on the same basis that I use to claim that another's property may not be stolen (that it would make impossible any pursuit of happiness if he were continually insecure in his possessions) might I not also claim that it is impermissible to acquire so much property that I make it effectively impossible for another to acquire the means to pursue his own happiness?

All I want to suggest here is that the issue at stake here – what is sometimes called the problem of "negative" versus "positive" freedom – is not resolved by the "essential ends" form of reasoning. Indeed we are still left with the danger, even with these qualifications defined in terms of the ends of humanity, of a "moral busybody state," or exactly what Kant's grand division in the *Metaphysics of Morals* is to allow us to prevent. For example, the maxim of selfish acts, when considered as a universal law, would certainly interfere with the freedom of individuals in the sense that such acts work to deny (effectively) others the means to pursue their own happiness, all essential ends of humanity, according to Murphy's interpretation. Public sarcasm or vulgarity, if considered universally, as general practices of a society, also seems to injure directly another's free pursuit of happiness. Of course, Kant wants to consider all such duties in the *Tugendlehre,* and to discuss the way in which they violate our duty to treat others as ends in themselves in terms, not of the acts themselves, but of willing the acts. And he also is completely silent about injuries to the essential ends of humanity throughout the *Rechtslehre,* implying, I think, that the treatment in the *Tugendlehre* is the only relevant way respect for autonomy can be connected with these ends. If we leave the situation as Murphy does, I cannot see why acts of avarice or even disrespect should not be said to be "serious" injuries to freedom. We know that individuals ought to be allowed to pursue their ends fully, so long as, to quote Murphy again, "these ends do not include the denial of freedom to others to pursue their essential ends – happiness and perfection." The examples cited previously, though, force a further qualification question, What counts as the "denial of freedom to others?" How seriously must my avarice affect someone for "interference" with the freedom of another to have the means to pursue his happiness, or for "frustration" of that freedom, to count as a "denial"? Murphy begins to discuss this issue by discussing whether homosexual acts can be said to injure my freedom to pursue my ends without disgust, but that case is too easy, as is the sloppy dress case earlier. He does not explain why, on his own criterion, in more obvious cases involving direct effect on the freedom of others like avarice, one should not warrant, say, "Silas Marner laws" prohibiting selfishness and rewarding or even demanding beneficence.

V

However, as indicated earlier, construing Kant's derivation of duties of justice from the moral law as a derivation from the duty to treat others as ends in themselves looks far too promising an interpretation to give up. It looks quite a plausible interpretation of the *Metaphysics of Morals* to suggest that treating others as such ends involves refraining from interfering with their autonomy (or conversely, ensuring that the autonomy of each be secured from injury), as well as developing our own talents and assisting others to achieve their goals. The end-in-itself formula also still looks like a promising way to explain why this distinction in types of duties corresponds to that between "legally enforceable" versus "ethically binding, but not legally enforceable." We can make this distinction by showing that although we can prohibit (or indirectly prohibit, through fear of punishment) actions that are incompatible with autonomy, we cannot (logically cannot) compel the adoption of ends or a policy to help others or develop our talents, and so these latter duties, although they are derivable from the end-in-itself formula, must be left outside the realm of law.[41] All of this seems quite close to Kant's intentions, and, as far as it goes, quite sound. Our problem has continually been to understand how Kant wants to defend a derivation of a class of duties that not only *can* be enforced, but ought to be, and we have suggested that we must settle that issue first before we can begin to understand which duties belong in this class. The "essential ends of humanity" qualification, though on the right track, did not do that, and so we need an alternative, if we wish to preserve the general schema sketched.

I believe that Kant has provided us with this alternative, and that the strategy involved there is more defensible than those surveyed previously. Kant himself, in what is his first mature public statement of his initial *Rechtslehre* (the 1793 theory–practice essay), gives us a clear indication of this

---

41 Kant regularly points out that an agent coerced to pursue some goal or policy cannot be said to have adopted such an end in the morally relevant sense.

alternative. In a context where Kant is discussing the basic issue we are interested in, the relation between moral and political theory, he says the following:

> And the necessity of an ultimate end posited by pure reason and comprehending the totality of all ends within a single principle (i.e., a world in which the highest possible good can be realized with our collaboration) is a necessity experienced by an unselfish will as it rises beyond mere obedience to formal laws and creates as its own object the highest good. The idea or the totality of all ends is a peculiar kind of determinant for the will. For it basically implies that *if* we stand in a moral relationship to things in the world around us, we must everywhere obey the moral law; *and to this is added the further duty of working with all our power to ensure that the state of affairs described above (i.e. a world conforming to the highest moral ends) will actually exist* [my emphasis].[42]

Kant seems to be saying here that we can understand our political obligation (and, thus, conversely, the state's authority) in terms of this "further duty" to pursue or work to ensure the "highest good" (*summum bonum*). And it should not be surprising that Kant would mention this duty to pursue the highest good as part of his derivation of specific, human duties. Five years earlier, in the second *Critique,* he went even further in insisting on the importance of the duty to pursue this end:

> But these truths do not imply that virtue is the entire and perfect good as the object of the faculty of desire of rational finite beings. For this, happiness is also required, and indeed not merely in the partial eyes of a person who makes himself his end but even in the judgment of an impartial reason, which impartially regards persons in the world as ends in themselves.[43]

He even writes, though not without some inconsistency with other passages,

> Since, now, the furthering of the highest good . . . is an a priori necessary object of our will and is inseparably related to the moral law, the impossibility of the highest good must prove the impossibility of the moral law also. If, therefore, the highest good is impossible according to practical rules, then the moral law which commands that it be furthered must be fantastic, directed to empty, imaginary ends, and consequently inherently false.[44]

42 *TP,* p. 65; *AA,* p. 280.
43 *CPrR,* p. 114; *AA,* p. 110.
44 *CPrR,* p. 118; *AA,* p. 114.

However, before trying to show the relevance of this claim to the political context, and before examining the textual evidence to support such a claim for its relevance, it must be admitted that the claim itself is problematic. Commentators have long been puzzled by such passages. The idea of the highest good, it has been argued, might be relevant in Kant's philosophy of religion, or of history. There, given Kant's controversial argument for the "primacy of practical reason," reason might be said to require us to hope, or expect, or think that there is such a highest good, all as a practical condition for continuous moral activity. It is the notion that we are required to *do* something to promote this end that has caused the puzzlement. In the first place, as with the often-criticized notion of postulates of practical reason, such a claim seems to introduce a concern with happiness directly into reflection on moral obligation, and, as every sophomore exposed to the *Grundlegung* knows, such an introduction sounds decidedly un-Kantian. Second, a famous criticism by Lewis White Beck charges that this purported duty is actually vacuous. Beck asks:

> For suppose I do all in my power – which is all my moral decree can demand of me – to promote the highest good, what am I to do? Simply act out of respect for the law, which I already knew. I can do absolutely nothing else toward apportioning happiness in accordance with desert – that is the task of a moral governor of the universe, not of a laborer in the vineyard.[45]

It is, I think, instructive that Beck argues that the task of promoting the highest good is to be assigned to a "governor." In fact, I want to argue, not

45 Lewis White Beck, *A Commentary on Kant's Critique of Practical Reason* (Chicago: University of Chicago Press, 1960), pp. 244–5. There are a number of responses to Beck's criticism. Perhaps the most well known are John Silber's articles, "The Importance of the Highest Good in Kant's Ethics," *Ethics* 73 (1962–3): 179–97, and "Kant's Conception of the Highest Good as Immanent and Transcendent," *Philosophical Review* 68 (1959): 469–92. I agree with the general structure of Silber's reconstruction, as when, in the former article, he writes, "It is the need of a human will for an object that forces Kant to this consideration of ends and to the extension of the law beyond its own limits alone to the condition of man." But I disagree with his neglect of the *Metaphysics of Morals* (as a way of finding out just what this "extension" involves and why), and thus believe he leaves far too vague his final conclusion, that we are "to strive for the realization of happiness in proportion to virtue in the lives of all men" (p. 195). Likewise, in the latter article, although Silber defends well the general relevance of the highest good to Kant's thesis, he again leaves unclarified just what we are supposed to do and why. (There is also no discussion here of the difference between the derived duties of *Recht* and *Tugend*.) The same problem (what am I to do, even if there is a further, immanent duty to pursue the highest good?) is even more apparent in Yirmiahu Yovel's book, *Kant and the Philosophy of History* (Princeton: Princeton University Press, 1980), pp. 104–5, 172, 189.

only is our duty to promote the highest good not vacuous in Kant, but the content of that duty directly involves our governing our own universe, our "collaboration" (a word Kant often uses when mentioning our duty to promote the highest good) in instituting and supporting a *Rechtsstaat*. Basically, what I want to claim is that once we understand why Kant thought that our duty to obey the moral law entails a moral interest in the coincidence of virtue and happiness, we can then understand how specifically political duties can be said to fulfill *that*, if you like, secondary or derived obligation.

Recall again that there are two initial problems with Kant's more extravagant statement about our duty to pursue the highest good. The first is, given Kant's famous insistence on the unconditioned nature of moral obligation, how he can go on to posit a moral interest in the coincidence of virtue and happiness; the second, why such an interest should involve the state. The first problem can be solved if we pay attention to what Kant says about the *necessity*, in any action, of what he calls a "material" end, or, loosely, an interest in happiness. For example, in the second *Critique*, he writes:

> Now it is certainly undeniable that every volition must have an object and therefore a material; but the material cannot be supposed for this reason to be the determining ground and condition of the maxim.[46]

He goes on in *Religion Within the Limits of Reason Alone* to write:

> But although for its own sake morality needs no representation of an end which must precede the determining of the will, it is quite possible that it is necessarily related to such an end, taken not as the ground but as the [sum or] inevitable consequences of maxims adopted as conformable to that end. . . . It is true therefore, that morality requires no end for right conduct. Yet an end does arise out of morality; for how the question, *What is to result from this right conduct of ours?* is to be answered, and towards what, as an end – even granted that it may not be *wholly* subject to our control – we might *direct our actions* and abstentions so as at best to be in harmony with the end: these cannot possibly be matters of indifference to reason [last two emphases mine].[47]

It is, of course, obvious in the preceding that Kant still insists that in a morally worthy action this end not determine the will. But if we, and Kant, remained with this insistence, then, to use now the relevant example, the

---

46 *CPrR*, p. 34; *AA*, p. 34.
47 I. Kant, *Religion Within the Limits of Reason Alone*, trans. T. M. Greene and H. H. Hudson (New York: Harper, 1960), p. 4; *AA*, VI, pp. 4–5.

moral status of political life would be hard if not impossible to assess. Our moral attention would be limited solely to assessing whether we were obeying the moral law or not, and it would, I think, be most unclear what our duty would be if it turned out that many other individuals were *not*. In that case, *I* might still be able to obey the moral law, and although I might strongly disapprove of the wholesale moral chaos going on around me, and might be most unhappy about the disasters that befall me as the one honest man in town, I would have no normative basis for any action other than my own continuing obedience.

Rather, I suggest, it is because Kant realizes that we cannot be indifferent to our pursuit of our own ends (or happiness) and to the consequences of the social practices of others that he argues that respect for the moral law itself (the only true incentive), when thought of together with the necessary characteristics of volition, generates a secondary "duty of justice," a duty that involves not only our own individual respect for the freedom of others, but allegiance to a legal institution that compels that respect, at least formally, from others. Again, the core of this argument is that, although, in any one act of volition, I *can* remain effectively indifferent to my material end (which I nonetheless still desire), I cannot *continually* remain indifferent to being able to achieve my ends in concert with others achieving theirs, all subject to the condition that no one violate the moral law in doing so. (That is, I cannot simply obey the moral law, without having some interest that my pursuit of my own ends is not thereby endangered or frustrated.)[48] If I tried to argue that way, to remain content with being some perpetually tragic moral hero, indifferent to his own ends, only concerned with doing the right thing, I would in effect be denying, or at best ignoring, what Kant takes it we have just admitted: that each action necessarily presupposes a material end. In other words, as Kant pointed out to Garve, not only am I not forever condemned to excluding consideration of my happiness in my pursuit to be "worthy" of it, but I *cannot* be indifferent to the possibility of a coincidence of happiness and moral worth.[49] What I am claiming here is that this impos-

---

48 The modality issue here is complex and insufficiently discussed by Kant. I can always simply do the right thing according to Kant (the right remains the *supremum bonum* in Kant, the condition of all other value). But *once* that is admitted, I cannot ignore my empirical nature, or leave wholly unconsidered the possible coincidence of happiness and virtue. My interest in moral worth must lead to an interest in whether or not pursuit of this worthiness is Sisyphean.

49 "Nor had I omitted to point out at the same time that man is not thereby expected to *renounce* his natural aim of attaining happiness as soon as the question of following his duty arises; for like any finite rational being, he *simply cannot do so*" (my emphasis). *TP*, p. 64; *AA*, p. 278.

sibility is what is most of all at work in Kant's transition from morality to politics.

Such a suggested transition is not yet effected, and the argument itself still has to be spelled out in more detail, but the basic form of Kant's argument for what he had called, in the 1793 theory–practice essay, the "further duty" to promote the highest good should be clear. Assuming that I have a duty to respect others as ends in themselves, then, Kant is arguing, I cannot be indifferent to others' *not being* so treated, to their being treated as means in the pursuit of material ends. This, though, does not mean that I must attempt to coerce others to give up their pursuit of those ends, in order to ensure this respect. I know, for one thing, that such a pursuit *cannot* be given up. In other words, I have the "further duty" of creating a situation where such a moral ideal of autonomy is actualized, and I know that one of the conditions of any such actualization is pursuit of happiness. And, I believe, Kant thinks a state can most effectively ensure that obedience to the law coincide with the possible pursuit of happiness: or, stated negatively, that I and others are not "victims" or "means" for others just because we respect autonomy, and do not lie, cheat, rob, or embezzle.

Now clearly, nothing in his argument claims that the state or any agency must actually bring about happiness. Kant realizes that no one can create happiness any more than one can create internal or truly moral obedience to the law. But my moral interest in a just polity is, I think, best explained in Kant by means of this *summum bonum* form of reasoning. Also, it is clear, just from the architectonic division of the *Metaphysics of Morals*, that Kant does not think that all moral duties to others are the subject of legislative coercion. He must defend only a restricted set of "minimal" or "essential" duties to others as so subject. If we look now at Kant's entire system of moral duty, reconstructed in the way I have suggested, we can see clearly where this restriction becomes most important.

(i) Given Kant's "critical" demonstration of the possibility of morality, he grounds all moral obligation on reason, so interpreted in the practical realm that it virtually means autonomy (in the literal sense of self-legislation). (ii) The law relevant to such self-legislation can only be the categorical imperative. (iii) The "*typic*" of the moral law for human beings is a "law of nature," understood as a harmony of beings pursuing their ends, where human agents are ends in themselves. (iv) Our obligation to treat other rational beings as ends in themselves entails a further obligation – to do what we can do to establish the most favorable conditions under which others are treated as ends in themselves. This obligation stems from the impossibility of continual indifference to achieving our material ends, consistent with the moral law and with others' achieving their material ends (happiness). (v) When we specify what we can do to fulfill (iv), we find two types of obligations: (a) to collaborate in civil society by prohibiting actions that, considered universally, would render impossible any agent's pursuing his own ends in conformity with the moral law (i.e., with respect for agents as ends in themselves), and (b) doing what we can as individuals actually to promote and aid others in achieving their ends, and the development of our talents.

Clearly, within this overview, one wants to know how to use this duty to pursue the highest good to help make out the distinction between (iva) and (ivb). But before addressing that issue, I also want to stress the textual evidence for using this approach. Its role is even apparent in passages where Kant seems to contradict it – where he sounds his most rigoristic. For example, in the 1793 theory–practice essay, he writes:

> But the whole concept of an external right is derived entirely from the concept of *freedom* in the mutual external relationships of human beings, and has nothing to do with the end which all men have by nature (i.e. the aim of achieving happiness) or with the recognised means of achieving this end.[50]

Or, even more directly, "No generally valid principle of legislation can be based on happiness."[51] But in these passages, Kant is arguing against an attempt to legislate in order to promote some particular view of "what makes men happy." He is not discounting the relevance of a concern for happiness to our interest in politics. Again, without this relevance, given only our moral duty to respect others as ends in themselves, political institutions would, at best, be consistent with that duty, not required by it, as the *Rechtslehre* teaches. Indeed, just after the last quotation, Kant writes,

> The doctrine that *salus publica suprema civitatis lex est* retains its value and authority undiminished, but the public welfare which demands *first* consideration lies precisely in that legal constitution which guarantees everyone his freedom within the law, so that each remains free to seek his happiness in whatever way he thinks best, so long as he does not violate the lawful freedom and rights of his fellow subjects at large.[52]

50 *TP,* p. 73; *AA,* p. 289.
51 *TP,* p. 80; *AA,* p. 298.
52 Ibid.

Such a claim seems to me perfectly consistent with the interpretation presented here of our duty to promote the highest good.

Moreover, at several places in the body of the *Rechtslehre* itself, Kant's own formulations frequently echo just this form of reasoning about the conditions for autonomy. Most clearly, in section 41 he writes, "A juridical state of affairs is a relationship among human beings that involves the conditions under which alone every man *is able to enjoy his right*."[53] Passages like these confirm that, in deliberating about the structure of political institutions, we are deliberating not only about the normative issue of right, but, to a larger extent than is often realized in discussions of Kant, about the empirical conditions that allow the *exercise* of rights.

It is undeniably true, though, that when Kant speaks most directly about the practical conditions of the moral law being respected, he mentions either the religion postulates, or his conjectural philosophy of history (i.e., what we ought to believe in order to "keep faith" with the law). Such remarks, unfortunately, not only cloud the picture concerning Kant's reasoning about the highest good, they introduce a good deal of tension into that theory. (If the existence of a benevolent deity and the immortality of the soul can be practically established, then my necessary interest in happiness is *fully* reconciled with my striving for moral worth, no *practicum absurdum* issue need arise, and, as in Beck's criticism, there is nothing for me to do to promote the highest good. The "governor" of the vineyard will see to it, ultimately.)[54] Even with this problem admitted, though, it is most important to stress that even in these contexts, the general form of practical reasoning at work in all Kant's moral philosophy is visible. To cite the two most important elements stressed here: (i) that obedience to the moral law entails more than doing the right thing in any individual action, but that such duties

---

53 *MEJ*, p. 69; *AA*, pp. 305–6. Cf. also Kant's note, *Reflexion* 6631, *AA*, XIX, p. 119: "Principium formale identitis in moralibus. Materiale: felicitas publica." I am thus disagreeing with the interpretation presented by Klaus Düsing in his "Das Problem des höchsten Gutes in Kants praktischer Philosophie," *Kant-Studien* 62 (1971): 5–42, although this article in general is an invaluable guide to the range of different uses to which Kant put his "highest good" doctrine. See also the lucid discussion by Otfried Höffe, "Recht und Moral: Ein kantischer Problemaufriss," *Neue Hefte für Philosophie* 17 (1979): 1–34. Höffe approaches this problem by pointing out how Kant mediates the traditional opposition between the natural right and positivist traditions, agreeing that *Recht* and *Moral* do not coincide (and that *Recht* requires compulsion), but insisting on the necessity, nonetheless, of a normative foundation for *Recht*. Like so many commentators, however, Höffe leaves unexplained how this distinction is to be defended, and what in particular follows from it.

54 See Allen Wood, *Kant's Moral Religion* (Ithaca: Cornell University Press, 1970), pp. 1–99, especially pp. 25–33, for a fuller discussion of the moral foundations of Kant's philosophy of religion.

themselves are duties only because of general duty to respect a certain ideal of human autonomy, an ideal we cannot take seriously without also acting to promote it, to see to it that it is respected; and (ii) that the central issue at stake in doing what we can to promote that ideal is reconciling it with desire for our happiness. Kant just wandered a bit, all over his moral map, as he tried to come up with either arguments that would make this ideal theoretically reconcilable with our empirical nature or more specific duties tied to this general obligation to promote the ideal of autonomy.

As final textual support, I would also argue that, without this component's being taken seriously as part of Kant's political reflections, there is no way, aside from armchair psychologizing, to explain why the theorist who perhaps most radically defended the absolutely inalienable, moral character of rights should have been such a cautious reformist, such a resolute anti-revolutionary. Our first derived duty is to be in civil society, for Kant, the *minimum* empirical condition for any protection of rights. As we shall see, just how the pursuit of material ends and the protection of human autonomy as an end in itself can be reconciled is remarkably wide open in Kant (all much to the irritation of later Kantian political theorists like Gentz and Rehburg, some of whom tried to develop a theory of human nature to pin this down more concretely).[55] But, for the moment, all I can claim here is that this interpretation at least systematically explains this prudential reformism in Kant.

VI

Although this reconstruction of the moral foundation of political duty differs from others presented here, it still faces the "ranking" problem involved in the *Recht–Tugend* distinction. We have at last seen that for Kant our obligation to the state stems from our obligations to ensure respect for the freedom of all, and we know that, for human beings, the crucial consideration in such ensuring is allowing the possibility of the pursuit of happiness, coincident with respect for others as ends in themselves. We now want to know what formal principles of a state *do* ensure this, as opposed to what we as individuals must do privately in respecting the autonomy of others and in furthering their being so respected.

That is, we still have to ask about more specific actions ranked close together as all violations of the moral law, but still significantly different.

---

55 Cf. *Über Theorie und Praxis*, ed. by Dieter Henrich (Frankfurt am M.: Suhrkamp, 1967), especially the introduction by Henrich, "Über den Sinn vernunftigen Handelns im Staat."

What makes my use of another as a means in one context unjust and so prohibitable (like violating the provisions of a contract), in another somewhat immoral (like withering sarcasm or greed), and in others morally neutral (as when I gleefully exploit my opponent's backhand in tennis, knowing that it embarrasses him and that I am using him only as a means for my own pleasure)? These questions are quite involved and go to the heart of many contemporary disputes about such issues as the relative rank of market freedoms versus the freedom to develop distinctly "human potential." But the interpretation offered here at least gives us a clear Kantian way to approach them (although I am not sure that it gives us a way to resolve them). Given what has here been identified as the foundation of the duty of justice, what we must show, in order to show that an act that treats others as means is unjust, is that the act (or maxim) when considered universally would make a civil society of autonomous agents *impossible*. It would thereby violate the *fundamental* duty of justice – to enter and remain in civil society, the one clear empirical condition for ensuring that human autonomy is minimally respected. Such acts could be shown to be different from treating others as means in ways that make achieving their (and our) goals difficult (but not impossible) and that thus I could not rationally will to universalize. (This distinction also corresponds to what can be prohibited, actions, versus what cannot, goals or objects of the will.) More precisely, this ranking principle includes prohibitions against acts that make the continued existence of civil society impossible, such as the use of the institution of private property to exploit and destroy natural resources.

To be sure, it might seem that we still do not have a clear criterion by which to define which acts would, if permitted, render a civil society of autonomous agents impossible. In clear cases it is not hard to see how the pursuit of any material end would be impossible if cheating on contracts or robbery were allowed, or how the very ground of the duty to enter civil society in the first place would be contradicted if institutions like slavery were allowed. Given that no one could pursue any plan of life without life, some security in the means necessary to pursue his ends, and sufficient freedom from authority to form such a plan and act on it; and given that the whole point of civil society is to make possible pursuit of such ends, in uniformity with the moral requirement to respect others' freedom to do likewise, a civil society that made such a coincidence impossible would be incoherent, from Kant's point of view.[56]

---

56 This reasoning about ranking is similar to one suggested, but not used, by Rawls in *A Theory of Justice*, p. 42. At least in this book, Rawls prefers a ranking principle more in line with his

However, can anything more specific be said about these conditions? What are the externally legislatable (and only externally legislatable) means necessary to secure individual pursuit of happiness consistent with respect for autonomy? Kant is notoriously brief in answering this question in the *Metaphysics of Morals*. With respect to "private law," he deals mostly with property rights; in the section on public law, he briefly argues for the separation of powers, a vague version of republicanism, and the necessity that citizens be free, equal, and independent; he denies the right of revolution, and discusses public welfare, public offices, the right to punish, and some issues in international relations. It would take far more space than I have left here to attempt to assess whether Kant's discussion of all of these issues can be defended along the general lines suggested here. I want to close by discussing one of them – property rights – as a way of raising a serious problem remaining in Kant's account. A full "Kantian theory of institutions" will have to await a future discussion.

I have been arguing that, although there is a fundamental connection between Kant's moral and political theory, there is also an important principle demarcating each realm. That is, political duties are just those moral duties to others that it is not only permissible but obligatory to compel. Said another way, political sanctions involve only the protection of rights. I have further argued, incorporating some of Kant's brief remarks on external legislation and perfect duties, that the criterion that defines which duties ought to be compelled must involve Kant's argument about our "further duty" to promote the highest good, that is, to prohibit those actions or institutional practices aimed at a material end in a way incompatible with respect for human autonomy and/or the minimal condition required for that autonomy to be respected: the rule of law. Now, putting all this together, it would not be difficult to show, as indicated earlier, how, for a modern, or even eighteenth-century, European society, this view would condemn slavery or endorse some standard list of basic liberal rights. Moreover,

contractarian argument, which he calls a "lexical" ordering principle. However, putting aside for the moment complications introduced by his later Dewey Lectures, I would argue that the interpretation offered here is closer to the requirements of Rawls's theory than some of his own formulations. As stated in *A Theory of Justice* (sect. 40, "The Kantian Interpretation of Justice as Fairness") and in "A Kantian Conception of Equality," *Cambridge Review* (1975), I do not think Rawls can justify the priorities of his original contractors on *Kantian* grounds. The situation is rather as if Hobbesian egoists were forced into a situation with Kantian restraints. See here the criticism of Andrew Levine, "Rawls' Kantianism," *Social Theory and Practice* 3 (1974–5): 47–63. Put another way, I think that the interpretation defended here better explains a "Kantian" interest in the material conditions of freedom stressed in Rawls's second principle (and also helps correct the standard view of Kant used against Rawls by such commentators as Levine).

one could also easily show that certain rights, like free speech or vigorous expression of disagreement, are essential to respect for autonomy and that they thus may not be abridged for the sake of any general moral duty we have to aid others in their quest for happiness and so refrain from public vulgarity or sarcastic criticism. But the point at issue now is, Do these considerations not only legitimate the "rule of law" *überhaupt* but also help specify the kind of laws that may be adopted? For example, what should be the permissible extent of ownership and use of property?

Not surprisingly, at least not surprisingly given the preceding interpretation, Kant deals with such an issue only in a highly abstract way, leaving a very good deal, too much I shall argue, open to contingent legislative decision. For he argues not that property rights are directly derivable from the duty of justice, and certainly not that any particular institution of property is. All he thinks he can claim is that ownership of some property is a "postulate" of justice. Generally, he means by this (i) that ownership of property in some form is not inconsistent with the duty of justice and that it is thus permissible (a *lex permissiva* or *Erlaubnisgesetz*); (ii) that the idea of rendering *any* object a *res nullius*, the property of no one, would be inconsistent with the exercise of freedom, for, "in that case, freedom would be robbing itself of the use of its will in relation to an object of the same will inasmuch as it would be placing usable objects outside all possibility of being used;"[57] and (iii) that, therefore, it would be unjust to prohibit this permissible exercise of freedom.

In the body of his discussion, however, he is mostly concerned with two more general issues: to show how and why de jure possession, or what he calls *possessio noumenon*, is possible, and through the use of this concept, to show that if there is such noumenal possession, interfering with it would be a violation of justice; second, to show how this de jure possession is possible only in civil society, not in the state of nature.[58] He thus only claims, as a conclusion, "It is a duty of justice to act towards others so that external

57 *MEJ*, p. 52; *AA*, p. 246.
58 There is thus no natural right to property in Kant, nor any natural entitlement to property improved through our labor, and so forth. This is so because without an institutional framework, there would be no way to distinguish empirical possession, which is not, according to Kant, even having property, from noumenal possession. The latter depends on the possibility of possessions being recognized, to use the Hegelian notion, as property by citizens. That possibility is what makes possession property. However, this just requires some *public* rule specifying what property is so that I can be assured that, if I am subject to these rules in the acquisition of property, others are too, equally. It does not presuppose that all do agree (or implicitly agree), as a general will, on what these rules are. This point is badly confused by Howard Williams in "Kant's Concept of Property," *Philosophical Quarterly* 27 (1977): 39. See *MEJ*, pp. 64–5; *AA*, p. 256.

objects (usable objects) can also become someone's [property]"[59] (my emphasis).

This argument, on the one hand, confirms much of what has been said here about Kant's political philosophy, but, on the other, stops curiously short of extending that reasoning into more detail. That is, Kant discusses the general issue of property rights in a way we would, by now, expect: as a condition for the exercise of autonomy. I cannot value freedom so highly without ensuring that there be some means for my exercising my freedom, and the use of objects without threat of theft is just such a means. Even at this level, though, Kant's claims are empirically unstable, since he nowhere argues that private ownership alone is an indispensable means for the exercise of such autonomy (as, for example, Hegel does).[60] He does not consider (although he admits the possibility of) collective, legally defined ownership of land.

But more to the point here, Kant has very little to say about the extent to which the general duty of justice might impose limits on the possible legislative acquisition of further, more specific property rights. He can show that if there is de jure possession in civil society, violation of this possession is an injury to human autonomy, but he has little to say about whether justice requires any specific social institution of private property. Given the case presented, we might expect him to be able to argue that property rights are rights at all only if they can be shown to be morally permissible and empirically necessary to the exercise of autonomy. But that case defends the value of private property only because of a prior commitment to the moral ideal of autonomy itself. Thus we would also argue that the institution of private property is limitable: no use of private property may be inconsistent with the very ideal that legitimates it. More concretely, we might then argue that no claim about rights of ownership in, say, a restaurant, given why that right is a right, can be consistent with the exercise of that right to deny persons use of that restaurant on the basis of some claim that denies universal autonomy, such as race. We might even argue that the use of property for profit is, especially in an economic system where there is little or no option about employment for wage earners, inconsistent with dehumanizing, mechanical labor. Of course, even in such an argument, we would need to be mindful of Kant's concern with securing the minimal empirical conditions

59 *MEJ*, p. 60; *AA*, p. 252.
60 G. W. F. Hegel, *Philosophy of Right*, trans. T. M. Knox (Oxford: Oxford University Press, 1967), pp. 40–57; *Grundlinien der Philosophie des Rechts* (Hamburg: Felix Meiner Verlag, 1955), pp. 55–79.

for the pursuit of any material end, but, for all his formalistic rigor, Kant is almost excessively concerned with this latter issue.

Thus, for example, when discussing in the 1793 theory–practice essay the moral ("a priori") requirements of equality in civil society, Kant admits:

> This uniform equality of human beings as subjects of a state is, however, perfectly consistent with the utmost inequality of the mass in the degree of its possessions[61]

and he goes on to state the classical liberal formulation of equality as equality before the law alone. However, he also insists in this passage that no one may "stand in the way" of another's equal opportunity for advancement by means of hereditary privilege. Such inheritance of *authority* would be inconsistent with the freedom of all. But Kant simply allows that a subject "may hand down everything else"[62] and thereby "create considerable inequalities in wealth among members of a commonwealth."[63] He just does not consider the issue raised so often in the nineteenth century, whether this inequality alone just as effectively "prevents" equal opportunity of advancement as inherited authority. That is, he does not consider whether his own argument about hereditary privilege should lead him to deny an unrestricted right to bequeath property. Given that property rights, as interpreted previously, are not directly included within the duty of justice, but are only argued for as "a condition" of autonomy, various empirical and historical factors might convince one that some particular institution of property impeded rather than promoted such universal autonomy, and so violated our duty to promote the highest good.[64]

This hesitation to deal with the details of the empirical conditions of autonomy is visible in several other passages, particularly in those in *Perpetual Peace* where Kant insists on perpetual peace as a moral ideal for statesmen, but condemns any "precipitate" means toward that ideal, endorsing a notion of prudence so vague as to be almost meaningless (or, at best,

---

61 *TP,* p. 75; *AA,* p. 292.
62 *TP,* p. 76; *AA,* p. 293.
63 Ibid.
64 Of course, those who because of unrestricted economic competition are too poor to make use of their "equal opportunity" would, although still free to do so, find this freedom valueless. And Hart is right to point out in "Are There Any Natural Rights?" p. 75, that these are still two *different* evils, not to be confused. Nevertheless, given the argument presented, once we know why economic freedom is a right, that reasoning might just as well convince us that this other worry is a politically relevant wrong and hence an object of legislative concern.

Burkean).[65] If the interpretation presented here is at all correct, then his own case for the general duty of justice provides him with the theoretical resources to extend his reasoning about the conditions of right in ways far more detailed than he attempted.

That is, in sum, he need not have restricted himself, in either of these cases, to his famous legalism. Since, as we have interpreted the argument, our obligation to the laws of civil society is based on general obligation to promote and secure the conditions under which the pursuit of material ends is consistent with respect for autonomy, a theoretical consideration of the social institutions within which this quest for material happiness takes place could certainly be far more detailed, and less open to simple contingencies, than Kant allows. If what we might loosely call the "highest good" form of reasoning is inherently involved in why duties of justice are duties at all, then the famous post-Kantian extension of a concern for justice into social as well as political institutions could be seen as wholly consistent with Kantian premises.

A good deal more methodological and historically relevant detail would have to be provided before this extension could be fully defended, but the structure of such an argument is inherent in Kant's own case, or at least in any successful general reconstruction of it. Providing this detail, that is, would just be to take seriously Kant's own words quoted earlier: "What is to result from this right conduct of ours . . . cannot possibly be matters of indifference to reason."[66]

---

65 I. Kant, "Perpetual Peace," trans. H. B. Nisbet, in *Kant's Political Writings*, p. 122; *AA*, VIII, pp. 377–8.

66 See note 47.

4

HEGEL, ETHICAL REASONS,
KANTIAN REJOINDERS

I. Rousseau's Problem

The term *ethical reason* is not a Hegelian term of art, but it highlights a problem Hegel clearly must address. He is well known for claiming that a worthy or good life involves achieving some sort of identification with various modern social institutions. It is only by participating in such institutions, by adopting and affirming the central modern social roles, that a good life with others can be led. However, Hegel does not believe that this process of identification is wholly psychological or a social fact of the matter. The basis of the reconciliation is, in some way, reason.

Traditionally, this has often been understood to mean that the central modern institution for Hegel, the state, represents some sort of necessary manifestation or coming to self-consciousness of World or Cosmic Spirit. Various modern institutions are rational because of the role of such institutions in the unfolding of reason itself, logos, or the word of God. My purpose in the following is to show that Hegel ought not to be understood as advancing any such theodicy or cosmic claim, that he means pretty much what he seems to mean when he says such things as in "the ethical world" it is "reason" that has "power and mastery," or that "the science of right" will "conceive and present the state as something in itself rational," or, in Gans's addition, "In right, man must meet with his own reason."[1] This all seems to

---

1 *PR*, pp. 7; 4; *PR*, 15; 11; *PRG*, 17; 224. For the most part, all references to the *Philosophy of Right* (*PR*) will be to *Grundlinien der Philosophie des Rechts* (Hamburg: Felix Meiner Verlag,

mean and, I think, does mean, that it must be possible to demonstrate that any modern agent would have good, in some cases overriding, reasons ("*his own* reasons") for affirming what is required in a modern society: as a family member, a participant and competitor in civil society, and a citizen of a modern state. Since Hegel is pretty clear that I am not morally obligated to engage in such roles, and that these reasons are not the result of an implied contract, or of any attempt at the maximization of my self-interest or even the exercise of prudence, he is obviously obliged to tell us what such reasons could be. And that is just what he is trying to do throughout the *Philosophy of Right.*

No full defense of such a notion will be possible here, but I want to indicate what motivates Hegel's claim that there are such reasons, why they are not moral or prudential, and just what else would have to be defended in any claim that there are ethical reasons to act in contemporary society. I shall be especially interested in the distinction between moral and ethical reasons, and in whether many recent discussions of Kant succeed in undermining or avoiding Hegel's objections to the moral point of view.

To understand Hegel's strategy, we need first to recall that Hegel inherits a tradition that begins with Rousseau.[2] This is especially so since Hegel will make a case for such reasons by arguing that it is only as such a social participant that I can be a free subject, truly self-determining, and thereby be able to recognize myself in my deeds and practices. And this way of thinking about the problem can be traced to a famous passage at the end of the *Second Discourse,* where Rousseau introduces us to the great disease of modern civilized life.

> The Savage lives in himself; sociable man, always outside himself, is capable of living only in the opinion of others; and so to speak, derives the sentiment of his own existence solely from their judgment.[3]

1955) and, where possible, will refer to paragraph number or the Remark (R) to the paragraph. Any page numbers will be followed by a reference to Hegel's *Philosophy of Right* trans. T. M. Knox (hereafter *PRE* 2) (Oxford: Clarendon Press, 1967), which I have relied on, though often altered. For the additions of Eduard Gans, see *Grundlinien der Philosophie des Rechts* (hereafter *PRG*) (Berlin: Akademie Verlag, 1981).

2 I note that Hegel's own remarks on Rousseau do little to make clear the positive nature of his relation to Rousseau. He stresses instead Rousseau's individualism, to such an extent that he seems to confuse (or not to believe that Rousseau can defend) the crucial distinction between the "will of all" and the "general will." See the comments in *PR* §29R, and §258R.

3 Jean-Jacques Rousseau, *The First and Second Discourses and Essay on the Origin of Languages,* ed. and trans. by Victor Gourevitch (New York: Harper & Row, 1986), 199.

In the midst of such a miserable dependence, we are

> forever asking of others what we are, without ever daring to ask it of ourselves, in the midst of so much Philosophy, humanity, politeness, and Sublime maxims, we have nothing more than a deceiving and frivolous exterior, honor without virtue, reason without wisdom, and pleasure without happiness.[4]

This famous concern creates Rousseau's famous problem, a problem much at issue in different ways in the later German tradition, and, as we shall see, especially important for Hegel. On the one hand, savage or primitive independence is actually, Rousseau argues, chance isolation from, and ignorance of, others: not true independence from them. Further, no such savage is truly self-determining because so ignorant of self.[5] (They are not dependent, without being truly independent.) On the other hand, what we eventually establish as marks of independence in society – property, prestige, all the other consequences of amour-propre – and the self we end up caring so much about, everywhere involve a slavish dependence on the "opinions of others." In society independence is always fragile and suspicious, and, ironically, establishing such independence seems to require acknowledgment by, dependence on, others.

What then will count as the achievement of freedom in a social setting? Once we come to see ourselves as others see us, able to evaluate ourselves no longer absolutely, but only relatively, how might we ever return to ourselves? We seem forever unsure of the worth of our own desires, and so desire that others affirm us as we want to be seen; we need that in order to be sure that we are who we take ourselves to be. In such a situation, in what sense is "independence" ever possible?

We might claim that this all involves far too extravagant a requirement, that the independence required to be truly free involves unsatisfiable stan-

---

4 Ibid.
5 Each savage may have "considered himself master of everything," but only because of his "weakness and ignorance." In reality, by having no understanding of others outside their family, "*they did not understand themselves.* They had the concept of a father, a son, a brother, but not that of a man." Rousseau, *Essay on the Origin of Languages,* pp. 261, 262 (my emphasis). Rousseau's claim is that it is chance alone that helps create new sorts of desires, the sociable and deeply ambiguous desires alluded to previously, and which so much comprise the subject of Rousseau's work. In this charming, if often incredible account of the origin of language, this chance event (at least for southern languages) is the uneven distribution of water supplies for livestock and household use, and the chance encounters of the boys and girls from entirely different families who must congregate at these watering holes and confront a truly distinct Other. Reading the account, one would not guess that Rousseau is as much describing the origin of slavery as of human love. See especially p. 271.

dards for finite creatures like us. It might be enough for us to be relatively unconstrained by others in the pursuit of our wants, and to have some sort of second-order relation to these wants, to be capable of thinking about and altering them. Rousseau and many after him, for the first time aware of the great depth and often the sheer contingency of modern socialization, do not settle for such a notion of freedom. Rousseau, and others of the same period (like Herder), realized that they lived in very different sorts of societies, societies that were themselves, for the first time, so powerfully influential and formative that any future talk of the strictly natural requirements of man, the nature of our sympathies, the predictability of our passions would be dangerously simplistic. From now on, it was clear that if we were to be consistently free, we must be autonomous, directing life in a way wholly self-imposed and self-regulated.

Rousseau's attempt to formulate a political satisfaction of this criterion will lead to several larger themes at stake first in Kant, and then in Hegel, and so back to the theme of ethical reasons. Simply put, Rousseau believes that we must *completely* achieve civic virtue for this problem to be resolved.[6] Most famously this means subjecting ourselves to the "general will"; more complexly it means coming to understand ourselves, our individual egos, in a wholly new way, as intimately bound up with the will of all other citizens. The *moi individu* is both the source of the self-serving egoism that generates the anomie, fragmentation, and chaos Rousseau sees as typical of modern political life, and is itself illusory. Once we are socialized, the very sentiment of our own existence, so thoughtlessly esteemed by us, in which we take so much pride, is not ours, but depends on others. However, to be dependent on the civic unit or state, on the whole as general will, is not to be dependent on others, but, finally and truly, on ourselves.[7] Acting for ourselves in the usual sense (egoism) is acting in the service of what others (or brute circumstances) have taught us to want. Only by freely subjecting ourselves to the general will, by identifying ourselves with the general, wholly objective good,

---

6 I pass over the tension between the solution proposed in such works as the *Second Discourse* and the *Social Contract* and that suggested by *Reveries of a Solitary Walker.* The latter intimate that the former would be, but cannot be, a solution. On the character of Rousseau's utopianism, see Judith Shklar, *Men and Citizens: A Study of Rousseau's Social Theory* (London: Cambridge University Press, 1969). See also David Gauthier's remarks about the "post-social" self in his "*Le Promeneur Solitaire:* Rousseau and the Emergence of the Post-Social Self," *Social Philosophy and Policy* 8 (1990): 35–58, especially p. 55.

7 This is the infamous, paradoxical claim of the *Social Contract*, bk. I, ch. 7, that such a "giving of each citizen to the country," or the ominous "forcing him to be free," "ensures him against all personal dependence." *The Political Writings of Jean-Jacques Rousseau*, II, ed. C. E. Vaughan (New York: John Wiley & Sons, 1962), p. 36.

not the preserve of any one or group, can we be self-determining agents. (Or at least, only in this way can we *ensure* that we are *not* other-determined.) And at this point the problems, ambiguities, and *aporiai* tumble from Rousseau on every page. What appears to be a radical democratic claim, with everything depending on the equal will of each, turns out to be less a theory of will than a procedure for confirming or recognizing the common good. (Democracy is the only form of sovereignty, but aristocracy is the best form of government.) Man is born free, but if he is to live free in society, his sentiments must be strictly educated on every significant issue. (He must be "forced to be free," in this as well as other senses.) The achievement of such civic virtue, such an identification (rather than sacrifice) of self with the common good, seems to depend for its realization on an odd condition: that it has already been achieved. The possibility of transforming particular will and self-love into an identification with the general will requires individuals already socialized in a community governed by the general will.[8]

And then there is the immense problem of the "legislator." It is due to his work that individuals can come to appreciate the only condition under which they can truly be the subject of their own deeds, can be free from the opinions of others, and can "become who they truly are," virtuous citizens of the republic. As such subjects they achieve freedom in appreciating the vanity and so dependence of egoism and self-love. But the educator himself seems to have a divine, inhuman status; his own coercive, deceptive powers (especially with respect to civil religion) seem almost unlimited. Most importantly, his work seems never done, just as Émile and Sophie seem permanently dependent on their Tutor, supposedly the source of their final independence.[9]

Genuine independence, then, involves a puzzling condition. It requires an independence of or even alienation of the self from itself, an ability of a subject to stand above everything he or she has come to care most deeply about, not as a way of realizing more coherently something most of all or supremely cared about, but to determine, as if *ab initio,* what should be

---

8 On this and other points in this paragraph see the discussion by Patrick Riley, *Will and Political Legitimacy: A Critical Exposition of Social Contract Theory in Hobbes, Locke, Rousseau, Kant, and Hegel* (Cambridge: Harvard University Press, 1982), pp. 98–124, especially p. 110.

9 Cf. the uses to which David Gauthier puts this important point in "The Politics of Redemption," in *Moral Dealings: Contract, Ethics and Reason* (Ithaca: Cornell University Press, 1990), pp. 77–109. Gauthier is surely right that Rousseau has not identified any successful political redemption, any way out of the secular "fall" into dependence and egoism. Whether, therefore, "we *must* live, unredeemed," p. 109, is another matter. On the cultural and historical problem of autonomy see my *Modernism as a Philosophical Problem: On the Dissatisfactions of European High Culture* (Oxford: Basil Blackwell, 1991).

cared about at all, or at least what should be done. For some, this kind of attempt to ensure that my projects and goals are mine, that I pass judgment on the cares and interests that have formed my character and so, in effect, reform myself reflectively, ironically requires a loss of any genuine or concrete self. This adoption of an impersonal, reflective standpoint ("what any rational agent would value," the general will) would appear to increase self-alienation rather than resolve it (assuming that the legislator cannot succeed in reforming our souls), and to generate a host of "moral motivation" puzzles.

The problem at issue, then, is, Under what conditions can I view what I resolve to do as truly self-determined? The question implies a suspicion, a denial that simply being able to get what I want counts as an instance of such self-determination, and a demand that links freedom with some sort of rational self-reflection and self-rule. And the question's very formulation has seemed to many to suggest the problematic solution just described: I am a free agent only by conforming to some universal rule of reason, and so by sacrificing, by not counting as important, all the particular cares and wants that make me *me*.[10]

II. Hegel's Promises

Hegel's language in his many different accounts of "objective spirit," although idiosyncratic, clearly reveals that he accepts this way of framing the problem and believes he has resolved it. Freedom is understood as the greatest human good (the "goal" of any "free mind" (*PR* §27)), and is not only understood as a kind of independence, but seems at first glance like a fantastically extravagant autonomy. In his view, the achievement of human

10 It would clearly introduce many more issues than can be managed here, but formulating the problem this way already highlights a difference between those influenced by (generally) Hume, for whom any reason to act could be a reason only if it offered some sort of (not necessarily causal or efficient) *means* to the satisfaction of desires, "the passions," or, much more broadly, a prior "subjective motivational set" and those influenced (roughly) by Rousseauean worries about the origin of such a "set," and so the problem of autonomy. See Bernard Williams, "Internal and External Reasons," in *Moral Luck* (Cambridge: Cambridge University Press, 1981), pp. 101–13, and the brief discussion later in note 16. Also highly relevant here are the issues brought out by John McDowell, "Are Moral Requirements Hypothetical Imperatives?" *Proceedings of the Aristotelian Society* 52 (1978): 13–29. His attempt to distinguish between considerations that motivate me to act only when coupled with an independently identifiable desire and considerations, or views of the world, that motivate me to act on their own is relevant to Hegel's attempt to understand ethical reasons on a model neither Humean nor Kantian, although exploring that issue would be a major discussion in itself.

freedom, a freedom in which the will has become "truly infinite" and "has itself as its object" (*PR* §22), means achievement of a state where the will is "absolutely with itself (*schlechthin bei sich*), because then it is related to nothing except itself and thereby involves no relation to anything other than itself" (*PR* §23).

This language of "being with self" is clearly motivated by many of Rousseau's concerns about a non-alienated self-determination. It could be expressed by saying that I must be able to "identify" with my actions, and those of my desires and needs and interests that actually motivate actions. Hegel's metaphorical formulation is

> There is an action at all only through the fact that the subject is *in it*. . . . But drive and passion is nothing but the vitality of the subject, through which [the subject] is *in its ends and their execution*.[11]

The Introduction to the *Philosophy of Right* makes clear that Hegel understands this possibility in, at least partly, a traditional way, one that resonates with Platonic and (especially) Spinozist, as well as Rousseauean and Kantian, themes. This identification is understood by noting that I must judge that what I am inclined to want or avoid should be desired or avoided, if I am to act freely in satisfying such inclinations and wants. It means that my ends be pursued for some reason, and that I understand and affirm such reasons.

This does not mean that everything I do, every end set or choice made, counts as self-determined only if it is the direct result of some rational reflection. Like Kant's, Hegel's interest is in the general principles or criteria of evaluation presupposed in any deliberation and choice, however implicit or rarely formulated as such. *These* principles are mine only if genuinely self-imposed, prompting the question of under what conditions such self-imposition could occur.

By contrast, if I act thoughtlessly, unreflectively, or in mere conformity to prevailing conventions, I have declined to become the subject of my own deeds, allowing the direction of my life to be charted by others and by a complex of contingent psychological factors. I achieve this status – "subject" – by being able to evaluate my inclinations and needs, by being directed by good reasons that I recognize as such. The great dispute, in this tradition and throughout the modern enterprise, is, What will *count* as such

---

11 *Enzyklopädie der philosophischen Wissenschaften: Die Philosophie des Geistes*, §475R, in *Werke* (Frankfurt a.M.: Suhrkamp, 1970), Bd. 10.

rational self-determination; especially, what sort of self-legislation will not thereby create a self-alienation? I want to explore Hegel's answer to this question in what follows. Doing so will eventually lead to his account of what I am calling ethical reasons. This account is characterized by two interesting and controversial claims.

(i) First, Hegel argues that such reasons, or self-imposed principles of action, cannot be understood in the way suggested by his famous competitor, as moral demands I make on myself, as obligations, duties, or moral reasons.[12] Ethical reasons are not, like these, radically discontinuous with my sensible, natural being; nor are they expressions of my real or pure or better self or part. As we shall see, such reasons are reasons because of the way in which what is thereby recommended realizes or completes my sensible, or natural, will. Hegel claims that the rational institutions of right, property, contract, morality, ethical life are all implicit in an original natural will, that such a will implicitly aims at becoming a fully free will, and so realizes itself in the institutions that make possible and realize such freedom.

This ambition is clear enough in the Introduction to his *Philosophy of Right*. Hegel signals there that he means to derive his fundamental ethical and political claims from premises describing a minimal original situation, a single agent attempting to satisfy a variety of wants efficiently and coherently. He describes what he calls a merely "natural will," one whose content is a "multitude and manifold (*Menge und Manigfaltigkeit*) of impulses, each of which is in general mine, alongside other impulses also universal and undetermined, all with any number of possible objects, and satisfiable in any number of ways" (*PR* §12). This "immediate" or "natural" will is said to be implicitly (*an sich*) *a free will*, and that ultimately means free in the fully "actualized" Hegelian sense, free only within ethical life and especially the "system of right" (*PR* §4). Hegel promises to show that any such agent, once reflective and consistent, must be "implicitly" and finally explicitly committed to the institutions of "abstract right" (property, contract) and some moral regard for the other, and that he ultimately would come to understand himself as an *ethical* being, someone whose very identity and whose ties to others are "institution-bound" in a certain sort of modern

12 "Everything in nature works according to laws. Only a rational being has the capacity of acting according to the conception of laws, i.e. according to principles. This capacity is will. Since reason is required for the derivation of actions from laws, will is nothing else than practical reason." *Grundlegung der Metaphysik der Moral* (hereafter *GW*), in *Kants gesammelte Schriften* (hereafter *AA*) (Berlin: de Gruyter, 1902), Bd. 4; *Foundations of the Metaphysics of Morals*, trans. L. W. Beck (hereafter *F*) (Indianapolis: Bobbs-Merrill, 1959); *AA*, 412; 29.

society. Thus already implicit in the "natural will," somehow, is "the rational system of the will's volitions," and the argument of the *Philosophy of Right* is to make good that claim.[13]

That argument has a general form. As we begin to reflect on which objects will be pursued in the satisfaction of such wants, and which wants will have priority, we begin to invest this content with the form of rationality, and so universality. Stated more simply, since we cannot satisfy all our desires, and must determine the sorts of objects to pursue in such attempts, we must begin to think about such satisfaction and settle on more general *principles* in our action. Of course, utilitarians, welfarists, contractarians, and Kantians would still have no quarrel with such generalities. Hegel's position begins to become more distinctive when he claims that through "resolving" such matters,[14] the will also begins to reveal the subject as a determinate individual, set off against others by virtue of these particular decisions and the general principles they begin to reflect. Some such principles can help reveal and help determine a self or agent; others invoke some sort of rational reflection "too late," accepting as given some set of preferences, passions, or a subject's "motivational set." Initially, though, this individual is merely "abstract . . . not yet filled with its free universality" (*PR* §13R), but it is by virtue of these acts of resolving and choosing and reflecting that I can begin to see myself, determinately, "in" my actions.

However, ultimately, various "contradictions" (*PR* §17) and "demands" (*PR* §19) arise from any such attempt at a self-conscious, reflective evaluation and satisfaction of desires, and these lead to a "process of absorption in or elevation to universality," "what is called the activity of thought" (*PR* §21R). This process, as often called a "purification" of impulses as their "absorption," results in achieving the standpoint of a "universal will," universal "because all restriction and particular individuality have been absorbed within it" (*PR* §23). Thus it is only when I have achieved this standpoint, when I determine my actions as a universal subject, not as a mere particular

---

13 The same sort of claim is prominent in the *Phenomenology of Spirit,* especially where Hegel introduces the ideas of Spirit and "ethical substance." There the language of identification is quite prevalent: "the obedience of self-consciousness is not the serving of a master whose commands were arbitrary, and in which it would not recognize itself. On the contrary laws are the thoughts of its own absolute consciousness, thoughts which are immediately its own (*welche es selbst unmittelbar hat*)." *Phänomenologie des Geistes* (hereafter *PhG*) (Hamburg: Felix Meiner Verlag, 1952); *Hegel's Phenomenology of Spirit,* trans. A. V. Miller (Oxford: Oxford University Press, 1979), (hereafter *PhS*), 310; 261.

14 Cf. Hegel's comments in the Remark to §12 on *etwas beschliessen* and *sich entschliessen*.

ego, that I am a truly free subject of my own deeds, that the will is "with itself absolutely" (*schlechthin bei sich*).

And, to complete a very programmatic summary, this occurs when (and only when) I understand myself as an "ethical" being, a member of "the substantially ethical" (*PR* §144) or "ethical life" (*Sittlichkeit*). The "authority" of such "ethical laws" (*PR* §146R) is not

> something alien to the subject. But one's spirit bears witness to them [such laws] as to its own essence, in which it has its own self-feeling [*Selbstgefühl*], and in which it lives as in one's own element, something not distinguished from itself. (*PR* §147)

And again, the intriguing, even if suspicious, quality of this claim is that Hegel clearly thinks he can show how the achievement of such a universal will does not (ultimately or finally) involve the familiar (essentially Christian) divided self so familiar to moral theory.[15] The appeal to what is already implicit in the natural will, and the metaphors of absorption, elevation, and purification, rather than those of opposition, struggle, and renunciation, suggest some sort of self-reconciliation and harmony whose appeal is hard to deny, but whose promise seems extravagant.

This means that Hegel accepts the argument so prominent in Rousseau and Kant that true self-determination requires rational self-legislation, but that he cannot accept that such rational self-determination involves an identification with the general will, or a subjection to the categorical imperative. One is a false harmony; the other, a permanent dualism. Everything in his position must then hinge on what he means by acting on reasons. Now it turns out that he means quite a great many things by such a notion, as he explores, partially rejects, transforms, and carries forward various candidates for the general principles agents would need to adopt in their quest for the realization of freedom, their being able to recognize themselves in their deeds.[16]

---

15 The qualification ("ultimately or finally") is necessary because Hegel *does* think that a certain separation of an agent from himself, or self-alienation, is a necessary stage on the way to a full reconciliation. That is a longer and different story from the one I want to sketch here.

16 Hegel is thus both affirming that a reason to act can be a reason only if it could come to count as such a reason to an individual agent, if it could motivate the agent, and denying that this amounts to acceptance of some Humean principle that reasons must be in the service of passions, or, much more broadly, "internal" in the sense defined by Williams,

(ii) Second, Hegel denies that this construal of ethical reasons, which preserves what he calls "the right of particularity," "the right to be satisfied," and which satisfies the condition that "moral consciousness cannot forego happiness and leave this element out of its absolute purpose," is a doctrine of *individual prudence.*

In the first place, he clearly does not believe that the reasons justifying my participation in an ethical community are simply prudential or are rightly described as, exclusively, reasonable for an individual satisfying his wants or life plan, or even some end viewed as an objective good for all human beings. Let us assume that a prudential reason is "a reason for adopting a certain way of acting as a rule . . . if and only if it fits into the agent's projects and experiences so as to make sense."[17] It might then appear that Hegel, by virtue of, or as a consequence of, his rejection of the moral point of view is justifying the institutions of ethical life prudentially, in this sense. We have good reasons for participating in such institutions because, so it would have to be argued, they are essential to the realization of any reasonably coherent individual project in the modern world.

However, as we have been seeing, the notion of prudential reasoning must assume that the life plans and projects that form the baseline of justification *are* in some genuine sense mine, are plans and projects I do not simply have, or have not arrived at in dependent ways, but are ones with which I can genuinely identify. Any worry about that sort of issue will lead us to a sense of reflection and justification that cannot be prudential. It will very likely introduce some notion of what ends and projects I originally ought to pursue in order that I be a self-determining subject. It is only after

"Internal and External." See the claims made by Christine Korsgaard, "Skepticism about Practical Reason," *Journal of Philosophy* 83 (1986): 5–25, especially her argument that, even under Humean assumptions, there may be reasons for an agent to act that are not motivating for some pathological reason, but are still reasons, and her suggestion of the "possibility that reason could yield conclusions that every rational being must acknowledge and be capable of being motivated by" (p. 22). This all remains an important criterion for Hegel. If we need to be able to show not that a reason must *be* motivating for it to count as a reason, but still must be able to show that it *could* be, then, from Hegel's point of view, compared with Kant's project, we should admit that we are launched into a far more complex inquiry into the conditions (social and historical, as well as psychological) under which this could occur. It is not, according to Hegel's critique, a criterion satisfiable by a theoretical demonstration that pure reason can be practical. For a very interesting "neo-Aristotelian" perspective on these same issues, see Jonathan Lear's account of "objective" reasons in "Moral Objectivity," in *Objectivity and Cultural Divergence,* ed. by S. C. Brown (Cambridge: Cambridge University Press, 1984), pp. 135–70.

17 Rüdiger Bittner, *What Reason Demands* (Cambridge: Cambridge University Press, 1989), p. 117.

some sort of relation between my will and my own projects and ends is established in a way that can ensure this identification that prudential reasons could count as genuine reasons for me. Hegel's interest in this prior issue accounts, I am suggesting, for the continuing language of duty, even while it is couched in the promise of "liberation."[18]

Such formulations certainly introduce their own questions into Hegel's account, even apart from issues of prudence. He is clearly claiming that some principle can as a matter of fact be "my reason" for acting; it was in fact the reason I gave myself, and it did motivate me. And I could as a matter of fact "identify" with such a reason; I could fully affirm such reasons as the sort that ought to be determinative in life, and so regard the principle as self-imposed. A person could oppose abortion because the Catholic church teaches it is wrong and could sincerely regard that as a reason, indeed as the best reason. As we have been noting, Hegel would deny that such an allegiance could be truly self-determined, and he would no more consider this a genuine example of "identifying myself" in my actions than he would the infamous "happy slave" who identifies with his life, perhaps even after rational reflection. As we shall see, what will be essential for Hegel's evaluation of such principles will not be the sincerity or thoroughness of an individual's self-examination. The question of whether what I end up doing reflects me as a *subject* of my deeds is, he shall claim, a question about social institutions and what is or is not possible within them.

That is, the notion of an *individual* deliberating about what principle of action fits in with ongoing projects, and so deliberating about participation in an institution, wondering about the justification for such participation, is quite foreign to what Hegel claims actually occurs. Hegel also wants to show that the true realization of freedom, or the achievement of genuine subjectivity, occurs when I "see myself *in an other.*"[19] This appears to mean that "taking others into account" in self-determining actions is not limited to coordinating actions successfully, or to refraining from impermissible wrongs, or to understanding how some social relation "fits in" with my

---

18 See *PR* §149. There is a great deal more to be said on the differences between Hegel and a defender of the primacy of prudential reasons. Bittner, for example, in *What Reason Demands*, is quite right to refer to a pivotal discussion in the *Phenomenology* on "die Sache selbst," and Hegel's argument there for the necessary "completion" of "reason" in "spirit" (pp. 140–57). I disagree with his account there of Hegel's notion of "contingency." See my discussion of the problem of "transitions" in the *Phenomenology* in the *Cambridge Companion to Hegel,* ed. by F. Beiser (Cambridge: Cambridge University Press, 1993), pp. 52–85.

19 Cf. the very good discussion in Allen W. Wood, *Hegel's Ethical Thought* (Cambridge: Cambridge University Press, 1990), pp. 44–52.

projects. It means that the force or appeal of an ethical reason requires that I have already come to identify myself and my good with others and with some collective good, that what I recognize as rationally compelling *for me* involves my already having to come to understand *myself* as a social being of some sort, as a mode of "the ethical substance" (*das sittliche Wesen*).

By now all this could seem too good to be true. Hegel's attack on the alienated character of moral life, together with his rejection of consequentialist, egoistic, or prudential models of rationality, calls to mind an infamous history of ethical thought designed to highlight the "have your cake and eat it too" quality of Hegel's promises. On this account Aristotle could show what a reasonable person would want to do, but not why such a goal would be a compelling reason, why one ought to do what such a man would want to do. Kant, on the other hand, could show what any rational agent ought to do, but not why he would want to do what he ought to do. And along comes Hegel, who can demonstrate what we ought to do, and why we would want to do it.[20] As unfair as this history is to everyone involved it raises a good question: How could Hegel have possibly understood the twin promises just discussed, and how could he have meant to defend them?

III. Moral Reasons

Hegel is well known for arguing that striving to realize human freedom cannot be fully understood as striving to realize a moral ideal. He rejects as insufficient or incomplete the notion of a universally binding requirement to respect all others as ends in themselves, and he attacks any notion of moral worth that esteems only actions done from a duty to fulfill such a requirement. In his account, it is not by virtue of this universal moral respect for the freedom of persons that "freedom is actualized." Such a respect and such a notion of a person, while not false or ungrounded, are far too abstract and indeterminate. We come to understand what counts as the realization of freedom only by understanding the institutions and social rules that, in a particular, modern historical community, are essential to the exercise of such agency. And we come to see a rational social system realizing such agency as essential to our own agency, although again only in a certain sort of social context.

The charge of abstractness or emptiness is stated in a number of more specific formulations by Hegel. The categorical imperative is itself empty,

20 I owe this version to Terry Pinkard.

merely a dressed-up law of non-contradiction, not usable as an action-guiding principle, ruling in or out too much or too little. Or a purportedly moral will is empty; when we attempt to act from duty alone, there is nothing we could do. We either refrain from action (the beautiful soul), or profess this moral will hypocritically, or "dissemble," disguise from ourselves and others the particular interests that always must lie behind particular actions. And all such formulations (some far less fair to Kant than others) have stronger or weaker versions. Hegel sometimes seems to imply that the categorical imperative could in no sense be a guide to action; at other times that it is an incomplete guide, that the idea of respecting a kind of "moral equality" is fine, but, from the moral point of view, leaves unspecified what, in particular social settings, will count as such respect. Sometimes, Hegel appears to argue that any attempt to act on a general principle or any notion of a dutiful action will introduce a kind of alienation that will forever obscure the sense in which such a principle or call to duty could be a reason for me to act. At other times, as we have already seen, everything depends on the nature of the principle or call to duty.[21]

Of the scores of issues raised by such claims, I am only interested in how the morality critique raises the dilemma cited; how to do justice to that critique and still explain what Hegel means by ethical (non-prudential) reasons. To do so, we need first to clear away the general inaccuracies in the received, or textbook, picture of this Hegelian attack on morality, and then deal with the somewhat distorted picture Hegel gives of Kant.

This common view is influenced by Hegel's well-known denial that his own exposition of the right and good should be understood as an account of ideals, ideals to be formulated by reason and imposed on a recalcitrant reality.[22] On this reading, if Hegel is right that the language of moral obligation is alienating and paradoxical, then his own position would appear committed to the claim that ethical reasons, our sense of *why* we ought to fulfill the expectations inherent in participation in various practices and to acknowledge their claim on us, do not involve an "ought" of any kind, but rather simply embody and express some sort of already shared, social self-understanding. "Morality is a matter of something like custom, not of de-

---

21 In the *PR*, an indication that Hegel thinks of his own theory as a development of the incompleteness of morality is the Remark to §135. See also the comment in §207 about the sphere wherein "morality has its proper place." The tone in the discussions of *Moralität* in the *PhG*, although still developmental, is harsher. For more on the difference between the youthful *PhG* and the mature *PR*, see Terry Pinkard, *Democratic Liberalism and Social Union* (Philadelphia: Temple University Press, 1987), pp. 186–7.

22 *PR*, pp. 15–16; *PRE2*, p. 11.

mands: shared ways of life, learned by example and imitation."[23] Such a view does not seem contradicted by such typical remarks as

> In this way the ethical substantial order has attained its right, and its right to validity. That is to say, the self-will of the individual has vanished together with the private conscience that had claimed independence and had opposed itself to the ethical substance. (*PR* §152)[24]

Such a "vanishing" is, of course, immediately problematic. We can and often do become dissatisfied with our shared way of life, and we do so well before some other common orientation is historically relevant. It might be possible in many instances of such social criticism to show that the criticism is internal; that the substance of the dissatisfaction arises concretely in internal tensions in a common self-understanding and that such criticism therefore still expresses the dynamics of custom, of how we go about things (and how we go about changing things). Perhaps this is how Hegel understood the Sophists, or Plato. But it would be question begging simply to insist a priori that all such criticism must be internal in this way. We are, for example, not satisfied to excuse the racism, sexism, or brutality of other cultures by reference to their way of life; not content to wait, to foreswear criticism, until tensions and conflicts within such frameworks arise.

So, we do go about things collectively in shared and often deeply unreflective ways, but since it is always possible to wonder whether our practices are acceptable, there is no reason to see subjects as so embedded in their communities that everyday, recognizably moral calls of conscience are ruled out of court as abstract or empty. Indeed, if this characterization were to be pursued, it would be hard to see how any sort of question about the rationality or justification of these practices could be raised. If "self-will" is submerged in "ethical substance," I have become what my community requires;

---

23 Bittner, *What Reason Demands*, p. 5.
24 When the notion of *Geist* is introduced in the *PhG*, the same language predominates. In "spiritual being," "laws are the thoughts of its own absolute self-consciousness, thoughts which are immediately its own." It thus "recognizes itself" in the commands of such a law, (pp. 310; 261). In this context, though, it is clear that Hegel is introducing the first or immediate form of ethical life, in which such an identification with a community's mores is far too immediate and unreflective, as in the famous account of the tragedy of Antigone. Cf. the standard statement of the objections to such a supposedly conventionalist position in Alan Donagan, *The Theory of Morality* (Chicago: University of Chicago Press, 1977), pp. 12–17, and the rejoinder by Allen Wood in *Hegel's Ethical Thought*, ch. 11, especially the description of Hegel on pp. 196 and 207. See also the introductory discussion of these issues by Andreas Wildt, *Autonomie and Anerkennung: Hegels Moralitätskritik im Lichte seiner Fichterezeption* (Stuttgart: Klett-Cotta, 1982), p. 18.

there is no distance between me and it within which such a question could arise. Any question I raise is simply a reenactment of the community's practice.[25]

However popular it has recently become to invoke Hegel's authority in communitarian, hermeneutic, aretaic, or conventionalist attacks on morality, this sort of general understanding of the opposition between the "moral point of view" and "ethical life" is quite misleading.

In the first place, such a characterization of Hegel assumes something at issue: that morality itself can be understood other than as a kind of custom or shared way of life. Hegel clearly believes that the moral point of view, one that ties moral evaluation to the purity of intentions and admits as good only intentions to obey the moral law, is itself a particular historical practice, and not one that simply discovers at a certain time what pure reason determines is obligatory.[26] What Donagan called "the" theory of morality is, as he also realizes, a product of Jewish and Christian culture,[27] whose social appeal and whose justification rest on the shared assumptions of a particular historical community.[28] This may all be a wrongheaded account, and a pure

25 Michael Theunissen has pointed out a number of ambiguities in Hegel's account of ethical life in his "Die verdrängte Intersubjektivität in Hegels Philosophie des Rechts," in *Hegels Philosophie des Rechts: Die Theorie der Rechtsformen und ihre Logik*, ed. by Dieter Henrich and Rolf-Peter Horstmann (Stuttgart: Klett-Cotta, 1982), pp. 317–81. He is especially interested in the tensions between a more metaphysical, even premodern, notion of the "ethical substance" in Hegel's account of ethical life, and a notion of genuine "inter-subjectivity." I think at least some of the problems Theunissen points to can be avoided if Hegel's central account of the "will willing itself" (*PR* §10) is first understood by referring to its Kantian origins, than by immediately invoking Hegel's speculative logic. The same concerns are expressed by Vittorio Hösle in his *Hegels System* (Hamburg: Felix Meiner Verlag, 1987). See my "Hösle, System and Subject," *Bulletin of the Hegel Society of Great Britain* 17 (1988): 4–19, and Chapter 6, this volume.

26 In fact, Hegel, by claiming that "Right" and "Morality" are abstractions, that they both already presuppose modern *Sittlichkeit* (cf. *PR* §141R), is introducing what would be a familiar left-Hegelian claim. Given that the central institution of ethical life is civil society, Hegel is claiming that the notions of persons as rights bearers and as moral subjects are essentially "bourgeois" notions. For him, of course, this is hardly a criticism. See the excellent discussions by Theunissen, "Der verdrängte Intersubjektivität," and by Rolf-Peter Horstmann, "Über die Rolle der bürgerliche Gesellschaft in Hegels politischer Philosophie," in *Materialen zu Hegels Rechtsphilosophie* ed. by Manfred Riedel (Frankfurt a.M.: Suhrkamp, 1975), pp. 276–311.

27 Donagan, *Theory of Morality*.

28 In a much more secularized Christian community (a religion of pure reason), morality's claim to rationality depends essentially on claims about the absence of "natural" standards, attacks on standard versions of teleology, and an awareness of the contingency and mutability of various central social practices in a community. Only under such conditions could the moral point of view, with its demand for a purity of intention and a strictly universal law, claim the authority it does.

justification may be given without reliance on this historical phenomenology of the Christian community, and in a way stronger than Hegel's wholly comparative assessment of the rationality of such a practice, but that should not be assumed from the start.

Second, as we have already seen, Hegel does not believe that individuals simply embody some sort of communal spirit. "Ethical life is a subjective disposition" (*subjektive Gesinnung*) (*PR* §141R) as well as an objective custom.[29] This means that what is required of individuals be rational, and that individuals be able to understand and affirm what is rationally required of them. He is not at all hesitant about using some notion of "duty" to describe the requirements involved in various social practices.[30] This alone presupposes what Hegel must have believed to be obvious: that individuals can certainly come to experience some sort of tension between their individual lives and what various social roles require of them, and a tension among the demands of one's multiple social roles. Although he claims that, in a rational social order, ethical life is indeed mostly experienced as custom (*Sitte*) (*PR* §151), he admits it is not always so even there. In his remark discussing this sort of duty (which he calls *Rechtschaffenheit*, rectitude), he discusses how virtuous conformity to such duties does occur sometimes in situations of "collisions" among "relations" required in ethical life (*PR* §150R).[31]

Finally, the passage cited (*PR* §152) is very carefully worded and does not collapse ethical life into custom or convention. The only thing that has vanished into ethical substantiality is "self-will," or some essentially private self-understanding (*Eigenwilligkeit*), not individual will and reflection itself, and it is not subjectivity or conscience itself that has been superseded, but a certain individualistic, self-certifying notion (*das eigene Gewissen des*

---

29 Cf. Wood, *Hegel's Ethical Thought*, ch. 12.
30 Just what would satisfy this requirement for a "subjective" affirmation is a matter of some controversy in Hegel. See my "Hegel's Political Argument and the Problem of *Verwirklichung*," *Political Theory* 9 (1981): 509–32.
31 All of which would seem to reopen the Kantian possibility of an alienated self, now merely described in other terms. The reason that ought to be of overriding importance for any free agent, an intention to further the good, might still seem, precisely because universally binding, an impersonal principle, overriding the particular desires and interests that might incline me to other sorts of actions.

   Hegel would certainly not deny that I might experience a conflict between my "subjective interests" and what might be required by my ethical role in society. But, as we have seen in several contexts now, he would not interpret this as a conflict between impersonal duty and private interest. He thinks he can show that such ethical duties are themselves "self-realizing," linked to my true self-satisfaction, even if not free of conflict, confusion, and ambiguity. There is a good discussion of this issue in Wood, *Hegel's Ethical Thought*, ch. 12, especially pp. 210–11.

Einzelnen) of conscience. And, coming again to the sort of claim paradigmatic for Hegel's understanding of ethical reasons, he claims that an individual's "dignity" and the "stability of his particular purposes" are understood to be "grounded" in such ethical substantiality, that he "knows" this and knows that his purposes and dignity become "actual" in such an ethical life. There is thus good reason for him to participate actively in such institutions and practices. He is an autonomous, self-determining agent, *himself:* only by virtue of such participation, but not because pure practical reason demands this of him, nor because it is prudentially wise for him to participate.

So much for what is not being said in, or as a result of, the morality critique. What is being said has been the subject of several books and ranges over a number of issues. In the context developed, we can first note a similar approach to the issue of what can count as a practical reason. Generally stated, Hegel's position, as introduced here, will argue that the best reason for an agent to engage in an action, a course of action, a practice; to adopt a policy; and so on, is that such an action or practice best allows the agent *to be an agent,* a free or self-determining agent. Such a reason has a supreme priority in practical matters, because no particular course of action could be of value to me unless such a condition were satisfied, unless I could be assured that the action or policy formulated and executed was mine, that I had truly determined such a policy. As we shall see, Hegel thinks such reasons obtain only in a certain sort of social situation, by virtue of coming to maturity within certain established relations to others. It is only in such a context (called *Sittlichkeit*) that I could be a self-determining agent and that there would be good reasons for me to identify with these social institutions. It is in this sense that freedom involves "being with self in an other."

Stated so generally, though, it is possible to claim that Kant would agree with major elements of this approach (the link is, again, the Rousseauean worries mentioned earlier). Obviously, both Kant and Hegel believe that whatever will turn out to be a compelling practical reason will be independent of an agent's contingent (or what Hegel would call "immediate," natural) wants, whatever as a matter of psychological fact an agent experiences as a pressing desire, need, or impulse. They both agree that it would only be rational for me to pursue the satisfaction of such wants if I determine that they ought to be satisfied, if they pass what Taylor has called "strong evaluation."[32] And this means for both that any such pursuit, or any other, must

---

32 See "What Is Human Agency?" in *Human Agency and Language: Philosophical Papers,* I (Cambridge: Cambridge University Press, 1985), pp. 15–44.

satisfy this self-determination, or freedom condition. Kant writes quite strongly about this in a passage from the *Lectures on Ethics*.

> Man must give [the] autocracy of the soul its full scope; otherwise he becomes a mere plaything of other forces and impressions which withstand his will, and a prey to the caprice of accident and circumstance.[33]

And this all brings the differences between them to a relatively fine point. It could be said, with some qualifications, that both agree on the best practical reason for acting, on what sort of reason is always overriding. Reflecting their common debt to the Rousseauean considerations introduced earlier, both could be said to agree that no practical reason, or hypothetical imperative, could be a compelling reason to an individual unless the end to be realized, the desire to be satisfied, the self-interest to be maximized, and so forth, were themselves products of the individual's will, were *his own* ends, desires, or needs. Thus, anything that would ensure that this self-determination condition was met must count as a supreme or overriding practical reason. I must be free to act, to direct or lead a life I can recognize as mine; the best practical reason is thus any recommendation to adopt a policy or project that would realize or ensure such freedom. Even if I come to care little about the origins of my desires, and come to value only their intensity and satisfaction, I have presupposed that these factors are what have come to matter to me; I have identified with such a project, and I thereby inherit the presumption that the conditions under which this could in fact be claimed can be defended.

Kant of course believes that this autonomy condition can only be satisfied in one way, only by acting rationally, on one sort of principle; can ensure, by so acting rationally, that I am freely determining my action, or that it is mine. This principle is the categorical imperative, and acting "on" such a principle must be acting "from" duty.

The qualifications mentioned earlier are necessary because Kant would object to portraying autonomy as some sort of ideal or good that needs to be realized, and would be uncomfortable with the slightly hypothetical tone of any talk of "moral reasons." We are autonomous as rational beings; we are unconditionally obligated to the moral law, and so the best reason to act is, We are duty-bound to act. However, as the third section of the *Groundwork* and the discussion of "material principles" in the *Critique of Practical Reason*

---

33 Immanuel Kant, *Lectures on Ethics*, trans. Louis Infield (Gloucester: Peter Smith, 1978), p. 140.

make clear, the arguments by which Kant tries to establish that we are in fact bound to the moral law unmistakably evince the Rousseauean appeal noted previously. In different ways he often tries to insist that no agent can truly act except "according to the conception of laws" or the idea of freedom. In the Introduction to the *Doctrine of Virtue*, Kant claims that "the less a man can be controlled by natural means and the more he can be constrained morally (through the mere thought of the law) so much the more free he is." And in a familiar formulation, he claims that a person "proves his freedom in the highest degree by being *unable to resist* the call of duty."[34]

The general form of this sort of claim is that in any act we are "practically" presupposing an idea of freedom, or independent self-determination, a negative capacity, and that this capacity can only be realized by imposing on ourselves a strictly universal principle.[35] And that form makes clear that Kant is justifying such obedience by arguing that only thereby are we actually the self-determining agents we presume to be in any action.

Further, when Kant says that nothing can be good without qualification except a "good will," he is certainly supposing that everyone, as a rational agent, is capable of good willing and subject to a self-imposed practical law. But he realizes we are also finite, sensible, even radically evil creatures, not inclined to obey such a law. As we shall see in more detail shortly, there are things we can do to make the realization of such a capacity more likely and we are in some sense bound to pursue such goals. And, given such a knowledge of our own and others' finitude, there are ends we must adopt as general policies, if we are fully to realize such a capacity. Such language at least allows and sometimes invites a translation into Hegel's account of ethical reasons, justifications based on the notion of a self-realization, or "concrete" autonomy, in a finite world.

IV. Kantian Counters

These similarities and differences raise a number of difficult issues that must at least be introduced and briefly discussed.

---

34 *Grundlegung zur Metaphysik der Moral (Tugendlehre)* (hereafter *TL*), AA, IV, *The Doctrine of Virtue* (hereafter *DV*), trans. Mary J. Gregor (Philadelphia: University of Pennsylvania Press, 1964), pp. 381; 39 (my emphasis).
35 See Thomas Hill, "Kant's Argument for the Rationality of Moral Conduct," *Pacific Philosophical Quarterly* 66 (1985): 3–23; Henry Allison, "Morality and Freedom: Kant's Reciprocity Thesis," *Philosophical Review* 95 (1986): 393–425; and Allison's discussion in *Kant's Theory of Freedom* (Cambridge: Cambridge University Press, 1990), pt. 3.

As we have seen, Hegel, by criticizing morality, is not adopting the institu-
tionalism or complete anti-subjectivism with which he is sometimes associated. And much more to the point, Kant's own position cannot be fairly
criticized as demanding that we forgo pleasant or self-satisfying activities;
nor is he grossly underappreciating the values of love, commitment, or
solidarity in any good, worthwhile life; nor is he requiring that we merely
conform to legalistic constraints, just do nothing impermissible, in our pursuit of any and all material, even low-minded or crass ends.

First, although it is often thought of as more grist for Hegel's mill, Kant
was clearly not indifferent to the appearance of rigorism and struggled to
formulate some way in which our inevitable interest in our own happiness
could be coherently harmonized with what pure practical reason demands.
Kant was obviously concerned with the claim that such demands can appear
to be a practical absurdity, like a demand that "I not be me," and thus be
forever willing to prescind in principle from the pursuit of the ends I care
about. However ultimately problematic, his account of the *summum bonum*
and the postulates, his philosophies of history and religion and education,
all evince such an interest. But Hegel always pounces on such attempts, and
treats them as a kind of concession. He claims that it proves that a so-called
moral agent is not sincerely or "seriously" committed to morality, and is
always secretly interested in self-interest and the promise of reward.[36] And
such accounts do not, finally, show us any way of producing a genuine
harmony, or any realizable goal.[37] If they are not promises of rewards for
good behavior, they are only vague expressions of what we might hope
about the future, and of what we must concede to our sensible natures in
such hopes. And if Kant uncharacteristically does seem at points to make
the possibility of highest good or the postulates a *condition* of a coherent
moral life, then Hegel's "lack of seriousness" charge will have some bite.[38] A
prudential condition will have entered the sphere of supposedly unconditioned duty.

36 *PhG*, p. 437; *PhS*, pp. 376 ff.
37 Cf. Lewis White Beck, *A Commentary on Kant's Critique of Practical Reason* (Chicago: University
    of Chicago Press, 1960), pp. 244–45.
38 Cf. *Kritik der praktischen Vernunft, AA*, IV (hereafter *KdpV*) pp. 110; 114; especially pp. 114;
    118 ("the impossibility of the highest good must prove the impossibility of the moral law");
    Über dem Gemeinspruch . . . , in *Werke*, Bd. VI, ed. by W. Weischedel (Frankfurt a.M.: Insel
    Verlag, 1964), pp. 131; 132; *On the Common Saying: 'This May be True in Theory, but It Does Not
    Apply in Practice,'* in *Kant's Political Writings*, trans. H. B. Nisbet, ed. by Hans Reiss (Cam-
    bridge: Cambridge University Press, 1977), pp. 64, 65; cf. my discussion in Chapter 3, this
    volume.

It is also true that Kant's reflections on what I must do in order to ensure that I have the continuing capacity to do what the moral law demands are not limited to these general considerations about what it is rational to hope. Although he never officially classifies them as such, he does appear interested in a broad class of what he called "indirect duties."[39] Such duties concern a major aspect of virtue: strength of character, fortitude, or even the development of moral "courage." He reasons that if I have an unconditional obligation to obey the moral law, I must also do what I can to ensure that I will discharge this duty, that I will acquire the right moral sensitivities ("he who wills the end wills the means"). The most important consideration here is again my knowledge of my necessary interest in my own happiness, and so my needing some life plan that pursues a kind of moral perfection and strength of character in a way that takes my desires and passions into account. I must, for example, do such things as visit the poor and sick in order to generate the feelings of sympathy that I know, given how subject I am to the pull of my emotional life and the pleasure I take in satisfying such desires, will aid me in doing my duty to aid others in need.

But such reflections, like the conditions issues raised previously, introduce their own tensions into Kant's account. The picture of someone visiting the sick, imagining others in distress, training his moral sensibilities by some regimen of uplifting reading, and so forth (all in the realization that he might need their aid in his own quest for moral perfection) suggests again not a life lived in a way animated in some substantial sense by a moral ideal, but a life not lived but "employed" in the service of this ideal, and so a life not itself a realization of freedom, but a kind of preparation for what is, always, the only true realization of such freedom, moral autonomy. It is thus a life not one's own, a mere means to an ever more effective obedience to an abstract ideal. It is one thing to note that the status of such indirect duties as love, charity, and self-development is not absolute: that they must always conform to some general notion of the absolutely morally worthy. It is another to consider them of no intrinsic value, mere educational aids or emotional props to greater moral self-discipline.

The same cannot be said, however, for another crucial dimension of Kant's theory that Hegel does not discuss, an area that will help highlight further their similarities and differences. For if it is fair to point to their shared concerns with freedom as the highest human good, and their shared appreciation of the link between such freedom and reason, with what any

---

39 This phrase is introduced in the *TL* without much fanfare and concerns a range of duties aimed at "the preservation of my moral integrity" (pp. 387; 47).

agent would have to be committed to if he is to be a self-determining agent, it would be extremely surprising if this commonality led to a disagreement wholly based on Kant's supposed formalism and rigorism. Such a focus would have to ignore or seriously underplay the Rousseauean interest, the moral ideal, as it were, that motivates both their projects.[40] This is particularly clear when one considers that Kant's moral theory is by no means exhausted by his attempt to formulate the practical law binding on all agents, and by his argument that moral worth, goodness, can only be attributed to acts done from duty alone. For Kant does not restrict himself to discovering the criterion by which *actions* can be judged as permissible, obligatory, or forbidden. He argues that we have duties not only to act or refrain from acting in various ways (and that performing or refraining from such actions is morally worthy only if we act out of an intention to obey the moral law) but *to adopt maxims, to set ends.* This means that his moral theory is misrepresented if it is portrayed as primarily concerned with a limiting condition in our pursuit of our material ends, or portrayed so negatively. There are things we must do, positively, if we are fully to discharge our duty; there are duties of virtue, not just of right; and this should prompt some reconsideration of Hegel's criticism and the Hegelian alternative so deeply motivated by that criticism. This is especially true since a good deal of recent discussion by Kantians, much of it motivated by the rigorism charge (and by Alasdair MacIntyre's and Bernard Williams's recent books),[41] refocuses so much attention on these more substantial, more emotionally rich and culturally sensitive aspects of Kant's position.

The important distinction of course is that just discussed in the prior chapter: between perfect and imperfect duties, very roughly, between the *Rechtslehre* and *Tugendlehre*, between duties that may be "legally" discharged

---

40 For a fine discussion of the deep similarities and equally profound differences between Rousseau and Kant see Richard Velkley, *Freedom and the End of Reason: On the Moral Foundations of Kant's Critical Philosophy* (Chicago: University of Chicago Press, 1989).

41 Alasdair MacIntyre, *After Virtue* (South Bend: University of Notre Dame Press, 1981); Bernard Williams, *Ethics and the Limits of Philosophy* (Cambridge: Harvard University Press, 1985). I should emphasize how important this issue is for Hegel's critique of Kant. Allen Wood, for example, states the core of Hegel's disagreement well when he writes: "But Hegel maintains that abstract right and morality are actual in modern society only to the extent that their abstract conceptions of the individual are given real embodiment through modern social institutions." *Hegel's Ethical Thought*, p. 197. On the face of it, any Kantian who takes seriously Kant's theory of moral judgment, and the spirit of his *Doctrine of Virtue*, would not have anything to disagree with in such a claim. But, I shall argue, that appearance is quite misleading. This issue is especially important for Wildt, who in *Autonomie und Anerkennung* exaggerates, I think, Kant's reliance on "legal" duties and neglects Kant's *Doctrine of Ethics*, where it would be most relevant. See, e.g., p. 120.

even for prudential reasons (the object of most of the attacks on Kant) versus duties that can be fulfilled only by adopting the right maxim.[42] As noted earlier, the distinction also seems to correspond to different tests or criteria for duties: whether a maxim is even conceivable without contradiction as a universal law versus whether I could *will* that all adopt the maxim as a law. Lying to extricate myself from unpleasant circumstances could not be conceived as a universal law of nature. That no one aid others could be so conceived, but, knowing that I am a finite agent and might eventually need aid from others, *I* could not consistently will that all adopt such a maxim. I would be contradicting myself, given what I know I might require.[43]

Now Hegel often tries so hard to prove that it would simply be in principle impossible for any agent to know what he is to do if he were to attempt to obey a universal, formal, moral principle that he neglects to examine in any detail Kant's attempt to show just what would follow from such an attempt, and why it would follow that such an agent would be duty-bound to set certain substantive ends.

This neglect is significant, because Kant argues that one of the ends I must pursue is my own self-perfection and the other is the happiness of others. Since both of these count as imperfect duties, there is no specific action required in satisfying such a duty. At least on one account of imperfect duties,[44] this means that any act performed in my attempt to realize such an end is not *itself* required by duty, and so I can fulfill a duty without being directly motivated by an intention to do my duty. I don't have to save my wife from the burning building because it is my duty to render aid, and so Kant needn't be said to undervalue love and friendship for the sake of duty. I get full moral credit if I save her even if I do so because she is more important to me than anyone else in the building, because I love her, as long as I have established, and my actions reveal that I really have established, the

42 Perfect–imperfect, narrow–wide, legal–ethical, contradiction in conception–willing, are not for various reasons all strictly parallel. See my discussion in Chapter 3, this volume.
43 The clearest formulation of this distinction, described as between "narrower" and "broader" duties, occurs in *GW* p. 424; *E*, pp. 41–42. The most influential modern discussion of the distinction can be found in Onora O'Neill, *Acting on Principle* (New York: Columbia University Press, 1975). See my discussion of her interpretation in "On the Moral Foundations of Kant's *Rechtslehre*," sect. 3.
44 Cf. Barbara Herman, "Integrity and Impartiality," *Monist* 66 (1983): 233–49; "On the Value of Acting from the Motive of Duty," *Philosophical Review* 90 (1981): 359–82; Marcia Baron, "The Alleged Moral Repugnance of Acting from Duty," *Journal of Philosophy* 81 (1984): 197–220; Thomas Hill, "Kant on Imperfect Duty and Supererogation," *Kant-Studien* 62 (1971): 55–76; Karl Ameriks, "The Hegelian Critique of Kantian Morality," in *New Essays on Kant,* ed. by Bernard den Ouden and Marcia Moen (New York: Peter Lang, 1987), pp. 179–212.

end of beneficence. This act of beneficence, even motivated as it is (subject to certain general conditions),[45] helps satisfy such a duty.

Kant's doctrine of imperfect duties thus neither requires that all our helping relations to others, or all relations of love, be deemed worthy only if done directly from duty nor ignores the great significance of love, solidarity, or even the value of reconciliation or non-alienation in any morally worthy life. He does deny that there is anything morally worthy about a spontaneous dedication to others, or love for another, or social solidarity, that could not be overridden by a concern for the morally right, but that is surely a qualification worth preserving.

And he makes clear in several places that, as subjects of the moral law, we must be concerned with more than individual acts of duty. In the first place, he even suggests in spots that if the basic issue is whether we are in fact acting from duty alone in a particular action, we will be misled in answering such a question if we try to settle the issue by looking within ourselves as deeply as possible at the moment of action, by trying to find what single motive actually caused the single action.[46] We might not be able to determine whether or to what extent we are truly motivated by moral obedience unless we look over a longer stretch of time and allow in, as relevant, information about the agent's emotional life, the "frame of mind" with which he acts. Judging that an individual *actually has adopted*, made his own, a maxim might require knowing a good deal about the agent's deeds over time and his reaction to various circumstances.[47]

---

45 See Marcia Baron, "Kantian Ethics and Supererogation," *Journal of Philosophy* 84 (1987): 237–62. I certainly could violate a duty to myself if I rush into a hopeless situation, not to mention my duties to, say my two small children, and others. There are all sorts of circumstances where it would not be difficult to hesitate in praising such "unconditional" love, where it is a good thing indeed to "have one thought too many."

46 I am concentrating here on the ways Kant and Hegel believe that human freedom is linked to rationality, and so on the formalism and application issues raised by Hegel's critique. But they also disagree over the proper account of action itself, and so about such issues as the way to account for or explain an action. See Wood's discussion of the motivation–intention (or "internal reason") issue, *Hegel's Ethical Theory*, ch. 9, and Allison's response, *Kant's Theory of Freedom*, pp. 184–91. I discuss this issue, and offer some further criticisms of Kant's position, in "Idealism and Agency in Kant and Hegel," *Journal of Philosophy* 88 (October 1991): 532–41.

47 This position is at least implied in Kant's famous note, responding to Schiller, in *Die Religion innerhalb der Grenzen der blossen Vernunft, AA*, VI, pp. 23–4n; *Religion Within the Limits of Reason Alone*, trans. Theodore M. Greene and Hoyt H. Hudson (New York: Harper, 1960), pp. 18–19n. He seems to deny there that an individual doing his duty with a "fear-ridden" and "dejected" temperament could really be said to have adopted as his maxim a maxim of duty, that it reveals an actual hatred of the law (even if there is still some sense in which I could be said to have "adopted" a maxim I hate, and even if Kant still is worried about the

Moreover, such duty itself presupposes some general end in life, a moral ideal that requires training, a certain sort of socialization and community, and ultimately a religious community.[48] Thus, even in my attempt to fulfill perfect duties – say, in general, to respect others as ends in themselves – I know that I can adopt policies that (i) make it more psychologically difficult for me to perform such duties and (ii) tend to make me less sensitive to what Barbara Herman has called the "morally salient" features of a situation.[49] I have an imperfect duty to perfect myself, and this seems to open up a good deal of "free play" (*latitudo*) for Hegel's concerns. I need to know what counts in various cultures as genuine marks of respect, what various social practices esteem and condemn in this regard; whether in certain modern Western cultures, various social roles and social possibilities have come to be indispensable in respecting others' autonomy or even in attempting to attain their own happiness. I need to be attentive to features of my own and others' moral education and socialization. And I need to be concerned about my own character, about not just doing my duty in this or that instance, but about adopting as my end the development of a character committed over a long stretch of time, a lifetime, to a moral sensitivity and a kind of moral disposition. This goal too would presumably require attention to various aspects of my society: say, nowadays, the corrupting influence of

"moral fanaticism" threatened by Schiller's position. See Allison, *Kant's Theory of Freedom*, pp. 180–4.) In the second *Critique* we are also told that the kernel of laws is to strive toward "practical love," where "to love one's neighbor means to like to practice one's duties towards him," *KdpV*, pp. 83; 86; elsewhere he remarks that we cannot really count on duty "to any great degree unless the command is accompanied by love." *Das Ende aller Dinge. AA*, VIII; *The End of All Things*, trans. T. Humphrey in *Perpetual Peace* (Indianapolis: Hackett, 1983), pp. 338; 101. See also Ameriks, "Hegelian Critique of Kantian Morality," pp. 185–92; and Barbara Herman, "What Happens to the Consequences? Some Problems of Judgement in Kantian Ethics," in *The Practice of Moral Judgment* (Cambridge: Harvard University Press, 1993). Onora O'Neill also points to such considerations in "Kant After Virtue," in *Constructions of Reason: Explorations of Kant's Practical Philosophy* (Cambridge: Cambridge University Press, 1989), p. 153.

48 A very good discussion of the role such imperfect duties play in Kant and of the relation between such duties and moral alienation can be found in Karl Ameriks's "Hegelian Critique of Kantian Morality." See especially Ameriks's discussion there of the moral motivation problem in the development of Kant's theory, and the way in which his theory of "respect" opens up a range of issues relevant to Hegel's attack.

49 Barbara Herman, "The Practice of Moral Judgment," *Journal of Philosophy* 82 (1985): 414–36. This account suggests a number of ways in which one might identify resources within Kant's theory that could be used to respond to Hegelian worries. She admits that rules of moral salience are not self-imposed by adults. They are the products of a particular socialization process, and so reflect presuppositions of particular moral communities. I am not sure that the Kantian notion of autonomy would be consistent with such claims, but that is a longer story.

mass culture, the manipulation of political and ethical sensitivities by advertisements, the commercialization of the aesthetic, and so on, all recognizable left Hegelian (perhaps post-Kantian?) sorts of concerns.

It would appear that such claims do accommodate many of Hegel's concerns. They seem close to saying, It is true that I can exercise my autonomy and be genuinely self-determining only as a rational being. But it must be admitted that there are social and historical and psychological conditions for the exercise of such autonomy. It is always theoretically possible to subject myself to the moral law in any circumstance, but (we might imagine Kant himself conceding) that in itself is an abstract and empty claim. I could not rationally will a world in which ever more favorable conditions were not realized, and so I must adopt as my end that realization, and therewith must will what will make possible my own self-perfection and the happiness of others. There are good reasons, derived from our duty to obey the moral law, for coming to understand and appreciate what will count as a respect for others as ends in themselves in the community I inherit, and for perfecting myself within that community, complemented by a knowledge of social and individual psychology. And this does not imply that every act in the fulfillment of these ends is to be done from duty. Just the contrary; that would evince a misunderstanding of the difference between perfect and imperfect duties.

Should all these things – Kant's account of "the good," his sensitivity to the issue of moral feeling (respect), his expanded discussion of the conditions under which a realization of the moral ideal is possible, his flexible account of moral judgment and its central role in moral life, his attention to the moral importance of the religious community, and his emphasis on the importance of love, beneficence, and self-perfection in his *Tugendlehre* – count as a rejoinder to Hegel's famous rigorism charge?

That is a large issue, and each of the topics listed merits its own discussion, but we can at least introduce here what would be, I think, Hegel's general reasons for saying no.

The basic reason is that, given Kant's dualism and incompatibilism, the foundations of his moral theory will not support any claim stronger than the legalistic, constraining ones so prominent in Hegel's attacks. That foundation cannot tell us, beyond ruling out the impermissible, ruling in vast areas of the permissible, and requiring the juridically obligatory, *what to do* in order to be able to identify with our deeds and practices. Were Hegel to address these ethical dimensions of Kant's theory, then, his response would have to be, Nice work if you can get it, but you *can't* get it (even if you try).

Consider first the issue of imperfect duties, or duties to adopt maxims, actually to set ends, as opposed to negative duties, to refrain from impermissible ends. Kant introduces such a distinction in the *Groundwork* by means of the "contradiction in willing" test discussed earlier, and his most famous application of the principle concerns the "end" of beneficence. Presumably, a person could not will as a universal law of nature a maxim of non-beneficence (could not have as an end non-beneficence) knowing that "he would need the love and sympathy of others," a love and sympathy he would have "robbed himself of" by so willing.

We may pass by the well-known problems with this example and focus simply on what follows from the argument if it goes through. Clearly it only establishes the impermissibility of a certain sort of end (a complete selfishness); it prescribes ends only in the negative sense. This means that the duty required can clearly be satisfied by my not having a policy of non-beneficence, rather than by "making others' happiness my end." And, in turn, my actual policies will count as so satisfying that requirement if I do something to aid others, sometimes. And this sort of duty to beneficence, to "make beneficence my end" by not avoiding as a policy matter opportunities to aid, is pretty thin gruel.[50] It is in keeping with the more legalistic and rigorous approach of the *Groundwork* (at least as compared with the *Tugendlehre*), and Kant's general account of the way humanity itself functions as an end in itself, that it "must serve for every maxim as a condition *limiting* all merely regulative and arbitrary ends."[51] He does of course go beyond such formulations, and also insists that "the ends of a subject who is an end in himself must, if this conception is to have its full effect on me, be also, as far as possible, my ends,"[52] but nothing in the *Groundwork* tells us very much about what is entailed by this (beyond conscientiously obeying the law), or *why* such a more positive end would be required. The contradiction in willing test still leaves us only with general constraints on our pursuit

---

50 Since Kant believed that the "contradiction in willing" test did establish that beneficence was a morally required end, in however limited a sense, he must have believed that beneficence and nonbeneficence were *contradictories*, and so that not having a policy of non-beneficence amounted to having a policy of beneficence. It seems plausible that this is wrong, that I may have neither policy. But Kant seems to have believed that since it is possible to attribute to someone a maxim, even if that person has never formulated a "policy" as such, we are entitled to say of someone who does not, or even rarely, gives aid, that he does have a policy of nonbeneficence. In the *Doctrine of Virtue*, however, Kant appears to think the two goals are contraries and so he needs a different and stronger argument to show why we must adopt "as our end" beneficence. See *TL*, p. 389; *DV*, p. 49. (I am grateful to Henry Allison and to Allen Wood for conversations and correspondence about many of these issues.)

51 *GW*, p. 436; *E*, pp. 54–5, my emphasis.

52 *GW*, p. 430; *E*, p. 49.

of ends, establishes an end we must "have" only in a very weak sense (an end whose realization we may not ignore), and so leaves us with a position in which I can truly recognize my own agency in a very limited, still essentially negative, context.[53]

In the *Doctrine of Virtue*, it is at least clear that Kant *wants* to defend something much stronger than the impermissibility of non-beneficence. He is much clearer that he wants to defend "ends which are also duties," or obligatory ends, ends I must have and seek to realize: positive, not negative ends. I must make the (permissible) ends of others "*my own ends as well.*"[54] The stronger claim is present even though there are still many references to the weaker contradiction-in-willing test earlier used to defend ethical duties. (See Section VI.)[55] However, several other arguments are also present.

Many of these are introduced quickly and not developed much. It is very much as if Kant were exploring considerations, rather than presenting a well-worked-out approach. In explaining why we have a duty to develop all our talents (not just those that would better enable me to obey the law), Kant asserts that I must attend to my education and correct my errors in order "to be worthy of the humanity" in any person.[56] He does not explain why the development of an intellectual talent is itself a duty (as opposed to something simply of value and, as we might expect, of value only in relation to the development of my moral capacity, the true source of my worthiness), or whether, say, the duty means I may not ignore an obvious scientific talent

---

53 Marcia Baron, "Kantian Ethics and Supererogation," points to the distinction between avoiding a policy of nonbeneficence and having a maxim of beneficence, or making beneficence my end, but she neglects to reconstruct any Kantian argument for the latter position. As I shall argue in a moment, there is no successful argument in the *Tugendlehre*, although Kant there is clearly interested in the more substantial "obligatory end," and at least appears worried by exactly the difference Baron is pointing to. See *TL*, p. 389; *DV*, p. 49.

54 *TL*, p. 387; *DV*, p. 47.

55 One discussion of beneficence makes use of the stronger claim, but replays the *Groundwork*'s reasoning. We are said to know that our own unavoidable self-love "cannot be divorced from our need of being loved by others (i.e. of receiving help from them when we are in need)." Since I must make it my maxim to count on being "an end for others," I must make others my end to prevent an inconsistency in willing. *TL*, p. 392; *DV*, p. 53. But Kant is here simply changing the terms, not defending better what the argument allows him to say. Since I cannot know when or how much aid I will need, all I know a priori is that I will need *some* aid, and I cannot will a maxim that would make it a universal law that there be *no* aid. This does not require that I make others' happiness my end, something I must be committed to and do whatever I can to promote.

56 *TL*, p. 386; *DV*, p. 46.

in favor of meager aesthetic ones, if I happen to find the latter more personally fulfilling.

At another point, he claims that reason must set substantive ends for us to pursue,

> For since the sensuous inclinations tempt us to ends . . . which may be contrary to duty, legislative reason can check their influence *only* by another end, a moral end set up against the ends of inclination, which must therefore be given a priori, independently of the inclinations.[57]

One might have thought, from the rest of the Kantian corpus, that an awareness of obligation itself was sufficient to "check" the temptation of inclinations.

Other, somewhat more distinctive arguments for the claim that there are obligatory ends are just as brief and confusing.

> Now there must be such an end (obligatory) and a categorical imperative corresponding to it. For since there are free actions there must also be ends to which, as their object, these actions are directed. But among these ends there must also be some that are at the same time . . . duties. For were there no such ends, then all ends would be valid for practical reason only as a means to other ends; and since there can be no action without an end, a categorical imperative would be impossible.[58]

Although it is true that the existence of a categorical imperative is inconsistent with *all* actions aiming at relative ends, all this means is that I cannot make the realization of such ends an overriding policy goal, a super end or goal. Rather, I must always be committed to the absolute priority of obedience to the moral law, no matter what relative ends I pursue. Again Hegel's intuitions about the moral point of view, and the strictly negative implications it generates, would be confirmed.

Later Kant tries a different formulation with similar results. Pure practical reason cannot be "*indifferent* to ends" and must "prescribe them a priori" if reason is actually to guide action. Such a rationally prescribed end would thus be an obligatory end.[59] But as Kant himself had demonstrated, reason can "take an interest in ends" and so determine the maxims for actions directed at ends, without having to tell us *what* ends we must pursue. There

---

57 *TL*, p. 380; *DV*, p. 37.
58 *TL*, p. 284; *DV*, p. 43.
59 *TL*, p. 394; *DV*, p. 56.

is no reason given to support the conclusion that pure reason cannot be practical, that there cannot be an action-guiding categorical imperative, if reason does no more than forbid impermissible ends, and in that sense prescribes a supreme "end" in life: doing nothing contrary to the moral law.

And even if all these arguments were successful, we would still be a long way away from any defense of the claim that there are just *two* obligatory ends, at least not without a kind of regression into teleological assumptions incompatible with the critical enterprise as a whole.[60]

Many of these considerations also make it unlikely, I think, Kant can be characterized as a "virtue theorist," that Kant "offers primarily an ethics of virtue rather than an ethics of rules," as Onora O'Neill has suggested.[61] The heart of such a reading brings together many of the Kantian counters we have been considering.

> Maxims can have little to do with the rightness or wrongness of acts of specific types, and much more to do with the underlying moral quality of a life, or aspects of a life. In adopting maxims of a morally appropriate sort we will not be adopting a set of moral rules at all, but rather some much more general guidelines for living. To have maxims of a morally appropriate sort would then be a matter of leading a certain sort of life, or of being a certain sort of person.[62]

Such a position has a number of problems as an interpretation of Kant. For one thing, it seems to eliminate Kant's own obviously important interest in duties of justice, and in rules that do eliminate, strictly, as impermissible, whole classes of actions.[63] For another, it is fair enough to distinguish maxims, or deeply underlying principles, from specific intentions in individual actions, and to focus our moral evaluation on such general principles (whether explicitly formulated by the agent or not). But, as we have now seen in some detail, Kant's criterion of evaluation still seems to be, whether I am leading the sort of life, or have become the sort of person, who is progressively better able to check the effects of inclination and to obey the moral law more regularly and consistently.

---

60 Cf. Jeffrie Murphy, *Kant: The Philosophy of Right* (London: Macmillan, 1970), and Bruce Aune, Kant's *Theory of Morals* (Princeton: Princeton University Press, 1979), and my discussion in Chapter 3, this volume.
61 O'Neill, "Kant After Virtue," p. 154. She has later emended tbe claim to the assertion that Kant has an "ethics of principles."
62 Ibid., p. 151
63 Ibid., p. 158: "Kant's picture of right action is inadequate."

O'Neill tries to block such a familiar characterization by describing Kant's moral ideal in a way more friendly to the worries of virtue theorists, and so more positively. The import of "accepting the Categorical Imperative" is supposed to be that we "accept the moral reality of other selves," and "hence the possibility (not, note, the reality) of a moral community."[64] But it is too radical a reconstruction of Kant to say that, for him, "The good life for man is one of projects that invite and never preclude the collaboration of others."[65] Kant is quite clear that the good life is the one that best realizes human freedom, the distinctive human capacity worthy of respect. Since this freedom can best be realized in subjection to a universal, rational principle, "community" is simply a result of such necessarily equal subjection. We relate to each other by virtue of our relation to the moral law; certainly an indirect, a more "Leibnizian," one might say, than Aristotelian or Hegelian "community." And there is quite a gap between doing nothing that precludes such a community and "inviting" or positively pursuing community. As with many previous examples, the principle, Do nothing to make a community of rational agents impossible, is not equivalent to, Promote, as an ethical ideal, as necessary for the realization of freedom, a community. I see no argument in Kant for the latter as a moral ideal, and I do not think O'Neill provided one.[66]

And finally, insisting on the importance of moral judgment in the work of practical reason, and so on the particular social and historical context within which what is morally salient and insignificant arises, introduces problems Kant's theory cannot handle. Since we are obviously capable of reflecting on whether or not the standards and practices we have inherited conform to reason, either this reliance on a kind of phronesis simply returns us to a higher-order, quite familiar Kantian reflection, whether the practices violate the moral law; or we need a much broader assessment of the relative "rationality," the relative success of our ethos in the full realization of freedom, in a complex narrative of a historical tradition. If a culture regards it as a deep mark of respect for the dignity or even self-determination of women

---

64 Ibid., p. 156.
65 Ibid., p. 159.
66 Richard Eldridge, in a recent book, *On Moral Personhood* (Chicago: University of Chicago Press, 1989), has made use of the spirit of Hegelian criticisms of Kant to suggest that it is the issue of moral judgment that is crucial to Kant's enterprise (at least in meeting these objections), and that such judgment must be informed by a sensitivity to a good deal of social and historical information. Eldridge suggests how much modern literature would be of help in understanding what is or is not essential in modern society for any respect for others' dignity as rational beings, their autonomy.

("as women") to keep them in purdah or considers that open economic competition with, necessarily, big losers and big winners, is necessary for the exercise of individual freedom, will a Kantian ethical evaluation be able to assess such claims, or must it accept them as what counts to a culture as the realization of Kantian ideals?[67] I suggest that here is where we would need to introduce something much more like Hegel's historical assessment in order for there to be an assessment at all.

V. Ethical Reasons

A belief that any subject, in initiating some intentional action, must be presumed to intend that the action satisfy conditions under which it can truly be his action, can be freely self-determined, and that this condition is best met by the self-imposition of a rational principle, unites Kant and Hegel.[68] But Hegel denies that such a condition of rational self-legislation can be satisfied by an individually conceived agent attempting to realize this condition negatively, by not counting his contingently formed desires and needs as primary, by adopting a principle whose chief recommendation is that it is not tied to the fulfillment of these motives, and so can be simultaneously willed by any agent, no matter what ends he seeks.

As we have seen, this disagreement can be understood to come at Kant from two different directions. Hegel himself suggests that what comes to count as satisfying such a self-realization condition, and so what counts as the reasons relevant to it, change. Various social conditions, and developments in intellectual and religious history, are indispensable in understanding what could, at some period, count as such a satisfaction, and in understanding what wins out, what at least relatively best satisfies such a condition. Without such a phenomenology, it would also be impossible to understand why an individual agent, within some particular social setting, would come to understand not just "what any purely practical agent would impose on himself as a principle," but why that agent would understand himself as

67 O'Neill is certainly right in "Ethical Reasoning and Ideological Pluralism," *Ethics* 98 (1988): 705–22, that no formulation of principles can be expected to eliminate the need for moral judgment and a necessarily imprecise, non-algorithmic response to cases. But too much free play or *latitudo*, one not informed by a reflection of wider scope than one limited to an assessment of individual sincerity or moral consistency, is as problematic as some sort of rule fetish.

68 At least it does on the interpretation I am defending here. Others distinguish Kant and Hegel on freedom by distinguishing the question of the "rules that the will gives itself" (Kant) and the proper "objects" of the will (Hegel). See Terry Pinkard, *Hegel's Dialectic: The Explanation of Possibility* (Philadephia: Temple University Press, 1988), p. 122.

bound to that version of rational agency, why, under what conditions, he would see *his own freedom* as realized *only* in that way.[69] There is no "fact of reason"; there is only what has come to count for us as such agency and why it has come to count.

On the other hand, if we simply start with Kant's position, without worrying about such origins problems, we won't get much out of it. There may be much in a life determined by the Kantian moral law that is permissible and enjoyable, perhaps much of some value in preparing me to obey more readily, but little that can be said to reflect me substantively, as a self-determining agent; little beyond my ability to prescind from my ends and enact some empty demonstration of my own negative autonomy.

These considerations commit Hegel to a good deal that is quite controversial. The idea of a wholly internal notion of historical rationality has been controversial enough.[70] But his general claim about modern institutions commits him also to an ambitious defense of many individual arguments: that modern institutions such as property, contract, civil law, moral practices, legally sanctioned punishment, some form of free market competition, association in corporations, some form of representative political life (in a constitutional monarchy), and a world order of states, all best realize this autonomy ideal in modernity. These are supposed to be the indispensable modern social roles within which an agent can actually act as a free agent among other free, determinate agents. They are thus the true "objects" of a rational will (a will situated in the modern epoch) and have a claim on our allegiance and participation.[71]

---

69 Cf. Dieter Henrich, "Das Problem der Grundlegung der Ethik und im spekulativen Idealismus," in *Sein und Ethos*, ed. by P. Engelhardt (Mainz: Matthias Grünewald, 1963), pp. 350–86, and my "Idealism and Agency in Kant and Hegel."

70 See my "Hegel and Category Theory," *Review of Metaphysics* 43 (1990): 839–48.

71 These twin claims – that Hegel thinks he can demonstrate that one can be an autonomous agent only as a social agent, and that Hegel fully accepts the obligation to justify the assertion that only certain modern social insititutions realize such autonomy – should be stressed again, in the light of the constant association of Hegel with modern conventionalist and communitarian and relativist attacks on morality. Onora O'Neill, for example, in "Ethical Reasoning and Ideological Pluralism," frequently refers to "neo-Hegelians" (p. 710), *Sittlichkeit* (pp. 714 ff.), and "Hegelians" and "most deeply Hegelian liberals" (p. 715) in such a conventionalist and anti-universalist way. It is of course Hegel's own fault that he is both portrayed in such a "pluralism of *Sittlichkeiten*," conventionalist way, and, among some of the French, as the reverse, as the epitome of Enlightenment universalism, even "totalitarian," "imperialist" thinking, but I hope to have shown that he attempts a recognizable account of ethical reasons aptly described by neither label. See also my *Modernism as a Philosophical Problem: On the Dissatisfactions of European High Culture* (Oxford: Basil Blackwell, 1991), ch. 3.

Underlying all such claims is a general thesis: that I cannot successfully lead a free, self-determining life except as a social subject, or, as he had put it in his early discussion of property in the *PR*, "This relation of will to will is the true and proper ground in which freedom is existent" (§71). I am free as an individual only "in" others, only if my own self-realization is essentially and concretely tied to the self-realization of my fellow family members, co-workers, and fellow citizens. The claim for such an ontological sociality is so strong that a consequence is that my own self-actualization must itself be understood as a social goal, something that can only be collectively realized. That is, we must not only avoid principles that make a community impossible; we cannot "be who we are" except as social beings.

These are familiar claims, long associated with Hegel.[72] And although it has always been clear that Hegel regarded himself as having demonstrated such conclusions, it has not been so clear how that demonstration was supposed to go. As we have been seeing, these paradoxical formulations have, at least partly, a Rousseauean and Kantian origin, an origin that begins to decrease the air of paradox. The rational reflection that ensures my genuine independence or *Selbstständigkeit* is, by virtue of its very rationality, universal. I must take into account what any agent would do in acting as I do, and thereby at least an "abstract" notion of social subjectivity, or "spirit," is achieved (the kingdom of ends).

However, by denying that this criterion could mean "what any agent would do in the efficient satisfaction of these contingent preferences," or "what any agent would do, independently of any ends or preferences he might have," Hegel has proposed a conception of rationality in such reflection that is *essentially* social and historical, rather than rule-governed, or only ideally communal, or social and historical in "application" only. What I am doing in identifying what is rationally required for me, for my own self-determination, is appealing to what would be required for any concretely represented agent, and thereby representing *what has to count* as essential to a historical community as indispensable to such agency (e.g., voting, choosing my own spouse) versus what is marginal or insignificant. Hegel (i) thinks he has identified what social functions have come to be essential in modernity to such a realization (here his most controversial claim: that modern societies require wholly new sorts of legal relations among private individuals, or "civil society," as well as a genuinely public life, a common identifica-

---

72 And long influential in the post-Hegelian intellectual and social history. Cf. Karl Marx, "Zur Judenfrage," *Frühe Schriften*, I, ed. by H. J. Lieber and K. Furth (Darmstadt: Cotta Verlag, 1971), p. 473.

tion or citizenship in a state, and that these realizations of freedom are not inconsistent, but continuous, even require each other), and (ii) believes he has shown why only that sort of historical interpretation and this historical notion of the rationality of these practices can explain and justify what it is to realize human freedom.

Now, partly, this all also depends on a very ambitious, even deeper, claim that links any possible determinate self-consciousness with recognition by others. On that account, most famously presented in the *Phenomenology of Spirit*, I come to understand who I am, what is required for me to realize some conception of myself, only in a complex relation to, and struggle with, others. I identify myself, what is of essential significance to me, only through others. And partly, as Hegel tells us in the *PR*, this whole claim depends on his category theory, or his logic. The "details," he says, of the transition to ethical life "are made intelligible in logic," especially the logic of "limitation" and "ought" (*PR* §141A), and the "universality" claimed for any individual will in ethical life clearly presupposes Hegel's intimidating notion of a "concrete universal."[73]

Both claims are obviously beyond the scope of this discussion. But we have seen enough to be able to note how radically Hegel wants to transform the conception of practical rationality, and why. Within the details of his exchange with Kant, there is already evidence to warrant renewed attention to his proposal for a "third way" between prudential and moral reason.[74] At least it is now clearer, I would hope, what sorts of claims he would have to defend to make good on his positive case, why the details of historical narrative and philosophical analysis are so intertwined in such a case, and how we might understand such influential, if idiosyncratic, claims as the one that ends Hegel's account of "Morality" in the *Phenomenology*.

---

73 Cf. sects. 6 and 7 of Theunissen, "Die verdrängte Intersubjektivät," and my discussion in *Hegel's Idealism*, ch. 10.

74 Obviously, a reconstruction and defense of Hegel's position on *Sittlichkeit* cannot rest content with such a programmatic argument. There is good reason to believe that Hegel's own claims of "rationality" for the nineteenth-century patriarchal family, his hopes that modern civil society would promote various forms of ethical association (e.g., corporations), his faith in the stability of modern class relations, and his underestimation of the roles of religion and nationalism in modernity should all prompt a major revision in any account of the contemporary possibility of *Sittlichkeit*. That will clearly not be easy: MacIntyre may well be right, and there may be no such possibility, consistent with modernity itself. My only claim here is that these limitations in Hegel's case can be admitted without damage to his general position on what would be required for such a reconstruction. Any final assessment would have to depend on what could be said about the "ethical life," if any, of the contemporary family, civil society, and modern state.

The reconciling Yes, in which both I's release their opposed existence, is the existence of an I which has expanded into a duality, and therein remains identical with itself, and, in its complete externalization and opposite, possesses the certainty of itself; it is God appearing among those who know themselves as pure knowledge.[75]

75 *PhG*, p. 472; *PhS*, p. 408.

5

AVOIDING GERMAN IDEALISM:
KANT, HEGEL, AND THE REFLECTIVE
JUDGMENT PROBLEM

In the following, I want to suggest two different ways of understanding the relation between Kant's *Critique of Judgment* and the later German Idealist tradition. The first might be considered the received or standard view about that relation. I shall summarize it in Sections I and II.

The second presents a different picture, and I shall begin defending it in the remaining sections. The main issue raised by both possible directions is whether they represent internal developments of Kantian arguments in the third *Critique*, or whether they are motivated by non-Kantian, even non-"critical" commitments of Schelling and especially Hegel. My claim will be that the suggested alternate formulation of Kant's influence does rely on an internal criticism and development. That claim will require a defense of the reading of Kant's text suggested by that appropriation.

I

Many German philosophers of the last decade of the eighteenth and the first decade of the nineteenth century interpreted the *Critique of Judgment* in the light of what they perceived to be the great problem created by the Kantian revolution in philosophy. That problem, as they saw it, was, once "inside" the Kantian project, to find one's way "out" again.

To enter the project seemed to many simply unavoidable. It was to share in the spirit of Kant's revolutionary modernism, to destroy dogmatism, to assert the autonomy of human reason, its sufficiency in being a law unto itself. To be able to see all conscious, intentional relations to nature or any normative relation to others as primarily a "self-determination" in relation to nature and others would establish that free self-determination as the supreme condition of intelligibility and action.

Finding some way out, however, quickly seemed necessary to many. The main problem: Kant's transcendental skepticism, his denial that any knowledge of things in themselves was possible; that, instead, we knew only appearances. For some, taking their bearings from Kant's own remarks at the end of the first *Critique*,[1] this restriction still left the possibility of "Spinozism" unacceptably open and so did not sufficiently secure the ideal at the heart of the Idealist aspirations: the absolute reality of human freedom. For others, this restriction meant that Kant's account of the merely subjective conditions of experience could not finally be distinguished from an epistemologically inconsistent and still unsystematic psychologism; that philosophy had not really advanced much beyond Locke,[2] and that it must. For still others, Kant's skepticism meant that the essentially practical proof for the efficacy of pure practical reason, and the transcendental case for the subjective conditions necessary for nature to be a possible object of experience, could be integrated into no systematic whole. And without such a systematic account, Kantianism amounted to faith (*Glauben*), not knowledge (*Wissen*), finally just an expression of faith that the whole is as it must be, if we are to be able to act as we ought.

For the young Fichte, the young Schelling, and the young Hegel, the prominent charge that there was finally no way out of Kant's skepticism (most memorably formulated by the devious Jacobi)[3] was much more a

---

1 A803 = B831. For a good sense of the importance of these problems for the early Idealists, especially the Spinozism issue, see Karl Ameriks, "Kant, Fichte, and Short Arguments to Idealism," *Archiv für Geschichte der Philosophie* 72 (1990): 63–85.

2 It had of course advanced to some degree, since Kant proposed what later Idealists would characterize as an "immanent" account of the origin and interrelation of concepts. He had insisted on the nonderived status of pure concepts (without a theory of innate knowledge) and so had at least proposed a theory of synthetic a priori knowledge. See the quotation from Locke in *Glauben und Wissen*, (hereafter *GuW*), *Gesammelte Werke*, IV (Hamburg: Felix Meiner Verlag, 1968), p. 326; *Faith and Knowledge* (hereafter *FK*), trans. W. Cerf and H.S. Harris (Albany: SUNY Press, 1977), pp. 68–9; and Jean Hyppolite's helpful discussion, "La critique hégélienne de la réflexion kantienne," *Kant-Studien* 45 (1953–4): 86ff.

3 Friederich Heinrich Jacobi, a major figure in the German counter-Enlightenment, formulated many of the most influential early criticisms of transcendental philosophy, for example, that its skepticism was inconsistent with its own claims to ground knowledge, that it was inadequate to the explanation of organic life, and that it dangerously undermined the centrality of religious faith in human life. Rolf-Peter Horstmann, in *Die Grenzen der Vernunft:*

challenge than a damning criticism, an invitation to formulate an internal criticism of Kant that accepted central aspects of his anti-empiricism and his attack on transcendental realism, but that avoided these putative skeptical problems.[4] They shared none of Jacobi's counter-Enlightenment, religious worries about transcendental philosophy; preferred to see themselves, in the biblical terms first formulated by Reinhold, as avoiding the "letter," but embracing the "spirit" of Kant's philosophy; and were all spectacularly confident of success.

But everyone seemed to see a different sort of way out of the Kantian wilderness, and, eventually, a different philosophical promised land. Tickets were soon being sold to an *Elementarphilosophie*, a *Wissenschaftslehre*, an *Identitätsphilosophie*, a *Wissenschaft der Logik*, and so on. In my own view, the most interesting and philosophically suggestive of these journeys began with Fichte's radicalization of Kant's claims about the apperceptive or self-conscious nature of human experience and action. The direction of this transformation would eventually lead to a revision of Kant's founding distinction between spontaneity and receptivity (as one between conceptual and wholly non-conceptual content) and so to an anti-skeptical argument for the "absolute" (or unconditioned, not exogenously limited) status of the mind's spontaneous self-positing. This direction, formulated by Fichte roughly between 1790 and 1797 or so, would form a key element, even, I think, the heart of Hegel's eventual absolute idealism.[5] (It is also, we shall see later, a key element in Hegel's understanding of the third *Critique*.)

Eine Untersuchung zu Zielen und Motiven des Deutschen Idealismus (Frankfurt am M.: Anton Hain, 1991), narrates the history of post-Kantian philosophy in a way that reveals the importance of Jacobi. See also Frederick Beiser, *The Fate of Reason: German Philosophy from Kant to Fichte* (Cambridge: Harvard University Press, 1987).

4 One strategy for achieving this goal: to rethink and radicalize the Kantian beginning, the supreme epistemic condition without which there could be no experience, by explication of which a variety of determinate conclusions about possible objects of experience could be derived. This is roughly the strategy adopted by Fichte and Reinhold. Another strategy would be to follow more closely what I am calling here "Kant's own way out of Kant" in the third *Critique*, or his reflections on the necessity of an intuitive intellect. This is the path pursued by Schelling and Hegel. See the summary in Horstmann, *Die Grenzen der Vernunft*, ch. 4, "Kant's 'Kritik der Urteilskraft' im Urteil seiner idealistischen Nachfolger," pp. 191–221.

5 Cf. my *Hegel's Idealism: The Satisfactions of Self-Consciousness* (Cambridge: Cambridge University Press, 1989). The idea that Hegel's position is best assessed in terms of his interpretations of, and his claims against, Kant is not, of course, a novel one and is prominent in much of the best contemporary work on Hegel, such as that by Klaus Düsing. See his *Hegel und die Geschichte der Philosophie* (Darmstadt: Wissenschaftliche Buchgesellschaft, 1983), pp. 196–242, and "Aesthetische Einbildungskraft und intuitiver Verstand," *Hegel-Studien* 21 (1986): 87–128. Traditional and contemporary accounts like Düsings's have not, though, in my view, done full justice to the philosophical quality of Hegel's Kantianism, and that is especially

But this Kantian–Fichtean heart is not the whole Idealist body.[6] And it is also true that the publication in 1790 of Kant's *Critique of Judgment* convinced many that *Kant himself* had found a way out of Kantianism, that Kant had conceived a way of defending a systematic or holistic position within which the possibility of moral agency and of living or organic beings, as well as of law-governed, dynamically moving matter, could all be understood consistently. Somehow, our ability to appreciate natural beauty (in a "subjective" but "universally valid" way) and the indispensability of our "estimations" of life could help defend the possibility of the systematic philosophy devoutly pursued by the post-Kantians.

However, although there is widespread agreement that Kant's position in the *KU* was at least as influential in the development of later Idealism as his theory of self-consciousness, transcendental deduction, or theory of autonomy, and substantial consensus about the terms and issues that formed the core of that influence, there does not, at least on the surface, appear to be much in the consensus account that is very philosophically interesting. The question, in other words, has pretty much become a wholly historical one, a question simply of the proper formulation of an episode in *Ideengeschichte*, an episode without much contemporary or perennial relevance. This is so because the standard picture looks like this.

Both Schelling and Hegel directly identify the passages and themes that are supposed to mark out Kant's way out of Kant. They both cite two sections from the Dialectic of Teleological Judgment, sections 76 and 77, which attempt to explore the implications of the unavoidability of the appeal to purposiveness in explanations of nature, or the unacceptability of the radical and infinitely detailed contingencies we would have to face in wholly mechanistic explanations. To have to conceive of nature as purposive is to conceive of parts as existing "for the sake of" wholes (or to think of the effects of causes as also the causes of those causes) (sections 63 and 64), or is simply to conceive of nature as intelligently designed. (Or, perhaps said in a more Schellingean way, as intelligently designing itself.)[7] When Kant comes to explain what thinking of nature this way amounts to, he says that,

---

true, I want to show, with respect to the question of his appropriation of third *Critique* themes.

6 In Hegel's case, for one thing, a final account of his trajectory would obviously also have to include his complex commitments to various elements of classical Greek philosophy and to Christian theology.

7 Kant himself says, "Nature organizes itself," but he is quick to stay clear of the hylozoism he would see in Schelling's formulations. See *Kritik der Urteilskraft* (hereafter *KU*), AA, V, p. 288. In this chapter, I have mainly consulted the translation by Werner Pluhar, *The Critique of Judgment* (hereafter *CJ1*) (Indianapolis: Hackett, 1987), though I have often made

reason forever demands that we assume something or other (the original basis [*den Urgrund*]) as existing with unconditioned necessity, something in which there is no longer to be any distinction between possibility and actuality. (402)

This "necessity" appears to require that nature be conceived as the product of an "intuitive intellect" (406); not, like ours, an understanding that must discursively judge, organize, and systematize "material" that pure thought itself cannot supply, but an absolutely "active" intellect, a "complete spontaneity of intuition" (406), an *intellectus archetypus* (408) or "intellectual intuition" (409)[8] whereby "wholes" are not thought as dependent on, or as aggregations of, prior "parts," but parts as dependent on, only intelligible in their existence and functioning by reference to their relation to, already thought "wholes."[9]

changes. (Page references to the unpublished introduction are to Bd. XX of the *Akademie* edition.) See, also, p. 374. For a study of the relevance of the pantheism, life philosophy, and hylozoism controversies to the composition of *KU*, see John H. Zammito, *The Genesis of Kant's Critique of Judgment* (Chicago: University of Chicago Press, 1992).

8 Kant uses the *intellektuelle Anschauung* phrase rarely; this is the only occurrence in these famous passages, although, largely thanks to Schelling, it would become the term of art for stating this problem and so come to play a large role in Fichte's 1797 *Introductions* and in Hegel's Jena writings. See Schelling's *Abhandlungen*, in *Sämtliche Werke* (hereafter *SW*), ed. by F. W. J. Schelling (Stuttgart: J. G. Cotta'scher, 1856–61), I, p. 402, and the discussion in Horstmann, *Die Grenzen der Vernunft*, pp. 210–19, and notes pp. 102–3. (Horstmann points out that although many of Schelling's criticisms of Kant's first *Critique* were common currency at the time, Schelling alone insisted that the third *Critique* notion of intellectual intuition could remedy those supposed deficits, see p. 212. Cf. also the heady pronouncements in the 1800 *System der transzendentalen Idealismus* (hereafter *STI*), *SW*, III, p. 368: "Intellectual intuition is the organ of all transcendental thinking." *System of Transcendental Idealism* (hereafter *ST*), trans. Peter Heath (Charlottesville: University of Virginia Press, 1978), p. 27.

9 In other words, a merely "strategic" purposive creator, with an intellect and will much like ours, but extremely powerful, could not explain the organic unity of nature and natural wholes. For the appeal to a creative intelligence to fill the great gap created by mechanistic explanations, "wholes" must really *be* prior to "parts" for such an *intellectus archetypus*, and that means it must create what it thinks immediately, rather than rely on some "material" to create for the sake of some causally motivating end. In the latter case we would not have appealed (even negatively and by contrast with our discursivity) to a purposively designing intelligence but to a mind and will empirically motivated like ours and so would be back with the contingencies problem, which undergirds the claim that "it is just as indubitably certain that the mere mechanism of nature cannot provide our cognitive power with a basis on which we could explain the production of organized beings" (p. 389; see also the famous remark on a "Newton for a blade of grass" at p. 400). Kant himself is clear about the only possible realization of this idea: "Es is schwer zu begreifen, wie ein anderer intuitiver Verstand stattfinden sollte als der göttliche." *Reflexion* 6048; *AA*, XVIII. Cf. also the discussion in Henry Allison, "Kant's Antinomy of Teleological Judgment," *Southern Journal of Philosophy* 30, suppl. (1991): 25–42.

Now on one reading, this could all certainly sound as if Kant might be claiming that human reason can determine what there really is or must be (the *Urgrund*); that it must be a living, self-organizing nature, and so in some sense a "spiritualized" nature. This approach would defend a conception of such an "original basis" or *Urgrund* that transcended the great Kantian dualism of *Geist* and *Natur* (such a nature must exhibit a purposively designing intelligence). And this direction would appear to have greatly revised the first *Critique*'s picture of reason's subjectively regulative function. We now appear, in other words, not to be making some claim about how "we must think" of nature such that our explanatory demands can be met, but how nature must be, such that our conceivings and demandings, not to mention our very "living," could be possible in the first place.[10]

This version of the direction is especially stressed by those (like Burkhart Tuschling) who are particularly worried about the development of Kant's views about systematicity (after around 1787) and who see in Kant's own work increasingly strong claims that a non-human intuitive intellect is required to account for empirical concept formation, organic unity, and a system of scientific laws.[11] Tuschling even, rather startlingly, suggests that these claims in sections 76 and 77 represent the beginnings of a major turn in Kant's thought, leading him toward an acceptance of a Schellingean self-positing divine mind or "absolute," and culminating in the *Opus Postumum*'s otherwise bewildering affirmation that transcendental idealism is a "Spinozism," or that its "present" is represented as much by Schelling as its past is by Spinoza.[12]

10 As we shall see, the exact difference between these formulations, of crucial importance to Schelling's insistence that the "system of idealism" include *both* a philosophy of nature and transcendental philosophy as coequals, is extremely difficult to formulate. Cf. Schelling's attempt in the preface to *STI*, III, p. 330; *ST*, p. 1.

11 Tuschling takes his bearings from passages in the published introduction to *KU* that make claims like "particular empirical laws, must, as regards what the universal laws have left undetermined in them, be viewed in terms of such a unity as if they too had been given by an understanding (even though not ours) so as to assist our cognitive powers by making possible a system of experience in terms of particular natural laws" (p. 180). See his account in "The System of Transcendental Idealism: Questions Raised and Left Open in the *Kritik der Urteilskraft*," *Southern Journal of Philosophy* 30, suppl. (1991): 113.

12 See the quotations from the *Opus postumum* in Tuschling, "System of Transcendental Idealism," pp. 121–2, and see also his "Intuitiver Verstand, absolute Identität, Idee. Thesen zu Hegels früher Rezeption der 'Kritik der Urteilskraft." In *Hegel und die 'Kritik der Urteilskraft,'* ed. by Hans-Friedrich Fulda and Rolf-Peter Horstmann (Stuttgart: Klett-Cotta, 1990), pp. 174–88. In the latter, Tuschling discusses a number of important differences between Hegel and Schelling on the "logic" of such a self-positing intellect, but as will be clear later, I disagree with the way he ropes Hegel and Schelling together. Moreover, when

What is clear is that the young Schelling, in the *Ich-Schrift*, was certainly very much excited by this version of a third *Critique* revision of the first: "The completed Science does not rely on dead faculties, which have no reality and exist only in an artificial abstraction; it rather much more relies on the *living unity of the I,* one which remains the same in all the external manifestations of its activity; in it all the different faculties and activities, which philosophy has always set out, become only one faculty, only one activity of the same identical I."[13] Hence no transcendental skepticism; no unsystematic dualism, or lifeless mechanism, or mere faculty psychology; but a holistic, speculative philosophy; a nature conceived of as actively intuiting itself (purposively organizing itself) with human thought as a manifestation of this activity, not a classifying, legislating machine, operating on "dead," passively received matter.

Hence, too, the great enthusiasm in commentaries on these passages. Here is Schelling again:

> There have perhaps never been so many deep thoughts pressed together on so few pages as occurred in the Critique of Teleological Judgment, paragraph 76.[14]

In an 1801 letter to Fichte, Schelling formulated his own "idea of the Absolute" as the "identity of thinking and intuiting," about which he says that this is "the highest speculative idea, the idea of the Absolute, the intuiting of which occurs in thinking, the thinking of which occurs in intuit-

Tuschling asks whether this whole direction represents a "regress" into a pre-critical metaphysics or an "ontologization" of logic, he answers no, for two reasons, neither of which seems to me persuasive. First he claims that, internally, Kant himself had not solved the problem of the "determinability" of the empirical manifold, as if this alone in some way supports the Divine Substance solution. Kant's difficulties could be addressed in any number of ways, as we shall see, apart from a full-blown, metaphysical philosophy of nature, and, anyway, there is no philosophical justification for any claimed connection between Kant's putative failure and a romantic metaphysics solution. The second reason Tuschling presents is that we should not understand Hegel's metaphysics as a kind of absolute apriorism, or as the derivation of analytic truths from concept analysis. The concept is supposed to be demonstrated as the "immanent structure of empirical existence," which "unites in itself the moments of identity with itself and relation to others" (p. 187). This might suggest that the *sort* of metaphysics to which Tuschling's analysis commits Hegel is unprecedented, but that, as far as I can see, does not address the "regress" question that would be raised by a Kantian (which is an epistemological problem).

13 *SW,* I, p. 238.
14 Ibid., I, p. 242. See also *SW,* I, p. 181.

ing," and that he is, in articulating this idea, simply "relying" on paragraph 76 of the *KU*.[15]

Hegel too, in *Glauben und Wissen*, identifies sections 76 and 77 as the place where Kant expresses most fully "the idea of Reason," the basis for a truly speculative, not merely reflective philosophy. He too notes with great enthusiasm that Kant was "led" (by the internal logic of his own position) to the idea of an "intuitive intellect" and led to it "as an absolutely necessary idea."[16] And he goes on to claim:

> So it is he himself who establishes the opposite experience, that of thinking a nondiscursive intellect. He himself shows that his cognitive faculty is aware not only of the appearance and of the separation of the possible and the actual in it, but also of Reason and the In-Itself. Kant has here before him both the idea of a reason in which possibility and actuality are absolutely identical and its appearance as cognitive faculty wherein they are separated. In the experience of his thinking he finds both thoughts. However in choosing between the two his nature despised the necessity of thinking the Rational, of thinking an intuitive spontaneity and decided without reservation for appearance.[17]

It is clear from these and from many other enthusiasts (especially Schiller) that many post-Kantians were not content to interpret the *Critique of Judgment* as a limited critical account of the "conditions for the possibility" of some possibly objective status for distinctive sorts of pleasure–pain responses to the world, or as a kind of expanded account of how we must, subjectively, think of nature if an appreciation of its beauty and an estimation of the living beings within it are to be possible. Aside from Schiller's insistence on its importance in supposedly revising Kant's moral theory, the direction suggested by these quotations points to the even more ambitious belief that Kant's analysis implied revisions and expansions in Kant's core transcendental project. As we have seen, that claim rests on putatively revisionary implications of the "necessity" for postulating an "intuitive intellect."

Hence the questions, *Do* these remarks by Kant in sections 76 and 77 suggest such revisions and expansions in any central doctrines of the Transcendental Aesthetic and Analytic of the *Critique of Pure Reason*? If they do, what are such revisions? And even if they do, do those revisions lead in any

---

15 Quoted in Horstmann, *Die Grenzen*, pp. 214–15.
16 *GuW*, p. 341; *FK*, p. 89.
17 *GuW*, p. 341, *FK*, pp. 90–1.

interesting philosophical direction, or instead toward a romantic meta-physics, even a hylozoism, or a panlogicism or wild apriorism, and so on?

II

Officially of course the answer most prominent in the text itself is no. The idea of an intuitive intellect serves a very limited, still basically regulative, subjectively required function. It may indeed be that Kant, in his account of teleological judgments and reflective judgments in general, is going further than the first *Critique*'s account of regulative ideas, treating the problem now not just as one of the organization of the results of empirical inquiry, but as involving a different sort of formation, subsumption, and application of concepts. Appeals to nature's purposes are not ways of systematizing the results of our empirical inquiries about efficient causation, and are not heuristic principles necessary to regulate such inquiries. There are phenom-ena, he now claims, that will never be adequately explicable mechanistically. The problem is not now just systematization, but the possibility of subsump-tion under concepts in the first place, and a new model for such subsumption.[18]

And he may be "upping the stakes" in introducing this topic, beyond what was claimed for similar issues in the appendix to the "Dialectic of Pure Reason," suggesting now that without a legitimate warrant for such re-flective judgments (its "a priori principle"), "our empirical cognition could not thoroughly cohere to form a whole of experience" (23).[19]

But whatever argument Kant presents for the "necessity" of teleological explanation, and however he resolves the apparent dialectic of teleological and mechanical judgments, the invocation of the idea of an intuitive intel-

---

18 For discussions of this difference, see Paul Guyer, "Reason and Reflective Judgment: Kant on the Significance of Systematicity," *Nous* 24 (1990): 17–43; Hannah Ginsborg, "Re-flective Judgment and Taste," *Nous* 24 (1990): 63–78; George Schrader, "The Status of Teleological Judgments in the Critical Philosophy," *Kant-Studien* 45 (1953–4): 204–35; L. W. Beck, "Kant on the Uniformity of Nature," *Synthese* 47 (1981): 449–64; Christel Fricke, "Explaining the Inexplicable: The Hypothesis of the Faculty of Reflective Judgment in Kant's Third *Critique*," *Nous* 24 (1990): 45–62; Rudolf A. Makkreel, "Regulative and Re-flective Uses of Purposiveness in Kant," *Southern Journal of Philosophy* 30, suppl. (1991): 49–71; Max Liedtke, "Der Begriff der Reflexion bei Kant," *Archiv für die Geschichte der Philosophie* 48 (1966): 207–16.

19 All of which was no doubt involved in the remarkable transformation of the planned, limited "Critique of Taste" in 1787, and the virtual invention of the topic of "reflective judgment." Cf. Rolf-Peter Horstmann, "Why Must There Be a Transcendental Deduction in Kant's Critique of Judgment?" in *Kant's Transcendental Deductions*, ed. by E. Forster (Stanford: Stanford University Press, 1989), pp. 157–76.

lect appears of narrow, explanatory significance. In the first place, it can be introduced this way only because Kant is clearly wedded to a general intentional model of teleology, on the strict model of an agent doing A in order to achieve B. When he considers teleological functions in organisms, since hearts do not act in order to circulate blood, he must revert to that model by requiring that the heart be intentionally designed by an agent in order to circulate blood. And he claims that the analysis of such an intentional designer reveals it must be a non-discursive intellect.[20] In other words, Kant's position seems designed more to avoid the metaphysically idealist direction than to invite it.

Where then (where, at least in Kant) is Schelling getting the idea that by introducing this idea of an intuitive intellect Kant has also reformulated his notion of human subjectivity itself, proposed a new view of "the living I," or even an unconditioned condition of all intelligibility, an absolute, the "producings" of which involve a collapsing of the key Kantian distinction between thinking and intuiting?

Where especially is Hegel basing his even more extravagant assertion that Kant's discussion in sections 76 and 77 has something to do with *the human intellect*?

> Kant also recognizes that we are necessarily driven to the Idea (of a nondiscursive intellect). *The Idea of this archetypal intuitive intellect is at bottom nothing else but the same idea of the transcendental imagination that we considered above.* For it is intuitive activity, and yet its inner unity is no other than the unity of the intellect itself, the category immersed in extension, and becoming intellect and category only as it separates itself out of extension. *Thus transcendental imagination is itself intuitive intellect.* (My emphasis)[21]

It might be possible here to detect in this take on the issue of an intuitive intellect something vaguely Kantian, an echo of the first edition of the first *Critique* and its suggestion of "a common root" out of which, or by original reference to which, the dualism between understanding and sensibility can be understood, a common root suggested to be the "productive imagina-

---

20 There is not, I think, any particularly good reason for Kant to think that all such teleological explanation must be cashed out in the intentional sense. Aristotle did not and Hegel's Aristotelianism provides him the basis for several effective criticisms of Kantian or subjectivist teleology in the *Science of Logic*. See Willem de Vries's article, "The Dialectic of Teleology," *Philosophical Topics* 19 (1991): 51–70; Klaus Düsing, "Naturteleologie und Metaphysik bei Kant und Hegel," in *Hegel und Die' Kritik der Urteilskraft,*' pp. 141–157, and especially his *Die Teleologie in Kants Weltbegriff* (Bonn: Bouvier, 1968).

21 *GuW*, p. 341; *FK*, p. 89.

tion."²² But a vague echo is the most that could be said, and the standard view of this *point d'appui* for German Idealism would seem confirmed. Whether the move in question is to a divinely productive nature, or to some even more obscure claim about our divinely productive intellect, the moves seem motivated by non-Kantian commitments and non-critical expectations. This view is well stated by Düsing, who in summing up the issue writes,

All the foundational principles and doctrines of Kantian aesthetics in the *Critique of Judgment* are accordingly transformed and exported into a different metaphysical system of meaning [*Bedeutungssystem*]. The critique made against Kant is therefore not immanent, but presupposes the soundness of Hegel's own conception, which Kant, as the opponent of doctrinal metaphysics, would have criticized.²³

III

So, it appears that one way of thinking about the possibility of a purposively ordered world (as intelligently designed by an intuitive intellect) is somehow being inflated into a thesis about the supersensible substrate of nature itself (i.e., Kant's warnings about the subjective, regulative character of this thought seem contemptuously swept aside), and even more importantly it is being treated as a thesis of direct relevance for the basic mind–world relation at stake in Kantian philosophy. Such an inflation would appear to rest

22 For an exploration of the position on the imagination that emerges from the first and third *Critiques*, see Rudolf Makkreel, *Imagination and Interpretation in Kant: The Hermeneutical Import of the Critique of Judgment* (Chicago: University of Chicago Press, 1990), pt. 2. Makkreel's general position is that whereas Kant claims that the human understanding categorially sets the conditions for the possibility of an experience of nature, and that reason self-imposes laws for action, it is a reflective imagination that makes possible the apprehension of a wholeness and so an overall meaning in experience (this by way of what is called "reflective specification"). Makkreel links this orienting activity, especially in the apprehension of life, to the hermeneutical tradition. Hegel is close enough to Kant still to link such possible "meaning apprehension" with truth, and so is interested, with Kant, in the nature and basis of the claim that all others ought to appreciate the beautiful and estimate life (or "orient themselves meaningfully") as I do. Cf. also the discussion in J. M. Bernstein, *The Fate of Art: Aesthetic Alienation from Kant to Derrida and Adorno* (Cambridge: Polity Press, 1992), about the various ways in which the reflective judgment doctrine strains the basic faculty divisions of the first *Critique*, pp. 44–55.
23 Düsing, *Hegel und die Geschichte*, p. 112. See also, "Er [Hegel] nimmt hierbei die idealistischen Weiterführungen der Kantischen Konzeption der Vermittlung und des Übergangs von der theoretischen zur praktischen Vernunft, von der Natur zur Freiheit auf und schmilzt sie ein in sein spekulatives Identitätsprogramm" (p. 110). Another good summary of the position I am trying to oppose (at least with respect to Hegel) can be found in the conclusion to Zammito, *Genesis*.

on some independent commitment to the view that Kant's transcendental
account must already rest on a prior theory of some absolute world process
posing or dividing itself from itself and then identifying with itself in some
act of supreme self-realization, as in many standard views of Fichte, Schelling, and of course Hegel. Why else, apart from such a commitment, would
sections 76 and 77 be read in this way? Düsing's view would appear
confirmed.

What is noteworthy, however, about Hegel's treatment of these passages
in *Glauben und Wissen* is that he does not frame his discussion of sections 76
and 77 in any way informed by the specific problem of mechanism and
teleology or even the philosophy of nature in general.[24] As we have seen, the
issue that seems to be suggesting to Hegel some "inflation" of the importance of the idea of an intuitive intellect is not the problem of organic
wholes or functional explanation. In a way that can indeed be said to follow
Kant's treatment without distortion, what interests Hegel throughout these
passages is what is involved in *our* capacity to "estimate" (*schätzen*) nature as
living (and, originally, to appreciate it as beautiful). His remarks make clear
that it is *this* capacity for estimation and appreciation, and the relation
between such a capacity and our capacity for determinative judgment and
discursive systematization, that will require a revision in the intellect–
sensibility relation originally proposed. This is why he says that it is the issue
of *reflective judgment* (*not* "nature") that "exhibits the most interesting point
in the Kantian system"[25] wherein the "reality of reason" (not its subjective
regulation) is demonstrable, exhibiting as its "subjective side" the aesthetic
judgment, and as its "objective side," organic nature.[26] *Our capacity to experience a beautiful and living nature* is what requires a revision in understanding

---

24 Because I am interested here in the question of the early reception of *KU* in German
idealism, I shall concentrate on Hegel's *Glauben und Wissen* comments. In Hegel's
posthumously published *Lectures on Fine Art*, he interprets *KU* in both a more friendly and a
more critical way and concentrates (appropriately) more on the aesthetic theory itself than
on its implications for his own systematic philosophy, which is the topic I want to pursue
here. His account there does, though, make clear the importance to him of the way in
which "ideas" can be said to be "embodied" in, rather than applied to or derived from, art
or the beautiful. See G. W. F. Hegel, *Werke in zwanzig Bände*, ed. by Eva Moldenhauer and
Karl Markus Michel, XIII (Frankfurt am M.: Suhrkamp, 1970), pp. 11–99; *Aesthetics: Lectures on Fine Art*, I, Trans. T. M. Knox (Oxford: Clarendon Press, 1975), pp. 1–90.

25 *GuW*, p. 338; *FK*, p. 85.

26 "The objective side is the nonconscious intuition of the reality of Reason, that is to say,
organic nature. In his reflection upon it in his 'Critique of Teleological Judgment,' Kant
expresses the Idea of Reason more definitively than in the preceding concept of a harmonious play of cognitive powers. He expresses it now in the idea of an intuitive intellect, for
which possibility and actuality are one" (*GuW*, p. 340; *FK*, p. 88).

the general relation between "the empirical manifold" and the "absolute abstract unity." And this is why he suggests that it is in our being driven or required to think of the possibility of an aesthetic appreciation of nature, and our being driven or required to think through the implications of a living nature, both in ways with some binding normative status, that the idea of reason as organizing or systematizing data breaks down, and, let us say, the idea of a reason (non-arbitrarily, non-subjectively) *determining its own data,* or an intuitive intellect, becomes unavoidable.[27] What is also interesting is that so much of what Hegel discusses in *GuW* is inspired by Kant's discussion of *aesthetic* experience, aesthetic judgment, and "aesthetic ideas," topics that, in Kant's presentation, stand far away logically and textually from sections 76 and 77. The Hegelian claim is the following:

> This [Hegel has been exploring various versions of the "authentic idea of Reason" in Kant] shows that the Kantian forms of intuition and the forms of thought cannot be kept apart at all as the particular, isolated faculties which they are usually represented as. One and the same synthetic unity . . . is the principle of intuition and of the intellect. (70)

Clearly Hegel is claiming that Kant is introducing something in his treatment of aesthetic judgments that in a fundamental way alters the empirical realism–regulative idea theory of the first *Critique;* that this claim requires an intellect that does not only conceptualize data in a passively received manifold or organize the results of empirical inquiry in a system, but can itself be conceived as intuitive; and that this alternative way of conceiving the mind–world issue is most visible in Kant's doctrine of the productive imagination, Kant's "truly speculative idea" (71).

It is of course still true that Hegel is in some sense conflating what Kant is saying about the *idea* of nature's origins and a putatively *divine intellect* with a claim about the proper relation between the *human intellect* and sensibility. But this sort of claim about the divinity of the human is certainly not foreign to Hegel's idiosyncratic theology, and it is at least clear that the issues of life and beauty raise directly for Hegel questions about the Kantian concept–sensibility relation, and *not* about the possibility of a pre-subjective *Urgrund*

---

27 Kant himself of course is famously given to remarks about how "reason" in investigating nature is really "investigating itself." And in the first *Critique,* his concept–intuition divide does not prevent him from calling apperception itself an "indeterminate intuition." Cf. B422n.

expressing itself in human actions and thinking.[28] And he is also at least purporting to point to issues in Kant that *justify* this turn to the broad problem of our cognitive capacities.

IV

On the face of it, this is still a sort of "frying pan into the fire" interpretation. It does not seem to help matters much to argue that Hegel is not leading us "out of Kant" toward a romantic monism, but is instead making use of the analysis of aesthetic judgments to establish that our intellect really is intuitive.

If we focus on what seems of most relevance to Hegel, the Kantian account of beauty, the questions suggested by this version of "the influence of sections 76 and 77" are straightforward. (i) Of what consequence for the core Kantian position on the intellect–sensibility relation is the general case for the "subjective universal validity" of aesthetic judgments? (This question is really dual; it involves the direct issue of the possibility of such intersubjectively valid judgments, based as they are on sensible pleasures, and the separate issue of the implications of such a possibility for Kant's position on the general possibility of the intelligibility of the world for a human mind. It may in other words be possible that aesthetic objects are simply *uniquely* intelligible.) And (ii) assuming Kant got something right about the radical and general implications of aesthetic intelligibility, did Hegel get something right in extending the implications in the way suggested? These are the questions involved, at any rate, in such typical Hegelian claims as the following:

---

28 These two questions are of course not incompatible and Hegel could be raising both issues, but the body of evidence, I am suggesting, shows that he only considers such an *Urgrund* in terms of our intellectual activity. The question is treated differently by Schelling and would require a separate treatment. On the one hand, in a work very much like Hegel's *Difference* essay, his 1797 *Treatise Explicatory of the Idealism in the Wissenschaftslehre*, Schelling also stresses the way in which Kant himself was supposedly led to the idea of *our* actively intuitive faculty and really did not intend, for us, any "utter separation of the understanding and sensibility" (*SW*, I, p. 359; *Idealism and the Endgame of Theory: Three Essays by F.W.J. Schelling*, trans. Thomas Pfau [Albany: SUNY Press, 1994], p. 73); on the other hand, he begins to stress that in order to account for such an activity, we must assume a "productive force" inherent in all things (pp. 387; 93); and so "it is a fundamental mistake to attempt a theoretical grounding of theoretical philosophy" (pp. 399; 101). Hegel never gave up such a goal. In general the issue of Schelling, and the relation between Schelling's and Hegel's positions, is too complicated to discuss here. The "Hegelian direction" I am defending here is not, though, in any great opposition to the early Schelling, as is clear from pt. 6 of *STI*.

Since beauty is the Idea as experienced, or more correctly, as intuited, the form of opposition between intuition and concept falls away. Kant recognizes this vanishing of the antithesis negatively in the concept of a supersensuous realm in general. But he does not recognize that as beauty, it is positive, it is intuited, or, to use his own language, it is given in experience. (87)

In this extraordinary phrase – "the form of opposition between intuition and concept falls away" – Hegel's overall interests begin to emerge. He is interested in the possibility of some intelligible appreciation of nature, *understanding* nature we might say, even, in general, grasping a meaning, all with some normative validity, without that normativity (= "all others, suitably situated, ought to understand in the same way") being a function of the application of a concept (or the imposition of an ideal) to a passively received manifold (or "on" a set of empirical concepts or regularities), and he is apparently interested in the implications of such a possibility for intelligibility as such.[29] If, in other words, a common intelligibility, a shareability of experience, is possible in some way inconsistent with the general critical model of conceiving a passively received content, and if that intelligibility requires a different model for the engagement of our intellectual activity in such an intelligible experience, then, so goes this "direction," we are in effect proposing a different critical model of the relation of thought to reality in our experience, one of potentially wide relevance.[30] (Or: as we might expect in a Kantian idealism the content of aesthetic experience itself should not be cleanly distinguishable from *our* actively "making sense" of what is occurring to us, or from the aesthetic judgment and its shareability. To be in a mental state, even to experience a feeling of pleasure, is to have taken up a position, to have evaluated or judged. But now, it is being sug-

29 "Intelligibility," in this context, admittedly covers a very great deal of territory. It is a more general term for what a Kantian would recognize as the question of the possibility of experience or a possible representation of content at all, where experience is understood as the possibility of judgments, and understanding such a possible judgment is understanding what it would be for a judgment to be true. Cf. the best account of this dimension of the Kantian theory in Gerold Prauss, *Erscheinung bei Kant* (Berlin: de Gruyter, 1971).
30 The general suggestion toward which such revisions in the classic Kantian picture is leading is familiar: that what it is for any thinking to be about something, to be constrained in a way common to all, cannot be said simply to be the result of, or based on, the direct impingement of the external world, or "its" just occasioning in some distinct way a pleasure. Since even receptivity or the passivity of aesthetic experience requires the activity of spontaneity, that constraint and so shareability is a matter of integrability into some whole. See the recent book by John McDowell, *Mind and World*, (Cambridge: Harvard University Press, 1994), especially his criticisms (in what seem to me a Hegelian spirit) of Davidsonean holism, on the one hand, and "bald naturalism," on the other.

gested, the possibility of the latter no longer can appeal to concept application, to regulation, or to an empirically given, common, non-conceptual content.)

Now, this reading, as we shall see, highlights something clear from the surface of Hegel's remarks. He does not comment much on the problem of pleasure, or the affective dimension of Kant's case, suggesting that it is in appreciating, or in being reflectively aware of, the harmony of our faculties that we experience pleasure, thus shifting a great deal of weight to the reflective evaluating supposedly going on *in* aesthetic experience.[31] Hegel does not note that this all implies that it is by means of this reflective appreciation that we are taking pleasure *in* the formal suitability of nature to our rational ends, or that pleasure can be intentional, and that we are therewith evaluating our experience in a way that can be shown to be universally subjectively valid.[32] Since there is conflicting evidence about Kant's meaning, with many passages suggesting that, for him, harmony simply produces pleasure, that pleasure is a qualitatively identical, non-intentional state, and that subjective universal validity involves an expectation about another's feeling, and not a claim about a warranted evaluation of nature, this is all extremely controversial if considered as an exercise in Kant scholarship.[33] My own view is that Hegel is very much on the right track in reading Kant, but I can only sketch the case for that here.

Such a sketch must at least indicate what reading of the deduction of aesthetic judgments Hegel must have had in mind to suggest this direction. And posed this way, with so many issues at play, it is hard to see how any sort of economical discussion is possible. We can, I think, begin to defend the extension Hegel is pursuing, but that will first require some giant steps over

31 This emphasis is what allows him to shift attention somewhat from Kant's concern with the more formal issue of the exercise of our faculties in aesthetic experience, the "play" of the imagination and the "striving" of the understanding, to the concepts or ideas supposedly expressed in such "material." This shift is especially obvious in his treatment of Kant in the *Lectures on Fine Art*, trans. T. M. Knox (Oxford: Clarendon Press, 1975), pp. 55–68.

32 A way of explaining the intentionality of pleasure, one of much relevance to this "direction," is presented by Richard Aquila, "A New Look at Kant's Aesthetic Judgments," in *Essays in Kant's Aesthetics*, ed. by Ted Cohen and Paul Guyer (Chicago: University of Chicago Press, 1982), pp. 87–114. See also the useful formulation by Jens Kulenkampff, *Kants Logik des ästhetischen Urteils* (Frankfurt am M.: Klostermann, 1978), p. 88.

33 I defend the broader reading of Kant's strategy in "The Significance of Taste: Kant, Aesthetic, and Reflective Judgments," *Journal of the History of Philosophy*, forthcoming. The narrower and wider views also reflect what would become, in the post-Kantian European tradition, basic differences about the autonomy of art, on the one hand, and its ever accelerating cognitive, moral, and political significance in later modernity on the other: all of which are the subject of Bernstein's valuable study, *Fate of Art*, especially pp. 1–65.

much contested terrain. Consider first the famous details of Kant's accounts.

According to Kant, the claim "This is beautiful" has a misleading surface structure. It appears to be a standard application of an empirical predicate to an object, but it is not. It really involves the claim that

(i) I am in a certain mental state, I feel something in the presence of an object, and, Kant wants to show, by being in such a state, under certain conditions, am ipso facto warranted in claiming all others would be too, "if they had taste" (as I am justified in assuming they could).

(ii) That state is a *pleasure* ("consciousness of a representation's causality, with respect to that state, so as to keep me in it").

(iii) It is *disinterested* (does not incite any desire directed at existence of the object occasioning such a state).

(iv) This pleasure is attendant to, or in Kant's somewhat clumsy phrase "attaches to," a reflective awareness of a *harmony* of cognitive faculties (the imaginative reproduction of a manifold in harmony with what would have been required by the understanding for its unity).

(v) Since there is such a harmony without the application of a concept, this harmony should be seen as a "free play" of such faculties, although Kant also claims, in some way that remains the subject of much controversy, that our appreciating a beautiful object must involve the activity of reflective judgment (the attempt in general to find a universal for a given set of particulars, although in this case without any real prospect of, or progress toward, such a concept).

(vi) This is a reflecting occasioned by and in some sense directed upon the *formal properties* of the occasioning object(s), experienced in such judgmental striving to be purposively suited to our cognitive ends, without such a discovery's requiring any specific discovery of "a" purpose ("purposiveness without a purpose"),

(vii) all occasioning the delight that accompanies the attaining of my cognitive ends, here unintentionally, not as a result of some conscious project.

(viii) In the most important aspect of this argument for our purposes, Kant goes on to claim that, in engaging in such a reflection, what I am doing is attempting to situate myself, or orient myself in experience "as anyone else would," to take account "of everyone else's way of representing" (293) and am, in feeling pleasure in this way, relying on a *sensus communis*. The universal communicability of such a state thus presupposes a common set of cognitive faculties and a shared ability, reflective judgment guided by, in some way, such a common sense. This assumption, he argues, is warranted because experience itself would not be possible without such a capacity.

I am therefore entitled not only to assume the universal communicability of my mental state, but to demand (*fordern*) that all others appreciate the beautiful, that they "ought" to find this beautiful ("as a duty, as it were"). The experience of beauty, in other words, involves a norm, binding on all with subjective universal validity. And again, for the purposes of our discussion, the important point is, Without such normativity involving the *application* of a norm *to a content,* nor the *idea* of a possible norm that we "must think" applies.

These are the bare details. And, with this skeleton of the theory in mind, it is not hard to find passages, particularly in the published and unpublished Introductions, that show that Kant himself did believe that such an analysis was relevant to the larger issues that Hegel summarizes as the "authentic idea" or "reality" of reason. Those passages are all based on the claim that aesthetic judgments are a species of "reflective" judgments (given the particular, find, formulate, construct the universal) as opposed to determinative (where one has a concept and seeks to apply it) and on the general claims made on behalf of reflective judgments. The principle of such judgments is "purposiveness" and the claims made are very great. The Kantian language also calls to mind Hegel's remarks about our own reason's spontaneously "giving itself its content," as if an intuitive intellect. For example,

> Judgment . . . provides nature's supersensible substrate (within as well as outside us) with determinability [*Bestimmbarkeit*] by the intellectual power . . . and so judgment makes possible the transition from the concept of nature to that of freedom. (37)

Although Kant often claims that our intellectual powers "determine" nature, thus leading to the skeptically Idealist claim that we should consider nature only as determined by us, this sort of claim about our originally providing (*verschafft*) nature *with* "determinability" in the first place is unique, as far as I know, to the third *Critique* and later works.[34]

34 See again Tuschling's claims about the *Opus postumum* in the articles cited previously. In the first *Critique* Kant does say that "reason thus prepares the field for the understanding," A658 = B685, although how that is supposed to happen (as opposed to reason's systematizing the results of the understanding's work) is not explored.

And the direction of these remarks suggests that in appreciating the beautiful, we are providing ourselves with a sort of original "orientation" in experience that is not like reason's subjective self-regulation (again we don't "impose" a demand on nature but appreciate nature's suitability to our demands) and not like empirical apprehension (since we are talking about an original orientation required for there to be coherent empirical apprehension). It is the relation between a subjectively universally valid pleasure in the beautiful and this self-orientation that forms the core of Hegel's suggested direction. Perhaps the fullest Kantian statement of this direction occurs in the unpublished Introduction:

> Hence we must consider aesthetic judgment as a special power, necessarily none other than reflective judgment; and we must regard the feeling of plea-sure (which is identical with the representation of subjective purposiveness) as attaching neither to the sensation in the empirical representation of the object, nor to the concept of that object, but as attaching to – and as con-nected with, in terms of an a priori principle – nothing but the reflection and its form (the essential activity of judgment) by which it strives to proceed from empirical intuitions to concepts as such. (249)

Now, in his 1786 essay *Was heisst, sich im Denken orientieren?* Kant, discuss-ing spatial orientation, had noted, "To this purpose, I require above all the feeling of a difference in my own person."[35] These remarks on the reflective character of aesthetic judgment, and on the function of reflective judg-ment, suggest that by the time of the third *Critique*, Kant had also realized that a more fundamental "orientation" in all the "activity of life" is needed, and cannot be the result of any inference or application of, or even obe-dience to, a rule.[36] It turns out that this fundamental orientation is also achieved by a "feeling," although Kant still insists on a "critique" of such a feeling and so on its universal normative force. Since, in sections 76 and 77, Kant appears to claim that the subsumability or general suitability of particu-lars to the application of our concepts is itself the result of the original, non-determinative, active engagements of our judgment power (an original

---

35 *AA*, VIII, p. 134.
36 Howard Caygill, in *Art of Judgment* (Oxford: Basil Blackwell, 1989), connects Kant's account of this orientation with very broad themes in the role played by considerations of taste in earlier political and civil society traditions, and he concludes with characterizations of Kant's position that sound very much like those of the later Idealists (see ch. 5 especially and, for example, p. 299). Whether the historical Kant could accept this position (and the enormous implications that follow from it) and remain the historical Kant is, I think, another question, not settled by Caygill's speculation.

"self-orienting"), he seems to have at once conceded the general priority of
such reflective activity in any account of the possibility of experience, and, as
Hegel and Schelling suggested, to have undermined his own strict distinction between the divine and the human intellect. The broadest claim is at p.
404:

> Were the power of judgment not able to recognize purposiveness with respect
> to particulars, were it not to have its own universal law [the law he identifies as
> purposiveness] under which to subsume particulars, *it could not make any deter-*
> *minate judgment about particulars.*[37]

But now we come to the most specific of the difficulties involved in trying
to read Kant in this Hegelian direction, this link between the normative
status of the experience of the beautiful, and this reflective activity, an
activity that supposedly undermines or bypasses the standard Kantian picture of normativity (the application of a concept or principle). As alluded to
earlier, the problem with such passages and claims has always been to understand the role of such reflection *in* aesthetic judgments, which, on the face
of it, seem so much a matter simply of sensible pleasure, albeit occasioned in
a unique way in the case of the beautiful.[38] There is no question that Kant
himself goes very far in linking the experience of such pleasure with "reflective activity" and so, apparently, with the themes Hegel is interested in.
But the question has always been whether he is entitled to such claims.

For example, in section 4,

> A liking for the beautiful must depend on the reflection, regarding an object,
> that leads to some concept or other (but is indeterminate which concept this
> is). This dependence on reflection also distinguishes the liking for the beauti-
> ful from the agreeable, which rests entirely on sensation. (207)

37 The sentence in which this claim occurs is extremely complicated. Pluhar has tried to help
   by rearranging its order fairly radically. The quoted passage begins by saying that we would
   have no distinction between the mechanism and the technic of nature, "wäre unser Verstand nicht von der Art, daß er vom Allgemeinem zum Besondern gehen muß, und die
   Urteilskraft also in Ansehung des Besondern keine Zweckmäßigkeit erkennen, *mithin keine*
   bestimmende Urteile fällen kann, ohne ein allgemeines Gesetz zu haben worunter sie jenes
   subsumierien könne" (my emphasis).
38 The most influential contemporary accounts skeptical of such a connection are Jens
   Kulenkampff, *Kants Logik des ästhetischen Urteils* (Frankfurt am M: Kostermann, 1978), (cf.
   p. 28 ff.) and Paul Guyer, *Kant and the Claims of Taste* (Cambridge: Harvard University Press,
   1979), pp. 33 ff., inter alia.

In section 8 Kant calls our aesthetic sensibility the "taste of reflection" to distinguish it from a mere taste of sense, and to emphasize further the role of our intellectual activity in the possibility of such pleasure (beyond, that is, some sort of passive "activation" of the understanding and the imagination) he notes that this capacity, taste, can be cultivated, indeed, in section 32, that

> taste is precisely what stands most in need of examples regarding what has enjoyed the longest-lasting approval in the course of cultural progress in order that it will not become uncouth again . . . and taste needs this because its judgments cannot be determined by concepts and precepts. (283)

This "taste" is defined in section 40 "as the ability to judge something that makes our feeling in a given presentation universally communicable without mediation by a concept" and that "taste is our ability to judge a priori the communicability of the feelings that (without mediation by a concept) are connected with a given presentation" (295–6).

Kant is undoubtedly very aware that by linking in this way aesthetic experience and the possibility of a distinct pleasure in the beautiful to some sort of reflective awareness of natural purposiveness, however non-standard and indeterminate such an awareness, he is in danger of intellectualizing the experience again (the "we get out of nature what we put there" model), or of making it very hard to see how, without a concept, the normative or common significance of such a vague appreciating can be preserved.[39] As noted, in addressing these concerns, he suggests that such a reflecting activity is not based on the a priori needs of reason, nor on a putative common "content," but is already and originally oriented from a "common sense," as if in appreciating the beautiful we already are appreciating its shareability. This "sense" is

> a power to judge that in reflecting takes account (a priori), in our thought, of everyone else's way of representing, in order as it were, to compare our own judgment with human reason in general, and thus escape the illusion that arises from the case of mistaking subjective and private conditions for objective ones. (293)

---

39 He makes his concerns very clear in no. 9, at p. 218, insisting that it is most definitely not "intellectually, through consciousness of the intentional activity by which we bring these powers into play" that we "become conscious, in a judgment of taste, of a reciprocal subjective harmony between the cognitive powers." I discuss this passage in "Significance of Taste."

Most famously, these considerations are concentrated in the passage Kant calls "the key to the critique of taste," section 9, where the question is "whether in a judgment of taste the feeling of pleasure precedes the judging of the object, or the judging precedes the pleasure," and the answer, causing great difficulty to many commentators, but consistent with the direction Hegel is pursuing, is the latter. That section is quite a tangle, and although a detailed consideration of its claims is central for the direction Hegel is suggesting, I want to conclude with a more general consideration of the issues Kant himself raises with these claims about the role of reflective activity in our appreciation of the beautiful.[40]

V

The point at issue is the suggestion of a "reflecting" activity that is not the conceiving of a content, but an activity already engaged in the taking up of a manifold and so not checked by some externally received content, a thinking or "ability to judge a priori the communicability of the feelings that (without mediation by a concept) are connected with a given presentation," which thinking somehow reveals this "a priori communicability" of our feelings and so the normative status of the experience of the beautiful. According to Kant, "we have a merely aesthetic power of judgment, *an ability to judge forms* without using concepts and to feel in the mere judging of these forms a liking that we also make a rule for everyone, though our judgment is not based on an interest and also gives rise to none" (300; 167).

Since this sort of reflective appreciating is not an application of a concept, nor a response necessitated or directed by some sensory impingement, nor a postulated ideal, Hegel claims it is like a *self*-orienting in relation to nature and others,[41] or a kind of "intellectual intuition," intellectual be-

---

40 As noted, the interpretive problem stems from those passages, as in sect. VII of the published Introduction, or at p. 224 of the first, where Kant seems to claim that judgments of taste are based on a sensation, which is itself just "brought about " [*bewirkt*] by the harmony of faculties. What I am suggesting is that Kant is not claiming that this harmony simply causes a pleasure, nor that it is "through" or by means of pleasure that we attend to this harmony, but that it is *in* appreciating such a harmony as purposive that we feel pleasure. This implies that without "taste," a certain harmonious play could occur without pleasure in the beautiful, or could be appreciated only as the agreeable. I try to defend this reading independently in "Significance of Taste."

41 When, in the "General Comment" after no. 22, Kant defines taste as "an ability to judge an object in reference to the free lawfulness of the imagination," he calls the activity of the imagination "productive and self-active [*selbsttätig*]," or says that it is "free and lawful of

cause actively established, and intuiting because not the projection of an ideal, but an experience, an orienting "in" an experience.[42]

I have already noted where, in the reading of Kant implied by Hegel's remarks, the controversial points of interpretation lie. They mostly have to do with the relation between reflective judgment and aesthetic experience itself, and each would require an extensive separate discussion. It is also true that the general significance of aesthetic experience for the "system" problem so important to later Idealists, or the way in which the possibility of universally valid aesthetic judgments implies a possible, comprehensive account of morally free agents, mechanically moving matter, living beings, and scientific systems, is only suggested by this emphasis on the priority and centrality of such a reflective self-orienting, and its a priori principle, purposiveness, for any and all of these accounts.

In the *KU*, of course, the specific "systematic" problem is the link between aesthetic and teleological judgments, and here again, Hegel only makes a suggestion: that the Kantian "sense" of purposiveness required in both appreciating and estimating is not the postulation of an idea that we "require" in our experience of nature, nor the application of a concept to a manifold or set of empirical regularities. To be oriented in this way, to take up the natural world in its purposiveness, suggests that we are both responsive to what nature requires if we are to explain it, as well as "reflectively" active in such responding. To him this sounds like being "intellectually intuitive."

But, finally, besides these continuities with Kant suggested by this sketch of the direction opened up by sections 76 and 77, there is clearly a major discontinuity. As Kant himself implies when he discusses the kind of "sense" involved in the role of a common sense in appreciating the beautiful, and when he associates such a sense with everyday good sense, or prudence, or

itself [*frei und doch von selbst gesetztmäßig*]," pp. 240–1; see Makkreel, *Imagination and Interpretation*, ch. 8, for a discussion of the hermeneutical aspects of such an "orientational" view of reflective judgments. Cf. also Caygill's remarks in *Art of Judgment*, ch. 5. As noted earlier, Hegel would not agree with the reliance on an indeterminate "common sense" to explain such common orientation and claims to be able to provide determinate content to such common orientation, a topic that would lead to his theory of conceptual change and to his "logic." Cf. also Zammito's discussion of this "orientational" issue, *Genesis*, pp. 237 ff., especially on the relevance of Kant's "Was heißt: sich im Denken orientieren" essay.

42 To quote Hegel, "*Kant himself recognized in the beautiful an intuition other than the sensuous.* He characterized the substratum of nature as intelligible, recognized it to be rational and identical with all reason, and knew that cognition in which concept and intuition are separated was subjective, finite cognition, a phenomenal cognition" (my emphasis) *GuW*, p. 343; *FK*, p. 91.

other examples of a capacity for judgment for which no rule can be given,
this reflective activity is always indeterminate.[43] It yields no determinate
concept or concepts of purposiveness in this aspect or that, just an orienting
and pleasing "sense." He does say in the Solution to the Antinomy of Taste
that "a judgment of taste must refer to some concept or other," but this
concept is "intrinsically indeterminate and inadequate for cognition" and is
only the "concept of a general basis of nature's subjective purposiveness for
our power of judgment" and may be considered the concept of the "supersensible substrate of humanity" (340).

It is in commenting on such passages that Hegel objects to this "merely
negative" conception of the supersensible and insists that Kant does not
appreciate his own doctrine, that Kant

> does not recognize that as beauty, it [the supersensuous] is positive, it is
> intuited, or, to use his own language, it is given in experience. Nor does he see
> the supersensuous, the intelligible substratum of nature without and within
> us, the thing in itself . . . is at least superficially known when the principle of
> beauty is given an exposition as the identity of nature and freedom. (88–9)

Because, supposedly, Kant does not see a way of integrating what his
exposition required into the standard transcendental Idealist picture, he
retreats, and claims

> that the supersensuous, insofar as it is the principle of the aesthetic, is un-
> knowable; and the beautiful turns into something strictly finite and subjective
> because it is only connected with the human cognitive faculty and a harmo-
> nious play of its various powers. (88)

Exactly as one might expect, Hegel is much more interested in that side
of Kant's exposition of aesthetic experience that does allow for the possibility of some reflective grasp of determinacy, the expression of *aesthetic ideas* in
fine art.[44] In Kant's presentation, although the "expression" of Juliet's love
or Iago's jealousy allows for a great deal more determinate "play" in our
"reflective powers," the possibility is still understood on an analogy with
natural beauty and so an indeterminate play of such reflection is still all that
is allowed. The aesthetic idea remains a representation of the imagination
for which no conceptual exposition or definition can be given, just as an
idea of reason is one for which no demonstration can be given, "demonstra-

---

43 Cf. the claim at p. 340.
44 Cf. the discussion in no. 49, pp. 314 ff.

tion in the Kantian sense being a presentation of a concept in intuition" (87). Hegel goes very far in summing up what he thinks can be derived from the implications of Kant's case, contra Kant's official line: "As if the aesthetic idea did not have its exposition in the Idea of Reason, and the Idea of Reason did not have its demonstration in beauty" (87).

At this point, such a claim remains a promissory note, a promise to be able to show that certain sorts of rational "self-determinations" in relation to the contents of experience are, in their various determinate forms (which we might imagine as the categories of Hegel's *Logic*), not "empty forms" (but the famous "concrete universals"),[45] any more than aesthetic ideas or organic wholes are empty forms or subjective regulations. This promise already suggests the problems we appear headed toward: (i) an extreme coherentism, a network of categories and principles "unchecked" by intuitions or the pure forms of intuition because our intellect itself is already, supposedly intuitive, and (ii) how to explain the determinacy in such self-determination if we take the idea of such an "unboundedness of the conceptual" seriously.

These are serious problems, still very much with us in any of the many forms of philosophy that could be called post-Kantian by virtue of a common rejection of any comprehensive empiricism or "absolute" realism or naturalism. My point in this chapter has been to show how Hegel must have been reading the *Critique of Judgment* in order to see such a promise implied in our capacity to appreciate the beautiful and to estimate life, and to suggest that his reading has a great deal to be said for it.

---

45 There is an interesting discussion of the relation between the Kantian notion of "aesthetic object" and Hegel's "concrete universal" in G. Wohlfahrt, *Der spekulative Satz: Bemerkungen der Spekulation bei Hegel* (Berlin: de Gruyter, 1981).

Part Two

CRITICAL MODERNISM

6

HEGEL, MODERNITY, AND HABERMAS

I

Hegel's pre-Jena and early Jena writings partly reflect what Nietzsche called a kind of German "homesickness,"[1] a distaste with Enlightenment "positivity," and an appeal to the models of the Greek polis and the early Christian communities (and, to a lesser extent, to art) as ways of understanding, by contrast, the limitations of modern philosophic, religious, and political life. In these texts, the Enlightenment victory over religion is portrayed as Pyrrhic, as the idealization of a calculating, fragmenting model of rationality, all in a way that merely transferred an oppressive, alien lawgiver from without to within. This Enlightenment is a "hubbub of vanity without a firm core," a purely "negative" reaction to custom and religion that tries to "turn this nothingness into a system."[2] On such a familiar view, Hegel represents, together with Schiller, Schelling, and others, a "romantic reaction" to modernity continuous with Rousseau's *Second Discourse*, united in various attempts to reject the abstract, materialist, "dehumanizing" nature of modern institutions, without a regression into premodern forms of thought.

1 In no. 419 (1885) of the notes collected as *Der Wille zur Macht* (Stuttgart: Alfred Kröner Verlag, 1964), p. 284.
2 G. W. F. Hegel, *GuW*, p. 316; *FK*, p. 56. In the *Phenomenology of Spirit* Hegel treats the struggle between Enlightenment and faith as itself a religious or sectarian struggle.

157

Yet, it is also well known that during his stay at Jena, although never wholly abandoning these Hellenic and Christian sensibilities, Hegel came to reject a critique of the Enlightenment based on either nostalgia or aesthetic experience. Hegel's reading of political economy and his growing attention to what he theorized for the first time as "civil society" convinced him of the uniqueness and superiority of modern forms of social and economic life. Moreover and more significantly, the problem of modernity broadened. In addition to his famous analysis of the "alienated" character of modern society, Hegel started paying greater attention to uniquely modern forms of "reason," of account giving and justification. Especially, his rapidly growing interest in the theoretical problems raised by Kant's first, and not just his second and third *Critiques* transformed his understanding of the nature of modern philosophy and its role in modern institutions.[3]

He still formulated the "modern problem" in much the same way. Now it was the paradigmatically modern notion of reason, Kant's self-legislating or self-grounding pure reason, that is said to end up "alienated," merely "posing" itself as an unsecured supreme authority, cut off from nature, or things in themselves, and so haunted by skepticism and a psychologizing of philosophy, and in perpetual opposition to inclination, or the contents of the heart. Such a notion of reason, so important to the distinctly modern hope for full "autonomy," was said to be unacceptably "finite," formal, empty, critical without being positive, and so unsatisfying. The problem of modernity remains the well-known if obscure Hegelian problem of some sort of reconciliation between individuals and modern institutions, but the solutions proposed now claim to be ultimately based on completions and so overcomings of modern "*philosophies* of reflection." Modern philosophies have "recast the dogmatism of being into the dogmatism of thinking," and have thereby reached the fundamental modern *aporia*, which Hegel will now resolve. "True philosophy," he claims, will now appear *out* of this com-

3 On the issue of Hegel's development in Jena, see Otto Pöggeler, "Hegels Jenaer Systemkonzeption," and "Hegels Phänomenologie des Selbstbewusstseins," both in *Hegels Idee einer Phänomenologie des Geistes* (Freiburg: Verlag Karl Alber, 1973); Rolf-Peter Horstmann, "Probleme der Wandlung in Hegels Jenaer Systemkonzeption," *Philosophischer Rundschau* 19 (1972): pp. 87–118; H. Kimmerle, *Das problem der Abgeschlossenheit des Denkens. Hegels System der Philosophie in den Jahren 1800–04* (Bonn: Bouvier, 1970), H. S. Harris, *Hegel's Development: Night Thoughts* (Oxford: Clarendon Press, 1983), on the point at issue, especially pp. 3–73; I. Görland, *Die Kant Kritik des jungen Hegel* (Frankfurt am M.: Klostermann, 1966), especially p. 15; and Klaus Düsing, "Spekulation und Reflexion: Zur Zusammenarbeit Schellings und Hegels in Jena," *Hegel-Studien* 5, (1969): 95–128, and his *Das Problem der Subjektivität in Hegels Logik* (Bonn: Bouvier, 1976); and the discussion in ch. 4 of my *Hegel's Idealism: The Satisfactions of Self-Consciousness* (Cambridge: Cambridge University Press, 1989).

pleted philosophy of subjectivity, and this philosophic revolution will thereby help establish the central modern idea, the "idea of absolute freedom."[4]

For many commentators, this typical Hegelian insistence on having one's cake and eating it too saves Hegel from the charge of nostalgia only at the price of a deep, probably fatal obscurity. For, as the familiar criticism goes, the only way he can do all this, consistent with the premises of modern subjectivity and reflection he now accepts, is by means of a theory of *absolute subjectivity*, an account of how the opposition between subjective certainty and self-satisfaction, on the one hand, and objectivity and sociality on the other, is finally "sublated" within some single "macrosubject," or self-conscious God; by means, that is, of some theoretical denial of all "otherness" and so the "totalization" of a self-conscious subject as "the whole."

Habermas has recently expressed this standard view by claiming that Hegel's solution "conceived of reason as the reconciling self-knowledge of an absolute spirit,"[5] and that it "overpowers every [finite] absolutization and retains as unconditional only the infinite processing of the relation-to-self that swallows up everything finite within itself."[6]

Or, Hegel "solves the initial problem of a self-reassurance of modernity, but solves it too well."[7]

Now Habermas has his own reasons for characterizing Hegel this way. He wants to affirm the intuitions of the younger, more nostalgic Hegel in order to suggest that Hegel was then at least working his way toward a theory of a "communicative action" or at least intersubjectivity, a theory only finally realized by Habermas himself.[8] In Habermas's influential account (which I shall return to in the last section of this chapter), Hegel, for all of his

---

4 *GuW*, p. 414; *FK*, p. 191.
5 Jurgen Habermas, *The Philosophical Discourse of Modernity*, trans. Frederick Lawrence (Cambridge: MIT Press, 1987), p. 84.
6 Ibid., p. 36.
7 Ibid., p. 42.
8 The most affirmative of Habermas's discussions of the young Hegel is his famous essay, "Labor and Interaction: Remarks on Hegel's Jena *Philosophy of Mind*," in *Theory and Practice*, trans. John Viertel (Boston: Beacon Press, 1974), pp. 142–69. See especially his familiar claim about Hegel's "abandonment" of his early insights about labor and interaction in favor of a philosophy of identity. Fred Dallmayr is right to point out that later, especially in the *Discourse* book, Habermas does not merely affirm the young Hegel's social theory, since even in those works there is supposed to be some sort of reliance on a "premodern" notion of social life. See "The Discourse of Modernity: Hegel and Habermas," *Journal of Philosophy* 84 (1987): 682–92. See also the discussion of Habermas's position in my *Hegel's Idealism*, pp. 282–3, 292–3.

160 CRITICAL MODERNISM

gestures toward the "transformation of epistemology into social theory,"[9] represents the epitome of the modern "philosophy of consciousness," the attempt first to doubt, and then to secure the subject's claim to represent objects, or judge objectively, the claim that a subject, consciously representing to itself, can successfully refer to and make claims about objects other than its own conscious states. Hegel supposedly "missed" the opportunity to revolutionize the very problem of modern philosophy; he only flirted with the notion that the fundamental question was not the possibility of representation of objects (or objective judgment, or reference, or intentionality, or all the familiar post-Cartesian problems) but the possibility of communicative activity, the linguistic achievement of *Verständigung*, intersubjective understanding. Representing objects could then have been seen as basically dependent on social, linguistic activities; all meaningful claims about objects, deeds, others, and so on, could have been understood as *functions* of socially redeemable "validity claims," and the conditions of such redemptions (for categorially different types of validity claims) in ideal speech situations could have been spelled out. The subject–object model could have been displaced from its primacy by the subject–subject model and all the modern problems of skepticism and alienation ("homesickness") could have been prevented.

These kinds of general criticisms of Hegel's theoretical position have become quite familiar since the Left Hegelians and throughout the critical theory tradition.[10] They echo an even more polemical characterization once provided by Adorno. Playing armchair anthropologist, speculating on the atavistic impulses of idealism, he remarked in *Negative Dialectics* that

Idealism – most explicitly Fichte – gives unconscious sway to the ideology that the not-I, *l'autrui*, and finally all that reminds us of nature is inferior, so the unity of the self-preserving thought may devour it without misgivings. . . . The system is the belly turned mind, and rage is the mark of each and every idealism.[11]

9 Cf. Habermas's discussion in *Knowledge and Human Interests*, trans. Jeremy Shapiro (Boston: Beacon Press, 1971), pp. 3–24, and the helpful exposition by G. Kortian, *Metacritique: The Philosophical Argument of Jürgen Habermas* (Cambridge: Cambridge University Press, 1980).
10 The most extensive recent treatment of this theme, particularly the problem of subjectivity and intersubjectivity in Hegel, is Vittorio Hösle, *Hegels System: Der Idealismus der Subjektivität und das Problem der Inter-Subjektivität* (Hamburg: Felix Meiner Verlag, 1987). For a summary and critique of his position, see my "Hösle, System, and Subject," *Bulletin of the Hegel Society of Great Britain* 17 (Spring/Summer 1988): 5–19.
11 Theodor Adorno, *Negative Dialectics*, trans. E. B. Ashton (London: Routledge and Kegan Paul, 1973), pp. 22–23.

However polemical, this interpretation would seem to correspond directly to Hegel's claim in the *Encyclopedia Logic* that "the tendency of all man's endeavors is to understand the world, to appropriate and subdue it to himself: and to this end the positive reality of the world must be as it were, crushed and pounded [*zerquetscht*], in other words, idealized."[12]

So, the evidence would suggest that Hegel means to affirm what he identifies as the theoretical principle of modernity – variously called self-consciousness, or subjectivity, or more usually, absolute freedom – only by defending a position as extreme as that attributed to him by Habermas, Adorno, and before them many others, the late Schelling, Kierkegaard, Marx, and Schopenhauer. Theoretical and practical freedom might not be possible on the Baconian mastery model, by a manipulation or control of otherness, but it still involves a kind of typically modern rage against such contingency or otherness, a denial by a speculative "devouring," a reinterpretation of what had appeared contingent or other, as really a posit of freely self-determining spirit. I want to defend here a different view of Hegel's theoretical modernism, and so my question is whether there is any other way to understand formulations like the one just quoted, or such extraordinary claims as the following from the *Difference Essay*: "That the world is the product of the freedom of intelligence is the determinate and express principle of idealism."[13]

II

To understand what Hegel might mean by such claims, we have to understand first that he accepts a Kantian rather than a Cartesian version of the "self-grounding of modernity," and that they are very different programs. The Cartesian ideal of self-sufficiency, a radical self-grounding, was understood to begin with the self's apprehension of the indubitable, the incorrigibly given contents of its own consciousness, and to proceed "outward" by methodologically rigorous means. It cannot mean anything like that for Kant since, for him, simply being in a mental state does not even count as an experience, much less a foundational one. The prior question concerns the rules under which a subject could determine "for itself" what such contents are taken to be. The key, difficult point is, The mind is a "spontaneity," not a

12 *Die Wissenschaft der Logik. Erster Teil, Enzyklopädie der philosophischen Wissenschaften*, in *Werke*, ed. by E. Moldernhauer and K. Michelet (Frankfurt am M.: Suhrkamp, 1970–1), VIII (hereafter *EL*), p. 118; *Hegel's Logic: Part One of the Encyclopedia of the Philosophical Sciences*, trans. W. Wallace (Oxford: Clarendon Press, 1975) (hereafter *EnL*), p. 69.
13 *D*, IV, p. 43; *Diff*, p. 130.

"mirror of nature," not even a mirror of itself.[14] Ultimately, once such a point is appreciated, it will mean that there is no such thing as "*the* philosophy of consciousness," or at least that the differences between the program common to Descartes, Locke, Berkeley, Hume, and Husserl, on the one hand, and Kant's philosophy of subjectivity and its descendants, on the other, are far more important than their similarities.

For it was by means of this insistence on the subject (or "mind") as a spontaneous activity (and not as a substance to be inspected or seen clearly), that Kant introduced into what we now call epistemology the political language of freedom, self-determination, even "autonomy." The Kantian principle of modernity is not Cartesian certainty, but "the autonomy of reason," the demand that reason determine for itself what it shall accept as evidence about the nature of things, and that it determine for itself the rule under which it shall evaluate actions. Reason thus emerges as the supreme self-legislator, in Kant's crucial, anti-metaphysical phrase, "occupied with nothing but itself" (B708 = A680),[15] "commanding" and "legislating" to nature, "framing for itself with perfect spontaneity an order of its own according to ideas, to which it adapts the empirical conditions" (B576 = A548).

As is well known, Kant himself hedged his bets significantly and greatly qualified these claims about autonomy with other claims about the restrictions created by the forms of sensible intuition, by reason's natural architectonic, by the need for postulates in practical reason, and so on. And, aside from the exuberant first generation of Idealists, the story of post-Kantian philosophy is the story of a full-scale retreat from such claims about reason's independence, the story, that is, of various attempts to modify or qualify such claims about reason's supreme authority, out of either a desire for some sort of ultimate court of appeal in empirical experience; some more pragmatic view of human rationality; a suspicion that what passes for reason can often reflect political, economic, or psychological motives; or just some general sense of the contingency and fallibility of reason's pronouncements about its own requirements.

It is in this context, the one created by Kant, and so frequently criticized by later philosophers, that Hegel does seem to stand alone as such a final extravagant version of idealism. However, the standard emphasis in such accounts on the metaphysics of Hegel's "identity theory," and on what appear to be the obvious implications of such phrases as "Absolute Knowl-

---

14 For a fuller discussion of this issue, see Chapter 2.
15 *Critique of Pure Reason,* trans. N. Kemp Smith (New York: St. Martin's, 1929).

edge" or the "actualization of absolute freedom," has all greatly obscured the original radicality of Hegel's position, his attempt to think the principle of modernity through to its conclusion. Hegel's formulation can sound so extravagant, I want to claim, because he is not, as it were, hedging any bets, because his enterprise stands as one of the most rigorous attempts to avoid completely any form of "dogmatism" or what would later be called (in the Critical Theory tradition) "positivism." The Hegelian experiment, we might call it, involves entertaining and thinking through the view that, in accounting for the fundamental elements of a conceptual or evaluative scheme, there is and can be no decisive or certifying appeal to any basic "facts of the matter," foundational experiences, logical forms, constitutive "interests," "prejudices," or guiding "intuitions" to begin or end any such account. We can appeal only to what we have come to regard as a basic fact or secure method or initial, orienting intuition. Although at some level it seems obvious that we have come to rely on a kind of methodology or a certain sort of evidence and pattern of inference because it has proved reliable, or because of some sort of non-controversial success, at what Hegel identifies as a categorial or notional level, this sort of appeal to external constraints on thought is said to be unavailable. Instead for Hegel the task of philosophy can only be an account of the progressive "self-determination by thought" of what comes to count as a constraint or success. Thus the extravagant claims, such as, in the *Encyclopedia Logic*, "This pure being-on-our-own belongs to free thought, to it in its free sailing out on its own, where there is nothing under it or above it, and where we stand in solitude with ourselves alone."[16]

III

There is good news and bad news about the prospects for this Hegelian radicalization of modern philosophy. The good news is that Hegel is acutely aware of the obvious problems and, despite the passages already cited, takes great pains to deny that he has the "Great Devouring Maw" theory of subjectivity described by Adorno and Habermas. The bad news is that his most elaborate defense against such charges is couched wholly in the language of the *Science of Logic*. Unfortunately, his way of putting his position is to say such things as "Therefore, what reflection does to the immediate, and the determinations which issue from reflection, are not anything external to the

16 *EL*, p. 98; *EnL*, p. 52.

immediate but are its own proper being."[17] Or, "In so far, therefore, as it is the positedness that is at the same time reflection-into-self, the determinateness of reflection is *the relation to its otherness within itself.*"[18]

These passages, although they at least hint at a position that maintains that the "determinations of reflection" are not "external" to reality, and preserve a "relation to otherness within itself," also land us hip-deep in Hegelian speculation, and we can only make our way to the relevant claims by taking some rather quick, giant steps across some very contested territory.

In the first place, the only way we can make sense of these and many other passages in the *Science of Logic* is to assume that the "Notions" discussed in the work (these ultimate "criteria" for discrimination and explanation) can be said to be "independent" and "freely determined" only in the sense that they are independent of "*empirical* determination." Or, the discussion only assumes that empirical discrimination in a self-conscious experience requires, at some level, concepts that originally prescribe what could count as an object of experience in the first place.[19] So the natural question is, Whence such concepts? In the *Logic*, Hegel's project looks to be an exploration of which non-derived concepts might have to be involved in the conceptual discrimination of "anything at all"; he begins, that is, with the notion of "being," and tries to show what further "thought-determinations," as he calls them, would have to be minimally involved if anything could be successfully discriminated, could be identified as a determinate thing, in a self-conscious experience.[20]

Moreover, since the *Logic* is clearly as developmental a work as any other of Hegel's, it is important to note that he does not propose an architectonic or structural answer to this question of our conceptual scheme. So, for example, there was a time in the history of thought when only the categories of a realist metaphysics, quality, quantity, and measure, appeared available

---

17 *Wissenschaft der Logik,* II (Hamburg: Felix Meiner Verlag, 1969), (hereafter *WL*), p. 19; *Hegel's Science of Logic,* trans. A. V. Miller (London: George Allen & Unwin, 1969) (hereafter *SL*), p. 405.

18 *WL*, p. 22; *SL*, p. 408.

19 For a fuller defense of this reading of the "thought on its own" passage cited earlier, see my Hegel's *Idealism,* ch. 9. I realize of course that this brief summary does not justify the reading of Hegel I am proposing. Such an interpretation would require a defense of the way Hegel read Kant, and a philosophic reconstruction of his own work in the light of this reading of Kant. I have provided the details of such a reading in *Kant's Theory of Form,* (New Haven: Yale University Press, 1982), ch. 2, "Kant on the Spontaneity of Mind," and throughout *Hegel's Idealism.*

20 On the issue of interpreting the *Logic* this way, see my "Hegel and Category Theory," *Review of Metaphysics* 43, no. 4 (June 1990): 839–48, and Terry Pinkard's "How Kantian Was Hegel?," *Review of Metaphysics* 93, no. 4 (June 1990): 831–48.

as categories, and their true status (as, actually, "self-determinations of reason," rather than "ideal entities," as conceived in the realist tradition) was
only dimly understood, if at all. There was a time when reason determined
for itself (at the time, "correctly") that objects could only be understood as
behind a veil of perception, or when the modern understanding of the
"essence–appearance" distinction came to supersede and qualify the realist
picture.

Among the many issues that all of this raises are, The theory of social
integration and reproduction implied by this account (bound to be very
controversial since Hegel obviously places a great deal of explanatory weight
on the role basic criteria or "norms," let us say, play in socialization and
social struggle); how we should understand this notion of an "internal
deduction" of the forms of thought; and what implications might follow
from Hegel's approach. The *Logic,* of course, is not the full answer to this
question because the analysis undertaken there presupposes so much, or in
Hegel's language, presupposes already that we have come to understand its
"standpoint," or why we should be attending so intently to these internal
kinds of conceptual change.

The larger picture of "thought's self-determination" looks something like
this: Hegel's answer to the question of why we have come to think about
things as we have, to categorize our experience and evaluate our activity in
ways so fundamental that they cannot be said to be due to what we have
learned or discovered about reality, but can be shown to be presupposed in
any attempt to learn or discover or justify, is that we have come to think
some way or other because of prior attempts at such categorization (keeping in mind yet again the controversial account of this "we," and the role of
"Notions" and the process of self-reflection in its formation and
reproduction).

One of the ways in which Hegel frequently makes this point is by appealing to a very general principle that runs throughout much of his mature
philosophy: that the question of the justification for what comes to count as
an authoritative explanation of objects and events, an acceptable classificatory procedure, and so forth, can never itself be resolved by simply using a
more comprehensive classification, or by invoking some higher order rule
or axiom or regulative ideal or argument strategy. There are no rules to tell
us which methodological rules we ought to follow in regulating our discursive practices, no intuitions certifying the axioms out of which such rules can
be constructed, and no transcendental arguments justifying *the* necessary
conditions of experience. What we always require is a historical account of
why we have come to regard some set of rules or a practice as authoritative

or even indispensable. In Hegel's *Phenomenology* that account appeals to a complex prediscursive context, a social "experience" tied to various norms and principles (sometimes called simply "life"), as the origin of various concrete epistemic and discursive practices. That is how "reason" will account for these sense-making practices and their rules. Such practices are regarded as responses and solutions to *aporiai* experienced in the "life of Spirit," and so the justification of our most authoritative claims to knowledge is "dialectical," not logical or formal.[21]

At this point, it is extremely important to understand that Hegel does not want merely to appeal in a general and vague way to such a dialectical origin; he is committed to an account of this apparently chaotic swirl of contingent, "experienced" variables. He rejects attempts both to formalize or to find a "structure" or a language in such practices and to rest content with any discussion-ending appeal to "the way we happen to talk."[22] Rather the shared intuitions, we might call them, especially the intuitive sense of "the whole" within which this or that practice alone seems acceptable, are themselves always already historically mediated, products of prior attempts at historical self-understanding. Intuitions, or experiences, or dissatisfactions are always results, the products of principles and rules so deeply shared as to become almost unnoticeable. And Hegel thinks he can describe, without falsifying or rendering overly abstract, these "mediations," and the general process of mediation.

---

21 Cf. here the discussion by Stanley Rosen, "Logic and Dialectic," in *Ancients and Moderns: Rethinking Modernity* (New Haven: Yale University Press, 1989), pp. 118–59, especially p. 155.

22 This is an admittedly unfair compression of Richard Rorty's position in, for example, his *Contingency, Irony and Solidarity* (Cambridge: Cambridge University Press, 1989). Rorty is in favor of some version of Hegelian "dialectic," understood as "the attempt to play off vocabularies against one another, rather than merely to infer propositions from one another," or as a "partial substitution of redescription for inference," but he considers this practice just a "literary skill" rather than an "argumentation procedure" (p. 78). However, even though Rorty indicates, in his criticism of Habermas, that we still require some sort of "replacement" for religious and philosophic accounts of a ground for modern institutions, and that a "historical narrative" (p. 68) will provide such a replacement account, he also undermines the possibility of any genuine narrative by insisting throughout on a kind of radical contingency in conceptual and social change. That Europe simply "lost the habit of using certain words and gradually acquired the habit of using others" (p. 6; see also pp. 9, 14, 16), or that the use of a new language "with luck . . . will also strike the next generation as inevitable" (p. 29), makes it very hard to see how such a narrative could be a narrative (rather than a list of social events) and how it could function in the way Rorty suggests on p. 68. From Hegel's point of view, the appeal to chance or luck or contingency is simply another species of dogmatism, an appeal to "the positive" or "what simply happens," as if such an appeal were possible.

So, as noted, for Hegel all the significant activities of members of a social community presuppose, at some level, a self-conscious application of these sorts of commonly held criteria for discriminating and evaluating experiences. Said more obviously, Hegel is an Idealist; communities are the way they are fundamentally because of how they have come to regard and evaluate themselves. Principles and criteria govern activity in the relevant institutions because participants, again at some level of self-consciousness, collectively take the principles to be legitimate, and for a variety of reasons. The fundamental institutions of a society are understood to be sustained by a kind of ongoing implicit consensus, a consensus that depends on various forms of "self-legitimation," and that, for reasons Hegel thinks he can describe, periodically break down.[23]

Moreover, the centrality of such norms and principles is such that it forms the basis for Hegel's controversial "holism" and so his attempt to sketch a possible, ultimate reconciliation between reason and sensibility in modern institutions, a non-alienated life. Even to "feel," on this account, is to have been educated in a certain way, to value or abhor within a certain community itself made possible by collectively held, historically specific norms. An ongoing, and in some sense finally successful self-reflection about such principles is thereby tied to more than intellectual self-satisfaction, to a kind of social and psychological integration as well. And philosophy is that social institution wherein these attempts by subjects to organize and explain their experiences and regulate their activities gains its highest or most self-conscious expression and assessment.[24]

23 Thus, to state a complex issue simply, it is true that Hegel does not have a theory that gives epistemological and ethical pride of place to an *original* "intersubjectivity." Whatever human collectivity there is, is treated by Hegel as a *result*, a product of the social struggle and dissatisfactions of individuals. But he does have an account of the radical insufficiency of individual self-determination and wholly subjective attempts at "certainty," and that account meets, I think, objections based on reading him as still a "philosopher of consciousness." See *Hegel's Idealism*, ch. 7, and my discussion of Hösle, "Hösle, System, and Subject," pp. 5–19.

24 This connection, between the success or failure of rational self-reflection and the often very different sorts of "success" relevant to human action, introduces the endlessly complicated "theory–practice" problem, and so the link between the original Kantian meaning of epistemological "critique" and the different sense of "critique as practical negation" so powerful in the young Hegelians and the early Marx. See Rüdiger Bubner, "What Is Critical Theory?" in *Essays in Hermeneutics and Critical Theory*, trans. Eric Matthews (New York: Columbia University Press, 1988), pp. 1–35; and "Habermas's Concept of Critical Theory," in *Habermas: Critical Debates*, ed. by John B. Thompson and David Held (Cambridge: MIT Press, 1982), pp. 42–56. Habermas, in his "A Reply to My Critics" in that volume, denies that in his position there is any confusion between the two senses.

Obviously, such a radicalization of Kant's notion of categoriality raises a large number of questions that cannot be addressed here. Given many parallel contemporary concerns, however, we should at least briefly note the philosophical issues that arise in such a contemporary context. We might especially ask about Hegel's strategy for *justifying* various conceptual changes, and so about his general case for the rationality of this "process." Once, that is, Kant's complicated transcendental way of tying down logically possible forms of thought to real possibility and so objectivity is rejected, but some general anti-empirical strategy about categories is retained (a denial that the manifold of impressions alone could be responsible for the conceptual apparatus with which experience is to be discriminated), why not just opt for some now popular conceptual scheme or framework or paradigm relativism, together perhaps with some sort of contingent or sociological ground for "what we can't seem to get along without," and be done with it? Why shouldn't that be the legacy of Hegel's historical radicalization of Kantian modernism?

We have already seen, however, that Hegel would immediately claim that such explanatory appeals to causal origins or functional correlations are themselves embedded in complex, historically specific theoretical projects, and so are unavailable as a straightforward *explicans* for the conceivings and justifying we sanction at one point or another. Such ways of looking at the issue require their own "phenomenology" and logical reconstruction, if one is possible (so, no sociology of knowledge, no genealogy of the play of power, and so on, at least, again, not without a "logical" reconstruction and deduction of the Notions presupposed in such strategies. Anything else would be a regression to positivism).

This sort of response, however, could simply provoke a more radical rejoinder. Let us assume that Hegel has successfully linked the question of the rational justifiability of various cognitive and evaluative principles with something like their historical sufficiency, with an account of how such principles emerged as resolutions of an experienced and logical crisis in a community's self-understanding. Let us also assume that in making his case for this progressive view of conceptual change Hegel is not, as stated in the Hegel literature, "presupposing the Absolute," or justifying this claim for progression by appeal to some theory that just presupposes that basic conceptual change is to be understood as a process of some monistic subject's self-enlightenment. Given the preceding rejoinder to more sociological or empirical accounts of conceptual change, and, now, a denial of any "metaphysical" foundation for a faith in teleological progression, why should we believe that there could be any overall progression, or even that we could account for such conceptual change at all? Perhaps such changes are in a general sense historically motivated, are responses to historical *aporiai*, but maybe any determinate resolution is just one of many that could have emerged then, and these basic shifts are just fundamentally contingent, and so *alogos*, not subsumable under any single narrative.

Indeed, looking at the issue this way provides a good means for understanding much of later European thought. For, Hegel's claim that human history is dialectically and progressively self-transforming was (apart from the obvious case of Marx) much less influential than his general historicization of Kant's transcendental enterprise. A great deal of the thought of later European philosophers could be categorized by understanding their differing sorts of opposition to Hegel's account of the progressive logic of conceptual change and his case for the significance of that conceptual change in social, religious, political, and aesthetic practices. If history turns out to be as purposeless as nature (the "slaughterbench" Hegel himself described), unavailable as some whole within which to orient and assess collective and individual possibilities, then the agenda facing Kierkegaard, Schopenhauer, Nietzsche, and Heidegger appears on the horizon.

Again, although we shall return to this issue in more detail in the next section, we have already seen something of the spirit of Hegel's response to such suspicions. In the first place, he would be quite critical of any account that implied that communities could suddenly, in some radically contingent way, "change the subject," could simply invent a new agenda or basic self-description. Communities ("Spirit") don't just "have" or "adopt" such agendas; the authority of basic principles and criteria is linked to shared assumptions about the justifiability of such norms, and we could not arrive at any account of the determinacy of a new agenda without some accompanying account of what went wrong in such a consensus and why that going wrong would lead to this resolution.

Moreover, Hegel's own account of the *telos* or end point of such a process does not conclude with any substantive theory of the basic principles of all account giving. In the third book of the *Logic*, his interest is much more focused on the process by which any such principle is established and he everywhere implies that self-consciousness about such a process is all that the vaunted "Absolute Knowledge" is all about. In fact, it is especially important to note that Hegel's formulation of this final self-consciousness expressly denies any sort of systematic closure or static finality. Indeed, Hegel goes so far as to say:

The *identity* of the Idea with itself is one with the *process;* the thought which liberates actuality from the illusory show of purposeless mutability and trans- figures it into the Idea must not represent this truth of actuality as a dead repose, as a mere picture, lifeless, without impulse or movement, as a genus or number, or an abstract thought; by virtue of the freedom which the Notion attains in the Idea, the Idea possesses within itself also the *most stubborn opposi- tion;* its repose consists in the security and certainty with which it eternally creates and eternally overcomes that opposition, in it meeting with itself.[25]

Perhaps the most controversial of the questions introduced by such a reading is what this new form of self-consciousness about internally self- legislated systematic principles will mean for *future* reflection, and for the way we understand the current systematic organization and explanation of nature and human activity. In the interpretation I am suggesting, much of the *Encyclopedia* represents a search for those modern institutions and forms of self-understanding that can be said finally to embody this anti-realist, historicized self-consciousness, and much of his philosophy of history and religion tries to tell the same developmental story about the role of such "absolute negativity" in the genesis of modern political life and religious communities.

But the problem at issue here is Hegel's modernism, and the question now is whether this sketch is of any help in figuring out what one should say about that issue. I have tried to argue that Hegel's affirmation of modernity, his modernism, does not involve any monism or any premodern teleology or any "reconciliationist" moment that involves a World or Cosmic Spirit directing human history to some pantheistic self-understanding. In the con- text sketched, what, then, is Hegel's modernism?

IV

Consider first Hegel's famous dissatisfactions with modernity. It should be clearer now that there is a continuity between Hegel's often sympathetically received critique of the modern notion of practical freedom (best ex- pressed in Kant's and Fichte's moral theory) and his critique of modern accounts of theoretical enlightenment, something that, prima facie, might be hard to see.

For, in the practical context, the idea that "acting rightly" requires that duty alone be the determining ground of the will is apparently criticized by

25 *WL,* II, p. 412; *SL,* p. 759.

Hegel, in effect, for its severity, for the impossible demands it places on the role of reason in human life. When it comes to thought's speculative self-determination, however, reason's attempt to determine the conditions of acceptable claim making about any sort of object, the spirit of Hegel's criticism of Kant and Fichte seems to be directed at their skepticism and hesitancy. They don't go far enough.

However, in both cases the criticism is based on a common claim that a residual positivism or dogmatism reemerges, an attempt, as it would later be characterized, to "reify" the subject's relation to the moral law and to systematic principles, and so to avoid considering the developmental and (broadly construed) social context within which the moral law, and much else besides, would come to appear as the formula for rational self-legislation, and within which various systematic principles would come to appear as superior to any competitors. In Hegel's language it was this overly "finite" view of subjectivity that generated the modern problems of alienation and skepticism, as modern subjects struggled to understand the significance of their moral lives and cognitive activities without the larger (again "developmental") context or whole necessary for such reflection.[26]

Put another way, it is precisely *because* Hegel is insisting so radically on the autonomy of thought that he ends up with this theory of the always situated, or historical, nature of human reflection. The consequence of Kant's Idealist revolution really does mean that there can be no "anchor" for thought's self-legislation in a "beyond" or "immediacy," or "pure form." For Hegel, Fichte was the first to see this but he drew the wrong conclusion when he tried to discover an original "transcendental positing" somehow responsible for the "I's" relation to the "not-I." There is no such original activity; the

---

26 The best discussion of the link between the German Idealist project and problems in Kantian moral theory is Dieter Henrich's "Das problem der Grundlegung der Ethik bei Kant und im spekulativen Idealismus," in *Sein und Ethos*, ed. by P. Englehardt (Mainz: Matthias Grünewald, 1963), pp. 350–86. Henrich concentrates on the "Copernican Revolution" in ethics, on Kant's argument that in moral life objects do not determine the will, but the will its own objects, if "pure reason" can be "practical." But many of the problems that emerge for the Kantian account of "self-determination" in that context parallel the issues involved in the pursuit of a full or "absolute reflection." This is especially true of a problem that long bothered Kant: how to account for the relation between the recognition of a universal moral law and the obligatory force of that law, its bindingness. Without an account of why we would come to regard such a law as binding, we have, as Henrich puts it, only an "Autognosie" of reason and not the "Autonomie" of reason, cf. p. 356. I am arguing that from Hegel's point of view, the same is true of the "binding power" of any criterion for a rational practice, and especially for Habermas's account of the *Bindungskraft* of "norms." See also Seyla Benhabib's charge, in *Critique, Norm and Utopia* (New York: Columbia University Press, 1986), about Habermas's "rationalistic fallacy," p. 317.

transcendental perspective is itself but a solution to a concrete, earlier problem.

We can sum up this interpretation of Hegel's account of the principle of modernity – "thought's autonomy" – by noting that it introduces two distinct problems. There is first the more general point about the necessarily "self-determined" nature of reason giving or justification. As I have interpreted it here, this is meant to deny the availability of any external or intuited or certain ground as *explicans*. What comes to count as verifying or restricting or disconfirming a claim is viewed as the result of a historical consensus, one that can only be measured and assessed "against" historical (and equally "self-determined") predecessors or historically available competitors for such a consensus. That is all there is or can be to a rational assessment.

But this general historical idealism is not, for Hegel at least, the whole story. As already noted, he also wants to explain how various moments in the formation of such social consensus can be understood as teleological or purposive, more than just constantly shifting and differing, even if "concretely rational," responses to various intellectual or social crises. Hegel's claim is that, once the full dimensions of the "self-determined" status of such principles are understood, we can then better understand the nature of the failure of all past categorial schemes. The theory is simply that such basic failures are always due to the denial of such conceptual autonomy, to various forms of pre-Hegelian reliance on "the positive," or the traditionally metaphysical. Hegel tries to show that there cannot be a coherent organization of experience and practices that suppresses or denies this element of collective autonomy or the role of social self-determination in the formation and reproduction of Spirit. The proof for that claim is the exhibition, or description, of such failures.[27]

Human thought, of course, although inherently self-negating and purposive in this way, is not "fated" to reach any such self-comprehending *telos*. The internal confusion and skepticism created by such an unsuccessful moment of dogmatism may simply be ignored by the community in ques-

---

27 Cf. the following sorts of claims: "The Absolute Idea has for its content only this, that the form determination is its own completed totality, the pure Notion" (*WL*, II, p. 485; *SL*, p. 825); "Since, however, it [the consciousness of the Notion, or the method] is the objective immanent form, the immediacy of the beginning must be in its own self deficient and endowed with the urge [*Trieb*] to carry itself further" (*WL*, II, p. 489; *SL*, p. 829); "The advance consists rather in the universal determining itself and being for itself the universal, that is, equally an individual and a subject. Only in its consummation is it the absolute" (ibid.).

tion, as it busily plunders its neighbors or enslaves its citizens. But once and if such a *telos* is reached, this reconstructive understanding is possible.

It is, I think, quite unlikely that most of this ambitious reconstruction can be defended. It is unlikely that so much, from the exhaustion of Greek tragedy, to the paradoxes of Roman law on property, to Leibniz's failed monadology, can be linked to a developing self-consciousness about the very possibility of "positions" or "theories" or philosophy. The most one can say (and it is still a great deal) is that such an account can often be right and helpful about the failures of human consensus, about unjustifiable, "dogmatic" appeals to the external authorities of religion or objective expertise, and so forth, and that Hegel can powerfully motivate his own position on such a possibility by accounting for the problems encountered when his own position on such autonomy is implicitly or explicitly denied.

Indeed, one final way of seeing this is by returning to quite an explicit denial of that idealism, one complicated by a somewhat tendentious interpretation, but that engages Hegel's idealism in a way that will allow us a final point of view on Hegel's affirmation of "the autonomy of thought." Consider again Habermas's alternative picture of modernity and the following question. I have argued that Habermas and others are correct in attributing a great immodesty or extravagance to Hegel's idealism, but that they mislocate the source of that extravagance by attacking Hegel's supposedly "all-consuming" theory of subjectivity. If, rather, Hegel's immodesty simply is the immodesty of modernity itself, its notion of a "self-grounding," carried to a kind of consistent extreme, or if the preceding interpretation is roughly correct, what is the Hegelian response to Habermas? On the interpretation I have sketched, it is unlikely that their disagreement over the status of modernity has much to do with the differences between a "self-reconciled, Absolute Subject" and an open-minded "discourse community." The important issue has to do with differences about the nature of appeals to reason in modernity, especially between Hegel's account of a collectively self-grounded subjectivity and Habermas's of a procedurally regulated intersubjective discourse. What does this difference amount to?

V

Like Hegel, Habermas has always been eager to present himself as a modernist. In the Critical Theory tradition, especially after the work of Marcuse, Horkheimer, and Adorno, this has meant finding a way to affirm the great technical and scientific dynamic of modernity, the control of nature for the satisfaction of interests. But Habermas has also always been concerned to argue against the confusion of this "instrumental" notion of rationality with other forms, and especially to claim that the distinct nature of communicative activity, the attempt to arrive at a genuinely mutual, intersubjective understanding, be respected and not be reduced to agents manipulating or strategically influencing each other. Again, as for Hegel, for Habermas, the problem of modernity is not primarily an ongoing and still incomplete technical problem (e.g., scarcity) and not, at least not fundamentally, a wealth-distribution problem, but involves the nature of cultural reproduction and socialization, particularly given modernity's weakening of tradition and religion.[28] Habermas's own proposal about this problem amounts to demonstrating how modernity can be said to have made possible a variety of new "communicative" forms of such social integration.

In other words, Hegel and Habermas stand together in affirming the extraordinary Enlightenment attempt to promote the new integrative and socializing function of "reason," in both public life and theoretical discourse, and they agree that this goal requires a conception of reason significantly different from the "instrumental" rationality of Bacon, or the "strategic" rationality of Hobbes. The key question is the nature of this expanded or more adequate notion of reason.

And this is all too long a story to summarize adequately here, but the basic idea is simple enough.[29] According to Habermas's latest version of the issues, we do not need a Hegelian, romantic notion of an organic, integrating or reconciling reason, a "macrosubject" recognizing itself in nature and

28 In other words, the central question for both involves fulfilling the modern promise that collective, coordinated social activity could be made possible and sustained by an appeal to reason, by collective allegiance to principles that are and are understood to be genuinely universal. They both are interested in how that promise comes to be distorted and unfulfilled in modernity; they both tend to hold a narrow and unsatisfying notion of "reason" largely responsible for this failure (*Verstand* in Hegel, Weberean *Zweckrationalität* in Habermas); so they both insist, in a distinctly "idealistic" way, on the importance of "self-reflection" or self-consciousness in any genuine emancipation (although Habermas has always relied on the model of psychoanalysis, rather than the *Phenomenology of Spirit*, to make this point).

29 For good summaries of Habermas's position and its history, see the account by Stephen K. White, *The Recent Work of Jürgen Habermas: Reason, Justice and Modernity* (Cambridge: Cambridge University Press, 1988), especially pp. 39–47, and the very useful study by Axel Honneth, *Kritik der Macht: Reflexionsstufen einer kritischen Gesellschaftstheorie* (Frankfurt am M.: Suhrkamp, 1985). There are, of course, many different stages in the development of Habermas's theoretical position, but he has always been concerned to contrast the norms and ends of "work" and those of "interaction" and to resist the totalization of the former domain. His later "linguistic turn" only extends and deepens his insistence on the distinctiveness of "symbolic interaction" and, as I think Honneth shows decisively, is fully consistent with the concerns of, say, *Knowledge and Human Interests*.

spirit, but an adequate theory of communicative reason. This general theory of communicative activity is intended by Habermas to sketch out a middle-ground position between alternatives that have bedeviled the post-Kantian tradition. He describes these often as an oscillation between "pure transcendentalism," on the one hand, and "pure historicism," on the other,[30] or between a notion of reason that "stands abstractly over against history and the complex of social life," or one that "falls prey" either to historicism or to sociology of knowledge.[31] These alternatives can be avoided, he claims, by a theory that reconstructs the ways in which everyday practices of communication *already* embody implicit and unavoidable appeals to reason.

This reconstruction, first, assumes the obvious teleological character of communication, that people can be assumed to engage in it in order to be understood. Habermas then argues, far more controversially, that we manage to understand these speech acts of others when we know the conditions under which they could be accepted as *valid* for any hearer.[32] So just trying to communicate, to be understood, implicates us in claims on each other (different types of validity claims) that, just by speaking, we are obligating ourselves to being able to "redeem." These claims all presuppose a commitment to a certain sort of rationality, and are in fact rational if, within some approximation of an "ideal speech situation," consistent with the type of validity claim made, we can either produce convincing arguments and evidence, or be convinced by the force of the better argument.

These notions of different types of validity claims, and of a formal or procedural definition of rationality, are the cornerstones of Habermas's modernism. He insists with Kant, via Weber, that modernity's greatest achievement lies in the differentiation of these domains of discourse (or "worlds"), the realization that norms inherent in different speech acts are heterogeneous and cannot be subsumed under a common standard. When we make a claim about an objective fact of the matter, or when we assert a moral judgment or express aesthetically a subjective state or feeling, we make claims that all have different "logics" of redemption, and confusing them leads to a "distorted" situation, either a "moralization" of aesthetic issues, an "aestheticization" of moral problems, or, most often in modernity,

---

30 J. Habermas, "Questions and Counterquestions," in *Habermas and Modernity*, ed. by R. Bernstein (Cambridge: MIT Press, 1985), p. 193.
31 J. Habermas, "Reply to My Critics," p. 232.
32 The most concise defense of the claim "Communicative actions always require an interpretation that is rational in approach" occurs in vol. I of *The Theory of Communicative Action*, trans. Thomas McCarthy (Boston: Beacon Press, 1984), pp. 102–41. The quotation is on p. 106.

an objectification of communicative and expressive issues, a marginaliza-
tion of moral and aesthetic issues as "irrational."[33]

To be sure, Habermas admits, too often in modernity the ideals we are
implicitly committed to in such claims are further distorted by the general
influence "of money and power."[34] Government bureaucracies, medical
institutions, mass media, and so on, often address their audiences in ways
designed to confuse different types of validity claims, and so to create a false
or unfree consensus or to deny the possibility that a consensus is relevant,
given the supposedly specialized knowledge of "experts." The "life-world" is
"colonized" in modernity, all for the sake of the advancement of strategic
self-interest. The chief social phenomenon of modernity might be said to be
the extensive distortion of the communicative practices of the "life-world"
by the demands of "systematic" functions and strategic considerations.

But, for Habermas, modernity's achievement lies in distinguishing these
different validity spheres, a realization that and why they must not be confused with each other, and especially a denial that there is any philosophic
science that can legislate the contents of any claim in any such domain. He
frequently denies, against his Hegelian critics (such as Rüdiger Bubner),[35]
that the "discourse ethics" implied by his approach posits some utopian goal
of a free and rational consensus about everything. He claims unequivocally
that all substantive questions of the "good life" or "personal values," and so

33 On this scheme the full "rationalization" of society requires (a) the connection of these
"three cultural value spheres" with "corresponding action systems," (b) a "passing on" of
the "cognitive potential developed by expert cultures" to the "communicative practices of
everyday life," and (c) a "balanced" institutionalization of the spheres to ensure that none
is "subordinated to laws intrinsic to heterogeneous orders of life." See ibid., pp. 239–40.
See also the summary diagram on p. 238 of the fundamental formal–pragmatic relations
between actors and their worlds.

34 I pass over here a complex issue dealt with very well by Honneth in *Kritik der Macht*, chs. 8
and 9, where he argues that Habermas often "reifies" the opposition between "system" and
"life world," and tends to forget that any theory of socialization, social power, and social
evolution must appeal not simply to "systems" or to "money" or to "power," but to historically concrete social groups, unified around concrete interests, struggling with one another for control of the social agenda. See the important distinction he draws on p. 273
between possible directions for a Habermasean theory of social conflict, and the implications he claims result from Habermas's neglect of these alternatives, pp. 290, 296, 299.
What this also means is that the influence of "systematic" and instrumental issues in
modernity is itself a historical *explicandum*, requiring a complex and rather ambitious
narrative, and that, as I am presenting the issues, is a Hegelian point.

35 See R. Bubner, "Rationalität, Lebensform, und Geschichte," in *Rationalität*, ed. by H.
Schndelbach (Frankfurt am M.: Suhrkamp, 1984), pp. 198–217, and Habermas's reply in
the same volume, "Über Moralität und Sittlichkeit – Was macht eine Lebensform 'rational'?" pp. 218–35.

forth, are not subject to any universal rationalization. These issues remain local and contingent (contrary to the way Habermas is often characterized by his postmodern critics), and the moral point of view concerns *only* "justice," only questions that arise when one's pursuit of one's norms begins to affect others who do not share them. Philosophy can then describe what is rational to do, and in what sense we are bound to do it. Even so, though, on the other hand, Habermas maintains "an outrageously strong claim" that "there is a universal core of moral intuition in all times and in all societies," and this because there are "unavoidable presuppositions of communicative activity."[36]

There are obviously some similarities between this general intersubjective, communicative approach and Hegel's rejection of "the understanding" as adequate in accounting for the dealings of human spirit, but there are (at least) two great differences between them that will help focus the issues raised. First, Habermas has always had trouble convincing his critics that these communicative norms are "presupposed" in so much human activity, that we simply cannot, under pain of a "performative contradiction," engage in such activity without a commitment to such norms.[37] Contrary to his Frankfurt colleague, Apel, Habermas has backed away from any claim about "transcendental pragmatics," and has preferred to call what he is doing an empirical, fallibilist, reconstructive enterprise. This basically means that he is trying to construct "hypotheses" about the rules that subjects must be assuming in various activities in order for us to be able to explain various competencies and their successful coordination of activities.

This methodological issue of presupposition introduces its own problems, but it still leaves unresolved the most difficult "Hegelian" issue. Even if Habermas can show that such norms are effectively presupposed in current cognitive, practical, and aesthetic practices, that analysis alone will not get us to any claim about "the" conditions for linguistic activity as such, and certainly not to any claims about what is rational or even to what is superior or affirmable in our practices. It certainly might be the case that there are or were forms of social life and linguistic activity, and assumptions about acceptable claim making, that involve no such "ideal speech situation" norm, and such societies functioned. For Habermas to claim what he does about "universality," and "rationality," and the like, he shall have to show, for

---

36 See the interview "Life-Forms, Morality and the Task of the Philosopher" in *Habermas: Autonomy and Solidarity*, ed. by P. Dews (London: Verso, 1987), p. 206.
37 Cf., for example, Allen W. Wood's very helpful discussion of the *Verständigung* thesis in "Habermas' Defense of Rationalism," *New German Critique* 13 (1985): 145–64.

example, that such alternate activities created (or would create) some sort of crisis or failure that in some way "led" (or would lead) to the realization of these modern differentiated spheres and their various conditions. And with this sort of justification, we are now getting much closer to Hegel.[38]

Habermas has tried to sketch such a developmental story (what he once called a "reconstruction of historical materialism"),[39] but to this point, he has relied very heavily, in different contexts, on the psychological models of moral development in Kohlberg and the "genetic structuralism" of Piaget, and these models have rightly proved very disappointing to critics. They suggest a naturalist understanding of "developmental stages" that begs most of the serious questions at issue (e.g., whether a certain stage is superior or not) and, so far, has not been determinately applied with any success to the actual history of social communities (apart from some very brief remarks about mythic cultures).[40] Although Habermas is willing to admit that these "models" need to be supplemented by his own theory of communicative activity, and although he admits that Kohlberg especially too often (in his last "stage") confuses philosophical claims with developmental progression, Habermas himself adopts the language of "heightened capacities for learning" and "greater reflexivity" as if they are matters of organic growth and maturation, and not controversial views about autonomy and emancipation, products of a still ongoing cultural debate.

And here all the Hegelian points are quite relevant. If there is some multifaceted norm for distinctively communicative activity, we shall need some determinate account of *why* we have collectively taken it to be such a norm, and particularly why it remains such a controversial, still not fully

---

38 Habermas admits that his theory does not predict that in a free dialogue we will be able to find any "generalizable interests," any ends that will be accepted by all affected. This will entail "compromise" rather than "consensus." He is concerned to show that this fact does not transform his theory into some bourgeois version of contractarianism because he still maintains strict conditions for the legitimacy of compromise, but I do not see how the general picture that emerges from this admission does not land us back in the problems of a radical Weberian pluralism. See White's discussion, *Recent Work*, pp. 75–7, and note 48, this chapter.

39 Cf. chs. 2, 3, and 4 in *Communication and the Evolution of Society*, trans. T. McCarthy (Boston: Beacon Press, 1979); *Moralbewusstsein und kommunikativen Handelns* (Frankfurt am M.: Suhrkamp, 1983), pp. 127–206; and the discussion in White, *Recent Work*, pp. 58–68, and pp. 94–95.

40 Cf. the discussion in *Theory of Communicative Action*, I, pp. 43–74, and especially II, ch. 5. See also the discussion by Anthony Giddens, "Reason Without Revolution: Habermas' *Theorie des kommunikativen Handelns*," in *Habermas and Modernity*, ed. by R. Bernstein (Cambridge: MIT Press, 1985), pp. 95–121, especially his account of "what would have happened" had Habermas relied on Lévi-Strauss for his genetic structuralism, and not Piaget, pp. 117–19.

acknowledged norm.[41] On Hegel's view, nothing could simply be a norm presupposed in a speech act. Communities might, in an implicit and very complex way, come to adopt and pursue such a norm, but that narrative will bear the weight of the justification of these norms, and without it, no empirical reconstruction can perform the critical task Habermas wants.

Said another way, Hegel would deny Habermas's version of the *Moralität–Sittlichkeit*, or the "morality–ethics" distinction. Habermas proposes these procedural norms as neutral on the ethical questions of the good life, highest values, and so forth, constraining only our "dialogue" about such issues.[42] But these norms already greatly restrict what could be a just substantive goal in modern social life, and so already themselves embody an ethical ideal, a vision of the major feature of the good life for modern agents – the public status of reason, and so, justice. Accordingly, some historical justification must be given for a collective commitment to these ideals, and on Habermas's own terms, it cannot be transcendental or "quasi-transcendental," or "empirically reconstructive," or simply sanctified as "developmentally advanced." For reasons clearly related to the Hegelian issues developed, Habermas needs something like a *Phenomenology of Spirit*, or some sort of way of accounting for the modern affirmation of the values of reciprocity and self-consciousness that does not rely so heavily on the meager philosophic resources of developmental psychology.

Habermas has responded to charges like these in the past, but not, in my view, in a way that answers the fundamental problem. To the question of how individuals could actually come to be "motivated" to adopt and act on the "universalist" moral point of view, Habermas responds by admitting that what Kohlberg calls the "postconventional" stage in morality (an ability to distance oneself from and criticize deeply entrenched sentiments and intuitions) can only come about in a certain "milieu," or under certain conditions, and that part of the task of moral education is to aid in the formation of this sort of "superego."[43] But the deeper issue does not concern how we might motivate an individual to adopt such a perspective, but how a society as a whole could come to be interested in such an end as a collective goal. That issue is not just a historical one, but concerns the reconstructive justification (if possible) of its historical significance.

---

41 Habermas, of course, addresses such an issue by invoking his "boundary war" account of the "system/life word" issue, but Habermas has, even by sympathetic critics like Honneth, rightly been accused of "overcategorizing" this relation.
42 See Habermas, "Über Moralität," p. 225.
43 Ibid., p. 230.

To the question of whether his promotion of the priority (in certain contexts) of the universalist point of view ignores the historical and cultural specificity of that principle, and so the possibility of its supercession in later cultures, Habermas has responded by denying that he wishes in some way to "prescribe" the content of the historically contingent "life-world." That is precisely what he does not want to do; he has conceded so much to the modern ethos about the radical plurality of views of the good, and to the fact that such substantive goals, although they could be said to be alienating, or healthy, or cruelly abstract, cannot be said to be rational or irrational, that he has focused on only a very specific issue for which the universalist perspective is required, roughly "justice."[44] But again, the basic issues do not concern the problem of what Habermas is not proposing, but whether he can justify the "all times and all places" universality of the principle he is defending. If he is not a "transcendentalist" about such principles, and does wish to avoid treating them as "standing abstractly over against history and the complex of social life," it is hard to see how the case for universality can be made (or, as Rorty has put it, why shouldn't one be able to follow Habermas up to the point of his universalism – admit that he has offered a good description of what we are, contingently, all about – and then "swerve off"?)[45]

Of course, Habermas has a great many other things to say about the consequences of the "distortion" of communication and the attendant "pathologies" of advanced capitalism, and these bring us to the second difference introduced earlier, the modern notion of autonomy and its connection with rationality. Habermas's ideal of *Verständigung* is clearly connected to the deepest original ideals of the German Idealist tradition. Linguistic activity itself, he tries to show, in some way commits us to the assumption that other participants in the linguistic community are to be understood as fellow subjects, not manipulable objects, and so in all cases as potentially rational subjects, freely capable of advancing or rejecting various claims made by subjects on each other. The argument with Hegel over this issue is supposed to concern (i) an intersubjective model of such autonomy, versus the idea of a collective subject or "group mind," originally in opposition to, and then reconciled with, objects; and (ii) Habermas's attention to the linguistic dimension of this autonomy, and Hegel's neglect of that dimension.

44 Ibid., pp. 232–4.
45 See Rorty's review of *The Philosophical Discourse of Modernity* (entitled "Posties") in *London Review of Books* September 1987, p. 12.

The latter is too involved even for the kind of sweeping summary I am engaged in, but one brief Hegelian response should be noted. Simply put, from Hegel's point of view, Habermas is wrong to look for the achievement of modern reciprocity and mutual recognition in the norms implied in the use of *language*. Such norms themselves (if they exist) *reflect* a more basic social achievement, the way in which modern societies have come to understand the relation between the very large issues Hegel calls the "independence" and "dependence" of self-consciousness, and the "struggle" for recognition.

With respect to the first issue, some familiar criticisms of Habermas's position again point back to a Hegelian issue.[46] In the first place, it is not clear why we should think that merely conforming to the procedural requirements of an ideal-speech situation could accomplish the kind of autonomous reflection Habermas has in mind, and so would produce results we should sanctify as "rational," or even, as Habermas appears to claim in cognitive contexts, "true." What counts as the "force of the better argument" in a given situation may be fully and freely recognized as such (as a matter of fact) by the interlocutors, and may actually be effective in the dialogue, and there would still be no reason to think that what is so understood, contingently, as the force of the better argument would be the force of the better argument, at least not without either some classically independent, philosophical assessment of those criteria, or, as in Hegel, some way of situating those concrete criteria, governing the content of the dialogue, within various failed alternatives or hypothetical alternatives.[47]

Thus, said all at once, a Hegelian could not view the rationality of such substantive conclusions as only a matter of their being produced in a procedurally correct way, since what is appealed to in such a procedure will already reflect a great many shared assumptions about the details of such deliberation, and these details, as Habermas himself admits, always are presupposed in and decisively direct any such dialogic deliberation.[48]

---

46 Cf. the discussion in Thomas McCarthy, "Rationalism and Relativism," in *Habermas: Critical Debates*, ed. by John B. Thompson and David Held (Cambridge: MIT Press, 1982), pp. 57–78.

47 For similar problems in the relation between Habermas's and Hegel's understanding of (in essence) the "dialectic of universal and particular," see the concluding remarks in the discussion by Frederick Olafson, "Habermas as a Philosopher," *Ethics*, 100, no. 4 (1990): 641–57.

48 This introduces another large, controversial topic in Hegel studies. The locus classicus of the discussion is Hegel's account of the "logic" of "civil society." At issue are the nature of the "universality" and so the legitimacy of the major economic institution of civil society. Such institutions claim to be universal by not being committed to any of the quite various

If this Habermasean picture could be made more concrete, and such shared assumptions could also be viewed as the cumulative result of some idealized process of collective deliberation, then much of what Habermas wants to say would be preserved. But these are the considerations, I can only suggest here, that led Hegel to a view of a "collective" or "already shared" subjectivity (*Geist*).[49] For Hegel, in other words, the presuppositions embedded in what Habermas calls the "life-world" cannot simply be viewed as "material" for rationalization, to be subject to challenge and deliberation. The norms embedded in such practices are necessarily involved in the practices of challenge and deliberation themselves, however "procedurally rational."

Habermas would clearly be concered about being forced into such substantive issues, into a distinctly philosophic reconstruction and assessment of the "history of spirit." The Hegelian spirit of the preceding objections, he would claim, implies a retreat to "metaphysics," an unwarranted teleological view of history, and a philosophic pretension to arbitrate from on high claims about the good life in modernity. Habermas has professed himself deeply skeptical "in the face of so many failed attempts to have one's cake

individual ends pursued by individuals, who are all presumed to be the ultimate origin of such ends in acts of "free choice." For Hegel this results in a merely "formal" and so empty universality, a mere coordination and so a kind of *replication* of such ends, rather than the achievement of something he calls the "concrete universal," a universal achieved not by abstracting from content, but by possessing a universal content. Although it has never been clear what this means, it is clear that and why Hegel would regard Habermas's proposals as such a typical replication of the *aporiai* of civil society.

Although Seyla Benhabib's discussion of Habermas, in *Critique, Norm and Utopia*, makes use of Habermas's own account of the "philosophy of the subject" (applied against his own project), and although I am disputing the usefulness of that framework in interpreting Hegel, there are obvious similarities between her criticisms of Habermas and those raised here. In my view, however, that problematic framework prevents her from adequately grounding the introduction of more substantive ethical concerns ("needs," concrete others, and so on); or, once Kant's position is rejected, and a Kantian view of the prior tradition accepted, the post-Kantian choices come down to, for all its difficulties, Hegel's narrative account of rationality, or, for want of a better label, Nietzsche.

49 Habermas himself links the formation of individual identity with "collective identity," something that, in the modern world, requires a very great "flexibility" in one's reflection on one's needs and desires, and that can be increasingly problematic, given the "cultural impoverishment" resulting from the intrusion of system on life-world. The question that emerges from a comparison with Hegel on this issue concerns the nature of this link between individual and collective identity, whether the individual constantly "reflects" on his or her "identity" under a kind of "pressure" to reach "agreement" with others, or whether the terms of such reflection must already reflect a shared social idea, where Habermas overstates the possibility of individual self-determination. See, inter alia, "Historical Materialism and the Development of Normative Structures," in *Communication and the Evolution of Society*, pp. 95–129.

and eat it too: to retain both Kant's insights and, at the same time, to return us to the 'home' from which these same insights have driven us."[50] But this skepticism, I have argued, is based on a traditional and very questionable reading of Hegel, one fashioned in the early "left–right" Hegel wars, and insensitive to the radicality of Hegel's modernism. In the view I have sketched here and defended more fully elsewhere, Hegel's position does not depend on the metaphysics of absolute spirit or a theodocical philosophy of history, and, more importantly, without invoking something like a Hegelian or narrative assessment of modernity and its implications, Habermas himself cannot defend a *critical* theory of modernity.

Of course it does not follow that such a detailed account can be given, that a narrative history of contemporary institutions and practices can defend a claim about the "historically sufficient" rationality of those institutions. If Hegel was wrong about the potential of Western political history and so especially wrong about the ethical status of the state, it may be that there is no more successful account, that there just are no "traces of reason"[51] to detect or reconstruct in such institutions. But this sort of account of the contemporary family, or market economy, or mass culture, or international relations, or a contemporary "Hegelian ethics" can at least be put on the philosophic agenda and given a run for its money without fear of the "philosophy of consciousness" or Cosmic Spirit metaphysics.

And doing so is potentially important in many contemporary contexts. In the later work of Rawls and Habermas, on the one hand, and throughout Foucault's career on the other, one can detect a common realization that many standard, long accepted strategies for justifying or legitimating modern institutions already presuppose much of the modern, Western European sensibility. This fact then either can serve as a kind of genealogical weapon, revealing the utter contingency of such institutions, the utter con-

50 Habermas, "Questions and Counterquestions," p. 211. Habermas is responding here to remarks in Thomas McCarthy's article, "Reflections on Rationalization in *The Theory of Communicative Activity*," in Bernstein, *Habermas and Modernity*, pp. 176–91. McCarthy had suggested that Habermas's acceptenace of an exclusively scientific view of the natural world could be supplemented without a retreat to metaphysics, as in the account given by Kant of teleology in the *Critique of Judgment*. My suggestion is that we do not need such a supplement, a new account of "man's place in the cosmos," as we do an account of the scientific attitude, or any view of the cosmos, as themselves results of a historically self-determining, collective subjectivity. That is the "whole," from the Hegelian perspective I am sketching, and investigating it would help us see something of the origin of the modern "self-differentiation" into radically different "value spheres," something Habermas has no account of.

51 "Spuren der Vernunft," Rüdiger Bubner's phrase in "What Is Critical Theory?"

tingency of modernity, and so their lack of legitimacy, or can push the question of legitimacy and justification back to a deeper level, to the vast question of the legitimacy of modernity itself.[52] My claim has been that Hegel, "the first philosopher . . . for whom modernity became a problem,"[53] is not merely a historical source or origin for such a discussion, but ought to be counted the most important participant in the "discourse of modernity" that Habermas and others have recently thrown open for discussion yet again.

52   I have attempted to provide a broader account of the relation between the German Idealist version of the "modernity problem" and similar issues in literature, art, social modernization, and the "postmodernity" discussion in *Modernism as a Philosophical Problem: On the Dissatisfactions of European High Culture* (Oxford: Basil Blackwell, 1991).
53   Habermas, *Philosophical Discourse of Modernity*, p. 43.

7

TECHNOLOGY AS IDEOLOGY: PROSPECTS

I. Technology as a Political Problem

It is an undeniable fact that a central feature in the history of Western modernization has been an ever increasing reliance on technology in the production of goods, in services, information processing, communication, education, health care, and public administration. This reliance was anticipated and enthusiastically embraced by the early founders of modernity (Bacon and Descartes, especially), and finally (much later than they would have predicted) became a reality in the latter half of the nineteenth century. Moreover, increasing technological power proved an especially valuable asset in liberal democratic societies. The great surplus wealth made possible by such power appeared to allow a more egalitarian society, even if great inequalities persisted; representatives of such technical power could exhibit, publicly demonstrate and so justify their power in ways more compatible with democratic notions of accountability; and a growing belief in the "system" of production and distribution as itself the possible object of technical expertise seemed to make possible the promise of a great collective benefit, given proper "management," arising from the individual pursuit of self-interest promoted by market economies.

Since that time such an increasing dependence on technology has been perceived to create a number of straightforwardly political problems and publicly recognized controversies. Commentators came to see that this reliance also had certain social costs, created difficult ethical problems, and began to alter the general framework within which political discussions took place. Such problems included the following:

(i) A greater and greater *concentration of a new sort of social power* in fewer and fewer hands. At least within democratic societies, such a concentration of power might easily become inconsistent with the ideal of democratic control of socially relevant decision making. As noted, although there are deep compatibilities between democratic values and such scientific canons as the public demonstrability of knowledge claims and the public benefits of the ends to which technology can be employed (e.g., public health, agricultural planning, communication), it is also true that the rise of expert elites posed a certain sort of threat. With the growing sophistication of science and technology, and the difficulties encountered by a lay public in understanding evidence, demonstrations, and the ambiguities and risks inherent in the pursuit of any end, such elites grow progressively less accountable in traditional ways for the exercise of their power, shielded as they are by the claim to greater technical competence.

(ii) A simultaneous and connected *de-skilling* of the labor force through automation, and more rigid, hierarchical forms of technically efficient administration. In such cases the imperatives generated by competition can promote an increased acceptance of technically efficient monitoring techniques (e.g., typists on centralized computers, whose backspace or delete key usage is closely monitored, and who thus can be held accountable not only for what they do, but what they could have done, or the zealous monitoring that the phone company exercises over its operators), job simplification, greater risks to worker safety resulting from conformity to more efficient machines, and a variety of organizational strategies, all relatively inconsistent with basic post-Enlightenment ideals of self-respect, dignity, and autonomy.

(iii) A connected and much noted phenomenon exhibited by writers like Arendt and Habermas: a narrowing of acceptable topics for "public debate," thanks to a greater emphasis on policy issues as technical issues.[1] This amounts to the *depoliticizing of public life*, such that much political debate becomes merely a war among competing experts, or an exercise in the manipulation of symbols, a wholly theatrical celebra-

---

1 Cf. Hannah Arendt, *The Human Condition* (Chicago: University of Chicago Press, 1958); Jürgen Habermas, *Strukturwandel der Öffentlichkeit* (Berlin: Leuchterhand, 1962).

tion of rival images and icons, all rather than a collective and substantive deliberation about a common societal direction.

(iv) A simple increase in the *extent of administrative power* over aspects of daily life. Foucault's claims for micropower and biopower are relevant here, and the simply massive character of the kind of power made possible by data storage in medicine, government, banking, insurance, et cetera.[2] A worrisome example to many recently has been the project to map the human genome. Armed with this information and new diagnostic techniques, eventually it may be possible for, say, insurance companies or potential employers to predict from a simple blood test, with some reliability, the chances that an individual will get a stroke, coronary disease, whether he smokes or drinks too much, or even, perhaps, eventually, whether he suffers too much stress, or is too neurotic or too unsociable, and so forth.

(v) An extraordinary new role for science and technology in *national security issues*, requiring diversion of vast resources to ever more expensive weapons research, a diversion that has seriously and perhaps permanently derailed hopes for welfare state capitalism.

(vi) Cultural complaints that the "technological tail" was beginning to wag the "human dog"; that too many areas of daily life were being modified to meet *the needs of technical efficiency:* complaints, for example, about being reduced to a number, about having to talk to answering or voice mail machines instead of people; excessively technological and so "dehumanized" environments for birth, illness, death; or complaints about the medicalization of mental health issues.

II. Technology as an Ideological Problem

Often such topics are discussed within some sort of cost–benefit framework and under the assumption of a kind of technological fatalism, that the clear efficiency of a reliance on technology makes such continuing or ever growing reliance more or less inevitable, or at least unproblematically rational. Amelioration of the social costs, and exploration of options with respect to ethical dilemmas, could, under such assumptions, only occur marginally, as a kind of moral hope, and only after the technological imperative had been basically satisfied (a situation especially obvious in a climate of worry about international competitiveness).

---

2 .Cf., inter alia, the essays in Michel Foucault, *Power/Knowledge: Selected Interviews and Other Writings*, ed. by C. Gordon (New York: Pantheon, 1980).

A more radical critique can be detected in those who understand technology itself as a kind of *ideology*. This notion is both a complex and a vague category, and its usefulness has suffered a great deal from an increasing use of the term to mean simply a philosophy or belief. But, as a critical concept, the notion was made possible by the Kantian revolution in philosophy and its central claim that there could be "forms" or "conditions" of experience not themselves derived from experience, but "constitutive" of the very possibility of experience. It was this notion of a priori constraints on empirical experience or, more broadly, belief formation, that set the stage for Hegel's historicization of these categories, Marx's social theory, and Lukács's use of the notion of "reification" in a full-blown "ideology critique."[3]

Within this tradition, a form of consciousness, or a general, comprehensive categorization of experience, can be ideological in any number of senses.[4] Ideological claims can be claims about the nature of reality, the significance of a social practice, the origin and legitimacy of an institution, the authority of a moral code, or many other sorts of things. To claim that any such general, fundamental orientation to the world is ideological means not only that some interconnected set of propositions about nature, others, or the cosmos is false, unsupported by evidence or argument, unproved or irrationally believed, but that such an orientation or form of consciousness somehow *prevents*, renders even unnoticeable, contrary evidence or argument. Consciousness itself, the way we originally take up and make sense of things, can be "false." (Of course, this resistance to criticism is not something constructed consciously and strategically, and so the question of whether there could be, or why there should be, this *sort* of blindness, rather than just mistaken, overly optimistic, or ethically inappropriate world views, is an important one for *Ideologiekritik*.)

It is controversial whether there are or ever have been "forms of consciousness" with these characteristics, but the notion, especially when applied to some sorts of religious or moral views, is, prima facie, plausible, and has also played a major role in deflationary critiques of technology (or technological rationality, or technological "promise"). (Nineteenth-century

---

3 Cf. the historical account in Norman Stockman, *Antipositivist Theories of the Sciences* (Dordrecht: Reidel, 1983), sect. 3.2, "Critical Theory's Critique of Positivism: The Kantian Background," pp. 43–51. Stockman's account should be supplemented by additional attention to the role of Lukács. See Andrew Feenberg, *Lukács, Marx and the Sources of Critical Theory* (Oxford: Oxford University Press, 1981).

4 See the three types of "pejorative" ideology critiques identified by Raymond Geuss in *The Idea of a Critical Theory: Habermas and the Frankfurt School* (Cambridge: Cambridge University Press, 1981), p. 13.

accounts of religion are probably the most familiar version of this sort of critique: Religious practices cannot be successfully explained by reducing religious propositions to unsupported empirical claims, motivated by compelling psychological states. Such practices could come to have the significance they do only within a certain context, one wherein human power over nature is required but unavailable, producing a projection of such aspirations onto a humanlike agent whose vast powers can be appealed to in support of human causes. The increase in real power thus helps explain the diminishing significance of religion in modernity, and so forth.) For the technology issue the question thus is, Has our "relation to objects" been so influenced by technical instruments, the power of manipulation and production, and so on, that our basic sense of the natural world has changed and changed so fundamentally that our reflective ability to assess and challenge such a change is threatened? Has our understanding of others and of social and political life become so shaped by technical imperatives in production, consumption, social organization, daily life, and politics that fundamental possibilities for social existence are seen only (in a "distorted," narrow sense) in terms of such technical imperatives?

Thus, in general, "ideology critics" are more interested in what is *undiscussed* in the modern experience of technology, what an extensive reliance on technology, which often is presented as a value-neutral tool, itself already hides, distorts, renders impossible to discuss as an option. To see technology as an ideology is to see an extensive social reliance on technology and the extensive "mediating" influence of technology in daily life, as already embodying some sort of "false consciousness": again, a way of looking at things not characterizable as simply a matter of false or problematic or narrow beliefs. And this means that such reliance reaches a point where what ought to be understood as contingent, an option among others, open to political discussion, is instead falsely understood as necessary (i.e., the relevant options are not rejected; they are not noted as credible options; hence the "false consciousness"); what serves particular interests is seen, without reflection, as of universal interest; what is a contingent, historical experience is regarded as natural; what ought to be a part is experienced as the whole; and so on.

III. The Classical Positions and the Classical Problems

This is all a large and much discussed issue, but in order to make the point I am interested in, I shall need to survey the general terrain from a fairly high altitude, and very quickly. I want first to set out briefly some typical sorts of claims that "technology is ideology," and some of the problems generated by such claims, before first introducing a general objection, and then focusing on one of the most influential recent arguments, Habermas's.

I begin with the most complex view, and one that does not use, and would deliberately avoid, all the notions of ideology critique, Heidegger's. Famously, Heidegger claims that technology embodies an "orientation to Being," and is "ideological" in the sense that, in such an orientation, Being is "forgotten." He claims that modernity itself is "consummated" or "completed" by a technological "en-framing" (*Ge-stell*), that technology exemplifies an understanding of Being, an absolutely fundamental orientation, that completes modern subjectivism and thoughtlessness.[5] (Technology is a "world view," or pre-theoretical "horizoning" of experience, a view also roughly maintained by Ellul.)[6]

Several commentators have objected to Heidegger's explanation of the "predatory" stance of the modern subject by appeal to an obscure "history of Being," in which, it appears, Being itself is responsible for its own obscuring or for our forgetting Being. Others dispute the way he dates modernity (as originating in Plato), or complain about the ambiguous practical consequences of his critique of modernity. My own view is that the central problem with Heidegger's approach is that the way it addresses the basic historical questions at issue is undialectical and even a bit moralistic. For him, the appeal of the modern emphasis on power, control, and the priority of the self-defining subject seems to be due to a kind of human *hubris*, a self-assertion that often sounds more like a theological account of the fall than a historical explanation. The possibility that the basic ontological dimension embodied in a technological world view (the subject–object split) could have been *provoked* historically, or was required in some sense, given the unavoidable and genuine deficiencies and dead ends created by the pre-modern tradition (understood in its own rather than later terms), is not considered by him.

To be sure, he has his own, infinitely complicated reasons for this neglect, having to do with his own understanding of the history of being, and how such a history, and his (Heidegger's) own role in the destruction of Western

5 This sort of theme appears in many of Heidegger's later writings, but I shall treat as typical such essays as "The Age of the World Picture," "The Word of Nietzsche: God Is Dead," and "The Turning," in *The Question Concerning Technology and Other Essays* (New York: Harper & Row, 1977), and the concluding lectures in the Nietzsche series, *Nietzsche*, IV, *Nihilism*, trans. by Frank A. Capuzzi (San Francisco: Harper & Row, 1982).

6 Jacques Ellul, *The Technological Society*, trans. J. Neugroschel (New York: Continuum, 1980).

metaphysics, play roles in the origin of modernity. But I simply note that his own position requires a historical narrative that has been, rightly, I think, the subject of much attack. (I have attempted a fuller assessment of Heidegger's position elsewhere.)[7]

I should also note that Heidegger's approach also ought to remind us of very speculative claims much discussed recently: that the modern fixation on technological power is not uniquely modern or a distortion of anything, but some sort of culmination of the deep connection between all knowledge and "the will to power" or a final revelation of the nature of power–knowledge (*pouvoir–savoir*).[8] These Nietzschean and Foucaultean themes, although continuous with Heidegger's approach, in some ways go much further than Heidegger, who always seems to want to preserve a contrast between the modern "age of the world picture" and some possible alternative. These approaches also raise their own famous questions about what sort of critique or critical knowledge is possible under such assumptions, but that would introduce in this context a major digression.

To return to positions more traditionally identified within the "ideology critique" tradition, we should recall the original Marxist attack: that the capitalist claim for its own "rationality," understood as technical efficiency, is ideological.

Marx focuses on the organization of production under liberal or so-called free market capitalism. What are asserted to be the imperatives of technical efficiency are "functionally" ideological in Geuss's sense. The claim for the efficiency of the capitalist organization of technology is only temporarily true. When maintained beyond the early phase of capitalism, such claims become a "socially necessary illusion," functioning to mask social contradictions, actually to impede the development of the forces of production and even greater technical efficiency, and to stabilize and sustain forces of domination that could not be sustained without such illusions.[9]

---

7 Robert B. Pippin, *Modernism as a Philosophical Problem: On the Dissatisfactions of European High Culture* (Oxford: Basil Blackwell, 1991), pp. 117–47.

8 See the references in note 2, and the useful discussion in David Hoy, "Power, Repression, Progress: Foucault, Lukes, and the Frankfurt School," in *Foucault: A Critical Reader* (Oxford: Basil Blackwell, 1986), pp. 123–48.

9 For representative passages, see Karl Marx, *Capital*, trans. Samuel Moore and Edward Aveling, ed. by F. Engels (New York: International Publishers, 1977), pp. 312–507; vol. I, pt. 4, "Production of Relative Surplus Value," especially ch. 15, "Machinery and Modern Industry." For the contrast between production under capitalism and after, see *Grundrisse*, trans. Martin Nicolaus (New York: Vintage, 1973), p. 488.

This position has been most often criticized for its historical limitation to the liberal phase of capitalism. With the onset of state intervention in and management of the economy, ideology critique could no longer be a critique of political economy alone. (There was no such thing anymore as "the economy" operating under its own laws. Or the model of a "base" supporting and, by virtue of its autonomous development, straining against, then being constrained by, superstructure, has been eclipsed with the arrival of welfare or state-interventionist capitalism.)

Second, the idea that the growth of productive forces is itself, inherently, emancipatory, or helps expose the ideological character of the justification for historically outmoded relations of production, has been rendered obsolete. The main contribution to growth in the forces of production now comes *from* science and technology, designed and implemented *by* managers and bureaucrats. Adherence to the imperatives of technical efficiency now helps legitimate the entire self-regulating social system.

Third, this notion of system now seems more relevant to social analysis than traditional class conflict notions. Genuine, clear-cut oppositions between class interests are now rarer. Allegiances are secured through a complex and efficient system of rewards and leisure time, and all perceive themselves to be helping to operate a system of benefit to all, rather than serving the interests of a discrete, identifiable group of others. This means, for someone like Habermas, that reflection can identify an emancipatory interest distorted or repressed in such a system, only as a *species interest,* as an interest of humanity, denied or regulated by such systematic imperatives. (Again, he wants to replace the class conflict and forces–relations of production model with what he calls a "work-interaction" model.)

Finally, the basic charge of suboptimization can be met on its own terms in later capitalism. State capitalism can easily claim to have solved that problem and to have regulated the cycles of early capitalism far more efficiently than other available historical models (certainly better than command economies).

In a radical extension of the scope of ideology critique, Horkheimer and Adorno connect the problem of technology to the "dialectic of enlightenment" in modernity in general, and so connect the mastery of nature to the mastery of others, and an attempted legitimation of domination, control, and psychological repression that, they maintain, is ultimately self-undermining and delegitimating.[10] The most well known form of such a

10 Max Horkheimer and Theodore Adorno, *The Dialectic of Enlightenment* (New York: Seabury, 1972).

critique (despite many differences) became Marcuse's attack in *One-Dimensional Man.*[11]

In the account given by Horkheimer and Adorno in *The Dialectic of Enlightenment*, the prevalence of technology in modernity should be understood as a central aspect of the "positivity" or "identity thinking" characteristic of the Enlightenment scientific revolution itself, characteristic, even, of the appeal to rationality throughout the Western tradition. Whereas Marx had understood science and technology as progressive forces, helping to create the material conditions for capitalism's self-overcoming, Lukács was the first to charge that science and technology also assume ideological functions in capitalism, contributing to an ideological distortion he called "reification." Horkheimer and Adorno (to a large extent developing a Nietzschean theme) radically extend this sort of critique.

What poses in modernity as a rationally enlightened attack on superstition, mythic consciousness, religion, and feudal social practices is presented by them as not only narrowing the arena of rational discourse (with great psychic costs, as in their studies of fascism), but as constituting a form of thought incapable of, and deeply resistant to, self-critique, and a way of linking rationality in the natural sciences and social sphere with total control and predictability, in a manner that again cannot assess or reflect on the ends served by such control. Incapable of such deeper reflection the Enlightenment thus itself becomes a myth or ideology, a promotion of control or power for its own sake, to the point of pathology. (Moreover, Horkheimer and Adorno especially do not treat this connection between rationality and domination as a historical phenomenon peculiar to capitalism and the predominance of the commodity form of labor power, as Lukács does. It seems to them characteristic of all attempts at integrative rationality, as visible in the Odysseus and Sirens story as in Faust.[12] This will mean that the critical contrast with such objectification and domination will have to be a rather romantic notion of "the natural" and a proposed reconciliation with nature that is, in Kantian terms, pre-critical.)[13]

Moreover, especially in Marcuse's account, such an ideology is far more

---

11 Herbert Marcuse, *One-Dimensional Man* (Boston: Beacon Press, 1964).

12 Cf. Max Horkheimer, *Eclipse of Reason* (New York: Seabury, 1974), p. 176.

13 This is, of course, not true of the position developed by Adorno in *Negative Dialectics*, but that is a longer story. See my discussion in *Modernism as a Philosophical Problem*, pp. 151–6, and Habermas's statement of his differences with the Horkheimer–Adorno approach in *The Theory of Communicative Action*, trans. T. McCarthy (Boston: Beacon Press, 1984), I, IV.2, "The Critique of Instrumental Reason," pp. 366–99; and in *The Philosophical Discourse of Modernity*, trans. F. Lawrence (Cambridge: MIT Press, 1987), ch. 5, pp. 106–30.

successfully *integrative* than any previously. Thanks mainly to the culture industry, what previous critics identified as signs of strain and potential contradiction in such integrative programs – the subjective experience of alienation, lack of reconciliation with others or such a system – have been eliminated. Individuals are progressively more reconciled, at a deeper, and more psychologically complex, and perhaps permanent level, to social authority.

There is a famous often-mentioned problem with such accounts. The criticisms vary, depending on one's interpretation of the position, especially the extent to which one takes its proponents to be offering an indictment of the structure of modern scientific method and technology as such. An attack on the modern relation to nature (and others) as essentially a relation of domination presumes that there are alternative models *in* the natural science tradition that could preserve the canons of objectivity, repeatability of experiment, testability of hypotheses, relatively clear confirmation relations between observation and theory, and so forth, but that did not embody the relation of domination. It presumes as well a model of technology not wedded to the notion of mastery of nature. It is not at all clear what a new science or new technology would be like.[14] (It is also not clear to what extent Marcuse is committed to such a notion.)[15] In the case of Horkheimer and especially Adorno, something like this problem produced the wholly "negative" notion of resistance so associated with their program. Simply resisting the transformation of social relations into managed, technically modeled, or bargaining relations, and of natural–aesthetic relations into manipulative, means–ends relations, seems to be touted as an end in itself. And for many such a conclusion reduces resistance to little more than a symbolic gesture.

This is of course not the final story of the approach suggested by Horkheimer, Adorno, and Marcuse. Worthy of note and much attention is a recent book by Andrew Feenberg (*The Critical Theory of Technology*) that attempts to revive some of Marcuse's insights, without the unacceptable utopianism and romanticism it appeared Marcuse was committed to.[16] This involves showing the ways that the *design*, implementation, and organization of technology are historically contingent; that they, at least partly, reflect the interests of "elites" who do the designing and implementing; and that some form of a democratization of the work force can make the best, most just

14 Cf. Stockman, *Antipositivist Theories*, pp.57–64, 240–46.
15 Marcuse, *One-Dimensional Man*, p. 154.
16 Andrew Feenberg, *The Critical Theory of Technology* (Oxford: Oxford University Press, 1991).

social use of the now critically revealed "contingencies" in design and implementation.

None of this, he argues, requires the familiar "trade off" between efficiency and justice sometimes said to be at stake in traditional debates. This approach historicizes the question of technology itself, such that there is no such thing as, simply, "technology," or *the* technological enframing; there is technology designed in a certain social period for various tasks, embodying various ends, organized under certain normative assumptions.

The "critical theory of technology" promoted by Feenberg has a number of virtues. It avoids the limitations of the instrumentalist account of technology (a tool is just a tool, a hammer a hammer whether used in carpentry or in banging a tree trunk in Samoa) and the excesses of the "substantialist" approach, wherein technology embodies a world orientation. To the former it points to the variety of contingent ways a particular technology for a particular purpose was designed, and how important political notions of administrative control and hierarchical principles of organization were inherent in such design. To the latter it makes the same point about contingency, that technologies represent complicated and often contradictory political decisions, even if it is still possible to maintain an essentially human interest in efficiency and productive power.

However, as Feenberg admits, there is no compelling reason to think that any sort of democratization of industrial organization and technology design will simply lead, thereby, to a substantially different form of production. It would certainly make such reform *possible* in ways not now possible; there are good reasons to think that various reforms enhancing autonomy, the chances of being the "subject" rather than the "object" of workplace technology, reforms enhancing interesting, diversified work and in general self-respect, are made much more difficult by the imperatives of power and control and *not* by considerations of efficiency.

But the problem here is deeper and will help introduce the larger problems facing ideology critiques. *Whoever* is in charge of the design and implementation of technology will be an agent deeply socialized in a modern ethos. And it is still not clear that such an ethos possesses the resources to sustain a political and ethical appeal to a reform that may result in a system just as efficient, but more humane and just. The press of the rewards now in place, and the fragmented, often unclear basis of a call to reform and to the social solidarity and sacrifice needed to implement it, may make it too risky an adventure for any modern agent. Democratizing may have a fair but dispiriting result: "relegitimation" rather than reform.

To some extent such a question is an empirical and/or a historical one, and, it seems fair enough to admit, the most a critical analysis can do is to set out the misleading or ideological character of claims about the "necessary" constraints of efficiency, or the "requirements" of technological rationality. But the problem just suggested raises a much larger issue.

IV. *Aporiai* in the "Technology as Ideology" Claim

Although it is true that a massive social reliance on technology can "blind" one to various social, ethical, and even potential "ontological" implications of that reliance, none of the preceding accounts succeeds in identifying what is fundamentally "unthought" in the ever increasing role of technology in modernization, nor what might be the implications of the changing social status of technology (our apparently declining confidence in the autonomy, or the methodological purity, or even the very efficiency of the "purposive rationality" it embodies).

Rather, one needs to understand the original social appeal of potential technological mastery as a central aspect of the *ethos of the modern revolution itself,* a revolution that is not, I have argued elsewhere,[17] essentially a bourgeois, or capitalist, or scientific revolution. To make a very long story very short, in that context, the right sort of doubt to have about the nature of the social and cultural promise of technological mastery is not a doubt about a change in our fundamental ontological orientation, or about who is really and unfairly benefiting from the payoff of the promise, or who is benefiting from ossifying and reifying one stage in the historical development of technology, or whether we are becoming the objects of the forces we were the original subjects of, or whether a form of rationality has been thoughtlessly totalized, or whether technology might have been designed differently, in ways more responsive to the social needs of those who labor, and so forth. These are all important questions in their own right, but they are not, I think, the fundamental one.

If we make a few rather vague, but relatively uncontroversial assumptions (at least for the sake of the present argument), the problem will have to be posed differently. Assume simply that there is some sort of fundamental connection between the original justification of the modern revolution itself and the "mastery of nature" promise so essential to the contemporary influence of technology. To be sure, technological power can assume a different kind of importance in any number of different social situations: early industrialization, nineteenth-century American optimism; totalitarian

17 Pippin, *Modernism as a Philosophical Problem.*

regimes, and so forth. But any very general worry about the relation between technological power and, for example, our understanding of nature, the nature of knowledge, or the possibility of democratic politics (the kind of subjects addressed by "ideology critiques") will require some attention to the uniquely modern understanding of the *necessity for* an ever *expanding* control over the forces of nature. There could have been such a technological orientation, or a supreme political and social significance to technological power, only when such mastery seemed both necessary and possible. And understanding the conditions under which that could occur requires, I shall try to suggest, a different sort of account than is presupposed in the standard versions of ideology critique.

So, by contrast with the modern promotion of mastery,[18] the premodern emphasis on contemplation, the belief that the best regime was a matter of chance rather than human will, the insistence on an accommodation to natural *tele*, the traditional horror at the prospects of mass, collective action, are all assumptions that can effectively be countered only if the likes of Bacon and Descartes can successfully attack and undermine the bases of such claims, and then fulfill the promise of a comprehensive alternative vision, a secure, repeatable "method" capable (according to Descartes) even of challenging God's own words to Adam, and of allowing us to "enjoy without any trouble the fruits of the earth and all good things which are to be found there."[19] Making this assumption simply means that if we want to understand the relative importance of growing technological power in modernity, its significance or meaning for modern societies, we need to understand the centrality of the technological promise to the possibility of a modern *revolution,* and so to the modern rejection of antiquity, and especially to the revolutionary notion that the future can be directed and controlled by human will. (And if this is so, *challenging* the role of technology in modernity, whether in terms of the straightforward political problems

18 I shall be assuming that the modern enterprise does not merely seize the opportunity to *extend* a "natural," species-characteristic interest in the control of nature through labor and tools, but that the early moderns began to reformulate the range of natural events that could be mastered, what could count as such mastery (given the new influence of mathematics, and a new attention to the problem of certainty), what such mastery was *for,* and the relation between such a goal and other desirable social ends. Given such a claim, understanding why such reformulations occurred cannot be answered by appeal to a mere extension of such a species-characteristic interest. I am thus disagreeing with, e.g., Habermas's account. See the following discussion.

19 René Descartes, *Discourse on Method,* in *The Philosophical Works of Descartes,* trans. Elizabeth Haldane and G. R. T. Ross (Cambridge: Cambridge University Press, 1969), I, pp. 119–20. Cf. Genesis 3:17.

noted, or in resistance to the orientation, conception of reason, alienating social relations, or false neutrality charged in ideology critiques, will require a reexamination of, assessment of, and alternative to *that* essentially modern imperative.)

For example, in traditional accounts of the function of the "legislator" or statesman, a common assumption was that one function of those who held political power was to create a common ethical sensibility among citizens. The reproducibility of a society, its ability to rally support and fend off attack, to maintain its identity over time, required an extensive political project, judiciously and wisely administered by leaders and educators with unique talents. Successful individual *self-mastery* for the citizenry was assumed to be a primary goal of political (or politico-religious) life.

One way of asking about the emergence of the technological imperative is simply to ask about the fate of such a goal when: (i) under the influence of Machiavelli, among others, such a policy comes to be seen as wildly utopian, when political history itself reveals which (usually base) passions always guide human action, no matter the motives we would like or hope would be determinative; or (ii) under the influence of Hobbes, the authority of the legislator's claims to "know" what virtues, or manifestations of self-mastery, are most important to promote, is challenged, when a devastating epistemological attack on the foundations of traditional politico-religious authority is mounted.

Under such conditions, political life or collective action in general, might come to look either impossible, or possible only under radically altered expectations. The successful mastery of nature might finally make possible our being able to face the fact that a trustworthy self-mastery is simply impossible. "Unredeemed," hedonistic agents might, though, still be able to secure common goods, as long as we (i) change our expectations about those securable goods (health, security, freedom from want, the chance for a commodious life), (ii) (and this is the absolutely crucial claim) are able to produce enough surplus to be able to appeal to such interests (the *only* reliable social "glue" cementing us together) and be able to "pay off," and (iii) if we assume that our legislator need not transform or ethically educate the souls of the citizens, but can just efficiently calculate what they will do, and so "manage" well rather than "rule." The possibility of modern democracy, under the assumption that human beings are egoistic, passion-satisfying engines, would thus depend *essentially* on a qualitatively improved, "world-historical" leap in technological power. And, as often noted, if the technology of management is sophisticated enough, we might eventually not only come to expect and rely on such an egoistic, hedonistic conception of agents, but promote and energetically encourage such activity, under the now familiar "private vices–public benefits" formula. (Or, ironically, an energetic technological optimism is required precisely because of a kind of philosophical pessimism, a great reduction in expectation about what sort of "guidance" philosophy might provide.)

Stated a different, broader way, we need to note that the kind of technical power that could make possible such a new politics is itself dependent on the successful promotion of a distinct, new sort of social ethos. In the most famous and disturbing case, the productive power necessary to generate the surplus that would make modern politics possible requires a culture of consumption and acquisition, indeed a culture of ever expanding, ever more "stimulated" consumerism. In such a context, the questions of who *controls* the productive capacity, how its surplus is *distributed,* who *designs* the technology, and so forth, although all important issues, do not touch the fundamental problem. The links in the modernization process have to be taken in all at once: (i) The collapse of the premodern understanding of the connection between individual virtue and public life itself leads directly and unavoidably to (ii) the emergence of the altered modern expectations about the narrow possibility of peaceful, coordinated activity, which in turn requires (iii) new, greatly expanded technological power, itself dependent on (iv) a socialization process, the "production of demand," that will itself decisively influence and constrain all modern political life. Once we understand the way in which the modern rejection of premodern politics was itself provoked by intellectual and social crises, an absolutely fundamental connection between such politics and productive or technological power, together with the "virtues" necessary to sustain it, comes into view, and appears permanently to "frame" any possible account of the significance of any new steering or distribution program for the productive forces.

In this sense, the proper question of technology would be the question of modernity itself: Is a distinctly modern epoch, one characterized by a radical attempt at a break with these sorts of traditional views, and by the attempt to achieve true collective self-determination, possible? Without such an enterprise, however diverse and hard to characterize, there could have been no *centrality* to technological power in modern life.

By contrast, ideology critique seems inevitably linked either to some controversial account of origins (agents' *true interests,* hidden until "reflection" exposes them), or, as we shall see shortly, to the notion of a sort of structural encroachment by one domain or "world" over another. The historical–social formation *of those interests,* especially the interest in autonomy; the control of destiny and of one's own body (originally but not exclusively embodied by property owners); and the historical sources for the growth of such "domains" (especially the historical reasons for the collapse of traditional, teleological world views; the emergence of "instrumentalist" models as the only publicly defensible notion of rationality), are, I want to claim, different and more important issues.

Or: the right metaphor for understanding the extraordinary and potentially distorting appeal of technological power in modernity is not a hunt for hidden origins, or a delineation of geographical boundaries, but attention to the *context*, the historical moment when mastery in general would have seemed, with some historical urgency, an unavoidable desideratum. If, I want to claim, we can understand the rising importance of technological mastery in such a broader context, we will be less inclined to see that rise as some sort of Faustian bargain, prompted by hubris, narrow class interest, confusion about different domains of rationality, or as a lust for power. Ideology critique tends toward such explanations of *why* what is now claimed to be hidden or unnoticed became hidden or unnoticed, and, although I cannot demonstrate the claim here, I want at least to suggest that such interpretations are implausible.

Still more simply put, the modern claim that the highest, publicly defensible good is a technically efficient mastery of nature, with all its implications for social organization, ethical relations, and public life, may be, in both historical and general terms, *rational*. Modern agents may not be confused by the implications of the "philosophy of the subject"; their preferences may not have been wholly formed in a situation distorted by the influence of money and power; they may not have confused the ends of work and those of interaction; they may not be falsely universalizing or naturalizing a particular historical epoch. At least we should not beg any questions in making such claims, and that will require the broader assessment I am suggesting, an assessment of the resources *within modernity* for understanding the possible narrowness of such a conception of a rational end, and the exclusion of others.

Such a broader view will also permit a more adequate understanding of the implications of the shifting social status of science and technology away from a privileged center, under the weight of various historicist, sociological, naturalist, and other critiques, something not well understood in the rather jejune contemporary fascination with a possible postmodernism.

All of which seems to raise the stakes for understanding the role of science and technology in modern life to an unsatisfiable level (the old Hegelian "You've got to understand everything to understand anything" problem). In order to motivate this way of looking at things, I want at least to defend the claim about the limitations of the ideological approach and hope the alternative I have in mind will begin to emerge. My example will be Habermas's well-known argument.

V. Habermas on Technology as Ideology

According to Habermas's famous account, the great problem with technological modernization has little to do with technology itself, but with the way in which the influence, scope, and success of technology in modern life have tended to authorize only "purposive" or instrumental and strategic notions of *rationality*, and to delegitimate (as unresolvable and subjective) genuinely practical or political questions.[20] The imperatives of "work," rational if efficient, efficient if productive, and "interaction," rational if the norms of successful, genuine communication are realized, have become confused, and the specific form of rationality inherent in communicative action has been overwhelmed by the demands of technical efficiency. The "life-world" has been "colonized," "steered," or encroached on by the demands of a self-regulating system.

This critique, according to which it is the totalization of the instrumental notion of rationality, its absorbing the categorially distinct forms of communicative rationality, that renders science and technology ideological, appears a sensible response to the historical limitations of Marx's original account, and appropriately cognizant of the undeniable benefits of technological power over nature and our own fate.

The account is largely motivated by a critical appropriation of Max Weber's original account of modernization as the progressive rationalization and so demystification of various spheres or subsystems of modern life. On this account control "from above," legitimated by appeal to cultural, religious, and mythic world views, constrains the development of purposive rationality in various spheres of life. The efficient satisfaction of basic needs, creation of surplus and so leisure and luxury, and so forth, are all impeded by such cultural (and basically irrational) constraints. This begins to change with capitalism and the creation of a purposive–rational system that demands its own continual expansion. Under the growing pressure of such expansion, traditional world views are transformed into private beliefs, incapable of functioning as universal or culturally stable forms of social author-

20 Especially in Jürgen Habermas, "Technology and Science as Ideology," in *Toward a Rational Society*, trans. J. Shapiro (Boston: Beacon Press, 1970) and in *The Theory of Communicative Action* II, trans. T. McCarthy (Boston: Beacon Press, 1987).

ity, and the legitimacy of the capitalist claim to productive efficiency and universal satisfaction of interests wins out in a kind of competition for social power. The West is modernized.

This success, however, a real advance when measured against "the systematically distorted communication" and the "fateful causality of dissociated symbols and suppressed motives" of premodern forms of communicative interaction, becomes itself repressive and ideological when it prevents any *reestablishment* of a genuinely interactive life among modern subjects, which is what Habermas claims happens, and why he claims this role for science and technology (in its presumption to be definitive of rationality as such) is ideological.

Habermas's approach generates the following problems, all of which return us to the general issues about modernization raised: First, Habermas does not treat the extraordinary acceleration of technological progress in modernity or the modern reliance on technology as unique historical phenomena. Following Gehlen, he interprets this as an extension of the basic structure of all human purposive–rational action. We are simply getting much better at "aiding" homo faber in what he has always been interested in doing: moving about better, seeing and hearing better, producing and regulating energy, governing our actions more efficiently, and so on. Work is a permanent, constitutive "human interest."[21]

But this claim leaves unanswered the question, *Why* (to use Habermas's language) work, or the imperatives of purposive–rational activity, became so much *more extraordinarily important* in the modern age; why the ideal of mastery began to occupy a qualitatively different position on the social agenda.[22] In terms of Descartes's rhetoric: We need to know why (rather suddenly in historical terms) we should have turned so *much* of our energy to the "mastery of nature." That image suggests not merely an *extension* of our human interest in successful purposive action. Even viewed within the domain of work, of being able to get done what we want to get done (ignoring for the moment whether this involves a wholesale new relation to nature, or world orientation, or understanding of Being), this image suggests a kind of urgency, a situation of insecurity requiring a military assault against an *enemy*, all not captured in Habermas's account.[23]

---

21 Habermas, "Technology and Science as Ideology," p. 87.

22 Cf., for example, his account of how "pressure" from the development of productive forces brings about, as if by hydraulic force, the end of traditional societies, ibid., p. 96.

23 Contrast the different account of the significance and unique characteristics of labor in the modern world in Arendt, *Human Condition*, ch. 3.

Second, Habermas supplements Weber's account of rationalization with his own picture of the competing requirements of work and communicative or interactive activity. He suggests a theory of modernity in which the premodern standards of communicative interaction, since they were prejudiced, distorted, products of repression, and so forth, "gave way" under the press of the successful expansion of productive capacity and the purposive–rational standards of rationality that go with it. It is unclear whether this account is limited to certain social and economic aspects of modernization or is meant to identify the basic origin of modernization. The latter is suggested by the frequent references to Weber, and to the larger intellectual, philosophical, and religious issues supposedly called into question by the "expansion" of purposive standards of rationality into numerous subsystems.

Such an account, in the first place, downplays the philosophical crisis brewing in the tradition since nominalism. It would be hard to understand why the *promotion* of utility, our development of interest in becoming "masters and possessors of nature," should have displaced the notion of knowledge as contemplation, or explored an account of knowledge (the "new way of ideas") subject to methodological rigor and control, unless such a philosophical tradition is taken into account.[24] For example, the importance of developments in technology could not possibly have risen to such a high spot on the social agenda without the essentially modern view that the source of most if not all human misery was *scarcity* (a new and quite controversial claim) and that scarcity was a solvable technical problem, nor without a new notion of "knowing as making," inspired by developments in mathematics.[25] The simple emergence of a new, more optimistic view of how much of the basic scarcity problem could be technically resolved would not be a deeply significant discovery had the classical view still held sway: that the central political problem is an unimprovable finitude; a basic, permanent distinction between the few and the many; and the unpredictable, wholly contingent congruence of wisdom and political power.

And the metaphor of one view pressing on or pushing aside another is not very persuasive. We need an account and an assessment of such a new

24 Among the many studies of this complicated intellectual development, see Hans Blumenberg, *The Legitimacy of the Modern Age,* trans. Robert Wallace (Cambridge: MIT Press, 1983), and Amos Funkenstein, *Theology and the Scientific Imagination from the Middle Ages to the Seventeenth Century* (Princeton: Princeton University Press, 1986). See also Chapter 10, this volume, and ch. 2 of *Modernism as a Philosophical Problem.*
25 Cf. the account in David Lachterman, *The Ethics of Geometry: A Genealogy of Modernity* (New York: Routledge, 1989).

view of the basic problem. Why did it arise when it did? Was it a rational thing then to believe? For whom? Under what conditions? The general picture that Habermas paints, with one version of rationality in a kind of boundary war with another, does not adequately account for the historical context in which they would have first been seen as competitors, and in which their competition would have been considered significant.[26]

The essential point is this: Without a sufficient understanding of that larger context, we shall be unable to understand the consequences of any sort of acknowledgment of the "limitations" of instrumental rationality. It wouldn't matter if claims about such limitations were based on an attempt to historicize scientific and technological procedure, or on an attempt to question the neutral, universalist pretensions of such procedures (by attention to sociological, psychological, or pragmatic origins), or an attempt to attack the "ideological totalization" of purposive rationality. We shall not be in a position to understand what such limitations amount to without quite a broad view of the historical landscape.

If, for example, what Habermas calls the displacement of practical by technical questions occurred because *any* version of practical politics must appeal to essentially premodern and no longer defensible notions of ends, teleology, nature, and so forth, or can be resolved only by a kind of strategic bargaining among agents with incommensurable goals, then there *are* no significant practical consequences of such claims about limitations. There just *would be no possible agenda* for the practical realm, and a growing lack of confidence in the standard or traditional claims of science and technology to provide unprejudiced or neutral means to satisfy any sort of ends would result only in a *greater* skepticism and social fragmentation, *not* emancipation.

Now Habermas claims in his own voice that there is such an alternative agenda, one based on freeing communication from arbitrarily imposed limits and distortions caused by the interests of money and power, and so promoting an "ideal speech situation." This claim has given rise to objections that Habermas's distinction between purposive and communicative rationality is often arbitrarily drawn. On such a view, Habermas has a curiously positivistic understanding of "science and technology," as if they really are, if restricted to the proper sphere, as squeaky clean methodologically as

26 See the criticisms of Habermas by Axel Honneth in *Kritik der Macht: Reflexionsstufen einer kritischen Gesellschaftstheorie* (Frankfurt am M.: Suhrkamp, 1985), and Chapter 6, this volume.

traditionally maintained.[27] Many recent discussions in philosophy of science, from historical and sociological studies of scientific practice to issues raised by a new generation of scientific realists, have created a number of doubts about the possibility of such boundaries and at the very least raise as a possibility that there is no methodological way to isolate the purposive–rational dimension of science and technology and preserve it safely in its own domain. Admitting that the institution of science, its organization, hierarchy, criteria of success, or criteria of good or central, as opposed to bad or marginal science, et cetera, and the design and implementation of technology, are everywhere *already*, themselves, "symbolically mediated"; that social values interpenetrate at every level, helping to define purposive effectiveness, need not mean we are committed to some contrary or new science. We may just have successfully pointed out the ever "embodied" nature of thought and the severe problems Habermas faces in trying to keep things in their proper boxes.

Habermas faces a similar problem if it can be shown that the significance of the modern emphasis on the form of rationality embodied in science and technology cannot be explained as a result of some sort of contingent (and reversible) displacement of interactive by purposive–rational norms. If there is some more comprehensive historical context within which both the abandonment of traditional value systems and the allegiance to an instrumental notion of rationality could be explained and motivated, then promoting open allegiance to rules of ideal communicative equality, within such a context or whole, might and likely would simply institute a formally fair way of *relegitimating* the substantial anomie, fragmentation, and dissatisfactions of modernity, forcing us, after our freely arrived at and communicatively fair interaction, back to the narrow confines of strategic and instrumental rationality as the best concrete, realizable hope we have for coordination.

Habermas of course disagrees, and thinks, first, that there would be some sort of pragmatic contradiction in a situation where agents, even while conforming to ideal speech conditions, sanctioned instrumental social relations, and power relationships justified only by instrumental efficiency, and, second, that a very great deal in modern social life would change if such an ideal speech situation were achieved. And his account is more sensitive to issues and more nuanced than I have been able to present in this summary. In many ways it remains a powerfully critical approach to many aspects of

27 Cf. Stockman's account, *Antipositivist Theories*, pp. 109–12.

modernization. But I think the basic strategy – the "separate into relevant spheres" approach – does not go deep enough into the modern origins of such original separations, and so leaves too unclear the implications of the Habermasean delimitations.

The most general and now quite familiar way to state these issues would be to say that Habermas and the whole ideology critique tradition remain bound by the Kantian assumptions that made it possible, still wedded to the hope that a formal account of communicative practice, or the conditions of interest formation, or reflexivity in general will provide us with the critical tools necessary to understand modernity. My claim has been, not that such a direction is misguided,[28] but that these issues need to be raised within a broader philosophic framework, one more sensitive to the substantive, historical, and practical issues at stake in the modern revolution itself, and so more responsive to the claim that modernity, and its technological implications, is, finally and decisively, "legitimate"; at the very least, in historical terms, "sufficiently rational."[29]

---

28 Cf. the development of this theme in my "Marcuse on Hegel and Historicity," in *Marcuse: Critical Theory and the Promise of Utopia*, ed. by R. Pippin, A. Feenberg, and C. Webel (London: Macmillan, 1988).

29 I am thinking here of Hans Blumenberg's strategy and terms. See his *Legitimacy of the Modern Age*.

Part Three

GREEKS, GERMANS, AND MODERNS

8

THE MODERN WORLD OF LEO STRAUSS

I

There are a number of very well-known controversies associated with Leo Strauss.[1] However, although arguable, it seems fair enough to claim that it is his complex and multifront attack on the insufficiencies of modernity that stands as his most influential legacy in America, both inside and outside the academy. This probably has something to do with the unique importance of the ideas of Enlightenment, religious tolerance, and scientific optimism in American political life, when compared to the more homogeneous societies of Western Europe. The very possibility and fate of an American nation state are tied deeply to the possibility and fate of Enlightenment modernity, and so Strauss's reflections were bound to find a distinct (and distinctly contentious) audience in the United States.

Moreover, the problem of Strauss's reception has become even more fascinating and confusing in the contemporary American academy. His attacks on the self-satisfaction of post-Enlightenment culture, his doubts about the benefits of technological mastery, about the attempted avoidance

---

1 I mean such things as his theory of esoteric writing; his passionate attack on the political science community, with its "fact-value" distinctions and "historicism"; his partisan support for what appears to be an antiegalitarian political agenda; his unusual, "classical" defense of liberal democracy; and his apparent ability to inspire a sectarian consciousness among followers.

of any public reliance on religion, and about the modern confidence in the power of enlightened self-interest in the formation of a polity, all often delivered in a rhetoric sometimes bordering on biblical prophecy, have now suddenly reappeared, more quietly but insistently, on the agendas of neo-Aristotelians, critical theorists, communitarians, and postmodernists. The literature on the newly rediscovered "problem of modernity," Strauss's central and, until recently, quite neglected problem, could now fill several shelves a year and shows no signs of abating. It has also created a different, and in many ways more receptive context for Strauss's claims. However, in the following I am mostly interested in the philosophical nature of Strauss's basic dissatisfactions with modernity and with the adequacy of his criticisms.

I shall focus attention on his noted "wave hypothesis," his claim that the modern experiment should be understood as occurring in three waves – a great instauration attributed mainly to Hobbes (though built on ground well prepared by Machiavelli),[2] a first "crisis" correctly diagnosed but not solved by Rousseau, and a second crisis, the continuing "crisis of our times," correctly diagnosed and ruthlessly explored by the thinker arguably more influential for Strauss than anyone other than Plato, namely, Nietzsche. In particular, I want to argue that Strauss's interpretation of the second wave (or first crisis) misinterprets and undervalues the alternatives presented by the German thinkers so influenced by Rousseau, the German Idealists, especially Kant, Fichte, and Hegel. Strauss had a number of reasons for the belief that this tradition must eventually result in a self-undermining historicism, one that intensifies rather than resolves the "modern crisis." I

---

2 Strauss's works will be cited as follows, using the abbreviations indicated: "A Giving of Accounts" (*Acc*), *The College* 22 (1970): pp. 1–5; "On Collingwood's Philosophy of History" (*C*), *Review of Metaphysics* 5 (1992): 559–86; *The City and Man* (*CM*) (Chicago: University of Chicago Press, 1964); "Correspondence Concerning Modernity" (*CCM*), trans. Susanne Klein and George E. Tucker, *Independent Journal of Philosophy* 4 (1983): 105–19; *Liberalism Ancient and Modern* (*LAM*) (New York: Basic Books, 1968); *Natural Right and History* (*NRH*) (Chicago: University of Chicago Press, 1968); "On Classical Political Philosophy" (*OCPP*) in *WIPP*: pp. 78–94; *On Tyranny* (*OT*), ed. by Victor Gourevitch and Michael S. Roth (New York: Free Press, 1991); *Persecution and the Art of Writing* (*PAW*) (Chicago: University of Chicago Press, 1980); *The Rebirth of Classical Political Rationalism: An Introduction to the Thought of Leo Strauss* (*RCR*) (Chicago: University of Chicago Press, 1989); Spinoza's *Critique of Religion* (*S*), trans. E. M. Sinclair (New York: Schocken Boules, 1965); *Studies in Platonic Political Philosophy* (*SPP*) (Chicago: University of Chicago Press, 1983); *Thoughts on Machiavelli* (*TM*) (Chicago: University of Chicago Press, 1978); "The Three Waves of Modernity" (*TW*) in *An Introduction to Political Philosophy: Ten Essays by Leo Strauss* ed. by Hilail Gilden (Detroit: Wayne State University, 1989), pp. 81–98; "An Unspoken Prologue to a Public Lecture at St. John's" (*UP*) *The College* 30 (1979): 30–1; *What Is Political Philosophy?* (*WIPP*) (Chicago: University of Chicago Press, 1959). Here, *TW*, p.84.

disagree with those reasons, and thereby disagree that there is some fatal
aporia within modernity finally and decisively revealed by Nietzsche.[3]

However, before addressing that specific controversy, I should admit that
Strauss's theory of modernity is very difficult to discuss as an isolated theme
in his work, and that something first must be said about both the Straussian
project as a whole and its complex reception in America.

This problem of reception and, because of it, what one might consciously
or implicitly bring to any discussion of Leo Strauss is quite complicated. For
opponents, Strauss is everything from a rebarbative crank to a dangerous
cult figure, and for many such critics he raises "the problem of modernity"
only because he is an anti- or at least a premodern thinker, wedded to a premodern view of natural hierarchy and a kind of religious sense of human
finitude, and so believes in the permanence of insoluble political problems.[4] Even his followers present him as both a pious natural law absolutist
and, on the other extreme, a closet Nietzschean; a sincere enemy of modern
relativism, or an opponent merely of the openness of the modern discussion
of the deeply conventional nature of moral and political life; a moral cru-
sader against modernity, or a sophisticated, dissembling zetetic.[5]

---

3 For one thing, such rational-will theories, in the work of Rawls, Habermas, and Gewirth;
   prominent Kantian theorists like Onora O'Neill, and attacks on Strauss like that by Luc
   Ferry, occupy a far larger area of the political theory stage than during Strauss's lifetime, and
   that fact alone suggests a modernist strategy in political thought that at least appears far
   more resilient, both culturally and philosophically, than Strauss seems to have anticipated.

4 This view of Strauss as an antimodern proponent of ancient thought has persisted, despite
   Strauss's many warnings against expecting classical "recipes for today's use"; his clear admission that modern political thought has produced a kind of society "wholly unknown to the
   classics," for which "classical principles . . . are not immediately applicable"; and his frequent defense of modern liberal democracy. Cf. *LAM,* pp. 4–5, 10, 23; 207–8; *WIPP,* pp. 27–
   8, 78–87; and *CM,* p. 11. There is, of course, still the ambiguity of that "immediately."
   Perhaps, it would be more accurate to see Strauss as a tentative supporter of Nietzsche's
   interpretation of those dissatisfied with modernity: "The main thing about them is not that
   they wish to go "back," but that they wish to get – *away.* A little *more* strength, fight, courage,
   and artistic power, and they would want to *rise,* not return!" *Beyond Good and Evil* (*BGE*),
   trans. W. Kaufmann (New York: Harper & Row, 1966), sect. 10, p. 17.

5 Cf. Thomas Pangle, Introduction to *Leo Strauss: Studies in Platonic Political Philosophy*
   (Chicago: University of Chicago Press, 1983); the review by Harry Jaffa, "The Legacy of Leo
   Strauss," *Claremont Review* 3 (1984): 409–13; and their subsequent exchange in *Claremont
   Review* 4: 18–24. Some support for a "Nietzschean" view of Strauss can be found in ch. 2 of
   NRH. Although Strauss sometimes slips into the voice of the position discussed, the remarks
   on p. 107 about the "fictitious" nature of the city are striking.

   Shadia Drury has presented the most extreme Machiavellian/Nietzschean/esoteric
   reading of Strauss in *The Political Ideas of Leo Strauss* (London: St. Martin's Press, 1988), pp.
   29, 36, 170–81. The idea of Strauss's "philosopher" as Nietzschean "superman," "creating
   values," is an absurd overstatement and misses a very central issue in Strauss's account, the

In the light of these controversies and this recent reemergence of the modernity problem, I need to begin with a few very general remarks about what Strauss understands by the modernity problem, the question to which his three-wave analysis is the response.

The least controversial claim one could make is that his modernity critique is everywhere motivated by one great opposition, or *gigantomachia*, the *quarrel between the ancients and the moderns*. The best-known implication of Strauss's understanding of such a fundamental clash, and the origin of by far the greatest scholarly controversy, is his claim about ancient and much of early modern writing. It is esoteric. Great thinkers do not say what they mean when they write publicly; they dissemble or write in a way that will not be easily and clearly understood by the many, the hoi polloi, and they indicate, deftly and most carefully, their true intentions "for those with ears to hear," for the few capable of following the hints and clues. This strategy is, first of all, prudential. If Straussianism were a religion, its central icon, rivaling the crucified Christ, would be Socrates drinking the hemlock. According to Strauss, it is by no means a mere contingency that the emergence of the first great philosopher coincided with his condemnation and execution by the city, and virtually everything Strauss (himself a political and "ideological" émigré)[6] wrote is in one way or another informed by that event. There is a necessary hostility between "the city" – any political unit that must rely on opinion, convention, and religion (that is, any political unit) – and "philosophy" – an enterprise devoted to inquiry about the universal and eternal and so inimical to the locally sacred and ancestral. However, this also means for Strauss that the philosopher writes secretly not only to protect himself but also to discharge his debt to the city; he knows his own danger, and knows how much his leisure accrues a debt to the city, and so acts beneficently by writing carefully.[7]

---

problem of nature, nowhere explored with any sensitivity in Drury's book. The crude characterization of Strauss as a "consequentialist" does not help matters much either. A much more subtle discussion of Strauss's "exotericism" and his relation to Nietzsche can be found in Stanley Rosen, *Hermeneutics as Politics* (Oxford: Oxford University Press, 1987), pp. 107–23. See especially his remarks on why the Straussian "hypothesis" is "*an act of will*, and hence a moral matter," pp. 111, 118, 119, 122, 125 ("My thesis is that Strauss is himself almost a Nietzschean"), p. 127, and the top of p. 133, where Rosen suggests his own position, a more dialectical relation between pre-theoretical intuition and discursive account giving.

6 Cf. Nathan Tarcov's discussion of how the "crisis of the West, of modernity," "was, for Strauss most clearly exemplified by the Jewish problem, which he [Strauss] regarded as 'the most manifest symbol of the human problem insofar as it is a social or political problem.'" *Epilogue to History of Political Philosophy*, 3d ed. (Chicago: University of Chicago Press, 1987), p. 909. The quotation is from *S*, p. 6.

7 Cf. *CM*, p. 52.

This hermeneutical issue already evinces Strauss's fundamental claim, a tragic view of the human predicament: Political life, its sacrifices, compromises, and effort, is worthwhile to the extent that it allows and helps promote human perfection, the distinctive, extremely rare excellence of the species, the philosophical life.[8] But no political community could be based on such an ideal: No call for sacrifice or effort for the sake of the "few" could ever hope to enlist the support of the "many," who love "their own," especially their own families, and can live together politically only by coming to regard the city as also "their own," itself an extremely difficult task. Although we tend to think of justice as a paradigmatic human good, Strauss often contrasts it (even if only understood as "doing good to friends as harm to enemies") with "the good," whose possession, if possible, is essentially private. If such claims are coupled with the assertion that such an excellent, or even a second- or third-best regime is wholly a matter of chance, then we should conclude, as he does, that the chief political virtue is moderation; the chief vice, idealism; the central modern folly: the promise that philosophy can play a public role, that by understanding ourselves as we truly are (and by relaying some of these truths to the Prince, or, ultimately, by publishing our results, speaking *als Gelehrte*), we will also be able to establish peace, conquer *fortuna*, rationally coordinate the pursuit of private ends in a public realm, achieve a social order and rule of law held together, defended, and reproduced by appeal to reason; or that we shall become, finally, the subjects of history.

Said a different way that will be relevant later, the modern promise could be stated in Hegelian terms: It is the promise of *Versöhnung* or a full reconciliation among fellow citizens. The modern demands for legal equality, politically secured self-determination, fair distribution of collective resources, all involve, when understood as ethical demands, the hope for a full reconciliation among fellow citizens. This will mean that the "realization" of each, whether as rational egoist or as free, self-determining agent, requires, and is understood to require, the realization or at least the possible realization, of all. There will then, thereby, be a full reconciliation between all citizens and their social, political, legal, and indeed religious institutions, all regarded as the products of, or at least rationally protected by, their collective, and so mutually reconciled will, and not merely required by chance, necessity, tradition, class power, or circumstance. Essentially, this is also the Christian promise: that there need not be masters and slaves, that, exactly

---

8 Cf., however, the remark in *CM* that "Socratic conversation" and "Platonic dialogue" are "slightly more akin to comedy than to tragedy," p. 61.

like Christ, each is both master and slave, ruler and ruled, father and son, at once. I think it is fair to say that Strauss's attitude toward such claims is exactly the same as Nietzsche's, even if he hides his contempt a bit better. The "ancient" position, by contrast (at least if we adopt Strauss's usual *façon de parler*, and abstract from the vast differences among Plato, Aristotle, the Stoics, and so on), is easy to state: no reconciliation.[9] The city or the public world of human affairs is a permanent cave. Even if the philosopher in the *Republic* can be persuaded (perhaps by the force of the argument that he owes the city a debt) or, paradoxically, can persuade the many to compel him to return, it is clear that he must rule in the dark. He cannot bring the outside light in, and it never seems to enter his mind to attempt to bring those inside out (apart from the select few).[10] By remembering the complex, censored education, and the control of images presented in the early books, we can even surmise that Socrates as ruler assumes the role of chief puppeteer, at least projecting salutary and philosophically informed shadows.[11] Both positions, when thought through, involve dialectical twists

---

9 Cf. Victor Gourevitch, "Philosophy and Politics II," *Review of Metaphysics* 22 (1968): 296.
10 I am alluding here to recent controversy created by M. F. Burnyeat's review, "Sphinx Without a Secret," *New York Review of Books* 32, no. 9 (May 30, 1985): 30–6. See also the exchange in 32, no. 15 (October 10, 1985), "The Studies of Leo Strauss: An Exchange." The problem of the philosopher's return to the cave in book VII of the *Republic* is the single philosophic issue at stake between Burnyeat and the respondents in Strauss's name. On the general issue of Strauss's reluctance to engage in the more "technical" aspects of Platonic philosophy, cf. the apposite remarks by Rosen, *Hermeneutics as Politics*, p. 121. But whether Burnyeat or Strauss is right about the interpretation of that passage seems to me to miss the larger point. The "unrealizability" of the city described in the *Republic* is a central, explicit theme *in* it. Not only does Socrates make very clear how unlikely its realization is, he goes on to claim that in the unlikely, chance event it were realized, it is *impossible* that it could survive beyond the first generation. (There is no knowledge of the "marriage number.") So, it is highly unlikely that such a city could be realized and, if realized, *impossible* that it could survive. So in what sense could the Republic be an "ideal" to be imitated? That is the only question important to Strauss's larger purposes.
11 This is all not because the philosopher "knows things" of great danger to the city. His only knowledge is knowledge of ignorance, and that is why he is so dangerous, or far more dangerous than if he represented a determinate set of claims. The radically skeptical, incomplete, or zetetic character of Strauss's version of Socraticism is what promotes a kind of homelessness potentially subversive in contexts where steadfast loyalty, faith, and dedication are the required virtues. See the very helpful discussion in Gourevitch, "Philosophy and Politics II," 304–11.
       Paradoxically this characterization also undermines somewhat Strauss's claims about "tension" since it suggests what is at least as manifest in Platonic dialogues as is the political problem of Socrates – the political irrelevance of Socrates, his being ignored, mocked, his not having a *techne*, and so being an *idiotas*, his lack of success in influence as well as in arguments.

that are important but cannot be explored in this context. That is, the promise of reconciliation in someone like Hegel famously requires and never overcomes (even while it "sublates") the modern experience of "alienation," a great diversity and opposition within civil society, and especially the loss of the natural world and even the family as "home," and the promise of a final reconciliation only within institutions produced by human will. For Strauss (and Hannah Arendt, incidentally, both decisively influenced by Heidegger), such a promise of a genuinely modern, "artificial" reconciliation of self with self, others, and world is a disastrous promotion of a self-defining subjectivity, connected with the thoughtless attempt to establish human dominion over the planet, and with the apotheosis, not the over-coming, of alienation or loss. It inaugurates what will become apparent in Nietzsche: a complete "measurelessness" for human deeds and a dangerous, vain, and finally apolitical (either moralistic or aesthetic) self-absorption. By contrast, Strauss (and again Arendt) regards a genuine rec-ognition of the finitude of "the human things" (or the "human condition"), or an acceptance of the permanently unreconciled "natural" condition of human life, as itself the realization of reconciliation, and so the beginning of a truly humane politics not based on hubris or resentment. As we shall see, many such issues in Strauss devolve from his understanding of Rousseau and, consequently, how he understands what is everywhere for him the central issue: the problem of nature in modernity.

These sorts of considerations introduce Strauss's sweeping claim that any form of this modern promise can be fulfilled only in one of two unaccept-able and ultimately incoherent ways. A fully mutual, common reconciliation among all citizens might be possible if we drastically "lower" our conception of the ends to be served by political life; if we actually find a lowest common denominator, minimally common to all persons and so a possible goal of rationally coordinated action; and if we treat such a goal as the whole of the political problem. Strauss associates this strategy first with Machiavelli, who rejected the ancient orientation from how men ought to be and took his bearings from how men are, and then, decisively, with Hobbes's "political hedonism,"[12] his beginning with what are in fact the most powerful pas-sions. And he regularly asserts that such a reconciliation based on en-lightened self-interest founders on the gang-of-robbers problem, or that the position must recommend non-cooperation and active defection when the

---

12 *NRH*, p. 169. Machiavelli had been "ancient" enough to recognize the importance of glory in any account of a stable, thriving regime. This drops out in Hobbes and, for Strauss, decisively distinguishes him from Machiavelli.

risk of detection is low, and faces insurmountable problems in situations like war or risk of life.[13]

Second, and more elusive, Strauss is aware that a principled form of reconciliation, a model for self-rule rather than ruler and ruled, would be possible if the basis of that reconciliation were the mutual recognition of a common capacity worthy of such universal respect and clearly capable of generating and sustaining such respect; if our mutual claims on and debts to each other were not based on a strategy of self-interest or self-preservation but on the realization that any act of mine (insofar as I am an agent) presupposes a like capacity in all such agents, and so I may not act as if it did not, as if I were a unique exception. Starting with Rousseau, of course, this capacity is "freedom," and a central hope in the modern tradition is that some non-egoistic principle of freedom could be the basis of a universally self-ruling, socially integrated, self-reproducing, or what I am calling a reconciled, political community.

Strauss strongly disagrees. In the first place, he often alludes to many familiar dissatisfactions with this option. Why is freedom only one among many competing goods, not at all a "supreme condition" of any other good's being a good? How could such a morally rigorous, even absolutist requirement ever serve as a guide to political life? How could a formal criterion of permissible action, a principle that rules out the forbidden and requires the strictly obligatory, ever substantively guide human life, provide a measure for what sort of life is worthwhile, the highest? More generally he is clearly most worried that any position that links right with what the will legislates for itself or produces quickly heads down the slippery slope toward legal positivism, historicism, relativism, and finally nihilism.[14]

He realizes of course that there is a difference between the beginning of a slope and the end point (that Rousseau and Kant intend to be universalists

---

13 Clearly, of course, from the modern point of view sights are raised, not lowered, particularly when the point of comparison is Scholasticism and papal or feudal politics. In the Kantian phrase cited earlier, *sapere aude!* See Stanley Rosen, "A Modest Proposal to Rethink Enlightenment," in *The Ancients and the Moderns* (New Haven: Yale University Press, 1989), pp. 1–21.

14 *NRH*, p. 17. I should note here that Strauss only asserts, "The historical school had obscured the fact that particular or historical standards can become authoritative only on the basis of a universal principle which imposes an *obligation* on the individual to accept." Depending on what Strauss means by "authoritative," such a claim either is a tautology or begs the question at issue. Some principle can be authoritative for me if in some situation it counts as a reason *for me* to act; to claim otherwise would require a much more serious confrontation with a figure Strauss (and, as far as I can see, most of his students) neglects: David Hume.

and rationalists), but his general position clearly assumes some sort of strict disjunction: Either there is a natural (non-conventional and non-posited) standard for right, or there is (ultimately if not initially) positivism, historicism, nihilism. Early modernity (pre-Rousseau) still preserved such an appeal to nature but at far too low and accommodating a level, one insufficient to sustain any genuine political community. Later modernity is too vulnerable to Nietzsche's challenges and Heidegger finally represents the "culmination," the "highest self-consciousness," of "modern thought."[15] These latter claims, about the "second wave" and its consequences, are what I want to explore.

II

Several ambiguities, often remarked, arise in what Strauss claims.[16] And these ambiguities are compounded by a more fundamental ambiguity: Strauss's hesitancy to say very much as a "political philosopher" in the modern, conventional sense. That is, his own account of political philosophy (apart from his historical studies of others' attempts to philosophize about the political matters) seems mostly concerned with the political problem of

---

15 *WIPP*, p. 57. Heidegger is not here mentioned by name, but there is little doubt whom Strauss means. For Strauss's comments on his own debts to Heidegger, see *WIPP*, p. 248; *Acc*, pp. 2–3; *UP*, p. 31. See also Pangle's somewhat Heideggerian characterization (or so it seems to me) of the role of "need" (or "care") in "shaping" awareness, Introduction, p. 5.

  Luc Ferry, in *Political Philosophy 1: Rights – The New Quarrel Between the Ancients and the Moderns*, trans. Franklin Philip (Chicago: University of Chicago Press, 1990), makes a very great deal out of the relation between Strauss's modernity critique and Heidegger's. See especially pp. 19 and 37, where he criticizes the results of this affinity for Strauss's political thought. Strauss subscribes to "the neoconservative [*sic*] tendency to sacralize natural inequalities," p. 21. Ferry nowhere addresses the enormous differences between Strauss and Heidegger over the nature of the "pretheoretical orientation" so crucial for Strauss and so underplays Strauss's vigorous attacks on Heidegger's historicism.

  Moreover, Ferry's criticism, which also takes up the post-Rousseauean or German Idealist themes introduced here, is limited by relying on a traditional and, I think, deeply flawed reading of Hegel (as a metaphysical "identity theorist," with a historicist theodicy) and by a reading of Fichte (essentially Philonenko's) that presents an elaborate, idiosyncratic interpretation of the *Wissenschaftslehre*, only to end up attributing to Fichte a Kantian position still vulnerable to many of Hegel's original worries. See my *Hegel's Idealism*, chs. 1 and 3, and *Modernism as a Philosophical Problem*, ch. 3.

16 Many of the most puzzling have to do with a central theme in his multifaceted worries about modern secularism and enlightenment, what he calls the Athens–Jerusalem theme, or the competing claims of reason and revelation. Cf. *NRH*, pp. 74, 75, 86; *S*, p. 30, and Richard Kennington, "Strauss's *Natural Right and History*," *Review of Metaphysics* 25 (1974): 69.

philosophy, or the political issue of a philosophic life, rather than a philosophy of politics.[17]

Moreover, Strauss's account sometimes slips into an indictment of the hubris or folly of the modern founders and so neglects the larger issue of the *motivations* for the modern revolt against antiquity. Any further consideration of that theme would introduce issues rarely mentioned by Strauss: the role of Scholastic controversies (especially nominalism, and the continuing problem of the Gnostic heresy);[18] the Reformation, and the transformation of political notions of right directly linked to Reformation ambiguities about church–state relations.[19] Moreover, although Strauss is clearly out to defend the classical notion of natural right, he never does so in his own voice, preferring to write historical studies. These studies sometimes seem to propose logical connections among ideas, or "necessary deteriorations" of positions, which commit Strauss to a complicated historiography only rarely discussed as such, and which leave the details of his own views, or his strategy for defending natural right, hidden in asides, allusions, remarks, marginal comments, and so forth.[20]

But there is a deeper issue involved in the way Strauss presents the ancient–modern contrast, one that will lead us directly to problems with his second wave. That problem has to do with his motivation for presenting the issue as a *quarrel* between the ancients and moderns. Given the obvious deep continuities between the traditions and the difficulties in understanding the connections between Christianity and modernity, what do we gain by viewing the issue this way?

17 In *OCPP*, he contrasts a "provisional" definition of political philosophy, in which philosophy is the manner of treatment and the political is the subject matter, with a "deeper" meaning, in which, "the adjective 'political' in the expression 'political philosophy' designates not so much a subject matter as a manner of treatment; from this point of view, I say 'political philosophy' means primarily not the philosophic treatment of politics, but the political, or popular, treatment of philosophy, or the political introduction to philosophy – the attempt to lead the qualified citizens, or rather their qualified sons, from the political life to the philosophical life," pp. 93–94.

18 As in, e.g., Amos Funkenstein, *Theology and the Scientific Imagination from the Middle Ages to the Seventeenth Century* (Princeton: Princeton University Press, 1986), and Hans Blumenberg, *The Legitimacy of the Modern Age*, trans. Robert Wallace (Cambridge: MIT Press, 1983). See "Blumenberg and the Modernity Problem," Chapter 10, this volume.

19 Cf., e.g., Quentin Skinner, *The Foundations of Modern Political Thought* (Cambridge: Cambridge University Press, 1978).

20 Interestingly enough, as Nathan Tarcov has pointed out, many of these standard criticisms of Strauss were first raised by Strauss himself in a 1946 review of John Wild. This introduces a new level of ambiguity, an ambiguity about how Strauss himself understood these ambiguities in his work. Cf. Nathan Tarcov, "On a Certain Critique of 'Straussianism,'" *Review of Politics*, 53, no. 1 (Winter 1991): 7.

Partly, Strauss thinks, this gain stems from our own historical situation. He writes that only "men living in an age of intellectual decline" have a sufficiently powerful and ultimately fruitful motive for a devoted reading of old books. In such a situation alone does history "take on philosophical significance." It is a profound dissatisfaction with our own situation that provides us with "good reasons for believing that we can learn something of utmost importance from the thought of the past which we cannot learn from our contemporaries."[21]

What is that "thought"? In "Political Philosophy and History," Strauss claims that modern historicism "creates an entirely new situation for political philosophy," one that raises "the most urgent question for political philosophy."[22] In a remarkable discussion of the "natural obstacles to philosophy" in *Persecution and the Art of Writing*, Strauss describes this situation with an image and tries to explain why it is novel. Using the classic Platonic image of the cave, Strauss suggests that it is as if people had "dug a deep pit beneath the cave in which they were born" and had withdrawn into that pit.

If one of the descendants desired to ascend to the light of the sun, he would first have to try to reach the level of the natural cave, and he would have to invent new and most artificial tools unknown and unnecessary to those who dwell in the natural cave. He would be a fool, he would never see the light of the sun, he would lose the last vestige of the memory of the sun, if he perversely thought that by inventing his new tools he had progressed beyond the ancestral cave dwellers.[23]

That is, our situation is "beneath" the natural obstacles (passion and superstition) described by Spinoza; "It is obvious that that situation does not exist in our time"[24] – where "that situation" is some "natural" experience of the nature of political life and its relation to philosophy. Instead, the "twin sisters," science and history, have conspired to render impossible anyone's taking seriously the possibility of a genuine account of "the whole" (and this especially has shaped, forever altered our direct experience of the "things around us"). Our "natural" experience has been thoroughly distorted by an unphilosophic science, and a weak competitor, unscientific, ever more "poetic" philosophy. Science still needs some sort of historical narrative to establish its authority, its progressive character, but this history now in-

---

21 *C*, pp. 576, 585 (my emphasis). See also Nathan Tarcov, "Philosophy and History: Tradition and Interpretation in the Work of Leo Strauss," *Polity* 16 (1983): 24.

22 *WIPP*, p. 57.

23 *PAW*, pp. 155–6.

24 Ibid., p. 156.

coherently replaces rather than introduces philosophy. Thus, in a remarkably sweeping conclusion, Strauss asserts that *there no longer exists a direct access to the original meaning of philosophy,* as quest for the true and final account of the whole. Once this state has been reached, the original meaning of philosophy is accessible only through recollection of what philosophy meant in the past, that is, for all practical purposes, only through the reading of old books.[25]

Our artificial tools are hermeneutical, linguistic, and, ironically, historical; our reward is at least to climb out of our artificial "subcave," and to confront the natural obstacles to (and, presumably, natural opportunities for) philosophy, as these were "originally" understood in classical philosophy. In such old books, we are said to experience what Strauss calls the "natural" understanding of political things,[26] or "the understanding of political things that belongs to political life."[27]

So, if we could recover this "natural" experience of the human things, we could at least understand and, presumably, perhaps, begin to defend the classic "natural right" doctrine, the claim that there is by nature a best life. And with such a promise we are introduced again to that most important and least developed of Strauss's themes, nature.[28] He does not deny that "natural right in its classic form is connected with a teleological view of the universe" at the same time that he freely admits that "the teleological view of the universe, of which the teleological view of man forms a part, would seem to have been destroyed by modern natural science."[29] He admits honestly that "an adequate solution to the problem of natural right cannot be found before this basic problem has been solved."[30] But there is no indication whatsoever that he thinks he solves it.

25 Ibid., p. 157 (my emphasis). See also *CCM*, pp. 106–7, 109, 114, especially the claims about our being "still natural beings with natural understanding" even though "the way of natural understanding has been lost to us."
26 *NRH*, p. 79.
27 *CM*, pp. 11–12.
28 "Strauss was dedicated to the restoration of a rich and concrete natural consciousness of the political phenomenon." Allan Bloom, "Leo Strauss: September 20, 1899–October 18, 1973," *Political Theory* 2, no. 4 (1974): 376. See also p. 379 and the reference to Kant. Cf. also, on the general problem of nature in Strauss, Kennington's "Strauss's Natural Right and History," which is indispensable.
29 *NRH*, pp. 7–8.
30 *NRH*, p. 8. See also *TW*, p. 85. Strauss's own reliance on teleology is quite limited. His concern is not with teleological explanation, and he certainly does not write as if final causes are also efficient. Moreover he has little to say about a complex natural hierarchy, or chain of being. It is only important to him that in some sense the human kind is not the highest, and that the nature of the human kind provides a "standard" for life, something Strauss most often interprets as a limit, as in *TW*, p. 86. This raises interesting questions

The problems are manifest already in Strauss's use of Plato's very image. In the *Republic*, Plato's depiction of the pre-philosophical situation makes it very clear that the obstacles to philosophy are both natural and artificial. The cave itself is a natural image, representative of our initial, natural ignorance, but that situation is made extraordinarily worse by very ambiguously presented artifices. Someone has chained the prisoners to the ground, preventing them from turning their heads; the light within the cave is wholly artificial, and the images they see on the wall are themselves many removes from reality, "shadows of artificial things" (515c). These are all presented as such powerful obstacles that it is hard to see why Strauss thinks he needs to add a new, artificial subcave to describe "our situation." The original pre-philosophical situation seems designed to show how effectively the possibility of philosophy in any sense, let alone some knowledge of "the whole," has been completely suppressed, and suppressed by opinions of various sorts, not necessarily those derived mainly from "passion or superstition." In fact, interestingly enough, the suppression seems politically motivated, as if to preserve the power of the puppeteers.

The situation is so bad, in fact, that it could be argued that the image presents a serious *aporia*. There is no explanation of how anyone might free himself from such chains (nor even why he would want to, given that he does not know that he is seeing images), and plenty of evidence that even after being freed by others, an ascent to the light would be too frightening and uncertain. Indeed, when considered in terms of the three great images that dominate the middle books of the *Republic*, the cave appears to be in a "metaphysical space" itself underneath the possible ascent captured by the divided line. There is no evidence of *eikasia*, the lowest and most important faculty described in the line image, the ability to see images as images. Thus, if we "work our way back" to the ancient experience of political life and its relation to philosophy, what we would seem to discover is a powerful image of the impossibility of any natural experience of each other, or our own political situation, obscured and mediated as such experience is by natural ignorance, political power, nearly insuperable barriers to our even coming to know that we don't know, and by the ever present chains of *doxa*.

Of course it is possible that Strauss may be quite wrong about some historically privileged and natural (rather than merely different, otherwise oriented) experience of "what belongs to political life" and still be right that

about his view of philosophy, the most immoderate of activities. Cf. *WIPP*, "For moderation is not a virtue of thought," even though "moderation is a virtue controlling the philosopher's speech," p. 32. Cf. also Gourevitch, "Philosophy and Politics II," pp. 290–3.

the classical alternative itself, even if indebted to unique and long lost conventions, is superior. But it is essential to the classical alternative itself, or at least to the critical force of Strauss's position, that we be able in some way to identify the "natural order of things," the situation of the human qua human.[31]

And this, above all, is what is so incompatible theoretically with post-Kantian critical philosophy and its political implications. Modern historicism, after all (assuming for the sake of argument that there is such a unified phenomenon), did not originate in the conservative reaction of the German historical school, and it does not primarily develop as a consequence of the modern emphasis on the "individual" (eventually the individual national character), so visible in Hobbes and Rousseau. The decisive modern book in philosophy, especially for *that* problem, is not Machiavelli's *Prince* or *Discourses*, or Hobbes's *Leviathan*, or Locke's *Essay*, or Rousseau's *Second Discourse*, or even, I would argue, Descartes's *Meditations*.[32] It is Kant's *Critique of Pure Reason* (again, particularly given Strauss's concerns with Weber, Nietzsche, and Heidegger, that is, with positivism and historicism), and none of Strauss's allusions to the recovery of a "natural" orientation, or of the human things, will be of much philosophic interest unless the Kantian attack on the entire rationalist and empiricist tradition, on the dogmatism of the classical notion of nature, is taken into account in philosophic terms.[33] After all, Strauss himself would point out that it is only after Kant that the discussions of "natural" right end. Machiavelli, Hobbes, Locke, and, though the decisive transitional figure, Rousseau still appeal to nature as a standard, even if a mechanistic, purposeless, or subhuman nature. That all becomes in a certain sense "impossible" after Kant. And, at least originally,

---

31 Rosen, in *Hermeneutics as Politics,* has rightly suggested that the better Straussean strategy (sometimes followed by Strauss) would be to try to show that the fundamental political problems emerge as the same *in all times.* "Then the Greeks as Greeks become irrelevant" (p.128). This would still, however, run afoul of the Kantian and post-Kantian objections to the *possibility* of such an identification of our "natural situation."

Rosen himself, in his own work, is not concerned with that problem, since he believes that such Kantian objections stem from a project that is in itself essentially practical, based on a kind of Nietzschean recommendation to "will" a different world, and so Rosen believes that Kant is not in a better theoretical position in his critical stance. Once there is no "natural standard," "all theory is construction." See p. 126, inter alia. I've the same problems with this "slippery slope" argument (here, in Rosen, from Kant to Nietzsche) as I do with Strauss's Rousseau-to-historicism slide. The ride is so fast that many potential safe stops on the way down are too hastily ignored.

32 See my *Modernism as a Philosophical Problem,* and "Hegel, Modernity, and Habermas," Chapter 6, this volume.

33 See the very brief reference in *NRH,* pp. 19–20.

one must take seriously the claim that the Kantian attack on nature is based on a theoretical attack on the very possibility of such appeals and on a complex, "transcendental," non-skeptical alternative.[34]

The Kant problem is especially important because Strauss himself sometimes suggests or at least alludes to a kind of neo-Kantian solution to his own great problem of teleology. That solution involves denying that a teleological understanding of ourselves and of nature is a direct competitor with non-teleological accounts, that they are not answers to the same question, and that each question, understood properly within its own domain, is a legitimate one. Strauss himself suggests this solution in language that seems to reflect his debt to Husserl and Heidegger, more than to the systematic reflections of Kant or Hegel. He invokes, often incidentally and without elaboration, the indispensability of a teleological perspective in any attempt to understand the "human experience of the human," the natural or lived world, as it is lived, for us, and as it forms the subject, say, of novels, drama, poems; the sine qua non of any adequate political reflection on human life, rather than an "object" of study artificially created by a methodology.[35]

However, unless we are willing to accept something like Husserl's methodology, with its suspensions, bracketings, and reductions, such a strategy will still not uncover, and would make much more dubious, any notion of a distinctive "natural" point of view, only later overlaid with scientific and historicist prejudices. The whole notion of a practical point of view, a life-world, or lived perspective is a descendant of the Idealist denial that an unmediated appeal to nature or any sort of immediate experience is possi-

---

34 I put it this way because it is open to someone sympathetic to Strauss to argue that Kant's own critical attack is motivated by a practical project not finally defensible discursively, but only intuitively. See Stanley Rosen's chapter "Transcendental Ambiguity" in *Hermeneutics as Politics*, pp. 19–49, and my discussion of Kant in *Modernism*, ch. 3. For a discussion of the "moral foundations of Kant's critical philosophy," see Richard Velkley, *Freedom and the End of Reason* (Chicago: University of Chicago Press, 1989).

35 Perhaps the most well known of such passages: the reference to the "simple experiences regarding right and wrong which are at the bottom of the philosophic contention that there is a natural right," and the surrounding discussion in *NRH*, pp. 31–2. For passages that resonate with Husserl's influence on Strauss's view of the natural attitude, see pp. 78–9. Of the many tensions in *NRH*, none seems to me more puzzling than the contrast between Strauss's claims about such a natural experience on p. 24, where the experience of "fundamental problems" is introduced, but immediately qualified by the claim "To leave it at this would amount to regarding the case of natural right as hopeless" and qualified by the argument that a philosophic *solution* of these problems must be possible, must be in view, if there is to be a philosophic issue of natural right; and, by contrast, p. 32, where "*no more is needed to legitimate philosophy* in its original, Socratic sense" than a grasp of these problems *just as problems* (my emphasis). Cf. Rosen's remarks on Strauss and Husserl, *Hermeneutics as Politics*, p. 131.

ble. There may be structural characteristics common to the possibility of such an agent-centered framework, but these are clearly logically formal and compatible with all sorts of content, and there is no way, without begging the question, to claim that the content of the classical experience of an ordered, natural hierarchy, even if not understood as a theory about objects, but as an articulation of an experience and a pre-theoretical orientation, is original or decisive.[36]

III

In his essay *Belief and Knowledge,* Hegel emphasizes a common theme in his account of modernity: The modern age is the realization of human freedom, indeed of "absolute freedom." But he also stresses that what makes this freedom possible is the experience of a great and terrifying loss: indeed the experience that "God himself is dead, upon which the religion of recent times rests."[37] However much this loss creates an "infinite grief, . . . dogmatic philosophies" and "natural religions . . . must vanish," there must be a "speculative Good Friday . . . in the whole truth and harshness of its Godforsakenness" before the modern "resurrection" can occur.

As we have seen, Strauss doubts that the loss Hegel speaks of – essentially, in his terms, the loss of nature as standard – will be followed by any resurrection; modernity is better described as a Good Friday with no Easter Sunday. Again, Strauss fundamentally agrees with this aspect of the Nietzschean critique of modernity. Once the human subject is understood as a self-legislating, even self-defining spontaneity, the German Idealist's hopes that such spontaneity would realize itself as "law" or "reason" were doomed. For Strauss, such an unmasking of a self-legislating reason as will to power is reason enough to return to the ancients; for Nietzsche, it is an unmasking of the ancients as well, and a situation that demands courage rather than moderation.

However, since Strauss realizes that the sort of "freedom" Hegel appeals to is not at all a species of the "early modern" liberation of the passions or restriction of the self to self-interest and of reason to calculation, the reasons for his doubts emerge only in his account of the "second" modern wave, that is, the first crisis of modernity. The most self-contained expres-

---

36 An experience can be pre-theoretical, but it can be pre-conceptual or wholly "unmediated" only if one is willing to buy into, say, more of Heidegger's program than Strauss, for other reasons, ought to.

37 *GuW,* p. 414; *FK,* p. 191.

sion of his interpretation of this issue is his account of Rousseau in *Natural Right and History.*

Naturally enough, Strauss concentrates a good deal of his discussion on Rousseauean themes central to Strauss's own project. No writer, after all, has had more to say about the "tensions" between individual and society than Rousseau, and no one wrote in more "glowing terms of the charms and raptures of solitary contemplation."[38] Of course, such contemplation is not philosophy, but the general issues replay the Straussian theme, with civil society "good" only for a certain individual, a type of man who "justifies civil society by transcending it," by "living at its fringes,"[39] even if in Rousseau "his claim to privileged treatment is based on his sensitivity rather than on his wisdom,"[40] and even if, for Strauss, such a criterion finally "lacks any definite human content."[41]

Nevertheless, Rousseau sees for the first time how much had been lost in the first modern wave, especially sees the Faustian bargain, how modern man had sacrificed virtue for ease, and had acquired freedom only freely to traffic in goods and money, to trade, to acquire, to lose himself in idleness. And Rousseau sees the potential hostility, not just the potential practical benefits, in the relation between the requirements of the small, Spartan, virtuous city and science, with its universalism and cosmopolitanism and skepticism. Nevertheless, however much Rousseau was drawn to the "classical view," he always "succumbs to the powers from which he sought to liberate himself,"[42] and remains a sort of conscientious objector within modernity, and not a genuine opponent.

The reason for this goes back to the theme we have been exploring in Strauss – the problem of nature. Rousseau is justly well known for his doubts about the attempt by Hobbes and other moderns to argue from the natural human condition. They have not, he claimed, identified the truly natural and appeal instead to contingent features of already socialized man (like pride, suspicion of others, vanity, even rationality itself). For this reason, their attempts to argue from the inherently unstable or self-contradictory situation in the natural state, justifying or requiring the sort of civil society that would resolve this problem, do not succeed. This at once opens up a great ambiguity in Rousseau, since it allows him both to appeal to a truly

38 *NRH*, p. 91.
39 Ibid., pp. 292–3.
40 Ibid.
41 Ibid.
42 Ibid., p. 262.

original state of nature as a critical weapon against all society, even as the sheer contingency of civil life makes possible a claim for such a great naturally unrestricted malleability that a far more perfected political situation becomes possible and desirable (i.e., more perfect than what Hobbes or Locke settle for, falsely constrained as they were by their illusions about nature). So Rousseau appeals both "from the modern state to the classical city" and "almost in the same breath . . . from the classical city to the 'man of nature,' the prepolitical savage."[43] "He presents to his readers the confusing spectacle of a man who perpetually shifts back and forth between two diametrically opposed positions."[44]

As he develops his picture of this tension, however, Strauss begins to stress only one, more romantic direction in his overall portrait of Rousseau. On the one hand, Strauss admits the strain in Rousseau in which, put paradoxically, nature still serves as a criterion for right only by being unavailable. "By thinking through" the appeal to nature, "Rousseau was brought face to face with the necessity of abandoning it completely,"[45] and so "showed that man's beginnings lack all human traits," that it was "absurd to go back to the state of nature in order to find in it the norm for man."[46]

But this is hardly a mere negative point; it has historic positive results. It means that "what is characteristically human is not the gift of nature but is the outcome of what man did . . . in order to change or overcome nature." And this very fact itself implies a new wholly modern notion of virtue, one according to which man is good or virtuous only as self-determining, free; that we owe ourselves and others respect only for what we have done or made. Although Strauss hints at his own objections to this doctrine (by implying that it confuses freedom as a condition of virtue with virtue itself),[47] he clearly recognizes that Rousseau is attempting to preserve the notion of public or civil right on a wholly new basis, by appeal, again, to the absence of a usable natural standard, and so by appeal to the only conditions under which the human will can exercise its distinctive function. This alternate account of the will is a "'realistic' substitute for the traditional natural law," according to which "the limitation of human desires is affected, not by the ineffectual requirements of man's perfection, but by the

43 Ibid., p. 254.
44 Ibid.
45 Ibid., p. 274.
46 Ibid.
47 Ibid., p. 278.

recognition in all others of the same right which one claims for one's self."[48]

Such a "substitute" for classical and early modern natural right should also be understood as grounded in the wider implications of Rousseau's still influential suspicions that any appeal to nature often disguises an already socialized, artificial situation. Such doubts wholly transform our notions of ends, desire, reasons, the whole structure of practical, intentional activity. One could say that Rousseau was one of the first to realize how deeply even what we feel, what feels immediately and most closely our own, may not be genuinely our own, may itself be the product of the desires of others, or the derivative result of our own desire to be desired by others. Or one might say that he lived in the sort of society for the first time powerful and influential enough to generate these worries. It doesn't matter here how one puts the issue; the result is the same. No matter how powerfully I feel drawn to an end or goal, how intimately important it seems to me, nothing about such an immediate orientation ensures that such a goal is indeed mine, truly expresses "me." Only some assurance that I have freely determined to pursue such a goal (an assurance, in the tradition Rousseau founded, provided by some sort of reliance on practical reason) will allow me to count the goal as mine. (This is the original meaning of the Hegelian doctrine of negation: Only by losing or "negating" my natural self can I become a genuine self, or self-conscious subject. Put another way, in its full Hegelian flourish: The true human "home" is a fully realized "homelessness," although when fully realized, no longer experienced as such.) Given such a worry, the "natural" in all the senses invoked by Strauss is "lost"; that "God" is dead.

This is not the first time in the history of philosophy that the subject would be portrayed as strange to, or ignorant of, itself, that I could "do the very thing I hate." But for the first time, this dissatisfaction cannot be solved by knowledge of some substantial self, knowledge of what the human soul really is, or what it by nature needs. The subject is now an agent, a self-determining will, and so a non-alienated form of self-realization will involve securing the conditions under which I can genuinely exercise such agency, wherein my deeds reflect what *I* determine. The politics of perfection has become the politics of self-determination.

But having made all these points, and having suggested the direction of this tradition, Strauss chooses to present Rousseau as one still requiring an account of nature. He denies that Rousseau finally conceived of the "law of reason" as independent of the "law of nature," and that he was afraid of a "doctrinairism" were he to do so.[49] Although Strauss admits that Rousseau himself "distinguishes true freedom or moral freedom" from "the natural freedom which belongs to the state of nature, that is, to a state characterized by the rule of blind appetite and hence by slavery in the moral sense of the term," Strauss nevertheless insists that Rousseau "blurs these distinctions." He notes that Rousseau maintains that in civil society "one obeys only himself and remains as free as before." However, Strauss interprets him to mean not that the citizen or moral agent simply does not lose his freedom, does not become "dependent" in imposing a law on himself. According to Strauss, Rousseau means to claim that man must be free in the same sense "as he was in the state of nature." And for Strauss, "this means that natural freedom remains the model for civil freedom." (I note that Strauss does not say a postcivil or postsocial freedom.) After having himself reminded us unequivocally that for Rousseau it was "absurd" to find a norm for man in nature, Strauss concludes his discussion of Rousseau by insisting that nevertheless "the state of nature tended to become for Rousseau a positive standard," and "hence Rousseau's answer to the question of a good life takes on this form: the good life consists in the closest approximation to the state of nature which is possible on the level of humanity."[50]

There is of course a great deal of truth to this characterization, but it seems to apply much more to *le promeneur solitaire*, a self-conscious and hardly natural refugee from civil society, and not to Rousseau's conception of a self-created political life. Or, it may be true as a statement about the good life, but it does not define the virtuous life, the only worthy or praiseworthy life possible for us. That is, Rousseau's great worry about civilized life already reflects a moral concern that makes it unlikely that Strauss's final characterization of Rousseau's position, or at least his final emphasis on one of the many aspects of Rousseau's position, could be accurate.

I suspect that Strauss wants to reemphasize Rousseau's romantic sentiments, his clear pessimism about the possibility of a modern, virtuous commonwealth, because Strauss has his own grave reservations that "moral and political ideals" can be established "without reference to man's nature."[51]

These reservations include a number of very familiar charges. First, Strauss clearly thinks that by relying simply on "reason," Rousseau's sweep-

---

49 Ibid., p. 277.
50 All quotations are from ibid., p. 282.
51 *TW*, p. 92.

ing reservations about political life invite the famous emptiness and rigorism charges leveled against Kant by Hegel.

> To have a reservation against society in the name of the state of nature means to have a reservation against society without either being compelled or able to indicate the way of life or the cause, or the pursuit for the sake of which that reservation is made.[52]

Second, Strauss believed that the central modern question about the realization of a regime based on such principles will now require not an appeal to men's interests and passions but an ultimately mysterious "historical process" or fate, independent of human will, something that leads necessarily to Heideggerean fatalism or some form of relativism.

Third, as already indicated, Strauss believes that assigning to politics the task of the protection of "the one natural right," liberty, confuses a necessary condition for the realization of virtue with its sufficient condition. This is particularly clear in his debate with Kojève in *On Tyranny*. The achievement of "universal recognition" is an empty historical achievement unless we know for what, for what great deed or achievement, individuals are being recognized. To recognize and value them for a capacity, without some natural measure for evaluating their use of that capacity, is pointless.[53]

Finally, at other places, as in his discussion of Weber in *Natural Right and History*, Strauss also implies that, without a substantial, natural theory of the human good, the appeal to reason will be unmotivated and arbitrary, suggesting some Aristotelian worries about Kantianism again very much in the news.[54]

However, although it is typical of Strauss to show that a certain position or tradition ends in a kind of *aporia* as a way of at least motivating an alternative position, he hardly gives this "replacement" notion of autonomy a run for its money, he nowhere establishes such an *aporia* as such, and, especially, he does not discuss the many reasons in Rousseau for resisting a natural standard for civil freedom.

---

52 *NRH*, p. 294. Strauss realizes that Rousseau intends to preserve a distinction between "liberty and license," but he implies throughout these concluding remarks that his theory does not have the resources to sustain that distinction. See also *WIPP* and his remarks there about "horizontal" as opposed to "vertical" limits on liberty, p. 53.

53 *OT*, pp. 177–212. See also *TM* on modern philosophy in general, p. 298, and the discussion by Michael S. Roth, *Knowing and History: Appropriations of Hegel in Twentieth-Century France* (Ithaca: Cornell University Press, 1988), pp. 125–46.

54 See Alasdair MacIntyre, *After Virtue* (Notre Dame: University of Notre Dame, 1984).

We have already seen a number of such considerations in our discussion of the *Second Discourse* in Chapter 3. Especially relevant to Strauss's claims is the discussion there of Rousseauean "independence." We should recall that Rousseau's attack on modern civilized life appears to stem from quotations like these.

> The Savage lives in himself; sociable man, always outside himself, is capable of living only in the opinions of others; and so to speak derives the sentiment of his own existence solely from their judgment.[55]

This claim is what, apparently, forms the basis of the critique. In society, we are

> forever asking of others what we want, without ever daring to ask it of ourselves, in the midst of so much Philosophy, humanity, politeness and Sublime maxims, we have nothing more than a deceiving and frivolous exterior, honor without virtue, reason without wisdom, and pleasure without happiness.[56]

But, if this is the problem, then, so stated, Rousseau cannot resolve it by trying to "make the state of nature a positive standard," not, at least, if savage independence is actually only a contingent result of a temporary isolation and ignorance of others. As noted in Chapter 4, no "savage" can be said to be truly self-determining because so ignorant of self. (Each savage may have "considered himself master of everything," but only because of his "weakness and ignorance." Again as noted earlier, it is by virtue of having no understanding of others outside their family that "they did not *know themselves*. They had the concept of a father, a son, a brother, but not a man.")

It is in terms of these sorts of considerations that Rousseau argues for a notion of autonomy wholly civil (subjection to the general will), however problematic that will turn out to be.[57] And admittedly, this is only the

---

55 Jean-Jacques Rousseau, *The First and Second Discourses Together with the Replies to Critics and Essay on the Origin of Languages*, trans. Victor Gourevitch (New York: Harper and Row, 1986), p. 199.

56 Ibid.

57 There is obviously much more to this story, especially with regard to the infamous general will and legislator problems. Strauss clearly shares, say, Hegel's worries that Rousseau cannot effectively distinguish such a general will from the will of all, that the "general will," is "for all practical purposes, the will of the legal majority." *NRH*, p. 286. But Strauss seems also to reject, without much consideration, the attempt by Kant and Fichte to extend what Strauss calls Rousseau's "horizontal" limitation of liberty (*WIPP*, p. 53) by insisting that this very appeal (the constraint of the will of others) itself represents a "vertical" ideal, a genuine "kingdom of ends."

beginning of the issue. Rousseau is clearly interested in such autonomy because he is also still interested in happiness, in the fullest or sweetest satisfaction of our passions. This all greatly complicates the Kantian direction of the foregoing remarks, and would take us far afield in the present context. Here I only mean to suggest that the concern with autonomy so prominent in Rousseau, and the necessarily accompanying "unavailability" of any politically relevant appeal to nature, is more thoroughly and consistently motivated in Rousseau than Strauss allows for, and generates a far more powerful and influential legacy in later philosophy than the romantic, "natural" sentiments (or classicist nostalgia) pointed out by Strauss.

Let me conclude by pointing to the line of reasoning inaugurated by Rousseau and, I am claiming, seriously underrepresented in Strauss's modernity narrative. The central foundational issue is entwined in complex epistemological and metaphysical issues and is difficult to state simply. Obviously, the sweeping Kantian and post-Kantian attack on the possibility of a rational or a priori account of "nature" (or "substance"), as well as its attack on the efficiency of any attempt at a radically empirical account, set the stage for a drastically altered context for ethical and political thought. Most prominently, such theoretical accounts of the role of an "active" subject in "forming" and "legislating" what could count as an appeal to nature or any fact of the matter ended up greatly influencing the way in which the "bindingness" or obligatory character of normative principles was understood. I can be so bound or obliged only if I bind myself, freely impose on myself a principle or norm. What I am by nature inclined to do, or what might be naturally satisfying or naturally flourishing and so forth, will henceforth count as reasons for action, only if they can be reasons for me, if I can count them as principles of action, under conditions that ensure that I am freely so counting them or self-imposing them.

Such an idealist attack on the possibility of givenness or immediacy or the "natural" as such thus creates the modern post-Rousseauean problem of freedom. Or: in what sense can I be said to impose a "law" on myself, such that I can be assured that I am freely legislating in such a way? Already in Rousseau, as we have seen, the problem of freedom is largely the problem of independence, and already such a good is what Kant would call a *supremum bonum*, a condition for any other good. Nothing could be said to be good for me unless I can recognize it as a good for me and pursue it as such. And already with him, such independence is crucially linked with rationality. In any case where I count as a reason to act some contingently produced or socially powerful desire or interest, I am acting in the service of others or the vagaries of nature, not as a self-determining agent. I can act as a self-determining agent only as a rational agent, only under principles equally applicable to all such agents.

And all of this introduced a rich and complicated set of problems, most of which have to do with (i) the sense in which such a notion of freedom can itself be said to be a substantive good (rather than a mere condition for the pursuit of any substantive good) and (ii) how the requirement of universality in any possible, genuine self-legislation (how the necessity of "taking others into account" in such self-legislation) is to be understood. These are controversial, much disputed claims, but I hope to have said enough to indicate that such a tradition remains an unexplored option in Strauss's account, or a modern "wave" that has not yet peaked or crested, much less crashed and dissipated.

9

BEING, TIME, AND POLITICS:
THE STRAUSS-KOJÈVE DEBATE

When Leo Strauss's study of Xenophon's dialogue *Hiero, or Tyrannicus* was republished in English in 1963, together with a review by Alexander Kojève and a "Restatement" by Strauss,[1] the resulting "book" had already become a curious stack of Chinese boxes. At the center seemed to be some Xenophonic teaching about the limitations and attractions of the tyrannical life, itself a variation on the central Socratic question: the best human life. But Strauss showed, in commonsensical, detailed remarks about the dramatic setting, the two personalities (the tyrant Hiero and the visiting poet, Simonides), and Xenophon's other works, that the text provided no clear access to that teaching, and certainly no justification for identifying what Xenophon wanted to say with Simonides' praise of beneficent tyranny. In fact, Strauss argued, once inside the dramatic setting, even once inside the implied assessment of the tyrannical and the private life, we come upon some of the most comprehensive and important issues in classical political thought.

In two important passages, Strauss went so far as to assert that the dialogue's treatment of the issue makes clear by contrast the great poverty of

1 Leo Strauss, *On Tyranny (Revised and Enlarged)* (New York: Free Press, 1963). Strauss's original study appeared in 1948, and the French edition, with Kojève's essay and Strauss's restatement, in 1954.

the modern or social scientific understanding of political affairs.[2] The modern attempt to understand political matters is a disaster; even tyranny cannot be recognized as such by "our modern sciences." If this result is, as Strauss often implies it is, the "inevitable result" of modern philosophy itself, then we are "forced" to consider a "restoration of classical social science" (177). Strauss claimed that modern philosophy deliberately turned away from a principled distinction between kings and tyrants with Machiavelli (in a way itself informed by Xenophon's *Education of Cyrus*), and that a "confrontation" between the *Prince* and *Hiero* was a necessary first step in understanding "modern political science" (24–5; 184–5).

Although such remarks are the principal justification for studying the dialogue, and introduce Strauss's chief concerns, they are not much explored, and the contrast between the classical (successful) and modern (failed) understanding of tyranny is approached indirectly. Strauss is clearly dissatisfied with etiological and analytical accounts of the distinctive twentieth-century uses of power by groups or individuals against others or the masses, dissatisfied with the categories "dictatorship" and "fascism" and "totalitarianism." He clearly assumes that to understand the perennial appeal of tyranny, or absolute rule without law or accountability (and so to understand *what*, in human terms, it is), we shall need much more than information about economic conditions, nationalist histories, or the politics of cultural despair. He never presents a theoretical defense of this sort of claim, here or elsewhere, but he clearly intends that a competing, classical account of "what tyranny is," one sensitive to the *ends* any tyrant must be pursuing, and to the relative *worth* of those ends, will manifest its superiority.

Kojève then placed all of this in yet another box, a historical point of view. He claimed to see in what Strauss had uncovered the great failures of all pagan thought: its utopianism, its misunderstanding of human work and satisfaction, of the human struggle for recognition, even indications of the potential "insanity" of classical philosophy itself. The classical project depended essentially on the autonomy and superiority of the philosophical life, a distinction between theory and praxis that the Hegelian Kojève rejects. He traced such failings, finally, to the largest issue, to the "religious" character of such thought, by which Kojève meant its reliance on a belief in the eternality of Being and the ordered, purposive character of nature.[3]

2 Leo Strauss, *On Tyranny (Including the Strauss-Kojève Correspondence)* (New York: Free Press, 1991) (*OT*, as previously), pp. 23 and 177. (All future page references are to this edition.)
3 Worries about pagan hubris; asceticism; the political implications of classical, cyclical views on temporality (fatalism, the "tragic sense of life," Stoic resignation, and so on); or even an

By the time Strauss had finished his last restatement, the issues had become the ancients versus the moderns, the "history of the Western world," and the political differences that follow from one's view on whether "there is an eternal and immutable order within which history takes place, and which remains entirely unaffected by history" (212). Xenophon's small, neglected dialogue finally seemed in some sense or other to be about, or at least to require a discussion of, the politics of the "Being and Time Issue": in the bluntest terms, either a politics oriented from a notion of cyclical, non-progressive time; the possibility of a higher or lower, better or worse, realization of fundamental human capacities (by reference to which, and only by reference to which, phenomena like tyranny could be intelligible); and a necessary reliance on a chance, natural distribution of these capacities; or a politics of historical time, a history subject, at least in part, to human will and collective effort, the conquest of chance and a project of self-making that could be understood as purposive and continuous.

(Now such alternatives obviously omit what has become the most prevalent modern orientation: neither nature, in the classical or hierarchical sense, nor history, but precisely the unavailability of such comprehensive standards should orient political discussion. This leaves us with the natural individual [or what results from modern naturalism or from "methodological individualism"] and so rational egoist or rights based political thought. And another point that makes the exchange between Strauss and Kojève so strikingly unusual is how confidently they ignore such options in this context.)

Victor Gourevitch and Michael Roth have repolished and restacked these boxes, producing now a still more layered, complex book by publishing (without editing) all the extant letters between Strauss and Kojève written between 1932 and 1965, many of which continue and deepen the exchanges on Xenophon first published in French in 1954. (The editors have also reviewed and corrected the translation of Xenophon, retranslated Kojève's review, and restored a crucial, sweeping statement of philosophical principle Strauss had originally published in the French version and some-

underlying ancient *ressentiment* against the human itself, are of course not new, nor limited to traditional Christian complaints (as the famous charges of Kierkegaard and Nietzsche show). What is so unusual about Kojève is that he does not raise such complaints in the name of a traditional post-Christian or modern egalitarianism, a different sort of elite or master morality, or a new subjectivist theology. As we shall see he proposes a *universalist* morality (neither master nor slave) in a "universal and homogeneous world state," based on a wholly atheistic philosophical anthropology, and completely indifferent to the liberal democratic concerns that often accompany worries about classical positions on aristocratic politics.

what mysteriously omitted from his own first English version.) The result is a complex and stimulating book, with its "parallel dialogue" between the University of Chicago professor and the French civil servant, a dialogue made all the more striking since both participants take such unusual, highly provocative positions, and so force readers to face substantial problems in what are often wholly unfamiliar, even shocking ways.

I. Strauss's Xenophon

As noted, Strauss is confident that there is nothing historically anachronistic in making use of a premodern understanding in an assessment of contemporary issues. It is true that some aspects of modern versions of "absolute rule without law" would be nearly incomprehensible to ancient commentators: the power of modern technology and communications, and so the scope of what could be controlled, the very idea of tyrannical rule for the sake of some idea, some vision of history or "ideology." But such novelties are, for him, marginal in any thoughtful ranking of possible kinds of lives (cf. 178).

Neither are the classical categories of assessment inadequate, however foreign they might at first sound to modern ears. Any adequate condemnation of the tyrannical life must just show it to be *unsatisfying* in itself, not a worthy or reasonable goal. A certain claim about pleasure and satisfaction in human life is implied by those who aspire to tyranny, and this claim is in error. This incompleteness, or even perversion of human possibility, is what is wrong with tyranny; it is why the harm done to others, the use of brute force to restrict their lives, and so forth, cannot be justified; it is in the service of an objectively unworthy end.[4]

The Xenophonic dialogue used by Strauss to pursue these issues can sometimes have an air of unreality or folderol, much of which is pointed out very concisely by Strauss. The poet–businessman–Sophist–perhaps wise

---

4 There is, of course, the option of arguing that by harming others the tyrant does harm to himself (as does a shepherd who harms his flock), but that can simply sound like advice to the tyrant to "fatten the flock" more efficiently, more cunningly (cf. *Republic*, 345b). In more modern terms, one could argue that there is no solution to that problem, that harm to others always invites or in principle sanctions harm to all, and so no rational egoist could affirm a tyrannical life, as in the Hobbesean equations. Or one could argue that "I" cannot be "me" apart from a certain relation to others, so that my flourishing and theirs are necessarily linked, a train of thought introduced by Aristotle (mediated by the notion of being fully human, or species-being) and extended by Hegel to the modern notion of individual identity.

man, Simonides, has traveled for unexplained reasons to the tyrant Hiero's city.[5] He defers to Hiero's presumed wisdom, and asks which is better, the life of the tyrant or that of the private man. (Hiero is supposed to have superior knowledge of this issue simply because he has experienced both; the necessity for good judgment is not mentioned.) Hiero responds in a complaining litany that often sounds like a rich person's grousing about the miseries of vast wealth, or a beautiful person's that no one understands him. He claims that tyrants really do have fewer pleasures, and more and greater pains, than private persons. Simonides finds this claim incredible, and the first half of the dialogue is under way. When it is over and Hiero's most interesting and believable complaint has been lodged – that the sweet pleasures of love (for Hiero, pederasty) are denied him, are always clouded by fear and compulsion – Simonides takes over and in the second part offers advice. He counsels Hiero to worry more about honor than love (it is a higher, more satisfying pleasure), and he shows him some simple (and obvious) means to encourage such admiration, and to avoid mere fearful compliance.[6]

So, although there can be no doubt that a good Socratic like Xenophon would indeed believe that a tyrant's life, despite appearances, is really miserable, he goes about establishing such a claim in an odd way. No Thrasymachean boldness here in defense of such a life; the tyrant himself, in an unbalanced and exaggerated way (the pleasures of tyranny are hardly mentioned), does all the work undermining the tyrannical option (even if with an air of protest-too-much insincerity), and it is Simonides, referred to

---

5 Strauss suggests a possible business transaction (p. 36), but, throughout his commentary, he adopts Hiero's view that Simonides is simply a wise man, and he often treats Simonides as some approximation to the Xenophonic Socrates (cf. p. 38). Strauss is obviously aware of the fact that Simonides is introduced in the dialogue as a poet (an issue that raises the sophistry–philosophy problem), and of his reputation for wealth, even "greed" (p. 33). He points out that Simonides should indeed be called a Sophist (p. 94), and that his advice to Hiero speaks a language the latter can understand; it concedes a good deal to hedonism, is amoral, and praises as highest not virtue, but happiness unmarred by envy. But what is important to Strauss is that Simonides preserves a distinction between the pleasant and the good as such (p. 95), and that the praise of honor leads Simonides (and especially us) "outside" the city and fellow humans (as finally insufficient in the pursuit of the highest) and even beyond the conventional understanding of honor. This Socratic reading of the implications of Simonides' advice begins with the discussion of friendship on p. 97. See also the apposite remarks by Victor Gourevitch in "Philosophy and Politics I," *Review of Metaphysics* 22 (1968): 79–82, and "Philosophy and Politics II," *Review of Metaphysics* 22 (1968): 309–10.

6 Cf. 66 on the first part as "pathology," the second as "therapeutics," together with the reminder that the reader must "add to and subtract from Hiero's and Simonides's speeches to lay hold of Xenophon's teaching."

as "wise" by Hiero, who must correct the account by reminding Hiero of the higher pleasures of honor or admiration, available to the tyrant if some elementary precautions and anticipations are managed. He thus appears to praise highly beneficent tyranny. He does not praise it as best simply, but the dialogue ends with the claim that a beneficent tyranny is at least one way to secure the "most noble and most blessed possession to be met with among human beings," that is, "while being happy, you will not be envied for being happy" (21).

Strauss points to a number of possible explanations for this drama, and draws out a number of implications taken up very critically by Kojève.[7] Hiero's somewhat overstated deprecations of the tyrannical life are not surprising, on Strauss's reading. The reasons for Hiero's eagerness to discourage any potential aspirations toward such a life by Simonides are stated explicitly by Hiero. Tyrants, he tells us, fear the brave, the just, and the wise; they must suffer the fact that they cannot enjoy the company of such virtuous souls because of this fear. They fear the brave "because they might dare something for the sake of freedom"; they fear the just "because the multitude might desire to be ruled by them"; and they fear the wise "because they might contrive something" (12). The indefiniteness of the last fear reveals that Hiero must fear the wise most because he understands them

---

7 Strauss clearly understood that the way the issues of love and honor (or "recognition") were raised by Xenophon and interpreted by him (Strauss) made Alexandre Kojève the only appropriate interlocutor. (For Strauss, Kojève was clearly history's most interesting and thoughtful "Hegelian," and their exchange was the result of Strauss's invitation and persistent encouragement.) In a note (125, n. 59) Strauss alludes to the fact that Hegel's later writings seemed to abandon his earlier "dialectics of love" for a "dialectics of recognition." He refers to Kojève's *Introduction à la lecture de Hegel* for support of this claim (Strauss refers to the work as *"Introduction à l'étude de Hegel"*) (Paris: Gallimard, 1947) and notes passages where Kojève discusses such a change in Hegel, pp. 187 and 510–12. These passages suggest that Strauss himself was much influenced by Kojève's distinction between love and the desire to be loved on the one hand, and the struggle for recognition, on the other. (See especially Kojève's discussion of a passage from the theological fragments on pp. 511–12). The insufficiencies of Hiero's desideratum are described in terms that parallel Kojève's invocation of Goethe's insight about the same issues on p. 512, and much of their debate is possible because both share Simonides' dissatisfaction with Hiero's desire to be desired, and both see similar implications for contemporary discussions. (They do, however, differ on some details; see pp. 199 ff.)

I mention all of this because their discussion is framed by certain Kojèvean assumptions about Hegel's position that so limit that position that it becomes a good target for many of Strauss's objections. As Hegel's remarks on forgiveness and reconciliation later in the *Phenomenology* show, there is no simple shift from a "dialectics of love" to a "dialectics of recognition." This will all become quite important in assessing Kojève's position later, and has a great deal to do with Kojève's thumotic, Greek, non-Christian reading of Hegel.

least.[8] He only knows that he doesn't understand them and that they possess what seems to many a good, a good he cannot achieve with all his power. (Strauss links this fear of the wise with the general, "vulgar" mistrust of theoretical types, with the suspicion that the wise will see no reason to compromise with or accommodate themselves to the non-wise, and so will aspire to tyranny, and that the skepticism of the wise can be subversive of civic life and religious piety. There is a "disproportion between the intransigent quest for truth and the requirements of society," and so "society will always try to tyrannize thought" (27).)

Simonides' advice and his ultimate praise of beneficent tyranny, although highly "rhetorical," and comprehensible only within this particular setting, lend some credence to that fear. Simonides does seem to "long for tyrannical power" himself (55), although, Strauss argues at length, not simply as an end in itself. Although Simonides praises what is productive of the greatest happiness without envy, this is not said to be the greatest good, and it must be somehow squared with Xenophon's other, much more Socratic remarks about virtue.

That is, Strauss argues that Simonides' praise of beneficent tyranny reveals (and is intended by Xenophon to reveal) its own limitations (68) (limitations beyond those required in any conversation with a tyrant by a visitor in the tyrant's hometown) and that such praise, by implication and suggestion, points to deeper concerns. Simonides has an interest in advising and especially moderating the tyrant's actions; he is cleverer even than Machiavelli in creating the rhetoric necessary to gain the ear of an immoderate man (he is simply silent about the amorality of the tyrannical; Machiavelli believes he must be more explicit about ruthlessness to establish his bona fides). But his words, limited and careful as they are, allow Xenophon to address *us* as well. These claims about the implied limitations of the tyrannical life and the positive implications suggested by those limitations will take us to the heart of the debate with Kojève and to Strauss's basic claims about the absolute (or "eternal") limitations of political life itself (not "Greek" political life), the absolute (or "eternal") tension between a philosophical or theoretical life and human, political concerns (and not just as an expression of alienated social relations in a particular society), and the impossibility and undesirability of a historically achieved, universal state within which free, mutual recognition is realized.

8 Hiero himself points out that the tyrant enjoys the "least share" of trust, and that he must regard everyone as a potential rival for his wealth (p. 11).

Strauss reasons this way. If Simonides is right that honor is a more worthwhile goal than love, then no tyrannical life can realize such a goal, despite the content of Simonides' advice. For one thing, the citizens of the tyrant, although they can be enriched by prizes, will always experience an "inequality of honors" in comparison with the tyrant. They cannot have the honor he has, and so cannot honor him without also envying and resenting him, no matter how elaborate the ritual of prize giving, the composition of the militia, and so on. The citizens, however subject to such measures, are not, after all, fools. This fact inevitably adds constant uncertainty and tension to the tyrant's rule. For another, Simonides offers no real solution to the problem of freedom raised by Hiero himself. Praise from others is the more pleasant the freer the bestower, but there is no situation with less freedom than tyranny, however beneficent.

It is at this point that Strauss pushes his interpretation well beyond the text itself. Rather than interpret, he begins now to think through the implications of the position within a much larger frame of reference. The key link in the reasoning is that, whereas "love has no criterion of relevance outside itself . . . admiration has" (89). For Strauss this already means that "Simonides's emphatic praise of honor cannot possibly mean that he preferred honor as such to all other things" (87). Honor, Aristotle reminds us, cannot be the highest good, sought for its own sake. (And so securing the chief condition for satisfying honor, freedom, cannot be essential to political life.) One is honored only by reference to some ideal or standard of excellence that one approximates. Such an ideal or good is not good because it is honored; it is honored because it is good. Thus, although appeal to the pleasures of acclaim and praise might moderate and render more virtuous a tyrant, the real issues are more complex. In fact, interest in honor, if it can be inspired and nurtured, can only be a transitional stage in education, leading to a more noble concern with that-for-which-one-is-honored, "in itself," as it were.[9] A beneficent tyrant might be able to pursue such a goal, let us say, virtue in itself, and, given the problem of freedom noted, not be able to enjoy in any satisfying way the praise of the citizens. But that would be important only if virtue were linked essentially to an honored life, or if a "virtuous polis" *required* free citizens. The former cannot be true for the Aristotelian reasons just cited, and Strauss points out that, at the very

9 Strauss claims that "the desire for praise and admiration as distinguished and divorced from the desire for love is the natural foundation for the predominance of the desire for one's own perfection" (p. 90).

least, Xenophon himself cannot have believed the latter, given his admiration for the "slavish" but virtuous young Cyrus (72).

Strauss is careful to point out here, as he does elsewhere, that this teaching about a *truly* beneficent tyranny (essentially the absolute rule of the wise) has a "purely theoretical meaning"; it is not a blueprint for action. Of course, a view that only the rule of the wise is legitimate, but that the rule of the wise is impossible, is a position that, however "theoretical," has many practical implications, some of them notorious. It might lead the young to "look down with contempt on the political order established in Athens"; it might be "embarrassing" for its supporters in "almost every city" and might have had something to do with the real difficulties experienced by Socrates and Xenophon (76). It might also serve as a prelude to the issue of the rule of law, although Strauss clearly regards even that "second best" solution as highly "problematic" (77).[10]

Hence Strauss's conclusion, that the dialogue intends to present us with a great contrast between two ways of life – the political life and the life devoted to wisdom (even though, Strauss admits, the *Hiero* itself is "silent about the status of wisdom") – and to "indicate" the superiority of the latter. Or, "when Socrates assumes that the wise man is just, he understands by justice trans-political justice, the justice which is irreconcilable with hurting anyone. The highest form of justice is the preserve of those who have the greatest self-sufficiency which is humanly possible" (91).

This is a sweeping conclusion with many assumptions, among them the following:

(i) There is a difference between better and worse regimes but there is no hope for some fundamental perfection of political life. That would require the rule of the wise, which is impossible since it would presuppose some reconciliation between the wise and the non-wise. This in

10 Cf. Leo Strauss, *The Argument and Action of Plato's Laws* (Chicago: University of Chicago Press, 1975). Strauss's commentary implies that, besides the notorious "blindness" of written laws, the "rule of law" is fraught with many dangers. In communities where the law is the highest authority, like Sparta and Crete, a Dorian-spiritedness threatens to take over; mere courage rather than moderation becomes most important; the ground of good law in reason and so nature must be suppressed in favor of a more politically persuasive theological authority (and this with unjust consequences: the wise must enter into compromise with the unwise); there must be many, many laws; and, for Strauss, there are many indications in the dialogue that what must be given up or moderated for a regime of law, free from Dorian imperfections, may be worse than those imperfections, that too much in the dialogue represents a compromise with the actual.

turn would be unjust to the theoretical person (the wise will never wish
to rule) and would require utopian and dangerously naive assumptions about the power of education and reason in human life. The
fundamental political fact is the few–many distinction, and it is a permanent consequence of the nature of things. Accordingly, the fundamental classical teaching on politics can be stated in one word:
moderation.

(ii) Philosophers are not wholly self-sufficient (only self-sufficient as philosophers) and could not lead philosophic lives without a division of
labor and the creation of sufficient wealth and leisure. So they must
attend to politics, but, essentially, only to make the political world safe
for the philosopher. Or,

> In what then does philosophic politics consist? In satisfying the city that
> the philosophers are not atheists, that they do not desecrate everything
> sacred to the city, that they reverence what the city reverences, that they
> are not subversives, in short that they are not irresponsible adventurers
> but good citizens and even the best of citizens. (205–6)

(iii) True philosophic self-sufficiency is possible. A philosopher's satisfaction in progress toward wisdom is completely autonomous and in no
way dependent on the recognition or, ultimately, even the cooperation
of others. Such a life is certainly not dependent on the social and
political character of one's fellow citizens; philosophy is not its own
age, politically, socially, religiously, culturally, "comprehended in
thought." "The wise man alone is free" (84).

(iv) If such a life is in fact best, it would be unjust to affirm political
principles that made the realization of such a life less likely or more
difficult, even if in the service of other, otherwise desirable goods, such
as maximizing the free self-development of each, or protecting the
natural right to liberty, and so forth.

(v) Philosophy itself, however, is not a doctrine or method or dogma. It is
an awareness, difficult to achieve and rare, of "the fundamental problems," and an awareness, equally difficult, of how little is known in
answer to such questions. Philosophy is radically zetetic, can never
become wisdom.

With magisterial self-confidence, Kojève sweeps aside all these claims and
proposes a radical alternative.

II. Metaphysical Politics

Regarding the issue, I can only keep repeating the same thing. If there is
something like "human nature," then you are surely right in everything. (Kojève to Strauss, October 29, 1953; 261)

The Russian émigré Alexandre Kojève, nephew of Kandinsky, lecturer at
the École des Hautes Études, trade negotiator and civil servant under de
Gaulle, has been called the "big secret of French philosophy," the force
"behind Sartre, Merleau-Ponty, Aron, and also Lacan, behind the thinking
which dominates France between '45 and '70."[11] In the early and more
revolutionary part of his career, Kojève's lectures on Hegel's *Phenomenology of
Spirit* (delivered between 1933–1939) convinced many French intellectuals
and philosophers that the great sweep of Western world history could be
comprehended as a whole, given some comprehensive philosophical point
of view, a kind of "wisdom" that Kojève professed to have, all in preparation
for a bloody final revolution, permanently establishing a universal and homogeneous world state.[12] Many a later "engaged" or even armed intellec-

11 André Glucksmann, interviewed in *Le Nouvel Observateur* (November 11, 1983), quoted by
Michael Roth in "A Problem of Recognition: Alexandre Kojève and the End of History,"
History and Theory 24 (1985): 293. See Bataille's representative description of the impression Kojève made on students, *Oeuvres complètes* (Paris: Gallimard, 1970), VI, p. 416, or R.
Queneau's "Premières confrontations avec Hegel," *Critique*, 17, no. 19 (1963): 195–9. For
a summary (insofar as one is possible) of the participants in the seminar, see the appendix
to Michael Roth, *Knowing and History: Appropriations of Hegel in Twentieth-Century France*
(Ithaca: Cornell University Press, 1988), pp. 225–7. Kojève claimed that, prior to taking
over Koyré's Hegel seminar, he had read the *Phenomenology* thoroughly four times and
hadn't understood a word. But when he read it in 1933 for the seminar, and got to chapter
4 it occurred to him that it was all about Napoleon and he was off, always lecturing
extemporaneously, without preparation. See the interview reprinted in *Vermittler: Deutsche-
französisches Jahrbuch I*, ed. by J. Sieß (Frankfurt am M., 1981), p. 121. For general accounts
of Kojève's influence see Roth, *Knowing and History*; Vincent Descombes, *Modern French
Philosophy*, trans. L. Scott-Fox and J. M. Harding (New York: Cambridge University Press,
1980), pp. 9–54; and Judith Butler's *Subjects of Desire: Hegelian Reflections in Twentieth Century
France* (New York: Columbia University Press, 1987), especially her summary of Hyppolite's
objections to Kojève, pp. 63–92.
12 In his later work, Kojève appears to have changed his mind, and argued that, essentially,
such a state had already come to pass, prompting a much more ironic tone in his style. Cf.
the helpful discussion by Roth, *Knowing and History*, pp. 134–46. This is perhaps the place
to point out that Kojève's claims about the "end of history" should not be understood as
another odd eccentricity in what has seemed to many an endless parade of such claims in
café society philosophy. Kojève is stating without compromise or hedge the self-
understanding and the "legitimation strategy" of *modernity itself*. He really believes the

tual drew his or her inspiration, wittingly or not, from this charismatic Hegelian.

These École lectures form the basis of the remarks made by Kojève in his "Tyranny and Wisdom" essay. Human existence, it is assumed, must be understood in a radically historical way; both the significance and the adequacy of present forms of life, practices, institutions, and so on, lie in a possible connection with some future realization (and not as measured against some eternal ideal of human perfection or some formal criterion of rational action). This realization or completion must be brought about in good left Hegelian fashion, by the deeds of finite historical agents; World Spirit does not necessarily unfold or manifest itself. So the full realization or completion of what is rationally implied by the first expression of a distinctly human (free) act may or may not come about. If it does, or if its general outlines and possibility become clear (as they do with Napoleon–Hegel), this can be retrospectively comprehended by a proper account of this distinctiveness and a proper reconstruction of its historical consequences.

This latter task is the heart of Kojève's project. Human being, and so human history, must be understood as the result of intentional human *action,* itself the expression of some original dissatisfaction, a *negation* of the actual for the sake of the possible. Human being is *desire,* but a form of negation distinctly or *self-consciously* human. To show in what distinctive sense, Kojève proposes a kind of philosophical anthropology much influenced by Hobbes and Heidegger as well as Hegel. Purposive human action cannot be properly understood by reference to some spiritual or otherwordly dimension. In this or our world, death is the first lord and master, and any account of the human struggle to achieve any end must take account of the conflict among such struggles and the willingness of some to risk all for success. Human deeds always occur in a distinctive setting or context – possible opposition among actors – and are always overshadowed by the further possibility of a complete indifference to life by one of the actors. Any introduction of a moderating or mediating assumption into this initial situation is often characterized by Kojève (in a Nietzschean voice) as "religious" (all of which makes the issue of the tyrant, or master, and the limitations of such a life, of supreme importance for Kojève).

So far this could simply serve as a prelude for an account of clever and/or

modern credo: Prior to modernity all philosophy and science was really religion; nature is to be mastered; there is nothing essentially new to *think* about in the postmodern world; a complete and universal human satisfaction is possible.

vicious animals. What changes everything for Hobbes are fear and the kind of future-oriented, egoistic rationality inspired by fear. Hegel–Kojève see no reason to assume such a universal fear. What finally distinguishes human desire as human is the desire for an end only another self-negating (acting) being can provide: recognition (*Anerkennung*). Human beings desire (and, in order to be fully satisfied, reassured, *must* desire) that the worth, prestige, and entitlement that their own risk of life warrants (or so they believe) be recognized by others; human desire is always desire for another's desire. Moreover, it is only in the risk of life, or the indifference to death, that even such "socially mediated" desire can be understood as truly human or free, more than a strategic satisfaction of an animal need for dominance.

All of this requires, initially, the fundamental human social relation: masters and slaves, those who are willing to take this risk, and those who are not. This situation, however, leaves the master at an "impasse": recognition is coerced and so is not true recognition. Even if recognition is freely given, the master would receive it from those whom he does not recognize as worthy. His only satisfying option is a life of constant war with other masters, dissatisfying at the moment of victory. The slave, on the other hand, *works*, and so by that work begins gradually to achieve control over nature and his own "slavish" devotion to natural life. To make a long story short, it is by such work, the realization of the slave's ideas and the mastery of nature, that the conditions are slowly created for the world historical possibility of genuinely *mutual recognition*, some institutional achievement of and securing of legal, civil, and, in general terms, political and social equality.

Thus, once we understand history in terms of this philosophical anthropology, understand the significance of human work and the political situation in which it has always occurred (unequal power), it will be possible to talk about the "end of history," or the full realization of the most distinctive and important element of human desire, the desire for recognition.

This also means that the profound disagreement between Strauss and Kojève occurs within some shared view of what the basic problems are and how they must be addressed.[13] For each, the basic issue depends on how one understands human desire and its possible satisfaction: for Kojève a theory of *negation*, an active doing or making, a response to an original insufficiency or not-being that reforms, shapes, even creates the only possible human home, an activity that essentially confronts and must eventually

---

13 There is a prima facie similarity in the fact that one defends a "prehistorical" and the other a "posthistorical" point of view, returning both to the ambiguous problem of nature.

include others;[14] for Strauss, a desire for *completion,* wholeness, or the eternal *possession* of the good, a perfection that requires the cooperation of others, but that is in itself silent and private.

This fairly breathless summary of many, many issues in *Introduction à la lecture de Hegel* at least makes it possible to see the great critical relevance of someone like Kojève for Strauss. For one thing, as noted, Hiero's complaint, and what it reveals about the inadequacies of tyranny, open up the Xenophonic and Straussean concerns to Kojève's major problems. "In describing his situation, Hiero describes the tragedy of the Master analyzed by Hegel in the *Phenomenology of Mind* (chapter iv, section a)" (142). Said in a more directly Hegelian way, this means that Hiero wants to retain and live out his own subjectivity (that his deeds be *his,* enacted *because* of him and his will); that he adopts a short-sighted, "Masterly" interpretation of what this should mean (that all be coerced into submitting to this unlimited claim to entitlement), and so finds that this subjectivity cannot be acknowledged as such, remains always in doubt, threatened, insecure, and so unsatisfying.

And, as we have also seen, according to Strauss, when Simonides attempts to correct this "impasse," and suggests that Hiero can be esteemed for the great deeds of his city, he begins to raise implicit questions about the goods for which honor is bestowed, and the qualifications of the bestower, questions that will eventually lead to the great contrast between the political and the philosophical life. This is precisely what Kojève rejects, and is the basis of his own defense of the moderns in the famous quarrel. So, thanks to Kojève's reading of Hegel, and his application of that reading to the ancients–moderns "history of the West," this issue, Simonides' advice, and what it implies, is the point in the dialogue where all the differences between them come to a very fine point.

Before pursuing it, though, it should be noted that Kojève tailors his own response to Strauss's essay, and so does not present a full defense or even account of his own position. First, Kojève refuses to be constrained by the way Xenophon has set up the issue between tyranny and philosophy. Kojève is out to make quite an extreme point: that the ends of the theoretical life and of the political life are ultimately the same and cannot be satisfied independently. Accordingly, he rejects the notion that the actions of the tyrant, Hiero, would make sense if he were motivated by a desire to be *loved,* that he wants to experience the *unqualified* regard of as many as possible. Neither his actions nor Simonides' would make sense were they out to have

---

14 Cf. the discussion and the "ring" image (much used later by Sartre) of the metaphysical assumptions of such a position in *Introduction à la lecture de Hegel,* pp. 485–7.

some "value attributed" to their very "being." "Love thrives in the family, and the young man leaves his family and devotes himself to public life in search not of love but of recognition by the State's citizens" (156).

Second, Kojève explicitly contrasts the "aristocratic" context of his discussion with Strauss–Xenophon and the " 'bourgeois' way of looking at things," which is neglected in their exchange (141). He is happy enough to discuss the implications of the human desire for honor (recognition) since it will allow him to make his central point: that there is no difference between what the tyrant wants and what the wise man wants. But this context obscures the importance of *work* in the final realization of such ends.

> A man can work hard risking his life for no other reason than to experience the joy he always derives from *carrying out* his project or, what is the same thing, from transforming his "idea" or even "ideal" into a *reality* shaped by his own *efforts* (140).

The pagan connection between deeds and glory must be "complemented" (141) by the "Judeo–Christian" renunciation of glory in favor of the humble laborer's point of view, the pride in accomplished work, especially as a manifestation of one's unique individuality. This all indicates that a full response to the "pagan point of view," or a fuller account of the historical conditions within which a satisfying form of mutual recognition could take place, would finally involve an account of the significance of labor, as both conquest of nature and realization of self, in the final content of that recognition.[15]

In this context, Kojève orients his discussion from an obvious point: Hiero never responds to Simonides' advice. He remains silent, and there is no indication that anything Simonides has said has persuaded Hiero of

---

15 In his "Restatement," Strauss denies that the dialogue implies praise for some pagan or aristocratic sense of "workless nobility" (p. 191). The position he is teasing out of Simonides' remarks concedes the fact of a "pleasure deriving from doing one's work well" (p. 190) but insists that this pleasure, to be truly satisfying, must be linked to the work's relation to "virtuous or noble activity." The point is not the praise of workless nobility, but a rejection of "ignoble work" (p. 191).

Kojève's remarks are subject to this criticism, but only because he does not clearly link the bourgeois notion of work with the highest bourgeois good, freedom or even autonomy. It is the value of work as the realization of free individuality that cannot be properly understood within a pre-Christian context. This alone will introduce moral distinctions (a safecracker's pleasure, p. 190, cannot count as a truly *free* expression of individuality) if a longer story is told. Kojève cannot tell this story because he interprets Hegel in such a Platonic or nonbourgeois way, and so does not place him in the Rousseauean–Kantian tradition in the right way. See Chapter 3.

anything. Simonides' proposal for a form of tyranny or coercion in which those on the street would nevertheless *"willingly* give way" hangs there at the end of the dialogue like the "utopian" faith it is.

> Simonides seems to have behaved not so much like a wise man as like a typical "Intellectual" who criticizes the real world in which he lives from the standpoint of an "ideal" constructed in the universe of discourse, an ideal to which one attributes an "eternal" value, primarily because it does not now exist and never has existed in the past (137).

This evocation of Hegel's famous remarks in the preface to the *Philosophy of Right* is meant to introduce a contrasting explanation of Simonides' failure. This failure is not due, as Strauss argued, to the fact that Simonides is moving the discussion toward the supreme good of the theoretical life and so is hinting at the eternal tension between the human goods of political life and that supremely self-sufficient good. For one thing, as Kojève will soon try to show, such a notion of the supreme good is incoherent. For another, he first argues, the possibility and desirability of a beneficent, theoretically enlightened tyranny depend on concrete historical and social conditions. It might take time ("centuries") before such conditions were appropriate, but there is no (non-question-begging) reason to rule out a priori such a possibility by appeal to human nature. If there exist conditions wherein massive suffering and injustice can be ameliorated only by absolute rule without law or accountability, genuinely in the service of such ideals, so be it. (In a famous reference, Kojève mentions Portugal's Salazar as a possible actualization of a modern "ideal" tyranny.)

Such hard-headed, "dirty hands" rhetoric, so reminiscent of intellectual and Party bravado from the thirties and forties, now seems simply naive.[16]

---

16 See the remark on p. 146 about when, "regretfully," the ruler would be "forced to kill 'the resistants.'" In principle both Strauss and Kojève affirm uncompromisingly the superiority of the rule of the wise (or the authority of some historically realized wisdom, in the latter's case). This means in principle a willingness to consider a possible suspension or transcendence of conventional moral constraints on political action, and so a consideration of possibilities that can sound shocking, or, as Strauss frequently points out, simply tyrannical. As noted, Strauss considers this a *wholly* theoretical issue, the utter unrealizability of which entails that moderation and the rule of law emerge as second best, a very high status on such a list. For Strauss, Kojève seems to stand for a kind of apotheosis of the modern, reckless disregard of such classical restraints, and so his praise of real tyranny is treated "theoretically" and prompts no "moral" outrage, cf. his understanding of their relation, p. 186 (Strauss is prepared to concede the Salazar issue, even though "one swallow does not make a summer," but he draws the line, still surprisingly gently, at Kojève's foolish allusions to Stalin, (pp. 188–9).

But Kojève's main point is the first: his direct attack on the ideal of philosophic self-sufficiency. In criticism, he argues against the assumptions behind the "Epicurean" ideal of a private "garden" for philosophers and Pierre Bayle's "Christian–bourgeois" notion of a "Republic of Letters," where intellectuals must work for a living, but "renounce all *active* interference in public affairs in return for being 'tolerated' by the government or the tyrant" (151).

In order to justify such a life, one must make a decisive assumption: that "being is essentially immutable in itself and eternally identical with itself," and that it is eternally accessible (151). In contrast to this "theistic" assumption, Kojève then briefly and often in bewildering terms proposes Hegel's "atheism," according to which "Being itself is essentially temporal (Being = Becoming) and creates itself insofar as it is discursively revealed in the course of history: revealed Being = Truth = Man = History" (152). Even for readers reasonably familiar with the Hegelian, left Hegelian, and Heideggerean background of such claims, this can all seem very elusive ("Being creates itself?"), especially since Kojève does not explain or attempt to justify this radically humanistic historicism. But regardless of his own position on ontology, the effect of his remarks is to cast rather traditional and quite pointed skeptical doubts on Strauss's isolated, egoistic wise man, self-certifying in his presumed wisdom.

For what Strauss praises seems to Kojève a recipe for incommensurable sects and the resulting sectarianism. It leads either to putatively self-certifying wise men who are indistinguishable from the mad (153), or a cloister, a closed society perpetuating prejudices and self-satisfaction, insulating itself from others in ways that cannot be challenged or moderated.

By contrast, Kojève proposes the necessity of some form of social confirmation even in the theoretical life:

From this perspective there is therefore *in principle* no difference whatsoever between the statesman and the philosopher: both seek *recognition* and both *act* with a view to deserving it. (156)

Since a man seeking recognition "should do everything in his power to make the number of those 'worthy' of recognizing him as large as possible" (157), the project of philosophic satisfaction essentially involves the project of politics, or of realization of those practices and institutions within which genuine and free mutual recognition is possible. *Only* such mutual self-reassurance can satisfyingly resolve philosophic, theoretical differences. Any criterion of evidence or experiment will itself be the product of such social recognition, and so our attention should be focused on decreasing the role of power and wealth in such social practices (which always lead back to "masterly" impasses), and increasing the "worth" (essentially the freedom) of potential "recognizers."

This does not mean that philosophers should act as political agents, or spend their time offering advice to tyrants. There is simply no *time* for such divided labor. But philosophical claims about the nature of human being, universals and particulars, essence and appearance, the virtues, and so forth, come to be, in Kojève's rather clumsy and misleading word, "verified" historically and only historically. Philosophical disputes can be resolved,

> only to the extent that they are played out on the *historical* plane of *active social* life where one argues by *acts* of Work (against Nature) and of Struggle (against men). Admittedly, Truth emerges from this active "dialogue," this historical dialectic, only once it is completed, that is to say, once history reaches its final stage [*terme finale*] in and through the universal and homogeneous state which, since it implies the citizen's "satisfaction," excludes any possibility of negating *action,* hence of all *negation* in general, and, hence of any new discussion of what has already been established. (168)

Philosophers in short are (*an sich* if not *für sich*) speculating always on the rational possibilities made available, brought to light, in their own age. Kojève is here assuming that in any age's comprehensive, philosophical self-consciousness,[17] what will always be at least implicitly at issue is human being as such, especially the *human-as-origin,* origin of criteria of truth, limits of knowledge, self-conscious agency, and so forth.[18] Such speculations are, it is further assumed, always also necessarily linked to a possible course of *action;* claims about nature or the human cannot be separated from proposals that agents can and should *act* in various ways.[19] In this sense, they are always aiming at what might finally be mutually affirmed within a universal and homogeneous state, without masters and slaves. And "history" itself determines the progressive realizability of such possibilities, and so their progressive truth. It is only when their speculations (their own political

17 Cf. the Introduction of Kojève's *Essai d'une histoire raisonnée de la philosophie païenne* (Paris, 1968), pp. 11–57, for an account of the distinctness of philosophic reflection.
18 To understand *why* Kojève believes this would be a much longer story, and would involve, at the center of such an account, the anthropological and systematic way Kojève reads Kant (especially the *Critique of Judgment*) in his posthumously published *Kant* (Paris: Gallimard, 1973). See the diagram on p. 75 for an indication of how involved such an account would have to be.
19 Cf. the remarks in *Introduction à la lecture de Hegel,* p. 95.

reality comprehended in thought or given the form of rationality) are "tested" by someone acting on the basis of such ideas, when an attempt to remake and create is undertaken in the light of some philosophic claim, that the idea can be established or discarded (cf. 174). (This all raises obvious problems not much taken up by Strauss, who has other interests. *Which* modern institutions realize mutual recognition, or are essential conditions for such realization, and why those? How does one determine what *counts* as "historical verification" or true "success" in this radically pragmatic theory of truth? Et cetera.)

By contrast, Kojève insists, Strauss's picture of the Platonic wise man or lover of wisdom renders *his* social activity incomprehensible, and makes it difficult to understand Socrates' activity in the marketplace. "Self-admiration," besides being an invitation to a sort of insanity and sectarian smugness, "is relatively worthless when compared with the pleasure one gets from being admired by someone else" (161). Socrates' own public activities, although not "motivated" by a desire for fame, appear to confirm Kojève's understanding. "If, as a consistent atheist, one replaces God . . . by Society . . . and History, one has to say that whatever is, in fact, beyond the range of social and historical verification, is forever relegated to the realm of opinion" (161).

III. Perfectionism, Actualization, and Hegel

> You have never given me an answer to my questions: a) was Nietzsche not right in describing the Hegelian–Marxist end as "the last man"? and b) what would you put into the place of Hegel's philosophy of nature? (Strauss to Kojève, September 11, 1957; 291)

Kojève has, in effect, defended a radical version of a modern claim: that the human is self-sufficient unto itself. Even under extreme finitistic, or "post-Heideggerean" assumptions about the human (atheism and the finality of death), a form of absolute or final satisfaction is possible, one also linked to an absolute or final *account* of such satisfaction.[20] The great hu-

---

20 Cf. Strauss's comments on p. 212: "On the basis of Kojève's hypothesis, absolute attachment to human interests becomes the source of philosophical knowledge; man ought to feel absolutely at home on earth. . . . On the basis of the classical hypothesis, philosophy requires radical detachment from human interests: man ought not to feel absolutely at home on the earth, but ought to be a citizen of the whole." This claim raises the question of what sort of "attachment" to the earth or the human is possible for such a cosmic citizen, an issue I address later.

man self-dissatisfaction, incompleteness, and restlessness characteristic of world and especially Western literature and philosophy, are always an expression of a concrete historical insufficiency orienting all human labor and thought, one that can be comprehended concretely by an adequate theory of human desire and satisfaction, and are an insufficiency that can be progressively overcome by that labor and thought.[21]

Kojève has left it more than a little unclear, here and throughout his work, why we should believe that this great disaffection (originating fundamentally in the implications of the master–slave dialectic) can be *progressively and continuously* ameliorated. (The "one damn thing after another" or "postmodern" school of historiography is owed a better response than the one implied in Kojève's work; e.g., that his own version simply will be or has been "proved" correct, or is correct to the extent that he can will or rhetorically create its own correctness in history.)[22] The metaphysical assumptions governing his project remain obscure and are delivered in a style that never goes beyond the oracular and hermetic. And the characteristics of life within the end state, the universal and homogeneous state, seem, alternatingly, hopelessly vague and terrifyingly banal.

None of this, though, prevents their exchange from illuminating a great deal about the fundamental alternatives they represent. Strauss is eager to bypass the many issues of clarification and expansion, and to jump right into the center of the basic dispute. At that center is Kojève's (and Hegel's) "miraculous" (191) synthesis of classical and biblical morality, a combining of two teachings on strict self-restraint that produces, ironically, Kojève's immoderation and "lax morality," a willingness to be satisfied at a low or vulgar level (universal, equal recognition).

Since, by contrast, Strauss's defense of the classical view denies that philosophic satisfaction can be said to require the "conditions for universal recognition," he is eager to respond to the images of egoistic, isolated, self-satisfied, or sectarian philosophers painted by Kojève. But his first attempts are disappointing. He denies that there is *either* some form of intersubjective reassurance available for philosophers *or* some essentially private,

21 Strauss explicitly rejects these assumptions and denies that "man is thinkable as a being that lacks awareness of sacred restraints or as a being that is guided by nothing but a desire for recognition" (p. 192). But this seems to rule out of bounds, a priori, the notion of restraints that restrain while not being "sacred," and it ignores that Hegel's desire for recognition cannot be realized without the historical realization of those capacities *worthy* of such recognition. Cf. Chapter 8, Section III.
22 See Stanley Rosen's discussion of Kojève's understanding of his own discourse and its status in *Hermeneutics as Politics*, pp. 95–107.

intuitive self-certifying. There is *no* sort of reassurance at all. Philosophy is "nothing but knowledge of one's ignorance," "nothing but genuine awareness of the problems; i.e. of the fundamental and comprehensive problems," and so is radically "zetetic" (196). No matter what the inclinations of "subjective certainty," the problematic character of possible solutions can never be ignored. Socrates founded no sects, and even the Platonic "school" was well aware of the *Amicus Plato* warning.

As it stands this is simply a hedge. No formulation of the fundamental problems or claim for their fundamentality can be so "solution-neutral." No ability to show the limitations of proposed solutions can itself be so problematic and zetetic. As Strauss well knows, knowledge of ignorance is an extraordinarily difficult thing to *achieve,* and a great deal must be excluded and rejected, on the basis of a great deal affirmed, before it can be achieved.

Strauss himself admits "Philosophy, being knowledge of our ignorance regarding the most important things, is impossible without some *knowledge* regarding the most important things" (201, my emphasis). This returns us to Kojève's charge again, and Strauss's more interesting remarks about the issue take up the challenge in a more strictly critical way. Whatever the problems are, they cannot be resolved by Kojève's theory of recognition. He has the relation between philosophic and political satisfaction all wrong, and his own account of the end state, the universal and homogeneous state, is internally incoherent on this notion of satisfaction.

To make the first point, we are returned to the issue of love and honor. Strauss wants to reject vigorously Kojève's human and social measure for philosophical satisfaction (recognition). So he rejects Kojève's attempt to ignore Xenophon's association of the tyrannical life with "love" (versus Simonides–honor–philosophy) and so rejects Kojève's argument that both the tyrant and the philosopher must be understood to be motivated by a desire for recognition. There *is* a fundamental difference between those who take their bearings from the concerns of the human and those capable of some radical "detachment" from the human, for whom the desire to be honored by a small minority is the first step toward a desire for the eternal possession of the good. The former attach an "absolute importance" to "man and human things" (198), and this must ultimately mean that "the political man is characterized by the concern with being loved by all human beings regardless of their quality," whereas the philosopher, in love only with the "eternal beings" or the "idea" of man, finds all human things "paltry and ephemeral" (ibid.).

This is all hardly a hedge, but now the problem is the extreme or exaggerated character of Strauss's distinction. Human love is characterized in a strangely egoistic, calculating way as "mercenary love" (202). (Xenophon's *Oeconomicus*, 20.29, is quoted: "'All men by nature believe they love those things by which they believe they are benefited,'" and Strauss had already claimed in his commentary that "love has no criterion or relevance outside itself" (89).) Although it may be true that one can love more easily one's own, or those who return one's love, there is no reason given to believe that one cannot love at all those whom one simply finds lovable, without "mercenary" benefit to oneself.[23] And even Strauss's own formulations indicate that it cannot be true that love has *no* criterion outside itself. Just in those cases where one loves in expectation of the good of being loved, one understands this good in some particular way or other, for some particular reason or other, and understands the "exchange" with another as involving some particular good for the other.[24] If one cannot see reflected in love from another *what* one loves in oneself, a content loved in a certain way for a certain reason, it would be hard to recognize love at all, as opposed to a desperate need to be affirmed on any terms at any price.

This would at least mean that there cannot be the *strict* divide between the political and philosophical life, and for a simple reason. To care for others (or for myself) is not to care for whatever they (or I) happen to want but for what they (and I) ought to want, for what good would make them (and me) fully satisfied, and one cannot care for that unless one also knows something about what is satisfying, and can find a way of reassuring oneself that things are as one thinks they are. This would then lead one to a wholly "selfless" concern with the good in itself only if one could distinguish the tangle of human motives far more than one can, or if the many doubts raised by the existence of competing sorts of goods, exemplified in competing individuals, articulated and defended by competing, often persuasive partisans, could be resolved by the intuitive self-certainty about which Strauss has already hedged.

And, on the other hand, the philosopher's "attachments" to other humans still look incomplete and dangerously closed on such a picture. All the elements of philosophical politics for Strauss, the need for others, for divided labor and wealth, the natural beneficence of the philosopher (not being subject to the normal, mercenary human concerns), the fact that the philosopher "cannot help" being drawn to potential interlocutors, and to well-ordered souls within which he might see an image of the eternal, and

23 This problem in Strauss's account is pointed out clearly by Victor Gourevitch in "Philosophy and Politics I," 71–84.
24 Cf. *Republic*, 437e–438b.

the fact that the philosopher can satisfy such requirements in all sorts of regimes, just or unjust, with only a select few and some privacy needed – all these simply reraise Kojève's basic point. That point was not about the strategic need to create as many smart interlocutors as possible, all to keep the level of discussion high. The point was essentially about modern *skepticism*, and the profound consequences of the modern discovery that, say, the science studied for millennia was a disaster, that the sun did not revolve around the earth, that God did not ordain who should end up princes and who peasants, or eventually that the universe was not eternal nor were species fixed in hierarchical order, and so forth.

Said more broadly still, modernity (going now beyond what Kojève said and to the Hegelian spirit of his enterprise) did not originate in a willful dissatisfaction with the moderation and self-constraint in the tradition, in fatigue at what was asked. It was provoked by an inability to affirm conscientiously the assumptions on which such a notion of self-constraint was built – nature's teleology, hierarchy, and species-characteristics, all accessible to unaided human reason. It would not be unreasonable to suspect that, after such a break, only versions of Kant's transcendentalism, Hegel's historical–dialectical account of reason, and Nietzsche's perspectivism would be on the horizon. In this situation, the great problem of modern reassurance about its own or any historical direction will require more than the chance discovery of like-minded souls.

This issue is not as clear as it might be in the Strauss–Kojève debate because Kojève's statement of Hegelian humanism is both so extreme and so undeveloped. Strauss is able to characterize matters in a Kantian way: as a contrast between a selfish, human-all-too-human self-absorption, and a selfless dedication to the highest in itself.[25] But Hegel himself rejects both Enlightenment humanism (which he thinks always does tend to lower the terms of recognition to "utility" and the immediately satisfying) and classical virtue theory (insensitive as it is to the self, to the ways in which "the" good can come to seem a good "to me"). He does this by denying that we should conceive of our relation to others in terms of some fixed "self" or stable set of desires that we seek to realize through or in spite of others, or that we must abandon for the good in itself (or the right, the moral law). The whole question of free subjectivity itself and its conditions must be properly raised before the claim for its necessary realization in modern, universal institu-

---

25 Cf. Gourevitch, "Philosophy and Politics I," 80–1, and Rosen, *Hermeneutics as Politics*, p. 122.

tions can be made out. And Kojève's "heroic,"[26] existentialist rhetoric does not allow that to happen.

The same issue can be stated another way. Strauss denies that anything remotely like the satisfaction promised by Kojève could, on the latter's own terms, be available in the universal, homogeneous world state. In the first place, if a state guaranteeing genuinely mutual recognition and "equal opportunity for all" were to come into existence, it would be hopelessly utopian to think that as a matter of fact everyone would be satisfied with such a state, and history as such would end. Men and women do not act reasonably; human passions are terribly powerful.

But this means that the citizens of the end state are only "potentially satisfied" (210)[27] and this is why Kojève still describes a *state*, or laws with teeth in them, not a stateless society. But then the ruler must engage in practices that, in effect, *force* people to be free. (See the chilling description of this "age-old drama" on 211.) And so much for mutual recognition and universal satisfaction. (Not to mention that Kojève's whole "historical verification" theory is in trouble if we are only talking about potential satisfaction.)

But the apparent susceptibility of Kojève's position to this reductio is a result of the incompleteness and vagueness of his account, and not to anything essentially Hegelian or modern in it. Hegel's account requires that some case be made that various concrete institutions in modernity (and not just the state) have achieved the legal, civil, and cultural conditions within which mutual recognition *is* possible, in which barriers to such recognition are not characteristics of the institutions themselves. (There must actually *be* such institutions for the Hegelian case against utopianism and moralism to go through, but the issue concerns institutions and what they make possible.) The serious objection to Hegel's position is not that, even so, there will still be psychologically dissatisfied, irrational individuals. It would be absurd to require of politics a kind of universally achieved divinity. All the Hegelian needs to show is that, for rational individuals (even if not wholly rational), there will be no *rational basis* for any dissatisfaction. The much more serious objection to Hegel's position is internal to his project, one that accepts his critique of Kantian moralism and classical "objectivism" but argues that no historical case has been made (or perhaps could be made) that any such modern institutions exist or are even on the horizon; that the modern

26 I borrow this term from Roth, "Alexandre Kojève and the End of History," 298, and *Knowing and History*, pp. 19 ff.
27 Strauss quotes Kojève as having admitted this and cites p.146.

family, market economy, and state cannot meet the demands of "ethical life" set for them, and so that a generally moral (or relatively apolitical) stance is all that is justified within modern assumptions. This issue does not arise in the present context because the only concrete *institutional* realization of the Hegelian ideal that Kojève discusses are the revolutionary activities of contemporary, mad tyrants (who he persuaded himself were, I suppose, World Spirit in limousines).

More serious is Strauss's objection that, on Kojève's own terms, there is not even a *potential* universal satisfaction in a final state. First, whatever the institutional character of the final state, there will remain a profound difference in degree between the kind of satisfaction available to the humble farmers, laborers, and civil servants of such a state, and Kojève's sage, or, perhaps, the chief of state. This means that there can never be a true mutuality of recognition; only the chief or sage will be "truly free" – a kind of "planetary Oriental despotism" (208) – and the satisfaction of such freedom is suspect because he is not, finally, recognized by those whom he recognizes. Moreover, by settling for equality of recognition, made possible by the elimination of most scarcity and the conquest of nature, Kojève describes an end almost identical to that Nietzsche characterized as the age of the "last men," men who had learned to desire the lowest but most accessible, the simplest kind of happiness; what could be successfully desired, and, once satisfied, were "nodding off" into a permanent cultural "sleep." To this Strauss responds, "Warriors and workers of all countries, unite, while there is still time, to prevent the coming of the 'realm of freedom.' Defend with might and main, if it needs to be defended, 'the realm of necessity'" (209).

This last remark is connected to the theoretical issue behind Strauss's objections to any sort of historically achieved satisfaction, an issue particularly clear in a letter Strauss wrote to Kojève just after reading Kojève's Hegel book (August 22, 1948, 236–8).[28] There is a very general reason why life in a final state of mutual recognition could not be fully satisfying. Unless we show by some deduction from a philosophy of nature that the historical process leading to and realized in such a state is the unique satisfaction of the most fundamental, comprehensive, essential human desire, then the chance events that led us to esteem such recognition so highly and to labor

---

28 Strauss's 1957 letter, quoted previously, is for the most part correct. Kojève does not take up the challenge in the correspondence. See, though, his letter of September 19, 1950, pp. 255–6, and the 1953 letter quoted earlier, pp. 261–2. Kojève's point that the classical account cannot do justice to human agency, subjectivity, action, and so ethical life is a frequent Hegelian charge.

so throughout time to realize it cannot be shown to be unique or uniquely satisfying. Another sort of history may start up tomorrow, given what appears to be Kojève's radical rejection of a philosophy of nature. And if his philosophical anthropology *is* a sort of philosophy of nature, then it is not "modern" or "atheistic" as promised, needs its own defense or nature's teleology, and so on. Further, that concession would imply that the only true satisfaction would be a comprehensive knowledge of such a nature and its implications, or, traditionally, wisdom. This sort of satisfaction would be available only to the few; however, the many would understand it, and it would be a kind of religion, unstable, unsatisfying, making "unavoidable" the "decline and fall of the universal–homogeneous state" (238).

These sorts of criticisms raise a number of issues relevant to the account of nature presupposed throughout Strauss's work, and about the adequacy of that conception.[29] Strauss's version of a philosophy of nature is a kind of Platonic perfectionism and seems committed to the problematic claim that the true perfection of a human being transcends the human as such. In a letter to Kojève on the issue (May 28, 1957, 276–80), Strauss notes that for a human being, "the end is complex because man is simply both a part of the whole (like the lion or a worm) and that unique part of the whole which is open to the whole" (279). Because of this, "man's form and end is articulated in such a way that justice can come to sight provisionally as simply transcendent and *in no way 'the perfection of man'* " (279, my emphasis).[30] But this is like saying that a "perfect" musical sonata could only be one whose mathematical relations were so beautifully complex that it could not be played by anyone with human hands or human brain. One could ask, In what sense is that a sonata? just as one could ask about a perfectionism that required the transcendence of the human altogether. If the human end is truly dual or complex, perhaps the natural perfection of the human is the maximum realization of both or all such ends, rather than the transcendant realization of the divine end? With that Aristotelian claim, we would be closer to the spirit of Hegel's theory of historical "realization" (*Verwirklichung*).

On the other hand, the criticisms of Kojève are indeed relevant to him, but mostly because he was only interested in those aspects of Hegel's posi-

---

29 See Chapter 8, this volume; Richard Kennington, "Strauss's *Natural Right and History*"; and Victor Gourevitch, "The Problem of Natural Right and the Fundamental Alternatives in *Natural Right and History*," in *The Crisis of Liberal Democracy*, ed. by K. Deutsch and W. Soffer (Albany: SUNY Press, 1987), pp. 30–47.

30 Cf. *Republic*, 472d–473a.

tion that could be placed in the service of his own claims about the risk of life, the centrality of the master–slave relation; the heroic, revolutionary action required to overcome such an impasse; and the final revolution or end state.

By contrast, first, Hegel himself did not simply reject a philosophy of nature in favor of a philosophy of spirit. He did argue that the "concepts" or "notions" presupposed in naturalistic accounts could be shown to be incomplete in a successful explanation of the doings and sufferings of complex natural beings; that reference to what such beings intend and make (*Geist*), and to the activities and projects made possible by the historical institutions that they make, was necessary in any intelligible rendering of the activities of such beings (and so progressively less reference to the strictly natural properties of such beings was necessary). And for Hegel, this claim is not the start of a slippery slope toward historicism or Kojève's inconsistent, "anthropological" reading of history.

It is true that in some sense Hegel is maintaining that human beings by nature can only realize or actualize themselves in history, but that is not a claim about the actualization of a species-specific potentiality. The character of such a historical realization is shown to depend, if it is to be rational, on what else has been done already, and for what end, and its direction is linked to what is claimed to be an emerging self-consciousness about the potential rationality of such enterprises.[31] Hegel needs to show that there is such an emergence and such emergent rationality is "real," linked "dialectically" to the forms of life actually lived out in historical periods. (The possibility that nature could provide different starting points, or that contingent natural events could drastically affect history does not bother Hegel. If the creatures left after such permutations or disasters are capable of historical memory and are rational – whatever their natural composition and immediate inclinations – Hegel claims to be able to show they must enact the only historical drama that historical and rational beings could enact.)

Second, Hegel's account of the *Rechtsstaat* makes no use of the language of ruler–ruled or degrees of satisfaction. His argument for the rational realization of those aspects of our lives that are influenced by love, are cooperative and competitive, is an argument for the historical realization of

31 On Hegel's understanding of the Spirit–Nature issue, see my "Idealism and Agency in Kant and Hegel," *Journal of Philosophy* 87, no. 10 (October 1991): 532–541; on the issue of historical rationality, see "Hegel and Category Theory," *Review of Metaphysics* 43, no. 4 (June 1990): 839–48.

those social aspects, full stop. Given the history of the West thus far, *this* "ethical life" is what would complete and realize "objective spirit." Absolute spirit is another matter, and although the full satisfaction of the philosopher presupposes a comprehension of this domain of ethical life, the reverse is not true. The state qua state needs no wise man or wisely informed chief of state. And the fact that citizens are less "satisfied" than sages is irrelevant to the satisfaction of citizens qua citizens.[32] Hegel is, again, an Aristotelian, not a Platonist, on this and many other matters.

Now Hegel may have failed in all of this. But Kojève's aristocratic insistence on the desire for recognition, and his Christian insistence that only a universal and homogeneous state can realize such an end, represent truncated and unsatisfactory jumblings of Hegelian ideas that get a better hearing in the original. It is commonplace among those who admire Kojève to grumble about the "Hegel scholars" who just don't get it when they criticize Kojève's eccentric reading, don't see that Kojève was no mere "professor" and was after world historical goals not limited by textual fidelity. But Kojève was a child of his own time, too, a time of academic exhaustion with the neo-Kantian and Bergsonian options in the French academy, and especially a time of lingering revolutionary hope and impending global war. Kojève's embodiment of such a finite *Geist* clearly limits and diminishes his work, particularly because it so limits what he can see in Hegel. Whether Hegel's more bourgeois confidence in the institutions, bureaucracies, administrations, in modern civil societies, is of greater historical moment, more sensitive to the rational potentials of history, is another matter.[33]

For Leo Strauss the legacy of that wave of modernity that begins in Rousseau and culminates in the revolutionary, Hegelian "historical subject" results in a relativistic and ultimately nihilistic historicism. Kojève's reformulation, with its anthropological interest in objective human satisfaction and end-of-history measure or standard, would, he admits, save that tradition from that fate, but only by counseling resignation to a last-man state of

---

32 This is not to say that Hegel's position is without ambiguity on the issue of the "subjective" realization of reason in the lives of citizens in a modern *Rechtsstaat*. See my "Hegel's Political Argument and the Problem of *Verwirklichung*," *Political Theory* 9, no. 4 (November 1981): 509–32.

33 Admittedly, given the complex history of Hegel's reception, it would take some time to establish that Hegel is just what Marx argued he was, the culmination of "bourgeois" philosophy, or that he belongs solidly in the modern legal, social, and political tradition, however critical of some aspects of that tradition. A number of recent works have begun to explore and defend such an interpretation. See Terry Pinkard, *Democratic Liberalism and Social Union* (Philadelphia: Temple University Press, 1987), and Allen W. Wood, *Hegel's Ethical Thought* (Cambridge: Cambridge University Press, 1990).

ironic animality ("educated apes") that, just so, cannot possibly be satisfy-ing, or "last." However, as argued, what makes their debate possible is an agreement about alternatives and categories of assessment that narrows and obscures the tradition at issue between them. That strain of Hegelianism that produced both "scientific" revolutionaries and existentialist heroes has now, it is safe to say, played itself out. Its limitations are clear and its limited and painful historical results also clear. And the great dangers (particularly political dangers) of that strain in Hegel that produced both a reactionary attack on politics itself and a kind of radical historical fatalism are also manifest. Whether all of this now finally makes possible a more substantive confrontation between the alternatives genuinely represented by the Kant–Hegel tradition, and the classical principles defended by Strauss, is still an open question.

Part Four

NARRATING MODERNITY

10

BLUMENBERG AND THE MODERNITY PROBLEM

C'est curieux comme le point de vue diffère, suivant qu'on est le fruit du crime ou de la légitimité.

André Gide

There is a great and confusing irony in what many regard as the culmination of the post-Enlightenment Western European tradition, the culmination of modernity. Sometime in the latter half of the nineteenth century, the story goes, the radically new rather suddenly seemed surprisingly old, outdated because self-deceived, unjustifiably self-satisfied, really an expression of an older, religious consciousness or of a premodern, even primitive will to power, or of an ancient forgetting of Being. In such a context, to be truly modern (here the confusion and the irony) was to be "modernist," to have seen modernity to its conclusion and to find it incapable of fulfilling its promise of a new beginning. As painter, or poet, or composer, or thinker, one could stand resolutely on the other side of a great historical abyss, across from which one could now see the continuity of say, Socrates and Bacon, or Augustine and Descartes; the historical collapse of the option they all represent; and could say good-bye to the whole territory.

In the long aftermath of such modernist suspicions about the still dominant "official" Enlightenment culture, the very title of the recently translated book by Hans Blumenberg is a bluntly direct invitation to controversy – *The Legitimacy of the Modern Age*.[1] For Blumenberg, when Giordano Bruno, condemned to burn at the stake in 1600, defiantly turned his face from a crucifix offered him as a last chance at redemption, the heroic gesture should be seen as just that, heroic and historically decisive, a rejection of the reality of the Incarnation, and the expression of a decisively new form of thought. "The Nolan" did cross a real threshold that separates modernity from premodernity (and Bruno from his counterpart on the other side of such a line, Nicholas of Cusa). The new, for Blumenberg *is* new, not belated, and what's more heretical still in our post-Nietzschean, post-Heideggerean world, *better* than the old. The "self-assertion" of modernity is, in a simple word, "legitimate."

When his book first appeared it provoked so much debate, and such spirited responses from Löwith, Gadamer, and others directly or indirectly criticized in it, that Blumenberg wrote an altered and expanded second edition (1976), and it is this version that is now translated. Much of the book still supports the weight of such a heavy academic exchange, but once Blumenberg moves from the details of his dispute with his opponents, he almost creates a kind of issue and argument for which there is no clear natural audience, whether in America or in Europe. He not only wants to legitimate the motives of the heroes of modern science (already a task beyond the scope of standard *Ideengeschichte*), but wants to define and defend the criterion of legitimation he uses. This latter goal leads him to propose an "anti-speculative" philosophy of history that is, nevertheless, an ambitious philosophy of history, although again one with no clear precedents. At his most ambitious:

> We are going to have to free ourselves from the idea that there is a firm canon of "the great questions" that throughout history and with an unchanging urgency have occupied human curiosity and motivated the pretension to world and self-interpretation. (65)

If this claim is correct, and, as it seems to imply, there is no independent way, either a priori, or naturalistically, or pragmatically, or through a methodological phenomenology (of a Hegelian, Husserlian, or Heideggerean variety), to determine which questions *must* be asked and so which are

1 The Gide quotation with which this chapter opens, from *Les Faux-Monnayeurs*, was the epigram to Blumenberg's 1966 version of *Die Legitimität der Neuzeit* (and does not appear in Wallace's translation). All quotations cited in the text are from Robert N. Wallace's translation of Hans Blumenberg's *The Legitimacy of the Modern Age* (Cambridge: MIT Press, 1983).

"legitimate," then it falls to Blumenberg to show us not only how a question becomes one that needs to be answered in some epoch, but also how and why that need should convince us that the question is legitimate, a criterion that seems to imply far more than historical urgency. These are the two issues I want to discuss in the following: Blumenberg's sweeping historical narrative and his much more philosophic "legitimation strategy." I shall argue that, for all of its value in challenging much modernist dogma, Blumenberg's now justly famous project does not succeed.

To make such a case it will be necessary to review a good deal of his historical narrative itself, since much of the proof for what he wants to say is in the details. And when one does begin to digest these details, particularly in the intimidating context of Löwith and Gadamer, Strauss and Arendt, even Nietzsche and Heidegger, Blumenberg's book, for all its six hundred and seventy pages, can look deceptively modest.

His approach to the "problem" of modernity, although clearly committed to defending the progressive nature of the modern enterprise, looks academic and narrow compared with the work of such colleagues. His focus is for the most part on the late Scholastic and early modern philosophic–scientific tradition and his goal remains throughout a demonstration that the very particular questions asked during this period were new, even if not autonomous questions, and that they were "legitimate." Again, though, there is always a larger dimension implied by such an approach and one often discussed explicitly: that is, the firm rejection of any "holism" that would engulf the origins of the modern intellectual tradition in some larger (either social, or historical, or ontological) origin. Blumenberg is quite clearly insisting that the question of the significance or meaning of the modern point of view, whether of knowledge, rationality, nature, or progress, can only be asked in a much more limited "dialogic" context than is often assumed. There are, his approach always tries to show, only *these* kinds of questions being asked in *this* context (and these only as a result of those, earlier), *these* difficulties encountered *within* such questions, and only these possible responses.[2] Or (I infer from his argument), the likes of Horkheimer and Adorno were wrong to look for the "dialectic" of Enlightenment within the concept of Enlightenment rationality; they could not

---

2 Cf. "In a cartoon by Jean Effel in *L'Express*, DeGaulle was pictured opening a press conference with the words, 'Gentlemen! Now will you please give me the questions to my answers!' Something along those lines would serve to describe the procedure that would have to be employed in interpreting the logic of a historical epoch in relation to the ones preceding it" (p. 379).

have possibly understood that concept without the details of the dialogue out of which it developed.[3]

In sum, Blumenberg's attack on perennialist, speculative philosophies of history obligates him to defend a criterion of legitimation that does not defend the modern intellectual revolution by comparing it to other attempts to answer the "great questions" (or by simply applying an ahistorical test of rationality to modernity and premodernity), and his isolation of the scientific revolution implies an interpretation of the modern tradition that insists on identifying the particular "dialogue of opposition" at stake in each sphere in modernity, and resists collapsing or reducing such a plurality of questions. There is no set of great questions that spans all of history, and there is no modern *Geist* or totality within which modern science is a subsidiary phenomenon. Or summed up more simply, much of Blumenberg's legitimation of modernity will come down to his being able to justify his own notions of "legitimation" and "modernity," notions that are challenging even if often elusive.

Of course, these more systematic issues cannot be pursued adequately without attention to Blumenberg's analysis. In the following sections I want to focus on the most controversial components in each of the four parts of his study, parts I will designate "Secularization," "The Christian Contradiction," "The Liberation of Theoretical Curiosity," and "The Epochality of Modernity."

I

Secularization. The entire book, in a way nicely consistent with its own theory, owes its own genesis to a specific 1962 "dialogue" with Karl Löwith concerning the origin and significance of the modern idea of "progress," more specifically concerning the modern notion that there is infinite progress *and* that such progress is the "meaning" of human history. At the heart of that dispute is the question of whether the modern belief that history is in all decisive respects progressive, not static, cyclical, or chaotic, is a "seculariza-

3 It is this aspect of Blumenberg's approach that, if successfully defended, would help support some of what Richard Rorty has recently been saying about how we ought to read the story of the modern intellectual tradition. Rorty has gone so far as to write about Blumenberg, "Those of us who agree with Nietzsche and Heidegger that the philosophical tradition is pretty well played out, with Carlyle and Foucault that the arts and the sciences have not been unmixed blessings, and with Marxists that we should not believe what the lying capitalist press tells us about the modern world, but whose highest hopes are still those of Mill, now have a champion." *London Review of Books,* June 16–July 6, 1983, p. 3.

tion" of Christian eschatology; whether the centrality of the modern belief
that our present effort will become one day "redeemed" by future success
could only come to acquire that meaning and centrality as a version of the
linear interpretation of history required by the doctrines of Incarnation and
Last Judgment. Moreover, as Blumenberg rightly points out throughout this
section, the problem of progress is only one example of a large array of
modern views and practices often casually attributed to the secularization of
Christian themes. From Western civilization courses, to sociology seminars,
to intellectual chitchat, one can hear frequently and authoritatively that the
capitalist emphasis on success is a secularization of Reformation doctrines
of predestination and salvation; that the modern work ethic is a secularization of Christian self-denial and the ethics of saintliness; that modern, self-
disclosive literature is a secularized version of pietistic, confessional literature; that the modern quest for epistemological certainty is a secularized
attempt at secure salvation; that the modern view of political equality is a
secularization of Christian equality before God. Or, in a different context,
one hears that many aspects of modern notions of political authority are not
derivable from modern principles of contract, right, and freedom and must
be regarded as secular versions of divine authority, or even that Marxist
notions of a communist millennium represent a secularization of the Last
Judgment, perhaps that science itself is simply "our" religion. And, of
course, all this represents, at first glance, a quite natural explanation of
much of modernity. We do see around us few "sacred" things, and yet much
"devoutly" believed, pointing us toward vestigial religious sources of belief
when we realize that the modern philosophical tradition has not produced
anything remotely resembling a universal "foundation" for much of the
modern project. Moreover, the Cartesian myth of modernity's founding, a
complete suspension of all prior belief and an autochthonous beginning, is
so extreme that historicist debunkings of this myth, pointing to the connections with premodern religiosity, were inevitable.

But Blumenberg's argument focuses a good deal on the issue of progress
and on Löwith's secularization thesis.[4] This focus does not allow him a very
wide range within which to pursue the large secularization theme itself. In
concentrating on Löwith he selects an author for whom demonstrating that
a modern notion is a secularized Christian one is, ipso facto, to "delegiti-

4 Cf. Wallace's helpful introduction and his article "Progress, Secularization and Modernity:
The Löwith/Blumenberg Debate," *New German Critique* 22 (1981): 63–79. As will be apparent in a moment, I do not agree with Wallace that Blumenberg has answered all of Löwith's
criticisms. Cf. Löwith's review of Blumenberg, *Philosophische Rundschau* 15 (1968): 195–201.

mate" it, to show that that aspect of modernity's self-understanding is a self-delusion. There are several secularization theorists for whom that is decidedly not the case (Hegel being the obvious example). Nevertheless, in a way typical of Blumenberg's approach, he does manage to say a number of things in his *Auseinandersetzung* with Löwith (and later in this section, with von Weizsäcker, Carl Schmitt, and others) that are clearly intended to address the general issue. His particular argument is simple. He presents evidence that Christian eschatology simply could not have provided the basis for modern notions of progress, and he argues that it is incorrect in general to suggest that eschatological notions of history somehow "entered" a growingly secular world and were transformed exogenously in that context. Rather "Instead of Secularization of Eschatology, Secularization *by* Eschatology"; or, the eschatological view secularized itself. In support of the former, he argues for disanalogy by pointing to the eschatological notion of salvation from without, whereas the idea of progress required an internal generation; eschatology looks to the future with fear or foreboding, not the hope of progress theories; and the notion of "infinite progress" could not have been a transfer of the divine attribute of infinity to human history, since the secular notion of an infinite or even indefinite historical task makes a *reconciliation* with that task more difficult, not easier; it ends up not rendering history "divine" but an occasion for a depressing form of resignation. In support of the latter claim, he points out that New Testament eschatology is not itself translatable into any concept of history since its true impact is to devalue history completely in favor of salvation. It was only with the growing evidence that Christ was not returning anytime soon that a new view of the world and human history had to develop (internal to the Christian tradition), and that is what Blumenberg means by claiming that the eschatological view, under the pressure of its own unfulfilled prophecy, "secularized" itself; that an attempt was made within that tradition to reconcile man to the continued existence of a fallen world.

What is surprising, though, about all of the arguments in part I of the book is that Blumenberg only rarely makes clear exactly what is at stake in this critique of secularization. After all, the disanalogies between the eschatological and modern progressive views should cause no great concern to Löwith. He is not claiming that the modern notion of progress is Christian eschatology, but just that no explanation of why the idea of progress became such a powerful one in Western intellectual history can dispense with a reliance on a Christian *assumption* that human history as a whole must have some redeeming point to it. The mere fact of progress in astronomy or physics is insufficient to explain that assumption; it is hardly a perennial human presupposition (the Greeks did not have it), and so must be due somehow to a lingering effect of the Christian tradition. Now Löwith, with his own Greek and Nietzschean agenda, does often breezily assume that pointing out this necessary Christian "horizon" is enough to delegitimate, expose as self-deceived, the claim that the modern belief in progress is wholly modern and therewith rational, but not much of Blumenberg's critique really goes to the core of what Löwith wants to say; his arguments seem rather like marginal qualifications.

More surprisingly, when the issues are expressed carefully enough, Blumenberg agrees with a good deal of what Löwith and others claim. For all his criticism, he agrees that the modern view of progress as the "significance" of history as a whole is a remnant of sorts of the premodern tradition, and is an inappropriate, even illegitimate one, one that cannot trace its parentage to modernity itself. He argues, though, that there is no secularization of a premodern *content,* just a "reoccupation" of a territory that the Christian tradition had mapped out, and that modernity ("tragically") could not resist trying to invade in a new way.

> Thus, as we know, the modern age found it impossible to decline to answer questions about the totality of history. To that extent the philosophy of history is an attempt to answer a medieval question with the means available to a post-medieval age. In this process, the idea of progress is driven to a level of generality that overextends its original, regionally circumscribed and objectively limited range as an assertion. (48–9)

Given this, however, a reader might wonder what could possibly be at stake in "secularization" versus "reoccupation" models, or just what in modernity is being "legitimated" if so much of the territory modernity "reoccupies" is, it is admitted, not its own. But again, this problem exemplifies much of what is so interesting in this book, since a very great deal turns on what seem to be such microscopic or semantic issues. The real issue has little to do, I think, with Löwith, or von Weizsäcker or Schmitt. The nature of, and motivation for, conceptual change within a tradition is much more important for Blumenberg. As noted earlier, he is out to construct a completely internal narrative of one decisive change, a narrative that shows how the "assertions" of the modern epoch were the only possible responses to the deep, contradictory problems created by the Christian intellectual tradition, and he is out to assert (mostly to imply) that his approach is the only way that questions about continuity, or paradigms, or legitimation, or even just "our way of looking at things" can be posed. (In this sense, recalling Hegel's account of his own denial of the possibility of a priori, or "external" formal epistemologies and critiques, one could call Blumenberg's narrative an internal narrative or phenomenology of "epochal" change.) It seems to me that this will commit him to some explanation of *why* "the modern age found it impossible to answer questions about the totality of history," or what Blumenberg means by the "non-negotiability" of certain inherited questions, and why he thinks the intellectual tradition can be isolated in an almost pristine independence. But for the moment, his task is to show the Christian tradition itself generated a variety of hopeless dilemmas, all as a prelude to a modern "solution."

The Christian Contradiction. The story Blumenberg has to tell here is as fascinating as it is difficult to summarize, or rather summarize adequately. He begins the section himself by stating his whole theory in a wonderfully concise, although intriguingly hermetic claim: "The modern age is the second overcoming of Gnosticism" (126). What could this possibly mean? Indeed, it is one of the great achievements of the book to make this bizarre thesis quite plausible though the extremely detailed evidence for the claim cannot be summarized here. Roughly, the argument can be divided into two parts.

First, Blumenberg treats Gnosticism as Christianity's most challenging heresy, primarily because, for all of its own problems, it is more consistent with essential tenets of the early Christian tradition than "non-heretical" officialdom. Given the enormously difficult problem of reconciling God's absolute power as creator with the existence of evil, Marcion and others enjoyed an enviable theoretical advantage by arguing that God simply was not responsible for the evil of the material world; the "bad" demiurge was. Obviously, in order to reconcile God the omnipotent creator with God the Redeemer (with a God who "needed" to redeem the world he had himself omnipotently erected), official Christianity had to hold on to the notion of God "supreme," and come up with an alternate explanation of evil. Hence the enormous importance of Augustine and his "first" overcoming of Gnosticism by making man, not God or the demiurgos, responsible for evil and this through his freedom. But, as Blumenberg tells it, this was a resolution bought at the high price of continuing to hold to the notion of God's absolute sovereignty and omnipotence, an explosive notion that came to grow more and more unstable as it worked its way through the Middle Ages; this especially because the correlate of this notion of omnipotence and human evil is the beginning of the disappearance of the idea of any "divine" order in the world. When the implications of the notion of divine omnipotence are worked through to their logical conclusion, and any claim for a rational coherence or plan or point to the world comes to be regarded as an unacceptable *limitation* on God's power, then this *Ordnungschwund* has prepared the possibility for the modern "self-assertion." ("The destruction of trust in the world made him for the first time a creatively active being, freed him from a disastrous lulling of his activity" [139].)

This account raises several questions. Many of the scholarly issues are the most important, and the most difficult to discuss briefly. Did the legacy of the Gnostic challenge "live on" within the Christian intellectual tradition in as dominating and infecting a way as Blumenberg suggests? Did the ever accelerating requirements of the notion of an omnipotent God play as decisive a role in the destruction of the possibility of teleology, the growth of nominalism, the "hiddenness" of God, and the "abandoned" character of the world? Did all of this contribute decisively to the origin of the modern "retrieval" of the world under the banner of human "self-assertion?" How much of this is a story of actual historical influence, and how much a kind of "ideal" phenomenology of the logical relation of issues? Many of the more speculative interpretive issues are so compressed that it would be difficult to engage Blumenberg directly on them. Is he portraying the origin of the modern concept of nature (matter in motion, eventually as mere material, *Stoff,* to be controlled or "mastered") as *tied* to a theological tradition, such that the notion represents, or can only be understood as a "reoccupation" of, a *theologically* defined territory (even if that territory is located at the dead end of that tradition)? I find this one of the most interesting, though undiscussed issues in the book. There are hints of how Blumenberg would respond in his brief use of Nietzsche's argument that the modern scientific enterprise could not free itself from its Christian, especially teleological assumptions.

But, in keeping with the context developed here, the central question that can be asked is whether Blumenberg's account – assuming its scholarly plausibility – can contribute to an understanding of the decisive origins of the modern point of view, whether he can defend his general claim that there is neither a "gap" between the epochs (of a Cartesian or Kuhnean or Foucaultean kind) nor a repetition of the Christian thematic. To advance this large claim, he adopts an intriguing strategy in the second major claim of this section. He tries to show the importance of this Christian–Gnostic problematic by raising the issue of why the motivation, goals, and world view we now associate with modernity did not arise prior to the Christian project, indeed, when it might seem most likely to have arisen, as a consequence of Epicurus' atomism.[5]

What he tries to show is how very different the revival of Democritean atomism was in, on the one hand, the context of Epicurus and Lucretius and, on the other, in the context of divine absolutism, voluntarism, and the world's uncertainty that the theological tradition had created. Without the latter context, Epicurus could, in effect, "afford" to attempt simply to "neutralize" man's relation to the cosmos. His goal was a view of nature that would legitimate the possibility of indifference to nature, the Stoic *ataraxia*. This clearly assumed that if a mechanistic atomism was correct, that would be all that would be required to promote or make reasonable that nature was "neutralizable," intellectually unthreatening enough so that all Epicurus needed to do was to "exclude uncertainties," not "create certainties" (182). However in, for example, Descartes's case, the historical developments that had led to a lack of any rational connection between the world and God (as well as the expectation that there ought to be) had rendered the insecurity, uncertainty, and potential deceptiveness of nature far more pressing and threatening than in the Stoic context. Thus, for Descartes, the materiality of the world *had* to mean something different. In fact, "Reduction of the world to pure materiality is not primarily a theoretical proposition, which would have to compete with a traditional truth, but rather a postulate of reason assuring itself of its possibilities in the world – a postulate of self-assertion" (205–10).

The theological tradition had in effect created the fear that *anything* was possible in the material world, and one who asserted the explicit postulate of materiality could not, now, afford to be "indifferent" to the practical consequences of that materiality; he had to protect himself from this fear and uncertainty. He had to *master* nature, and it is only in that context that a mechanistic atomism, or any potentially scientific view of the world, generates a research project, that there is any motivation for a continuing inquiry into the details of material events.

All of this creates an unusual but, I think, welcome picture of early modernity, especially of Descartes. It does not take his foundationalist metaphysical project at face value, and grounds many of Descartes's theoretical

5 Readers interested in a much more focused example of Blumenberg's method should consult his *Die Genesis der Kopernikanischen Welt* (Frankfurt am M.: Suhrkamp, 1975). There Blumenberg also tries to show how Copernicus did not simply revolt against a tradition full of mistakes and illusions, but that that tradition itself created the "possibility" of Copernicus (and so can explain the impact of Copernicus as opposed to, say, Aristarchus).

claims in a practical intention; he argues that that intention, understood in its historical context, is the legitimation of Descartes's project, rather than the surface candidates for such a foundation, the cogito–clear and distinct ideas–God structure.[6] It would be interesting here to compare Blumenberg's account with a similar emphasis on the practical origins of modernity – that of Leo Strauss. Although the issues are in some cases complicated by the problem of esotericism, in Strauss and Straussean interpretations, that practical intention is often a kind of political scientism, a "will" to mastery for which metaphysics or first philosophy of any kind is either wholly post facto, a Trojan horse, or otiose. However, often, within the "quarelle des anciens et des modernes," the origin of that "will" is explained by Strausseans just by contrast with antiquity, as if the rejection of antiquity is the necessary and sufficient condition of this "will." Blumenberg's forceful insistence on the importance of the Middle Ages as more than a mere middle, and so on the intellectual problematic that generated the motivation for modernity and blocked a return to antiquity, is an important contrast to that interpretation.

However, for all its value, Blumenberg's approach continues in this section to attribute enormous power and influence to the complications, contradictions, and resulting solutions within the intellectual tradition, perhaps more than it can bear. It's not as if he is simply trying to argue that the contradictions of divine absolutism and voluntarism contribute something to the modern motivation to view nature in a different way. It is the only source of motivation he appears to want to credit.[7] Why a question comes to be a question that needs answering, or most needs answering, may have a good deal to do with the questions that were asked "before" it, but it seems strikingly odd to suggest that a variety of other historical, social, political, or even personal, psychological factors do not play a role. One does not have to be a crude reductionist, a sociologist of knowledge, a Nietzschean genealogist, a Foucaultean archeologist, or whatever, to be at least skeptical that the interplay of "questions" and "answers" can account for so much of the motivation that went into the founding of modernity. Surely the problematic aspects of medieval court culture, *Bildung* (to refer to Hegel's account

6 Clearly, the practical and theoretical issues are not inconsistent, but the important issue is that of priority, and given some decision on the issue, how one reads the totality of the Cartesian texts.
7 Among many examples, cf. his explanation of Ockham's nominalism (pp. 188–9), his subsequent criticism of Heidegger, or his argument that much of what happens in history can be explained by attention to the "questions" human beings ask and try to answer, and not to any hidden agenda (pp. 191–2).

of the origin of modern *Geist*), both social and political, as well as the influence of personal will and genius, have some role to play. It has always been difficult to know how to put such pieces together (or even whether they can and ought to be "put together"), but, at least on this issue, it seems to me that Hegel's account of *sich entfremdte Geist* in his *Phenomenology* is more on the right track toward a full explanation.

But pursuing this line would be a major digression indeed. Given the way Hegel is often interpreted, to pursue his approach means to be committed to an unwieldly metaphysical apparatus with "Cosmic Spirit" revealing itself in time, "necessary" stages in a historical march toward wisdom, and the destruction of difference and individuality within a "closed" identity theory. This theological and metaphysical reading of Hegel has recently become popular again and so Hegel's voice is even less often heard in contexts like Blumenberg's than it might. However, showing his relevance (without the metaphysical baggage) is quite another story.

The Liberation of Theoretical Curiosity. This section, called the "Trial" of curiosity by Blumenberg, is the longest in the book and ranges over figures from Socrates and Epicurus to Voltaire, Kant, Feuerbach, and Freud. In this next stage of the story, the issue is how, within the prepared context detailed previously, modern theoretical curiosity came to define, understand, and legitimate itself. Why did it become a worthwhile thing to be "curious," indeed intently, almost obsessively curious in a way not tied to traditional assumptions about the "value" of knowledge? If the paradoxes of divine absolutism and voluntarism rendered the world so uncertain and God so *absconditus* as to create a pressure for explanation and security that "faith" alone could not handle, then how did the modern notion of curiosity come to relieve that pressure?

And again, Blumenberg's narrative has a proto-Hegelian, that is to say dialectical, ring to it: "In the perfection of Scholasticism, the potential for destruction is already latent" (336). In this case the perfection–destruction dialectic involves how the history of attempts to argue for an "economy" of theoretical curiosity, that is, to argue against unrestricted curiosity in favor of a higher good or a more important, more comprehensive goal than curiosity's satisfaction could achieve, finally contradicted itself. The argument for this progression involves a dual denial of alternate accounts. First, he denies the claim that the motivation for scientific knowledge, our sense of its significance, originates in "natural" necessity, a survival necessity. Science may have historically made itself indispensable for survival, but that fact is no argument for its natural necessity and is no explanation of the specific origin and self-understanding of modern curiosity. Moreover, such a naturalistic pragmatism does no justice to the original promise of those who pleaded for the liberation of curiosity from external restraints: It would make men *better,* happier, not just "possible." Second, Blumenberg denies any postulation of an eternal, comprehensive "desire" for all knowledge that incorporates philosophy, natural science, mathematics, religion, art, and so on. It was not the case that such a natural desire was arbitrarily suppressed by the Middle Ages, constantly struggling against these chains of superstition until finally freed in the "Renaissance" (cf. 233). What human beings wanted to know and why they wanted to know it were always much more specific than that, and no justice is done to the significance and motivation of the medieval enterprise if almost all of it is written off as superstition, ignorance, and faulty argument.

Blumenberg's alternative account is a fine example of what he calls looking for the questions that an epoch was struggling to answer. Sometimes it is not clear just what questions are behind an "epochal" enterprise, and in this case it takes Blumenberg a great deal of space and detail to sketch the context within which the proponents of modern curiosity would have had to stand. He begins by making much, far too much I think, of Socrates' *deuteros plous,* his famous "second sailing" away from the natural philosophy of Anaxagorous, toward "the human things." For Blumenberg, this begins the traditional argument against the independent value of theoretical curiosity and the simultaneous assertion of a higher value for practical ends. He sees this argument extending through Stoicism, skepticism, Augustinianism and much of the Christian tradition, given its emphasis on the priority of salvation to all other goals. Blumenberg might even have made more of the case against curiosity by the greatest modern Augustinian, Heidegger. There is much in this story that is valuable, and much in the tensions it makes for itself that contribute persuasively to what Blumenberg wants to claim about modern curiosity, but there is also, here more than anywhere else in the book, much that is forced together in ways that raise a number of questions.

For example, to speak so abstractly about Socrates' "rejection" of "natural" philosophy in favor of human *pragmata* adopts too quickly a crude Ciceronean perspective (cf. 248). It could, I think, be more easily argued that Socrates did not reject inquiry into nature but challenged the *sufficiency* of the naturalist notion of *aitia,* claiming that their accounts were incomplete, not simply wrong, and required a completion in speculative philosophy. Moreover, it could also be more easily argued that Socrates did not so much turn away from naturalistic inquiry in favor of self-knowledge as to argue that the issues are inseparable, that what is recovered in *anamnesis* is not "the" self, or even the soul, but the Ideas, and so the really "natural." Ironically, when Blumenberg notes this other side of the Socratic enterprise (and indeed, it is so prominent he could not fail to note it), he chooses to rest content with his categories and blame the Platonic Socrates for violating them. "Still the foundation of the visible world in the world of Ideas, which remains [in the Platonic Socrates] cannot be easily reconciled with the Socratic position's exclusion of cosmological theory" (254). I would have thought that this unreconcilability might have given Blumenberg pause about his hasty inclusion of Socrates in this narrative of the history of the "economy" of theory.

This narrative line in Blumenberg's story is clear enough. Beginning with the Socratic insistence on the priority of self-knowledge, through the Epicurean priority of indifference to nature, the skeptical and generally Hellenistic priority of philosophic therapy over theory, to the early and late medieval insistence on such points as God's "right" to the secret of his own creation, the Tertullian restriction of the value of knowledge to those things relevant for salvation, and the general suspicion that the temptation to know the material world risks the loss of one's soul, the ancient and medieval restrictions on curiosity created a highly problematic self-understanding. This problem is visible, first, in the heresy problem (i.e., a certain amount of theoretical speculation and investigation is necessary to answer the heretics), second, in the growing dependence on science, even for religious purposes (fixing the date for Easter); it is especially clear when Augustine tries to explain the physical possibility of eternal punishment to an unbeliever and tries to avoid an ad hoc invocation of omnipotence.

> The inconsistency of Augustine's argumentation is itself very significant: on the one hand he can provide himself with a basis on which to deal with unbelievers and with their concept of the cosmos only by making a point of holding to the regularity of the world and regarding supposed miracles as appearances due to regularities unknown to us; on the other hand, he fears a lawfulness to which appeal can be made, which would give legitimacy to the human inquisitive drive and would leave behind it, on account of its insistence on rationality, only a restricted acknowledged part of God's free will. (320)

This is only one of many examples of the ironic problem, What, theoretically, must be known in order to know how insignificant and potentially dangerous is the need for theoretical enlightenment? Moreover, the very attempt to denigrate the importance of theoretical knowledge and to challenge the possibility of an adequate knowledge of the fallen world makes it that much more difficult to expend much energy in arguing *against* theoretical activity itself. (Why bother if reason is so impotent?)

> Raising theology to its maximal pretension over against reason had the unintended result of reducing theology's role in explaining the world to a minimum, and thus of preparing the competence of reason as the organ of a new kind of science that would liberate itself from the tradition. (347)

But none of this pressure for the liberation of curiosity meant that curiosity was simply self-justifying. The growing lack of coherence in the arguments against an uninhibited curiosity made possible the "self-assertion" of curiosity, but the modern epoch still required its positive legitimation of that assertion, and it found that criterion in the concept of utility. In contexts ranging from Bacon to Descartes to Voltaire, utility was capable of safely being invoked to repeat the Scholastic charges against vain, idle, metaphysical speculation, and to offer a defense of what seemed a greatly reduced pretension to know. Here the story of modernity's restriction of speculative pretension for the sake of infinite real power over nature is a familiar one. However, as Blumenberg proceeds with his explanation of how this legitimation unfolded, his own attitude is much less clear than in the secularization discussion. To some extent, he seems to regard any demand that a pretension to knowledge be justified as itself a reoccupation of a Scholastic problematic, as if modernity could not forget its Socratic and Christian heritage (although it should have) and had to try to defend itself in their terms, which were inappropriate to the rest of modernity. That is, Blumenberg seems to think that the epoch illegitimately committed itself to beliefs in the possible finality of the scientific enterprises, progress toward that goal, and its utility, and so forth, and that these beliefs are dangerously anachronistic. When exposed as exaggerated or double-edged, they can seem to delegitimate *science itself* – and this unfairly, given that the justification demand is as anachronistic in modernity as wondering how modernity will answer the question about the point of human history. As noted, Blumenberg's own position is not as clear here as in the former case, but he is also not finished.

He points out how the claims for an enlightened, useful liberation of curiosity created their own problems. For one thing, it was hard to see what kind of limits on unrestrained curiosity could be argued for in this context, as in Maupertuis' suggestions about performing experiments on live human beings. For another, the spheres within which the results of scientific activity were to be useful became progressingly harder to define, and the exact relations among medicine, morals, politics, and metaphysics could not but become a serious problem.

In short, the stage was set for Kant. Blumenberg's discussion of Kant is brief, but quite important. For, it was Kant who "brought the 'trial' of theoretical curiosity to a close that, as a systematic explication, was not to be superseded or revised again" (p. 433). Presumably, this means that Kant's (finally dualistic) understanding of the status of reason's "need" to know is still ours, and although it is easy to agree in a broad way with such a claim, it is not clear exactly what is involved. That is, one of the great ambiguities in the Kantian project is that the same book that looks to be a radical critique of the pretensions of both speculative and theoretical–scientific philosophy promises that this limitation is also a *satisfaction* (*Befriedigung*) of our knowledge desire (*Wissbegierde*). The book concludes with the promise that we can achieve

> before the end of the present century what many centuries have not been able to accomplish, namely, to secure for human reason complete satisfaction in regard to that which its appetite for knowledge has occupied itself at times, though hitherto in vain. (A856 = B884)

Kant thus argues *both* that a fundamental human curiosity can be satisfied and that the very pursuit of that satisfaction involves reason in a self-critique that completely and finally restricts metaphysical pretensions; or, Kant has successfully rejected the old Socratic–Augustinian terms for the whole problem: either outward and dangerous curiosity *or* inwardness and self-knowledge. For Blumenberg, part of the early modern difficulty in legitimating theoretical curiosity was its acceptance of those alternatives – hence the early, somewhat apologetic defenses of common sense, utility, practicality. It was Kant who broke the hold of this assumption, and showed

> that these are not the alternatives at all but instead that the motive of curiosity itself, consistently pursued, by reaching for the totality of the conditions of objectivity, finally makes self-knowledge its necessary subject. (434)

This argument made possible the unrestricted actual pursuit of scientific knowledge by showing that that pursuit was not in competition with self-knowledge, but required a kind of self-knowledge as its legitimating condition and could not be perceived as a metaphysical threat to our moral autonomy.

Here again, Blumenberg seems to me to run a number of separate issues together. To associate Augustinian self-knowledge with the formal self-knowledge of the Transcendental Analytic is quite anachronistic, and misses a crucial point in Kant's transformation of the issue – that there is little room left at all for the possibility of traditional humanistic self-knowledge. Certainly the tasks of empirical psychology, *Anthropologie,* or even moral self-examination bear little resemblance to what was considered so important in the Socratic, Christian, and romantic traditions. Moreover, as Blumenberg himself notes, Kant's critique of the metaphysical pretensions of science ironically renders completely autonomous and unrestricted our investigation of phenomenal nature. Although Blumenberg's later chapters try to tie Kant's subject of knowledge with the later investigations of Feuerbach and Freud into the historical and psychological subjective sources of inquiry, he is associating Kant far too quickly with later developments only loosely tied to his. It might be more accurately said that the Kantian legitimation of scientific curiosity accomplished its goal by *neutralizing* the origin and practice of such inquiry, not by tying that practice to a kind of self-limiting self-knowledge (hence the great emphasis on the formality of the critical enterprise, as I have argued elsewhere).[8] Thus the later discussions of Feuerbachean and Freudian subjects are, strictly speaking, incoherent in the Kantian context, and would require a great deal more detail from the Fichtean and Hegelian *critique* of Kant before the line Blumenberg wants could be drawn. In sum, Blumenberg is right that Kant has avoided an opposition between theoretical curiosity and self-knowledge, or between science and salvation, but he did not do so by connecting the two themes. Indeed, he avoided this framework by even more decisively separating the realms, by "detaching" the subjective "conditions" for knowledge from the human, *acting* subject, and that separation is far more his legacy to the contemporary world.

The Epochality of Modernity. The core of Blumenberg's case is given in parts II and III, in the story he tells about how the "immanent rigorism" (465) of the Christian tradition provoked its own self-destruction over the issue of omnipotence and worldliness and how modern scientific curiosity came to understand and legitimate itself in that context. Part IV is mainly a recapitulation and reassertion. He recapitulates his historical thesis by examining how Nicholas of Cusa, on the medieval side of the modern "threshold," began to see clearly the problems that that tradition had created and

8 Robert Pippin, *Kant's Theory of Form* (New Haven: Yale University Press, 1982).

tried to solve them without crossing that threshold. He failed. By Blumenberg's account, he failed necessarily. Then he examines how Giordano Bruno resolved those problems, but only by rejecting that tradition and being wholly modern. Throughout, he reasserts this methodological claim by criticizing again "historical substantialism" (466) and any other view that would deny the true epochality of modernity, and by again insisting that this epochality does not mean radical novelty, discontinuity, or incommensurability. To make this point, he discusses Kuhn and claims that (a) there *are* "reference-frames conditions" that span epochal change (I think he means "common questions" even if different answers); (b) that these questions have a kind of durability that outlasts transformations or revolutions in the content of thought (though they are not perennial and eventually are perceived as illegitimate, as not needing to be answered); and (c) that Kuhn just avoids explanations of any kind for *why* new paradigms arise. Note how odd it is to hear Blumenberg, of all people, argue against Kuhn that something analogous to Kant's "first analogy" is a necessary condition for the possibility of historical explanation. That principle asserts the permanence of substance (cf. 466). Of course, the heart of Blumenberg's disagreement with Kuhn is the former's claim that the Cusan's attempt to hold together various elements of the medieval world view had to fail, that his failure was not an example of the problems any "research project" continually encounters, but one that rendered that project incoherent.

The details of the story Blumenberg tells about this failure are intriguing, though I doubt that they will convince any Kuhnean that inconsistencies in academic theology were so devastating as to make the continuance of that tradition impossible. What is of more interest, though, is the way this last section nicely and finally makes explicit the methodological dimensions of Blumenberg's challenging picture of the modern point of view. As suggested earlier, the most important elements of his project, his account of legitimation itself and his isolation of scientific rationality as *die Neuzeit,* are both clearly on view in this last section, and prompt a final comment.

II

As indicated throughout, Blumenberg's intention is to isolate a specific historical dialogue: The way in which the demand for a certain "self-assertion," the need and right to inquire freely into nature, arose, was resisted, and finally prevailed. His argument is that this epochal event is not a *revolutionary* break with the assumptions of premodern culture. That culture is what produced the demand and is the criterion by virtue of which the demand is "legitimate," is a "better" resolution of various late Scholastic problems; yet it is a break, it does propose a new set of answers – so new that, in some respects, the enterprise illegitimately "reoccupies" a framework of assumptions that these very solutions will eventually invalidate. As demonstrated, this involves a somewhat tortuous dialectic (or occasionally, a hedging of bets), but the philosophically challenging aspect of Blumenberg's case is his insistence on the specificity of the issue of legitimation, and so of progress.

Somewhat ironically, in his attempt to carry out this program, Blumenberg has produced a book that is just as much a "legitimation" of the pre-modern world, since he is always claiming that any assessment of the progressive qualities of modernity can only be made in specific comparison with preceding options, and in terms of the criteria of *that* preceding tradition. Thus he claims to have shown such a legitimation for the modern version of independent theoretical curiosity, utility, self-knowledge, progress in research, and so on. But, of course, that remains a legitimation with quite a specific accusative. It is and can only be directed to the premodern world, and this historically bound context implies a de facto acceptance of *those* legitimation criteria. Moreover, at those points where the research program of modern astronomy and physics *does* begin to look wholly discontinuous with the assumptions of the prior epoch, where some old questions cannot be "answered" because the new answers to other old questions entail the rejection of the questions (the "point" of history, the justification of curiosity), Blumenberg changes gears, in effect, invokes his reoccupation thesis, and seems to admit that those discontinuous, wholly new elements cannot be legitimated in the same way. He appears to believe that the progress demonstrable on so many specific issues is what, in *this* kind of case, legitimates the rejection of such reoccupied "question-frameworks." But if that is so, then many of the most interesting questions about the legitimation of *modernity* seem to be avoided.

This is just to suggest that Blumenberg leaves rather hazy the issue of what is to count as a central or defining feature of modernity and why, and to offer the suspicion that he picks those phenomena that fit his own theory of the internal self-destruction of the Christian, Scholastic tradition, and those elements of the early modern tradition that don't are marginalized by the reoccupation theory. To put all this another way, I finally do not see why "modernity" itself is "the second overcoming of Gnosticism." Of course, if it is, then Blumenberg has done a great deal toward showing that it is "legitimate," that it does overcome *that* problem.

Further, the claim for "legitimation" is as puzzling finally as the claim about modernity. If the book had been called "The Historical Appropriateness of Some Elements of the Modern Enterprise," it would be hard to quarrel with what Blumenberg does here. But *The Legitimacy of Modern Age* is quite another matter. With that announced intention, Blumenberg's case is vulnerable to two very different kinds of attack. Someone like Strauss (or, to pick a strange bedfellow, Nietzsche) would clearly want to know how much is involved in the claim for legitimacy. After all, although we are nowhere yet close to realizing, to thinking through to the end, what it means for the "scientific image" to be the dominant force in "official culture," we do know that there are several possible implications of that centrality that have to be assessed (because we must decide whether to pursue them or not). These are vast issues in politics, law, medicine, education, and many other areas. In that context, when the full implications of the modern project are considered, it does not seem helpful to hear that modernity is legitimate because of its resolution of late Scholastic contradictions (unless of course, one is talking with someone encouraging a return to a premodern, theological culture). Blumenberg may demur that he's only talking about and legitimating a narrow range of scientific and philosophical issues, but this would unreasonably restrict the domain properly covered by these "issues," and would "legitimate" them only at the price of triviality. In more Straussean terms, a legitimation of modernity, if successful, must legitimate the kind of life promised by the modern project, must demonstrate that it is a good life, not just better than that implied by Nicholas of Cusa. Simply to assert that a demand for some conversation about a better or worse life is an anachronistic "reoccupation" by modernity of premodern issues, or that if the issue can be discussed, it cannot be raised except in a narrow specific historical dialogue, begins to sound like one of the oldest stories in the new enterprise – positivism.[9]

9 This points to another danger in Blumenberg's notion of "sufficient rationality," his claim that any assessment of modernity can only be a comparison between it and the "ancient" and "modern" options. This approach can easily either lead one into using facile, textbook categories in dealing with these epochal options or restrict one to the epoch as historically appropriated, to the way its "questions" have been made a part of some historically specific agenda. In that case, one might be able to show, for example, that the *historical* "Greeks," the ones in terms of whom the medieval intellectual tradition began to define itself, are not *the* Greeks who might represent *the* ancient option. If that is so, Blumenberg's legitimation procedure will not work. And one does not have to be a member in good standing of any ideology–critique camp to suspect that the historical Plato (or Descartes, or Hegel) may represent only a portion of, or distortion of, the Plato, say, who represents the ancient epoch.

Second, someone like Hegel would want to know how we can accept the theological tradition as a necessary component in our legitimation of modernity if we do not know the full story of the motivation of that tradition. The particular story of the relation between modernity and any premodern crisis does not legitimate anything unless that premodern tradition is itself, somehow, legitimate. Predictably, Blumenberg wants to tell that story by isolating the dialogue of questions and answers that defined the relation between the ancient and early Christian traditions. But at some point it becomes fruitless to look for the motivation of some question in another question. Blumenberg has done an ingenious job in showing how much can be learned by doing so, but I see no reason to think that that approach exhausts various important questions about the significance and historical authority of Greek culture, or Christianity, or the Enlightenment. Hegel's great contribution to this issue, his claim that the self-understanding of individual historical agents, or the self-images of various historical cultures, can be shown to be inadequate bases for explaining various actions and events and that much more can be explained if we assume a common historical project in which individuals and societies participate without explicit acknowledgment may have been much abused in later manifestations (or by Hegel himself) and may always be a dangerous invitation to speculation about "hidden hands." But in Hegel's hands, or Marx's, or Nietzsche's, or Freud's, or Heidegger's, or Gadamer's, the interpretive power of such an assumption does allow us to recover and render intelligible a tremendous amount of our own past culture as our own, as something that can illuminate our own "motivation." At least, that strategy of interpretation can potentially tell us more about ourselves than that we have failed to answer a set of questions.

Of course, Blumenberg's book does not engage these large issues often. But again, given the explicit claims he does make about how to "legitimate" modernity, there is enough to make one worry that, despite the work's many splendors and its intimidating scholarship, some of those convinced by it, particularly those frustrated by the ambiguities and abuses of more speculative approaches, will take from it a justification of another familiar phenomenon of modernity – and all other ages – willful myopia.

11

MODERN MYTHIC MEANING:
BLUMENBERG CONTRA NIETZSCHE

> Nothing surprised the promoters of the Enlightenment more, and left
> them standing more incredulously before the failure of what they
> thought were their ultimate exertions, than the survival of the con-
> temptible old stories – the continuation of work on myth.
>
> Hans Blumenberg, *Work on Myth*, p. 274

I

Burkhardt relates an "incomparably remarkable story" in Apollodorus. The
story helps represent the peculiar powers and limitations of Zeus, and so
might be said to be typical of "mythic thought" in general. It represents Zeus
as "just powerful enough to help fate, which has gotten totally muddled, on
account of two animals, to escape from its dilemmas" (143).[1] The Theban
fox was fated never to be caught, whereas the Athenian hound was fated to
catch everything that he pursued. Were such a world to be possible, were two
such creatures possibly to meet, a great threat to any worldly "significance"
would have to be entertained; no logos for or reliable judge of the world
would be conceivable (let us say). One can at least imagine the importance
attached to excluding or somehow confronting such a possibility. One can
also imagine the energies that might be expended in the Talmudic or

---

[1] All page references cited in parentheses in the body of the text and in the notes are to Hans
Blumenberg, *Work on Myth*, trans. Robert Wallace (Cambridge: MIT Press, 1985).

Scholastic traditions on such a problem; the energies that were expended on problems like omnipotence and omniscience. Zeus "solves" the problem differently. He turns both to stone.

What does it mean that the story would be recounted this way in a mythic context, would have made the peculiar sort of sense it apparently did, would have been in some sense satisfying or resolutive? Indeed what is the general point of considering such puzzles and such resolutions as subjects of stories? What function is served by reading about Ahab and his god-defying hunt for the white whale? by Eliot's reoccupation of Fisher King territory, Joyce's of Homer's? What is added to Mary Shelley's Frankenstein by its subtitle, The Modern Prometheus, and so on? Why should it have been the case, as it seems to have been, that the introduction of monotheism (or a shift from "mythos" to "dogma") would have meant a move away from such a mythic, almost defiant refusal of "explanation" toward a secure chronology, a linear, non-repeatable history organized around a singular event and an apocalyptic ending; an invocation of a god's agency that answers questions, however difficult and paradoxical, rather than defying such interrogation, rendering unquestionable?

"Stories are told," according to Hans Blumenberg, "in order to kill something. In the most harmless, but not least important case: to kill time. In another and more serious case: to kill fear" (34). The claim that "stories" can "kill time" and "kill fear," and that they can and must do so perennially, not as vestigial traces of some premodern, frightened, powerless creature, introduces all at once the distinctive and controversial elements of Blumenberg's bold, sweeping theory of mythic meaning.

In the course of the telling of stories about the origin of, and forces within, the cosmos; about retribution, justice, death, and afterlives; about male and female, harmony and disorder, various human communities and traditions fix on, retell, refer to, and, most importantly for Blumenberg, alter and adjust a repeated store of possible narratives and images. Significance or meaning (or at least one form of sense making, *Bedeutsamkeit*) is understood by Blumenberg as a kind of familiarity or a secure anticipation, and revolves around questions of power and limitation of power. The world cannot be obliterated; suffering will ultimately end; there is no single, absolute divine force to be feared. These aspects of mythic accounts, a trusted expectation of repeatability, formal coherence, and limitation, are contrasted with any appeal to real causes, natural origins, or divine purposes and plans. Myths do not explain anything; they do not render the obscure clearer, or the unintelligible intelligible; they do not tell us what really happened, or who really did what to whom. They are not "believed in."

Instead, they orient and console. Civilized life might be a defiance of god, infinitely risky, and it might incur, necessarily, great suffering. But the source of such suffering is not all powerful; Prometheus will be saved and Zeus too will fall.

These stories are thus said to serve a function, one that is necessary and ineliminable in human life.[2] Blumenberg describes this function in terms of a very general species-characteristic: that the course of human evolution has produced a species with capacities that fit no predictable, secure biological niche. Supreme adaptive success produced the maladaptation of Protean powers and too great a possible array of survival tactics. Too malleable, adaptable, haunted by an excess of imagination, we became an essentially futural creature capable of anticipating a disorienting variety of possibilities. As a result of such a "sudden lack of adaptation," we emerge as creatures always shadowed by a great anxiety about what Blumenberg calls the possible "absolutism of reality," an awareness of an absence of control, predictability, or cosmic place. To explain what he means by such a fear, Blumenberg associates it with Freud's description of "the complete helplessness of the ego in the face of overwhelming danger," the core of the traumatic situation, the source of the child's early demand for love as "compensation" for such helplessness (4–5).

Quite simply, in Blumenberg's account, myths function as such a "compensation," to reduce this anxiety, or to "transform" it into a manageable fear. *Names* are given to forces, already a massively comforting introduction of familiarity. More importantly polytheism is everywhere a feature of mythic thought. No deity or force is absolute and so absolutely to be feared; each is opposed by others and none can ever completely triumph. The "fund of the monstrous and the unbearable recedes" before a mythic representer, and myths function to produce a great "distance from the quality of uncanniness" (117).

Thus, there are two very controversial elements in Blumenberg's theory: "Mythic thought" (which is opposed both to religious or "dogmatic thought," as well as to theory, science, or "Enlightenment") should be understood to mean what it means functionally. And myths can be said to have a rational and perennial function. Second, such a function for mythic thought is not to be understood in some fateful opposition to logos, as in the familiar account of human progress as proceeding from mythos to

2 "Nothing is more instructive than to observe the repeated performance of the 'final over-coming' of the absurd and the abstruse in history, from which one can learn at least that it is not so easy to overcome," pp. 17–8.

logos. (For Blumenberg, this is not true, as we shall see with respect to either the original, Greek enlightenment, or the modern, sixteenth- and seventeenth-century revolution.) "That the course of things proceeded 'from mythos to logos' is a dangerous misconception" (27). It "does not permit one to recognize in myth itself one of the modes of accomplishment of logos." There is no great "leap forward" from mythos to logos, after which there is only continuous progress in logos; both the mythic and theoretical accounts represent alternate sorts of leaps. The account that the earth rests on the ocean or rises out of it and "the so much paler universal formula that everything comes out of water and accordingly is composed of it" both serve "the same interest," differing only in the means by which that interest is served.

Accordingly, *Work on Myth* supplements and to some extent alters and reframes Blumenberg's most important contribution to *Ideengeschichte*: his analysis and assessment, and most controversially, "defense," of the distinctly modern epoch in European history.[3] Whereas in his account the nature and "legitimacy" of *die Neuzeit*, or the modern age, Blumenberg had insisted on the genuinely "self-assertive" or truly revolutionary and superior aspects of modernity in the modern–premodern divide (even while also denying modernity's official self-understanding of such a break, as if completely autochthonous, or wholly self-grounding), the emphasis here is different. There he had stressed again and again the conceptual dead end created by late Scholasticism, its inevitable provocation of the "liberation of theoretical curiosity." Here he qualifies somewhat this picture, now focusing on historically evolving mythic sense making as perennial, indispensable, *not* something surpassed by the modern liberation, as was Scholasticism. By extension, modernity itself, when conceived as some grand narrative about the gradual mastery of nature, in the service of universal enlightenment, perpetual peace, and maximum health, is neither some "secularized" version of Christian eschatology, nor the inauguration of some secular myth (now overcome in the "postmodern" age).[4] Modernity is legitimate, and not inherently "demythologizing," even though, in the greatest complication of Blumenberg's position, its reoccupation of big questions, or grand narrative positions, like the one just mentioned, is illegitimate. The characteristic features of early modern thought, its anti-teleological, anti-hierarchical

3 Hans Blumenberg, *The Legitimacy of the Modern Age*, trans. Robert Wallace (Cambridge: MIT Press, 1983).
4 Cf. J.-F. Lyotard, *The Postmodern Condition: A Report on Knowledge*, trans. G. Bennington and B. Massumi (Minneapolis: University of Minnesota Press, 1984).

character, its reconception of nature and human passion, were all simply "sufficiently rational," appropriate resolutions of *aporiai* created within the Christian, Scholastic tradition and in the classical thought appropriated by it. And that is all they were. But that is not all, apparently, we "needed."

This book, *Work on Myth*, indicates that although Blumenberg still wants to defend his controversial claim that the modern tradition should not be understood as a "new" answer to some eternal "big question," that its significance requires no appeal to "secularized" religious notions, he nevertheless does not think that sufficient rationality is, as it were, a sufficient framework, or narrative scheme, within which the practices and results of the modern enterprise could be fully understood, could "have meaning." (There is a "principle of *insufficient* reason" involved in mythic thought, one Blumenberg even associates with the possibility of tolerance and freedom, precisely not dogma and prejudice.)[5] Modern success at a certain sort of mastery does not solve the biological niche problem noted: It just provokes a distinct sort of anxiety, a distinct set of imagined contingencies and anticipations that can never be resolved by method or technique, and that will always require some sort of mythic orientation and reassurance. Given the continual threat of an "absolutism of reality," a sense-making practice neither modern nor premodern must be said to accompany any intellectual and social adventure of the human species: "work on myth." (This Blumenberg distinguishes from the "work of myth," indicating that mythic meaning and resolution go on even in intensely self-conscious, literary contexts, where, in effect, mythic frameworks are more mentioned than used, even though not simply as subjects of analysis or reflection. A good deal of his extensive discussion of Goethe deals with and explains this sometimes elusive point.)

As noted, Blumenberg advances these claims while avoiding any mythicization of logos itself (as the preceding considerations might seem to suggest), or any relativism that would treat scientific practices as our rituals and scientific results as our myths. His position thus occupies its own niche in much contemporary debate. We are, that is, familiar enough these days with the legacy of attacks on the sufficiency of some supreme authority granted to "reason" alone. Romanticism originally, then life philosophy, Nietzsche, Heidegger, existence philosophy, several currents in modernist literature, Gadamerian hermeneutics, different relativist strands in the social sciences, and the suggestion of a "postmodern condition," have all contributed to a well-known "great suspicion." Many suspect that location of the significance of the new discoveries in astronomy, mathematical physics, and, eventually,

5 Cf. pp. 230–1.

physiology and chemistry, as well as the collapse of the authority of hier-archical and teleological notions of nature, within some "grand narrative" of progress, liberation and demythologizing, merely reinvoke some heroic myth, the "species" now as the new Prometheus, religious and traditional authorities as the Olympians.

In some quarters, such a suspicion has led to an intense attention to what might be called the "pre-rational" conditions necessary either for the claims of reason to have any purchase on human agents, or necessary for a sort of significance or orientation in existence different from and perhaps prior to any cognitive sense. This in turn has reinvigorated a study of mythic mean-ing, and a denial that such sense making is primitive, vestigial, or dispens-able. But in Blumenberg's theory, the differences between "mythic thought" and "dogma," on the one hand (religious, unrepeatable, singular eschatol-ogy; scriptural meaning), or theory (nomic regularity, explanation, etc.), on the other, are rigorously respected, even while primitivist and reductionist accounts of myth are resisted. The permanence of mythic meaning is de-fended, but, in the book's major conclusion, not as opposed to, or in spite of any demythologizing enlightenment, nor because "enlightenment's dialec-tic" reveals it to be *itself* mythical, but because myth is a "functional" ally of enlightenment, in the service of the same ends, necessarily complemen-tary.[6] Moreover he advances these claims without hope for identifying any fundamental origin of mythic stories, or any universal, common, sense-making structure in myth. Cassirer and Lévi-Strauss are as much his oppo-nents as Freud and Jung.

That is, in what is probably the most interesting aspect of his case, all mythic sense making is treated as radically historical. There is no common, underlying savage mind; no archetypical sense making, no ever reemerging species-characteristic divisions and classifications in experience. What we take up, use, alter, and expand in some standard narrative always represents a "working out" of a historically particular version of the fears and anxieties Blumenberg has identified as unavoidable in human experience.[7]

---

6 See p. 163. Blumenberg both concedes that it is often rational not to demand secure rational foundations where none can be given but cautions that mythic expressions of this state of affairs are far too "risky," with quite ambiguous pragmatic implications, even while he also cautions that these ambiguities never justify the kind of wholesale jettisoning, in the name of critical reasoning, prominent since Descartes's suggestions that the best way to build cities rationally was to raze the old ones completely.

7 This is not to retract, as the translator, Robert Wallace, points out in his Introduction, Blumenberg's famous denial of perennial or fundamental questions in *The Legitimacy of the Modern Age*. As he somewhat elusively argued there, a common "territory" or set of concerns

Throughout his account, the central example of such historical work on, or receptions of, myth is the Prometheus story, and how a kind of "selection of traits" in such a story of defiance of God can be traced in the evolution of the myth's telling and retelling. But he also provides a useful overture to such a treatment. The Homeric *Odyssey* originally evinced, in its presentation and what must have been its reception, a great anxiety about a violation of order and place, and so, by contrast, celebrated the restoration of rightful authority and hierarchy, especially against great resistance and temptation. It is, in many ways, *the* great myth of civilization itself, celebrating the rocky, hard island of Ithaca and the restoration there of natural order, against the social chaos of the suitors' presumptions; the formless, unmeasurable sea, and the great enemy Poseidon, and the "soft" temptations of Kalypso, Kirke, and the Phaiakians. But for the Stoics, the same story had ceased to mean that; it had come to be about the sheer persistence of Odysseus, the will to continue and triumph in the face of essentially senseless sufferings. By the Middle Ages, as the story is incorporated in Dante, the hope for a this-worldly resolution of Odysseus' homelessness has vanished. The hope itself is mere vanity and Odysseus is a sinner, a paradigm of excessive worldly curiosity, dissatisfied with Penelope, destined to sail again, and again, and finally to perish. By the time of Joyce's appropriation, the story itself has become a mere "story," accessible only at a metalevel; the wanderings and homecoming themselves essentially meaningless except in their calling to mind significances lost and now available only by contrast and in memory, in the irony of replacing the faithful, ever waiting, incomplete Penelope with the monologic Molly. The tragedy and nobility of life itself have been replaced with the "nobility of the desk," an internal, self-referential modernist literature, written for scholars and aesthetes, in an age, presumably, when anxiety about the absolutism of reality has become internalized, the "absolute reality" at issue the absolute opacity of meaning itself; also a psychological experience, potentially uncontrollable and absolute without the naming, repetitive, familiarizing stories of modern selfhood: internal homecoming, self-realization, romantic fulfillment, autonomous expression, and so forth.

can be occupied and reoccupied by various strategies and approaches, without a common question or problem emerging. In this case, what counts as a possibly absolute reality, in what sense uncertainty and anxiety are produced by such an awareness, what would count as a resolution of such, and anxiety and so on, all cannot count as "common" questions, in search of a more successful answer throughout time. All of which is not to claim that this reoccupation claim (made most famously with respect to Christian eschatology and Blumenberg's denial of the secularization thesis) is not without its problems. See the discussion in Chapter 10.

II

Throughout his treatment of these and similar issues in the first two, more theoretical parts of his book, Blumenberg pushes ahead very fast, eager to get to what he must consider a kind of test case for his claims in the latter parts, that magisterial examination of the reception and transformations of the Prometheus myth and the complex role of such "work on myth" in the German romantic and Idealist traditions. He thus leaves relatively unexplored such questions as the general theory of "significance" (*Bedeutsamkeit*) he is appealing to in his analysis, for example, under what conditions a story, merely as a story, not a pseudoscience or ersatz philosophy or religious hope *can* succeed in rendering the world less uncanny, more familiar, as opposed to instances of failure, marginal narratives authoritative only in cults or minor sects. (Actually, he appears to deny that there can be such a theory of significance. The answer to any question of the "possibility" of such mythic success is simply the historical actuality of that success. Selection over time and some historical stability just thereby tell us what worked and what didn't. That persistence alone is enough to account for what narrative frames or forms are significant; no archetype, or collective unconscious, etc.)[8] Blumenberg also concentrates so much on the opposition between the different functions of myth and either dogma or theory, insisting that there really is in myth no "account" given of phenomena, no distinct sort of intelligibility, that he comes close to making it very hard to understand *how* "mythic thought" could perform the reassuring, anxiety-reducing function it is supposed to.[9]

But there is quite a lot of theoretical apparatus introduced in part II and it should be noted before the major details of his analysis are introduced and assessed. In general, Blumenberg's response to such questions is to deny that there is much value in focusing much attention on the origins of, or motivation for, or common structures to, mythic accounts (all of which accounts for his disagreements with well-known treatments by Cassirer and Lévi-Strauss). Although he rarely uses the word in this way, Blumenberg's

---

8 Cf. pp. 161–71.
9 Cf., for example, this typical claim: "Myth is, precisely, not a theology, because the punishing god does not explain himself and because he rejects every opportunity for a theodicy. . . . Myth is not the preliminary stage of logos, a stage in which one is not yet capable of it, but is instead the most intolerant exclusion of it" (pp. 599, 600). Such opacity might reassure by being able to "head off" any temptations to theodicies that will fail and explanations that will founder, but a plausible response to that line is simply, some reassurance. One needs a more positive view of the modality involved in holding or invoking a myth other than not believing, not explaining with it, and so on.

approach to the problem of significance is always pragmatic. So, the "problem" at issue for him is the problem of the "specific acceptance in history" of some mythic account and its various transformations. (The problem of meaning is thus linked, as in more well-known accounts, with the problem of "*reception.*") This acceptance is tied to the apotropaic (or "ill averting") function of myth, something accomplished through rendering the world familiar, and the natural forces within the world finite and self-opposed, not absolute, even if not explicable; all by contrast with any project of infinite mastery or complete, unified explanation.

Not only does mythic thought or sense making reassure, orient, "signify" in a way distinct from explaining the evidence, or providing details; it must also be distinguished from that other equally weighty root of modern history, also tied to stories and images, the biblical or "dogmatic" accounts.[10] Here the modalities involved in invoking a myth, versus a scriptural account, are central. Mythic stories appear to have been invoked as relevant, appealed to, but, famously, not "believed in," not disputed as dogma. Several stories of Dionysus, or Odysseus' conduct, or of Prometheus's actions could coexist peacefully. But scriptural accounts are written down, in one sacred text, and are invoked as accounts of what happened, where to know what happened is necessary in understanding what we now face. Consistency is necessary. And, as Heine noted, tragedy disappears with this demand for unity and consistency, that is, in monotheism (225). And, pace Voltaire's remark that theogeny caused no disturbance of the peace, getting the facts right about God's creation and will, all as the truth of truths, necessarily begins to wear away at tolerance and ambiguity.[11]

Blumenberg has denied that the modern epoch should be understood as some replacement narrative, as if some sweeping myth of the eventual mastery of nature and slow enlightenment toward individual self-interest were the new "meaning" of history, replacing reliance on providence, salvation, and the second coming. This means that he is disputing, to some extent, the

---

10 See p. 184 on the difference between myths as dispelling uneasiness and discontent, rather than "answering questions." It is not entirely clear in Blumenberg's account *how* such functions can operate if not by explaining or illuminating. This is particularly true once the historical experience of stories and storytelling occurs alongside dogmatic or scriptural stories and theoretical explanations. On Blumenberg's own premises, our experience of such stories would then change; whether they could function as myths once identified *as* "*mythic*" is a question he does not much pursue.

11 Cf. a parallel remark about science and dogma as well: "If one examines the historical experience of the modern age, one finds the incomparable lesson, which is seldom taken to heart, that could have been drawn from the possession of the sciences and their historical form: to see the nonpossession of truth as what – in contrast to the promise that the truth would make people free – still comes close to such a liberation" (p. 230).

actual self-understanding of many early modern thinkers themselves, maintaining that their "reoccupation" of traditional, eschatological questions is vestigial and inconsistent with the emerging project of modern "self-assertion." On his view modernity is neither radically discontinuous with its past, a self-grounding, nor a secularized repetition of religious themes and hopes, however much it feels itself compelled to reoccupy such territory. This also means that Blumenberg is creating troubling questions about his own ability to identify "modernity" as such, and is in danger of legitimating some "idea" of a modern epoch, but not the epoch we happen to be in, founded and motivated by the intentions of its real founders.

Here he notes that such a modern self-assertion and self-reliance did create a need for some mythic significance or reassurance, and he does not treat such work on myth as illegitimate or simply premodern. Such an orienting, reassuring work has some function. Consistent with modernity's own pretensions, however, such mythic work also ultimately aims at "bringing myth to an end," not by being the final demythologizing, but by being the final myth.

This "myth" we call "German Idealism" (266). It is an illusion to think, according to Blumenberg, that there *could* be a myth that "fully exploits, and exhausts" (266) the form itself, but the project of German Idealism, in his reading, exemplifies, in spite of this illusion, a good deal of what Blumenberg wants to say about work on myth in general. Descartes, in this reading, introduced what is called "the last monster" into the modern world, the *genius malignus,* or evil genius. Given the modern notion of world or object as idea, or representation, as experienced, a new "absolutism" threat intrudes; absolute uncertainty or doubt about the sufficiency of the subject's founding acts, makings, or graspings, in securing such an intended world as reliable, or secure. Descartes's own resolution, or apparent resolution, in the *ens perfectissimum,* satisfied no one.

> There was only one way by which to remove this last monster from the world, for the cognitive subject to make itself into the authority that is responsible for the object it knows. Thus Idealism's "final myth" is a way of establishing distance from a terror that is now only mental, and now strikes deep only into the theoretical subject. (267)

Thus Schiller's description of Fichte to Goethe: "To him the world is only a ball that the ego has thrown and that it catches again in 'reflection'" (266) and thus also Schopenhauer's complaint about Fichte: "I am trying to explain how this whole fairy tale arose in Fichte's brain" (268). This claim for a self-grounding by the subject is treated as myth and as an attempt at final myth because Idealism "drives out the desire to ask for more and to invent more to add" (288); it aims at a final resolution of the modern subject's sense of the contingency of its founding, its being unable to be the source of itself. And, "under the conditions of the modern age, which cannot invent gods – even allegories – any longer," new and highly abstract titles serve their mythic function: the "I," the world, history, the unconscious, Being (288). All of which introduces the chief functional category for Blumenberg – something like "mythic reassurance" – and the twin questions of when an appeal to a comprehensive principle, whether the ego, or extended matter moving in space, or Being, or the eternal return of the same, should be regarded as a "mythic" invocation and when not, and in what sense, under what conditions, such accounts could be said to be *reassuring.*

This characterization of the German Idealist response to the issues of modern philosophy also begins to raise a number of questions that will eventually focus his disagreements with Nietzsche over many of these issues, disagreements that will suggest several problems (decisive problems, I think) in his account. For, Blumenberg has suggested a self-consciously *Cartesian* view of the significance of German Idealism within the modern tradition. The "new way of ideas," methodological solipsism, and the foundationalist search for subjective certainty, all did indeed introduce the great "monster" of skepticism. Within that context, a demonstration (or "myth") establishing the necessity of the subject's constituting role in all experience might look like a sort of solution and might look like what German Idealism was all about (in mythic terms: If the world is a dream or a phantasm, at least we can assure ourselves that we shall not wake up).

But this narrative ignores the issue at the top of the agenda for Kant, Fichte, Schelling, and Hegel. The problem was not skepticism so much as "dogmatism," or "transcendental realism," and so the incompatibility between the only accounts of nature sanctioned within modern methodology (materialist, deterministic, etc.) and, first, the conditions for the possibility of such a knowable nature (for the Idealists, the subject's apperceptive activity) and, second, and deeply related for many after Kant, the possibility of some notion of freedom compatible with such conditions and such nature. Some sort of notion of autonomy is the problem and compatibilism, or some sort of consistent whole, not so much Cartesian security, is the desideratum.[12]

---

12 For a more extensive discussion of the relation between the German Idealist and modern philosophical tradition, see *Modernism as a Philosophical Problem: On the Dissatisfactions of*

Of course, the possibility of both *Geistes-* and *Naturwissenschaften* emerged from such debates primarily as an epistemological and metaphysical problem. But as Blumenberg himself suggests in some places, the characteristic claims of modern theory inevitably create a different and far more hostile climate, not so much against "story telling" as such, as against any sort of *reliance,* in any practically significant sense, on such stories. The "conditions" under which such stories could "function" are inevitably affected by the social power of other methods for securing the future and protecting the present. Not for nothing have we begun to study stories, representations of human agents and the social interactions unique to human beings, as "socially constructed documents," or literary and mythic meaning in terms of social and psychological agendas. Only studied this way can the authority of the most authoritative modern notions of method and sense making be respected. The German Idealist problem is not the same as the old quarrel between philosophy and poetry, or the compatibility of logos and mythos, but neither is its issue rightly understood as strictly the "problem" of freedom and determinism.

The reason it is important to quibble about this issue is that Blumenberg always tries to avoid some suggestion of a deep incompatibility between the implications of the modern intellectual and especially scientific revolution, and essential components of both traditional and modern notions of human praxis or agency, notions familiar to and essential to, mythic narrative.[13] In *The Legitimacy of The Modern Age,* he had tried to do this by, in effect, reducing the extension of the notion of *die Neuzeit* (the modern turn was "the second overcoming of the Gnostic heresy"). It was not answering any big question and so threatened no list of big answers. Here, in this work, he suggests a "compatibilism of function" between mythic and theoretical practices and so simply maneuvers around the great issues and great fears at the heart of the post-Kantian German tradition. He discusses the issues in terms of Cartesian reassurance and not the Third Antinomy. As we shall see, the same maneuvering occurs in his attempt to avoid or deflate what Nietzsche called the "eternal *conflict* between the theoretical and the tragic world view" (Nietzsche, 1956: 104; Nietzsche, 1972: 107).[14]

European High Culture (Oxford: Basil Blackwell, 1991).

13 One can make this point more simply just by pointing to the popularity of the contempt phrase "folk psychology."

14 In this chapter, I refer to Nietzsche, *The Birth of Tragedy and the Genealogy of Morals* (*BT*), trans. F. Golffing (New York: Doubleday, 1956); *Werke. Kritische Gesamtausgabe,* (hereafter *GT*), ed. by G. Colli and M. Montinari (Berlin: de Gruyter, 1972).

III

It appears to have been conceded, in the original accounts of the story of the theft of fire by Prometheus, that unaided human beings are neither capable nor worthy of existence. At the origin of their central attempts at any self-sufficiency, both their technical power and their civilized form are a gratuitous divine act, and one that is illegal (unjust? a violation of what is due, appropriate?), a theft. What is stolen, fire, itself evinces the fragility and contingency of civilized life; it could easily go out, its secret lost. Civilized life seems to exist as a result of some risky defiance of the divine, one that can provoke great vengeance and suffering, even if, in the myth, such suffering can end in a Herculean redemption. Such anxieties are familiar to biblical stories as well; Cain's sacrifice, agricultural products, or the result of craft and techne, are unpleasing;[15] cities are dangerous places, which promote a false sense of self-sufficiency; the demand that God show himself in forms familiar to us, idolatry, seems an inevitable temptation; an impious tower of Babel needs to be destroyed; the Hebrews must demand a king: They are not content with their hidden, nameless god, and the transition from Samuel to Saul, much less to David, seems a move in a more Promethean and hence the more dangerous, defiant direction of reliance on techne, and a hoped for self-sufficiency. It was not until Rousseau that such anxieties about the artificial and conventional were expressed without the language of impiety and transgression against the divine, but the mythic implications of Prometheus' theft, the constant work on myth that is inspired by it, are everywhere, with or without the theodicy problem, in Blumenberg's survey.

Throughout this survey, the appeal of the Prometheus story to Blumenberg himself and to his own resolutely historical way of looking at everything human is also apparent. In chapter 2 of part III, the Promethean problem seems to figure the great natural anxiety at the center of Blumenberg's own picture of human existence. In the classical context, Prometheus appears as some sort of affirmation of the sophistic view, and by extension, much of what Blumenberg himself wants to say.[16] In this picture, "man is a creature who is fundamentally left in the lurch by nature" (329). "Culture is a necessity of nature itself" (329) because nature provides nothing much of what we need to survive and flourish and thereby creates (allows us to evolve into)

---

15 Cf. the summary of the dispute between Erasmus and John Colet (p. 368).

16 "As the protagonist of a theory of the origin of culture that was specific to a school, Prometheus, for Sophism, came into the neighborhood of allegory for the first time. This was to be one of his future destinies" (p. 329).

a profound uncertainty and disorientation. The gratuity in the bestowal of fire and craft, and its illegality, emphasize not only the nomos–physis gulf, but the radical differences between Plato and Aristotle, on the one hand, and the sophistic tradition, on the other. The former, in essence, gave human beings nothing much to do but to recognize and conserve. Their metaphysics affirmed "reassuringly, that there remained nothing essential to be done in the world. The decisions had already been made in the realm of the Ideas or the forms – in other words, by nature" (331). For the latter, everything of significance is to be done or made (even if a crime against nature), most importantly, by the political art. (Plato's response can be seen in his own version of the Prometheus myth in the *Protagoras*, where *aidos* and *dike cannot* be stolen from Zeus, are due only to his gift. No making can be successful without such qualities, yet, contrary to the basic sophistic–Promethean claim, they cannot be stolen, or by implication, bought, traded, taught for money.)

This all will introduce, within the framework of a Promethean–sophistic versus Socratic contrast, a dispute with Nietzsche over his own tragedy–Socrates opposition, and thereby one that reraises many of the fundamental questions of Blumenberg's account, especially the mythos–logos, myth, and Enlightenment questions at issue throughout the work.

This large issue, and the opposition to Nietzsche, is also relevant to the most complex analysis presented in the study (a discussion that concludes with another round with Nietzsche and that itself concludes the book). Blumenberg notes, as if marginally, something curious about the initial provocation of one of the most famous and influential controversies in the German struggle about Enlightenment and counter-Enlightenment. Blumenberg, that is, agrees with Goethe's guess that the Prometheus myth is "priming powder for an explosion" (407). The occasion for the explosion was Jacobi's July 5, 1780, visit to Lessing. Jacobi, preoccupied with finishing his correspondence, offered Lessing Goethe's "Prometheus" ode to read over while he was waiting. Lessing volunteered that he greatly admires the poem, that the poem's point of view was his own, that orthodox conceptions of divinity were not for him. Jacobi appeared stunned and when they resumed the discussion the following morning, Lessing uttered the famous sentence around which so much of the discussion of the German Enlightenment swirled: "Es gibt keine andere Philosophie, als die Philosopie des Spinoza" (There is no philosophy but the philosophy of Spinoza) (411).

Jacobi, in one of the most renowned hermeneutical fights on record, takes this as evidence that philosophers like Lessing and Mendelssohn are on a treacherous, Enlightenment slippery slope; that the views of mind and nature and man to which they are drawn must ultimately lead to a kind of pantheism, a denial of the transcendence and so benevolence and providence of God, which, for the orthodox, would be indistinguishable from atheism.[17] Mendelssohn, of course, and many others, disputed Jacobi's understanding of what Lessing had said or meant, but the general significance of the controversy, and its Promethean frame, were set.

In Blumenberg's reading, the fate of the poem and myth helps us to understand the course of modern self-understanding, or at least those aspects confined to "work on myth." *Sturm und Drang*'s defiance of the gods turned into romanticism's "transcendental identity" with God (414). Later, when it was realized that Kant, despite being a "critic of pure reason," was the supreme modernist, that he had only intensified the Promethean break with nature and revelation in favor of a radical self-consciousness, even a self-grounding and complete autonomy, the terms of the original debate were carried forward and intensified (however difficult it is to see Kant as a Spinozist, as Jacobi continued to maintain). That the human mind is wholly sufficient to reveal its own relation to Being as a whole, and that that relation was, after Kant, constitutive, a spontaneous activity, now "occupied" the space opened up in the Jacobi–Mendelssohn dispute. The myth and the dispute were now about human defiance of the place of god, and a self-divination – the final myth. This means for Blumenberg that Idealism should be assessed within that space, mythically, as a story that reassures against contingency, that secures the subject, as source, within itself; a mythic function that only intensifies when this subjective activity begins to be discussed in more aesthetic and less psychological and transcendental terms.

All of which is not to say that Blumenberg believes such a myth (precisely in its pretensions to finality – or what they called systematicity and necessity) could succeed. The myth of Idealism has a "poetic weakness," which

> makes it evident why Idealism of any kind could not satisfy the new century. It makes unintelligible the core of a self-consciousness that sees the irrevocability of its own achievements as the guarantee of its historical invulnerability. (576)

Again, though, this reads the issues of German Idealism in some sense through the lenses of the German counter-Enlightenment, as if a divine self-sufficiency or great impiety were the story. I have already suggested why I

---

17 Jacobi tries to draw a line of descent beginning with Bruno: "Pantheism is the unavoidable consequence of combining the concept of creation with the attribute of infinity" (p. 412).

consider this a misleading picture. But it is now time to consider the famous claim that "the modern myth" might involve neither divine assistance, defiance of God, nor an identification with God, but "the death of God."

IV

Blumenberg's account of the necessary persistence of myth has a clear ancestor, an ally, and an important opponent – Nietzsche, especially his own "explosion," the 1770 *Birth of Tragedy Out of the Spirit of Music*. Both Blumenberg and Nietzsche deny what Nietzsche would have called the hope for any self-sufficiently "Socratic" view of human existence; to attempt any demythologizing, or reductionist, or psychologizing, or historicist "debunking" of myth (or the "tragic point of view") is to ensure some remythologizing self-understanding "somewhere else," and to engage in a self-deceived and ultimately futile attempt at a pure Socraticism, or "enlightenment."

They obviously differ over how mythic thought (or "the tragic view of existence") functions (although Nietzsche would never use that word that way),[18] a difference that also introduces a great difference over the legacy of modernity. Put simply, Nietzsche was one of the first within (or roughly within) the tradition to attack Socrates, and not simply as having misunderstood tragic myth. There is no way to meliorate a great struggle (*Kampf*) between the tragic and theoretical point of views. They are not complementary or alternative versions of some function, and the Socratic is inferior.

Nietzsche, of course, denies, like Blumenberg, that we should understand either the classical or modern enlightenment as a progression from mythos to logos; the tragic presentation of ethical dilemmas, character, fate, politics, and so forth, is not the result of, or expression of, a "pre-critical" position, inadequately thought through, tested, and dialectically transformed. Socrates is not an enlightener, or liberator, who puts an end to such dangerously incomplete notions of human finitude, divine conflict, and fate, in favor of the "unity of the virtues," "virtue is knowledge," "no one does evil knowingly," "only the virtuous are happy," and so on. There is even some

---

18 There are, though, similar formulations. In the 1886 "Versuch einer Selbstkritik," Nietzsche remarks that his question was why the Greeks found tragedy necessary, why they needed it (die Griechen . . . gerade sie hatten die Tragoedie noethig?) or what Greek art was for (*BT*, p. 3; *GT*, p. 6). But see *BT*, p. 50, *GT*, p. 52; and the reference to the "metaphysical solace" (*metaphysiche Trost*) "with which, I wish to say at once, all true tragedy sends us away, that, despite every phenomenal change, life is at bottom indestructibly joyful and powerful." "Tragic myth" in this sense does not make life bearable, but affirmable in some sense, and, as we shall see, this notion of affirmation and its connections with ethical life are missing from Blumenberg.

sense in which, in Blumenbergean language, both the tragedians and Socrates could be said to have confronted the same consolation and reassurance problem. In the world of what Nietzsche calls "tragic myth," "the
Greeks had to construct these deities" "in order to live." "The gods justified
human life by living it themselves – the only satisfactory theodicy ever invented" (*BT,* 30; *GT,* 32).

But, in Nietzsche's characterization, Socrates represents a symptom, a
sign of decline (in other works, a "weak," or "plebeian" response to such an
original realization, simply an incapacity, because of such weakness, to rest
content with "tragic strength" in the face of the unredeemable qualities of
human existence).[19] The classical enlightenment represents a failure of
nerve, as well as a self-deceived, life-denying distaste with existence itself.
Socrates, in the most astonishing conclusion of the book, represents decadence, a claim that obviously already implies that what he represents should
be understood as a proposal about a kind of life, a proposal to construe the
human soul, the polis, the gods, nature, in a different, and for Nietzsche,
weaker, less "healthy" way.

> Might it be that the "inquiring mind" was simply the human mind terrified by
> pessimism and trying to escape from it, a clever bulwark erected against the
> truth? Something craven and false, if one wanted to be moral about it? Or, if
> one preferred to put it amorally, a dodge [*eine Schlauheit*]? Had this perhaps
> been your secret, great Socrates? Most secretive of ironists, has this been your
> deepest irony? (*BT,* 4–5; *GT,* 6–7)

These claims are all, obviously, occasions for much interpretive controversy, but at a first pass, it is easy to see the nature of Blumenberg's
disagreement with someone otherwise his ally. Socrates, or the kind of classical enlightenment he represents, should also not, for Blumenberg, be understood as some sort of rational realization of myth, but also most definitely
not as some sort of cultural decline. For Blumenberg, he simply represents
another form of "work on myth," a different, not a competing nor a progressive version of such myth. According to Blumenberg, Nietzsche goes wrong
here for several reasons.

First, Nietzsche is said to have a kind of "heroic agent" view of history, as if
"Socrates, Euripides, and Aristophanes are capable of making Dionysus fall

---

19 In sect. 15 of *BT,* the moral and political nature of Socrates' project are less on view than in
    later works. The problem is simpler: Socrates is presented as a "mystagogue" of science and
    his confidence is criticized for its naive optimism. This will ensure its "shipwreck."

silent" (337). Second, "Nietzsche does not permit work on myth as a great and burdensome effort" "to make life possible" for differing historical generations (ibid.). Tragedy itself, in Blumenberg's view, already represents some historical attempt to take into account "something itself unmythical," "the uncanny, the unfamiliar, reality as absolutism" (ibid.). The reception of that attempt would already have altered the conditions of its possible future and would ensure some transformation and "selection of traits." "Work on myth" is always necessarily historical and a matter of reception in differing contexts, and not a matter of "metaphysics" or "metaphysical solace," to use Nietzsche's word. Nietzsche, by contrast, admires the tragic position of irremediability, some permanent irresolution or Dionysian abyss, because it heightens the importance of a dramatic (or musical) consolation. True "justification" is "aesthetic," and this requires a metaphysical, rather than historical view of the "Dionysus–Apollo" contrast. Particularly given the Wagnerian direction of *The Birth of Tragedy*, it was important, presumably, for Nietzsche to deny that the tragic self-understanding could have, by virtue of its own exhaustion of form and new *aporiai*, "provoked" the alternate "consolation" of the security of consciousness, lucidity, tying authority to reason giving and worth to self-knowledge. This must represent a kind of deluded cheerfulness and optimism, all so that genuine renewal of tragic fortitude could come, after Kant's and Schopenhauer's puncturing of this optimism, with a new spirit of music, Wagnerian opera.

There is also a good deal of straightforward hermeneutical disagreement with Nietzsche, and in this context some very telling points are made. Nietzsche is said to simplify the mythic presentation of the divine. The crucial importance of oppositions among the gods is underplayed. Nietzsche treats the Prometheus story not as a story of a "fall," but as a self-elevation, man raising himself up to the certainty of himself. But this confuses issues in Aeschylus, who presents them as chiefly a drama among gods and only incidentally between gods and man. (Nietzsche concentrates so much on the suffering god that the original question raised by the drama, the unworthiness of man, even to exist, is not dealt with adequately.) Similarly the theft cannot be described as some heroic "sacrilege." Zeus' acts toward Prometheus are not expressions of divine honor insulted, but of a prudent ruler who will change his mind instantly when it is in his interest. And Nietzsche gets wrong his comparison with the biblical Fall and denigration of its story as "feminine." Actually, Adam and Eve risked everything for a kind of dazzling equality with God, not for tools and fire. (Thus, the "anti-bourgeois affect" that "sustains" Nietzsche's book also has its ironic side. What Prometheus' heroic (and so presumably anti-bourgeois) act provides is simply the possibility of the "normal state of existence, at its lowest limit." "The anti-bourgeois affect produces the bourgeois mode of life" (617).)

But these criticisms do not much affect the general animus against Nietzsche as having misunderstood the function of tragic myths, as having underestimated the historical "work" necessary for myths to be effective and "received," and his misunderstanding of the conflict with Socrates. Although all of these issues raise many others and involve questions about reason and enlightenment far too unmanageable to address here, there are, I think, Nietzschean counters to these major issues, and they all raise some questions about Blumenberg's general enterprise.

On the first point, Nietzsche himself complains about the shadow of Schopenhauer's "pessimistic" and metaphysical theory across his early work and admits that he did not state well his views about tragic negativity (*BT,* 12; *GT,* 13). Tragedy does not inspire a kind of pessimistic resignation, nor Blumenberg's humanization and familiarization. It is precisely the absence of any familiarization or reassuring sense of the limits of Prometheus' and Oedipus' suffering that confronts us in tragedy, and precisely the absence of any "defeatism" (but rather affirmation) in the tragic attitude that is uniquely expressed in tragic art. Aesthetic "delight" (*Urlust*) is a kind of pain (*BT,* 143; *GT,* 148). In Nietzsche's account it is a despair at the possibility that a secure, distinct "Apollonian individual" should be capable of emerging from some Dionysian wholeness and survive as an individual. There is no possibility for such individuation, but the attempt "must" occur anyway, even if it "must" fail.[20] To think that this struggle, by Prometheus or Oedipus or Orestes or Ajax, would only be possible if tragedy "consoled" us somehow about its possibility, reassured us that the failure of such self-assertion was not absolute, is to miss the whole point of tragedy. We are "consoled" precisely in spite of the recognition of the inevitability of such failure, precisely because the unresolvable Dionysian–Apollonian "reality" *is* "absolute."

It is not so much that Nietzsche maintains this for "Wagnerian" reasons, because he clings to the hope for some elevated power for art. He wants to

---

20 Clearly there are volumes implied in the claims of such a "must." I don't mean to pretend to have suggested any account of Nietzsche's theory of tragic affirmation or aesthetic justification. The point here is only to note his rejection of Schopenhauer's and Blumenberg's views and to suggest that he is trying to formulate a different evaluative category in our assessment of human deeds (the "tragic"), one not tied to having good reasons or appropriate intentions, but rather like the kind of "must" involved in claiming that a person "must" act in such a way or cease to be "who he is." See also W. Müller-Lauter, *Nietzsche: seine Philosophie der Gegensätze und die Gegensätze einer Philosophie* (Berlin: de Gruyter, 1971), pp. 51, 81.

challenge the ethical assumptions with which, from the "theoretical" point of view, tragedy is often interrogated, as if only either a reason for the suffering, or a promise that it can be contained, could explain the affirmative delight we take as spectators, or could account for its function. It is Blumenberg who has raised the problem of tragedy and myth as linked (to use his word) with the bourgeois problem of security. Prometheus is not, though, part of any "strategy" to help man, any more than Aeschylus is out to console us. Prometheus' defiance is not originally, or ever, rational or strategic. To look at it as, therefore, unmotivated or irrational defiance is to miss the whole point of the Apollonian moment, at least in Nietzsche's account.[21]

Moreover, as to the second point, Nietzsche does not portray this Dionysian–Apollonian dilemma in as static or metaphysical a way as suggested by Blumenberg. Tragedy, and in Nietzsche's famous theory, the use of music and the chorus in tragedy, transformed the archaic myth of Prometheus and "endowed myth with a new and profound significance."

> For it is the lot of every myth to creep gradually into the narrows of superstitious historical fact and to be treated by some later time as a unique event of history. . . . It was through tragedy that myth achieved its profoundest content, its most expressive form; it arose once again like a wounded warrior, its eyes alight with unspent power and the calm wisdom of the dying. (*BT*, 68; *GT*, 70)

And that last phrase, about the wisdom of the dying, does not only refer to the dying hero in tragedy, but to tragic wisdom itself, always already dying. For Nietzsche goes on in the next section to claim something inconsistent with any hope for an aesthetic retrieval, through Wagner's music, of the classical, tragic point of view (although he admits in the later preface that he mistakenly wandered close to such a hope). "Greek tragedy perished in a manner quite different from the older sister arts: it died by suicide, in consequence of an insoluble conflict" (*in Folge eines unloesbaren Konflikt*) (*BT*, 69; *GT*, 71). This does not mean only that a "tragedian," Euripides, finished off tragedy with a new attitude, but, as the claim asserts, that the nature of the conflicts presented in tragedy ensured some eventual exhaustion and variation.[22] In later remarks about how even Sophocles begins the process

---

21 For a more extensive discussion, see my "Nietzsche and the Origin of the Idea of Modernism," *Inquiry* 26 (1983): 151–80.
22 There is not in this work a detailed account of the instability and fragility of tragic affirma-

of tragic disintegration, Nietzsche presents the history of Greek drama as itself a Promethean tragedy: the struggle to achieve Apollonian individuality and distinctness, by its very success, ensured its own destruction, the disintegration of the chorus into individuals, and of the hero into a mere person. Tragedy is presented as an attempt to conquer and to forget the threat of Dionysian disintegration, one that succeeds so well that the failure to secure such individuality would be misunderstood, would have to seem arbitrary, Euripidean (*BT,* 89; *GT,* 91). The same historical points are suggested in the striking claims about what Nietzsche views as Plato's attempt at a new form of aesthetic justification, his invention of "the novel" or dialogue, a "new art form" that created a "new status of poetry" (*BT,* 88; *GT,* 90), as well as in the suggestions that the limitations of the "theoretical point of view," present now in the post-Kantian age, will create the *historical* conditions for a new tragic sensibility.

Nietzsche came to abandon the revolutionary, transformative rhetoric of this early work, but the language of an "eternal struggle" between the tragic point of view (and its various emanations later in his work) and theory, enlightenment, or philosophy would remain. This means that he is denying what amounts to the heart of Blumenberg's two-front attempt (i) to restrict the scope of the theoretical attitude, and so deny any "mythos–logos" opposition, and (ii) to explain the possibility of mythic meaning in a wholly functional, non-cognitive way and so to portray mythos as no rival to logos. In doing so, Nietzsche points to Socrates' own suspicion of and even "war" with the poets, and so Socrates' own view that what he is proposing is not compatible with what the poets do. Nietzsche thus suggests that the insistence on lucidity, consciousness, and the link between virtue and knowledge would not be wholly intelligible in the Socratic turn except in the conflicts and *aporiai* and tensions created by the tragic attitude, requiring some transformation, or in Blumenberg's terms, "work on myth."

Blumenberg, no doubt aware of Cassirer's own reversals and hesitations upon witnessing the Nazi use of mythology and the contemporary prominence of political mythology, is appropriately hesitant to draw any pragmatic implications from mythic meaning. But, given his views on the persistance and power of "mythic thought," his justification for this hesitancy remains, at least to me, obscure, for many of the reasons discussed. Moreover, for both Socrates and Nietzsche, what Blumenberg calls mythic

tion, or, in other words, an explanation of tragedy's suicide. There is certainly nothing that plays the same role as Nietzsche's account of the self-undermining role of the notions of honesty and intention in Christian moral psychology.

thought cannot function in *any* way without being relied on in action, in some way or other. In fact, Nietzsche tends to treat the possible role of such an orientation, or reassurance, or resignation in action as fully and wholly expressive of the meaning of such attitudes. They, the tragic or Christian, or even the theoretical stance all *are* already "modes of action," not evidence or data that count as reasons for action. And in those terms, where the problem to be solved is how to live well, not the fear of absolutism, an "eternal conflict" between any mythic sense of finitude or tragedy and "Socratic optimism," is inevitable.

Part Five

MODERNISM AND NIHILISM

12

TRUTH AND LIES IN THE
EARLY NIETZSCHE

I

Nietzsche is well known for a critique of the classical philosophical tradition. But there is an obvious problem in understanding this critique. At points it seems completely dismissive to hold that philosophy itself is pathological, always a symptom or sign of a kind of spiritual and ethical degeneration, a self-destructive hatred of life. (Just as there cannot be a "good" version of alchemy, astrology, or misogyny, there cannot be an improved or better version of such a sickness.) At other points, this critique only seems aimed at essentialist or metaphysically realist, or dualist, or Platonic–Christian philosophy, naturally raising the question of the Nietzschean philosophical alternative, the nature of the authority with which Nietzsche proclaims it, and the relation of such an alternative to the much criticized asceticism.

There are scores of ways of considering Nietzsche's texts in order to raise this question. I shall concentrate on an early version: the contrast between the tragic and the Socratic point of view, and its implications in Nietzsche's work of the early 1870s. I raise this question because of some dissatisfaction with many widely known and influential characterizations of Nietzsche's relation to traditional philosophy. These include various characterizations of Nietzsche:

The last metaphysician of the Western tradition. By being wedded to a radical and unprecedented metaphysics of the will to power, according to Heidegger, Nietzsche supposedly reveals the underlying assumptions of all modern philosophy and so the unavoidable nihilism that is the fate of all post-Platonic philosophy.

A psychological "underminer," and therapist. This is the Nietzsche who reveals the true or secret motivations of philosophical activity; perhaps even a naturalist, an instinct therapist.

An aesthete or litterateur. This Nietzsche understands philosophical world views and normative claims as, let us say, poems, matters of taste or style, and whose final normative assessments of life are and must be based on aesthetic criteria.

There is Nietzsche as some sort of *armchair cultural anthropologist* or ethnologist, for whom philosophical and religious claims and the political and moral practices they sustain are the mere integrating, conformity-inducing tribal rituals or mythic practices of our clan; an ethnologist who can reveal the essentially practical function of such rituals in our community.

A provocateur, experimenter, shock therapist, dismantler. This is a Nietzsche capable of revealing the immoralism of all morality, the cruelty in Christian pity, the fear and cowardice in modern egalitarianism, not because of any grand theory of immoralism or cruelty, but just because of an intense sensitivity to the actual cruelty in Christianity, the immoral arbitrariness and brute contingency in moral evaluation. This Nietzsche is as internalist a critic as there ever was; the Nietzsche who merely wears masks, assumes roles, inhabits philosophical views more authentically and intensely than their adherents can. A deconstructive force of nature, if such a thing is possible: at once "every name in history" and "dynamite."

There is finally the surface meaning; that Nietzsche is not a critic of philosophy, but himself *a philosophic critic;* not someone dissatisfied with metaphysics as such, but only a metaphysics bewitched by the stability of language and logical form; himself an exponent of a metaphysics of radical flux, of unstable, shifting, provisional identity; a proponent of cyclical, mythic time (the Nietzsche of Löwith, Klossowski); the Deleuzean Nietzsche of active forces; the theorist of *Macht quanta,* of life as the senseless and ceaseless expression of force (Günther Abel's quasi-Leibnizean); the linguistic and conceptual Idealist and relativist epistemologist so favored by anglophone commentators; the moralist whose own moral recommendations seem grounded on how things really are, not how we would like them to be.

This last Nietzsche has a theory of forces, or drives, of Dionysian reality, of values, of language, of will, of appearance, lots and lots of theories, and no general position against theory. The tragic point of view relies on the philosophy of the Dionysian; genealogical critique on the nature of any possible evaluation and on human nature in general; psychological critique on a displacement of naive and distorted views of human desire and the soul, in favor of a true view.

By contrast, the more radical, contemporary Nietzsche is anti-theory and anti-philosophy altogether, an enemy of the ascetic ideal and suspicious of any value to truth, simply because, for this Nietzsche, there just is no truth.

Moreover, there is also the merely *philosophic Nietzsche* who is no "master thinker," or great philosopher, just generally philosophical, perhaps even slightly subphilosophical. This is the Nietzsche who belongs with Voltaire, LaRochefoucauld, Heine, Emerson, Carlyle, Huxley, even Spengler; as powerful an essayist as ever there was, but essentially a moralist; a Camus, not a Heidegger; as a philosopher, a Schopenhauerean–Wagnerian echo, not some new voice, some Wittgenstein.

But the question of these various Nietzsches, raised like this, would have to lead into the complexities of Nietzsche reception, and the function "Nietzsche" has served in modern European intellectual history; it would require a compilation of the many valuable books now appearing in what seems to be the "Nietzsche in . . ." series: Nietzsche in Germany, in England, in France, in Italy, in Russia (I think there are books with all those exact titles).

My own view is that there is ample textual evidence, in the standard scholarly sense, to support any of these versions. I hope to make some progress in exploring in what sense they could all have come to be influential by exploring the contrast mentioned in detail. My orienting question is the one that emerged in Nietzsche's explosive first work and remained with him throughout his life: what it means to see philosophy (and eventually science, morality, and art) all "*from the point of view of life*," and especially from the point of view of a "possible" (or by contrast, "impossible") life. Although Nietzsche would not pursue the "artist's metaphysics" he originally proposed as the most adequate to the possibility of life, he never abandoned as his central concern the question of what was necessary for an affirmable or sustainable life, and never abandoned his claim that traditional philosophy, religion, and the moral point of view had turned out to be inadequate answers to such a question. (It is typical of Nietzsche that the most concentrated statement of his own final answer occurs only parabolically, in the tension between Zarathustra's two "mistresses," "life" and "wisdom," the original contrast with Socraticism set up in *BT,* and that what appears to be

Zarathustra's resolution of this issue is "whispered into life's ear," and that we are never told what Zarathustra said!)[1]

But framing the issues this way forces us to ask just what the question to which Socraticism was an inadequate response is, this question of the possibility of life. As I hope to begin showing, Nietzsche's view of this matter is far more complex and elusive than it might first seem.

Accordingly, I propose simply to plunge right in by first simply summarizing what appears to be the thesis of *BT,* at least the thesis relevant to us and to this question.

That thesis concerns the origin and demise of Greek tragedy in the classical period, a familiar and profoundly interesting question (Why, under what circumstances, what does it mean, that at some point in the orgiastic and largely feminine rites associated with Dionysus, the goat dance or goat sacrifice, *tragoidia,* an individual character would begin to speak as the great suffering god Dionysus? Why would then, eventually, the practice of coming

---

1 In the remaining chapters, references to the German texts of Nietzsche's works are to the *Kritische Studienausgabe* (hereafter *KSA*), ed. by Giogio Colli and Mazzino Montinari (Berlin: de Gruyter, 1967–77, 1988) and are abbreviated as follows: *Also sprach Zarathustra* (hereafter *ASZ*), IV; *Die Fröhliche Wissenschaft* (hereafter *FW*), III; *Götzen-Dämmerung* (hereafter *GD*), VI; *Die Geburt der Tragödie* (hereafter *GT*), I; *Jenseits von Gut und Böse* (hereafter *JGB*), V; *Menschliches Allzumenschliches* (hereafter *MAM*), II; *Morgenröte* (hereafter *M*), III; *Vom Nutzen und Nachtheil der Historie für das Leben* (hereafter *VNN*), I; *Zur Genealogie der Moral* (hereafter *ZGM*), V; and *Der Wille zur Macht* (hereafter *WM*) (Stuttgart: Alfred Kröner, 1964). English translations and their abbreviations: *Beyond Good and Evil* (hereafter *BGE*), trans. Walter Kaufmann (New York: Vintage, 1966); *Daybreak* (hereafter *Da*), trans. R. J. Hollingdale (Cambridge: Cambridge University Press, 1982); *Human All Too Human* (hereafter *HAH*), trans. R. J. Hollingdale (Cambridge: Cambridge University Press, 1986); *On the Advantage and Disadvantage of History for Life* (hereafter *AD*), trans. Peter Preuss (Indianapolis: Hackett, 1980); *On the Genealogy of Morals* (hereafter *OGM*), trans. Walter Kaufmann and R. J. Hollingdale (New York: Vintage, 1969); *Philosophy and Truth: Selections from Nietzsche's Notebooks of the Early 1870's* (hereafter *PT*), ed. by Daniel Brezeale (Atlantic Highlands, N.J.: Humanities Press, 1979); *The Birth of Tragedy* (hereafter *BT*), trans. Walter Kaufmann (New York: Vintage, 1977); *The Gay Science* (hereafter *GS*), trans. Walter Kaufmann (New York: Vintage, 1974); *The Will to Power* (hereafter *WP*), trans. Walter Kaufmann (New York: Vintage,1967); *Thus Spoke Zarathustra* (hereafter *TSZ*), trans. Walter Kaufmann (New York: Viking, 1966); *Twilight of the Idols* (hereafter *TI*), trans. R. J. Hollingdale (Baltimore: Penguin, 1968).

I refer here to what is, in effect, the climax of *TSZ*, the last two sections of pt. III, "Der andere Tanzlied" and "Die sieben Siegel." When Zarathustra whispers whatever he does in "life's" ear, she says only, "Du weisst Das, oh Zarathustra? Das weiss Niemand. – " (*ASZ*, p. 285, *TSZ*, p. 227). Cf. Michael Platt, "What Does Zarathustra Whisper in Life's Ear?" *Nietzsche-Studien* 17 (1988): 179–194. See also the account in Lawrence Lampert, *Nietzsche's Teaching* (New Haven: Yale University Press, 1986), pp. 238–40. As both claim in different ways, Zarathustra does appear to be finally "affirming life" even as he acknowledges his own mortality, but that does not help much in unraveling the mystery of what is involved in affirming life, or in apparently turning from "life" to "eternity" in the Seven Seals.

together in the dark, in some continuing sense of religious sanctity and quiet, in order to watch human beings pretend to be all sorts of other human beings and gods, suffering horrible, painful fates, come to be a central cultural experience, to inaugurate the Western dramatic tradition itself?). Nietzsche presents his own answer to this question in relation to claims about music and contemporary culture that betray the deep influences of Schopenhauer and Wagner.

In a sense, thanks to these influences, the surface claims made by Nietzsche appear typical of late romantic disaffections. *BT* seems to celebrate the more deeply revelatory nature of pre-reflective, even pre-rational and pre-verbal primary experiences, an individuality-dissolving, Dionysian intoxication. He claims that living remnants of this original Dionysian, musical experience are present in the early function of the chorus and choral odes, and in the horrific failures of tragic heroes. Something in both the horror and the heroism of the excessive deeds that Agamemnon or Orestes must do, of Oedipus' failed attempt at wisdom, of Prometheus' suffering, figure what true *Ur-eine* chaos, arbitrariness, chance lies behind our feeble, if beautiful, attempts at order, nomos, intelligibility. (The true figure for Dionysian wisdom, requiring an indifference to all norm, or limit, is thus, as Nietzsche claims, Oedipus' incest, a desire he both must and cannot indulge. The same is true of Prometheus in Nietzsche's account, whose "sacrilege" is "necessary" but who must also, paradoxically, himself demand justice and measure. Hence tragic wisdom: "Alles Vorhandene ist gerecht und ungerecht und in beidem gleich berechtigt" (All that exists is just and unjust and equally justified in both) (*GT,* 71; *BT,* 72).

In fact, in Nietzsche's unusual "theory of acting," characters represented in front of the chorus are collectively experienced as the projections of this intoxicated mass; dreamlike images, whose instability, fragility, and even arbitrary inhabitability by all are actually experienced as such in the collective dramatic experience. This is all by contrast with the limitations and foolish optimism of the Socratic search for meaning through logos, definition, and the hope for an intelligible structure beneath or beyond the appearances. And, as noted, this appears a predictable contrast between the romantic–expressive lamp and the classical–reflecting mirror, between intuitive insight and the limitations of reflective or rational or empirical approaches.

But Nietzsche goes well beyond such standard polarities by treating the tragic itself as a complex ethical category, by understanding the dramatic experience in terms of very broad questions of affirmation and evaluation, the very sustainability of life itself. (The word he uses to characterize tragedy's function is *Rechtfertigung,* justification, and for reasons that will soon become clear, it is important to recall the resonances that term would call to mind in Nietzsche's German audience: *Rechtfertigung durch die Gnade* or *im Glauben,* or the sense of justification relevant to Luther and the justification or "live-ability" of existence by grace and faith, not some notion of a metaphysical or philosophical foundation.)[2] There is, in his account of tragedy, hardly just intoxicated selflessness in an unstable tension with dreamlike individuals and resolutely if irrationally cheerful Olympian gods. There is also a full tragic point of view, a way of appreciating and judging that is best understood by contrast with the Socratic and eventually the moral point of view. These evaluative issues involve the problem of suffering and justification in the largest sense. The question he takes tragedy to be answering is, he says, a possible response to the Silenus wisdom: Silenus, who says, the best is never to have been born; next best, to die young.

This is all what will lead him, as we shall see, to such a radical contrast with Socratic philosophy. The contrast shall turn on questions significant for the rest of Nietzsche's work: the problem of appearances or illusions (here the question of aesthetic justification, and an artist's metaphysics) and the larger question introduced by Socrates, in contrast to such justification, what Nietzsche calls "the value of truth."

II

Historically, *BT* is cobbled together from three essays that Nietzsche, the twenty-six-year-old *Wunderkind,* gave as public lectures in Basel in 1870 and then worked up into his momentous first book, "The Greek Music Drama," "Socrates and Tragedy," and the "Dionysian World View."[3] Because Nietzsche, the much heralded student of the great Leipzig scholar Ritschl, was supposed to be the next great name in German philology, the spectacularly unorthodox nature of the claims in classical scholarship, and its unprecedented form (no footnotes!), dominated the book's disastrous reception.

This was especially true because of Nietzsche's refusal to accept those aspects of Greek culture that for so long seemed to comfort German intellectuals, the *edle Einfalt and still Grösse* of Winckelman. Not simplicity, form, clarity, sculpture, architecture, and light (order) made the Greeks Greek for

2 Cf. the discussion in Volker Gerhardt, "Artisten-Metaphysik: Zu Nietzsches frühem Programm einer ästhetischen Rechtfertigung der Welt," in his *Pathos und Distanz* (Stuttgart: Reclam, 1988), p. 48.
3 Cf. the discussion in Graham Parkes, *Composing the Soul: Reaches of Nietzsche's Psychology* (Chicago: University of Chicago Press, 1994), pp. 60–83.

Nietzsche, but sex, violence, blood lust, alcohol, orgies, music, and the darkness of the human soul (excess). Nietzsche took extremely seriously the historical origins of tragedy in *Dionysian* festivals, linked the meaning of tragic experience to these orgiastic intoxications, and made use of Schopenhauer's theory of the will, the collapse of the *principium individuationis* into pure, selfless will, and the experience of music, to explain what such a Dionysian experience would be like and what its significance might be.

In making these points, *BT* would introduce a major player in the Nietzschean drama from now until his last days of sanity, Dionysus, the greatest god of the Hellenistic Greek world, celebrated at hillside orgiastic festivals, largely by women, the Maenads (frenzied ones). Dionysus was the patron god of the two great Greek dramatic festivals, the *Lenaea* and the *City Dionysia,* or eventually, comic and tragic drama festivals, and the stories of his origin were unusual, even by Greek standards. In one, Zeus had impregnated Semele. Hera disguised as nurse found out from Semele that Zeus was the father; she pretended to refuse to believe it unless Semele could persuade Zeus to appear in true form; Semele complied but was blasted into nothingness. (Dionysus was thus born as a result of the impossibility of life without illusion. We can tolerate the undisguised Zeus as little as a wholly Dionysian life, something that would dismember us.) Zeus, though, plucks Dionysus from Semele's womb before death and inserts him into his thigh, using it as a womb. (The story is thus full of ambiguities about male–female and life–death dualities that will show up again in Nietzsche's major Dionysian–Apollonian duality; it also means that the source of our *Zerissenheit* can also be the source of our birth.) Other accounts also stress the twice-born character of Dionysus (Demeter, impregnated by Zeus, is destroyed by Hera, but the heart of Dionysus is saved and eaten by Semele, who eventually gives birth to him). Dionysus is thus a figure of death and dissolution who can nevertheless produce or sustain life, something important both in the ritual eating of the sacrificed goat at the festival and in Nietzsche's account of tragic affirmation.

Likewise, in his account of Apollo Nietzsche insisted on something common in much nineteenth-century German treatment of Greek religion: that it was fundamentally an aesthetic, not a doctrinal or sectarian phenomenon. The Greeks experienced the Olympian world as a delightful as well as frightening dream world; sacrifices and rituals were more a communal aesthetic festival, where notions of a god's will, appeasement, forgiveness, and so forth, could not have played the roles they were to play later in the West. (A point in Nietzsche's favor, made by Blumenberg, among others:

There is no evidence of doctrinal or scriptural controversies. Several differing accounts of Prometheus, Dionysus, Odysseus, Pandora, and so on, could coexist comfortably, with no evidence that anyone was much concerned about which one was true.[4] This is exactly what seemed to upset Socrates in the *Republic* so much: Poets could say whatever they wanted about the gods and no one seemed to mind, no one seemed to *care* what was "true." As we shall see, on this and the issue of Socrates' criticism of imitation, of poets pretending effectively to be whoever they please, Nietzsche will claim that Socrates makes a gross category mistake, failing or refusing to see that poets are not bad or incomplete philosophers.)

What got Nietzsche into so much trouble was this suggestion in *BT* that the Greek tragic experience was not fundamentally religious or politically cautionary, not a way of depicting excess, in order to reconcile us to limits. It was just the opposite! Where Aristotle might see in Prometheus or Oedipus excess as hubris, Nietzsche saw a "titanic love of man," and "excessive wisdom" that could not be restrained or avoided (at least not without the consequences of the moral point of view he will come to hate); "The 'titanic' and 'barbaric' were in the last analysis as necessary as the Apollonian" "Excess [*Übermass*] revealed itself as truth" (*GT*, 41; *BT*, 46). (The nature of this *necessity* is really the main issue of *BT* and in its treatment of Socrates.) Tragedy was treated as a way of revealing the inevitable, necessary (even in some sense welcome) dissolution of limit, form, even the very sustainability of individual characters, and yet a way of affirming life anyway, a "once more, *de capo*," in spite of all that, a heroic pessimism.

Tragic drama was thus said to involve the perennial opposition between two natural drives, or "art impulses," the Dionysian and the Apollonian, representing both the inevitability of the Greek dream world of the plastic arts, sculpture, and the heroic attempts by individuals to establish identity, norm, measure, limit, within such dreamlike orders, as well as the inevitable disintegration of such illusory stability, reclaimed by Dionysian formlessness. The tragic experience itself, by refusing to deny or avoid such inevitability, both revealed and helped create a distinct mode of courageous affirmation, a tragic affirmation, even an aesthetic justification of existence.

Finally, to complete this brief summary (I shall pass over the "rebirth of tragedy," Wagnerian issues beginning in section 16), Nietzsche also proposes an account of the end of tragedy, and the loss of cultural authority, for

---

4 Cf. Hans Blumenberg, *Work on Myth*, trans. Robert Wallace (Cambridge: MIT Press, 1985), and the discussion in Chapter 11, this volume.

the tragic point of view. The main villain is of course, Euripides, though his decadence is frequently traced to Socrates.

> To separate this original and all-powerful Dionysean element from tragedy, and to reconstruct tragedy purely on the basis of an un-Dionysean art, morality, and world-view – this is the tendency of Euripides as it now reveals itself to us in clear illumination. (*GT*, 82; *BT*, 81)

What is sometimes described as the sexual coupling of the Dionysian and Apollonian, or the "expression of two interwoven artistic impulses," is now perceived as unacceptable or impossible. The Dionysian risks, religious fervor, heroic excess of Oedipus, Prometheus, Antigone, now look, from a wholly Apollonian, "cool" perspective, simply irrational, imprudent, unjustified, and so unjust. Chance, random suffering, the pre-history one inherits and cannot control, now appear simply unjust and unacceptable, now a reason, if unopposable, unredeemable, to accept the Silenus wisdom. The Dionysian is "scared off the stage" by a "demonic power speaking through Euripides": Socrates.

Even the "shining" images of the Apollonian dream world now appear as mere "lack of insight and the power of illusion" from which Socrates infers "the essential perversity and reprehensibility of what exists" (*GT*, 89; *BT*, 87). Virtue must now be knowledge, formulable in definitions; the unexamined life is not worth living; no one does evil knowingly.

> After Socrates, the mystagogue of science, one philosophical school succeeds another, wave upon wave. . . . The hunger for knowledge [*Wissensgier*] reached a never suspected universality in the widest domain of the educated world, became the real task for every person of higher gifts, and led science onto the high seas from which it has never again been driven altogether. . . . We cannot fail to see in Socrates the one turning point and vortex of so-called world history. (*GT*, 99–100; *BT*, 96)

III

As noted, the important aspects of this contrast with Socraticism, to return now to the critique of philosophy theme, have to do with two themes, and the relation between them is not clear-cut.

The first concerns the general question of the *possibility* of Socraticism. Let us assume there is something like tragic wisdom: some distinctive sort of appreciation of Dionysian instability and "real" disorder in the cosmos; a kind of enjoyment, delight in the formative Apollonian activity of human culture, a delight that can, by virtue of the kind of attachment and allegiance to existence it promotes, be called a *Rechtfertigung* or justification.[5] Its replacement presupposes the possibility of some sort of philosophical truth claim. Actually, it presupposes two things, both that a reasoned logos, informed in some way by what there truly is, can be achieved, *and* that achieving it is essential in the justification and the ultimate sustainability of life itself; the examined life and only the examined life is "worth living."

Nietzsche is often taken to have denied this possibility and to have done so by making a number of philosophical counterclaims in his own voice. He is somewhat cautious about his doubts concerning Socratic optimism in *BT*, though. That is, he makes a more historical than theoretical point: that the post-Socratic philosophical tradition has undermined *its own optimism* (he makes clear later that he is talking mostly about Kant): "Logic coils up at these boundaries and finally bites *its own tail* – suddenly the new form of insight breaks through, tragic insight, which, merely to be endured, needs art as protection and remedy" (*GT*, 101; *BT*, 98). But in other works of this period, one of which we shall look at in a minute, he appears to attack Socratic optimism more directly. No philosophical language *could* be adequate to (unstable, chaotic, formless) reality as it is in itself; language is a tissue of metaphors and linguistic tropes in no possible way adequate to the real; terms are always metaphors whose metaphorical character has been forgotten; every claim to say something true in some philosophically useful sense, the sense Socrates requires, is, by the criteria Socrates accepts, false. He appears even to claim that *any* truth claim is necessarily false. (This counter-Socratic metaphysics would appear to be invoked in *BT* in passages where Nietzsche speaks of the "Olympian magic mountain opening up" revealing its "*roots* to us." "The Greeks knew and felt *the* terror and horror of existence. That he might endure this terror at all, he had to interpose between himself and *life* the radiant dream birth of the Olympians." He goes on to talk of "*the* titanic powers of nature" [*GT*, 35; *BT*, 42].)

But the other question implied by Nietzsche's doubts about Socraticism is different. It addresses not so much the question of the inherent possibility of the Socratic quest itself, but what we think it will all do for us, what sort of

<hr>

5 I do not claim that the question of *how* such an experience can accomplish such a justification has been answered. In fact, as the *Selbstkritik* indicates, Nietzsche himself came to believe that he could not answer it within the assumptions he accepted at the time. Art alone, certainly Wagner's art alone, cannot accomplish such a reorientation unless much, much else also changes.

redemptive function, knowing what Socrates wants us to know, will or could serve. This question, the one I think Nietzsche is overwhelmingly most interested in, despite many appearances and rhetorical flourishes, he calls the question of the "value of truth." Trying to understand what Nietzsche means by a "justification" that is not "Socratic" will depend a great deal on which sort of question one takes to be paramount in the development of Nietzsche's remarks about "philosophy" (the very possibility of Socraticism, or the possibility that Socraticism could achieve the redemptive and sustaining function claimed for it).

To state my own view baldly, I think that even when Nietzsche wants to raise the question of the possibility of truth, he does so much more phenomenologically, internally, and historically, asking about the "fate" of the Socratic promise, rather than about its intrinsic possibility. I don't think he believes in any such "intrinsic possibility" or transcendental question, as classically conceived, because of how he understands the relation between assessments of such questions (the possibility of truth) and "evaluations of life," commitments and attachments to what he loosely called "values" *in* any such assessment. His main, overarching or master question is always *the value of truth,* or what we think "the truth" will accomplish, and more generally always the question of the various ways in which attachments to various possible lives come to be and are sustained.

Admittedly, these two questions are hard to keep separate and seem, in Nietzsche's works, logically implicated in each other. After all, one good reason to attack the Socratic proposal (to replace tragic wisdom with self-knowledge) as naively optimistic is that it *is* simply impossible; not that, even if it were possible, it could not do for us what Socrates promises. Or, to come back to the usual paradox, there is finally no way to explore what could serve what sort of function in "life" without a "true account of life," and *its* "conditions," perhaps not true in the Socratic realist sense, but true in some sophisticated post-Kantian, anti-realist, satisfaction-of-our-best-cognitive-criteria, fallible, perspectival-but-not-necessarily-false-just-the-best-we've-got sense of truth; perhaps not true in the sense of the great nominalizations and substantializations he objects to in post-Platonic philosophy, but true in a way that still leads us away from the radical implications of the attack on *the value of truth itself* (such as those expressed in part III of *OGM*) and back to Nietzschean truths, the will-to-power-radical-flux metaphysics, eternal return cosmology, and self-aggrandizing, power psychology, those "truths." I don't think either such suspicion accurately reveals the problem Nietzsche is dealing with (the paramount nature of the value of truth question), but defending that will take some time.

IV

We can begin by noting that the Nietzsche-as-counter-Socrates philosopher-of-Becoming does not fit well with *BT*. For one thing, the passage just quoted from section 3, about the "Olympian magic mountain" opening before us and "revealing its roots," is itself presented at least somewhat conjecturally and as an image. It reveals its roots, *gleichsam*, "as it were." For another the Dionysian side of things in *BT* is treated, to use Nietzsche's later language, perspectivally. The Titanic gods are as much aesthetic artifices as the Olympians, and the Dionysian is never presented as "life in itself," but, as he puts it, as a "terrifying view of the world" (*Weltbetrachtung*) (*GT,* 37; *BT,* 43). The point Nietzsche makes against Schiller's view of "naive" poetry is meant to be a general one about an aesthetic experience: "It is by no means a simple condition that comes into being naturally and as if inevitably" (ibid.). Indeed from the beginning of the essay (section 2), the Dionysian is treated as an artistic energy or power (*Kunstmächte*) or art impulse (*Kunst-triebe*), not the state of "things in themselves" unsuccessfully resisted temporarily by Apollonian formative powers. As Nietzsche's invocation of these mythic powers proceeded in later years, any appeal to the distinct force of the "Apollonian" dropped out, and both the *necessity of and resistance to form* in the sustainability and "justification" of life were, he obviously concluded, capturable in a single term: Dionysus (something that makes the view of art proposed in *BT* remarkably modernist, in even the post-Impressionist sense, as has been noted by some recent German aestheticians).[6] There is no invocation of an "original," chaotic "real life"; all life, the suggestion is, is and must be *lived,* or as we say "*led*" (even, in *TSZ,* "whipped"), only in its being justified in some way or other; intoxicating festivals, together with the making of music, are ways of leading a life and so justifying.

But the main evidence for denying that Nietzsche is essentializing Dionysian reality, or treating such a "view of the world" as *the* horrifying "truth" that Socrates is simply fleeing in some bad faith creation of a counterworld, can be found in the way Nietzsche describes the demise of tragedy. His basic view is not, contrary to most readings and the surface of many of his own formulations, that Socrates and Euripides are somehow personally responsible, thanks to their decadence, or thanks to what we would now call their

---

6 Cf. Volker Gerhardt, "Nietzsches ästhetische Revolution," in *Pathos und Distanz,* pp. 12–45, and Dieter Jähnig, "Die Befreiung der Kunsterkenntnis von der Metaphysik in Nietzsches Geburt der Tragödie," in his *Welt-Geschichte: Kunst-Geschichte* (Cologne: DuMont Schauberg, 1975), pp. 122–60.

bourgeois timidity, for killing off tragedy and undermining the tragic point of view. From their point of view, it might be possible to see the issue as one of "scaring" Dionysus off stage, and post facto it is possible to claim that it appears that "Euripides combated and vanquished Aeschylean tragedy" (*GT*, 83; *BT*, 82), but a much greater transformation must have taken place earlier for such a contestation to have been possible. Nietzsche states the nature of this prior transformation directly at the beginning of the turning point of the essay, section 11.

> Greek tragedy met an end different from that of her older sister arts; she died by suicide [*Selbstmord*], in consequence of an irreconcilable conflict [*unlösbaren Conflictes*]; she died tragically, while all the others passed away calmly and beautifully at a ripe old age. (*GT*, 75; *BT*, 76)

The "event" of Euripides is called the "long death struggle" of tragedy itself. In the previous section, Nietzsche had already treated the Dionysian myth, and its sense-making and justifying function, as possible at a time, for a time.

> For it is the fate of every myth to creep by degrees into the narrow limits of some alleged historical reality and to be treated by some later generation as a unique fact with historical claims. . . . For this is the way in which religions are wont to die out . . . the feeling for myth perishes and its place is taken by the claim of religion to historical foundations. . . . Through tragedy the myth attains its most profound content, its most expressive form; it rises once more like a wounded hero, and its whole excess of strength, together with the philosophical calm of the dying, burns in its eyes with a last powerful gleam. (*GT*, 74; *BT*, 75)[7]

(This is the same sentiment expressed much later in the discussion of "The Problem of Socrates" in *Götzendämmerung*: "The old Athens was coming to an end. – And Socrates understood that all the world had need of him – his expedient, his cure, his personal art of self-preservation" (*GD*, 71; *TI*, 32).)

Whatever Nietzsche wants to claim is unduly optimistic about Socraticism; it does not appear to have much to do with a metaphysical truth Socrates is avoiding or distorting. However, it might appear from other works of the early 1870s that Nietzsche's deep skepticism about Socrates is based on a general view about the nature of things in themselves and the

---

7 Nietzsche is not entirely consistent in these characterizations. Right after the passages quoted, he says both that the myth was itself dying, and that it died under Euripides' *gewaltsamen Händen* (*GT*, p. 74; *BT*, p. 75).

inevitably "false" or "distorting" effects of all language, or on claims, much quoted in many recent works, against "truth," not just against "faith in truth."

Many of these are concentrated in the 1873 essay, "On Truth and Lies in a Nonmoral Sense." Here it might appear that Nietzsche is presenting a sweeping rejection of the possibility of any true proposition, claiming that there is a world in itself that we could never capture in language, which is itself only a practical instrument in no sense capable of corresponding to the world. Thus,

> It is only be means of forgetfulness that man can ever reach the point of fancying himself to possess a "truth" of the grade just indicated [*in dem eben bezeichneten Grade*. I note the qualification on the kind of "truth" Nietzsche is interested in]. (*WL*, 878; *TL*, 81)

> We believe that we know something about the things in themselves when we speak of trees, colors, snow, and flowers; and yet we possess nothing but metaphors for things – metaphors which correspond in no way to the original entities [*Wesenheiten*]. (82–3)

And finally the most famous passage:

> What then is truth? A moveable host of metaphors, metonymies, and an-thropomorphism: in short, a sum of human relations which have been poet-ically and rhetorically intensified, transferred, and embellished, and which, after long usage, seem to a people to be fixed, canonical, and binding. Truths are illusions which we have forgotten are illusions; they are metaphors that have become worn out and have been drained of sensuous force, coins which have lost their embossing and are not considered as metal and not as coins. (*WL*, 880–1; *TL*, 84)

Well, if "truths are illusions which we have forgotten are illusions" then Socrates' attempt to justify life by understanding it, by appealing to the truth, would certainly be a non-starter. But if this is the basis of Nietzsche's proposal for some alternate "justification" of life, then, first, that basis seems to be simply bad philosophy, rather than an alternative to philosophy. There is no very good reason given in the essay to believe that just because there is a metaphorical dimension to language, quite reliable truth conditions for the utterance of expressions cannot be given. There is no particular reason to think that one needs some direct realist theory of reference or any theory of reference or even of meaning to establish truth conditions, and certainly no good reason to believe that we *know* that what we say is and must be "false." That possibility seems manifestly inconsistent with the thesis itself. And, second, it seems grossly inconsistent with Nietzsche's later work, which, say in his *Genealogy*, claims to have discovered many "unpleasant" truths about the origins of morality.

We can deal with the latter problem in the usual way of scholars: There are different periods in Nietzsche's development, he changed his mind; ceased to believe there was a truth in itself that no one could get at or that all assertions had to be "false"; in some perspective relative sense, some things could be said to be true, in some sense of improvable warranted assertability, and so on (Maudemarie Clark has gone about as far, in as much detail, as one can go in this direction, arguing that the decisive break comes in 1882, in 54 of the *Gay Science*, where the very conceivability of any thing in itself is rejected).[8]

But already in this work Nietzsche claims that "The 'thing in itself' is likewise something quite incomprehensible [*unfasslich*] to the creator of language and something not in the least worth striving for" (*WL*, 879; *TL*, 82). (Strictly speaking, this already means that the claim that language must get things, things in themselves, wrong, is already itself "incomprehensible.") As in much other work of this period, however, the object of his attack seems not to be a general theory of the possibility of truth. It is concentrated on the sort of truths that "the man of truth, the scientist, the philosopher" (ibid.) want to establish, and why they want to establish them, and that provoke Nietzsche's scorn and skepticism. Some realist claim about "essential qualities" and the redemptive hopes for knowledge of the real, not the appearances, remains his target throughout, and he particularly takes aim at those who think that such truths can be established by examining linguistic commitments.

It is philosophical and potentially redemptive (or life-"justifying") truths that are better understood as "really" a "movable host of metaphors," and so on. It is by virtue of such aesthetic qualities, he continues to argue in this essay, that they can justify (in the unique sense in which "life" can be justified), although we "forget" that and try to link such claims about "honesty" and "essence" to use two of his examples, to real properties in the world. Without such reassurance and realist confirmation, the redemptive function of such truths would, we have come to believe, or have been led to believe "after Socrates," fail.

8 Maudemarie Clark, *Nietzsche on Truth and Philosophy* (Cambridge: Cambridge University Press, 1990).

This is the point, after all, of the parabolic beginning to the essay, which I shall quote from the full 1872 version for Cosima Wagner:

> Once upon a time, in some out of the way corner of that universe which is dispersed into numberless twinkling solar systems, there was a star upon which clever beasts invented knowing. It was the most arrogant and mendacious minute of world history, but nevertheless only a minute. After nature had drawn a few breaths the star cooled and solidified, and the clever beasts had to die. The time had come too, for although they boasted of how much they had understood, in the end they understood to their great annoyance that they had understood everything falsely. They died and in dying cursed truth. Such was the nature of these desperate beasts who had invented knowing. (*PW,* 759–60; *PT,* 65)

Like *BT,* this passage speaks of a kind of natural (or historical) death for the Socratic hopes for knowledge. One minute of knowledge and we find that we do not know *what we need to know in order to live,* and we die cursing truth. In this and many other essays of this period, Nietzsche's attention is directed to the expectations for philosophical knowledge and his comments always try to show that, *insofar* as such claims can fulfill redemptive, justifying functions, respond to Silenus; answer the basic question *Wozu leben?,* they do so aesthetically, not by providing some cognitive answer. It is, in other words, only under the assumptions common to the Socratic–philosophical tradition, that a redemptive knowledge of reality in itself, and so of the Idea of the Good, is what most needs attaining, that *such* claims would eventually have to look "false."

That this is the issue that interests Nietzsche – what sorts of "truths" could "do" what Socrates claims for them, make life worth living; and whether *such* truths are possible – is apparent from the other discussions of this period. In his 1872 essay on the Philosopher ("Reflections on the Struggle Between Art and Knowledge"), Nietzsche writes:

> The philosopher of tragic knowledge. He masters the uncontrolled knowledge drive [the *entfesselten Wissenstrieb* often identified as the problem with philosophical hopes, not the drive for truth itself], though not by means of a new metaphysics. He establishes no new faith. He considers it tragic that the ground of metaphysics has been withdrawn, and he will never permit himself to be satisfied with the motley whirling game of the sciences. He cultivates a new life; he returns to art its rights. (*P,* 11–12)

Later in the essay:

Man's longing to be completely truthful in the midst of a mendacious natural order is something noble and heroic. But this is possible [and I note emphatically that according to Nietzsche, it is possible] only in a very relative sense. That is tragic. That is Kant's tragic problem! Art now acquires an entirely new dignity. The sciences, in contrast, are degraded to a degree.

The truthfulness of art: It alone is now honest.

Thus, after an immense detour, we again return to the natural condition (that of the Greeks). It has proven impossible to build a culture upon knowledge. (*P*, 28–9)

V

But, finally, *how*, by contrast, could some aesthetic or religious or non-philosophic "justification" be the basis of a "culture?" Why "now," a question that requires some attention to Nietzsche's treatment of Christianity? These are questions that lead us again to the general issue: what Nietzsche thinks the possible justification of life involves and what is especially involved when it fails. A few points in his approach are clearer, though too few are clear. It is clear enough that Nietzsche is treating the problem of a possible life (a life that can be affirmed, sustained "strongly" over time) as a general problem of practical teleology and so of purposiveness. To "lead" a life is to have some comprehensive sense of what is worth enduring, risking, sacrificing, and so on, a sense that can provide hierarchy, make decisions coherent. (Again the clearest example is for Nietzsche the strangest: philosophers, who desire intently, their whole lives, what may not even exist, wisdom, and who thus can be said to love death, what must be after or beyond life, not life.) It is also very clear that he does not think that this orienting "sense" can be a principle or a rational norm or achievable by some philosophical truth. To quote *Götzendämmerung* again:

Judgments, value judgments concerning life, for or against, can in the last resort never be true: they possess value only as symptoms – in themselves such judgments are stupidities. One must reach out and try to grasp this astonishing *finesse, that the value of life cannot be estimated.* (*G*, 68; *TI*, 30)

It is, though, still only initially clear why Nietzsche thinks that such principles, moral laws, rational norms, philosophical insights into natural hierarchy *could* not provide this orienting sense. For one thing, he thinks the evidence is in, historically. They have *not* been able to fulfill such an orienting and so life-sustaining function. And after Kant, the prospects are much worse. The Socratic experiment has terminated in nihilism. For another, he implies, it is only if, *already*, how "things really are" or what the nature of universals is or what God really wants, has come to matter to me, that such an enterprise *could* sustain and help affirm my "life." Knowing what law could be said to be unavoidably binding on all rational agents might be something interesting to determine, but there is nothing *in* such a determination, Nietzsche keeps insisting, that would explain why such a result should matter to me. (In fact, he always suggests, if we try to explain such "mattering" in *such* cases, we always detect, or smell, a psychopathology; we are forced to the language of fear, resentment, cowardice, and so on.) And it is also, finally, clear that at least Nietzsche's intention is to frame this problem of how purposes and *tele* could come to matter not "naturally" or "individually" but in broad cultural and historical terms, in terms of the Greeks, or the West, or Christianity.

The aesthetic language of his early essays suggests that he thought there must be some kind of distinctive "aesthetic effect" in the experience of tragic drama, a "showing" or presentation or appearance that was orienting and "justifying" *of itself*; in participating in such experiences and only in so experiencing could there be such an experience of the sense of things; and that he thought that no moral or political principle could be "effective" or motivating without such an "effect" (without what Schiller and even Kant promoted as the *Versinnlichung* of ideas).

So in the *Second Untimely Meditation*, "On the Use and Abuse of History for Life," there is said to be a way in which our own understanding of history can be "for life" or hostile to or irrelevant to life, and Nietzsche struggles to make clear that this has nothing to do with what we would like to be true about the past, as if we could pretend that some events occurred or didn't, and nothing to do with any general skepticism about objectivity in history, or with any claim that all writing of history is merely a matter of exercising power in the service of a particular view of life. In fact, antiquarian and monumental history require us to be able to get a great deal right about the past, and critical history must be able to be genuinely liberating to be critical. The problem concerns the function of a "historical sense," or occurs when some attitude about the past begins to function in some "life-justifying" way, to assume a role that is not justified or undermined by any fact about the past, or when the historical sense begins to function "aesthetically," in the same way as the "tragic point of view." Accordingly:

> The historical sense, it rules without restraint [*ungebändigt*] and unfolds all its implications, uproots the future because it destroys illusions and robs existing things of their atmosphere in which alone they can live. Historical righteous-

ness, even when it is practised truly and with pure intentions [I note that Nietzsche conceded the possibility of such virtues] is a terrible virtue because it always undermines the living and brings it to ruin: its judging is always annihilating [*ihr Richten ist immer ein Vernichten*]. (*VNN*, 295; *AD*, 38)

When "justice alone rules," he goes on, "the creative instinct is enfeebled and discouraged," and, especially, "*only with love*, however, only surrounded by the shadow of the illusion of love, can man create." "Each man who is forced no longer to love unconditionally has had the root of his strength cut off," and "Only if history can bear being transformed into a work of art . . . may it perhaps preserve instincts or even rouse them" (*VNN*, 299; *AD*, 40). This "atmosphere" that must "surround every living thing" for it to live, a "mysterious circle of mist" or "enveloping madness . . . a protective and veiling cloud," is not treated as wishful thinking, or self-projected illusion, but is presented in the language of organic growth, of what will "nurture" or help "ripen," and so as the problem of eros, not will or creation in the romantic sense. The problem is a problem because, Nietzsche keeps suggesting, the basic "possibility of leading a life" turns fundamentally on the issue of eros, and we understand so little under what conditions desire can be roused and sustained. It is clear enough that it is not by arguments that such eros is excited and sustained and clear enough that Nietzsche wants to invoke again the old Platonic contrast between justice and eros, conceding that there is some deep (or tragic) incompatibility between them, but insisting that this cannot be simply "resolved" in the *Republic*'s fashion, in favor of justice, without the poets, with naked exercising, eugenics, marriage numbers, with eros assumed to be the "many-headed monster" of book IX.[9] Even for this, he suggests, we require an eros for justice, for greatness, for an absolute measure, which eros itself cannot be justly measured, but must be spontaneous, *daimonic*. Hence again the deepest truth of these early works:

All that exists is just and unjust and equally justified in both.

9 It is just as important to realize that Nietzsche does not resolve this issue the other way, by "banishing" the historians here, by banishing, that is, the "just," or the objectivists more generally. Even though the very title of the essay can lead to the belief that Nietzsche means to encourage some unhistorical spontaneity as necessary for life, the text makes clear that "to be human" is to be "the remembering" or the historical animal, and that although "action" can never be simply based on a proposition about history, it can never for that reason be "unhistorical"; it must take place within the "horizon" of some kind of historical connectedness with the past and some "stretching forward" into an imagined future. How one might think of the "uses" as well as the "disadvantages" of history for life is explored in a valuable essay by Volker Gerhardt, "Leben und Geschichte: Menschliches Handeln und historischer Sinn in Nietzsches zweiter 'Unzeitgemäßer Betrachtung'," in *Pathos und Distanz*, pp. 133–62.

13

NIETZSCHE'S ALLEGED FAREWELL: THE PREMODERN, MODERN, AND POSTMODERN NIETZSCHE

According to a widely discussed recent book by Jürgen Habermas, Nietzsche's thought represents the "entry into post-modernity";[1] Nietzsche "renounces a renewed revision of the concept of reason and *bids farewell* to the dialectic of enlightenment."[2] This "farewell" to the hopes of the Enlightenment is seen as the decisive European "turning point" that sets the direction for the divergent "postmodernist" paths of (in Habermas's unique scheme) Bataille, Lacan, and Foucault, on the one hand, and Heidegger and Derrida, on the other. According to Habermas's somewhat tendentious history, the European dissatisfaction with the Enlightenment comes down to the failed attempt of Hegel and the post-Hegelians at a "dialectical" reformulation and completion of such hopes, and a "Nietzschean" inauguration of "irrationalism" and therewith a complete rejection of such hopes.

Habermas believes this because he believes many things about Nietz-

---

1 Jürgen Habermas, *The Philosophical Discourse of Modernity*, trans. Frederick Lawrence (Cambridge: MIT Press, 1987), p. 85.

2 Ibid., p. 86. I pause here to note the obvious: that a sensitive account of the very terms *modernity* or *Enlightenment* would be required before this sort of discussion could properly get off the ground, especially in the face of critics who deny there is any such decisive or epochal moment in history, or who think the phenomena are too diverse to be discussed together. There is, however, a conventional understanding of the terms current in much contemporary discussion, and I shall rely on such assumptions in what follows. See also my discussion in *Modernism as a Philosophical Problem: On the Dissatisfactions of European High Culture* (Oxford: Basil Blackwell, 1991), pp. 1–8.

sche's views that are, I think, compeletely inaccurate. (I mean his treatment of Nietzsche as a psychological reductionist in *Erkenntnis und Interesse,* and the simplistic position on genealogy and truth that Habermas ascribes to Nietzsche in essays like "The Entwinement of Myth and Enlightenment: Re-Reading *Dialectic of Enlightenment.*")[3] There is, however, something quite apposite in Habermas's pairing of Hegelian and Nietszchean dissatisfactions with modernity, an opposition that surfaces too in works of other influential writers, like Deleuze.[4] In order to address Habermas's concerns, and to consider Nietzsche's understanding of modernity, I would, though, introduce the whole matter somewhat differently.

Both Hegel and Nietzsche directly engage, and either radically transform or appear to reject, the great problem of all post-Cartesian or modern philosophy. The problem that began in Descartes – how to justify the adoption of a new, rigorous method – quickly became the perennial modern problem: some sort of comprehensive *self-reassurance* about the modern orientation itself; at once the academic problem of epistemological skepticism and the cultural and political problem of legitimate authority. In the face of the spectacular scientific errors of the premodern tradition, and the collapse of the Christian religion and its political authority into sectarian warfare, we now needed some comprehensive reassurance about the new resolve to treat only the mathematizable properties of nature as substantial or real, the resolve to replace contemplation as the *telos* of inquiry with mastery, the resolve to begin political reflection with the "natural" individual. The nearly pathological sense of insecurity that prompts Descartes's radical doubt and methodological resolve, and the great narrowing of what will count as reliable in the empiricist tradition, speak to such a pretheoretical need. (As moderns, we could at least resolve to restrict ourselves to foundations that we *can* reassure ourselves about: the immediate, the incorrigible, what is a safe foundation because not "due to us"; or, what was later, wonderfully, even religiously named, "the given.")

The first crisis in this attempt at reassurance, the crisis that produced Hegel and Nietzsche, was the book aptly titled *The Critique of Pure Reason,* and its attack on the early modern strategies of reassurance as still dogmatic

3 Cf. Jürgen Habermas, *Erkenntnis und Interesse* (Frankfurt am M.: Suhrkamp, 1970) and "The Entwinement of Myth and Enlightenment: Re-Reading *Dialectic of Enlightenment," New German Critique* 26 (1982): 13–30. A very persuasive statement of the case against Habermas's interpretation can be found in Raymond Geuss, "Nietzsche and Genealogy," *European Journal of Philosophy* 2 (1994): 274–92.

4 Giles Deleuze, *Nietzsche and Philosophy,* trans. H. Tomlinson (New York: Columbia University Press, 1983).

and uncritical. Eventually Kant's own suspicions of dogmatism were turned against him, his accounts of transcendental necessity, a fixed table of categories, a "natural" architectonic of reason, and so forth. The "critical spirit" had begun to devour itself and the project of reassurance was in trouble again.[5]

Hence the nineteenth-century crisis with which Habermas begins his account: either a wholly new form of such collective reassurance – a Hegelian narrative of what sanctioning principles or justificatory criteria *it has turned out* we could not seem to do without (and so, implicitly, an appeal to some social model of collective self-reassurance)[6] – or, apparently, a spectacularly new beginning, an attempt to imagine a form of life *wholly* without reassurance, in which the very search for such consolation, philosophy itself, was best understood as a slavish failure of nerve, not the one thing always needful.

These options are what, eventually, are supposed to have led to a common problem. Both Nietzsche and Hegel, given their attacks on transcendence (what Hegel called *Jenseits* philosophy) and their denial of the classical opposition between a noetic or true or substantial world and a sensible, unstable world of appearances, their denial of the distinction between Being and Becoming, are supposed to have created a common post-Kantian problem (one that Habermas is intensely sensitive to): some unacceptably affirmative stance toward, especially, the historical, human world of "becoming." In Hegel this is traditionally the problem of *Versöhnung* or reconciliation, an "immanentism" that amounts (supposedly) to a virtual divinization of human history; in Nietzsche the great watch word is *keine Rache,* no revenge, especially against time, and so an acceptance of the impossibility of revolutionary change, some profound acknowledgment of "the eternal return of the same."[7]

Before exploring such putative problems one should also not deny that the Nietzschean version of the modernity problem, now so popular and influential, is also tremendously controversial and possibly wrong-headed from the start. The Enlightenment, whether understood (with Kant) as the

---

5 Cf. Pippin, *Modernism as a Philosophical Problem,* pp. 46–79.
6 At least this is the way I would state the alternative. For a different view, cf. Rolf-Peter Horstmann, "Metaphysikkritik bei Hegel und Nietzsche," *Hegel-Studien* 28 (1993): 285–301.
7 Cf. my "Selbstüberwindung, Versöhnung, und Modernität bei Nietzsche und Hegel," in *Nietzsche und Hegel,* ed. by M. Djurić and J. Simon (Würzburg: Königshausen/Neumann, 1992), pp. 130–145, and Daniel Breazeale's article, "The Hegel-Nietzsche Problem," *Nietzsche-Studien* 4 (1975): 146–64.

final achievement of human maturity ("autonomy") and as the discovery of a certain, truth-producing methodology, or more pragmatically as simply our collective best bet for a better future life (with Rorty), may simply still be incomplete on its own terms, in need of no dialectical overcoming or bold farewell. ("We just need more time.")

But for anyone who rejects this appeal to "delayed fulfillment" as an explanation for the persistent lack of fit between the original promise of the Enlightenment and the contemporary payoff, the centrality of Nietzsche's thought for all so-called post-Enlightenment reflection is clear and makes all the more compelling an attempt to understand in detail what we might call Nietzsche's own historical self-consciousness, the modernity problem he called "nihilism." There are, after all, all sorts of ways to "say good-bye." If that is indeed what he is doing, what, I want to ask, is distinctive about Nietzsche's supposed "farewell"?[8] And what exactly does he take himself to be leaving behind?

I raise this issue by examining the three obvious historical categories relevant to Nietzsche's understanding of this problem: his complex relation to modernity itself (or the question of his own "modernism"); the common suspicion that his attack on modern self-satisfaction must betray an atavism, a premodern celebration of aristocratic politics and the heroic virtues of nobility and strength; and the recent fascination with his supposed post-modernism, his attempt to write, propose, and affirm, without consolation and without "revenge"; to play, perhaps even to anticipate, the attempt to write *sous rature*.

I. Modernity as a "Physiological Self-Contradiction"

The canonical treatment of Nietzsche as an anti-Enlightenment thinker can be confusing, since "the Enlightenment" or "modernity" is not itself of central importance in Nietzsche's treatment of major contemporary institutions. Indeed Nietzsche's remarks on the modernity issue tend to pull in two

---

8 It is also true that conceiving of the problem in terms of such an abstract opposition leaves out a number of other options and is itself incomplete without a wider discussion of the historical context within which the whole "Enlightenment problem" developed. This latter detail would have to include the theological–romantic challenges of Jacobi, Hamann, and Herder, among others; the Idealist appropriation and transformation of such a reaction; and the "left–right" post-Hegelian discussions. To raise the issue of modernity in Nietzsche in a manageable way, though, we shall here have to start with this admittedly crude distinction.

different directions. On the one hand, the problem he calls nihilism, although certainly of relevance to the major institutions of modernity – natural science, liberal democracy, skepticism, religious tolerance, and so forth – is a crisis he discusses within a *much* broader historical context, one that identifies "Platonism" and "Christian humanism" as the major targets of interest. Somewhat puzzlingly, for Nietzsche, modern politics is in many ways as Christian as feudal politics (perhaps even more so); modern scientists are *priests;* they pursue the "ascetic ideal" as vigorously, if not as self-consciously, as do recognizable priests, and modern "free thinkers" express as much *ressentiment* as their more devout brethren.

Yet, on the other hand, for Nietzsche there is something *distinctive* about the post-Enlightenment period in Western history, something not merely a repetition of Platonism and Christianity. Modernity represents some sort of epochal, unique "twilight," or "decline," or "degeneration," or "exhaustion," to use his frequent descriptions. At the heart of Nietzsche's theory of modernity is a complex, elusive characterization clearly meant to confront the optimism and self-satisfaction still prominent in much of modernity's self-understanding: The modern age is, uniquely, *the advent of nihilism.*[9]

These claims for both the *repetitive* and the *distinct* nature of the modern epoch can be summarized this way. On the one hand, Nietzsche's account, particularly when compared with the numerous, post-Hegelian theories of modernity, is rather tame, and does not make much, by comparison, out of the theoretical notion of "the modern." He stresses instead the continuity between Enlightenment thought and the prior tradition, but he often notes that modernity is mostly distinctive in its smug *confidence,* its ambition to complete the ancient "will to truth" and the identification of the truth with the "good in itself." It is this modern insistence on a successful resolution of Platonic and Christian "incompleteness" that makes the failure of such an attempt ("nihilism") more prominent and more significant. Modernity's dream of Enlightenment is so extreme, and, according to Nietzsche, fails so utterly, that it helps reveal this dreamlike illusion in all post-Platonic thought, and it allows us a distinct opportunity to understand that failure. Hence Nietzsche's images of modernity are physiological images of a final or decisive exhaustion and sickness, "symptoms" that finally allow a correct

9 Clearly this is meant to be a historical as well as a critical comment, and this fact raises the difficult issue of Nietzsche's views on history. Cf. *AD,* pp. 8, 24–6, with *TI,* p. 35. See also nn. 3 and 4 in my "Nietzsche and the Origin of the Idea of Modernism," *Inquiry* 26 (1983): 175, for a fuller discussion and fuller references to other treatments of Nietzsche's notion of history.

diagnosis, or poetic images (bows that have completely lost their "tension") that make the same point.

To begin to sort out these claims, we first need more details from the surface, the more accessible features of Nietzsche's attack on modern culture. For the most part, and somewhat surprisingly, this surface attack, the object of Nietzsche's "farewell," concerns the *self-understanding* of the modern enterprise. In keeping with the unusually idealistic maxim he had announced in *Beyond Good and Evil,* that the "greatest events" of an age are its "greatest thoughts" (*BGE,* 227),[10] Nietzsche's analysis of the major institutions of modernity is directed to the "Christian–moral *interpretation,*" the "thought" claimed to be responsible for the nihilism crisis (*WP,* 6). And "what does nihilism mean? *That the highest values devalue themselves.* The aim is lacking; 'why' finds no answer" (*WP,* 9). Somehow the Christian "faith in morality," its "cultivation of 'truthfulness'" (ibid.), has undermined the possibility of affirming a "goal," has itself "devalued" the values that make such an affirmation possible.[11] As expressed in *Thus Spoke Zarathustra,*

> Humanity still has no goal.
> But tell me my brothers, if humanity still lacks a goal – is humanity itself not still lacking too? (*TSZ,* 60)

Indeed, humanity, man as a self-overcoming creature, is lacking. Because "man will no longer shoot the arrow of his longing beyond man," or "will no longer give birth to a star," we are confronted with the "most contemptible," the "last man," "who makes everything small," who says "we have invented happiness" and "blinks" (*TSZ,* 17).

The way in which the "Christian–moral interpretation" has *itself* created this state of "goallessness" is among the most interesting, most obscure, and certainly most neglected of Nietzsche's claims. The unmistakable pride with which Nietzsche, or let us say, the official Nietzsche, unmasks self-delusions, points to the hidden, low origins of the high, and so forth, is everywhere

---

10 This paragraph, no. 227, besides bringing Hegel to mind, also represents a Nietzschean analogue to Hegel's famous "Owl of Minerva" passage. Here, the light from a star, a "great thought" in this case, perhaps the thoughts of the philosophers of the future, take many years to reach an observer, and until then we deny that there is such a star. Although Nietzsche's dissatisfactions with modernity appear in many works, he tells us in *Ecce Homo* that we should look to *Beyond Good and Evil* "in all its essentials" for a "critique of modernity" and some "pointers" to the contrary "noble, yes-saying type." *EH,* p. 310.

11 One of the terms Nietzsche uses most frequently to describe our discovery about "the Christian interpretation" is that it is "counterfeit" (*Falschmünzerei*). See *GS,* p. 308.

matched by what appears to be an insistence that he is not doing anything. He is pointing out to us what *we* have done to ourselves, what we are beginning to require ourselves to face, now. There is no doubt, in other words, that he means his project to be as much a phenomenology as a genealogy, and that he recognizes the methodological and self-referential problems generated by a naive faith in genealogy alone.

This large problem, what we might call Nietzsche's puzzling, common reliance on *the first person plural,* itself suggests connections with Hegelian themes introduced earlier. Nietzsche actually knew very little about the grand philosophical tradition he battled. Had he, his own approach to the *aporiai* of modernity would have immediately suggested his common cause with the revolution effected by the Introduction to the hated Hegel's *Phenomenology of Spirit.* It was that work that first proposed that all institutions, even scientific practices, philosophic schools, moral institutions, were to be treated as themselves "*appearances,*" "shapes of Spirit," or cultural practices.[12] Their possibility and adequacy were not to be unlocked by some exogenous method, or tool, or genealogical procedure, or research paradigm (themselves all mere "appearances"). There is no such external point of view, and so "we," ourselves inheritors and products of such self-transformations, must understand how such institutions and practices have come to assess themselves, what sort of reassurance they have achieved, how satisfying they have turned out to be, how they have led to "us." That is all there can be to understanding and assessing ourselves, at least for many of the "post-Kantians."[13]

Since Nietzsche himself is well known for insisting that all philosophy or

---

12 Cf. the famous account of science itself as an *Erscheinung,* why science itself "must *free itself* from this seeming (*Scheine*)," and how the *self*-education of "consciousness" results from this, all in Hegel's *Phänomenologie des Geistes* (*PhG*), pp. 66, 67; *PhS*, pp. 48, 50. Why these phenomena should have to be treated this way is a longer story but involves similar issues in both Hegel and Nietzsche and derives from the Kantian revolution. See ch. 5 of my *Hegel's Idealism: The Satisfactions of Self-Consciousness* (Cambridge: Cambridge University Press, 1989).

13 There is little in Nietzsche's self-understanding that connects him to the critical or post-Kantian tradition. But there is much in Nietzsche's work that evinces such a connection malgré lui, particularly the problems that develop when Kant's attack on the possibility of realism is accepted but the possibility of a transcendental or a priori method is rejected. Indispensable in understanding this connection: W. Müller-Lauter, "Nihilismus als Konsequenz des Idealismus," in *Denken im Schatten des Nihilismus,* ed. by A. Schwan (Darmstadt: Wissenschaftliche Buchgesellschaft, 1975), pp. 113–63; and Otto Pöggeler, "Hegel und die Anfänge des Nihilismus-Diskussion," *Man and World* 3 (1970): 143–99. I develop this point in *Modernism as a Philosophical Problem,* ch. 4.

theory is continuous with, an expression of, or a strategy wholly internal to "life" (a "confession" of its author); that it cannot be an external tribunal, with "life" as some *object* of study,[14] it should not be surprising that Nietzsche should need to restrict his account of modern failures and possibilities to "who *we* have become," "what *we* face," and so on. He has of course misled many readers on this point by means of his many personae or masks, as "philosopher of the future," "genealogist," "philologist," a man "philosophizing with a hammer," and so forth, but that raises rhetorical issues I shall address later. For now we need only note the similar strains in Hegel's and Nietzsche's reliance on this "we," at once neutral, descriptive, and yet also critically, contentiously narrative. (Hence also the similar ambiguities in a claim about the supposed modern "*self*-contradiction.") This is the emphasis that produces what Nietzsche calls in the *Twilight of the Idols* a state of "physiological self-contradiction" (*TI*, 95), apparently some sort of "double-bind" state in which we must still actually direct our conduct, choose, exclude, affirm, and so forth, but, given our Christian inheritance, and what we now understand to be the conditions of such esteeming, we cannot.

This general story of this historical fate (one wherein the Christian emphasis on honesty about intentions and motives plays a large role in its own self-undermining) then forms the basis for a wide-ranging discussion of many modern phenomena, including Nietzsche's attention to the complex dimensions, even paradoxes, of his own phenomenology (of "what is happening to us"). Nietzsche clearly realizes, especially throughout *Thus Spoke Zarathustra,* that by far the most telling "manifestation" of nihilism is its *non-manifestation,* the thoughtlessness with which this deflationary moment is actually embraced. "'What is love? What is creation? What is longing? What is a star?' thus asks the last man, and he blinks" (*TSZ,* 17).

This misinterpretation of enervation, the decline of the instincts and collective goallessness, as the "achievement of freedom," is characteristic of Nietzsche's famous attacks on modern mass society ("herd morality") in *Beyond Good and Evil* (section 202) and in the "Criticism of Modernity" in *Twilight of the Idols.*

The entire West has lost those instincts out of which institutions grow, out of which the *future* grows: perhaps nothing goes so much against the grain of its

---

14 This point is made very clearly in *TI*: "When we speak of values we do so under the inspiration and from the perspective of life: life itself evaluates through us *when* we establish values" (p. 45).

"modern spirit" as this. One lives for today, one lives very fast – one lives very irresponsibly: it is precisely this which one calls "freedom." (*TI*, 94)

We interpret the "loss of instincts out of which institutions grow" *as* our institutions.[15] In what has by now become a familiar Tocquevillean warning about modern democracy, Nietzsche suggests that such modern ideas as the respect for individual worth, the attempt to think universally, the putting of oneself in the position of the other ("pity") merely betray an anxiety about possible domination by the strong, a fear of (inevitable) inequality, and so reflect a desire to be safely and anonymously absorbed into a herd. The new modern idols, like the state or humanity or reason, are thus interpreted not as genuine goals, capable of commanding a genuine instinctual allegiance, but as counterfeit, filling the teleological void by a tranquilizing normality, commonalty value, and so are symptoms of the degeneration of man into a creature who can only will to do "what all others do."

It is this sort of Nietzschean dissatisfaction with modernity, with its language of failure, crisis, and self-contradiction, that has naturally suggested to many the *anti-modernism* long associated with Nietzsche, and, given the tenor of his contempt, an atavistic premodernism, the spectre of the familiar "premodern" Nietzsche of traditional interpretations; the elitist, patriarchal "blond beast" enthusiast; the Nietzsche who simply *celebrates the absence* of consensual or even minimally communal life, promoting not a social unity (always "the herd"), but a stern "order of rank" created ("bred") and maintained from above.

II. Premodern Origins

For those who read Nietzsche this way, much of the motivation for Nietzsche's farewell to the modern tradition appears to stem from a famous analysis of "the origins" of the Platonic, other-worldly, Christian, life-denying perspective at the heart of modernity's internal decay, an interpretation given in one of his most exciting and accessible books, *The Genealogy of Morals*. As noted, this is the story that has seemed to many to celebrate the premodern, and to encourage, if not a return, then something like a rebirth.

The story Nietzsche tells about such origins has become very well known, a kind of staple in undergraduate survey courses and history of ethics textbooks. The still dominant (but tottering) moral distinction "good versus

15 Cf. also *GS*, p. 304.

evil," a distinction between an act motivated by selfless, altruistic motives, an act done for the sake of the good in itself, or, more broadly, an act in which one's own good is never primary but measured in concert with the good of others,[16] versus an egoistic act, asserted with complete indifference to others or its effect on others, must be understood as a "reaction" to a very different distinction, one already in place, from which it degenerates. That "aristocratic" distinction is between the good and the "base" (*Schlecht*), a distinction virtually the mirror image of the good–evil standard. This divides acts and characters that are noble, beautiful, or fine (*kalos*), from the ugly and common; acts done with the supreme self-confidence of the agent, with the agent's own sense of a worthiness simply to *decree* how he shall act, and those done in weakness, and self-doubt, requiring the reassurance or consolation of an eternal value or rational criterion or the approval of others. In Nietzsche's typological account, the good–evil distinction so central to modern political and moral life represents a "reaction" by the "slave" type to such confident legislation; the whole Socratic and Christian point of view should be considered the "slave revolt in morality," a revolt fueled by *ressentiment* against the powerful by the powerless.

Further, in order for the slave to deny consistently the worth or significance of the very real power exercised by the master over him, a metaphysical and moral system begins to unfold in order to make possible the justification of an inner, private world, a metaphysics wherein intentions, and intentions alone, can determine what an agent is truly responsible for, and wherein soul, or a true self, can be distinguished from the "external" body so obviously subject to the will of the master. In the Second Essay, this genealogy of the subject is continued, as Nietzsche tries to account for the variety of ways a subject would have to come to think of himself, how he would have to train himself to be, in order to complete successfully the slave revolt. All of post-Christian metaphysics is thus read as a practical strategy, the construction of an edifice within which the illusion of strength, an *unassailable* exercise of true power, or of "the will" itself, could be defended and esteemed.

In the last essay, Nietzsche generalizes his account of morality and the moral understanding of subjectivity and focuses on many of the issues we

---

16 Nietzsche clearly does not think modern forms of utilitarianism are distinctive in this regard. Although they may not judge the act by reference to the intention of the individual agent, the overall evaluation of the act still invokes some sort of ideal of selflessness, that the act is unworthy unless it can be shown to benefit the many, not just the agent. See especially, *BGE*, no. 201. Moreover, "The Utilitarians are naive" (*WP*, no. 291), since they mistakenly believe that they can identify both the consequences of an act and "what is useful."

are interested in. The basic moral phenomenon in question, Nietzsche claims, should be broadly construed as an "ascetic ideal," an ideal that, although most visible in the priest or moralist, is, he tries to show throughout, also pursued by philosophers, artists, and scientists. It is a paradoxical ideal, one that requires a subtle interpretation of its meaning. For the ascetic priest, in all his manifestations, encourages us to "turn against life," to deny life itself, view it as a "wrong road," a "mistake that is put right by deeds" (*OGM,* 117). This "monstrous mode of valuation," apparently grossly self-destructive, has produced an "ascetic planet,"

> a nook of disgruntled, arrogant, and offensive creatures filled with a profound disgust at themselves, at the earth, at all life, who inflict as much pain on themselves as they possibly can out of pleasure at inflicting pain – which is probably their only pleasure. (Ibid.)

We have, however, made ourselves into such a "life-inimical species" "*in the interest of life itself,* that such a self-contradictory type does not die out" (ibid.). What must be denied at all costs, overcome by postulating a better, different life to come, by good works, a "narcosis" of the spirit, and so forth, is what Nietzsche variously calls the *horror vacui,* the reign of mere chance in the universe, pure becoming, and especially the unredeemable character of suffering (all the deepest concerns of the "slave" or the slavish, the type we now call "bourgeois").

But this self-preserving strategy seems to have played itself out. The illusions under which it prospered have been exposed. Where there used to be monasteries, churches, even salons and museums, testimonials to the sanctity and primacy of the inner citadel of will and intention, there are now "really" only madhouses and hospitals, concessions to the modern view of the always conditioned, arbitrary, contingent character of such "unowned," chaotically formed inner lives. On the other hand, much of the modern exposition of itself, much of this "modern spirit" itself, *is still as committed to the ascetic ideal as what it exposes.* And this charge is what raises all the interesting questions about Nietzsche's alleged "farewell."

When Nietzsche asks about these supposed modern "counter-idealists," who deny the ascetic ideal, the "nay-sayers and outsiders of today," he is uncompromising.

> All these pale atheists, anti-Christians, immoralists, nihilists; these skeptics, ephetics, hectics of the spirit . . . ; these last idealists of knowledge in whom alone the intellectual conscience dwells and is incarnate today – they certainly

believe they are as completely liberated from the ascetic ideal as possible. (148–50)

They are wrong, though, these self-proclaimed "free spirits," because "*they still have faith in truth*" (*OGM*, 149–50). This attack on modernity critics (which really starts in the beginning of *OGM* with the discussion of the English genealogists) immediately turns upside down any reading of Nietzsche himself as a sort of Darwin or Freud, proposing some resigned reconciliation with the natural or primitive being we truly or originally are. He strictly distinguishes his own voice from that of the predominant skeptical, secular institution of modernity, modern science, which still derives its "flame from the fire" of Plato's divine truth and from Christianity. It still encourages an ascetic enterprise, one tied to the need to secure mankind from contingency, to reassure him *by means of truth.*

This sort of attack on the ascetic ideal, on any sort of scientific genealogy, then raises the obvious questions: In *what* sense has a great "devaluation of values" in modernity been *shown?* In what sense has a "transvaluation" been prepared for? If Nietzsche does not claim to have discovered premodern or less corrupted origins, what has he proposed?

Put the problem this way, in his terms: Nietzsche may have famously proclaimed that by "abolishing the true world, we have *abolished* the apparent." We are not skeptics who must resign ourselves to the phenomenal, the inaccessibility of the real amid the play of interpretations. Everything looks different when the assumptions behind the "will to truth" have been exposed and undermined. This is a difficult point for Nietzsche to state properly, since his favorite metaphors for leading one's life without delusion invoke the images of "masks" and the task of "interpretation." These terms naturally involve the logic of originals and texts, even as Nietzsche insists that there *is* only "masking" in human action; no texts, only interpretation.[17]

But even if this paradoxical play on the "essential" character of the "appearances" could be clearly understood, it would not end the problem of gathering up and holding together, "reading," the phenomena rightly, *as* they show themselves. Nietzsche may, as is often said, be trying simply to "legislate," to create or will the authority of his own narrative with the force of a great auteur, but this claim simply raises the stakes *for him;* it just puts in

17 An important essay on the history of Nietzsche's use of the notions of *Schein* and *Erscheinung,* especially sensitive to the internal tensions developing in his later understanding of the "true" world and the "apparent": Robert Rethy's "*Schein* in Nietzsche's Philosophy," *Nietzsche and Modern German Thought,* (London: Routledge, 1990), pp. 59–87.

starker relief the problem of *his own* reassurance that he is legislating or creating, not merely imitating or following. (In Hegel's terms, self-consciousness is not a mere species of self-perception. It is always originally only an orientation, a self-regarding that projects one's activities forward, and so is always unstable, challengeable by others, redeemed – reassured – more by future activity and the reflection of others, or what one does, than by some depth of present insight. The Nietzschean actor can likewise claim no privileged access to a unitary, true self, or to some decisive interpretive frame or context within which to understand the various dimensions of one's doings and sufferings.)

The familiar Nietzsche who responds to such doubts and questions with aristocratic indifference, or by proclamation of some aesthetic reassurance, is only a preliminary or surface Nietzsche. The more interesting Nietzsche is not at all divinely immune to such an internal tension, and not indifferent to what such doubts might require.

III. Postmodern Prospects

To discover what Nietzsche does think of himself as doing, we need to attend again to some of the odd rhetorical details of his self-presentation, especially the peculiarities of Nietzsche's style, his way of raising these issues. When we do, we can see that the issue of Nietzsche's self-understanding, and therewith the nature of his proposal for a form of (supposedly) "postmodern" life, is hardly straightforward.

To return to the phenomenology problem raised earlier, *OGM* oddly begins with Nietzsche's identifying *himself with* those who would be the object of attack in the third section, the "men of knowledge" who, as noted, *still* believe in the ascetic ideal: "We are unknown to ourselves, we men of knowledge" (*OGM*, 15). (In the passages quoted from the third essay, Nietzsche's remarks are often made in the first person plural. Just as in the preface, he writes, with some sort of irony, as "we men of knowledge," and refers, with even more irony, to a type some commentators associate with a Nietzschean ideal, the "free spirits.")[18] In the preface, however, Nietzsche not only refers ahead to his claim about the wholly practical, even Christian motives of any quest for knowledge, but also claims, as he begins a book that professes to discover "the" origins of the moral point of view, that "we are

---

18 Pt. 2 of *BGE* makes frequent use of the expression "we free spirits" even as Nietzsche struggles to dissociate such a class from all "goodly advocates of modern ideas" (p. 55).

necessarily strangers to ourselves," that "we *have* to misunderstand ourselves," "we are not men of knowledge with respect to ourselves" (ibid.).

The creation of such an odd rhetorical voice for the work is not the only peculiarity of its form, but it is enough to raise a number of thematic as well as interpretive problems. In particular, it returns us to Nietzsche's claims about modernity's "devaluation of *itself*," its "*self*-contradiction," and the nature of Nietzschean interpretation. If Nietzsche *is* identifying himself with the "men of knowledge" ascetics identified in the Third Essay, then not only would Nietzsche, somewhat bizarrely, be accusing himself of the futile, self-destructive pursuit of an ascetic ideal, he would clearly be contradicting his own genealogy of the "will to truth" in, among many other places, the first chapter of *Beyond Good and Evil.* If, as is much more likely, the identification is ironic, if he is trying to parody the form of the work (a scientific genealogy) even as he makes use of it, and so to forestall our interpreting the work as a "new" form of *knowledge,* then the obvious question returns again: What *is* he doing and why the irony? Are we now engaged in the indirection, ellipsis, the self-cancelling "play" of "postmodern" discourse?[19]

Some of the reconstruction suggested previously begins, I think, to answer that question. Consistent with the assumption that the modernity crisis, nihilism, is a wholly historical crisis, one that originates within the self-understanding of modernity, *because* of the pursuit of modern ideals, then Nietzsche would be proposing that *OGM* should be read as the "dawning" self-understanding *of* "men of knowledge," or "free spirits." *OGM* is then to a large extent the self-revelations of "we [who are] modern men" (still not fully "known to ourselves") who "are the heirs of the conscience-vivisection and self-torture of millennia."

Nietzsche's irony, the absence of a complete identification with such "scholars," is something he himself remarks on, elliptically and evasively, in *Ecce Homo.* He calls *OGM* "uncannier than anything else written so far," and tells us that it is a "beginning *calculated to mislead:* cool, scientific, even ironic, deliberately foreground, deliberately holding off" (*EH,* 313, my emphasis). This irony appears to be a result of his sensing the *incompleteness* of the self-revelation concerning the contingency of moral institutions. "Men of knowledge," still convinced that traditional claims about the possibility of valuing hold, conclude that the consequences of their unmaskings would be willlessness, and, since man "would rather will nothing than not will," they convince themselves of the "truth" of their claims about "nothingness," take

19 Cf. Peter Dews, *Logics of Disintegration: Post-Structuralist Thought and the Claims of Critical Theory* (London: Verso, 1987), pp. 200–42.

pride and solace in their courage and their science, but end up a mere "decaying, self-doubting present" (*OGM*, 96). This is the step Nietzsche will not take, the move to what he calls "weak" or "passive nihilism."

This hesitancy is evinced by stylistic devices that are, as far as I know, ignored in the Nietzsche literature.[20] In the first essay, Nietzsche mysteriously switches narrative voices, and suddenly (in section 9) speaks in the persona of a plebeian, "free spirit" democrat, who complains that the genealogist's worries are irrelevant. The mob has won; why worry about origins? Nietzsche explains this frustrated interruption as an understandable response to *his* (Nietzsche's own) "silence" (even though we are now nine sections into the book). He simply notes that, whoever the character presenting the genealogy, it is not, or not wholly, Nietzsche. *He* has had "much to be silent about" (*OGM*, 36). And at the conclusion of the Second Essay, he oddly again mentions his own "silence" at points in the narration, suggesting that he is both presenting a genealogy, and distancing himself from its surface claims to truth or ahistorical correctness. ("But what am I saying? Enough! Enough! At this point it behooves me only to be silent" (*OGM*, 96).[21]

Of course, Nietzsche's account of origins, even if construed as some sort of ironically qualified phenomenology, not grounded in a theory tied to the "will to truth," but a representation and radical extension of our own "dawning" historical perspective and its current fate, is still far from unproblematic. He must still be able to make the proper distinctions and draw the appropriate conclusions within, let us say, his phenomenology of *the genealogy we have begun to write for ourselves.*

Here the obvious problems emerge for someone like Habermas. If this whole issue of Nietzsche's "farewell" comes down to his reliance on some form of radically historical hermeneutics, then, Habermas has often asked in a number of contexts, in essays on Nietzsche, Horkheimer and Adorno, and Gadamer,[22] what constitutes a possible resolution of *disputes* about such issues, disputes about who "we" really are? Without some account of the conditions of such interpretive activity, some standards or measure to sepa-

---

20 This is not to say that the general issue of Nietzsche's literary style has not assumed major importance in contemporary commentary. See the essays in *Nietzsche's New Seas*, (Chicago: University of Chicago Press, 1988); and in *Reading Nietzsche*, ed. by Robert Solomon and K. Higgins (Oxford: Oxford University Press, 1988), and especially Eric Blondel, *Nietzsche: The Body and Culture*, trans. Sean Hand (Stanford: Stanford University Press, 1991).

21 There is a very interesting reference to the value of silence in Nietzsche's discussion of Socrates' last days in *GS*, no. 340.

22 See especially Habermas's "Entwinement of Myth," p. 28.

rate the wheat from the chaff, then, the charge would go, the question involved in a possible farewell to the Enlightenment is begged. And this in turn provokes the obvious Nietzschean countercharge (one evident in much of the furious French and francophile response to Habermas's book): that it is the very possibility of such a reliance on transcendental (or "quasi-transcendental") conditions, identified by reason with some sort of necessity as governing *any* possible dialogue, that is being challenged by genealogy. Any suspicion about the "all too human" origin of a hope for such a possible reassurance would unfairly be foreclosed from the start, if we also needed some original rational reassurance that *the suspicion were warranted*. It would then be Habermas who begs the question by presupposing the necessity of such "criteria" from the start.[23]

However, I would like to conclude by suggesting that the situation need not be left at this kind of "begging the question" standoff. For, Nietzsche's radically "internalist" version of any assessment of socially sanctioned practices, his denial that philosophy could have "life" as an "object" and is always itself the expression of a form of life, should mean, quite consistently, that Nietzsche has no abstract, metalevel response to the kind of justification demanded by Habermas. As the details of the preceding summary of his position make abundantly clear, he has a proposal, a possible interpretation of what the demand for objective consensus within post-Platonic, Christian modernity means for us. As we have seen, Nietzsche is proposing an interpretation of the contingent social meaning of modern attempts at rational or universally binding consensus, collective reassurance. This interpretation is straightforwardly based on the notions of *ressentiment,* weakness, pity, and the contingent facts of European social history, and it should be possible to examine, in a way internal to Nietzsche's own assumptions, that interpretation and its implications for the question of the authority of Nietzsche's claims.

At least it is possible to begin an examination of such an issue here and to suggest a last, internal problem in Nietzsche's account (i.e., one subject to no question-begging charge). As we have seen in several contexts (to focus now on the issue of most relevance to Habermas), Nietzsche regards this

---

23 Nietzsche is famous for his apparent indifference to Habermas's question and does seem inclined to the response sketched. "Supposing that this also [Nietzsche's claim about the totality of interpretation, the absence of 'text'] is only interpretation – and you will be eager to make this objection? – well, so much the better" (*BGE,* p. 31). And in *Thus Spoke Zarathustra:* "'This is my way; where is yours?' – thus I answered those who asked me 'the way.' For *the* way – that does not exist" (*TSZ,* p. 195).

commitment to an ideal of some sort of intersubjective acceptability for one's "evaluations" as a "sign" of weakness, and a latent expression of fear of those who need no such support. It is a requirement that arises, that makes sense, only within a certain sort of social arrangement and historical experience. Such "pitying" concerns for others' views is to be contrasted with those who simply "seized the right to create values" out of a "pathos of distance" (*OGM*, 26). (See also *BGE*, section 261, and the "characteristic right of masters to create values," 209.) Bodying forth such a sense of their "distance" from others,

> The "well-born" *felt* themselves to be the "happy"; they did not need to establish their happiness artificially by examining their enemies, or to persuade themselves, *deceive* themselves, that they were happy. (*OGM*, 38)

For all of the rich complexity of Nietzsche's historical and psychological interpretation, it is *this* basic, somewhat crude contrast between "self-assertion" and the "weakness" of social dependence that forms the core of all his claims about a great many of the insufficiencies of modernity, its origins in the premodern, and of his hopes for a new, "postmodern," distinctly self-assertive type. And, even when all the methodological and stylistic subtleties of Nietzsche's approach have been conceded, there are still serious, unresolved tensions in Nietzsche's account.

Consider in conclusion one small passage in *OGM* where many of these issues can be brought to a very fine point, and consider again the issue of Nietzsche's interpretation of the need to rely on some universally binding justification, the needs, supposedly, of the reactive, ascetic "Enlightenment" type. In section 10 of the First Essay in *OGM*, he begins his concluding comments by noting first that the counterideal, Nietzsche's "noble creator," would be "incapable" of "taking his enemies seriously" for very long; he acts, with premodern glory and postmodern possibility, nobly, in supreme indifference to others, and without the "pity" characteristic of modern humanism. But then a curious dialectic, for want of a better word, takes over the passage. If, Nietzsche reasons, one *is* indifferent to one's enemies, to the "others" who oppose one's evaluations, then one can be *supremely* indifferent, can forget one's slights and be in the best position, not simply to ignore, but actually to *forgive* one's enemies. But then, as Nietzsche seems to get carried away, if one's relation to enemies is not determined by *ressentiment* and fear, one can not only forgive but actually enjoy one's enemies, indeed, "here alone genuine 'love of one's enemies' is possible" (39). And finally, as we have moved very far from "not taking one's enemies seriously,"

How much reverence has a noble man for his enemies! – and such reverence is a bridge to love. – For he desires his enemy for himself, as his mark of distinction; he can endure no other enemy than one in whom there is nothing to despise and very much to honor. (ibid.)

This disintegrating passage comes very close to associating the possibility of the master's self-esteem, his "distinction," the issue Nietzsche worries so much about in modernity, with "recognition" by the other. (Why else would a master "*desire* his enemy for himself"?) Such a notion would seem to link the possibility of the creation of value with a "self-consciousness" about the presence of others and a conflict with *their* "creation." And his rather abrupt shift in tone in describing this conflict, from "indifference" to "love," suggests an important ambiguity in his account of modernity.

As we have seen, Nietzsche's most frequent description of the modern situation is that Western Europe has become a mass or herd society. Stimulated by the secularism of modern social life and the theoretical attitude of modern science and philosophy, the dawning awareness of the contingency of traditional religious, metaphysical, and moral ideals has begun to make such ideals unavailable as bases of social cohesion and order. A vacuum has been created, and in its confusion and panic, "modernity" fills that vacuum with a sterile, timid conformism (*BGE*, 30; cf. also section 14).

However, even if there is something true about this picture of modernity, in the now rather standard claim that modern societies must face the prospect of collective evaluation and action without reliance on grand views of the cosmos, God, or the "good in itself," some of Nietzsche's own texts begin to suggest that this prospect does not mean that the alternatives open are some form of premodern heroic individualism (with its accompanying aristocratic code of war and primitive honor), or modern conformism, with its bourgeois ideals of security and prudence. The problem of a *collectively self-determined ideal,* one *based* wholly on the absence of natural ends or natural hierarchy, is as typical a *modern* problem as anything else. Nietzsche tends to focus attention on such forms of modern sociality as contract, or a collective ensuring of the basest, most "slavish" form of self-affirmation – self-interest. But there are many other accounts, motivated by a skepticism about metaphysics or objectivism as deep as Nietzsche's, that all attempt to account for a cooperative social existence and political ideals without such a narrowing of the issue of self-determination (for example, those philosophers who represent alternatives to both modern natural right and rational egoist traditions, or the "rational will" theorists; Rousseau, Kant, Fichte and Hegel all come to mind).

Indeed, Nietzsche himself seems to concede in the previous passage that one can never *be* radically independent or never wholly "active." Given simply the presence of others and so the possibility of conflicting interpretations of what one is doing, and given the simple possibility of *self*-deceit, one is always "*self*-reactive," despite Nietzsche's talk of an "active forgetting," or a "kind of second innocence." And given this concession, it is not hard to see how the conflict he points to could be historically transformed, need not be permanently violent or unresolvable. Surprisingly the passage at least suggests an account of the *social* basis of an ultimately necessary appeal to a universal or mutually agreeable reassurance (perhaps a final mutual recognition of those who have come to regard themselves as equals or "masters") that is only *originally* and not finally fearful and "slavish," and is familiar to readers of Hegel's *Phenomenology of Spirit.*

This is not, of course, Nietzsche's theory. The previously expressed "desire" (*verlangen*) for the enemy as the master's mark of "distinction" (*Auszeichnung*) is directly contradicted by a typical passage in *Daybreak*, attacking any desire for "distinction" (*Streben nach Auszeichnung*) as necessarily leading to the dreaded "ascetic ladder of rank" (*Da*, 113) and for the most part Nietzsche keeps up the fiction of master morality as wholly autochthonous and socially indifferent.

However, this passage in *OGM* is not the only place in the corpus where this fiction of a wholly self-reliant or self-created master is undercut. A great deal in *Thus Spoke Zarathustra* is simply incoherent unless such points as the apparently unbreakable link between Zarathustra and his disciples, even between him and the grim city of the Many-Colored Cow, the status of Zarathustra's equivocal "love of man," as well as his constant wandering between solitude and community, are all reconceived in ways that would finally undermine any heroic ideal of independence, the "pathos of distance."[24] One of the least traditionally heroic, least independent of the personae in all of Nietzsche's work is Zarathustra. He talks rather than fights, and worries frequently about his reflection in the souls of his disciples. The work itself begins and ends with a dramatic rejection of solitude or indifference, with Zarathustra's leaving his cave.

All of which introduces a much larger topic. Nietzsche's confusing remarks undermining his own anti-modern ideal, his suggestions that the noble man cannot live an independent life and must seek worthy enemies to "love," does not by itself go very far, or suggest much more than a social elite

---

24 Cf. "Irony and Affirmation in Nietzsche's *Thus Spoke Zarathustra*," in *Nietzsche's New Seas*, pp. 45–74.

of mutually worthy antagonists. But the tensions in Nietzsche's account can help throw a different light on his response to the modernity crisis and can begin to undermine the simplicity of any picture of Nietzsche as a pre-modern or postmodern thinker.

If, that is, it turns out to be impossible for Nietzsche to promote some wholly active, noble ideal by which the modern failure is to be measured, then we will have good, even Nietzschean reasons for rejecting an interpre-tation of the "slavish" origins of so much of the post-Socratic and modern tradition. First, whether that claim represents a discovery of Nietzschean genealogy or "our" own disenchantment with Enlightenment optimism, the noble–base, active–reactive contrast at its core turns out to be an unstable one, its boundaries hardly as fixed or as obvious as Nietzsche sometimes suggests. Nietzsche himself seemed to realize that Christian self-subjection can be a brilliant strategy for mastery, and that, as in the classical account of tyranny, mastery can be a form of slavery.

This result should suggest that the modern demand for some sort of methodological self-reassurance is misread if understood as a bourgeois or slavish failure of nerve, a timid conformism. That problem arises *necessarily* once a vast distrust of our pre-theoretical experience; our "natural, "lived" orientation; the "human experience of the human," begins, and once we think of ourselves as requiring a secure or honest or reliable way to *reestablish* some connection with that lost world and with other agents. That Nietzsche himself inherits this modern sense of loss, and so necessarily, in spite of himself, inherits all the problems and implications of the self-critical form of modern self-consciousness, helps to confirm Heidegger's otherwise baffling remark that Nietzsche is a Cartesian.[25]

It is this absence of any distinct premodern or postmodern ideal that suggests that the issue of Nietzche's "rejection" of or "farewell" to modernity is badly posed. In many passages he clearly regards himself, to use again Heidegger's phrase, as the "culmination" (*Vollendung*) of modernity, and, somewhat in spite of himself and his explosive rhetoric, does not intend to free himself from "our" modern problems of reflection, and the social consequences of "our" legacy. Thus on this reading, the unresolved tensions in Nietzsche's account, or the position of his Zarathustra, homeless both

25 Martin Heidegger, *Nietzsche*, IV, *Nihilism*, trans. Frank Capuzzi (San Francisco: Harper & Row, 1982), sect. 19, pp. 123–35. A fuller treatment of this point would raise a number of other issues: how we should understand the historical "provocation" that led to such a loss; whether the Hobbesean and Cartesian "reaction" was appropriate to the provocation; if somehow inappropriate, whether a form of philosophy (premodern, classical, fundamen-tal) that does not share such assumptions is possible without being "uncritical."

when in isolation and noble indifference and when wandering among the mankind he finds himself inextricably attached to, would represent the still unresolved problems of the resolutely self-critical modern age itself, rather than evidence of any revolutionary turn. Nietzsche is not bidding modernity farewell; he is the first, finally and uncompromisingly, to understand its implications and to confront its legacy.

14

MORALITY AS PSYCHOLOGY, PSYCHOLOGY AS MORALITY: NIETZSCHE, EROS, AND CLUMSY LOVERS

"Das Thun ist Alles"

JGB, p. 279

Der Glaube "so und so ist es" zu verwandeln in den Willen "so und so soll es werden."

WM, section 593

I

In section 23 of *Beyond Good and Evil*, Nietzsche encourages us to "clench our teeth," "open our eyes," and "keep our hand firm on the helm." We are to make a voyage that will entitle us to demand that "psychology be recognized again as the queen of the sciences, for whose service and preparation the other sciences exist. For psychology is now again the path to the fundamental problems."

The claim for the priority of psychology leads in many directions. It leads first to the familiar view of Nietzsche as a deflationary critic, exposing "human all too human" origins, or the "low" origins of the "high."[1] This enter-

---

1 Especially in the books of the late 1870s and early 1880s, like *Human All Too Human* (1878) (where a "History of the Moral Sensations" is proposed as "psychology," sect. 2) and *The*

prise, if etiological, appears to be about real, if hidden, psychological motives; if hermeneutical, about real, if hidden, psychological meaning.
Whether writing in the style of earlier French psychologists (as if Nietzsche
is radicalizing Montaigne, Voltaire, LaRochefoucauld) or anticipating modern reductionist claims about religion or mores, Nietzsche clearly means to
explain the motivations behind, and the meaning of, philosophical, religious, and moral phenomena, in non-philosophic, non-religious, and non-
moral terms. His summary label for such an account is "psychology," and
that suggests something that looks right at home in the "left Hegelian" or
"post-Feuerbachean" or "pre-Freudian" side of things in the late ninteenth
century, especially when the themes are religious or moral.

But one can follow this direction only so far before it begins to turn back
on itself. For one thing, Nietzsche regarded familiar forms of deflationary
psychologizing (like those cited) as themselves aspects of Christian
egaliatarianism, a "leveling" and self-abasement inspired by *ressentiment*, and
he wanted no part of it. This suggests a still deeper complexity, one that
arises when we try to take into acccount Nietzsche's critique of "dogmatism,"
or his affirmation of "perspective" (i.e., Nietzsche's denial that there could
ever be a true logos of the psyche). At his most radical Nietzsche seems to
suggest that psychology, or any view of motivation and action, is already itself
a kind of "moral" or normative affirmation, an assessment or evaluation of
ourselves. He certainly thinks this is true of Platonic and Christian psychology, the "invention" of the divided soul. He does not treat the basic modern
assumption that "intentions" explain action as simply a theory, even a bad
theory. For him, to frame the problem of explaining action by reference to
"individually owned" intentions is originally linked to what we want to be
able to expect of each other, to the problems of guilt and the gods, not just
beliefs and desires.

But the point is also made very broadly, in all sorts of contexts. The
"English" genealogists who are discussed at the beginning of the *Genealogy of
Morals* believe that a certain utilitarian calculation has been behind the
evolution of moral institutions. But Nietzsche does not proceed to ask
whether what they said is true, or to counter with his own theory. He asks
about them, "What do they want?" as if to ask, How would they have us live,
regard ourselves?[2]

Dawn (1881) (especially, "In this book, you will discover a 'subterranean man' at work, one
who tunnels and mines and undermines," preface, p. 1).

2 This sentiment is everywhere in Nietzsche. In an early essay, "The drive toward knowledge
has a moral origin" (*PT*, p. 35); in a late note, the distinction between "theoretical" and

Contrary to any appearance of psychological reduction then, Nietzsche's enterprise, even when expressed as psychology, or even physiology, affirms some "priority of the *practical*," where the practical is understood as the evaluative and purposive. (What ideal, in some "original" way to be defined, is "at stake"?)[3] Somehow the task of Nietzschean psychology (contra all other psychologies) is to see *everything* in the light of the prior authority of *this* sort of "queen." The rough idea seems to be that only some sort of original attachment to some end or ideal or purpose would account for why we come to regard our motivational and intentional lives, as well as all else, as we do. Such an attachment must be original in some way, since any traditionally psychological explanation of it would, so such an account would go, itself evince another such attachment, or, as he says, "evaluation" of life.

The attack on any putative autonomy for philosophy or morality in the name of psychology can then quickly get complicated, since the nature of any appeal to psychological factors is itself characterized as a strategy of sorts, a contestation over kinds of lives and evaluations of such kinds. This can make for very compressed passages and confusing implications. In *BGE*, the "conscious thinking" of a philosopher is said to be "guided and forced into certain channels by his instincts," but the psychological reductionism suggested is then undercut by the fact that these instincts are identified not with impulses or passions but with "valuations," *Wertschätzungen*, a qualification itself complicated when these valuations themselves are then re-described as "physiological," although, to complete the circle again, not physiological forces, but demands (*Forderungen*) for the "maintenance of a certain *type* of life" (11; 17).

But this direction too can quickly become quite unsettling. When Nietzsche, in the *Gay Science*, criticizes the possibility of contemplation as a "delusion," he denies that we are ever "spectators" and "listeners" of the "great visual and acoustic spectacle that is life"; the contemplative type "overlooks that he himself is really the poet who keeps creating this life." By contrast, "we who think and feel at the same time are those who really continually fashion something that had not been there before" (section 301). This

---

practical" is "dangerous," since there really is no difference between "judging the value of a way of life" and the "value of a theory" (*WP*, p. 458).

3 It would require a major study to set out the various things Nietzsche means by the "practical" (*das Thun ist alles*) and its "priority." As a general summary, it can at least be said that Nietzsche is trying to show that evaluation and explanation always express some prior attachment to an ideal, requiring as a central question something like the conditions (historical and social, as well as general or comprehensive) for the possibility of such "attachment."

appears to run together those considerations relevant to, motivating ("reasons for," norms regulating) *actions* (including makings), and considerations relevant to, constraining ("reasons for"), *beliefs* about what is the case. Considerations relevant to a course of action are relevant because actions are for the sake of goals, are teleological. In acting we believe we ought to influence the world in a certain way, often no matter how the world actually is. If the world doesn't match up to the way we have determined it "ought to be," we just act more vigorously. But in pursuing the truth, we want, as much as possible, for our beliefs to match the way of the world. So, most simply put, what we have a reason to believe is true (as opposed to what we have reason to believe we should do, what goal we should seek) cannot be any sort of function of "what we would like" to believe, of the goals we want to realize.

In other words, on the one hand, Nietzsche's psychologism could just be telling us *the facts* about the motives behind human doings and sufferings and projects and aspirations. He would then look like an eccentric species of the genus introduced by Shaftesbury, or Hume, or even eventually Freud, someone who *extends* psychological explanations (in his case, with a particular emphasis on power) far beyond traditional bounds, into morality, politics, religion, intellectual life. On the other hand, his attack on the possibility of truth and his tendency to treat all account giving as a manifestation of some deeper pursuit (the "affirmation" of life itself or the "will to power") force one to confront the charge that Nietzsche is engaged in quite a confused and wrong-headed defense of wishful thinking, as if we could want or will to believe what will count as true.

I do not think that Nietzsche is guilty of such confusions. Explaining this will eventually require attention to an oddly neglected topic in Nietzsche – his account of desire, especially "love," and more especially love of one's ideals, and so why he thinks cognitive inquiry, the authorization of criteria for inquiry, experiment and resolution of problems, and so on, all express a love and striving for an ideal.

II

The large question at issue is, in Eric Blondel's formulation, the meaning of Nietzsche's second "Copernican revolution." What does it mean to see "life" as the condition of the possibility of experience, of science (here even psychology), and morality, traditionally understood? Isn't life the object of psychology, what is judged by morality, not the "subject" of such activities, whatever that could mean?

The way Nietzsche talks about this "life" (in its evaluative, practical aspects) as some sort of condition for the possibility of anything else is both a factor in his claim for the "perspectival" character of all human projects (conditioned everywhere by an attachment to some sort of possible life), and itself, as a claim or a kind of sense making, presumably an *instance* of such a view of "horizons." To get to the question of life and psychology, then, we need to go through the daunting question of perspectivism. That is not my main interest here, but since the esteemings, evaluatings, or erotic attachments are, for Nietzsche, necessarily "perspectival," it is an unavoidable theme. So I shall try simply to summarize a few of the central claims.

Perspectivism is treated in *BGE* more as a kind of metaphor than as a claim, heavily indebted to the familiar visual image – that how things look, or even, in the metaphorical extension, what might appear valuable, *depends* essentially on a *limited* point of view, how things look from a certain angle or point of view at a time, with a history or disposition or expectation behind it.

For our purposes, what is important are a few implications. I skip many details and note only what is essential for our purposes. First, seeing things from a point of view (or any rendering intelligible, asserting truthfully, evaluating) inevitably promotes a "forgetting" of the perspectival character of such approaches. "Untruth," as he says in a famous phrase, the untruth, partiality, and contingency of any perspective, is a "condition of life." We simply "go on as we do," and, inevitably, it being only "*our* way" of going on recedes from prominence, or must, if "our way" is to survive and flourish.

But this "forgetting" can mean two things.

(i) A certain *narrowing* of focus and relatively "unjust" *self-asserting must* go on, without constant skeptical undermining, for there to be a human practice at all. In the language of his 1874 history essay,

> Every living thing can become healthy, strong, fruitful only within a horizon; if it is incapable of drawing a horizon around itself or, on the other hand, too selfish to restrict its vision to the limits of a horizon drawn by another, it will wither away feebly or overhastily to its early demise. Cheerfulness, clear conscience, the carefree deed, faith in the future, all this depends, in the case of the individual as well as of a people, on there being a line which distinguishes what is clear and in full view from the dark and unilluminable; it depends on one's being able to forget at the right time as well as remember at the right time. (*AD*, 10)

Nietzsche goes on to admit that this is in a certain sense "unjust" but he tries to show that the question of simply "being just," or remembering everything, always attentive to the partiality and contingency of one's practices, and, on the other hand, being "just *to life*" (and so also "unjust") is considerably more complicated than an abstract opposition will allow. As we shall see, those complications are really at the heart of the problem of Nietzschean psychology, the problem of seeing everything in the light of "the possibility of life." (Life itself is here given one of its few direct characterizations: "that dark, driving, insatiably self-desiring power" (*sich selbst begehrende Macht*) (*AD*, 22). This prefigures the summary in *BGE:* that life is "estimating, preferring, being unjust, being limited, wanting to be different" (*BGE*, 15).[4]

(I should note, as an aside, that this point, Nietzsche's resistance to the idea of any complete historical "justice" as, in effect, anti-erotic, debilitating, and the earlier point about his objections to deflationary or reductionist psychologizing, both make the adoption of Nietzsche as source by modern archaeologists, deconstructors, and genealogists quite problematic.)

(ii) But second, Nietzsche also means to point out that another sort of simplifying and forgetting occurs that promotes an *absolutizing* of such a perspective, or the dogmatism he inveighs against so famously. (This appears to be something like a completely successful forgetting; not an experimental or perspectivally self-conscious forgetting.) As the point just made should demonstrate, Nietzsche's perspectivism is not meant to invite some playful shifting of perspectival points of view, as if one can, suitably enlightened, treat one's participation in some practice *ironically*, as a game of "masks." Nietzsche's frequent insistence on what is necessarily involved in the possibility of such a practice or perspective (the necessary discipline, sacrifice, "obedience") naturally invites, however, the dogmatic solution, as if the authority of any "way of life" could not be secured without traditional, realist notions of truth or moral objectivity, and some success in meeting such criteria. His denial that this is so, or his denial both that there *could* be such a form of social authority, and that there *needs* to be, returns us again to the kind of problem "the problem of life" (requiring an "injustice" that is not "dogmatic") will turn out to be.

There are some particularly beautiful, if very elusive, passages in *BGE* where he tries to explain what it means to be "attached" to one's perspective

---

4 The key term in almost all the accounts of the problem of life is "esteeming" (*schätzen*). See *TSZ*, "On the Thousand and One Goals," "No people could first live without esteeming," and "therefore he calls himself 'man', which means 'esteemer'" (pp. 58, 59).

The same point is made more dramatically in *BGE* in no. 188 and Nietzsche's attack on any *laisser aller* and affirmation of a kind of tyranny. "Consider any morality with this is mind: what there is of it in 'nature' teaches hatred of the *laisser aller*, of any all-too-great freedom and implants the need for limited horizons and the nearest tasks – teaching *the narrowing of our perspectives*, and thus in a certain sense stupidity, as a condition of life and growth" (*BGE*, pp. 101–2).

non-dogmatically, in the way implied by the quoted passages. It means first of all something apparently skeptical, not "to be *stuck*," not to be stuck to some person, or to a fatherland, or to a science, but also,

> *not to remain stuck to one's detachment,* to that voluptuous remoteness and strangeness of the bird who flees ever higher to see more below him – the danger of the flier. Not to remain stuck to our own virtues and become as a whole the victim of some detail in us, such as our hospitality, which is the danger for superior and rich souls who spend themselves lavishly, almost indifferently, and exaggerate the virtue of generosity into a vice. One must know how to conserve oneself: the hardest test of independence. (*BGE,* 52)

In section 226, the same point is made differently.

> We immoralists! – This world that concerns us, in which we fear and love, this almost invisible and inaudible world of subtle commanding and subtle obeying, in every way a world of the "almost," involved, captious, peaked, and tender – indeed it is defended well against clumsy spectators and familiar curiosity. We have been spun into a severe yarn and shirt of duties and cannot get out of that – in this we are "men of duty," we, too. Occasionally, that is true, we dance in our "chains" and between our "swords"; more often, that is no less true, we gnash our teeth and feel impatient with all the secret hardness of our destiny. (*BGE,* 154)

However elusive, such passages at least begin to make clear the sort of question Nietzschean psychology will address. (The tone of such passages should also be constantly called to mind as qualification for the received view of Nietzsche – he of the glowering eyes, the ridiculous moustache, the supposed will to create and dominate, the celebrant of indifference and cruelty.) In the first place, Nietzsche does tend to pose the issue of the possibility of some organized, self-regulated, and self-sustaining perspective as a contrast between those who view the possibility as tied essentially to the possibility of "truth in itself" and "the good in itself" (and here he refers to almost everyone descended from the Socratic and Platonic attack on "tragic" answers to such questions) and his own, relatively unprecedented, alternative.

However, the context for such a discussion already shifts the nature of the question Nietzsche wants to ask about truth. Remarks like those quoted turn the basic question away from the problem of truth, and do not simply answer it, negatively or positively. The point of his insistence on perspective, in other words, is not so much to counsel humility or skepticism. It is intended to prepare for the question Nietzsche is most interested in: not the possibility of truth, but, to the extent of the social function of the "will to truth," or our collective hopes for, the "value of truth" (and of all of this by eventual contrast with a way of being attached to our practices which does not rely on realist or dogmatic hopes). We have convinced ourselves that success in understanding how things really are will be in some sense re-demptive, will change everything; that virtue is knowledge; or knowledge the power we most need. As a matter of emphasis, Nietzsche's counterclaim of perspective is much more concerned with this optimism about the value of knowing the truth, about what we have believed the truth will make possible, help promote, and so on, than it is, primarily, a matter of epis-temology. Now of course, the questions of the possibility and the value of truth are not wholly distinct, since one of the chief reasons for doubting optimistic hopes for the value of truth has to do with the general impos-sibility of securing any such redemptive truth. Nietzsche clearly believes that a sense of such an impossibility has become widely established after Kant, and is beginning to have devastating consequences. But it is the inevitably perspectival and so unsecured, unreassured, estimate of value which tradi-tional philosophy and science must assume, without admitting it, naively, and in a self-deceived way.

This topic reintroduces the main theme of my discussion, which can now be formulated as, *how* we should understand *why* some such "way" comes to have the authority and significance it does, given that any appeal to discov-eries, real success in coping with nature, truth, and so forth, is excluded. This is the question that introduces Nietzsche's moral–psychological lan-guage ("what we want"). And how does Nietzsche think that his own pro-posals for a new "way," and so his own understanding of the conditions now pertaining, "psychological" and historical conditions, must be understood? (What are *we* supposed to "remember" and "forget"? How?)

III

There is no theory of, or extended essay about, such a connection. For the most part, there is a famous image.

> Assumed: truth is a woman – what then? Are there not grounds for the suspi-cion that all philosophers, insofar as they were dogmatists, have been very inexpert about women? That the gruesome seriousness, the clumsy obtrusive-ness with which they have usually approached truth so far have been awkward and very improper methods for winning a woman's heart? (*BGE,* 2)

So, philosophers are like lovers, suitors; better, in other passages, seducers. More to the point, philosophers should be understood as inexpert, clumsy lovers. Philosophers, or those committed to truth and some hope of moral objectivity, want something out of existence, something like a life worth loving, but they go about satisfying this desire inexpertly and clumsily. Presumably, if we understand this, we can also understand something of Nietzsche's own account of what it means to be "attached" to one's perspective or way of life, to limit and discipline oneself (or one's culture) in the service of some loved end, all without such overly optimistic, ultimately self-defeating, philosophic hopes.

The "psychology" of love is a useful window onto Nietzsche's psychology of the philosophical type. This is so because most of us do not think of romantic attachments to other people as simply caused by psychological impulses; we think of such attachments as expressive, revelations of the more important and worthy aspects of ourselves, and so as also partly evaluative, at least in this expressive sense. (Those whom we love must be "lovable" in some sense.) But we also do not think of such attachments as the product of deliberation and normative evaluation, as if consequent upon some mere list of worthy and unworthy qualities. Think of our attachment to some sort of ideal, some goal of satisfaction, in as complexly psychological a way (neither naturally caused, nor reflectively deduced), appears to be the suggestion here.

To emphasize how important the image is, we can also briefly note how *On the Genealogy of Morals* opens, again with an image.

> It has rightly been said: "Where your treasure is, there will your heart be also"; *our* treasure is where the beehives of our knowledge are. We are constantly making for them, being by nature winged creatures and honey-gatherers of the spirit; there is one thing alone we really care about from the heart – "bringing something home."

The quotation is from the passage in St. Matthew (6:21) where Jesus is claiming that we misguidedly store up the treasures of Mammon, believing from the heart in a this-worldly salvation that is both unjustifiably fearful and anxious, and unfulfillable. In the way in which Jesus contrasts the illusory hope for a secular salvation with a heavenly one, so Nietzsche contrasts our misguided hopes for, love of, knowledge, with a truer salvation, a kind of "self-evaluation" wholly absent from our lives. He also, in a brilliant piece of irony (given that this book is one of the most famous and often vicious attacks on Christendom on record), is invoking Jesus' soothing ad-

vice not to rush to secular things out of so much fear and self-doubt. ("See
the birds of the air, they neither sow nor reap nor store in barns, yet my
father feeds them . . . Consider the lilies of the field, how they grow; they
neither toil nor spin; yet I tell you, even Solomon in all his glory was not
arrayed like one of these.) Our attempt to store up knowledge, to secure
truth is, he suggests, similarly driven by a self-induced, slavish anxiety and
fear. By contrast, apparently a wholly different sort of knowledge is what we
might want, an answer to the simple question, Who *are* we really?

These beginning images of eros and the heart, which Nietzsche returns
to again and again throughout his works, are not novel or revolutionary, as
Nietzsche, the old philologist, no doubt realized. He would clearly have
recalled that it was Plato who first characterized philosophy as essentially a
kind of love, as erotic, even divinely, insanely erotic, and he is no doubt
trying to invoke that memory ironically by suggesting that traditional philosophers, as conceived Platonically, are actually clumsy, amateurish lovers.

However ironic, though, the image aligns Nietzsche with Plato in an
important sense. He does not treat the desire to know, or the emotional and
affective aspects of interest in knowledge, in a more familiar, modern sense,
as provoked negatively, just by the pain of ignorance. We could consider
human beings as motivated by the usual assortment of passions and fears
produced by a functioning body, experiencing the kind of resistance to the
satisfaction of such passions human beings naturally encounter, not to mention the anxieties produced by a functioning imagination, the anticipation
of suffering, the fear of death. And so we could imagine these creatures as
suffering, provoked to understand the great nature machine so as to master
it, provoked to look beyond the satisfaction of their immediate interests to a
more rational, long-term strategy in predicting and dealing with others.
Even speculative philosophy might be understood as a similar kind of reaction to the pain of ignorance and uncertainty, the same sort of quest for
security and reassurance.

At least to some extent like Plato, however, Nietzsche treats philosophical
desire as originally *erotic,* not merely reactive, or passion-driven. There is
something that "philosophers," or lovers of wisdom, want that they want
independently of any attempt to lessen pain or ignorance.[5] Of course, all
unfulfilled desire is painful in some sense, and so all striving seeks the
pleasures of satisfaction. But by beginning *BGE* with the image of philosophical lovers, and *OGM* with the problem of where one's "heart" ought to be,

5 In this sense "philosophers" here do duty for any of the types who have bet so heavily that a
   common life could be made possible, self-sustaining, and vital by a faith in truth.

Nietzsche is pointing to a striving that is not satisfied merely in the absence of pain and the establishment of security, but one that always anticipates the satisfactions of a possibly better life, not the one that one happens to be leading. Nietzsche's question, in other words, remains Socratic, even if his answers don't: *Wozu das Leben?* Or even, *Warum das Leben?*[6]

The stress on eros in Plato suggests that the natural (unaided, untutored) human situation is a lack, a fundamental insufficiency.[7] We cannot "live naturally," not because nature is threatening and insecure but because our nature, at least in its most familiar, immediate manifestations for humans, does not clearly "tell" us what is worth securing and defending. In Nietzsche's rather different terms, nature is "indifferent," and living is "wanting to be other than this nature" (*BGE*, sect. 9, 15).

In the Platonic presentation, though, such a lack can, at least in principle, be satisfied, and there is a structure to its possible satisfactions. There *are* natural objects of human desire and a sort of coherence among the kinds of human wantings and satisfactions. Indeed, for Plato, many of the most important manifestations of human desire already reflect this coherence and intimate the proper satisfaction. Most famously (and controversially) the love of a beautiful body, sexual excitement at the sight of another human being, is already an instance of the desire for the eternal possession of the idea of the good. In the *Symposium*, Diotima establishes this striking claim by getting Socrates to agree that everyone who loves anything wants the *possession* of that thing, and does so in the belief that the possession will be good. In her famous "ascent," she concludes that contemplating beauty itself is really that for the sake of which all other desires really desire (211d). Philosophers may begin their careers as lovers in the

---

6 Nietzsche is so often treated as if interested in reduction and deflation, even as a "pragmatist," that it is important to stress this point. In the 1872 essay "On the Pathos of Truth," he speaks quite movingly about those whose "love of life" does not depend on a mundane attachment to existence; whose eros does not depend on the hope for some redemption, some "solution to a problem." The higher types all "bequeathed one lesson: that the person who lived life most beautifully is the person who does not esteem it. Whereas the common man takes this span of being with such gloomy seriousness, those on their journey to immortality knew how to treat it with Olympian laughter, or at least with lofty disdain. Often they went to their graves ironically – for what was there in them to bury?" (*PT*, p. 62).

7 As is often the case, Nietzsche's only substantive discussions of such issues occur in very stylized images and metaphors, impossible to discuss economically. In *TSZ*, in pt. II's "Dancing Song," Zarathustra engages in a kind of lover's triangle with two women, his "life" and his "wisdom," each obviously jealous of the other, with Zarathustra unwilling to break with either. What this means about how one could (or could not) be said simply to "love life" is not clear from this passage alone and would require an extensive interpretation of the work as a whole.

standard sense, but they come to experience the instability and flightiness of human experience, and the good they admire in the beloved is only a relative and uncertain good. To love the beauty of a beautiful body is to want to possess that beauty, something that cannot be achieved if we remain attached to the swiftly degenerating body in which it appears. What anyone wants in the beloved can better be found in the beauty of all bodies, the beauty of souls, or good laws; finally in beauty itself.

The completion of this philosophical quest is not, however, some sort of passive contemplation; it really is, in many famous Platonic accounts, *itself* an erotic fulfillment. In the *Republic,* the "lover of learning" always strives for "what is,"

> and he does not tarry by each of the many things opined to be but goes forward and does not lose the keenness of his passionate love nor cease from it before he grasps the nature itself of each thing which is with the part of the soul fit to grasp a thing of that sort; and it is the part akin to it that is fit. And once near it and coupled with what really is, having begotten intelligence and truth, he knows and lives truly, is nourished and so ceases from his labor pains, but not before. (490b)

The descriptions in the *Phaedrus* of how the student of wisdom "throbs with ferment in every part" when he begins to feel his "wings grow" and the "flood of passion" when joined with that which is beheld, make the same point even more dramatically (251c).

Now Nietzsche's point against Plato can be made more economically. In the *Symposium,* Diotima virtually treats the desire for a beautiful body as an instance, an example of the philosophical desire for the ideas. This is part of the importance of the topic of beauty. Our appreciation of the beautiful is an initial manifestation of the reality of the Forms in the sensible world. All erotic striving is thus also noetic, and intimates the contentment and fulfillment that result from the full philosophical contemplation of the beautiful in itself.

Her defense of such a claim rests on something that Nietzsche is most concerned to attack: the assumption that no one could find sexual satisfaction in such a body, or any finite, limited delight in the beautiful, ultimately satisfying. Such a desired object cannot be possessed over time, and the necessary question of its goodness provokes a different sort of attachment, to more universal, less corporeal objects. The whole possibility of a continuous "ascent" in Diotima's famous account requires some explanation of our dissatisfaction at the lower levels, the provocations that inspire the continuous ascent of eros. Once at 204d, she had Socrates say that the love of good things must be a love for their possession; and at 206a, that "love loves the good to be one's own forever"; or at 207a, that love is really always of immortality, then the ground is laid for the claims of an ascent. Our attempts to understand the world and ourselves are not provoked merely by the pain of ignorance or the need to satisfy wants and passions. The beautiful, for example, draws us to it, promising a greater good, not a means to avoid the bad or satisfy the necessary. But, under Diotima's assumption, we also see many instances of the beautiful in changing and degenerating bodies (207d and e), and so by being excited by such beauty, come to love the beauty of souls, just laws, and the form of beauty itself.

This assumption is what Nietzsche is disagreeing with, what he is calling clumsy and obtrusive. There is no reason to believe, he is implying, that such an original eros would be experienced as dissatisfying if it could not be redeemed by the kind of security and reassurance promised by Diotima. It is in this sense that philosophers look like amateurish or insecure lovers, as if they demand guarantees, rest, a final respite from insecurity, eternal possession. (They can seem like young lovers who must constantly demand from each other pledges of eternal love, as opposed to more "experienced" lovers, who can love passionately, and not cynically, without such delusory hopes.) The so-called ascent described by Diotima is not an ascent but a diversion of eros, away from what can only be enjoyed with great risk and uncertainty, toward what will satisfy souls already so fearful, even contemptuous of time and finitude. Only under a certain "evaluation" of life itself, essentially a negative or ascetic one, would they come to experience desire as they do. (All of this, as an instance of Nietzsche's inversion of the usual psychologizing, is why his remarks about the Platonic account are not "false" or "unsupported," but clumsy, amateurish, inexpert, and so on.) Likewise the erotic anticipation of wholeness or completeness, so crucial to the Platonic account, would be similarly read in such an account, as a hope for the end of instability and unavoidable transitoriness of human desire; in the famous phrase, as "revenge against time."

Now at this point, several extended qualifications would have to be made in any fuller assessment of the Platonic position and Nietzsche's treatment. For one thing, Nietzsche's account of Socraticism and Platonism is always "resistant" (to use what seems the appropriate psychological word) to the manifestly aporetic character of Platonic thought, to the insistence throughout the dialogues that the satisfactions spoken of by Diotima are forever *impossible,* that whatever slight ascents there might be are always followed by descents, but that eros is sustainable anyway. For another, at the end of the ascent passage (at 212a), Diotima claims that whoever beholds beauty itself "breeds *eidola*," images of excellence. As in the *Republic* and *Phaedrus*, the satisfaction of eros is pregnancy and birth. She is of course, here and in other passages, thinking of beautiful speeches, but the image still stands in marked contrast to Nietzsche's insistence on possession and security. Nothing could contrast more with the hope for eternal security than having children, even if for the sake of immortality.

But these points would lead us quickly into many issues in Plato. I mean only to show here that Nietzsche, by contrast, takes himself to be inverting Plato, and is treating the desire for the eternal possession of the truth as itself an instance or an example of a different sort of original erotic attachment, already expressive of an evaluation and perspective, not the natural situation of human beings, objectively dissatisfied by corporeal eros. Although there are no footnotes or references, I am sure Nietzsche must be returning to this way of expressing his disagreement with Plato in section 194 of *BGE*, when he remarks that "the difference among men becomes manifest not only in the difference between their tablets of goods . . . it becomes manifest even more in what they take for *really having and possessing something good.*" He goes on to reintroduce his original image:

> Regarding a woman, for example, those men who are more modest consider the mere use of the body and sexual gratification a sufficient and satisfying sign of having, of possession. Another type . . . wants subtler tests. . . . A third type does not reach the end of his mistrust and desire for having even so; he asks himself whether the woman, when she gives up everything for him, does not possibly do this for a phantom of him. He wants to be known deep down, abysmally deep down, before he is capable of being loved at all; he dares to let himself be fathomed. He feels that his beloved is fully in his possession only when she no longer deceives himself about him, when she loves him just as much for his devilry and hidden insatiability as for his graciousness, patience and spirituality. (*BGE*, sect. 194, 107)

If "truth is a woman," then this last, more sophisticated, unclumsy love at least gives us some sort of trope, a figure, with which to pursue the question of how Nietzsche's "philosophers" will continue to "love their truths" (*BGE*, sect. 43): not on the condition that some sort of security and stability can be achieved, based on the eternal possession of truth, but not as a mere lust for power, or domination or a brute exercise of will or even in the way an artist loves what he makes. (We can recall too the language of section 226 about how we love "our world," "involved, captious, peaked, tender.") Here the attachment to one's way of going on, one's perspective, is, although not based on "truth," always *"truthfully" (or without security, "insatiably") lived.*[8]

The question posed for Nietzsche earlier was, how we should understand why some perspective or other comes to have the authority and significance it does, given that any appeal to discoveries, real success in coping with nature, the truth, and so on, is excluded. The answer now appears to be, Such attachments are reflections of what we could love; but such a love can be satisfied only, we now find, under certain conditions, neither by simply dominating everyone else, by winning, nor by the realization of some "amateurish," clumsy hope that what one loves can be confirmed (by everyone) as objectively, universally lovable and eternally desirable.

IV

Nietzsche obviously invites metaphorical flights like this. Can the points just made be brought to bear on a more prosaic, accessible issue? I'll close with a brief look at his "psychological exposure" of a famous perspective, in the hope that the journey just taken through some of his many figures and images might now be helpful. The issue is the Nietzschean "psychology" of *morality itself*, understood not in general as "valuation," estimation, and life, but as the Christian institution so dominant in Western thought, the morality of good and evil. Nietzsche proposes his own version of a psychological account of why we became attached to such an institution: It is expressive of *ressentiment* against masters, and so helps complete the "slave revolt in morality." And he thereby begins also to intimate what else we might be capable of being attached to, of loving, now.

Nietzsche understands the institution of morality as presuming, among other things

(i) a central normative opposition, between the good, understood as selflessness, or at least some sort of suspension of the priority of one's interests, and "evil" understood as egoism, the absolute assertion of such a priority, and

---

8 Like this issue of Nietzschean "practicality," this topic, "living without the reassurance of the truth," is obviously at the heart of much of what Nietzsche wants to say and is difficult to discuss briefly. The passage just quoted, for example, despite its talk of the *gründlich*, does not seem to promise, as a "test" of love, some "real" revelation, or deep honesty, as if there were such hidden, unpleasant "truths," but some acceptance of *Unersättlichkeit* (no. 194).

(ii) the morally responsible, individual subject, the agent whose individual decision or will, and whose will alone, produced or caused the deed to occur.

According to such precepts, one acts well if one acts with the right intention. The worthiness of the action is to be assessed by considering the real motive that caused the deed (whether selfless or egoistic), something that also gives us a way to understand what element of what occurs in the world as a result of one's act one is to be held *responsible* for. One is only responsible for, roughly, what one intended to have happen, given reasonable expectations. And under these assumptions, only one sort of intention gets you moral credit: unegoistic or disinterested motives. The most worthy acts are those in which you do not prefer your own stake, and where you prefer to sacrifice such a stake for the welfare or happiness of others, or in acknowledgment of the claims of moral equality as a principle. Nietzsche is particularly interested in how important, within this picture, *proving* your own selflessness is, to the point of self-sacrifice, to the point of "that ghastly paradox, the God on the Cross."

As the last rhetorical flourish indicates, Nietzsche presents such an institution as inherently mysterious or paradoxical, since its central icon and core moral ideal promote self-denial and self-sacrifice, something prima facie strange. Even in its more secular, Kantian form, the moral ideal still involves a striving to act "as any rational agent would act," and not to act for myself, unless I am lucky enough to desire what any rational agent would want. And this is still paradoxical; why would a moral project come to be so taken with the ideal of selflessness, so oriented from a suspicion of the singular, desiring, affective self? Why would this moral ideal come to have so dominated the West?

Nietzsche tries to understand such an institution as a reactive phenomenon, a revolt within a Jewish community dominated and oppressed by Roman conquerors, the epitome of singular, indifferent, self-promoting subjects (this, although the ground for such a revolt had already been laid by Socrates and Plato, in their own reaction against and fear of "the tragic point of view"). Reformulating the moral agenda as an opposition between egoism and selflessness is a strategy, a way of opposing an agenda already firmly fixed by an opposition between nobility, indifference, and *strength* against baseness, commonness, and *weakness*.

Moreover, he goes on to argue, for this revolt to be a revolt, and not merely a reformulation of where things happen to stand, the masters must be held accountable in some way for their evil, and the slaves must have achieved, must be responsible for, the qualities that make them slavish, or in their terms, paragons of the virtues of equality and brotherhood. Hence the invention of the moral subject and the notion of responsibility. It was this sort of strategy that made possible further refinements of the slave revolt, such as the moral view that all human beings are perpetually and inescapably guilty, in bad conscience. Although such a view of what Kant called radical evil, and others called original sin, helped further suggest the radical equality of humankind (all dependent on a super master, all equally unworthy, and so forth), it also helped account for, make more acceptable human suffering, something otherwise intolerable to the slavish type. We know we should not act simply for ourselves, but also know we always do and so are guilty. Our own suffering, though, is thus intelligible and tolerable; it is divinely just, we deserve it, and those who seem now not to suffer for their injustice, like masters, will suffer eternally.

The details of this narrative are quite interesting but the point now is to understand the *kind* of account Nietzsche is trying to give of such an institution, since he is still asking of its participants his "psychological" question: What do they want? And that question is still elusive. Consider how Nietzsche contrasts a non-moral evaluation and assessment of human deeds.

In section 13 of the first essay of *OGM*, he portrays the slave revolt as the sort of morality that "lambs" would create in their struggle with "beasts of prey," and much of what he says restates the previous summary. But he explicitly here attacks the "seduction of language," which "conceives and misconceives all effects as conditioned by something that causes effects, by a 'subject'" (45). This is like what the "popular mind" does when it separates the "lightning from its flash and takes the latter for an *action*, for the operation of a subject called lightning." By contrast,

> there is no such substratum, there is no "being" behind doing, effecting, becoming; the "doer" is merely a fiction added to the deed – the deed is everything.

The central assumption in this contrasting picture is strength or a strong character "expressing itself" in (*sich aüssern*) an action, rather than some intention or motive causing the deed. This also, as in many classical tragedies, means that you cannot be said to be any wholly self-originating source of agency. What principles or motives seem consciously of great moment to you are not "up to you," but reflect or express who you have become, given the family, community, and tradition within which you "got to be you." This introduces such notions as fate, that you cannot avoid whom you have become, what as a family member you incur as debt just by being you, and it introduces a much different notion of what can be tied to you, your responsibility. (For both issues, the key example would obviously be Oedipus, though Agamemnon's dilemma would do as well.) It changes the notion of guilt or any self-recrimination based on a regret that one did not act as one could have, into something Nietzsche associates with Spinoza's theory: a sadness that one was not as one expected oneself to be; " 'Here something has unexpectedly gone wrong,' not: 'I ought not to have done that' " (83).

With at least this much of Nietzsche's depiction of the moral point of view and a contrasting one now on the table, we can return one last time to the question of Nietzschean psychology. As we have seen, to see such options *psychologically* is to understand what would be at stake in evaluating oneself one way rather than another. Seeing this is far more difficult than would be suggested by understanding "life" in terms of interests, problems, or mere survival. Seeing "life" in any such terms is already to have proposed one possibility among others, not to have reached bedrock. Nietzsche's proposal requires understanding both of the previous options in terms of "the way of life" *as a whole* suggested by such views of action and responsibility, and, at least minimally, whether such a way of life would be possible, could sustain itself. Indeed, although such a criterion, what would make life, the affirmation of some course of action, meaningful, possible, appears minimal, but it is a constant, deeply sounded note throughout Nietzsche's mature work. And, it appears to involve a very great deal – conditions for affirmation, sacrifice, sustenance over time, honesty, courage – that turn out to be harder to meet than might be anticipated. Or so we have found out. (For one thing, Nietzsche thinks it extremely probable that no such project or way of life will be possible under egalitarian assumptions, or without a few willing to discipline and form the desires of the many. Betting otherwise is likely to lead to a fatal, perhaps permanent "sleep," as the "last men" nod off.)

Both a "tragic" and a "moral–ascetic" ideal represent then something like a gamble, a bet, or experiment. The bet is, What will make possible a self-sustaining and affirmable civilizational project? What will make "willing" possible over time, a way of life that does not degenerate, undermine itself, or, in his apocalyptic word, end in nihilism? Each option has implications and possible permutations impossible to foresee, and each will lead to unexpected consequences in radically altered, future circumstances. One's uncertain situation in the gamble is thus exactly as Nietzsche describes for his "new species of philosopher," baptized with "a name not free of danger," "these philosophers of the future may have a right – it might also be called a wrong – to be called attempters (*Versucher*). This name itself is in the end a mere attempt and, if you will [as Nietzsche returns to the romantic image], a temptation" (52).

(Another, extensive digression would be required at this point to assess the direction of such an interpretation. There is already something faintly "ascetic" or anxious about insisting on what could be affirmed in a way sustainable, in common, over time, now. His own sense of what is possible "now" is so contestable, need not be the only reading that could sustain some action now, especially the Platonism as Christianity theme. His own images of eros and erotic completion are so non-generative; Zarathustra's famous metamorphoses are grotesquely unnatural, and the children spoken of at the end are unproduced, not generated but merely caught sight of. And so on.)

I only mean to suggest here that the preceding sketch is the way Nietzsche understands his "psychologizing." That this is so is evident from a number of unusual aspects of his treatment. For one thing, he does not treat the pre-moral, that is, the tragic or noble point of view, as either a possible option now, or, more strikingly, a glorious option that just ran out of historical luck. The tragic point of view turned out *not* itself to have been such a good bet after all. Indeed,

> Greek tragedy met an end different from that of her older sister-arts: she died by suicide, in consequence of an irreconcilable conflict; she died tragically, while all the others passed away calmly and beautifully at a ripe old age. (*BT*, 76)

And, aside from his many references to the impossibility of "going back" (*BGE*, sect. 10, 17), he does not hesitate to point out that, in the noble mode of evaluation,

> there is indeed too much carelessness, too much taking lightly, too much looking away and impatience involved in contempt, even too much joyfulness, for it to be able to transform its object into a real caricature and monster. (*OGM*, 37)

By contrast, the moral–ascetic point of view certainly does not lack such seriousness, and because of that was, comparatively, a better bet. The "Christian schema . . . however forced, capricious, hard, gruesome, and anti-rational, has shown itself to be the means through which the European spirit has been trained to strength, ruthless curiosity, and subtle mobility" (*BGE*, 101).[9] He is even more straightforward in *OGM:*

> For with the priests *everything* becomes more dangerous, not only cures and remedies but also arrogance, revenge, acuteness, profligacy, love, lust to rule, virtue, disease – but it is only fair to add that it was on the soil of this essentially dangerous form of human existence, the priestly form, that man first became an interesting animal, that only here did the human soul in a higher sense acquire depth and become evil – and these are two basic respects in which man has hitherto been superior to other beasts. (32–3)

Finally, this sort of question forces a great deal of emphasis on a certain "use" of history. For the question is, What is possible, possibly affirmed, loved, "now?" Contrary to many readings of Nietzsche, as epistemologist, pragmatist, truth theorist, or aesthete, but consistent with his constant emphasis on the history of Christianity, morality, modernity, and so forth, there is no possible answer, or wager about, the issue of what sort of way of life could attract allegiance now, unless we are able to put together some story of what fell apart and why. To some extent, this narrative too will be an "attempt," a kind of story that itself might make possible some sort of life now. But it cannot be wishful thinking, anymore than one can make oneself believe anything about a loved one. There may be no perspective-free account of the history of philosophy, Christianity, the Reformation, the Enlightenment, and so forth, but no perspective that tries to pretend that the constraints of memory don't operate at all could possibly promote some form of life.

It should be stressed one last time that this complex question – what makes life possible – does not simply trump or render irrelevant all questions about truth or truth–assertability conditions (as if defending the value of wishful thinking). Nietzsche, in the general reading I am presenting, is not at all denying that we must find some way of constraining what can count as an acceptable claim about what there is, and that such constraints must actually work in some way that can be counted on, reliably and predictably, in regulating our dealings with nature and each other. But there are a *variety* of such possible constraints; nature underdetermines ways in which we might comport ourselves reliably toward it. We are then turned toward

---

9 Nietzsche's famous praise of the Jews in *Human All Too Human* could also be cited, that people who "have had the most grief-laden history of any people," and yet whom "we have to thank for the noblest human being (Christ), the purest sage (Spinoza), the mightiest book and the most efficacious moral code in the world" (no. 475, p. 175).

Nietzsche's "psychological" inquiries into the appeal of some such constraints over others, but not as an account of matter-of-fact motivations, and not as if in preparation for our simply "picking" one. The question Nietzsche is asking is about the way attachments to ideals, ideals that orient our inquiry, make possible everything else, are themselves possible. They are not possible as results of reflection and deliberation, since the mode of reflection already evinces some ideal or other. Hence his questions about what is required for us to "love" our ideals, especially now. "What might be possible now" depends essentially on what we take to have happened, on ability to produce a "history" that will show us where we are and what might be appealed to now if we are to continue to "live." Coming to understand this, without *ressentiment,* is summed up in another famous Nietzschean reference to the problem of love: *amor fati.*

These questions – What is possible now? What sort of ideal could command allegiance, sacrifice? – are finally Zarathustra's in Nietzsche's magnum opus. (It is important to point out, though, that all three of Nietzsche's "big" books, *TSZ, BGE,* and *OGM,* begin directly with the problem of love, and so attachment to ideals: Zarathustra's "going down" for the sake of mankind, *BGE*'s account of "clumsy lovers," and *OGM*'s of where your "heart" should be.) The great problem with that difficult work, though, is that what Zarathustra seems to believe possible (without any hope for truth or universality or objectivity) is itself extremely unstable. It changes, is expressed with, eventually, great self-doubt and anxiety. Even the one clear and unavoidable premise of the work, the only assumption that would explain why Zarathustra goes down from his mountain, perhaps why Nietzsche himself wrote books in conditions of such pain and loneliness, has found almost no place in the long and complex reception of Nietzsche and now seems an incongruous, impossible, even sentimental assumption. I mean Zarathustra's answer when the hermit asks him a Nietzschean question, Why go down? "What do you *want* among the sleepers?"

Zarathustra answered: "I love man." (*TSZ,* 11)[10]

---

10 Cf. also the grand claim in *BGE:* "The philosopher as we understand him, we free spirits, is the man of the most comprehensive responsibility who has the conscience for the overall development of man" (p. 72).

Part Six

HEIDEGGER'S "CULMINATION"

15

ON BEING ANTI-CARTESIAN:
HEGEL, HEIDEGGER, SUBJECTIVITY,
AND SOCIALITY

I. Being-in-the-world and Not-Being-in-the-world

Contrary to Heidegger's own view, both Hegel and Heidegger are, I shall claim, anti-Cartesians. (According to Heidegger, Hegel was the greatest Cartesian.)[1] I shall not be concerned here with the historical Descartes, the comments of either about Descartes, Heidegger's peculiar reading of Hegel, or anything like a full exposition of each position. Rather I am interested in the theoretical implications both draw from being anti-Cartesian, where that notion is understood in the following limited way.

Hegel and Heidegger understand Cartesian philosophy traditionally, as arguing that the possibility of any cognitive or even intelligible relation to the world resides in mental episodes occurring in individual minds. The world and entities within the world are, originally, significant or meaningful only as a *result* of the occurrence of such subjective states, or of some subject's intending, or linguistic, or representing, or synthesizing activities. (Both, in other words, would regard naturalistic, neuroscientific, and psy-

---

1 See, inter alia, Heidegger's Cartesian reading of Hegel's notion of spirit in sect. no. 82 of *Sein und Zeit* (hereafter *SZ*), (Tübingen: Max Niemeyer, 1972), pp. 433–4; *Being and Time* (hereafter *BT*), trans. John Macquarrie and Edward Robinson (New York: Harper & Row, 1962), pp. 484–5. To facilitate reference, I shall refer to page numbers of the Macquarrie–Robinson translation throughout, but whenever there is a question or ambiguity, I shall indicate an alteration and/or insert the German expression.

chologistic accounts of such cognitive relations as still Cartesian, even if not wedded to the metaphysics of immaterialism. The key issue is whether representative success, or intelligibility in our dealings with the world, is something achieved by an individual subject's activity or processing, is a *result*. Although it might sound curious to put it this way, Mentalism, or some claim that significance is conferred by individual minds, is still mentalism, no matter what *mens* is said to be made of or how it works.)[2]

My suggestion will be that both Heidegger and Hegel want to advance an anti-individualist and anti-mentalist account of the *general* possibility of any sort of "meaning," of anything being intelligible at all (words, signs, tools, the conduct of others, and so on), whether tied to a linguistic expression or not.[3]

For both, that is, the central *explicans* for the possibility of the "world's being disclosed," in Heidegger's terminology, is not mind, or representation, or subject. That is, for both, to understand that something is a hammer, or that a speaker means hot by "hot," or that a gesture is an insult, is not for a mental state to occur, such as a belief or a belief about what everyone else believes, or an inference about what a speaker would do in other contexts. A hammer *is* a hammer in and only in a certain network of tasks and functions and I understand such a network by appropriately participating in it, not by representing it. Thus each philosopher invokes a term of art

---

2 The general shift in philosophy from "soul" to "mind," and then, perhaps in Descartes and certainly in Locke, to "person," or "subject," and finally to "self," as the central term linking epistemological, metaphysical, and moral problems, is obviously a longer story in itself. See Ludwig Siep, "Personbegriff und praktische Philosophie bei Locke, Kant und Hegel," *Praktische Philosophie in Deutschen Idealismus,* (Frankfurt a.M.: Suhrkamp, 1992), pp. 81–115. Also, I am assuming, along with almost everyone else nowadays, even the most ferocious materialist, that some bit of matter cannot *mean* anything all by itself, but only as an element within some sense-making activity or practice or structure. The point of the Hegel–Heidegger issues I shall be pursuing is simply that trying to explain "being an element within some sense-making practice" in terms of subjects conferring meaning by means of their activity, or even by virtue of a position within some causally interrelated network, won't get us anywhere.

3 The fact that the scope of this central question is so sweeping has some immediate implications for the relevance of their treatment to the many contemporary discussions of anti-Cartesianism (or anti-individualism, anti-mentalism) in the philosophy of language. For Heidegger and Hegel, the problems of linguistic meaning, understanding a speaker, assigning intentional content, and so forth, are all derivative, neither the primary phenomena nor fruitfully discussed in isolation from a theory of *Sein* or *Geist*. As we shall see, this has a special bearing on the way both treat the "norms" they think are fundamental in such a general theory. They may of course be quite wrong in such an approach; it has been hard enough lately to defend the claim that a philosophic theory of linguistic meaning is necessary or possible. But for purposes of this paper, I shall follow their lead.

immediately suggestive of some theory of sociality, rather than subjectivity in the Cartesian sense. Meaning is possible because of our participating in *Geist* in Hegel's case, *Dasein*'s being as *In-der-Welt-Sein* (ultimately *Geschichtlichkeit*, or historicity), in Heidegger's.

If this can be defended and explained in a way fair to both, the basic dispute between them will then come into view: Hegel believes that such a sociality, as origin, condition for the possibility of sense, can (ultimately if not originally) sustain itself and cohere among the subjects participating in it, only if somehow inherently "rational." Such sociality can function in making significance possible because it is governed by norms that are actively and in some sense self-consciously sustained by a community, as well as periodically undermined and altered. Such norms possess the authority they do because of some sort of progressively more reflective, ultimately more successful "self-authorizing" process. Even our ordinary "consciousness" (which Hegel calls "the immediate existence of Spirit")[4] always goes "beyond its own limits," "suffers violence at its own hands; spoils its own limited satisfaction." In a Heideggerian turn of phrase, he goes on, "When consciousness feels this violence, its anxiety may make it retreat from the truth, and strive to hold on to what it is in danger of losing. But it can find no peace."[5]

Heidegger has a different reading on anxiety and is deeply suspicious of any such claim about the possibility of sociality involving any such inherent rationality, much less any developing, teleological rationality. However, they share enough deep, common assumptions that we can ask fruitfully, I hope, What is the nature of this difference between them about such a central, even "primordial" sociality?[6]

Unfortunately, for the sake of any economy of presentation, there are many obstacles in the way of correctly "framing" this *Auseinandersetzung*. For one thing, Heidegger is probably right that they mostly and most fundamentally disagree about the ever elusive problem of "non-being." This

---

4 *PhG*, p. 29; *PhS*, p. 21.
5 *PhG*, p. 57; *PhS*, p. 51.
6 Such an emphasis on sociality in Hegel, and especially the term *anti-individualist*, can be very misleading, given the long history of criticisms of Hegel's "organicism," putative anti-liberal tendencies, and metaphysical monism. I mean here only to argue that Hegel rejects a "Cartesian" form of individualism, defined in the loose way suggested earlier. Hegel's own, full theory of individuality is obviously a complex and very long story, one that would require a separate discussion. (I am grateful to Rolf-Peter Horstmann for pointing out in discussion the many dangers implicit in associating the name of Hegel with the notion of "anti-individualism.")

disagreement is about how and why things simply *don't* make sense, "are not," are indeterminate, or how the possibility of making sense, and some failure of sense are "related." For another, especially in the United States, the anti-Cartesian theme has led to Wittgensteinean and neopragmatist readings of Heidegger more familiar to the American philosophical tradition. This in turn has pushed other interpreters down a well-known "anti-Cartesian slippery slope." The slope ends in insisting that what Hegel began and what Heidegger has almost brought to completion really amount to a denial that there is any great problem to be solved, that the philosophical question of how a linguistic utterance, or behavior, or comportment, or social practice, means anything, still betrays a residual Cartesianism or even a "Platonism." Practices just go on, texts just circulate, social scientists just observe, and so forth. Or philosophy should turn into a kind of cultural anthropology, cataloguing the interrelations among, and perhaps lawlike regularities of, various dispositions, responses, interactions, and so forth.

That is, the great attraction of post-Cartesian theories of the priority of sociality or social practices has arisen in the light of the skepticism that Cartesian theories of individualist mentalism seem prone to. This attraction could be called the appeal of *publicity* in theories of significance. And, as just indicated, it comes at a price. Cartesian theories may be prone to skeptical attack, but if individuals are representing something, grasping ideas, or are being caused to be in appropriate states, some possibility of explaining some individual's particular conduct is preserved. When we observe divergences in use and conduct, we don't have to say that someone is now going on in a new way, with a new concept. We can say that someone hasn't understood something.

Part of what I shall be arguing is that the Wittgensteinean and neopragmatist readings, those that greatly stress the publicity and sociality virtues, cannot be right about either Heidegger or Hegel; that they are wrong in a way that prevents the slippery slope slide; and that consideration of such issues suggests *aporiai* in Heidegger about the normativity issue that should reopen some issues in Hegel.

To begin, it will be important to risk oversimplifying Heidegger by summarizing aspects of his general project in *Being and Time,* and raising questions that will lead us, I think, to the Hegelian counterclaims.

"The question of Being" (*die Seinsfrage*) is Heidegger's question and in *Being and Time* especially, that question is understood as the question of "the *meaning* of Being in general." Since the methodological apparatus of *Being and Time* is still for the most part transcendental, the question is investigated by attention to the "conditions for the possibility" of any meaning of Being.[7] This way of framing the issue will lead Heidegger to the famous answer embodied in the book's title: "Time" is the horizon of all possible significance; human being, all Being, is radically historical; meaning or significance is something that happens (a *Geschehen*), even though what happens is not a result, or a subjective event, or a meaning conferral.

In raising the question of the possibility of the world's significance or intelligibility, Heidegger notes that, to deal with objects, other persons, social practices, and so forth, all the "beings" or "entities," is to be engaged in an always "disclosed" world, familiar and saturated with significance. Any sort of dealing, whether practical or cognitive, goes on "in the light of" such already present intelligibility, and ought to force on us the question of the possibility of such significance itself, or the meaning of Being in general. The fact that we are somehow intuitively inclined to ask this question as, What is the source of this sense making, how do we render the world sensible, make sense out of it, and so forth? has had, according to Heidegger, disastrous consequences since Plato, all in some ways especially visible in Hegel (though even more clear, later in the Heideggerean *Abbau*, in Nietzsche).

Heidegger proposes a kind of stalking horse as a way of getting to the general question of any possible significance (*Sinn*). He asks first, In what ways do we "make sense" *of ourselves;* what is the "meaning of *Dasein*'s being"; or, again, what are the conditions for the possibility that *Dasein* could make sense to itself, could, in his words, be "at issue" for itself? And this is what issues in the most well known anti-Cartesian claims in the book. *Dasein* is not primordially a signifying subject, but "being-in-the-world." The intelligibility of the everyday world, and our own familiarity with our unproblematic presence within the world, cannot be said to be a result of individual belief states, representations, linguistic competences, ideas, intending an object, or synthesizing intuitions; activities somehow simultaneously sustained in the minds of a plurality of individual consciousnesses. Several reasons are

---

7 In the 1936–7 Nietzsche lectures, Heidegger characterizes the "entscheidende Frage" at the end of Western philosophy as "die Frage nach dem 'Sinn des Seins,' nicht nur nach dem Sein des Seienden; und 'Sinn' ist dabei genau in seinem Begriff umgrenzt als dasjenige, von woher und auf Grund wovon das Sein überhaupt als solches offenbar werden und in die Wahrheit kommen kann." *Nietzsche* (Pfullingen: Neske, 1961), I, p. 26. For Heidegger's own account of *Sinn*, as "openness for self-concealment, i.e. truth" or "openness of Being" (not as sense of a word), see *Beiträge zur Philosophie, Gesamtausgabe*, 65 (Frankfurt am M.: Klostermann, 1982), p. 11; *Einführung in die Metaphysik* (Tübingen: Niemeyer, 1953), pp. 64, 67.

given to support such a negative conclusion. Such a representation theory is said to be phenomenologically inaccurate. We simply are perfectly capable of moving about within, coping with, dealing with, items and projects in the world in a completely unthematic, absorbed way, without first or simultaneously representing the world to ourselves as such and such, and without applying rules, calculating probabilities, or consulting beliefs. There is also no phenomenological way to account for how we would *come* to "take up" the world, thematically, as suggested by the representation theory. We are never in the position of being "worldless" subjects, "receiving" ideas and beliefs about the world from others or as caused by perceptual events and "then" believing them ourselves. And finally, too many *aporiai* result from the representation picture. There would appear to be no reliable way to find our way "back" to the undeniable, common, familiar meaningful world by trying to "get there" through representations. Chronic skepticism results, always, at least for Heidegger, in an indication of some methodologically generated, or "unreal" problem.

Accordingly, Heidegger simply rejects the problem of how subjects can be said to hook up with the world in determinate ways. The problem is to figure out the ways in which they are already hooked up within a significant whole world in any dealing or discriminating within the world. He puts the point sometimes in terms of tense modalities:

> When we speak of having already let something be involved, so that it has been freed for that involvement, we are using a perfect tense a priori which characterizes the kind of Being belonging to Dasein itself.[8]

Such claims against "subjectivist" accounts, however, should not be taken to imply an "objectivist" position. In an account of "the possibility of significance" in any of our dealings with entities, Heidegger clearly wants to formulate a position beyond such alternatives and that intention will prove of crucial significance in understanding his anti-Cartesianism and his relation to Hegel.[9]

8 *SZ*, p. 85; *BT*, p. 117.
9 This applies to both what we would call accounts of possible cognition and possible agency. In the latter, it is true, Heidegger denies that human deeds should be understood as caused by the presence of beliefs and desires in individual subjects; nor can they be accounted for as actualizations of natural potencies. Heidegger's own account of action comes to a head with his account of "resoluteness" (*Entschlossenheit*), which he denies has anything to do with any willfulness, or velleity. "Resoluteness does not first take cognizance of a Situation and put that Situation before itself; it has put itself into that Situation already. As resolute *Dasein* is already taking action" (*SZ*, p. 300; *BT*, p. 347).

There are two kinds of textual evidence, in *Being and Time*, and, I think, many other works, to support the claim that Heidegger's attack on the explanatory priority or foundational status of some sort of "individual mindedness" cannot be construed as an opening move in an eventual account of a wholly *mindless* maneuvering and coping within the world. First, there are simply the phrases Heidegger comes up with to describe the ways in which individuals (who do after all still exist in Heidegger's account) "go on" as they do within a social "network" of "assignment relations" and interconnected tasks, how *they* carry on such conventions and practicalities. The language is deliberately, even quite inelegantly, passive, but it cannot eliminate reference to some sort of *like-mindedness* and to some unusual quasi-intentional features of a taking up or sustaining a practice.

So, for example, for all the emphasis in *Being and Time* on a wholly unthematic, circumspective absorption (*Aufgehen*) or involvement (*Bewandtnis*) in, even what the English translators call a "submission" (*Angewiesenheit*)[10] to, a common practical world of "assignments," a network of already interrelated tasks and functions that one simply "carries on" in everyday life, the question of *how* one significantly does so forces some odd turns of phrase. For example, in understanding the sense of a sign, one does not "grasp" a sense or a ready-to-hand object. But one does not merely "respond" in an appropriately differentiated way (or merely use the sign appropriately). One "achieves an orientation" by means of the sign.[11] To make use of that metaphor, one does not achieve an orientation just by *ending up* pointed in the right direction; one must have some sort of "sense" of where one is going if the going is to be sensible at all. This "sense" is not private; one can be sensibly oriented "for oneself" only by being oriented within some common social horizon. But there is some such sense; the orientation does not merely happen. (I am conforming to a norm, not just getting it right as a matter of fact.) Or, trying to make this point without reintroducing intentionalist (Cartesian, meaning-as-result-of-my-activity) language:

> Letting an entity be involved, if we understand this ontologically, consists in previously freeing it for its readiness-to-hand within the environment. When we let something be involved, it must be involved in something; and in terms of this "in-which," the "with which" of this involvement is freed.[12] (117–18)

10 *SZ*, p. 87; *BT*, p. 121.
11 *SZ*, p. 79; *BT*, p. 110.
12 *SZ*, p. 85; *BT*, pp. 117–18.

(Heidegger even goes so far at one point in this giving with one active hand what he takes back with the other, passive hand, to say that our understanding does not make assignments; it "lets itself make assignments."[13]

Freeing something for its involvements, letting something be involved: The phrasing is tortuous but revealing enough to make unlikely that significance, awareness, and classification in Heidegger "must be given a social behavioral reading in terms of communal responsive dispositions"[14] or that our coping and engaging are properly characterized as "mindless" (a characteristic phrase in Dreyfus's recent commentary).[15] The various significance-constituting norms carried on in our unthematic engagements with the world do not simply operate, or as a matter of fact dispose us to respond; *we* must somehow, whatever it means, "let" such norms function; "free" entities for their involvement. If we formulate Heidegger's anti-Cartesianism in terms of one prominent issue inherent in this discussion of significance, following norms without representing and attending to the norm, the problem is obvious and not addressed only by noting that Heidegger rejects "Cartesian" answers, and prefers some account that makes central "being already situated unthematically within social practices." His own language indicates that the nature of this norm following – as something I must do, achieve, sustain, and so forth – still needs to be addressed. The point is, An entity is dealt with significantly not only when it is used appropriately (something that can happen without significance, were a *Dasein* to repeat ritualistically, or merely mimic, or even just "respond appropriately," "mindlessly"), but when it is used in the light of such appropriateness, in an oriented way, with implications for future activities. (Pressing Heidegger on this point is what will make necessary the return to Hegel.)

Second, and much more famously, this sort of problem is an important one in the relation between Divisions One and Two of the published fragment of *Being and Time*. On Heidegger's account, as we have seen, when *Dasein* "understands," is truth-disclosive, lets significance happen, and so on, its understanding is a kind of non-propositional, essentially practical orientation. And what it understands is roughly "how one goes on." Understanding is always an active "projection" in the light of one's thrownness in

13 *SZ*, p. 87. ("Das Verstehen läßt sich in and von diesen Bezügen selbst verweisen.") *BT*, p. 120.
14 Robert Brandom, "Categories in Being and Time," in *Heidegger: A Critical Reader*, ed. by Hubert Dreyfus and Harrison Hall (Oxford: Basil Blackwell, 1992), p. 53.
15 Hubert Dreyfus, *Being-in-the-World: A Commentary on Heidegger's Being and Time* (Cambridge: MIT Press, 1991). See, though, the differentiation of mindless and robotic behavior, p. 68 ff.

an established social community, or a matter of one's already having absorbed, and to be acting futurally, in the light of the relevant norms. However, Heidegger also insisted that, in all its dealings, *Dasein* is also, always, "at issue for *itself*"; its own meaning and significance are at issue in what it does. Another way of making the point that its dealings can never be wholly routinized or become wholly mindless would be to stress with Heidegger that these dealings or copings are not isolated, individual tasks, mere instances of respondings and appropriate initiatings. They make sense for that *Dasein* by all fitting in to some sort of coherent *purposiveness*. In some way, *Dasein* takes itself to be at issue *in* all its dealings and copings. The problem of its own significance for itself in its dealings cannot be ignored, nor, as we shall see, interpreted in the same conventionalist way as worldly significance.

As anyone who has heard anything about Heidegger has probably heard, such a carrying on or sustaining is itself to be understood primordially in terms of being-towards-death, and such a "being-towards" greatly complicates the general Heideggerean picture of one's involvement "in a world." *Dasein,* being about its tasks, oriented everywhere towards the future, also in a way has no future (will end) and also implicitly carries on everywhere in the light of the "possibility of such an impossibility" (even, for the most part, by evading it).[16] Because of this dimension, or because of what is ultimately "at stake" in all of *Dasein*'s practices, *Dasein*'s absorption in the world always also has the quality of "mineness" (*Jemeinigkeit*). This is not to reintroduce individualism, but to suggest that *Dasein*'s world, like a common language, can and must have its unique appropriations, irreducibly singular ways in which the common practices are carried forward.[17]

So, my everyday dealings, and the objects, practices, language, and events relevant to those dealings, make sense, fit together, all in some fundamental sense, in terms of, within the "horizon" of, my "being at issue for myself" in such dealings. This introduction of the theme of a practical teleology (or anti-teleology) into Heidegger's account obviously further complicates his

---

16 Looking at the whole issue this way prepares us a bit for the claim that authentic being-towards-death is the "hidden basis" of *Dasein*'s historicality. *SZ*, 386; *BT*, p. 438. In the largest and most comprehensive sense, all of civilized life itself for Heidegger is to be understood as a great recognition of, and avoidance of, mortality (and so not the repression of instinctual life; the collective realization of virtue; the struggle between masters and slaves; the exhibitions of amour-propre; the rational organization of the means of production, and so on).

17 Cf. the discussion in Frederick A. Olafson, *Heidegger and the Philosophy of Mind* (New Haven: Yale University Press, 1987), pp. 146–7.

anti-Cartesianism. For various reasons, according to him, I *cannot* just "go on" as "they" do with regard to the issue of my own purposiveness or "fundamental" temporality, my "stretching" of my existence on from past to future.

Now, in Heidegger's account, everyday activities *are* significantly purposive in the everyday way, within a network of already assigned possible tasks and functions. One gets into one's car, in order to drive to work, in order to teach one's class, in order to satisfy the conditions of one's employment, and so forth, where the interrelated network of cars, work, classes, status, employment, et cetera, is just unthematically "submitted to." In the everyday, *Dasein* "stands in subjection (*Botmässigkeit*) to others. It itself *is* not; its Being has been taken away by the Others."[18] And so begins the famous account of the dominance of *das Man* in modern public life.[19] But, as just indicated, and to get closer to the point where Heidegger's account begins to turn toward Hegelian issues, my "proximally and for the most part" understanding myself within such assigned functions and roles cannot be, however finally articulated, a sufficient answer to the "Who is *Dasein?*" question Heidegger originally asked. A tool "is" (is intelligible as) nothing but its role in such an assignment structure. That *cannot* be true of me.

One reason it cannot be so actually relies on the *first* of the two "anti-objectivist" points noted, and is more general than his existential attention to the problem of death. The question is, How am I taking up and *sustaining* sense-making practices, norms, if it is not by representing, calculating, or applying rules? In the language used with respect to my own Being, the question concerns what I allow or do not allow in what Heidegger calls my "falling" into the world, where "allowing" refers to some sort of a necessary "mindedness" in my activities even if not "Cartesian." In the passage where the issue is addressed with the fullest terminological flourishes, the problem is posed like this:

> Can *Dasein* be conceived as an entity for which, in its Being, its potentiality for Being is an *issue*, if this entity in its very everydayness, *has lost itself*, and, in falling, "lives" *away from itself*?[20]

18 *SZ*, p. 126; *BT*, p. 164.
19 Heidegger therewith continues the great shift in philosophically inspired criticism of modern culture that began with Nietzsche; away from the Hegelian problems of alienation and fragmentation, the lack of any "ethical place" *within* modernized societies, to a different though connected concern with mass culture "absorption," herd mentality, conformism, homogenization; with the absence of any ethical place *outside* such routinized wholes.
20 *SZ*, p. 179; *BT*, p. 223.

The prospect here sketched would indeed see a kind of mindlessness as a consequence of an anti-individualist and anti-mentalist, social theory of meaning. But Heidegger answers his question immediately, denying that this would be the right conclusion to draw.

> But falling into the world would be phenomenal "evidence" *against* the existentiality of *Dasein* only if *Dasein* were regarded as an isolated "I" or subject, as a self-point from which it moves away. In that case the world would be an Object. Falling into the world would then have to be re-interpreted ontologically as Being-present-at-hand in the manner of an entity within the world. [In the preceding discussion, this would be the mistake of interpreting "understanding" as "appropriate responding."] If, however, we keep in mind that *Dasein*'s Being is in the state of Being-in-the-world, as we have already pointed out, then it becomes manifest that falling, as a kind of Being of this Being-in, affords us rather the most elemental evidence for *Dasein*'s existentiality. . . . *Dasein* can fall only because Being-in-the-world understandingly with a state-of-mind is an issue for it.[21]

Or *Dasein* can only lose *itself;* it can fall only if it leaps. This claim, though, also means that Heidegger dangerously overstates his general position by interpreting *Dasein* as a kind of site or place or, most famously, clearing (*Lichtung*) where significance, Being, happens. *Dasein,* by virtue of the preceding claim, cannot simply "be" its there, be the site of disclosure. For there to "be" such a clearing, *Dasein* must "hold it open" in a certain way, attentive to certain norms and ends, purposively and in some sense, self-consciously. Heidegger has a tendency to try to outflank such points by insisting that whatever ways might be available to *Dasein* to sustain and reflect on its world's ongoing sense-making practices themselves always already reflect "how one goes on." Or, *Dasein* is radically "thrown" (*geworfen*), and there is no way to bring the "always already there" background context to the foreground, as if itself an object. But his own clarification of why *Dasein* cannot be said simply to *be* sensible in some socially assigned way ought to be a telling point for every form of *Dasein*'s disclosings. *Dasein* always is and is not its "there."[22]

---

21 *SZ*, p. 179; *BT*, 223–4.
22 Thus it need not be only a breakdown or a gap or obtrusiveness that can disrupt *Dasein*'s involvements and force a thematization of entities. A weapon or torture implement might not be "usable," not because it won't function and must be attended to in a present-at-hand way. One cannot "go on" as "they" do with such implements because one realizes one is not

HEIDEGGER'S "CULMINATION"

And, in language that has become familiar nowadays, if all of this is true,
it ought to raise the question of how we should account for our *conforming to
norms* in social practices. Knowing that we are not applying rules, and not
merely responding appropriately, mindlessly, and that the norm following is
possible and renders the world significant in the way it does only in terms of
human agency and purposiveness, is all not enough.

Now Heidegger has his own take on such issues and insists in his own
voice that no individual *Dasein* can ever "be" anything. *Dasein*'s being is "to
be," to exist. This is of course why he became, against his wishes, a famous
"existentialist." One of the most mysterious passages of *Being and Time* asserts the radical contrary, as he shifts attention from the world, and everyday
meaning in the world (where he tends towards a kind of social positivism, or
mindlessness) to the theme of authentic Being, where a kind of radical
absence, and so radical possibility, becomes the theme.

> Care itself, in its very essence, is permeated with nullity through and through
> [*durch und durch von Nichtigkeit durchsetzt*, or, literally, "shot through with noth-
> ingness"]. Thus "care" – *Dasein*'s Being – means as thrown projection, the
> (null or nothing) Being-the-basis of a nullity [*(nichtige) Grund-sein einer
> Nichtigkeit*].[23]

This claim again involves the importance of an ever impending death in
Heidegger's account of how *Dasein* can be said to be at issue for itself.
Everything "mattering" to me can provisionally be "handed over" to the They;
I can "allow" everything of such significance to be assigned. But my own
death and its significance for me, precisely as "mine," cannot be so handed
over, all prompting a kind of "anxiety" that undermines the solidity of all of
what has been handed over, all of *Dasein*'s familiar norms and practices.
However, that issue, and the associated themes of anxiety, guilt, the call of
conscience, authenticity, and resoluteness, do not shed much light on the
significance, subjectivity, and sociality issues we have been pursuing. We
might come to understand that much of what Heidegger has patiently
articulated as the structure of how things make sense for *Dasein* in everyday
existence is an evasion, a fleeing from death, and so cannot be any sort of
total absorption, free of such "negativity," but that all doesn't help us much

"one of them." One might imagine this happening in enough contexts to make it crucial to
understand *how* the norms of some "They" *are* sustained, and how some are not or cannot
be.
23 *SZ*, p. 285; *BT*, p. 331.

to understand the internal structure of such sustaining and reflecting. I conclude that what positive answer there is in Heidegger to the question of the possibility of a non-individualist, non-mentalist account of our sensible, norm-governed dealings with the world is undermined by his own analysis, and that we are only left with rejected alternatives.[24]

II. "The Awesome Power of the Negative"

Human nature exists only in an achieved community of consciousness [*nur in der zu Stande gebrachten Gemeinsamkeit der Bewusstseyn*].[25]

So, the question is, If the kind of anti-Cartesian position outlined previously is correct, what is it about the "*way* we go on," the way we *follow* social norms without "representations," that could explain my "distance," as it were, *from* the norm, my not merely responding and initiating appropriately, but in the *light of,* and so with some possible alteration or rejection of, such presumed shared sense of appropriateness? As we have seen, Heidegger's answer to this question requires a move into unprecedented topics in Western philosophy. The lack in such conventional sense-making practices of the ability to anticipate or make any sense of my own temporality, my being-towards-an-end, in effect radically disorients all continued participation in such practices. Such a shock to the everyday confronts me with the utter "nullity" or absolute contingency of the "ground of my Being." But this account of the "primordial" *absence* of sense leaves us just with a rather Manichean duality in Heidegger's account of the fundamental, world-disclosing practical activity at the heart of his whole account: a guilty, evasive falling, a fleeing from such an absence, and an authentic but famously empty "resoluteness," a resoluteness with "nothing" to be resolute about (the terms of resolute activity, content, are possible only in a socially structured world; only in "their" terms).

24 I am disagreeing here with Dreyfus's claim that one can simply distinguish a "positive" and "negative" function of the One (*das Man*), or between necessary conformity and slavish conformism, Dreyfus, *Being-in-the-World*, pp. 151–62. As noted, Heidegger clearly intends that the topics in Division Two are required if the account of "intelligibility" in Division One is to be successful. This is not to say that Heidegger's account of *das Man* is not without ambiguities. See Olafson's note on his early use in the *Prolegomena zur Geschichte des Zeitsbegriffs* (1925); Olafson, *Heidegger*, p. 266. In other words, Dreyfus is right that Heidegger's account of social intelligibility is not a theory of intersubjectivity, but that, I am suggesting, is part of the problem.
25 *PhG*, p. 48; *PhS*, p. 43.

Several controversial interpretive points would need to be established before what would have been Hegel's view about these matters could be fully discussed. There is first the claim that Hegel can be included under the non-natural kind invented here, anti-Cartesian. Here the critical text is obviously the *Phenomenology of Spirit*. I shall simply have to assume that that work, as its very title indicates, does indeed comprise Hegel's attempt to subsume the broad notions of consciousness (understood as any direct intending of an object), self-consciousness (understood as any reflective self-relation or practical self-determination), and reason (understood as the normative self-constraint of universality and necessity) all under what is argued to be the more comprehensive notion of *Geist* or spirit.

This is, of course, quite a complicated argument. There are two main components to it. The first concerns what Hegel means by Spirit's own "measure" of itself, its own Notion or criterion. Hegel thus tries to direct our philosophical attention to the criteria or *norms* that constrain the way we directly confront and take up the world, the criteria or norms that determine the nature and limits of our satisfaction of desire and comportment toward others, and the ideal criteria in any universally justifiable procedure for resolving disputes. Now there is difficulty enough here, in understanding what Hegel might mean when he identifies a *Masstab*, or *Begriff*, or shape (*Gestalt*) of spirit. In general, I shall understand him to be giving an account of the possibility of those human activities and interactions that are what they are *because* and only because constrained by norms in certain ways; the activities are constituted by such norm following. (I think Hegel, especially in the philosophy of objective spirit, uses the notion of right or *rechtlich* much as we would use the notion of norm.) So, an action is the fulfillment of a contract, the punishment of a criminal, a promising, an inheriting, or even a valid argument or acceptable evidentiality test, and so forth, only because the participants take themselves to be participating in institutions governed by certain rules. Were there "really" to be no such norms, or were they to perform the same body movements but without taking themselves to be following such norms, the actions would not be those actions. Second and more importantly, Hegel argues that such norms can only be adequately understood and accounted for as historically sanctioned *social* norms. On this reading the basic question for the *Phenomenology* is whether it has a persuasive case that such epistemological and ethical issues should be understood as manifestations of the history of spirit, or as historical social norms, and whether it has a good account of what it is for something to be a norm (a "shape of spirit") and what it is for such norms to be followed. Can there be an achieved *Gemeinsamkei der Bewusstseyn,* and can it account for so much?[26]

For our purposes, among the many controversies introduced by such claims, one is particularly relevant to our Heideggerean issues, and is particularly stressed in the preface to the *Phenomenology.* Hegel asserts that such a social subject, or "living substance,"

> is in truth actual [*wirklich*] only as the movement of self-positing, or is the mediation of its becoming other than itself with itself. As subject, it is pure, simple negativity, and thereby the division [*Entzweiung*] of the simple, or a doubling which opposes, which is again the negation of this indifferent differentiation and its opposition.[27]

This is, stated with all the systematic (and nearly incomprehensible) flourishes, Hegel's doctrine of the *Arbeit des Negativen,* the labor of the negative, and the justification for the claim that "the Absolute" is "essentially result, that it is first of all in the end what it is in truth, and therein consists its nature, to be actual, subject, the becoming of itself."[28]

Helpfully, Hegel also points out shortly after these remarks that "What has just been said can also be expressed by saying that reason is purposive activity [*das zweckmässige Tun*]." I take him to mean by this gloss that the norms that constrain and direct our cognitive and practical activities do so only if collectively authorized in some way, sanctioned, *rationally* legitimated, and that this collectively self-sanctioning process is necessarily developmental, that is, purposive.

All of which, especially the claim about the rational nature of these periodic dissatisfactions, breakdowns, and reintegratings, is controversial, especially in the eyes of a modern evolutionary epistemologist, skeptic, cultural anthropologist, and so on. For now the first important point for us is simply the extraordinary stress on "negativity," becoming other to self, doubling or division (something that reaches its high – or low – point in Hegel's famous and somewhat macabre claim "The life of Spirit is not the life that shies away from death and keeps itself untouched by devastation,

---

26 I try to defend such a reading in "You Can't Get There from Here: Transition Problems in Hegel's *Phenomenology of Spirit,*" in *Cambridge Companion to Hegel* (Cambridge: Cambridge University Press, 1993).

27 *PhG,* p. 18; *PhS,* p. 10.

28 *PhG,* p. 19; *PhS,* p. 11.

but rather the life that endures it and maintains itself in it. It wins its truth only when, in utter dismemberment [*Zerrissenheit*], it finds itself."[29]

It is this account of the self-undermining, self-negating aspects of collectively sanctioned norms that brings us to the same sort of point at issue in Heidegger's anti-Cartesianism. Our question throughout was how to understand an anti-individualist and anti-mentalist position on significance or intelligibility in a way that could still distinguish between matter-of-fact "appropriate responding" and some orientation achieved "in the light of" what is appropriate, to distinguish between an anti-subjectivism and a reductionist objectivism (i.e., a position that simply eliminated the "problem of the meaning of Being" at the outset). As we have seen, a large part of the answer for both Heidegger and Hegel has to do with attending to the conditions for our simply not being able to "go on as we do." For both, it is in understanding such a failure, or breakdown, that we can see more clearly how we were collectively sustaining the norms and conventions by means of which we were "allowing ourselves" to coordinate activities, understand each other, engage the world in a familiar, "circumspective" way, and so forth.

(And none of this, I should stress, returns us to individual mental episodes or beliefs as "where" such significance is "sustained." I can be said to be sustaining a practice in the way I act and move about within it, without my having resolved, or without my continually resolving, to sustain it. But that is another topic.)

Clearly what Hegel has denied in this context is that such failure can be as comprehensive, discontinuous, episodic, and "ecstatic" as Heidegger maintains. As we have seen from the limitations of Heidegger's case, there are good reasons to be so hesitant. By contrast, the general virtue of Hegel's position, at least the poorly sketched out fragment introduced here, is that such failure or negation is always *internal* to a practice and determinate. Our not being able to go on as we do in some way or other is as up to us or due to us as our so going on. We do not "come upon" an *Abgrund* in anticipating our death; in such a case, *we* go on, or fail to go on, as we have done or as we cannot any longer.

There are, of course, more accessible and better known examples of Hegel's theory of sociality, all of which help make the same point. So, for example, in political terms what this means is that the true or full exercise of agency by an individual, the possibility of realizing the modern norm of

29 *PhG*, p. 27; *PhS*, p. 19.

genuinely free activity without which a modern *Gemeinschaft* would not be possible, is only fully "realized" (*verwirklicht*), if the like capacity of all persons for such agency is recognized, if nothing in my deed implies the contrary, and if that mutuality of recognition is institutionally secured, ultimately in a *Rechtsstaat*. Hegel tries always to show that this is so by considering the implications of other candidate accounts of such norms of agency, beginning with the simplest sense of freedom understood as independence: my matter-of-fact ability to effect my will through sheer power alone. Such a putative independence is shown to involve a deep form of dependence inconsistent with any masterly norm, and the "master–slave" dialectic is under way.

And these sorts of claims are not of course limited to political philosophy alone. Hegel discusses the struggle to achieve some form of collectively sanctioned ("satisfying") like-mindedness as relevant to various philosophic and religious enterprises, to the European Enlightenment, the French Revolution, romanticism, and so on. And he agrees that such a like-mindedness is not sustained by individual acts of consent or by simultaneous beliefs or dispositions. Individual self-consciousness does indeed always evince such like-mindedness rather than constitute it. But we badly confuse the nature of such a shape of Spirit if we regard it as simply a network of tasks, how we go on, or who we happen to be, or what we are "absorbed" into. For the *possibility* of such like-mindedness is very much a question for Hegel in the way it is not for Heidegger and many of his followers. Given Hegel's claim that participating in a practice is a sustaining and affirming of a norm, such participation already presupposes the possibility of a collectively sanctioned norm. Our own practices carry with them the memory of failed attempts and new resolutions to achieve such a norm. There is no "form of life" as such, no *das Man,* then, only attempts to realize the successful like-mindedness on which individual self-determination and satisfaction rest. As is usually the case in his books, to show this, Hegel begins with the contrary assumption – that engagements with the world and others are radically individualist, unregulated by norms – and he proceeds to examine the kinds of conflicts that would have to occur for, and possible resolutions open to, such parties. By trying to show the "internal" insufficiencies of such resolutions as the exercise of sheer power, or mastery, a stoic withdrawal from or skeptical negation of the world, or a Christian, other-wordly dualism, he eventually tries to argue that a "satisfying" form of those activities by virtue of which the world could be disclosed at all must be governed by a universally sanctioned norm. In general this norm is described as a *complete* "mutuality of recognition" and, as noted, is most intuitively obvious in his account of a particular norm,

Recht. But the relevance of that norm, mutually affirming free subjectivity, to his accounts of modern religion, art, and philosophy is also evident.

Thus, I am suggesting that the right way to read the *Phenomenology of Spirit* is as an extensive attempt to expose the inadequacies of the very notion of a "mind–world" relation, and that these inadequacies themselves point to the primordiality of an historicized "subject–subject" relation. (This is shown to be so for any number of possible "objects," ranging from sense objects to ideas to the moral law to God.) However, with Cartesianism discarded, this subject–subject relation cannot rely on any suggestion of individual, self-inspecting agents confronting and negotiating in a social context, nor on any metaphor of submission to or lostness in *das Man*. Such relations have to be understood as mutually self-forming and self-authorizing in time.

So, a general way of looking at the problem developed so far would be this: Radically anti-Cartesian theories tend to support anti-individualist and anti-mentalist claims by appeal to the priority of participation in social practices in making possible the general intelligibility of the world, language, and others. But this sort of direction tends to treat questions of the authority or appropriateness of such practices for such agents as merely other aspects of "how we go on," as an issue itself raised and settled *within* a social practice, say an authorizing practice. And it can thus also lead to an elimination of any distinctly philosophical or normative assessment of such practices in favor of some replacement enterprise: hermeneutics, sociology of knowledge, cultural anthropology, or, in the Heideggerean case, a kind of anti-hermeneutics, an endless account of how practices break down, don't work, deconstruct, and so forth. (Not for nothing did Hegel produce his Marx and Feuerbach; Heidegger, his Gadamer and Derrida.)

But even such attempts to collapse all the traditional questions into questions about social practices or texts still confront our "Hegelian" problem: *how* such sense-making or authorizing practices are sustained and carried forward, or how and why the practices come to have and cease to have any social authority and are replaced. Whatever second-level, authorizing practice we come up with, supposedly as merely a component of the whole fabric of our "world," will itself raise the same problem and cannot be an "answer" to it. This is the problem we can call "negativity," the negative rather than absorbed relation between subjects and practice.

Heidegger's response to such issues involves, as we have seen, an account of the role of "anxiety" in the disfunction of such practices, or in general, an account of the radical finitude and contingency of any attempt to ground, reassure oneself about, such ways of going on. From the Hegelian perspective just sketched, this would look like a classic example of an "indeterminate negation," something Hegel thinks is only apparently possible. The insufficiency or breakdown of some sort of purposive, collective practice, let us say its loss of authority (e.g., when a religious doctrine of immortality comes to appear as a cowardly evasion of one's mortality), is possible only if the practice "fails" when measured against some end or point implicitly (or explicitly) posited by it. It could not be experienced as a failure if it were measured against some incommensurable, alien practice or standard. But if this is so then the failure or negation must always be determinate, insufficient with respect to X or Y, because of A or B. Unless Heidegger wants us to understand his own account of the disorienting consequences of anxiety, the disclosure of nullity, and so forth, merely as "how we go on about sense and authority" in twentieth-century, mass culture societies, his claims about the philosophical status and implications of such an experience would not, it would appear, be able to do justice to this point. If he does interpret them this latter way, then he is acting like an armchair anthropologist, whose only defense for his own way of regarding things is that he too simply radicalizes how we go on.

Several questions naturally arise at this point. For one thing, given where this path leads, one might be greatly moved to take a second look at the supposed insufficiencies of the post-Cartesian emphasis on the explanatory priority of individual minds or mental activity, with sociality, communicative success, and general intelligibility all quite rightly seen as a result of such activity. Methodological individualism might not have been such a bad idea after all. However if one is sympathetic at all to the Hegelian themes introduced and the problems they pose for Heidegger, daunting difficulties seem to lie ahead. At the very least one would seem to be committed to the following claims about social practices:

(i) All societies are best understood by understanding the norms authoritative in them. (Hegel is, after all, an Idealist.)

(ii) There is a difference between historical and non-historical societies.

(iii) There must then be a difference between the way in which some societies subscribe to and sustain such norms that makes possible a radical and continuous alteration of such norms, rather than a repetitive resanctioning with each generation.

(iv) Our own social practices – Geist – are best understood as the result of this sort of continuous historical transformation. Our sanctions and ideals are not just contingent results, however, merely our way of going on about things, but can be shown to be superior resolutions of internal insufficiencies in the status of norms in prior epochs of Geist.

(v) It is difficult to say, without a major book, what this distinctive, historically mutable way of sustaining norms is, but whatever it is, it has something to do with why Hegel thinks the transformations can be understood as progressive. For Hegel, this historicity occurred first in ancient Greece and it obviously had to do with the *norm's authority*, the way it functions, *not* resting on ancestral pronouncements, tradition alone, mystery, or brute power. (Heidegger's vacuuming up all such distinctions into *das Man* would be one of Hegel's great objections here.) The norm's sanctioning force has some relation to the intelligibility and universal justifiability or at least potential intelligibility and justifiability of the very claim to authority. (This doesn't mean that pre-historical or traditional societies live in dark unintelligibility or without sense. But Hegel is not a relativist. Lots of things that could make sense don't in such practices; much that would be intelligible isn't, all not because of what they haven't learned but because of what they do not allow themselves to understand.)

(vi) Such a shift in the kind of authority possessed by norms, however incomplete and inconsistent in earlier forms, can be said to imply its own eventual telos, or resolution (*Verwirklichung*). The only kind of norm that could be sustained in a way consistent with this new form of authority is, ultimately, one affirmed and sustained by actually free, mutually recognizing subjects within social institutions consistent with such freedom and recognition.

(vii) We have reached, or now could reach, such a stage. In a phrase, human history, the history of *Geist,* is indeed the history of the actualization of freedom. One was free; many were free; all are free.

Obviously, (i) to (vii) find few takers today. However, if one takes seriously that modern forms of anti-Cartesianism have a difficult time explaining the normativity of social practices, and especially the continuous and occasionally reconceived authority of such norms for the purposive agents who subscribe to them, then avoiding this general line of thought will prove difficult. One will be left, in trying to account for such subscription and purposiveness, either with Heidegger's revolutionary account of the absence of any such authority and his Nietzschean account of sociality itself as evasion, fleeing, concealment; or with accounts of "public" or naturalized meaning, confident that ordinary language is all right or that our practices just go on, but blind to the way such practices are at issue for participants and genuinely intelligible only if the way they are at issue is understood by an interpreter. Publicity and sociality without self-consciousness are blind; self-consciousness and purposiveness without sociality are empty.

16

HEIDEGGEREAN HISTORICITY AND
METAPHYSICAL POLITICS

In spite of the ascendant power of technology and of the universally technicized [*gesamtteknischen*] mobilization of the globe, hence in spite of a quite specific preeminence of an ensnared [imprisoned, *eingefangenen*] nature, an altogether distinct fundamental power of Being [*Grundmacht des Seins*] is on the rise; this power is history, which, however, is no longer to be represented as an object of historiography.[1]

I

In the following, I shall be mostly concerned to try to do two things. One is to explain, insofar as I understand it, some aspects of Heidegger's attack on the classical German philosophical tradition or "German Idealism."

I want especially to try to understand his account of the essay he seems to regard as the death knell for this Kantian program, and thereby, he insists, a death knell for the aspirations of modern philosophy itself: These are the lectures Heidegger gave in the summer semester in Freiburg in 1936 on Schelling's 1809 "Treatise on Human Freedom," the last essay Schelling

---

1 This remark is from Heidegger's 1937 Nietzsche lectures. *Nietzsche* (hereafter *NI*), (Pfullingen: Neske, 1961), I, p. 451; *Nietzsche*, II, *The Eternal Recurrence of the Same*, trans. David Farrell Krell (San Francisco: Harper & Row, 1984), p. 186.

personally prepared for publication (even though he was to live and lecture for over forty more years).

But, as already implied, for Heidegger, the stakes are very high in what appears to be a very abstract topic. The fact (if it is a fact) that the post-Kantian notions of subjectivity, self-consciousness, freedom, and so on, could not be defended or saved from various objections, is for Heidegger a reflection on the far deeper insufficiencies of all modern philosophy itself, and, indeed, those deficiencies reflect the inevitable nihilism of all post-Platonic philosophy. (Heidegger famously interpreted all of modernism and especially the German philosophical version as a failed attempt at human autonomy, an inevitable collapse into a meaningless willfulness he often summarizes with the single word that devours Plato, Descartes, and even Nietzsche in its condemnation: *technology*.)

In that context, the second thing I want to show is how the form of Heidegger's attack, or here the appropriation of Schelling's initial anti-idealism, should be understood as a kind of paradigmatic attack on what is itself a paradigmatic version of philosophical modernism (German Idealism), repeated many times after Heidegger, and that understanding the structure of this attack helps clarify its power, as well as its weaknesses and dangers. Heidegger was quite right to seize on Schelling as the first to appreciate this problem (which, as we shall see, is indeed a serious one), but that fact also helps one to identify what I think is the blind Schellingean alley (or overreaction) that Heidegger begins to wander into with his own doctrine of historicity, or the inevitably situated "happening" of any "thinking."

More simply: For the sake of argument I shall agree with Heidegger when he claims (later, in a 1941 seminar) that "Schelling's treatise is the acme of the metaphysics of German Idealism," and so the "highest expression of philosophical modernism"; even that "the essential core of all of Western metaphysics can be delineated in complete clarity in terms of this treatise,"[2] but that when Heidegger beings to formulate his own historicity doctrine in response to the problems Schelling identifies, he misreads his opponents and so "mis-reacts" in what remains a Schellingean form.

Before beginning, I should also note that the context for my remarks about Heidegger's views on historicity could be summarized as the large

2 Martin Heidegger, *Die Metaphysik des deutschen Idealismus, Gesamtausgabe,* 49 (Frankfurt am M.: Klostermann, 1991), pp. 2–3. Some of these remarks are translated in the appendix to *Schelling's Treatise on the Essence of Human Freedom* (hereafter *STE*), trans. Joan Stambaugh (Athens: Ohio University Press,1985), p. 165.

problem of the *political influence* of Heidegger, or even the emergence of what might be called "left Heideggereans."

With that label, I mean to identify a certain form of opposition to a number of central aspects of European modernity, or, if you like, to modern "bourgeois" culture: an opposition to such things as the very highly authoritative cognitive status of modern natural science (and the growing dependence of modern societies on the technologies made possible by such science); the supreme moral authority of individual conscience and so individual responsibility; the political authority of rights-based, liberal democratic institutions; or even the general European Enlightenment hope that the modern revolution would make possible a secular, an essentially rational, foundation for a collective life that could be relied on safely and rightly.

In this context, the link between these issues – the nature of Heidegger's attack on philosophical modernism, and his views on historicity – has recently taken on new meaning in the context of a putative postmodern political agenda (one supposedly not linked to the universalist aspirations of European modernism). At the very least, this sort of approach involves a radical dissatisfaction with the official culture of Western modernity, but one not tied to an analysis of modernity as essentially the culture of a self-contradicting capitalism, and more concerned to link all the universalist, moral aspirations of European modernism with a merely contingent, even necessarily contingent expression of mere self-assertion, "power," cultural imperialism, Euro-centrism, and so forth. To be sure, the people who might be linked together under this left Heideggerean label have profound differences, but the attack on the Idealist "philosophy of the subject" and of reason, on any possible "first philosophy," and the insistence on some sort of acknowledgment of the historicity or contingency of institutional life, even truth itself, does shape some common agenda for Rorty, Foucault, Reiner Schürmann, Jean-Luc Nancy, Philippe Lacoue-Labarthe, Gianni Vattimo, and others.[3]

II

In these lectures, as Heidegger struggles to explain the significance of German Idealism to Third Reich university students, one can find one of the

---

3 Among such others, see Fred Dallmayr, *Between Frankfurt and Freiburg: Toward a Critical Ontology* (Amherst: University of Massachusetts Press, 1991), and *The Other Heidegger* (Ithaca: Cornell University Press, 1993); Stephen K. White, *Political Theory and Postmodernism* (Cambridge: Cambridge University Press, 1991); Christopher Fynsk, *Heidegger: Thought and Historicity* (Ithaca: Cornell University Press, 1986).

most compressed and clearest of Heidegger's many accounts of the history of Enlightenment thought, all in formulations that make clear where contemporary "anti-humanisms" get their start.[4] It goes like this. The Enlightenment is to be understood

> as a liberation of man to himself. But what man is as himself, wherein his being a self should consist, is determined only in his liberation and by the definitely oriented history of this liberation. Human "thinking," which here means the forming powers of man, becomes the fundamental law of things themselves. The conquest of the world in knowledge and action begins. . . . Commerce and economy turn into powers of their own in the most narrow, reciprocal connection with the origin of technology, which is something different from the previous invention and use of tools. Art becomes the decisive manner of self-development of human creativity and at the same time its own way of conquering the world for eye and ear. . . . The idea of "sovereignty" brings a new formation of the state and a new kind of political thought and requirement. (31)

In particular, in the 1809 essay, Schelling focuses on what he regards as the "metaphysical reality" most inconsistent with the Idealist notion of freedom as autonomy and self-grounding, and so with the Idealist (or all mod-

---

4 Heidegger's Schelling lectures themselves evince a self-conscious political agenda. For example, Heidegger begins by telling his students that what is at stake in the topic he will pursue, the fate of German Idealism, is not a dispute among academic theorists, but the very "historical spirit of the Germans." Martin Heidegger, *Schelling: Vom Wesen der menschlichen Freiheit* (hereafter *SWMF*), *Gesamtausgabe*, XL; *STE*, p. 7; Heidegger had decided to begin his lecture series as a whole by reminding his students in great detail of the political setting when Schelling wrote and thereby implying that the fate of Germany and metaphysics or philosophy were linked (then and, we are obviously supposed to conclude, again in 1936). He reminds his students that in 1809 "Prussia had disappeared," that Napoleon had ruled since 1806 ("and that means here, he oppressed and abused Germany") (p. 1). And Heidegger had remarked on the "profound untruth" of the famous words Napoleon had spoken to Goethe at their meeting in Erfurt. Napoleon had told Goethe, in trying to persuade him to leave Germany and go to Paris, "Politics is fate." No, Heidegger tells his students, "Spirit [*Geist*] is fate and fate spirit. The essence of spirit, however, is freedom."

   Such cryptic remarks (wherein Heidegger sides with Schelling's rejection of "politics" in favor of "spirit," against the Idealist notion of freedom, in favor of the pre-institutional, presubjective, or even pre-political, perhaps *Volk*-ish "spirit") already point to the way in which some acknowledgment of the historicity of thought is meant in some sense to be relevant to politics, even in opposition (in the name of Spirit) to all traditional public life.

   More conventionally, of course, Heidegger sees the "subjectivist" understanding of freedom in Kant, Fichte, and Hegel (itself paradigmatic of modern aspirations) as "fated" to fail, sees that Schelling saw and appreciated that failure but could not resolve any of the difficulties caused by such a failure, so that Schelling's fate presaged the modern failure itself.

ernist) hope for a systematic or comprehensive account of any claim for the reality of freedom, *the reality of evil,* a topic I shall return to in the concluding section of this chapter.

Understanding and contesting such claims will require two preliminary steps. One concerns Heidegger's own project and the distinctive character of his claim about historicity or the presuppositions of his treatment of Schelling. The other involves some attempt at understanding at least the aspirations of the post-Kantian Idealist tradition that Heidegger, through Schelling, is attacking.

III

Heidegger's 1927 masterwork, *Being and Time,* was only published as a fragment, yet there is something deeply fitting about the question that ends the published version of the book. Its last sentence is "Does *time* itself manifest itself as the horizon of *Being?*"[5] The very title of the work already indicates that Heidegger had all along intended to offer an affirmative answer to this question, to defend a claim about the "historicity" of human existence and of "truth" itself, and therewith to begin the destruction of all Western metaphysics, a tradition understood by Heidegger to consist essentially in a refusal to acknowledge such a historicity.[6]

Yet, to come immediately to the question at issue in all "postmodern" appropriations of Heidegger: What *would* it mean to *acknowledge* such historicity and radical contingency, and so, if we follow Heidegger, *not* to think metaphysically, or even "philosophically," but in some new way informed by such an acknowledgment? If we pursue this issue in Heidegger's thought, we find mostly, over and over again, warnings, hesitations, indirections, allusions, neologisms, quotations from the pre-Socratics, from Hölderlin. Heidegger never tired of reminding his readers of just how profoundly difficult it was to understand what he wanted to say about historicity (*Geschichtlichkeit*) (even to the point of stating that his own formulations were necessarily "concealing," or deceptive).

He is certainly clear enough about the consequences of avoiding or forgetting the ontological dimensions of historicity and of aspiring to be the complete, self-determining subject of one's deeds and thoughts. "The es-

---

5 *SZ,* p. 437; *BT,* p. 488.
6 The relation between the notion of *Geschichtlichkeit,* which Heidegger inherited from Dilthey and transformed, and notions of historicism and history is a complex one. Cf. my discussion in "Marcuse on Hegel and Historicity," in *Marcuse: Critical Theory and the Promise of Utopia,* ed. by R. Pippin, A. Frenberg, and C. Webel (London: Macmillan, 1988), pp.71–3.

sence of modernity," he writes in a typical claim, "is fulfilled in the age of consummate meaninglessness."[7] Such a meaningless essence is said to involve "the securing of supreme and absolute self-development of all the capacities of mankind for absolute dominion over the entire earth." This impulse at a kind of predatory dominance is said to be the "secret goad" that "prods modern man again and again to new resurgences, a goad that forces him into commitments that secure for him the surety of his actions and the certainty of his aims."[8] The modern aspiration for an enlightened future, the hope that a secular foundation for moral and political life could be formulated and safely relied on, and that a kind of collective, self-legislating autonomy could be achieved, have all failed, according to Heidegger. The totality of "the essential possibilities of metaphysics" has thereby been "exhausted," and "European nihilism," most visible in Nietzsche's "culmination" of the tradition, is the result.

These claims all obviously depend on Heidegger's distinctive formulation of the basic problem of philosophy. "The question of Being" (*die Seinsfrage*) is Heidegger's question, and in *Being and Time* especially that question is understood as the question of "the *meaning* of Being in general." The question is not to be confused with the metaphysical questions of substance or degrees of reality or necessity, nor with traditional ontological questions: the kinds of beings there are, the basic categories necessary to articulate whatever there is. "Fundamental ontology," some pre-reflexive and everywhere presupposed "sense" of anything's "being" at all, is the theme. This requires at all costs respecting what Heidegger calls the "ontological difference," or not confusing this question of the meaning of Being with any question about beings or entities. This amounts to the problem of the possibility of our somehow always already being "oriented" in the world, originally having bearings of a sort.[9]

7 Martin Heidegger, *Nietzsche*, II (hereafter *NII*) (Pfullingen: Neske, 1961). "Im Zeitalter der vollendeten Sinnlosigkeit erfüllt sich das Wesen der Neuzeit," p. 24; *Nietzsche*, III, *The Will to Power as Knowledge and as Metaphysics* (hereafter *WPKN*), trans. Joan Stambaugh, David Farrell Krell, and Frank A. Capuzzi (San Francisco: Harper & Row, 1987), p. 178.

8 *NII*, p. 145. *Nietzsche*, IV, *Nihilism* (in this chapter, *EN*) (Pfullingen: Neske, 1961), p. 99.

9 In the 1936–7 Nietzsche lectures, Heidegger characterizes the "entscheidende Frage" at the end of Western philosophy as "die Frage nach dem 'Sinn des Seins,' nicht nur nach dem Sein des Seienden; und 'Sinn' ist dabei genau in seinem Begriff umgrenzt als dasjenige, von woher und auf Grund wovon das Sein überhaupt als solches offenbar werden und in die Wahrheit kommen kann." *NI*, p. 26; *Nietzsche*, I, *The Will to Power as Art*, (hereafter *WPA*), trans. David Farrell Krell (San Francisco: Harper & Row, 1979), p. 18. For Heidegger's own account of *Sinn*, as "openness for self-concealement, i.e. truth" or "openness of Being" (not as sense of a word), see *Beiträge zur Philosophie, Gesamtausgabe*, LXV (Frankfurt am M.: Klostermann, 1982), p. 11; *Einführung in die Metaphysik* (Tübingen: Niemeyer, 1953), pp. 64, 67.

As noted already, it is this way of framing the issue that will lead Heidegger to the famous answer embodied in the book's title: "Time" is the horizon of all possible such significance; the meaning of human being, all Being, is radically historical; the familiarity or disclosedness of "what is" *happens* (is a *Geschehen*), even though what happens is not a result of the beliefs or representations of subjects, or of any sort of a subjective event or meaning conferral. How such meaning or orientation happens, and why it cannot be some sort of result, or some event of matter-of-fact like-mindedness with sources, causes, explanations, and so on, is one of the great constant themes in Heidegger. (In fact, his position is so radical that even this fairly neutral language is misleading; "what" is disclosed is not a "what" but the utterly contingent event of disclosedness itself, what Heidegger calls *Ereignis*, "since 1936," he said, "the leading word of my thinking.")[10]

In *Being and Time* and in many other works, Heidegger claims that the fact that we are somehow intuitively inclined to ask any such question about our deepest pre-reflexive familiarity with the world as, What is the *source* of this sense making? How do *we* render the world originally sensible? *make* sense out of it? and so forth, has had disastrous consequences since Plato. Being is taken *to be disclosed, rendered* intelligible, by or because of us and so is made into a kind of standing or enduring presence by being so "measured" in our terms. We thus forget everything we would need to remember if we were to "think" fundamentally.[11]

Perhaps the way to say this is that Heidegger's conviction about the extraordinary elusiveness of the basic question for human thought means that any meditations inspired by the question must finally be distinctly non-philosophical, not "directed" by a subject toward an end, not a problem to be solved, an *aporia* to be addressed, or an opaque meaning to be clarified by some activity of ours. Heidegger's notion of historicity is thus not comparable to similar claims in the social or moral sciences, and this alone makes it (and his influence on the postmodernity discussion) extremely hard to understand. He is not trying to offer some transcendental case for the

10 From the *Nachwort* to the *Beiträge*, 512. Perhaps the most radical, and thus clearest formulation is from the end of the Nietzsche lectures: "What happens in the history of Being? We cannot ask the question this way, because then there would be a happening (*Geschehen*) and something which happens (*Geschehendes*). But the happening (*Geschehen*) itself is the only occurrence (*Geschehnis*). Only Being is. What happens? Nothing happens, if we are seeking for something that happens in the happening. Nothing happens; the event e-vents (*das Ereignis er-eignet*)" (*NII*, p. 485, not translated in the Harper & Row series).
11 The most economical summary of his position are the summaries given in the 1941 lecture series on Nietzsche, "Entwürfe zur Geschichte des Seins als Metaphysik," *NII*, 458–80 (notes not translated in the Harper & Row series). See also Chapter 15.

necessary conditionedness of thought, nor to point to contingent social determinants or interests behind or motivating the authority of various intellectual practices. He realizes that we inevitably take him to be offering a thesis about the historicity of truth, and he wages a lifelong battle to disabuse us of that response, claiming that his founding idea about ontological difference would thereby be ignored. He keeps insisting that he is actually trying *to think historically,* not to think about history. He knows we intuitively assume that an argument for the latter is necessary to justify the former, but that, he keeps saying, is the great error. There is no such argument, no place from which it could be made. There *is* just historizing thinking, whether acknowledged or not, whether in argument form or not. The key issue turns out to be the mode of acknowledgment. So, in writing about his own writing about the problem of finitude in *Kant and the Problem of Metaphysics,* he says:

> *The working out* of the innermost essence of metaphysics must *itself* always be basically finite and can never become absolute. The only conclusion one can draw from this is that *reflection* on finitude, always to be renewed, can never succeed, through a mutual playing off, or meditating equalization of standpoints in order finally and in spite of everything to give us absolute knowledge of finitude, a knowledge that is surreptitiously posited as being "true in itself."[12] (My emphases)

(This is not to say that Heidegger is not interested in motivating his own acknowledgment of this historicity, or that he just "poeticizes" historically. The acknowledgment begun by *Being and Time* is said to be provoked, even made necessary, by the "completion of metaphysics" in Nietzschean nihilism.[13] A very great deal thereby hangs on the sufficiency of Heidegger's

12 *Kant and the Problem of Metaphysics,* trans. James S. Churchill (Bloomington: Indiana University Press, 1962), p. 245.
13 It could also be noted that, since such a fundamental ontological orientation is not a result of or driven by insight or theories or beliefs, it is also a consequence of such claims that all politics inspired by an attachment to theories, beliefs, principles, or appeals to reason becomes suspect as naive, hiding instead of illuminating, falsely locating "the subject" and its reflecting activity at the center, all with political consequences that Heidegger wants to summarize as the technology problem. (He goes so far as to claim that the term *Technik* "reveals itself in its meaning with the designation: "completed metaphysics." "Überwindung der Metaphysik" [remarks collected together from 1936 to 1946], in *Vorträge und Aufsätze* [Pfullingen: Neske, 1967], p. 72.) At the "center" is rather a pre-subjective ontological site or *Lichtung,* a collective orientation, something with important consequences for any rights based or individualist politics, or any that take as supreme the sovereign, self-conscious, self-determining individual. (Heidegger's language varies in describing the

narrative of "modern thought," as is the case, I believe, with all "postmodernisms").[14]

Heidegger's own interrogative stance is thus itself some sort of expectation or an attentive waiting, or, in a frequent, obscure phrase, "repetition," not a thought or proposal in the traditional sense. (The later fascination with the *Dichten–Denken* and *Danken–Denken* relation is also crucial here, as is the formulation: *Gelassenheit*.) It could thus be itself called a poetic or theologico-political *engagement* of a sort, rather than the theory that would drive an engagement.[15]

nature of such a collective orientation. For an oft-quoted formulation, see the Hölderlin lectures of 1934–5 especially, and his claim, "The Fatherland is Being itself which from the ground up carries and ordains the history of a folk as one that exists," *Gesamtausgabe*, 39, p. 121. See also his claims in these lectures that "liberalism" is "deeply untrue," pp. 26–8, 99, and the reference to "der wahre und je einzige Führer," p. 210.) Since the meaning of Being *happens*, and happens in a *Volk*, in common (most especially, linguistically), it might be said that Heidegger's own program is itself an attempt at a kind of "political" reversal of the traditional priority of metaphysics (for him itself, inherently, already a political act, a "subjectivism"). Metaphysics is itself characterized as a "decision" (*Entscheidung*) in the Nietzsche lectures called "The Will to Power as Knowledge," *NI*, p. 476; *WPKN*, p. 6 (although, typically, Heidegger will also gloss such a decision as a "letting" be decided, to prevent the impression of someone just thinking something up and resolving). What is being displaced is the possibility of any contemplative a priori determination of substance, what has been called the "mirror of nature" view. Whereas, say, for Hegel any such determination already reflects spirit's practical determination *of itself in relation to the world*, for Heidegger, such a determination is also not primarily contemplative but a derivative expression of some *pre-reflective mode* of practical engagement, "care" and orientation that comprises the "event" of Being (as does his own hermeneutics, adding to the complexities). At least, it is with respect to this dimension of his thought that a comparison with Idealist humanism, and the corresponding notion of agency proper to it, can best eventually be made.

The "mirror of nature" phrase has of course been made popular by Richard Rorty. Any reference to him raises the question of his own answer to, *What* is displacing traditional attempts to get the furniture of the universe *right*, particularly those elements not sensibly apprehensible? Rorty rejects both any notion of a search for the normative requirements of some indispensable free activity and any original "event of Being," in favor of a Deweyan pragmatism. See especially the essays "Heidegger, Contingency, and Pragmatism," and "Wittgenstein, Heidegger, and the Reification of Language" in *Essays on Heidegger and Others* (Cambridge: Cambridge University Press, 1991). For objections, see *Modernism as a Philosophical Problem: On the Dissatisfactions of European High Culture* (Oxford: Basil Blackwell, 1991), pp. 70–4.

14 In the Schelling lectures, this sort of claim is quite explicit. Schelling and Nietzsche (called "the only essential thinker after Schelling") failed, their projects to realize and complete modern philosophy "fell apart," but this wasn't just a failure. It was the advent of something wholly different, even the "summer lightning flash" (*Wetterleuchten*) of the "new beginning of Western philosophy." *SWMF*, p. 5; *STE*, p. 3.

15 Here an enormous problem develops, perhaps the key problem in Heidegger. *Dasein is* its disclosedness, Heidegger tells us; it does not work toward disclosure by reasoning, reflect-

IV

It will not be difficult to contrast such a fundamental ontology with the original Idealist aspiration. As we have seen in several contexts in the preceding chapters, the idealism of German Idealism has little to do with ideas or representations in the rationalist or empiricist sense. The ideal is human freedom, understood as being a law wholly unto oneself. And philosophy is thus one dimension of a practical engagement, as it is for Heidegger. But where Heidegger strives for a kind of poetic receptiveness, the Idealists strive for a complete, universal, self-authorization. For the moment, we can understand this demand to mean, a kind of free self-determination, what Fichte called an *active* "positing" of one's stance toward nature and one's desires not originally determined or caused by one's relation to nature or such desires, or a kind of agency, spontaneity, activity, "purposive life," eventually a necessarily collective agency, is ontologically prior, "the condition for the possibility" of all relations to nature.

As we have seen before, in cognitive terms, the claim is a denial: that we can successfully explain the mind's intentional content, its holding possibly true or false knowledge claims, by appeals to the mind's being-determined by some independent content. In the simplest terms, in being aware that something is (or even could be) so-and-so, I am holding that it is; taking it to be so-and-so; making up my mind; taking a stand. The subject is not in a relation to the world; it takes itself to be, and is so always in absolute command of its conceivings and concludings. The same logic applies to action, where I can never be said to act for a pressing interest or desire, but only on the condition that I determine such interests or desires to merit acting on. In the extraordinary language soon developed, the I's relation to itself is "the Absolute," the unconditioned possibility of which explains the possible intelligibility of all else.

To a degree still, I think, unappreciated, the young Schelling quickly realized that the whole approach necessarily generated a basic problem. It

---

ing, contestations with others. These all already evince some original, disclosive event. This at least means that Heidegger's understanding of practical teleology, of *Dasein*'s acting "for the sake of its own possibility," cannot rightly be understood as acting *on,* or "having" reasons, as if it came to have its ends, or could see them as its own, only by virtue of such reasons (something much closer, I think, to the Kantian–Fichtean–Hegelian picture). This would be a secondary manifestation for Heidegger and would suggest an unacceptably subjectivist understanding of such activity (as if the subject were "origin"). What it then would be to *be* one's disclosure, or to wait or think or attend or dwell in some way *not* tied to "having come to think that one should think or dwell, etc.," is, I think, *the* Heideggerean problem (ultimately unresolved), at least after *BT.*

was one whose logic would first appear in the German counter-Enlightenment (especially in Jacobi) and then in many, many forms later (certainly in Kierkegaard, later in Nietzsche's account of "life," and thanks to Heidegger, in thinkers such as Gadamer and Derrida). The task had been to think through the implications of the claim that *being in* any cognitive relation to the world, to have disclosed any sense (or being the true subject of one's deeds) is necessarily *to have assumed such a relation actively,* to have determined *oneself* to be in such a relation. This does indeed make all the contents or objects of such a relation necessarily the results of some self-conscious self-determining. Yet we, as embodied agents in the world, are already natural or at least pre-volitionally situated beings, already thinking in a certain way, with a certain inheritance, with certain capacities we clearly share with non-human animals (like perception). It is only *in* being a kind of being, within a certain sort of world with kinds of beings, at a certain historical time, that we *could* be the particular self-determining subjects or agents. To view the issue of *this* sort of pre-reflective situation as itself a result, or in terms of "what we must *think*" to make sense of "our" conditions of intelligibility, seems to miss the point profoundly. (All of which simply invites the Idealist turn again, so visible in Hegel's early criticisms of Schelling: Except insofar as such a "source" or "origin" or finitude is self-consciously determined as such, for the subject, it is nothing; it is "the night in which all cows are black.")

Schelling thus in his 1800 *System* insisted that transcendental philosophy and a philosophy of nature were necessarily complementary, that the sort of living nature that could include a self-conscious subject must be thought through systematically before the transcendental conditions of such self-consciousness could proceed. Driven by his own realization that this could sound like a reversion to pre-critical dogmatism (an attempt to say how things in themselves are, without first establishing how we could know what they are), Schelling pushes forward (as if over a cliff) and insists that both nature or the object world and the self-conscious I, or the subject world, must be understood as "products" of a "producing force" not describable in either term, something he was driven to call an "identity of identity and nonidentity."

V

As we have already seen, in Heidegger's appropriation of Schelling's rejection of any such "priority" for subjective self-determination, some sort of lived acknowledgment of such an original situation is at issue, not a new intellectual realization or a different sort of system (all this to avoid the Hegelian rejoinder suggested earlier). In passages like section 74 of *Being and Time* (about "The Basic Constitution of Historicity"), the possibility of such acknowledgment is tied to anxiety, not insight, or systematic philosophy, Heidegger's early figure for the sorts of practical, lived dislocations, or breakdowns that *make* impossible just going on as usual (as if functioning anti-methodologically like Husserl's "bracketing" of the natural attitude). (Boredom, the violence of poetic language, world historical crises, and, as we shall see later, radical evil itself, can all function this way.) One *is* displaced in one's being-toward-death, does not just see something, and the acknowledgment is discussed as both a "taking over" of one's factual possibilities and a "handing down to oneself" of what has been handed down to one, a "*Dasein* existing fatefully in the resoluteness which hands itself down."[16] This will make assessing Heidegger's "reaction" to modernism extremely difficult, but I do think a general point can be made and explored in terms of the topic Heidegger himself focuses on.

If we understand German Idealism in this way, as linked to the aspirations of modernity itself in this way, and understand Heidegger's worries about historicity in this Schellingean context, we can understand something like the repeated, now almost perennial "logic" of the oscillations of the post-Kantian European traditions, especially the logic of the dissatisfactions with modernity that so overwhelmingly dominate that tradition (in a way largely absent from the Anglo-American tradition). Especially, some of the limitations of his approach can be seen in the great topic that engages him in the Schelling lecture, the problem of evil.

For Kant, Fichte, and Hegel, moral evil is generally understood as a supreme affirmation of an individual subjectivity, as if I alone am supremely "real"; all else counts for nothing. Such acts are themselves considered intelligible against the assumption of, by contrast with, what free agency really consists in. And, of course, in this tradition, morality is a matter of practical rationality; the realization of the highest value, freedom, is the realization of rationality. Immoral acts are themselves free, but only imper-

---

16 *SZ*, p. 384; *BT*, p. 435. Derrida accuses Heidegger of such a nostalgia for an *arche*, or first principle, but my own view is that that charge is hasty and unfair to Heidegger, as if what Schürmann calls the an-archic nature of Heideggerean thinking is to be trumped by the debating trick of calling the anarchic the Heideggerean *arche*. Cf. Jacques Derrida, "Différance," in *Margins of Philosophy*, trans. Alan Bass (Chicago: University of Chicago Press, 1982), pp. 1–27; and Reiner Schürmann, *Heidegger on Being and Acting: From Principles to Anarchy* (Bloomington: Indiana University Press, 1987) and the criticisms in my *Modernism*, pp. 142–7, 156–64.

fectly, incompletely, in some contrary to, conflicting with, one's own agency. Such acts appear within such a systematic understanding as a *failure* of true freedom, a failure to realize true freedom, and so as unfreedom, a deficit, a failure to be who you really are. (In fact, in Hegel's most notorious extension of this logic, the criminal actually wills *not* the crime itself, alone, but also, implicitly, his own punishment. He must so "will" on the assumptions necessary for him to be the subject of his own act.) Various possible realizations of freedom are, in such a view, obviously resisted or rejected by subjects, but this is due to ignorance, weakness, historical conditions (which can reach a point where an inseparability between good and evil is inevitable, as in tragic contexts), and so on. Such acts remain evil, even if intelligible, but can never be described as absolute negations. There is and can be no "absolute" evil in the world.

Schelling categorically rejects what he calls such a version of the *malum metaphysicum,* and insists that

> the basis of evil must therefore not only be founded on something inherently positive, but rather on the highest positive being which nature contains.[17]

This extraordinary claim implies a notion of "freedom *for* good and evil" or the claim that evil acting is not a kind of mismeasuring "through a glass darkly," or a failure, but a completely unmeasurable, or even unconditioned, unintelligible even if depressingly real human and metaphysical potential. (I should note immediately that even though Schelling formulates the issue often as a radical choice for good and evil, he has in mind no standard voluntarist picture. Such a "choice" enacts or evinces or in some sense merely expresses a pre-voluntary structure of significance or "Absolute.")

And Heidegger joins Schelling in the general worry about any comprehensively intelligible idealism, particularly as revealed by the problem of evil. In fact he goes quite far in his affirmative and sympathetic summaries:

> To demonstrate the possibility of evil means to show how man must be, and what it means that man is. After all this it becomes clear that the ground of evil is nothing less than the ground of being human. But this ground must be in God's innermost center. The ground of evil is thus something positive in the highest sense. (119)[18]

---

17 F. W. J. von Schelling, *Sämtliche Werke,* VII (Stuttgart: J. G. Cotta, 1860), p. 369.
18 *STE,* p. 119; *SWMF,* p. 208.

Now it is quite likely that Heidegger is not much concerned here with traditional (say, to cite one of his heroes, Augustinian) problems with moral evil. It is more important to him to insist on some notion of radical possibility in his account of historical happenings and of the pre-subjective origin of our collective practices and self-monitorings. Evil figures for him throughout these discussions as something necessarily unrecognizable as ours, not a finite and incomplete failure to fit in to how we go on.[19] Not acknowledging such a wholly negative possibility would be like regarding the nihilism crisis itself as still incomplete rationalization, or one's impending death as a possibility that will happen someday but not soon, or the failure of meaning in profound boredom as an accidental or pathological aberration in the meaning structures that are authoritative. In Heidegger's Schellingean version of such responses, we are always trying to reinscribe within the sovereign realm of the subject a phenomenon that actually wholly undermines the possibility of any such sovereignty.

So here again we have a version of Schelling's worries about the absolute status of a self-determining subjectivity, supposedly the source or condition for the intelligibility of all human thinkings and doings. Evil, so goes the largely implicit argument, cannot be rightly understood under such an assumption, as the privation or failure of practical rationality, without denying its status as evil (the assumption is that weakness, ignorance, or the mere influence of our passions fails to account for the reality of evil). For there to be evil, our capacity for evil must be original, not derivative from a potentially fully free agency, and for such evil to be an original possibility, self-determining subjects cannot be "Absolute." The Heideggerean "event" of Being must manifest itself originally "positively" and "negatively."

Our own determination for good or evil, in other words, is a kind of phenomenon or appearance, itself possible because of or by reference to "the self-positing of the Absolute." Since this origin is not, for reasons we have been initially exploring, a possible object of any account, it follows (for Schelling and Heidegger at any rate) that the reality of freedom, or ontological possibility, is absolutely *unlimited*. That is, there can be no system, no "whole," no "*philosophy* of freedom." (Kant's original argument that the mind must actively bring its thoughts and intentions into unity, and so under a norm, for there to be "my" thoughts and intentions is thus rejected, since such a spontaneity is argued to require, for its possibility, a dependence on some *arche* whose unity or coherence or intelligibility cannot be

19 His extremely compressed formulation of this point (italicized in the original): "*Die Größe eines Daseins zeigt sich zuerst daran, ob es im Stande ist, den es überrangended großen Widerstand seines Wesens zu entdecken und festzuhalten.*" STE, 105; SWMF, p. 183.

articulated.)[20] And if we are free in this sense, then Being cannot be accounted for by any notion or norm, and to live freely cannot hope to be a life commonly and justifiably measured by some norm. It must be some sort of *acknowledgment* of what cannot be measured without falsifying, covering over. A kind of mythic–poetic discourse seems to keep emerging as the appropriate mode of acknowledgment. (To some extent, as Heidegger shows, Schelling would agree with some formulation of the *nature* of evil as linked with an extreme individuation, but he insists that traditional interpretations of what Heidegger will call the "attraction" of such individuation have not been accounted for. Schelling, and Heidegger after him, attribute this attraction to the historical self-manifesting or disclosing process *of Being itself.*)[21]

Such claims all hearken back again to the radical dimensions of Heideggerean historicity – that he is not talking about *how we situate ourselves* within a tradition (or how we legislate the norms regulating our lives), but how we are, contingently and ineffably, *situated* in the revealing and concealing process within which "fundamental" sense is made. Our attempts to master and ground such contingency (to "conquer" it, he frequently says) are defeated in these breakdown situations, like anxiety or evil, wherein "being the null basis of a nullity" cannot but be acknowledged.

> Schelling's treatise has nothing to do with the question of the freedom of the will, which is ultimately wrongly out and thus not a question at all. For freedom is here not a property of man, but the other way around. Man is at best the property of freedom. (9)[22]

Or, "insofar as man is man, he must participate in this determination of Being, and man *is*, insofar as he brings about this participation in freedom."[23]

20 My own view is that the most important thing to appreciate about Hegel's project after 1807 is that he does not reject this Kantian beginning, as Schelling does, but tries to "realize" it.
21 Cf. *STE*, pp. 152–6; *SWMF,* pp. 264–71. Obviously in most of these passages, Heidegger is evoking his own claims about the inevitably "covering over" aspect of any "uncovering."
22 *STE*, p. 9; *SWFM*, p. 15. Cf. the discussion by Michel Haar, "The Question of Human Freedom in the Later Heidegger," *Southern Journal of Philosophy* 28, suppl. (1989): 1–16. The somewhat Spinozist strain in Heidegger's ontological sense of freedom (to live freely is to live "in truth," where truth is the happening of Being) is of course not foreign to the German tradition. See Ludwig Siep's "Der Freiheitsbegriff der praktischen Philosophie Hegels in Jena," in his *Praktische Philosophie im deutschen Idealismus* (Frankfurt am M.: Suhrkamp, 1992), pp. 159–71.
23 *STE*, p. 9; *SWFM*, p. 15.

VI

The path Heidegger is on, the way in which his distinctive oppositions set a direction for him, will lead to a number of complex, and I think, unresolvable *aporiai*. The most important consequence of the kind of anti-modernism we have been discussing will involve the resources Heidegger will have left himself in accounting for the possibility of the kind of pre-reflective intelligibility or finitude, the kind that, for him, renders so problematic the Idealist or modernist aspirations. To live "in" such "truth" after all is not merely to live truthfully, wholly unreflectively, as if a matter of luck or fact. It is to live in the light of the truth, ultimately the true place or status of human being, something that immediately opens multiple possible alternatives: whether as a rights-bearing individual, a morally responsible agent, a pious, thankful *ens creatum,* or an ontologically disclosive *Volk.* (We are thus back to our first question, how Heidegger can account for our acknowledgment of this historicity without some self-determination as historical, and I don't think we find, within Heidegger, a coherent answer.) Contrary to what Heidegger suggests, we do not simply participate or "dwell" within a "world" "framed" by such alternatives. We participate in a world only by also situating ourselves within it, either carrying on or contesting its own narrative about itself. Heidegger often seems to concede this point. He certainly distinguishes between an inauthentic falling within the practices of "the They" and an authentic resoluteness. And the light images, suggesting such an illuminated self-situating, are his. But he always paints his picture like one of those great seventeenth-century achievements, where the light shines from nowhere.

Admittedly, our own subjection to, and revision of, such norms is not easy to account for phenomenologically. We do, of course, inherit and pass on much unreflectively, or at least in a way that makes the language of self-imposition and justification look highly idealized. But the difficulty in stating that issue, and some general, well-justified reluctance to think of such norms in a non-historical and non-social way, as if a matter of "pure practical reason" alone, and so on, is no reason to throw the baby out with the bath water. If we do, we immediately confront the post-Heideggerean dissolution of subjectivity into the reifications of mentalités, epistemés, "discourses," "fields of power," and so on, terms that always suggest to me an arch, defensive neo-positivism.[24]

---

24 Such reification and neo-dogmatism are not foreign to Heidegger either. "Only a few, and they rarely, attain the deepest point of the highest expanse of self-knowledge in the

VII

The basic point I am trying to make is, The most important idea of modernity that Heidegger refuses to acknowledge is much broader than anything that can be captured by the Idealist notions of system or even the meaning of Being. It is a great confusion, for example, to treat the requirement within German Idealism for an "absolute" condition of intelligibility as somehow on a par with the notion of natural–scientific comprehensiveness, or an absolute *explanation,* as Schelling and Heidegger often do. (It is true to say that the Idealists made *das Ich* "the Absolute." But that involves a claim for the unavoidability and irreducibility of an active self-consciousness in the possibility of any cognitive claim or action. It is absolute as the supreme condition for thought and action, not itself "conditioned." This is a divergence from, not an instance of, the metaphysical notion of ground.) To assume otherwise would be to assume that the Idealist threat to the "reality" of evil were the same, as if, from a comprehensively informed point of view, the difference between the agent who acted wrongly and one who didn't could be *explained or predicted,* thus denying the metaphysical reality of evil. (As in, a sick body obeys the laws of nature as much as a healthy one; it is not any less real or complete.)

The original animus of the Idealist revolution, though, was so set against the problem of dogmatism that this sort of ideal could never emerge for it as an issue, and neither could any such realist question about metaphysical evil. We are never in any position to confront or reject or accept *the* reality of evil, and Heidegger's confusion about the problem of such a position tempts him to the same formulations he admires in Schelling. To comprehend the irruption of absolute subjectivity as a possible moment within, or permanent threat to, our own developing self-comprehension, and to understand it as a failure of such full self-understanding and so as unfreedom, is not to domesticate or deny it. *It is merely not to mystify it,* not to *pose* it as other, determine oneself in relation to such an event as a *malum meta-*

decidedness of one's own being. . . . That means that decidedness does not contract one's own being to an empty point of mere staring at one's own ego, but decidedness of one's own being is only what it is as resoluteness. By this we mean standing within the openness of the truth of history, the perdurance (*Inständigkeit*) which carries out what it must carry out, unattainable and prior to all calculation and reckoning" (*STE,* p. 155; *SWFM,* p. 269). For a different, but compelling criticism of "Heidegger's positivism" (p. 294) compare Stanley Rosen's *The Question of Being: A Reversal of Heidegger* (New Haven: Yale University Press, 1993). Rosen "reverses" Heidegger in the name of Plato, but not the textbook Plato of the ancient and modern schoolmen. See especially the first chapter, "Platonism Is Aristotelianism," pp. 3–45.

physicum, and then deny such positing, all of which, from the "Idealist" perspective, are being done in Schelling's response.

To make this point clearer, consider very briefly the contrasting treatment presented in Hegel's analysis of this theme in his *Lectures on Aesthetics.*

We should start with a statement of one of his general principles. In speaking of Greek tragedy in particular, he says, clearly at odds with the Schellingean–Heideggerean treatment: "*For evil in the abstract has no truth in itself and is of no interest.*"[25] In his earlier discussion of the moral dimensions of tragedies, he had conceded that agents can freely perform monstrous and barbaric acts, unrecognizable as "like us," transformed into some malignant, contingent force of nature. (Lear's insanity in the storm is alluded to. He also cites, wrongly I think, Goneril and Regan from *King Lear* as examples of such malevolent "forces," implying that Greek dramatists would never have had the bad taste to put such inhuman characters, or, say, Iago, on stage.) But there is, he also insists in a way that refers to his whole project, "*no truth*" and therewith no "interest" in such gross injustices.[26] There is only such "truth" in a more complexly *human* enactment of evil deeds, one in which the possible instability (or mere subjectivity) of the distinctions our norms establish between good and evil is evoked and confronted. (In his *Lectures on Religion,* he cites Milton's Satan as paradigmatic of this phenomenon.)

A full statement occurs later.

> For the purely negative is in itself dull and flat and therefore either leaves us empty or else repels us, whether it be used as a motive for an action or simply as a means for producing the reaction of another motive. The gruesome and unlucky, the harshness of power, the pitilessness of predominance, may be held together and endured by the imagination if they are elevated and carried by an intrinsically worthy greatness of character and aim; but evil as such, envy, cowardice and baseness are and remain purely repugnant.[27]

By insisting that there is nothing interesting or aesthetically worthy in a play about a tyrant mercilessly tormenting his subjects, Hegel is freely conceding that individuals may recognize but grossly ignore the norms that their actions presuppose, may act "against" their own free destiny, at the

---

25 G. W. F. Hegel, *Vorlesungen über die Ästhetik,* 15, *Werke in zwanzig Bänden* (hereafter *VA*) (Frankfurt a.M.: Suhrkamp, 1970), p. 543; *Hegel's Aesthetics* (hereafter *A*), trans. T. M. Knox (Oxford: Oxford University Press, 1975), p. 1212. My emphasis.

26 *VA,* pp. 276–7; *A,* 212.

27 *VA,* p. 288; *A,* p. 222.

same time that he is insisting that in many cases, and much worthier of thought, the "positive" and "negative" aspects of such actions are much harder to separate and so inspire a much more profound sort of "pity and fear," and bring the significance of evil deeds closer to home.

In his famous analysis of classical tragedies, this "instability" in the meaning of evil itself obviously has a historicizing implication, one that also ties the analysis of tragedy and evil to a social and historical theory. (His remarks on heroism and its possibility in modernity evoke similar themes.) But he is everywhere implicitly insisting that only by means of appeal to such a theory is the nature of the evil presented in such works intelligible, more than a mere "other." The theory is certainly not relativistic and never denies either the reality of such transgressions or the inevitable implications of transgressions in historical progress. His point is that the transgressions are understood as such within the self-understanding of a human ethical community, and ultimately that some formulation of the norms of such a community must resolve the conflicts evinced by the instability of those norms that made necessary various tragic impasses.

This introduces a number of issues that cannot be pursued here. The central distinction at issue, between a kind of collapse into the subhuman, which contains no "truth," and a recognizably motivated, complexly "positive" and "negative" evil, raises a number of questions. But it is clear that Hegel's approach *does* indeed foreclose the idea of some "pure" evil, or a "metaphysical" attraction to it, as evoked by Schelling and Hegel. But for Hegel, this only concedes that the conditions of human agency itself can "fail": A mad, unrecognizably human malevolence can occur. In the same way Hegel would object to the notion of some *absolute Nichts,* or event-like absolute failure of sense, evoked in Heidegger's account of death. Hegel would insist instead that our being toward death is a being toward a kind of death in a kind of community at a kind of time; in the same way he would object to the idea of "*the* modern" technological will to power, insisting that there is only a kind of technological reliance, within a community for a purpose; so he would object to the way in which Heidegger wants to evoke somehow what is beyond human self-determination or intelligibility as itself some negative measure for the human.

And so on, on into a refusal to mystify the notion of "what" we *must* face now, "*the*" retreat of the gods, our "fate," our "destiny," our "locatedness," our "origin," contingency, what we allow each other to get away with saying, "*the*" Other, "the" language of the Unconscious, "the" ineffable, textuality, "the" body, gender, and so on, through the list of postmodern "realities." By contrast, the Idealist version of modernism, as I am presenting it, imme-

diately trumps, as it were, or renders suspicious any claim about real origins
or about what is putatively "outside" our comprehension (like evil).

This is not an inviting prospect, since it promises a kind of unending
contestation about any fixed points or settled results, a modernity necessarily unending and unsettled.[28] It seems to require both a constant "boot-
strapping" (a reflective self-examination that is made possible by criteria
themselves suspiciously local, themselves always subject for such reflection)
and so a constant dissatisfaction with such incomplete and finite reflection.
Working out what such a modernist model of our intellectual and ethical
practices might look like will obviously not be easy. Finally, it might now
seem even more unlikely in this context to invoke the name of Hegel as the
champion of such a complete, if also therefore unsatisfying modernism,
since he is regularly taken to be the ultimately satisfied, systematically closed
thinker. But he does begin to bring his *Science of Logic* to a close with the
following:

> The Identity of the Idea with itself is one with the process; the thought which
> liberates actuality from the illusory show of purposeless mutability and trans-
> figures it into the Idea must not represent this truth of actuality as a dead
> repose, as a mere picture, lifeless, without impulse or movement, as a genus or
> number, or an abstract thought; by virtue of the freedom which the Notion
> attains in the Idea, the Idea possesses within itself also the most stubborn
> opposition; its repose consists in the security and certainty with which it eter-
> nally creates and eternally overcomes that opposition, in it meeting with
> itself.[29]

28 I discuss this notion in more detail in the last chapter of *Modernism as a Philosophical Problem*,
   and in a response to comments and criticisms of this book, "Hegelianism as Modernism,"
   Inquiry 38, no. 3 (September 1995): 305–27.
29 G. W. F. Hegel, *Wissenschaft der Logik*, II (Hamburg: Felix Meiner Verlag, 1969), p. 412;
   Hegel's Science of Logic, trans. A. V. Miller (London: George Allen & Unwin, 1969), p. 759.

Part Seven

HEGELIANISM

17

HEGEL'S ETHICAL RATIONALISM

I

Hegel claimed to have developed and defended a unique category of ethical assessment – "*Sittlichkeit*," or "ethical life" (*Sittlichkeit* might also be translated simply as "customariness"). Although he shares with many other modern philosophers the view that to live righteously is to live freely,[1] and with some classical thinkers the idea that the worthiest life involves an active engagement with others, Hegel adds to both positions the claim that to live freely is to participate in certain modern institutions, to *be* a social and political being of a certain sort.[2]

---

1 In the Introduction to the *Philosophy of Right*, the "system of right" is said to comprise the "realm of actualized freedom, the world of spirit produced from within itself as a second nature" (no. 4; *PR*, 28; *PRE*, 35). And in no. 29, "Right is therefore in general freedom, as Idea" (*PR*, p. 45; *PRE*, 58). In this chapter, references to the *Philosophy of Right* (*PRE*) will be to the English translation of H. B. Nisbet, *Elements of the Philosophy of Right*, ed. by Allen W. Wood (Cambridge: Cambridge University Press, 1991), which I have relied on, but occasionally altered. Also in this chapter, for the original of Gans' *Zusätze*, or the additions translated by Nisbet, I have consulted Band 7 of the *Jubiläumsausgabe in zwanzig Bände* (hereafter *GPR2*) ed. by H. Glockner (Stuttgart: Frommans Verlag, 1952), and the relevant volume of Ilting's edition of the lectures, as quoted in note 5.

2 The reference to modernity in this claim is not an idle modifier. In his *Phenomenology*, to cite one of many such references, Hegel makes very clear that an ethical community as such (one constitutive of freedom) is a distinctly modern, Western European accomplishment. It is not

Hegel's reasons for making this claim are complex, and many involve difficult issues in what he considered the logic of individuality and universality. But, like Rousseau and Kant, he also linked the possibility of free agency with a kind of practical rationality and based many of the things he wanted to say about the "priority of ethical life" on considerations arising from an analysis of the possibility of such rationality. Or so I want to claim in what follows.

However, appreciating Hegel's position on ethical life has been impeded, I believe, by two familiar characterizations of his case. First, the nature of Hegel's *ethical rationalism* has been obscured by his own spirited critique of moral rigorism, dualism of all kinds, the general *Zerrissenheit* of modern life, and so forth. Inspired by such passages, and what they might mean for Hegel's own account of moral motivation, some commentators classify him as a "romantic," along the lines of Schiller, and so try to equate a practically rational life with some sort of sensuous harmony with "the whole," or with *the rational,* "what there truly is." This has the effect of rendering Hegel, to use his own classification, a premodern rationalist in ethics, and so conflicts with his own enthusiastic modernism. (*My* reasons for acting, "my subjectivity," seem lost in any such account of being in harmony with, reconciled with, actuality.) Second, since Hegel's account of ethical life is a historical one, it is often assumed that his argument for the motivating (or non-alienating) power of modern ethical ideals, his claim that the rational (or any rational norm) is "actual," must rely on a sweeping, highly implausible historical theodicy, that the rationality of our participation in ethical practices stems from something like the divine rationality of history itself, and its resolution or culmination in modern institutions. I want to propose an alternative, although preliminary, reading of Hegel's general case for the rationality and priority of ethical life.

II

First, some qualifications are in order. Since this sort of claim for the priority of our social existence and for what might appear to be a kind of anti-

---

merely the "universal substance of all individuals (*die allgemeine Substanz aller Einzelnen*)"; rather, "ethical" or "true" spirit is a substance "known by these individuals as their own essence (*Wesen*) and their own work." It is not like some "essential light" that swallows up such individuals (in the manner of readings of Hegel's own account of the "divinity" of the state) but is the "free *Volk*" in which "custom" (*Sitte*) "makes up the substance of all, whose actuality and existence each and everyone knows as his own will and deed." *PhG,* p. 376; *PhS,* pp. 424–5.

individualism has had a complex legacy and has been associated with some disastrous political experiments, we should first note that Hegel does not argue that such sociality is all there is to an ethically worthy life. In the best known presentation of his practical philosophy, his *Elements of the Philosophy of Right,* he sides with those who argue that all human beings are bearers of "abstract rights." In his account, too, it is simply by virtue of being free agents that we are universally entitled to the ownership of some property and to the rights of transfer and exchange that this entails.[3] He also argues that responsibility may be attributed to free agents only by reference to their individual intentions and purposes (no blood guilt or generational curses can be *rechtlich*), and that we all stand under universal moral obligations to other individuals, whether members of our ethical community or not.[4]

However, the claims of right and morality are also argued to be "incomplete," and this is where the controversy begins. For example, "The sphere of right and that of morality *cannot exist independently* [*für sich*]; they *must* have the ethical as their support and foundation."[5]

To some extent, this sort of claim is meant to express only a reservation against believing that the question of a fully free and so worthy life can be *exhausted* by the protection of rights and the avoidance of moral harm. A fuller, more active and purposive collective pursuit of ethically worthy ends is, one might go on to argue, also important.[6] Such a gloss on Hegel's claim

---

3 To be sure, Hegel also argues, contrary to the contractarian or natural right tradition, that our being capable of mutually recognizing each other as equally rights-bearing, morally responsible individuals is itself a *historical* achievement, that such claims are relevant to *modern* agents. He recognizes too what this will sound like, and hastens to try to show that he is not thereby "excusing" past injustices, as the important addition to *PR*, no. 3 makes clear.

4 The general purpose of Hegel's practical philosophy is to describe the conditions for the possibility of being a free subject, or of "agency," and the results of that account are (i) be a "person" and respect others as persons (don't violate another's rights; respect legitimate claims of non-interference, above all with respect to property); (ii) be a "subject"; or be morally responsible for what you do and regard others, all other human beings, as morally responsible beings; and (iii) be an ethical being; affirm and sustain certain ethical institutions. Or in the conventional language: act legally, act morally, act ethically; respect rights; do what is morally obligatory and what is ethically good.

5 This is from Hotho's *Zusatz* to no. 141. *GPR2*, p. 225; *PR*, p. 186. Right and morality are said to have *das Sittliche zum Träger, zur Grundlage*. For the original notes, see G. W. F. Hegel, *Vorlesungen über Rechtsphilosophie 1818–1831* (hereafter *VRP*), III, ed. by Karl-Heinz Ilting (Stuttgart: Frommann-Holzboog, 1974), p. 478.

6 I don't mean by this that Hegel has in mind by such collectivity a common attempt to bring about substantive benefits or goods. Ethical life in general is not what Oakeshott has called an "enterprise" association, but a "civil" association. Cf. Michael Oakeshott, "On the Character of a Modern European State," *On Human Conduct* (Oxford: Clarendon Press, 1975), pp. 257–63. The ends we pursue consist of the arrangements of our relations to each other such

for the priority of ethical life (as a distinctive but the most important "realm" of right, or actualized freedom) would not be wrong, but it would clearly be incomplete. Hegel also maintains that "the ethical" is the "support and foundation" of rights-based and moral sanctions, and that claim also needs to be justified. Hegel is indeed claiming that the human good consists in being actively related to others within certain institutions. But he is also claiming, even more controversially, that it is only in being so linked that the nature, implications, and bindingness of other sorts of normative claims can be fully made out. He is especially claiming that it is only in being so linked that I can actually *be* an individual, rights-bearing, morally responsible, and therewith free individual.[7]

Ethical life, then, these "laws and institutions which have being in and for themselves," comprises what is called the "objective sphere of ethics," which is said to "take the place of the abstract good" and so to constitute "the living good" for human beings.[8] Hence too the familiar question: Why does Hegel believe that such social interaction is so essential to the human good (freedom) and that it is the "basis and support" of all other aspects of a worthy life?

III

Despite the recent, brief popularity of a "communitarian" spirit in ethical theory, skepticism about such a position is so widespread it is difficult to classify its various forms. Many doubt that there is any such thing as "modern ethical life"; on the contrary, the most manifest fact about the institutions, norm-governed practices, and religions of late twentieth-century life is the impossibility (and the danger, the potential injustice) of any attempt to define some comprehensively inclusive category for all of them. Hetero-

---

that any end might be pursued in certain ethically appropriate ("self-chosen") ways. The point being made here is that even such a "civil" ethical end involves much more than rights protection and the avoidance of moral harm, or more than institutions that guarantee the former and take account of the latter. They require a kind of civic life or political culture. What that might consist in and why it is the "rational" support and foundation of all "right" are the issues in Hegel's *Rechtsphilosophie*.

7 His best known reasons in support of such a claim for the priority of ethical life have to do with a broad, systematically based animus against what he regards as merely "formal" or wholly "negative" normative principles. Those considerations are quite important but I shall be reconstructing a version of Hegel's case here without direct reliance on such logical issues.

8 No. 144; *PR*, p. 142; *PRE*, p. 189.

geneity, pluralism, the fractured subject, incommensurable paradigms and practices, mere fragments of old traditions, and so forth, are all we've got.[9]

But the most familiar suspicion is that, when all is said in done, the category of *Sittlichkeit,* as one of ethical assessment, terminates in some version of a "my station, its duties" ethics, finally conventionalist and far too reconciliationist, or insufficiently attentive to the importance of some ethical detachment, the worth of individuality as such, and critical reflection in modern moral life.[10]

The standard response to this latter doubt is equally familiar and is pertinent to the first concern as well. Hegel's famous interest in the actuality of our social lives as the original expression of "the living good" is just as famously a claim for the "rationality" of such actualities. Not any "station" or social function counts as genuine ethical life, and the decisive criterion is clearly expressed in the *PR*'s preface. We cannot be content, Hegel writes, to stop at what is merely given as public law and public morality,

> whether the latter is supported by the external positive authority of the state or of mutual agreement among human beings, or by the authority of inner feeling and the heart and by the testimony of the spirit which immediately concurs with this.[11]

The task is rather to grasp what is "rational" in such institutions, so that it "may also gain a rational form and thereby appear justified to free thinking." A modern social norm "demands to know itself as united in its innermost being with the truth."[12]

---

9 The claim is that there is not in fact such fragmentation, that modern institutions possess the authority they do (if and when they do) because all aspects of the realization of a common norm, "freedom," are obviously something that can only be shown, if it can, in terms of some general theory of modernity and modernization, and by appeal to a detailed assessment of such institutions. A defense of a Hegelian reading of the former issue is sketched in my *Modernism as a Philosophical Problem.*

10 The phrase is, of course, F. H. Bradley's, from his 1876 essay, "My Station and Its Duties," *Ethical Studies,* 2d ed. (Oxford: Oxford University Press, 1927), pp. 160 ff. Even in Bradley's case, however, it would be a mistake to neglect his own insistence on the "inner side" of morality, the importance of the proper relation between an individual and an institutional role in order for that role to count as *sittlich;* see pp. 177 and 179. Cf. also the similar sentiments in T. H. Green: "To ask why I am to submit to the power of the state, is to ask why I am to allow my life to be regulated by that complex of institutions without which I literally should not have a life to call my own, should not be able to ask for a justification of what I am called on to do." *Lectures on the Principles of Political Obligation* (Oxford: Oxford University Press, 1895), p. 122.

11 *PR,* pp. 5–6; *PRE,* p. 11.

12 Ibid.

It is more widely conceded now than it used to be that such a claim is not based on an a priori justification of whatever happens in history, at least if the justification is supposed to mean that everything is deducible or derivable with necessity from the unfoldings of some World Spirit. (This consensus has been strengthened recently by the edition and publication of Hegel's 1819–20 lecture notes, where the rationality of the actual is stated much more cautiously, without such theodocical implications.)[13]

This is a simple point but it needs to be vigorously stressed. In the *PR,* Hegel never argues for the rationality of modern institutions simply by describing them and then insisting that, whatever they are, they must be rational because we know a priori that history is rational. However one interprets and defends the claim that "history" has produced these rational institutions, one is independently committed to some interpretation and defense of the claim that they are rational. Indeed, unless we are able to describe independently in what sense such institutions *are* practically rational, any case that some process of historical change produced them or even had to produce them won't have accomplished very much. More generally, it is very hard to see how any theoretical claim about the rationality of history could count for me as a reason to act, as *my* reason to participate in the institution. Since Hegel believes there are reasons to act, we shall have to look elsewhere.[14]

But what else could it mean to suggest that modern institutions are rational, can be "justified to free thinking"? A natural assumption would be that Hegel means to affirm only those "laws and institutions" that are in

---

13 Cf. G. W. F. Hegel, *Philosophie des Rechts. Die Vorlesung von 1819/20 in einer Nachschrift,* ed. by Dieter Henrich (Frankfurt a.M.: Suhrkamp, 1983) (hereafter *VPRN*), p. 51, and Henrich's remarks, pp. 13–17. In the *Berlin Encyclopedia,* Hegel also describes objective spirit as a world not only "brought forth" by spirit, but "to be brought forth by it." *Enzyklopädie der philosophischen Wissenschaften III* in Hegel, *Werke: Theorie Werkausgabe* (Frankfurt a.M.: Suhrkamp, 1970), no. 385. Cf. the discussion by Wood, *Hegel's Ethical Thought,* pp. 10–11.

14 This is not at all to suggest that Hegel's account of historical change is hopeless, or that it plays no role in a full case for the rationality of modern institutions. The twin claims (i) that agents, by acting at all, are implicitly committed to the realization of freedom, and (ii) that when such a norm is unrealized, institutions and practices cannot be sustainable (that this normative failure is a good historical explanation of breakdown and transition) is worth more rigorous attention than it has been given. I am only claiming here that it would be a gross oversimplification to collapse or reduce all dimensions of Hegel's claim for the rationality of modern *Sittlichkeit* into a general claim about the rationality of history. As we shall see later, Hegel will come to link the possibility of a rational norm, as well as the "actuality" of such a norm (which I shall interpret as its possibly motivating force), with a historical narrative. But he is also out to show the inescapability of such a historical self-consciousness in any ethical account, and that transcendental case needs to be clarified and analyzed first.

some sense "what all participants would rationally will." Only thereby could such institutions actually comprise the "objective sphere of ethics." Modern institutions simply happen to meet such a criterion.

This response raises a problem. Hegel clearly does maintain that modern ethical life is rational and that one distinctive feature of modern ethical life is that this rationality is the basis of both the normative claims for allegiance implied by such institutions and the actual participation and continued allegiance of participants. In the modern "ethical world" it is "reason" (not tradition or sentiment or religion) that has actual, motivating "power and mastery"; the science of right will "conceive and present the state as something in itself rational." And, "In right, man must meet *with his own reason.*"[15]

Such passages, together with Hegel's spirited attacks on sentiment, or national feeling, and the like, in accounting for ethical and political allegiances, do appear to support the view that by calling modern ethical institutions rational, he is simply appealing to the widely shared modern notion that they are the institutions that any individual would will, were she to will rationally. This of course opens a familiar can of worms: What conditions specify what would be a truly rational willing? Given that we are only imperfectly rational, why is it unqualifiedly better to do what pure practical reason demands of us? But it also does not help much in our attempt to understand the "priority" of ethical life. In such readings, it is hypothetically rational individuals who seem prior, and ethical life a consequence. And this simply cannot be right.[16]

So, to prevent resting everything on some contractarian view of the rational will, or on the *List der Vernunft* thesis, we need to begin with Hegel's general theory of practical rationality, of what, for him, makes some consideration, desire, social convention, and so forth, a justified reason to act, and

15 My emphasis. The first two quotations are from the preface to the *PR*, *PR*, p. 7; *PRE*, p. 13; and *PR*, p. 15; *PRE*, p. 21. The last remark is from Hotho's additions, *VRP*, p. 96; *PR*, p. 14. And, for Hegel, modern man is said to "meet his own reason" in a particularly enthusiastic, affirmative way. Such an ethical world, presumably in its rationality, "is not something alien to the subject. On the contrary, the subject bears spiritual witness to them as to its own essence, in which it has its self-sentiment and lives as in its element which is not distinct from itself – a relationship which is immediate and closer to identity than even faith or trust" (no. 147; *PR*, p. 143; *PRE*, p. 191).

16 Moreover the enthusiastic passages which begin the last section of the *PR* do not appeal to what a subject would approve were she rational in some hyperidealized state of nature, but to what "modern subjects" actually "find" in modern "actual" ethical "self-consciousness": that is, "its own substantial being" (cf. nos. 146, 147). And then there are also the famous claims in the *PR*'s preface, that philosophy does not propose "a world beyond which exists God knows where," and that philosophy "must distance itself as far as possible from the obligation to construct a state as it ought to be." *PR*, pp. 14–15; *PRE*, pp. 20, 21.

then with a case showing that a commitment to and participation in modern social existence, the family based on personal love, modern market societies, and republican regimes are defensible, are rational, in that sense.

Clearly many who worry about Hegel's possible conventionalism or historicism or collectivism (or who think that is what we are left with when Hegel's implausible theodicy is jettisoned) worry directly about this problem. They worry about why "how we have come to go on about this or that" could count as a reason, not to mention an overriding, or ethical reason, for me to act or refrain from acting. And Hegel clearly owes such skeptics an answer.

IV

Hegel's responses to such questions involve much contested claims about individuality and personhood, and about reason in general. In any full account of his position, one would have to include and assess his claim that the characteristics that define any possible individuality, or the various ways persons could understand themselves to be "bounded off" from and distinct from others, are historically distinct possibilities, and are necessarily results of what he called a "struggle for mutual recognition." As both a phenomenological and a logical issue, Hegel's claim is that self-definition is necessarily self-definition in relation to and even in unavoidable struggle with an other, and that no account of such a possible relation and result can ignore the inevitable problem of power inherent in such a relation. We cannot figure out what it is rational for anyone to do by pretending that life begins with relatively self-transparent, self-owning, determinate, adult, self-sufficient individuals. The ultimate Hegelian claim is that the problem of self-definition or identity is a problem of social power, not metaphysical truth, and that this process has a certain "logic" to it, and it is a book-length topic in itself.

Also part of any full picture would have to be Hegel's denial that "being rational" (which he agrees is the foundation of any possible agency or freedom) involves only the proper use of a faculty or competence. To be rational in this ultimate sense is to "fit into" the rational structure of the whole, to live "in truth," in the light of how "things in the broadest sense of that term hang together in the broadest sense of that term."[17]

---

17 The phrase is of course Wilfrid Sellars's, not Hegel's. See "Philosophy and the Scientific Image of Man," *Science, Perception and Reality* (London: Routledge & Kegan Paul, 1963), p. 1. Cf. also the helpful remarks by Ludwig Siep, *Praktische Philosophie im deutschen Idealismus,*

But there are also a number of levels and strategies in Hegel's large *Encyclopedic* presentation, and it is possible to understand his defense of the claim for the priority of ethical life and the rationality of modern social institutions in more limited ways, ways that derive from his general account of practical rationality. As I've tried to suggest, if the question is Hegel's case for the "rationality and priority of ethical life," that case breaks down into two parts. What conditions must some consideration fulfill in order to count as a *norm* in human conduct (on the assumption that only norm-governed conduct is free)? Second, why does Hegel's version of ethical or social norms best fulfill such conditions? As we shall see, a great deal of the work necessary for answering the second question derives from fully answering the first.

Consider first the more limited question of what it is for human conduct to be governed by a *norm*. Now Hegel's theoretical approach to the question of freedom is different than Kant's,[18] but both agree that it is practically necessary that, when I act, I act "under the idea of freedom," as Kant put it.[19] (All this need mean for the moment is, I cannot act as if my acts were determined unless I determine that I shall, unless such a principle becomes my norm.) And for both, this requirement cannot be satisfied if I act arbitrarily or wantonly. If the act comes about because of my determining that it should, then I am acting for some reason or other, some reason that it should occur. I am acting under a self-imposed norm. For both, to be a free agent is not to be *subject to* various motivational forces, but to be the *subject of* one's deeds, and for both the crucial issue in the possibility of such subjectivity is the possibility of acting on considerations that could be justified to all, or acting on reasons. For Hegel, the question of the possibility of such a norm is the same as the conditions under which a principle or goal or claim could play some role in an agent's justification of, reasons for, an action (and so in any third-person explanation of the action).[20] As in many philo-

---

(Frankfurt am M.: Suhrkamp, 1992), p. 308, and my discussion in "Horstmann, Siep and German Idealism," *European Journal of Philosophy* 2, no. 1 (April 1994): 96.

18 See "Idealism and Agency in Kant and Hegel," *Journal of Philosophy* 88, no. 10 (October 1991): 532–41.

19 *F,* p. 66; *AA,* IV, p. 448. Cf. Henry Allison, "Morality and Freedom: Kant's Reciprocity Thesis," *Philosophical Review* 95, no. 3 (July 1986): 395–424; and Christine Korsgaard, "Morality as Freedom," in *Kant's Practical Philosophy Reconsidered,* ed. by Yirmiyahu Yovel (Dordrecht: Kluwer, 1989) pp. 23–48.

20 Cf. Bernard Williams, "Internal and External Reasons," in *Moral Luck,* (Cambridge: Cambridge University Press, 1981): "If there are reasons for action, it must be that people sometimes act for those reasons, and if they do, their reasons must figure in some correct explanation of their action," p. 102.

sophical accounts, if the question is an explanation of why some agent did what she did, or "what motivated agent A to ϕ," a necessary component of the answer has to be "what reasons justified the act for A." We need to know what A thought she was doing, and why she thought ϕ should be done, or we will not know what action is being performed.

Now this situation immediately gets complicated because there is obviously a difference between someone's own "personal reasons" (sometimes glossed as simply "motives") for doing something, and genuinely justifying "reasons."[21] (People still have "their own reasons" for acting even when they act against their own interests, or irrationally, or imprudently; when there is no good reason in any sense to do what they do.) But if we assume, as I think we should, that anyone's individual reasons for acting must fit into some overall structure of justification, or that no one could have reasons for acting that weren't regarded by him as sufficiently justifying, then we are entitled to look for the explicit or implicit justificatory claim implied in anyone's acting as he does. This is what it means to say that the actions presuppose a commitment to some norm. (For the moment we can remain neutral on whether such a norm could ultimately be wholly "subjective" or personal.)[22]

Of course there are philosophers who hold that this account of norms or reasons is already quite misleading since it suggests that moral prescriptions, or prudential reasons, or even beliefs of any kind *could* function as the principal origin or motivation for actions. By contrast, "desires," say, could be better said to motivate "on their own," and just by virtue of their having "motivating power," or by causally producing actions. Or, one might argue that normative principles like those discussed might be formulated, but they

21 This issue has played a large role in the many contemporary discussions of duties, reasons to act, and "motivation." Cf. W. D. Falk's exploration of the ambiguities in "pure" oughts, and "formal–motivational" considerations in "'Ought' and Motivation," *Ought, Reasons, and Morality* (Ithaca: Cornell University Press, 1986), pp. 21–41. The original "internalism" problem in moral theory – the connection (or lack of it) between what I am obliged to do, or what pure reason requires, or what the divine law stipulates, and, on the other hand, what *I have a reason to do* – also arises in the Kantian and post-Kantian moral–ethical tradition, although that connection is rarely discussed as such. A hint of such a possible link between the two traditions can be detected in Dieter Henrich's remarks about "Autonomie" and "Autognosie" in "Das Problem der Grundlegung der Ethik und im spekulativen Idealismus," in *Sein und Ethos,* ed. by P. Engelhardt (Mainz: Matthias Grünewald, 1963). Cf. chapter 4, this volume.
22 Compare the controversial denial that they could be, by Thomas Nagel, *The Possibility of Altruism* (Princeton: Princeton University Press, 1970), chs. 10–13. And see his qualification and, to some extent, withdrawal of such a claim in *The View from Nowhere* (Oxford: Oxford University Press, 1986), p. 159.

could not play any role on their own in bringing about an action, not unless coupled with, or made relevant to an action, by a desire, ultimately an unmotivated desire.[23]

   This is one of many contentious issues that will arise, but for now we need only note that Hegel is not a partisan of such claims. He clearly considers it a condition on some event's being an action that it is norm-governed, that it is motivated by some consideration taken to justify the action. And he clearly believes that such norms need not and cannot be restricted to merely instrumental, prudential or "hypothetical imperatives."[24] Indeed the extent to which an agent can give and be motivated to act on reasons that do justify his action is the extent to which the action is free; or the extent to which someone could be said to have freely gone to a philosophy talk is not a matter of his having gone voluntarily, as a result of his own desires, without compulsion, but the extent to which he understood why he was there (including why he desired to go, what motivated his desire), or what norm governed his going, why he thought it better to go than not, and so on.[25]

---

23 Or one might count reasons as factors in psychological explanation, but as causes, mental states (beliefs) that, together with desires, explain action. Cf. Donald Davidson, "Actions, Reasons, and Causes," *Essays on Action and Events* (Oxford: Oxford University Press, 1980), pp. 3–20. This would, though, be, in effect, *not* to count such states as *reasons*, considerations whose motivational force depends on a complex of justificatory issues, or that cannot motivate by occurring, but only by fitting, in the right way, into the "space of reasons."
   The question, in other words, of how to explain the differing situations (i) an agent has reason to φ, and φ's and (ii) an agent has reason to φ, and does not φ, does not turn on (A) understanding how reasons were, contingently, causes in (i) and not in (ii), nor (B) on externalist accounts, because normative and motivational questions are stricly distinct, but (C) on some account that establishes (iii) that an agent for whom it is rational to φ could not but be motivated to φ and (iv) his not φ-ing must be the result of some "blocking" or "distorting" phenomena, or in Hegel's case, because of the particularity and incompleteness of the social conditions that would make possible the motivational effectiveness of such reasons. Accepting this requirement is what is involved in claiming that, in modernity, the rational, or *vernünftig*, is *wirklich*, what might be best translated as "effective," motivating, given the root in "wirken." Cf. Robert Derathé's translation, "Ce qui est rationnel est effectif," *Principes de la philosophie du droit* (Paris: Vrin, 1982), p. 55. Hyppolite's translation is the same.

24 For a discussion of how Hegel argues for the claim that any "natural will" (or any policy that seeks only to satisfy natural inclinations) itself commits a subject to a "fully free" or rational will (ultimately understood as embodied in collectively self-forming institutions), see Chapter 4, this volume. For a discussion of Hegel's objections to prudential notions of rationality, see my "You Can't Get There from Here: Transition Problems in Hegel's *Phenomenology of Spirit*," in *Cambridge Companion to Hegel*, ed. by Fred Beiser (Cambridge: Cambridge University Press, 1993), pp. 52–85.

25 To anticipate the entire conclusion of this discussion: The conditions under which this could occur, and so under which you could truly be a self-determining rights-bearer or morally responsible subject, are the social conditions that make possible this self-

The question of freedom in Hegel is not a question about what factor actually caused the action (a desire, or respect for the moral law, and so forth), but it is a question about the character and quality of the reasons that justify the action for you.[26] (There are thus wide "degrees" of freedom in Hegel's roughly compatibilist theory.)

To return to the general point, Hegel is quite explicit about a number of conditions necessary for a norm to be a norm in this sense. For example, for something to function as a norm, it must be *self-imposed*, even if, ultimately, in some way collectively self-imposed. In one sense, his theory of "objective spirit" is just an account of the possibility of those human activities and interactions that are what they are *because* constrained by such self-imposed norms in certain ways, constituted by such self-conscious norm following. An action *is* the fulfillment of a contract, the punishment of a criminal, a promising, an inheriting, and so forth, only because the participants in the relevant institutions "take themselves" to be participating in institutions governed by certain rules, and view these rules as in some sense justifiable. Said more speculatively, human beings are "in themselves" what they are "for themselves," or are collectively self-forming creatures. (This has nothing to do with what they individually believe, or the contents of their mental history. Such self-construals can be implicit, dispositional, revealed more in deeds than statements, and so forth. But that is another story.) The main point is, Were individuals to perform the same body movements without taking themselves to be following such norms, or if they took themselves to be conforming to other norms, the actions would not be those actions.

Stated perhaps more directly: There are and can be no straightforwardly "natural" or "divine" norms, no facts about the natural world, or revelations about God's will, or intuition of non-natural properties, that, just by *being* such facts or revelations, thereby constrain or direct my conduct. They could be norms only if they could count as reasons for me to act, and nothing about what nature is like or what God said, and so on, can show that.[27]

V

So, for Hegel, to act freely is to act under norms; this means to act on considerations taken to have justifying force; these norms must be self-

knowledge and rational action, and are not metaphysical or natural conditions.

26 Cf. the *Zusatz* to no. 15 in the *PR*. Allen Wood's discussion of this point in Hegel is among the best in his book; *Hegel's Ethical Thought*, ch. 2.

27 *Die Rechtgesetze sind Gesetzte, herkommend von Menschen* ("Laws of right are posited, made, something stemming from human being"), *VRP*, p. 93.

imposed, or must count as reasons *to or for* me, must actually motivate my action.[28] Before we move on to the issue of participation in ethical life as a condition of such a possibility, we should note that Hegel of course expresses what I have just said in his own language. Early in his philosophical career at Jena, in one of his first sustained treatments of "ethical life," an untitled work later called *System der Sittlichkeit* by editors (1802 or 1803), he returns to this sort of point over and over again, although the notions of fact and self-conscious self-imposition are often somewhat artificially forced into the language of intuition and concept, feeling and rational principle, nature and spirit. Here is a typical example.

In explaining what genuinely ethical relations comprise, Hegel tries to diminish the status or significance of relations perceived to be merely natural, or putatively a direct result of natural inclinations and desires. Ethical relations involve a "freedom" from such sorts of attachments, even their "cancellation." This is so because "absolute nature" as such does not "occur in a spiritual shape."

> Ethical life must be the absolute identity of intelligence, with complete annihilation of the particularity and relative identity which is all that the natural relation is capable of; or the absolute identity of nature *must be taken up into* the unity of the absolute concept and be present in the form of this unity. (My emphasis)[29]

The same point is made somewhat more straightforwardly in the philosophical psychology sketched in the Introduction to the *PR*. Instead of talking about what is "taken up into the unity of the absolute concept," Hegel discusses such a "taking up" in more directly psychological and motivational language, as he denies the possibility that, in self-conscious beings,

---

28 I mean "motivate" just in the sense of "must be capable of being the reasons I act on," not in the sense of "causally produce."

29 *System der Sittlichkeit*, ed. by G. Lasson (Hamburg: Felix Meiner Verlag, 1923), p. 460; *System of Ethical Life and First Philosophy of Spirit*, ed. and trans. by H. S. Harris and T. M. Knox (Albany: SUNY Press, 1979), p. 142. This passage goes on to talk about this ethical life, understood "conceptually" or self-consciously, as the "supersession of the natural determinacy and formation" of the natural individual, and so a "complete indifference of self-enjoyment." But this refers to the self-effacement of the natural or sensuous individual and should not be confused with a general anti-individualism. Cf. an earlier passage, for example: "Absolute ethical life cancels the individual's subjectivity by nullifying it only as an ideal determinacy, as an antithesis, but it lets his subjective essence persist quite unaffected. And he is allowed to persist, and is made real, as subject, precisely because his essence is left undisturbed as it is. In ethical life intelligence remains a subjectivity of this kind" (pp. 448; 131). It is this last sort of phrase that I am glossing as, Ethical norms count as reasons for an individual; they are motivating, and not just insofar as he has a rational will.

it could ever be true that an action was produced or caused by any desire or impulse, or any sort of mental state for that matter.

> The animal, too, has drives, desires and inclinations, but it has no will and must obey its drives if nothing external prevents it. But the human being as wholly indeterminate, stands above his drives and can determine and posit them as its own. The drive is part of nature, but to posit it in this "I" depends upon my will, which therefore cannot appeal to the fact that the drive is grounded in nature.[30]

(It is important to note here that when Hegel discusses why animals are not "free," he does not mention the issues of determinism and voluntarism. An animal is not free because "it does not represent to itself what it desires."[31] The character of the self-conscious relation of the doer to the deed is what is crucial, not the causal relation.)

He does not deny that an important component of someone's reasons for acting might indeed be some strong desire, but he does deny that the desire could play such a role just by occurring and having some causal force. The language he uses to make this point is striking. A desire must be "purified" if it is to play a motivational role "for me." That is, such desires

> must be freed from the *form* of their immediate natural determinacy, and from the subjectivity and contingency of their *content*, and restored to their substantial essence. The truth behind this indeterminate demand is that the drives should become the rational system of the will's determination; to grasp them thus in terms of the concept is the content of the science of right.[32]

Now, since the "content of the science of right" is argued to culminate necessarily in the structures of ethical life or a social existence, this all basically means that the claim just quoted must play a crucial role in justifying the "priority of ethical life" claim. Hegel, as I have presented him, is

---

30 *PR* 2, p. 64; *PRE*, p. 45.
31 *PR* 2, p. 52; *PRE*, p. 36.
32 *PR*, p. 39; *PRE*, p. 51. The same sorts of claims are made both in this work and in the much better known 1807 *Phenomenology of Spirit* about the very "first" manifestations of spirit. There a situation of some matter-of-fact superior power and possible coercion is distinguished from the normative status of master and slave relations. In this case, Hegel tries to distinguish between the ways in which a certain consideration, here the anticipation of my possible death in a struggle with another over prestige, might function as a causally effective impulse, "naturally" (with the outcome of the struggle fundamentally a matter of strength and psychological characteristics), and where such anticipations function for the subjects as norms, or motivating reasons, and the outcome is thus itself normative, a relation of masters and slaves, not simply stronger and weaker, victors and losers.

clearly making a number of Kantian assumptions. He too assumes that human beings can only act if they act "under the idea of freedom," that it is practically impossible to act as if we were determined. This means for him too that our actions presuppose the adoption or self-imposition of general principles (norms, maxims), even if for the most part in daily life, we just execute the norms we take for granted. And this also gets him to the question of what considerations could be relevant to the adoption of such norms, consistent with the practical requirement of regarding ourselves as free agents. So, the issue of "what could coherently count as a justifying reason for an action" is playing a large role in answering the question, Why does Hegel view the authoritative force of norms as dependent on social practices and institutions? The idea seems to be that the crucial condition for any consideration functioning as the coherent, effective norm for any free agent is a social condition, the existence of and involvement in certain social institutions. Or Kant thought such a condition for a fully justifying principle (and so a fully free act) could be satisfied only by one *kind* of formal principle. Kant's great worry was to show that considerations based on the satisfaction of desires could not be the only or fundamental norms that a free agent must adopt. Hegel is not, I think, disagreeing with such a claim, as much as he is disagreeing with the implications Kant draws from it, and with what Kant contrasts with such a possibility. He argues that Kant's moral principle (adopt *lawfulness itself* as your norm) does not satisfy Kant's own condition and tries to show why his (Hegel's) social arrangements do.[33]

VI

The reference to Kant also brings to mind what Hegel appears to regard as a more ambitious claim. So far all we know is that actions are those events that are explicable by reference to a subject's reasons for acting, that such rea-

---

33 Clearly, larger issues also loom between Kant and Hegel. If it is finally true that one is only truly free in "being recognized by another," or within certain sorts of social institutions, Kant would want to know how we should describe the poor fellow who must live unrecognized. Is he not still free, indeed still autonomous, however difficult and miserable his existence might be? That is, in one sense, Kant claims that autonomy is simply constitutive of human (noumenal) nature, eternally, for everyone, at any time, full stop. However, if that were the whole, rigoristic Kantian story, the philosophies of religion, history, politics, education would have to be extraordinarily marginalized. Or: it would clearly be a mistake to regard Kant's moral enterprise as exhausted by a theory of obligation. There *is* some theory of the good, even of the "whole" within which this good could make sense as a good, in Kant's philosophy. Hegel and many post-Kantians are clearly more interested in the latter elements.

sons always presuppose certain norms for action, and that such norms can be norms only as self-imposed, and so cannot be understood in what has come to be called some strictly "externalist" sense.[34] What we have said so far, though, is still compatible with someone's acting because he wanted to very strongly, and because his general norm, which he feels to be justifiable, is to do whatever he most feels like doing.

Now, as indicated, Kant famously argued that this sort of norm *could* not be fully self-imposed or ultimately justifying because such a subscription must itself be motivated by considerations not fully self-imposed, dispositions and desires true as a matter of fact of the individual, and that Kant called constitutive only of heteronomy, not autonomy. Only one sort of norm could be self-imposed and universally justifiable and so could constitute what it is for an act to be rationally motivated, and so freely performed: his famous categorical imperative.

Hegel's objections to this possibility reveal this other dimension of his account of practical rationality. He objects, that is, to the claim that an action is fully justifiable to all others, and so morally worthy, only if it is governed by a certain kind of norm, the categorical imperative. On the Kantian account, this means that an action is morally worthy only if performed "from duty alone," or only if I act in recognition of and am motivated by the bindingness of this norm. If I act because I fear for my reputation, or I want to secure my individual well-being, or I desire to satisfy an emotional need to act benevolently, I might end up doing what a purely rational agent would do because of the constraints of universal justifiability, but I get no moral credit. In such a case, my reasons for action, what Kant calls my maxim, express a principle that I have no reason to expect that others could share, or also find justifying, or could only expect them to

---

34 In Williams's formulation: "The whole point of external reasons statements is that they can be true independently of the agent's motivations." "Internal and External Reasons," p. 107. His example there is from a James story: Owen Wingrave's father insists that Owen has a reason to join the military even if Owen has no motivation to do so, his desires all lead in other directions, and he hates everything about military life and what it means. Very few philosophers have tried to affirm that there are external reasons in *this* sense. (In fact, as Williams himself seems to acknowledge, this is a strange example since it is very unlikely that Wingrave really *has* any good reason to give his son, one that could stand up to any scrutiny. The reason *this* isn't an external reason is, very likely, not because there are no such reasons, but because this is a bad one.) The rationalist response is usually to try to show that various considerations can meet the internalist constraint without being "relativized" to some existing, contingent "motivational set." In the recent literature, this response is common to Nagel and Korsgaard despite their differences. It is also common to Kant and Hegel, I am claiming, and the point then is to see how they differ on what *could not* be unmotivating, a matter of indifference.

share under contingent circumstances. (They just happen to want what I want, or fear what I fear, and so on.) I thus could not expect my reasons to act to count as reasons for him.

Hegel claims first that the categorical imperative, or the general principle to do only what all other rational agents could will to do, cannot be action guiding because so formal. It fails, as a norm, to rule in or rule out, with sufficient determinacy, kinds of actions or policies. It is empty.

I am not concerned with that objection here. But Hegel also claims that the criterion of moral worth is rigoristic, that no one could act as Kant demands. And that claim brings out what seem to be Hegel's implicit assumptions about the conditions under which *a principle could serve as a norm*, and so should point the way to the most important issues in his theory of the rationality of ethical life. That is, since we have been searching for the considerations that led Hegel to the view that the social norms of ethical life fulfill paradigmatically the conditions of rational agency, these objections to Kantian rigorism should reveal a great deal.

There are two loci classici for such claims, one in chapter 6 of the *Phenomenology of Spirit*, the other in the account of the moral point of view in the *PR*. In the former, Hegel argues that Kant's own moral system reveals that he himself acknowledges that

> the moral consciousness cannot forego happiness and leave this element out of its absolute purpose. The purpose, which is expressed as pure duty, essentially implies this individual self-consciousness; individual conviction and the knowledge of it constitute an absolute element in morality.[35]

But, Hegel argues, Kant's response to this recognition of the inevitably interested and individual character of our relation to any principle of action is, on the one hand, to condemn us as radically evil, incapable of ever fully realizing, but only at best striving for, what reason demands, and, on the other hand, to concede that human beings could not sustain the moral enterprise, could not fully make sense of its demands, unless it were also possible to believe in an all powerful moral judge, an immortal soul, and eternal reward and punishment.

This condemnation of our unworthiness and this concession about "postulates" reveal, according to Hegel, that in such a point of view, we are not "serious" about what morality requires, we "dissemble," or shift inconsistently from what we say we are requiring of ourselves, to what we concede we

35 *PhG*, p. 326; *PhS*, p. 366.

are able to do, and so we promote a kind of hypocrisy, a feature of Christian moralism that Hegel considers essential to it, not incidental.[36] "Duty for duty's sake," Hegel charges,

> is an unreality; it becomes a reality in the deed of an individuality, and the action is thereby charged with the aspect of particularity. No man is a hero to his valet; not, however, because the man is not a hero, but because the valet is – a valet, whose dealings are with the man, not as a hero, but as one who eats, drinks, and wears clothes, in general, with his individual wants and fancies. Thus, for the judging consciousness, there is no action in which it could not oppose to the universal aspect of the action, the personal aspect of the individuality, and play the part of the moral valet towards the agent.[37]

Clearly Hegel's proposition is that playing the role of this moralistic valet is pointless, that there is no point in formulating a view of the right that could not count for any real individual as a reason to act, and the same sort of point is made frequently in the discussion of morality in the *PR*. As in the claim,

> since the subjective satisfaction of the individual himself . . . is also to be found in the implementation of ends which are valid in and of themselves, it is an empty assertion of the abstract understanding to require that only an end of this kind shall appear willed and attained, and likewise to take the view that, in volition, objective and subjective ends are mutually exclusive.[38]

Hegel even thinks the moralist needs reminding that

> there is nothing degrading about being alive, and we do not have the alternative of existing in a higher spirituality. It is only by raising what is present and given to a self-creating process that the higher sphere of the good is attained.[39]

And finally:

> The right of the subject's particularity to find satisfaction or – to put it differently – the right of subjective freedom, is the pivotal and focal point in the difference between antiquity and the modern age. This right, in its infinity,

36 *PhG*, p. 334; *PhS*, pp. 376–7.
37 *PhG*, p. 358; *PhS*, p. 404.
38 *PR*, p. 112; *PRE*, p. 151.
39 *GPR2*, pp. 181–2; *PRE*, p. 151.

is expressed in Christianity, and it has become the universal and actual principle of a new form of the world.[40]

I am not here concerned with the obvious problem of whether all of this amounts to a fair criticism of Kant. One might dispute whether Kant's position relies on the postulates in the way Hegel claims, and one might insist that nothing Hegel says undermines Kant's considered or full argument to establish how pure practical reason can motivate action (perhaps, chapter 3 of part 1 of the *Critique of Practical Reason*). I want to focus attention only on what these remarks reveal about Hegel's own position and the general structure of his reasoning in support of it.

This is especially important because there are two different ways of drawing implications from these sorts of considerations, and Hegel's formulations often suggest what I think is the most misleading and ultimately un-Hegelian. On one interpretation, what Hegel is saying is that human actions can be shown to presuppose a certain motivational structure and that once we understand these constraints, we will be able to see that no recognition of what practical reason requires of us could fit such constraints, no consideration of what an impartial agent, motivated by no motives particular to him, would do, could ever be on its own a motivating factor in action. Presumably, we can show that human beings could only be motivated by desire for their own happiness and well-being, and so could be motivated to subscribe to norms only on this condition. On this reading, if the standard for a justifiable reason is a principle that makes no reference to any particular desires or ends; and the question is, Why should I care about such a principle? How could I come to see such a view of a purely rational agent *as a reason for me to act?* the answer is, I could not. Kant's own fuller position, so goes such a reading, shows this, since he concedes we could not, and either reminds us that we just are radically evil, or looks around for motivational support for that which could not on its own motivate (the "postulates").

This sort of an objection is a familiar one in attacks on rationalist conceptions of ethics and is most familiar in Hume's attacks on the possibility of any practical rationality. If we see Hegel's attacks on Kant in this light, and keep in mind our question about sociality, then Hegel begins to emerge, somewhat surprisingly, as sympathetic to these Humean concerns, but as substituting a kind of historical sociology for Hume's naturalistic psychology, in accounting for the true wellsprings of human motivation. It is our

40 PR, p. 112; *PRE*, p. 151. More poetically put: "The laurels of pure willing are dry leaves which have never been green." *PR2*, 184; *PhR*, 153.

affective and emotional dispositions, or our basic interest in our own well-being, that motivate what we do, but we are far more malleable than Hume realized. We can come to understand our own much-desired happiness in certain ways, by seeing our well-being as essentially linked to others, and so by subscribing to norms that others could fully share, but all this only in certain sorts of societies, with certain sorts of socially formative, desire-shaping institutions.))

As we have been seeing throughout, however, this *cannot* be the right conclusion to draw from Hegel's attack on Kant's rigorism. He is manifestly a rationalist in ethics and stresses this himself even when criticizing the moral point of view.

> The assertion that human beings cannot know the truth, but have to do only with appearances, or that thought is harmful to the good will and other similar notions, deprive the spirit both of all intellectual and of all ethical worth and dignity. – The right to recognize nothing that I do not perceive as rational is the highest right of the subject, but by virtue of its subjective determination, it is at the same time, formal; on the other hand, the right of the rational – as the objective – over the subject, remains firmly established.[41]

This must mean, contrary to the obvious readings, that Hegel is not denying that rational considerations can be motivating on their own (can count for an agent as reasons), or that *any* position that maintains this is positivistic or rigoristic. He must be objecting to the *kinds* of rational considerations that Kant thinks are compelling. (In other words, the claim is that it is Kant's version of an unconditionally overriding or categorical imperative, or his own formulation of an exclusive and singular principle of free action, that creates the rigoristic dualism between my core or autonomous self and the entirety of my contingent attachments. The appearance Hegel creates, that he is celebrating what Kant is decrying, self-love, hedonism, egoistic motivation, is what is misleading. Ultimately, Hegel is objecting to this characterization of non-moral motivation.)

Yet the results thus far are still puzzling. As we have seen, whatever Hegel believes about the content of norms, they are not binding simply because of who we are and what we happen to desire, or who we have become historically, and so because of what we cannot, as a matter of fact, help but esteem, but, still, they are binding because of what it is rational to esteem. Yet when Kant demands that we subscribe to norms that can be rationally self-

41 *PR*, p. 117; *PRE*, p. 159.

imposed, norms that are even abstractly "social" (in all acts we must take the other into account, as in the idealized Kingdom of Ends), Hegel complains that Kant is hard-hearted, ascetic, and that his account could not explain how we could be motivated to act on such principles, could count the categorical imperative as a reason to act.[42]

VII

Hegel is clearly no anti-rationalist, "whatever-my-community-says is-OK" conventionalist. To understand his case for this better, we need to put the passages we have been quoting into some sort of perspective. That is, we need to recall some classificatory issues. As the passages we have been quoting indicate, Hegel clearly believes that the possibility of motivation is a crucial condition for a norm's possible status as a norm. He does not, that is, believe that some consideration could count as a norm, and so a compelling reason for me to act, even if it could be shown that I could never act on such a reason. Indeed, this is the very sort of language he uses to introduce his notion of ethical life. He claims that it is "in ethical existence" (*an dem sittlichen Sein*) that self-consciousness has its "basis in and for itself" *and* its motivating purpose (*bewegenden Zweck*).[43]

Moreover, if he did not believe in this tight connection between a norm and its motivating force, there would be no point to his criticisms of Kant's rigorism. Kant could simply respond, Look, this is what we are supposed to do, full stop. The fact that we are so weak and so inclined to prefer our own case, that we cannot ever do what we are supposed to do, that we need so much motivational and religious help has nothing to do with *what we are supposed to do*. (I should note that Kant does sometimes sound like this. He is, after all, famous for claiming that nothing straight could ever grow from so crooked a timber as man. And, as just noted, Hegel's rejoinders can, in that spirit, sound as if he is simply approving rather than regretting the need for such motivational help. But this is not Kant's position and not central to

---

42 This means that the dispute between them does not concern a difference between Hegel's doctrine of "internal reasons" and Kant's commitment to a theory of psychological causation, as Wood claims, *Hegel's Ethical Thought*. I agree that Hegel believes in the possibility of motivational overdetermination for an action, and does not think moral worth could require the isolation of some "pure motive." But I don't think the reasons he believes this and why he objects to Kant's theory of moral worth have to do with views about reasons and causes in Kant. I agree here with Henry Allison's statement of Kant's own commitment to internal reasons, *Kant's Theory of Freedom* (Cambridge: Cambridge University Press, 1991), p. 189.

43 *PR*, p. 142; *PRE*, p. 189.

Hegel's objections. Kant does not believe that rational considerations cannot at all be motivating, or that that issue is irrelevant to such considerations' being reasons to act. In fact it is crucial to his case for the "possibility
of pure practical reason" that they can be motivating. But the fact that such
a principle "cannot but be motivating" does not mean it is decisive or
overriding, and in the weighing of considerations, we are always inclined to
allow other considerations more weight than would be justified.)[44]

Now it is not clear that anyone in the history of philosophy ever held a
completely externalist view of norms,[45] but someone who believed that we
ought to do God's revealed will because it was God's will, and also believed
that, because of our fallen natures, a consideration of God's will alone could
never motivate us to act (but that we still ought to; that the norm was
binding), would count. (In fact, one of the first indications of the importance to Hegel of the motivational aspects of any norm is his own investigation of the "positivity" of the Christian religion. Positivity in this sense, or
some disconnection with what could be motivating for a subject, is already
thereby an *objection* to the norm.) Sometimes J. S. Mill and G. E. Moore are
also named as philosophers who believe in some theory of the right and
good, independently of having to show why we would ever want or be
motivated to do the right or to promote the good.[46]

But, again, regardless of the complexities of this post-Humean controversy, the point to take our bearings from is simply that Hegel is manifestly on the other side. He accepts as a general constraint on the possibility
of a norm the principle P:

> For some fact, or state, or consideration to be able to count as a reason for S to
> do A, S's acceptance of, or having of, such a consideration must be able to
> motivate him to do A.[47]

Hegel's broad acceptance of such a principle is important to note for a
number of reasons, not the least of which are those that concern his influ-

---

44 Cf. Nagel, *Possibility of Altruism*, pp. 11–12, and the comments by Christine Korsgaard,
   "Skepticism About Practical Reason," pp. 10, 23–4. For a full treatment of Kant's views,
   especially on his earlier and later positions, see Henry Allison, *Kant's Theory of Freedom*, ch. 3.
45 Korsgaard, "Skepticism," p. 23.
46 Cf. Nagel, *The Possibility of Altruism*, ch. 2. See also W. K. Frankena, "Obligation and Motivation in Recent Moral Philosophy," in *Essays in Moral Philosophy*, ed. by A. Melden (Seattle:
   University of Washington Press, 1958), pp. 40–81.
47 This acceptance is the import, I take it, of the passages from *PR* quoted previously, as well as
   no. 132.

ence. For example, to conceive of an ethical community as "alienated," not "reconciled" to their own community's norms, is a kind of social criticism that presupposes an enthusiastic acceptance of such a criterion. It is possible to disregard the problem of alienation as an ethical problem; the fact that people do not "find themselves at home" in their own practices could simply be their fault, not the fault of the norms, all because of the corruption and irrationality of the human species. Why should anyone be surprised that we are alienated from ethical norms? To take this principle (P) seriously is to argue that at some level, a deep and persistent alienation *is* evidence that there is something wrong with the norm, that there is evidence that it *could* not be motivating, and in that sense *could not count as norm.*

But as noted, such a principle is most common in anti-rationalist and skeptical accounts. Philosophers who accept P are often Humeans, moral sense theorists, egoists, and emotivists. Given this, it can appear that the general debate is between those who, on the one hand, want to keep ethical considerations pure by keeping them strictly normative. The good *is* simply, say, the greatest happiness for the greatest number, even if the best of human beings, because of their selfishness and irrationality, could never act for the sake of such a good, or the good is some non-natural property in the world that we can apprehend, but could bring ourselves to realize and promote only if prompted by some view of our own self-interest. On the other side are those who find it hard to understand any view of the human good, or moral value, that was not originally oriented from some consideration of what human beings want and need, or oriented from what would have to be compelling reasons for persons to act. The former camp worries that we are thereby trimming our ethical norms to fit our most common natures; the latter worries that we are spinning tales of ethical perfection that not only take no account of our common humanity, but betray a kind of ascetic hostility to it.[48]

But this would all be too narrow a way of viewing the categories. As we have been seeing, plenty of rationalists in ethics believe in P and would never concede that they have trimmed their moral sails to fit our corrupt needs. Kant is one, and Hegel is another.[49] It would be a long digression to

[48] Cf. the concluding remarks of Frankena, "Obligation and Motivation," p. 81.
[49] Indeed, it is possible to be an objectivist of some sort and still accept it. One could hold that perceiving the world in a certain way *is* thereby already motivating, that discerning the morally salient features of a situation or possible goal thereby gives one an unavoidable

explore theses options in any detail. But it should at least be noted that, in the case of Hegel, one result of viewing the matter from this perspective is that it now helps clarify his famous denial that normative theory is about what merely ought to be, and so his celebration of the rationality of the actual. We can now see, I hope, that what is important in such formulations is what he is denying: that rational, normative principles could be considered norms apart from any demonstration of how and why they could be actual reasons for persons to act, or that some inspection of a quality or a good could function as a norm apart from such a demonstration of my "taking it up" and justifying "imposing" it on myself as a norm. To say that the rational is actual is just to say that some reasons *could not but be motivating;* that no person could be presumed to be "actually" indifferent to what they require. And to make such a claim is to attack any view of moral theory (e.g., many religious views) that ignores such a consideration.

So, finally, the decisive question is why Hegel believes *this,* a question that is one of the two decisive ones in our inquiry. The other is why he thinks only his version of "ethical norms" could satisfy this condition.[50]

motivation to act. One would accept the constraint suggested by P, but argue that it is a mistake to separate such moral discernment from, as a separate question, "what does the motivating" when I proceed to act on such perception. There is no way I could come to see it that way and experience any motivational gap. If I did, that would be good evidence that I hadn't seen what was there to see. (Irrationality is in the perceiving, or what clouds the perceiving, not in the willing or strength of will.)

50 As we have also already noted in the case of Hegel, the preferability of one course of action over another, or all "value," is something conferred, not discovered. A principle or goal can function as a norm, governing my evaluation of possible actions, only if self-imposed, a claim that forces the issue back to the conditions for a genuine self-imposition, or a truly justifiable valuing. (On this conception, that is, finding something valuable is not justified by being able to point to an inherently valuable quality of the thing, in the world, but by having reasons for the estimating or esteeming that do not rely on some consideration that is beyond justification or merely "given.") Just as in Kant, this in turn raises for Hegel the question of the relation between what, prima facie, might seem to be merely my own reasons for acting, reasons relevant just to me and my situation, or subjective reasons, and the general considerations I must appeal to in justifying those reasons to myself, or, ultimately, objective reasons.

That Hegel has this view of the problem in mind is signaled everywhere by the terms we have already quoted, and in many other places. He objects to what he regards as a Kantian opposition between subjective, or heteronomously determined, ends and objective, or autonomously determined, ends, implying that such objectivity is ultimately a condition of the justifying power of any consideration. He speaks metaphorically of our having to "take up" what is subjectively and contingently compelling, and "purify" it, "raising it up" to a level of "self-creating" "infinity" wherein our "subjective right of satisfaction" is completed in "rationality" itself, and so on.

These views, all of them shifting the question of the rationality of norms to questions of justifiability, and the relation between subjective and objective reasons raise their own

VIII

The most general result of trying to view Hegel as a rationalist can now be formulated. In a phrase, Hegel's concerns are, manifestly, not Schiller's. He is not portraying the problem as *primarily* one of psychic harmony, integration, or an inner alienation, as if what is originally wrong with the moral point of view is that it requires me to detach myself from all that I have come to care about, all that makes me "me." The question he is raising, *together* with Kant, is whether what you have come to care about really does reflect "you" as a *subject,* or it is about the conditions of *attachment* in the first place, such that these attachments truly reflect your subjectivity.[51] Kant thinks this is so if they pass the test of moral permissibility, are at least not logically *contrary* to what a spontaneous will could legislate. Hegel thinks that this an excessively limiting and unsatisfying view, and that the norms you must be committed to, such that any such attachments could come to reflect you and your subjectivity (such that you could be acting "under the idea of freedom"), involve social and institutional conditions wherein you can "meet with" your own reason.

The decisive issue his case, read this way, turns on is quite a general consideration. As we have seen, Hegel's interest in the role of motivational possibility in ethical theory does not amount to a claim that we must find room for hedonic or egoistic concerns in order to explain such motivation. He accepts the normative link between justification and autonomy, and then begins to look for some account of a *kind* of justification that would explain "*its* own" motivational force.[52] In his somewhat romantic language, finding such a consideration, one that does not *need* extrarational support,

problems. For one thing, such approaches tend to "oversolve" the problem and tend to treat all subjective reasons as reasons only if finally objective, thus grossly undervaluing the personal, or agent-centered, point of view. But at issue now is a final clarification of how Hegel's position on *Sittlichkeit* looks in the light of these considerations.

51 More generally, this is the problem with all "Humeanism" in ethics, or with any inclination to treat my "passions," desires, ground projects, or motivational set as a basic reason to act. Such a position must take account of the possibility, and ultimately the priority, of "motivated," or rationally induced, desires, not just "unmotivated desires." For a useful discussions of this version of the isssues, see R. Jay Wallace, "How to Argue About Practical Reason," *Mind* 99 (July, 1990): 355–85; Rachel Cohon, "Hume and Humeanism in Ethics," *Pacific Philosophical Quarterly* 69 (1988): 99–116; Michael Smith, "The Humean Theory of Motivation," *Mind* 96 (1987): 36–61; Philip Petit, "Humeans, Anti-Humeans, and Motivation," *Mind* 96 (1987): 531–3; Michael Smith, "On Humeans, Anti-Humeans, and Motivation: A Reply to Petit," *Mind* 98 (1988): 589–95.

52 "The subject is in its home; in that which is objective, it is in its element." *VPRN,* 122.

ensures that we have found "ourselves," that freedom as *bei sich selbst sein,* "being-with-self," can be assured. Like many others, his account comes down to what reasons could be given by a rationalist, or for that matter, by any "internalist," in satisfying such a motivational constraint.

This issue is complicated in Kant's case by the fact that the question of practical rationality is a question of imperatives, not "reasons" to act in the general sense. So what reason recognizes in Kant is that we stand unavoidably under a universal moral law, a requirement that we must act in a certain way. We experience the "fact of reason," that by acting intentionally at all we are bound by such a norm. (He then goes on to show what happens to us sensibly in recognizing this obligation, how we come to feel the pain of denying the priority of self-love and the esteem he calls "respect.") But it is in showing *that there is this obligation* that Kant, to his mind, shows that we could not be indifferent to what reason commands, could not possibly ask, Why should I care, want to do, what pure reason requires? If he can show what he claims, we have already been given the answer to such a question. Hegel will not agree that practical reasons are primarily imperatives, and he obviously thinks that Kant has formulated the inescapably compelling character of reason in an inadequate way, but the structure of this argument is what is important here.

That structure involves considerations in Kant and Hegel that are unavoidably metaphysical, at least in the general Kantian sense of a "metaphysics of the person."[53] It is at this level, I want to suggest, that Kant and Hegel are mostly disagreeing, and that the distinctiveness of Hegel's position begins to emerge. The common question is, What must be involved in acting "under the idea of freedom"? And this is understood to mean, What principle must govern the self-imposition of norms by such a freely acting agent? This appears to be asking about some putatively timeless event, "when" someone would, on purely rational grounds, impose such a principle ("self-love," or "lawfulness itself"). But the question asks rather, What principles are we already and unavoidably committed to just by virtue of acting under the idea of freedom? (This would mean, such that, imagining what it would be to repudiate such a consideration and still "act under the idea of freedom" would be incoherent.) To know what such a consideration is (or must be), we have to know what it must be to be such an agent. All the weight of the case for any principle (or for the social norms of ethical life) comes down to that sort of a consideration. (It is quite important to stress

53 Cf. Nagel, *The Possibility of Altruism,* pp. 14, 18.

that the same would be true for a skeptic, like Hume or Williams, who wants to say, *Given who we are, only* considerations relativized to what we already want, or are motivated to pursue, *could* count as reasons to act. And the same would be true of a strict contractarian, whose views on what could be justified to, or accepted by, another must be driven by some consideration of what could not but be compelling for anyone, given "who we are.")

We argue, in other words, that conceding that someone could be indifferent to some sorts of considerations, whether commands of reason or the goal of self-realization, would be tantamount to postulating a being wholly unrecognizable as us, someone who could not act on reasons at all. Because of this, such considerations could not be unmotivating (at least where all this means is prima facie motivating; I could not be indifferent to them, and still be me).

The same sort of account is visible in many other rational accounts, although with wide variations. Plato too argues that what pure reason determines to be the best social and political arrangement could not be such a norm, unless it could also be shown that "justice pays," that individuals could be motivated to subscribe to such a norm. Given "what it is to be a human being," and what the fulfillment and happiness of such a creature amount to, no one could help but be motivated to subscribe to the Republic, *if* (and here the decisive, massive "*if*") he could come to understand his own "good" or psychic health. He cannot, of course, and so we end up with the peculiar position (peculiar to moderns) that masses of people are as happy as they could be, if they live in the *Republic,* even if, subjectively, *they* might disagree, and prefer, imprudently, to live in a democratic regime.

And so on in Kant. Here the considerations rest on the metaphysics of agency itself, the "fact" that no one could deny that she is a free, responsible agent, and so could not possibly be indifferent to what is a priori required of any such agent. To deny that would be to try to deny that one is free, something that one must be free to be able to do. (It is, in all such arguments, supposed to be *impossible* to concede, I see what there is good reason for me to do, and still ask, Why should I do what there is good reason for me to do?)

The parallel claims in Hegel are terminologically idiosyncratic but the general strategy is still recognizable, as in the general account of *Sittlichkeit* found in *Die Vorlesungen von 1819/20 in einer Nachschrift.*

> In so far as individuals are in such an ethical unity, they attain their true norm (*ihr wahrhaftes Recht*). The individuals attain their norm in that in such a manner they acquire their essence. They would achieve thereby, as one says,

their destiny (*ihre Bestimmung*). . . . In that the ethical is actual in individuals, it is their soul in general, the universal mode of their actuality.[54]

And, "The common ethical life of a people is their liberation (*Befreiung*); in it they come to an intuition of themselves."[55]

IX

I have argued that we can locate Hegel roughly in this rationalist camp, and as broadly sympathetic to many aspects of the Kantian approach. By a "Kantian" approach (rather than, strictly, Kant's), I mean, the considerations Hegel is interested in defending, as the factors we could not but be motivated to realize, are not considerations based on perceptions of objective goods, or benefits, or values, but evaluations and esteemings (conferrings of value) whose *justifications* have a certain character.[56] Certain sorts of relations in which persons stand to their own activities are what is decisive in the possibility of "actions' being freely valued." In Hegel's account such justifications are rational in that they cannot merely appeal to or "deliberate from" contingent elements of "my motivational set."[57] This is because the evaluative issue at stake for a subject is precisely the bindingness or justifiability, as reasons to act, *of* any such element. It is only by means of the possibility of such an evaluative "elevation" and "purification" of my own motives that any such element could be said truly to belong to me, to be mine.[58] The basic Hegelian point is, This *desideratum* is not a condition I can achieve individually, by trying to "put out of play" all my attachments.

54 *VRPN*, p. 124. (I am indebted to Terry Pinkard for drawing my attention to these formulations.)

55 Ibid., p. 125.

56 There is a useful discussion of the ambiguities in Nagel on this score. Cf. Christine Korsgaard, "The Reasons We Can Share: An Attack on the Distinction Between Agent-Relative and Agent-Neutral Reasons," in *Altruism*, ed. by E. F. Paul, F. D. Miller, Jr., and J. Paul (Cambridge: Cambridge University Press, 1993), pp. 24–51.

57 This is Williams's language in "Internal and External Reasons." See also the notion of a "ground project" in "Persons, Character, and Morality," in *Moral Luck*, pp. 1–19.

58 The general issue of Hegel's disagreements with moral realism, and his own position on how values are conferred, and on the conditions for any such conferring, are obviously quite complex. But it might help to note that one of the models Hegel is probably thinking of here is Kant's for the justifiability of aesthetic judgments. There too the value, beauty, is conferred by subjects, not found; but there too not conferred contingently, as a result of dispositions and desires we happen to share. The expectation that others *ought* to find this beautiful rests on a general assessment of who they are, and so what they could not be unaffected by, if, as in most cases, it were not for something distorting or blocking such a reaction and conferring.

Accordingly, a summary of the points made thus far would look like this.

My argument has been that the core of Hegel's account of *Sittlichkeit* consists in a theory of practical rationality, or an account of what sorts of considerations count for Hegel as reasons to act. (Only within certain sorts of social arrangements could various considerations count for me as such reasons.) This is the crucial question because Hegel clearly believes that only a practically rational agent is a free agent, and he identifies an ethically worthy life with a free life.

Traditionally the question of the rationality of action has been limited such to views as that a course of action is rational if it is the most efficient means to some end; or, it is rational if conducive to an end unavoidable in *any* worthy or free life (some "human good"); or a course of action is rational if required by a principle no one could be presumed exempt from.

Hegel's general theory of action is teleological: All action is purposive, or for the sake of some end. But Hegel does not believe that such a premise commits him to any Humean account of motivation (where ends are set by "the passions"), or an Aristotelian theory of the human good (of essential ends). In Hegel's account, to pursue an end is to subject oneself to a norm; I pursue an end for a reason, a reason I take to have justifying force. This then raises the central question: the conditions under which my attachment to any such ends, any conferring of value, could be expressive of rational agency, "reasons we could share," to borrow a recent phrase.[59] These conditions are argued to be unavoidably social and historical, although a formal and general account of the adequacy of modern institutions in meeting such criteria can also be given. So the claim is that only within certain social conditions could individual attachments to a plurality of possible ends be established "non-idiosyncratically," in consideration of others and their attachments. Therefore I am a rational agent and so in that sense free only within *those* (rational) institutions.

If this much is accepted, the basic problem then comes down to how to determine the relevant conditions or constraints on any such attaching or conferring. As the passages quoted amply indicate, actions for Hegel are norm-governed, and, by being norm-governed, presume a commitment to the justifiability of such norms, and so to some rationality condition. We may not fulfill such a condition, and we may act irrationally or unethically, but we do not have to show why we would care about such possible justifications. Given who we are (our "essence" or "destiny" [*Bestimmung*] or our "soul"), we could not but be motivated by such a consideration. The content of any

59 See the reference to Korsgaard in note 56.

such norm comes down to our not being able to act as if we weren't who we are, and the adoption of any particular norm is not then uncomfortably constrained by such a general principle as much as that principle must be realized in any such norm. So the problem of what such an unavoidable rationality requirement amounts to comes down to who we unavoidably are. And this is where, given all the considerations so far advanced, Hegel's case for the priority and rationality of ethical life is made.

Although Hegel's reasons for claiming that we are collectively self-forming, socially dependent beings are too controversial to raise here, it is at least clear that he is objecting to a procedure for getting to such a basis that he describes as typical of "the understanding." We could *abstract* from everything that is particular and contingent, to arrive at a conception of ourselves "thin" and uncontroversial enough to justify those sorts of considerations to which no one could be presumed indifferent. We assume that the rationality condition requires that we ask ourselves what an impartial agent having no attachments, commitments, or, relying on, as it is said, no agent-relative reasons, could justify. This though would be the opposite mistake of thinking that such deliberation and justification must be based on some particular, contingent set of interests and desires or ground projects, on who we contingently are. That view is wrong, but it is equally wrong to conclude that we must adopt a criterion of justification based on so neutral and impartial a notion of a subject as to be quite problematically related to a real life of attachments, commitments, desires, and projects. In Kant's view the obligations that derive from so considering ourselves are supposed to be unconditional, to trump all other practical considerations, what might otherwise seem for us practical necessities. In Hegel's view, this could be shown (and so the motivational condition met) only by showing that all aspects of our lives not connected with such a core self, or set of obligations, could simply be "indeterminately negated," were mere appearances, "*not*" who "we are." The prospects for this in general are dim, and even if they were brighter we would be committed to some possible phenomenology of moral experience wherein this supreme attachment to a rational ideal could be shown to have some institutional and social dimension, some way in which it could be promoted and sustained. And the prospects for such an account are equally dim. Kant has some things to say about this, but given the moral ideal in question the prospects can look strange and counterintuitive.[60]

---

60 They include artificially manipulating our emotional dispositions; deciding to visit the sick to try to increase our sympathetic feelings, so that we can have some affective assistance when we discharge our duty of benevolence; or viewing marriage as a contract for the

Admittedly, thus far such considerations merely get us to a "neither the one nor the other" position, an affirmation that there is some reflective, deliberative condition necessary for our attachments and projects to be genuinely "ours" (for us to be "subjects," to act "under the idea of freedom"), but a denial that this can be satisfied by a merely prudential deliberation, or by the strict demands of moral rationality. It would be necessary, to complete the picture, to show how some worked out view of the fundamental or unavoidable character of our social attachments determines the character of this reflective or rationality condition.

It is, at least, not difficult to imagine how such an account looks for Hegel. In the simplest terms, everyone has parents, can reproduce the conditions of her existence only cooperatively, and is invariably subject to, or the subject of, decisions about the common good or the exercise of some sort of political power. We are not simply one agent among many, or all alike in being agents who can act on reasons. We are, but even in being able to recognize and act on such considerations, we require others, such that the socially formative and educational institutions that make possible such recognition and its realization are effective.[61] Or, although there are moral considerations in an ethical life, they are not unconditionally overriding considerations. In trying to determine whether and when such obligations may be superseded (as when a spy lies) we bring to bear on judgment the priority of ethical life as sketched here.[62]

---

mutual use of each other's bodies; and so forth.

61 One of the ways Hegel tries to show this concerns the problems of moral judgment, in cases when moral or rights-based claims are understood to be the claims they are by being formulated in terms of an abstractly conceived moral subject. Understanding the problem of moral justifiability in terms of avoiding treating myself as an exception, or avoiding a maxim that would deny others the standing of free agents, agents who can be motivated by reasons, and so on, will certainly end up prohibiting broad classes of action. But all moral life requires fairly fine-grained moral judgment, and although there are not application rules for such judgment, if the general orientation is provided only by such a "thin" conception of persons, the results, he claims, will be worrisome. Such a reliance will ensure, he argues, that I will have no criterion of judgment to rely on in deciding what counts as treating another as means or end except my own "conscience," or the depth of my personal conviction. And this, he tries to show, will ultimately allow everyone to claim some form of moral purity, agreement in moral principle, but widespread self-indulgence in moral practice. Preventing such a result will require some more complex view of our unavoidable, historically "thick," bonds with others, and *thereby* the kinds of reasons to act, or norms, which could not but be motivating, given such conditions.

Kant, of course, denies this and has a doctrine of virtue. I have tried to argue elsewhere that that doctrine does not meet this objection. Cf. Chapter 4, this volume.

62 This sort of limitation of morality is discussed in a Hegelian spirit by Williams in *Ethics and the Limits of Philosophy*, (Cambridge: Harvard University Press, 1985), ch. 10.

X

Hegel made a number of claims about modern ethical life. Modern institutions are said to embody the "differentiated" normative requirements of modern social life, and so to provide a rich "content"-laden answer to the question of what we ought to do. And he also claims that in modern ethical roles, there is no gap between the "objective" demands of "right" and what he terms the "subjective," what I have called the "motivating," aspect of such demands. (That is, I have argued that the Hegelian claim for a "unity of objective and subjective moments" amounts to his version of the satisfaction of a strong internalism requirement: that rational considerations be shown to be motivating. It is in this sense that the rational is, or has come to be, actual.)

In other words, Hegel accepts the condition that reasons for action must be able to motivate a subject to act, and tries to consider such possible reasons in the light of the general features of personhood and possible agency. What he adds is a simple but decisive insistence that whatever we are, we are not autonomously self-forming creatures. Everything, he argues, about both the content and the motivating force of reasons to act changes dramatically when we take account of this fact at some significant level. Such a realization shifts the focus of ethical issues away from two traditional areas and toward a third. It denies the priority or even the presumed ultimacy of "dispositions," "passions," or "ground projects" in our esteemings and evaluatings, raising large questions about what could be said to make up an "individual's *own*" inclinations, such that they could be decisive. But Hegel's ethical point of view does not do so under the assumption that the only condition that will realize such self-determination is some kind of radical detachment, a reflection "from nowhere," or a "pure," individual moral self-legislation.

These claims would open up a number of questions if we continued to explore how Hegel justified his view that certain pre-volitional attachments and dependencies (in the modern, Western European form he describes) are necessary conditions for a free, because practically rational, norm-governed life. My interest here has been to introduce the general form of his argument.

This form already suggests a number of implications, especially when considered in the light of Hegel's legacy. I mean especially the way in which contemporary ethical positions that insist on the priority of some sort of pre-volitional attachments or commitments, or ground projects in ethical life (prior in the sense of, necessary for any ethical deliberation to get started, but not themselves possible products of ethical deliberation), are sometimes casually referred to as neo-Hegelian. Such communitarian, or neo-Humean, or neo-Aristotelian, or pragmatist, or Burkean positions might be independently interesting, but not by way of what they lead to in Hegel. For Hegel, modern ethical life is not just ours; it is rational. It consists in practices and social attachments that make possible their own, rationally motivated and free affirmation. As in his theoretical philosophy, Hegel's vigorous attack on Kant can obscure the extent to which he is developing a position on practical rationality and freedom very much in the spirit of his predecessors in Rousseau and Kant.

It is also very much in the spirit of his successors, those "critical theorists" who claimed that no account of human norms would be possible without a general theory of society; that this theory could be "critical" without being moralistic or externalist; that it could discover the "real" emancipatory interests inherent in social forms and point the way to their realization. One way of making this point, and of seeing its origins in Hegel's attack on Kant's rigorism and on any externalist theory of purely rational "oughts," is to note that the underlying position for both is a kind of rationalist internalism, a way of showing why the norms constitutive of free agency could not but be ultimately rationally motivating for any real or "actual" agent. If we try to show this, goes Hegel's original account, we will be led back to social and historical dimensions of agency indispensable in being able to make such a case, and so to the question of what sorts of attachments and dependencies can be argued to be constitutive of a free life for a modern agent.

Moreover, other considerations also become immediately relevant and unavoidable. Not only are we not self-forming in our own lives, but we are collectively self-forming over time, or historical beings. For certain purposes, in certain contexts, it can be important to ask what we must acknowledge about each other apart from such considerations and realities. But Hegel objects to the priority given such abstraction in modern moral theory. No full account of what could be a reason to act, a reason that could motivate me, can be finally isolated from an account of what forms of cooperation, dependence, and recognition are required in my becoming and sustaining myself as the subject of my deeds. You can't be a rationalist in ethics without some commitment to this issue, but you certainly can be a cautious rationalist, concentrating on those considerations of personhood and agency that can be isolated from our social dependence and historical natures, and thereby searching for what could not but be motivating for anyone so conceived. But that agent is not really or "actually" us, and will only provide very general notions of what is impermissible (and so what is obligatory in that sense; refraining from the impermissible). To conceive of our whole moral life in these terms is to impoverish that notion, and to leave undiscussed the most important consideration of ethical discussion, What ought *we* to do?

NAME INDEX

SUBJECT INDEX